Popular Musicians

Volume 1
Abba - Donovan

Editor
Steve Hochman

Project Editor
McCrea Adams

SALEM PRESS
Pasadena, California   Hackensack, New Jersey

Managing Editor: Christina J. Moose
Project Editor: McCrea Adams
Acquisitions Editor: Mark Rehn
Research Supervisor: Jeffry Jensen
Production Editor: Yasmine A. Cordoba
Photograph Editor: Karrie Hyatt
Copy Editors: Lauren M. D'Andrea; Douglas Long
Research Assistant: Jun Ohnuki
Design and Layout: James Hutson

Library of Congress Cataloging-in-Publication Data

Popular Musicians / consulting editor, Steve Hochman ; project editor, McCrea Adams.
    p. cm.
    Includes discographical references and index.
    ISBN 0-89356-986-0 (set : alk. paper). — ISBN 0-89356-987-9 (vol. 1 : alk. paper). — ISBN 0-89356-988-7 (vol. 2 : alk. paper). — ISBN 0-89356-989-5 (vol. 3 : alk. paper). — ISBN 0-89356-990-9 (vol. 4 : alk. paper).
    1. Musicians — Biography — Dictionaries.   2. Musical groups — Dictionaries.
  I. Hochman, Steve, 1956-   .

ML105.P66   1999
781.64'092'2—dc21   99-11658
[B]   CIP

First Printing

Publisher's Note

The four volumes of Popular Musicians contain 532 articles on the lives and careers of musicians popular in the United States since the late 1950's. Arranged alphabetically, the set covers solo performers, bands, and vocal groups from Abba to ZZ Top.

Popular Musicians focuses on "pop music" performing artists to the exclusion of artists in certain other genres. Here one finds articles on performers in fields such as pop and its subgenres, rock and roll and its subgenres, rap and hip-hop, country, soul, disco, blues, and folk music. Composers of film, television, or theatrical music are not included; neither are modern classical composers or performers. Although jazz as a genre falls outside the purview of the set, its impact has undeniably crossed over into popular music. Fourteen articles on central, well-known jazz figures who have been widely influential are therefore included—among them Miles Davis, John Coltrane, Charlie Parker, and Charles Mingus, as well as fusion pioneers such as John McLaughlin and Weather Report.

Popular Musicians also focuses primarily on artists and styles popular in the United States since the late 1950's. Within that time frame, the set emphasizes what might be described as the music embraced by "baby boomers" and subsequent generations. Also included, however, are a number of artists—such as Jimmie Rodgers, Woody Guthrie, and Robert Johnson—from earlier generations who deeply influenced entire genres. The 1950's pioneers of rock and roll such as Chuck Berry and blues artists such as Howlin' Wolf are here, as are vocalists such as Frank Sinatra and Ella Fitzgerald whose popularity has spanned generations. Finally, although the set contains essays only on performing artists, many influential writers and producers are mentioned throughout the set, and their names may be found in the Name and Subject Index in volume 4.

The focus on performing artists allows Popular Musicians to give select artists more in-depth treatment than may be found in many biographical dictionaries or encyclopedias. The Beatles, for example, are treated extensively in a 5,000-word essay. A number of other popular artists who typify an era or a genre receive 2,500-word essays; among them are Garth Brooks, James Brown, Bob Dylan, the Grateful Dead, Jimi Hendrix, Michael Jackson, B. B. King, Led Zeppelin, Madonna, the Rolling Stones, Bruce Springsteen, Barbra Streisand, U2, and Stevie Wonder. Other articles range from about 600 words to 1,500 words, with most between 750 and 1,200 words.

All essays are uniformly formatted, allowing the user to locate information easily and quickly. There are two basic types of articles, those on individual artists and those on performing groups. Essays on individuals begin with birth and death information, the title and date of the person's first single or album release, and the artist's musical styles. Essays on groups begin with a listing of group members, including years of birth when available. Separate listings provide information on original members (considered those at the time of the group's first release), later members, and, when appropriate, the group's best-known configuration. As with articles on individuals, information on the group's first release and musical styles follows.

Within the text of each article, italicized subheads guide the reader. Chart positions of singles and albums are often noted in the text. Billboard magazine's chart listings are the most widely cited and used in the music industry, and when chart positions are listed they can be taken as Billboard statistics from the Hot 100 (singles) or Billboard 200 (albums) charts. (Some exceptions are indicated, most often for country or rhythm-and-blues artists; occasionally foreign chart positions, most frequently English, are cited as well.)

Articles conclude with the contributor's byline, followed by a select discography, select list of awards, and cross-references to other relevant articles in the set. The select discographies reflect the shift in relative importance of single versus album releases that began in the late 1960's: Discographies of artists whose major recordings were released before that time emphasize single releases, while those of artists after that time emphasize albums. Release dates given in the discographies are dates of first release, so some dates represent foreign release dates that precede the U.S. release. Dates of Grammy Awards, following the National Academy of Recording Arts and Sciences' own procedure, are not the year the award was presented but the previous year, when the work was in release.

Popular Musicians is liberally illustrated, with approximately 400 of the articles accompanied by photographs. The set also concludes with a number of additional reference features. A Glossary explains terms such as AM radio, cover song, demo, and EP, as well as genres of music such as disco, folk rock, grunge, and industrial. A Bibliography offers suggestions for further reading. A Time Line of First Releases provides a thumbnail historical overview; it lists, by year, the first album or single release of each artist in the set. A List of Artists by Musical Styles categorizes them by genre. Finally, there are two indexes: a Song and Album Title Index and a Name and Subject Index.

Salem Press thanks the many contributors—academicians, journalists, and critics—whose time and expertise made this set possible. We especially thank the set's editor, Los Angeles pop music critic Steve Hochman, for his guidance and many valuable contributions.

List of Contributors

McCrea Adams
Independent Scholar

Michael Adams
City University of New York Graduate School

Alyson C. Allison
Independent Scholar

Amy Allison
Independent Scholar

D. M. Frances Batycki
The University of Calgary

Alvin K. Benson
Brigham Young University

Karan A. Berryman
Andrew College

Wayne M. Bledsoe
University of Missouri, Rolla

Kevin J. Bochynski
Salem State College

Steve D. Boilard
Independent Scholar

Mark W. Bolton
University of Michigan, Flint

E. Douglas Bomberger
University of Hawaii at Manoa

Frank Bongiorno
University of North Carolina at Wilmington

Nila M. Bowden
Morgan State University

Kevin Boyle
Elon College

Tim Bradley
Independent Scholar

John A. Britton
Francis Marion University

Wesley Britton
Harrisburg Area Community College

Norbert Brockman
St. Mary's University of San Antonio

Karen M. Bryan
Arizona State University

Stephanie Brzuzy
Arizona State University

Thomas W. Buchanan
Ancilla College

Fred Buchstein
John Carroll University

Jeffrey E. Bush
Arizona State University

William M. Camphouse
Independent Scholar

Michele Caniato
Boston University

Lou Carlozo
Chicago Tribune

José A. Carmona
Daytona Beach Community College

William S. Carson
Coe College

Linda M. Carter
Morgan State University

David A. Clark
Rollins College

John W. Clark
Santa Barbara City College

Thomas Clarkin
University of Texas at Austin

Robert Clifford
University of Arizona

Jo Ann Collins
California State University, Fresno

Andrew Cook
Independent Scholar

Lauren M. D'Andrea
Independent Scholar

Frederick E. Danker
University of Massachusetts, Boston

Andy DeRoche
Community College of Aurora

Robert DiGiacomo
Independent Scholar

Joel Dinerstein
University of Texas at Austin

Douglas J. Dixon
University of Tennessee at Chattanooga

Margaret A. Dodson
Boise Independent Schools

David Allen Duncan
Tennessee Wesleyan College

Todd A. Elhart
Independent Scholar

Joseph J. Estock
James Madison University

Lawrence Ferber
Independent Scholar

Paul D. Fischer
Middle Tennessee State University

Popular Musicians

David Lee Fish
St. Andrews College

Inoke F. Funaki
Brigham Young University, Hawaii

Patricia L. Gibbs
University of Hawaii at Manoa

Elizabeth B. Graham
Independent Scholar

Rebecca Green
Independent Scholar

Shanna D. Greene
University of Wisconsin, Madison

Melissa R. Grimm
Independent Scholar

David Haas
University of Georgia

Roger D. Hardaway
Northwestern Oklahoma State University

Kerry Hart
Adams State College

Kim Heikkila
University of Minnesota

Arthur D. Hlavaty
Independent Scholar

Steve Hochman
Independent Scholar

Peter C. Holloran
New England Historical Association

K. L. A. Hyatt
Independent Scholar

Jeffry Jensen
Independent Scholar

Sheila Golburgh Johnson
Independent Scholar

Yvonne Johnson
Central Missouri State University

David Junker
University of Wisconsin

Cynthia R. Kasee
University of South Florida

Beverly Keel
Middle Tennessee State University

Charles Kinzer
Longwood College

Cassandra Kircher
Elon College

Joseph Klein
University of North Texas

Grove Koger
Independent Scholar

Benji L. Kreider
Valley Morning Star

Michael Lee
University of Oklahoma

Douglas Long
Independent Scholar

Roderick McGillis
University of Calgary

Edgar V. McKnight, Jr.
John A. Logan College

Jean McKnight
Independent Scholar

Joseph McLaren
Hofstra University

Bart MacMillan
Delta State University

David W. Madden
California State University, Sacramento

Lula Mae Martin
University of Alabama in Huntsville

Kevin M. Mitchell
Independent Scholar

Joseph D. Mixon
Lebanon Valley College

Josh Modell
Independent Scholar

Janice Monti-Belkaoui
Dominican University

Kimberly A. Morgan
Mt. Markham Central School

B. Keith Murphy
Fort Valley State University

Alice Myers
Simon's Rock College

William Nelles
University of Massachusetts, Dartmouth

Kurt C. Organista
University of California, Berkeley

Arsenio Orteza
Independent Scholar

James G. Pappas
State University of New York at Buffalo

Michael Pelusi
Independent Scholar

Benjamin Pensiero
Independent Scholar

Nicole Pensiero
Independent Scholar

Richard Pinnell
University of Wisconsin, La Crosse

J. P. Piskulich
Oakland University

John Powell
Pennsylvania State University, Erie

List of Contributors

Luke A. Powers
Tennessee State University

Maureen J. Puffer-Rothenberg
Valdosta State University

P. S. Ramsey
Independent scholar

R. Kent Rasmussen
Independent Scholar

P. Brent Register
Clarion University

Betty Richardson
Southern Illinois University, Edwardsville

Douglas W. Richmond
University of Texas at Arlington

Ernest Rigney, Jr.
College of Charleston

Deirdre Rockmaker
Independent Scholar

Joel Nathan Rosen
Georgia Southern University

Daniel Rothenberg
Independent Scholar

Kelly Rothenberg
Independent Scholar

G. W. Sandy Schaefer
University of Wisconsin, Oshkosh

Harriet L. Schwartz
Independent Scholar

Amanda Walzer Scott
Independent Scholar

Rose Secrest
Independent Scholar

Mark Sheridan-Rabideau
University of Illinois at Urbana-Champaign

Donald C. Simmons Jr.
Mississippi Humanities Council

Donna Addkison Simmons
Independent Scholar

Amy Sisson
Independent Scholar

Douglas D. Skinner
Southwest Texas State University

Jane Marie Smith
Butler County Community College

Ira Smolensky
Monmouth College

Mark J. Spicer
Elmira College

James Stanlaw
Illinois State University

Earl L. Stewart
University of California, Santa Barbara

Eric Strauss
Independent Scholar

Irene Struthers
Independent Scholar

James Sullivan
California State University, Los Angeles

Sandra A. Swanson
Independent Scholar

Warren C. Swindell
Indiana State University

Jeff Tamarkin
Independent Scholar

Leslie V. Tischauser
Independent Scholar

Don Tyler
Central Florida Community College

Erik Unsworth
Independent Scholar

Albert Valencia
California State University, Fresno

Ethlie Ann Vare
Independent Scholar

Marc E. Waddell
Morris College

James E. Walton
California State University, Fresno

Annita Marie Ward
Salem-Teikyo University

Gregory Weeks
University of Graz, Austria

Tyrone Williams
Xavier University

Mary A. Wischusen
Wayne State University

Contents

Popular Musicians

Popular Musicians

Abba

MEMBERS: Bjorn Ulvaeus (b. 1945), Anni-Frid "Frida" Synni-Lyngstad-Fredriksson-Andersson (b. 1945), Benny Andersson (b. 1946), Agnetha "Anna" Faltskog (b. 1950)

FIRST ALBUM RELEASE: *Ring Ring*, 1973 (as Bjorn, Benny, Agnetha, and Frida)

MUSICAL STYLES: Pop, disco

Formed in Stockholm, Sweden, in 1972, Abba consisted of two couples whose division of labor, like their marriages, seemed for a while to have been made in heaven. With the photogenic Agnetha (Anna) Faltskog and Anni-Frid (Frida) Lyngstad singing the catchy pop songs of Bjorn Ulvaeus and Benny Andersson, Abba went from being the first internationally recognized pop group from Sweden to being one of the most commercially successful pop groups of all time. Abba disbanded in 1983, several years after the dissolution of the group members' marriages. Nevertheless, its many original albums and hit collections would continue to sell millions of copies worldwide.

Sound and Eurovision. Prior to forming a songwriting and performing partnership that would lay the groundwork for Abba, Benny Andersson and Bjorn Ulvaeus enjoyed individual success as members of the Swedish pop groups the Hep Stars and the Hootenanny Singers, respectively. With Stig Anderson, who would eventually become known as Abba's fifth member, they established the company Union Songs and began writing, recording, and producing both their own music and the music of others.

In 1969, Andersson became engaged to Anni-Frid Lyngstad, and Ulvaeus became engaged to Agnetha Faltskog. Both Lyngstad and Faltskog were already established solo performers in Sweden, and eventually the two couples began performing and recording together under the name

Bjorn, Benny, Agnetha, and Frida. After failing to qualify as Sweden's entry in the 1973 Eurovision Song Contest with the song "Ring Ring," the group and Anderson began preparing for the 1974 competition. Shortening its name to the acronym Abba, the group wrote and recorded what would become the first of their many international hits, the 1974 winner of the Eurovision Song Contest, "Waterloo."

The Successful 1970's. Although "Waterloo" (1974) reached number 6 in the United States and number 1 in Great Britain, Abba appeared to be headed for the dubious distinction of "one-hit wonder" until the release of "S.O.S." Like "Waterloo," "S.O.S." was distinguished by the overdubbed vocals of Lyngstad and Faltskog and a wall-of-sound backing track featuring a sparkling blend of keyboards and guitars. The song's international popularity caused fans and critics alike to take the group more seriously and, as a result, to expect even more from them.

Far from being daunted, Abba rose to the challenge. Several popular singles later, "Dancing Queen" (1976) became the biggest hit of their career, reaching number 1 even in the United States. By 1977, Abba's worldwide sales were astronomical, and the band members had begun to feel the pressure of international superstardom. In response to the self-imposed challenge of continually outdoing itself, the group responded in 1977 with an album simply titled *The Album*, which included some of Abba's longest and most elaborate songs thus far. Viewed by many as a collection of only partially successful experiments, *The Album* was nevertheless treated kindly compared to *The Movie*, a feature-length film consisting largely of concert footage which, instead of cementing the group's superstar status, seemed to reveal its feet of clay.

Despite such missteps, however, Abba consistently enjoyed hit singles throughout the 1970's, even in the United States, where enthusiasm for the group's music had always been subdued in comparison with the enthusiasm with which it was greeted elsewhere. *The Album* eventually went platinum, and *Voulez-Vous*, which followed in 1979 and contained the hits "Voulez-Vous" and "Chiquitita," went gold.

Family Matters. Unlike the Beatles, whose dissolution was due in part to marriage, Abba began to break down as the result of divorce. By 1981, both Ulvaeus and Faltskog's seven-year marriage and Andersson and Lyngstad's three-year one had ended. Still, the end of the group was not immediately forthcoming. Amid the marital discord, Abba managed to record two of its best albums, *Super Trouper* (1980) and *The Visitors* (1981), both of which contained hit singles. However, when Lyngstad released her Phil Collins-produced solo album *Something's Going On* in 1982, and the group released no new music in 1983, rumors began to circulate that the title of their latest greatest hits collection, *The Singles: The First Ten Years* (1982), may have been too optimistic.

These rumors proved to be true. Faltskog's first post-Abba solo album, *Wrap Your Arms Around Me*, appeared in 1983. In 1984, the sound track to the musical *Chess*, on which Andersson and Ulvaeus had collaborated with lyricist Tim Rice, provided Murray Head with his first hit in fourteen years, "One Night in Bangkok." Meanwhile, all four group members had either remarried or established new live-in relationships. The 1986 *Live* album was the last album-length collection of previously unreleased Abba performances.

The Reissue Decade. When Polygram acquired the rights to the Abba catalog in the early 1990's, the company was able to capitalize on the

Abba (Archive Photos)

For the Record

By the late 1970's, Abba had become the most commercially successful pop act in the world, outselling even the Beatles. At the same time, the Stockholm stock exchange listed the group as its second-most lucrative corporation.

§

During the Stockholm, Sweden, stop of U2's 1992 "Zoo TV" tour, Benny Andersson and Bjorn Ulvaeus joined the Irish group onstage at the Globe Theatre for a performance of "Dancing Queen"; two years later, seventeen years after its initial release, the song (backed by a version performed by the Wedding Band Featuring Blazey Best) became the first single from the *Muriel's Wedding* sound-track album in 1995.

spotty availability of the group's albums by mounting a high-profile reissue campaign. Beginning with *Gold/Greatest Hits* in 1992, *More Abba Gold* in 1993, and the four-compact-disc *Thank You for the Music* boxed set in 1994, Polygram had, by 1997, rereleased all eight Abba studio albums, making them available on compact disc for the first time.

Some Abba enthusiasts have been too quick to spot the group's influence. Aside from the fact that both Roxette and Ace of Base, for instance, were also internationally successful Swedish pop exports, they have little in common with Abba aside from their homeland. There was, however, no mistaking Abba's influence on the British pop duo Erasure, who released a well-received four-song extended-play single of Abba covers titled *Abba-esque* in 1992. —*Arsenio Orteza*

SELECT DISCOGRAPHY
■ SINGLES
"Waterloo," 1974
"Fernando," 1976
"Dancing Queen," 1976
"Take a Chance on Me," 1977
"The Winner Takes It All," 1980
■ ALBUMS
Ring Ring, 1973
Abba, 1975
Voulez-Vous, 1979
The Visitors, 1981
Live, 1986
Gold/Greatest Hits, 1992 (compilation)
More Abba Gold, 1993 (compilation)
Thank You for the Music, 1994 (four-CD boxed set, compilation)

SELECT AWARDS
Eurovision Song Contest Award for "Waterloo," 1974
Broadcast Music Incorporated (BMI) Award for Most Played Record of the Year for "S.O.S.," 1975
Cashbox, named Top Album/Singles Artists of the Year, 1976

SEE ALSO: Collins, Phil.

AC/DC

ORIGINAL MEMBERS: Angus Young (b. 1959), Malcolm Young (b. 1953), Bon Scott (1946-1980), Phillip Rudd (b. 1954), Mark Evans (b. 1956)
OTHER MEMBERS: Cliff Williams (b. 1949), Brian Johnson (b. 1947)
FIRST ALBUM RELEASE: *High Voltage*, 1975
MUSICAL STYLE: Hard rock

AC/DC emerged from the culturally and geographically isolated 1970's Australian urban-club scene to become a cornerstone of contemporary hard rock. Known for raucous and explicit lyrics in songs such as "Big Balls" and "You Shook Me All Night Long" as well as for guitarist Angus Young's schoolboy uniform and spastic onstage gyrations, AC/DC captured a worldwide audience by remaining true to their basic twelve-bar boogie and wall-of-sound guitar barrage.

Let There Be Rock. AC/DC began with the demise of an Australian band known as the Easybeats. Former Easybeats Harry Vanda and George

Young struck out on their own as the Marcus Hook Roll Band with George Young's little brothers as guitarists. These sessions brought Malcolm and Angus Young together in the studio and led Malcolm to decide that he wanted to form his own band.

Malcolm put together a group including vocalist Dave Evans and, against his father's advice, his little brother Angus Young as a second guitarist. The name AC/DC came, at least in one version of the tale, as a suggestion from sister Margaret Young, who saw the term on her sewing machine. Apparently it was also Margaret who convinced Angus to wear his trademark school uniform on stage. In April of 1974, AC/DC recorded their first single, "Can I Sit Next to You," which was produced by Harry Vanda and George Young. The single became only a minor regional hit and the group disbanded.

Long Way to the Top. By September of 1974, Malcolm and Angus were reforming AC/DC. Despite the apocryphal tale that claims that AC/DC discovered Bon Scott while he was a member of their road crew, Scott was actually an experienced vocalist, and the band held a number of auditions before hiring him. Drummer Phillip Rudd and bassist Mark Evans were also added, completing the original AC/DC lineup. Only six weeks after adding Scott, AC/DC recorded their first album, *High Voltage*. Vanda and George Young served as producers. In February of 1975, *High Voltage* was released in Australia. The success of *High Voltage* led the band back to the studio in July of 1975 to record *TNT*. Both albums were laid down live with only vocals and guitar solos overdubbed. This method of recording created AC/DC's powerful and gritty sound.

During two years of touring, AC/DC built a phenomenal fan base in Australia. Confusion over the ambiguous meaning of the band's name made them a huge hit among Australia's gay communities. In February of 1976, *TNT* was released, selling eleven thousand copies in the first week. With a British tour set to begin in April, AC/DC returned to the studio. *Dirty Deeds Done Dirt Cheap* was recorded in February of 1976 and then shelved to be released when management felt it was needed.

For the Record

Bon Scott was rejected by the Australian army on the grounds that he was "socially maladjusted."

§

AC/DC's *Dirty Deeds Done Dirt Cheap* got its name from a character in the children's television show *Beany and Cecil*. The character in question was Dishonest John, whose business card read, Dirty Deeds Done Dirt Cheap, Holidays, Sundays and Special Rates.

In the spring of 1976, AC/DC's first British single, "It's a Long Way to the Top," was released in advance of their tour of the United Kingdom. This release was quickly followed by the release of the U.K. version of *High Voltage*. The band began their tour in May, opening for such bands as Back Street Crawler, but by June, AC/DC was headlining their own "Lock Up Your Daughters" tour. AC/DC's London debut coincided with the peak of punk rock. At first, AC/DC was mistaken, much to their chagrin, for a punk band. Their live shows, filled with Angus's bare-bottomed, mad-schoolboy theatrics and Scott's snarling vocals, provided London audiences with an experience that was even more outrageous than that of their punk competition.

In the summer of 1977, AC/DC began a grueling tour of American clubs to promote the international release of *Let There Be Rock*. An earlier attempt to tour the United States was derailed when AC/DC was refused visas due to Scott's criminal record. The 1977 club tour was followed by rapid-fire tours of Europe, Britain, and the United States, supporting such acts as Black Sabbath and Kiss. This incessant touring was increasing the band's fan base and their commercial success.

In 1978 AC/DC released *Powerage*, which became their first gold album. By the end of the *Powerage* tour, AC/DC had upstaged many better-known acts and were headliners. In 1979, AC/DC returned to the studio and Robert "Mutt" Lange was brought in to produce *Highway to Hell*, replacing Vanda and George Young. Lange convinced AC/DC to use more traditional recording techniques, allowing the band to make the transition from their early bar-band sound to a more musically mature and polished sound. The result was an album which cracked the Top 20 in the United States and became their first million-seller.

With the success of *Highway to Hell*, AC/DC seemed poised on the brink of global success until the early morning of February 20, 1980, when Scott was found dead. The cause of death was termed "death by misadventure," since Scott had drunk himself to death.

Back in Black. Less than six weeks after Scott's death, AC/DC hired former Geordie vocalist Brian Johnson. Johnson and AC/DC teamed up to record *Back in Black* (1980), which served as a tribute to Scott. By August, *Back in Black* had topped the British album charts and reached number 4 on the American album charts. *Back in Black* sold more than twelve million copies.

AC/DC continued their successful formula of album releases supported by a heavy touring schedule (with seventy dates in 1991 alone). By 1985 this formula had pushed AC/DC to the top, evidenced by *Billboard* magazine's naming them the best-selling hard-rock act ever, with sales of twenty-five to thirty million albums. As their success grew, the band faced a number of difficulties ranging from charges of Satanism, bisexuality, and drug abuse to the tragic death of three of their teenage fans at a 1991 concert in Salt Lake City, Utah. Antirock protesters were common sights at AC/DC concerts by the mid-1980's.

Pop Icons. Through endurance and popularity, AC/DC became icons in popular culture. This is evidenced by incidents such as the U.S. Army's 1989 attempt to flush Panamanian dictator Manuel Noriega out of his refuge at the Vatican embassy in Panama by playing "Highway to Hell" at top volume, and Butt-head's ever-present AC/DC T-shirt on MTV's cartoon *Beavis and Butt-head*. The band also received Grammy Award nominations for *The Razor's Edge* and the live sin-

gle "Highway to Hell." In 1995, an AC/DC tribute album, *Fuse Box*, featured Australian bands covering AC/DC standards, including Yothu Yindi's blend of aboriginal and rock music for their version of "Jailbreak." —*B. Keith Murphy*

SELECT DISCOGRAPHY
■ ALBUMS
High Voltage, 1975 (Australia only; international release, 1976)
TNT, 1975 (Australia only)
Dirty Deeds Done Dirt Cheap, 1976
Let There Be Rock, 1977
Powerage, 1978
Highway to Hell, 1979
Back in Black, 1980
For Those About to Rock We Salute You, 1981
Who Made Who, 1986
Blow Up Your Video, 1988
The Razor's Edge, 1990
AC/DC Live, 1992
Ballbreaker, 1995

SEE ALSO: Aerosmith; Black Sabbath / Ozzy Osbourne; Mötley Crüe.

Bryan Adams

BORN: Kingston, Ontario, Canada; November 5, 1959
FIRST ALBUM RELEASE: *Bryan Adams*, 1980
MUSICAL STYLES: Rock and roll; pop

Bryan Adams became Canada's reigning pop superstar in the 1980's and 1990's, recording a string of hit singles and successful albums. In addition to being a fine and distinctive pop-rock singer, Adams has a facility for writing melodic, anthemic ballads. With the release of his album *Waking Up the Neighbours* in 1991, he became Canada's most successful recording artist to date. By January, 1992, that album alone had sold seven million copies worldwide. Adams is also involved in the environmental movement, and he uses his position and his reputation as a solid concert performer to bring the environmental message to audiences around the globe.

Bryan Adams (Lissa Wales)

he graduated from high school, he bought a baby grand piano with the money his parents had saved to send him to college. In 1976 and 1977 Adams replaced Nick Gilder as the lead singer of the Vancouver-based group Sweeney Todd. In 1978 he met Jim Vallance of the group Prism, and the two began a long and productive songwriting relationship. Together, they wrote songs for groups such as Prism and Loverboy and for solo artists including Tina Turner and Joe Cocker.

Albums and Projects. In 1980 Adams released his self-titled debut album and, over the next five years, steadily made a place for himself in the pop music scene. In 1985 he became the first Canadian artist to receive the Diamond Award, for selling one million copies of his 1984 album *Reckless* in Canada. This album contained many Top-10 singles, including "Run to You," "Heaven," "Summer of '69," "One Night Love Affair," and "It's Only Love" (a duet with Tina Turner). The album also sold four million copies in the United States. The song "Heaven" went on to become the first Canadian single to reach number 1 on Billboard's Hot 100 chart since Anne Murray's 1978 hit "You Needed Me." Adams, with Vallance and David Foster, cowrote the Ethiopian famine relief anthem, "Tears Are Not Enough," which brought many Canadian musicians together at one time and place.

The raspy sensitivity of Adams's voice allows him to make the transformation easily from sad songs such as "Straight from the Heart" to raucous rockers such as "Hey Elvis." Adams has a knack for

Background. Adams is the oldest son of British-born Jane and Conrad Adams. His father, a member of the Canadian military, ran the family in a militaristic way. Conrad also verbally and physically abused both Bryan and Jane. He tried in vain to stop Bryan from playing rock-and-roll music. By the time Bryan was eleven years of age, he was seeing a psychiatrist three times a week. His parents separated in 1975, and Bryan moved to Vancouver, British Columbia, with his mother. When

creating memorable rock-and-roll tracks. Detractors have argued that his ballads are simplistic and his uptempo songs sometimes sound as though they were made on a production line. Yet few performers are so meticulous in their craft. Adams has very high expectations of himself and those who work with him. Other performers and music industry people have reported that Adams is uncompromising to work with. He has had creativity-inspired arguments with Tina Turner, Carly Simon, and a number of others.

Adams has written and performed several hit motion-picture songs. In 1991 he wrote "(Everything I Do) I Do It for You" for *Robin Hood: Prince of Thieves*, and in 1995 "Have You Ever Loved a Woman?" was included on the *Don Juan DeMarco* sound track. In 1996 he released a song that he cowrote, his duet with Barbra Streisand, "I Finally Found Someone," from her film *The Mirror Has Two Faces*. With these three songs, Adams was nominated for an Academy Award for Best Song in three different years. He has topped the charts in the United States four times with sound-track hits: "Heaven," "(Everything I Do) I Do It for You," "All for Love" (with Rod Stewart and Sting), and "Have You Ever Really Loved a Woman?"

Recognition and Charity Work. Adams has worldwide album sales exceeding forty-four million copies. By the mid-1990's he had become Canada's premier musical ambassador and had been awarded the Order of Canada and the Order of British Columbia from his home province for outstanding achievement as a Canadian citizen.

For the Record

In September, 1991, Bryan Adams broke a thirty-six-year-old record when his single "(Everything I Do) I Do It for You" hit number 1 on the British pop charts for the twelfth consecutive week. The previous record, long regarded as unbeatable, had been set in 1955 by Slim Whitman's yodeling rendition of "Rose Marie."

He was named Canada's "Artist of the Decade" by the Canadian recording industry in 1990. He holds the record of having had the longest-running number 1 single in Britain with "(Everything I Do) I Do It for You." His songs have achieved the number 1 position in over twenty countries. He has been nominated twelve times for Grammy Awards, winning in 1992 for Best Song Written for a Motion Picture or for Television with "(Everything I Do) I Do It for You."

Adams has been a longtime supporter of the environmental organization Greenpeace and has used his fame to gain attention for many of their campaigns, including saving the rain forests and establishing a whale sanctuary in the Antarctic. His work on Canada's African famine relief project, "Tears Are Not Enough," raised over two million dollars, an effort for which he was given a Harry Chapin Media Award. Adams also participated in Live Aid, the Amnesty International World Tour, and the Concert for Nelson Mandela. In 1987 Adams headlined the Prince's Trust charity pop concerts at Wembley Arena in London, England. He performed with former Beatles Ringo Starr, George Harrison, and Paul McCartney, along with Eric Clapton, Boy George, and Mark King of the British pop group Level 42, on three Beatles classics—"While My Guitar Gently Weeps," "With a Little Help from My Friends," and "Here Comes the Sun." He also joined in performance with Phil Collins, Paul Young, Midge Ure, and Dave Edmunds.

Adams does not give frequent interviews. He has a skin condition, a result of the stress he experienced as a youth, and so he prefers that pictures of him be taken from a distance. In the 1990's Adams was living in London with his girlfriend, actress Cecilia Thomsen. He also maintained a home in Vancouver, British Columbia.

—Patricia L. Gibbs

SELECT DISCOGRAPHY
■ SINGLES
"Cuts Like a Knife," 1983
"Straight from the Heart," 1983
"Run to You," 1984
"Heaven," 1985

"Summer of '69," 1985
"It's Only Love," 1986 (with Tina Turner)
"(Everything I Do) I Do It for You," 1991
"Let's Make a Night to Remember," 1996
"I Finally Found Someone," 1996 (with Barbra
    Streisand)

■ ALBUMS
Bryan Adams, 1980
You Want It, You Got It, 1981
Cuts Like a Knife, 1983
Reckless, 1984
Into the Fire, 1987
Waking Up the Neighbours, 1991
So Far So Good, 1993
Live Live Live, 1994
18 Til I Die, 1996
On a Day Like Today, 1998

SELECT AWARDS
Grammy Award for Best Song Written for a Mo-
    tion Picture or for Television for "(Every-
    thing I Do) I Do It for You," 1991 (wr. with
    Robert "Mutt" Lange and Michael Kamen)

SEE ALSO: Murray, Anne; Stewart, Rod; Streisand,
Barbra; Turner, Ike and Tina / Tina Turner.

Julian "Cannonball" Adderley

BORN: Tampa, Florida; September 15, 1928
DIED: Gary, Indiana; August 8, 1975
FIRST ALBUM RELEASE: *Presenting Cannonball Adder-
    ley*, 1955
MUSICAL STYLES: Jazz, hard bop, soul jazz

Julian Edwin "Cannonball" Adderley, nearly always called simply Cannonball Adderley, was an
alto saxophonist whose technique, style, and command of his instrument delighted audiences for
over two decades. As a skillful improviser, Cannonball demonstrated an exuberance for jazz performance as well as jazz education, and his unique
ability to communicate with audiences gained
him widespread popularity and success.

The Early Years. Cannonball Adderley was
playing saxophone in Florida as early as 1942. He
formed his first jazz group while still a student in
high school, where he studied both brass and
woodwind instruments. His father played the cornet, an instrument that Cannonball's younger
brother Nat eventually mastered. After attending
Florida A&M University, Cannonball followed in
the footsteps of his father and began a career as a
high school band director at Dillard High School
in Fort Lauderdale. He taught there from September, 1948, until 1950. His teaching career was
temporarily interrupted from 1950 until 1953
while he served in the United States Army. He led
several Army bands and fronted his own combo
in Washington, D.C., while at the United States
Naval School of Music. Adderley resumed teaching in 1953, but in 1955 he went to New York City
to pursue graduate music studies at New York
University and perform with his brother Nat. Nat
had recently gained some recognition through
his relationship with Lionel Hampton. After a jam
session with Oscar Pettiford's band at the Cafe
Bohemia, Cannonball gained immediate and sensational recognition that led to a recording contract with Savoy Records.

A Star Is Born. Although some listeners and
critics hailed him as the successor to Charlie
"Bird" Parker, the legendary bop alto saxophonist
who had died in March of 1955, Adderley did not
immediately give up his teaching career for the
uncertain life of a jazz musician. Only after serious
deliberation and the success of his first recording
did he move permanently to New York. In January,
1956, Cannonball formed a quintet that featured
his brother Nat, Junior Nance on piano, and Sam
Jones on bass. While the group found some success, it was forced to disband in September, 1957,
because of economic difficulties. Cannonball had
drawn the attention of trumpeter and bandleader
Miles Davis, however; Davis first heard him play at
the Cafe Bohemia. In October of 1957 Adderley
joined the Miles Davis Quintet, replacing tenor
saxophonist Sonny Rollins, who had departed in
September. Davis had a plan to expand the quintet to a sextet by adding tenor saxophonist John
Coltrane, and in December, 1957, the pairing of
Coltrane and Adderley on saxophones with Davis
on trumpet initiated the immortal Miles Davis
Sextet. Cannonball remained in the group until

For the Record

The nickname "Cannonball" is a modified version of "cannibal," a nickname given to Adderley by his teenage friends in Florida because of his love for food and his very large appetite.

September of 1959, performing on such classic recordings as *Milestones* and *Kind of Blue*. The two-year participation in the sextet was a major period in Adderley's musical development.

The Adderley Brothers Reunited. In September, 1959, Cannonball reunited with his brother Nat to form a second quintet, including Bobby Timmons, piano, Sam Jones, bass, and Louis Haynes, drums. One month later, the quintet recorded live at San Francisco's Jazz Workshop. The band became an instant success, primarily because of its performance of Bobby Timmons's sanctified waltz, "This Here." The piece introduced listeners to what came to be called soul jazz. "This Here" was followed by Timmons's "Dat Dere" and Nat Adderley's "Work Song," and for the next sixteen years the group recorded numerous other hits and achieved considerable success. Occasionally the band changed personnel, and through the years it included pianists/composers Barry Harris, Victor Feldman, Joe Zawinul, George Duke, and Hal Galper. Jones and Haynes, the original members of the rhythm section, were to be succeeded later by Victor Gaskin and Walter Booker (bass) and Roy McCurdy (drums). The addition of saxophonists Yusef Lateef and later Charles Lloyd made the group a sextet during the 1962-1965 period, but it then returned to the quintet format.

While it was under contract with Riverside Records (1959-1963), the quintet primarily recorded and performed soul-inspired hard bop. The collapse of Riverside resulted in Adderley's signing with Capitol Records, and the group's recordings gradually became more commercial. Zawinul's 1966 big hit, "Mercy, Mercy, Mercy," followed by "Why Am I Treated So Bad?" and "Country Preacher," won the Cannonball Adderley Quintet great acclaim and popularity. These compositions and several others became big hits in a largely noncommercial field. While Adderley's knack for interpreting funky crossover pieces such as Zawinul's "Mercy, Mercy, Mercy" led to steady work and commercial success, his musical philosophy always provided opportunities for experimentation as well as more mass-oriented works. The quintet's later recordings were highlighted by the use of electronics and greater emphasis on funky elements. In his last year, Adderley became somewhat reflective, and the album *Phenix* included new versions of earlier compositions. Adderley died in a Gary, Indiana, hospital from a stroke at the age of forty-six.

Performer, Educator, and Beyond. Although Adderley's fluid style and fiery technique were reminiscent of Charlie Parker's, he initially derived his style from swing-era saxophonists Pete Brown and Benny Carter. During the 1957-1959 period when he played with Miles Davis and John Coltrane, he reached a high level of creativity. Later exploration and development especially reveal the eloquence of Davis and the adventurous intensity of Coltrane. Although his stunning technique enabled him to negotiate fast tempos, Adderley also excelled in the playing of ballads, demonstrating warm and highly melodic playing. He was a master of the blues and funk, and his huge tone and ability to bend pitches and create earthy tone colors were his trademarks. Although his approach to improvisation changed significantly while he was with Davis, Adderley always seemed to convey a sense of humor or fun. He often would double the tempo and include short melodic fragments of pop tunes in his improvised solos, and an element of surprise is often apparent in his playing. By the mid-1960's he had begun to include elements of free jazz, and in 1969 he also performed on soprano saxophone.

Adderley's personality and love for teaching played important roles in the success of his quintet. He was one of the most articulate and engaging jazz personalities, and he both entertained and educated his audiences with commentary about the music and the players. In the late 1960's the quintet presented a number of jazz clinics and seminars at high schools and colleges. In addition, Adderley served as a prominent spokesperson for jazz through numerous television productions. Adderley also was responsible for assisting in the careers of several prominent musicians. He introduced Wes Montgomery to Riverside Records, helped produce Chuck Mangione's first album, and furthered the early career of singer Nancy Wilson.

An active supporter of the arts, Adderley served on the Jazz Advisory Panel of the National Endowment for the Arts. An advocate of civil rights, he was involved in the Reverend Jesse Jackson's Operation Breadbasket and participated in the Black Expos held in Chicago. A collection of materials commemorating Adderley's life and career has been established at the Black Archives and Research Center and Museum at Florida A&M University in Tallahassee, Florida.   —*Joseph J. Estock*

SELECT DISCOGRAPHY

■ ALBUMS

Presenting Cannonball Adderley, 1955

Somethin' Else, 1958

Things Are Getting Better, 1958

Milestones, 1958 (with Miles Davis)

The Cannonball Adderley Quintet in San Francisco, 1959

Kind of Blue, 1959; reissued with corrected pitch, 1997 (with Davis)

Cannonball and Coltrane, 1959

At the Lighthouse, 1960

Mercy, Mercy, Mercy! Live at "the Club," 1966

Country Preacher, 1969

Inside Straight, 1973

The Best of Cannonball Adderley: The Capitol Years, 1991

SELECT AWARDS

Grammy Award for Best Jazz Performance, Small Group, for "Mercy, Mercy, Mercy," 1967

International Jazz Hall of Fame, inducted 1996

SEE ALSO: Coltrane, John; Davis, Miles; Parker, Charlie; Weather Report.

Aerosmith

ORIGINAL MEMBERS: Steven Tyler (b. Steven Tallarico, 1948), Joe Perry (b. 1950), Tom Hamilton (b. 1951), Joey Kramer (b. 1950), Brad Whitford (b. 1952)

OTHER MEMBERS: Jimmy Crespo, Rick Dufay

FIRST ALBUM RELEASE: *Aerosmith*, 1973

MUSICAL STYLES: Hard rock, rhythm and blues

In the 1970's, one of America's premier hard-rock bands, Aerosmith, nearly self-destructed in the excesses of that era. After personnel changes and a reteaming of the band's classic lineup, they reemerged in the 1980's to engineer a successful comeback, relying on their talent for creating memorable tunes and witty, suggestive lyrics.

The Boston Sound. Boston has presented rock music with many talented performers, but perhaps none has had the enduring appeal of Aerosmith. Although identified with that city, the members of the band actually hail from places other than Boston. Still, they encapsulated the fervor and vitality of Boston's music scene while producing sardonic, hard-driving sounds loved by audiences throughout the world. Most media attention over the years has gone to frontmen Steven Tyler (vocals, harmonica) and Joe Perry (lead guitar). Riveting performers, the team projected the inner fantasies of young people (especially teenage boys) with tongue-in-cheek humor and blistering music.

Charismatic Steven Tyler was born Steven Tallarico into a family of classically trained musicians in New York City on March 26, 1948. He became interested early in the world of professional music, although hobbies such as hunting took up more of his time. Summering at the family's resort lodge in New Hampshire, he became an accomplished outdoorsman, earning money selling animal hides he had trapped and dressed. These were far happier times than those he spent in school, where he was a lackluster student and drew the ire of classmates who taunted him about his protuberant lips.

As Tyler was turning two, his destined musical partner, Joe Perry was entering the world in

Lawrence, Massachusetts, on September 10, 1950. Like Tyler, never a stellar student, Perry tried a stint at preparatory school before quitting formal education and laboring in a low-wage factory job. His family had not encouraged his early interest in popular music, but Perry maintained his devotion. After trying to make a career change (also relocating to New Hampshire), he met future Aerosmith bassist Tom Hamilton. The pair first played together in Hamilton's band, Plastic Glass.

By the mid-1960's, Tyler, then a drummer, had already played in his first band, the Strangers. Devoted fans of the Yardbirds, they faithfully copied the hits of their British role models. After the Strangers transformed into Chain Reaction, they enjoyed the thrill of their careers, opening shows for the Yardbirds during their 1968 U.S. tour.

Plastic Glass, now called Pipe Dream and soon to be the Jam Band, was performing steadily near Sunapee, New Hampshire, when Perry and Hamilton chanced upon Tyler. He was already an impressive performer and had the cachet of a rock star, even if he was playing regularly at Murray's Clam Shack in Vermont. It took little prodding to convince Perry and Hamilton that this was the kind of singer they needed, and Tyler liked the sloppy energy of the two players. When he joined the Jam Band, he brought in another guitarist, neighborhood friend Ray Tabano.

The group moved their base to Boston, where Tabano had a day job running his own leather-goods store. It was a stroke of luck when Joey Kramer, also an old friend of Tyler and Tabano, showed up at the store. In the ensuing conversation, he revealed that he was looking for a working band, one to which he could contribute his energetic drumming style. As Tyler had decided to be a full-time singer, a drummer was definitely an asset.

In the band's infancy, the members lived in squalid conditions, playing for very small fees in equally small venues. The band was experiencing internal dissent, possibly due to the trying conditions and the pressure to succeed. As a result, Tabano left the band, although he would soon return to work for his friends, first as a road crew member, later as a marketing officer. He was re-

placed on rhythm guitar by Brad Whitford, who had been noticed by the fledgling Aerosmith during his tenure in the Boston band Justin Tyme. Whitford completed the classic Aerosmith lineup, which would be responsible for nearly all of the band's future hit records.

Making It Big. As expenses climbed, Aerosmith found itself in need of financial guidance, which came in the personage of "Father Frank" Connelly, who arranged for the group to meet managers David Krebs and Steve Leber. Now all the pieces were in place for the launching of a hard-rock legend. Leber and Krebs scoured the record companies, trying to secure a contract for Aerosmith. They succeeded when the band signed with Columbia in 1972. *Aerosmith*, the group's first album, was recorded in less than two weeks and readied for a January, 1973, release date.

Aerosmith introduced the public to a band that wrote catchy songs and performed inspired cover versions of rhythm-and-blues classics with equal verve. Its centerpiece, "Dream On," is perhaps the most definitive Aerosmith song, though at the time it reached only number 59 on the *Billboard* charts. It remains a significant offering, embodying in its lyrics an empathetic portrayal of women's angst, a surprising feature of a band identified with adolescent-male perspectives.

To promote their album, on which Columbia was spending little marketing money, Aerosmith began nearly a full year of constant touring. Honing their craft in increasingly larger venues, they also fell victim to the dangers of life on the road, developing drug habits that would hound them for the next two decades. Their 1974 release, *Get Your Wings*, was also almost ignored by their record company, but fans across the nation were starting to pay attention. In particular, the album's first single, "Same Old Song and Dance," received a great deal of radio airplay. Aerosmith was earning the reputation of a band that made party music, and the rumors of their personal excesses lent credibility to that image.

Another nonstop touring schedule took up much of the band's time in the months following the release of *Get Your Wings*. Between these concert forays, Aerosmith went into the studio at the

Record Plant, producing their breakthrough album, *Toys in the Attic* (1975). The band's improvement, both as writers and as musicians, was visible. When *Toys in the Attic* debuted in the Top 20, Aerosmith became Columbia's best-selling artists, surpassing those whose efforts were receiving better marketing campaigns. The record-buying public was casting its vote for Aerosmith.

Whether on record or onstage, Aerosmith seemed to embody a hybrid phenomenon: Tyler was constantly compared to the Rolling Stones' lead singer, Mick Jagger, whom he resembled in both looks and high-energy performance style. Musically, Aerosmith was most frequently compared to Led Zeppelin, whom the band admired, but were not attempting to copy. The fans loved these aspects of the band, even if journalists too often focused their stories about Aerosmith on these two features.

Aerosmith also resembled other rock legends in the size of the audiences they were drawing. They graduated from playing in larger halls to playing stadiums, often teaming with other rockers such as Perry's idol, British guitarist Jeff Beck. With record sales soaring and concerts selling out, the members of Aerosmith were making a great deal of money for the first time in their lives. At first excited by and unbelieving of their good luck, they soon became used to the income, the luxuries it provided, and the other benefits of fame.

Aerosmith's Joe Perry, Steve Tyler, and Joey Kramer (Paul Natkin)

However, dangerous habits were fueled by their sudden wealth, and an endless stream of drugs, fast cars, guns, and beautiful women would soon lead to the unraveling of the friendships within the band.

If Aerosmith was beginning to come apart at the seams, that did not show on the records. The group continued to turn out popular songs, although critics disdained their open intent to write and play music for teenagers. Eventually, though, the group's business decisions began to suffer from their heavy reliance on drugs, particularly heroin and alcohol. (Tyler and Perry were even known as the "Toxic Twins" for their drug habits.) In 1978, Aerosmith agreed to appear in the film *Sgt. Pepper's Lonely Hearts Club Band.* Playing the Beatles' classic "Come Together," they portrayed the evil Future Villain Band. Their version of the song was innovative, but the plot of the film was silly, and it was a commercial disaster. It took Aerosmith a long time to live down their participation in the film, and their detractors seized on the caricaturish film portrayals as further evidence that Aerosmith was not to be taken seriously. This first commercial failure was a sign of things to come. Tempers flared within the band (and between band members' spouses), and the intensity of performing and recording made the situation worse.

Coming Apart. *Night in the Ruts,* Aerosmith's 1979 album, was also its initial swan song. While the music was still good, if less inspired than earlier work, the tension between Tyler and Perry had erupted into a full-fledged feud. After a poor showing at a concert in Cleveland, a fight broke out backstage, ending with Perry's leaving the band. He almost immediately launched the Joe Perry Project, which played its first show just one month after his departure from Aerosmith.

If the former friends were fuming over the collapse of their carefully crafted band, the fans were equally dismayed. Could Aerosmith continue without Perry's searing guitar solos? Did Perry think his musicianship would stand alone without the frenetic vocals and stage presence of Tyler? Graffiti expressing the fans' surly mood soon appeared on the outer walls of the Where-

house, a studio where the band frequently rehearsed and recorded. In the press, Aerosmith and Perry took aim at each other, escalating from remarks about musical differences to petty sniping. When 1980 saw the release of the Joe Perry Project's *Let the Music Do the Talking,* it met with some critical acclaim, but little support from Aerosmith's fans.

Certain the magical chemistry remained in the mix of Tyler, Whitford, Kramer, and Hamilton, they carried on as Aerosmith, adding lead guitarist Jimmy Crespo. In 1982, this new version of Aerosmith released *Rock in a Hard Place.* In concert, they put on a decent show, and Crespo was gaining confidence as a performing guitarist, but with Whitford's departure in 1981, and the subsequent addition of Rick Dufay, the touring Aerosmith was quite a different band from the one audiences had adored. A new element of Aerosmith's live shows was the tendency of Tyler to lose consciousness onstage. Staying awake for days at a time, traveling nonstop, playing under an army of hot lights, and living on a steady supply of drugs, Tyler was nearing the breaking point.

After nearly five years, time began to heal the wounds that the warfare between Tyler and Perry had caused. They began to yearn not only for the success of the original Aerosmith but also for their lost friendship. After jamming with one another and having several conciliatory phone conversations, they decided to reunite. Fans were ecstatic, but Aerosmith's decision to start fresh with new management threatened to stifle their plans to record and tour.

Rising from the Ashes. Lawsuits pending, the band went on the road again. They were on shaky ground professionally, hoping for a new record deal with a new company. They signed with Geffen Records in 1985, the year that saw the release of a comeback album, *Done with Mirrors.* It failed to earn the sales figures for which Aerosmith had hoped, but it forced the band to reassess their future. If they were going to climb to the top again, it would have to be on the strength of their tried-and-true rock formula, and it would require that they stop their drug and alcohol abuse.

In 1986, Tyler started the first of his several attempts at drug rehabilitation. As he did, the other members of Aerosmith congratulated themselves on not having habits as excessive as Tyler's, habits they were certain were under control. Although Perry agreed to undergo a treatment program, Whitford, Kramer, and Hamilton were not yet ready. Aerosmith was beginning to appeal to a whole new audience, young fans of rap music, spurred on by their teaming with rappers Run-D.M.C. on a remake of "Walk This Way." If they could just free themselves of their drug problems, new success awaited them.

Rehabilitation. Although plagued by relapses, the members of Aerosmith did eventually beat their drug demons. On subsequent tours, they employed the services of tour managers who specialized in working with bands recovering from addictions. Backstage areas were kept free of temptation, and close watch was kept on band members' room service orders to prevent liquor consumption. Even if they could have preached to other bands about the pitfalls of addiction, they chose instead to lead by example. For a band whose image was so tied up in years of excess, the new, drug-free Aerosmith was a force to be reckoned with musically.

From 1989's *Pump* (and the disturbingly sad tale of child sexual abuse and murder, "Janie's Got a Gun") to such hits as "Dude (Looks Like a Lady)" and "Love in an Elevator" on 1994's compilation *Big Ones* to the frantic riffs of 1997's *Nine Lives* (especially the title track), Aerosmith proved they had recaptured their mantle as America's quintessential hard-rock band. Perhaps more important, they regained their health, their friendship, and the enjoyment their music had always brought to them. —*Cynthia R. Kasee*

SELECT DISCOGRAPHY
■ ALBUMS
Aerosmith, 1973
Toys in the Attic, 1975
Aerosmith's Greatest Hits, 1980 (compilation)
Rock in a Hard Place, 1982
Permanent Vacation, 1987
Get a Grip, 1993

Nine Lives, 1997
A Little South of Sanity, 1998

SELECT AWARDS
Grammy Award for Best Rock Performance by a Duo or Group with Vocal for "Janie's Got a Gun," 1990
Grammy Award for Best Rock Performance by a Duo or Group with Vocal for "Livin' on the Edge," 1993
Grammy Award for Best Rock Performance by a Duo or Group with Vocal for "Crazy," 1994

SEE ALSO: Led Zeppelin, Rolling Stones, The; Yardbirds, The.

Air Supply

ORIGINAL MEMBERS: Russell Hitchcock (b. 1949), Graham Russell (b. 1950)
OTHER MEMBERS: Frank Esler-Smith (b. 1948), Ralph Cooper (b. 1951), David Green (b. 1949), David Moyse (b. 1957), Rex Goh (b. 1951), others
FIRST ALBUM RELEASE: *Air Supply*, 1976
MUSICAL STYLES: Rock and roll, pop

The Australian-based group Air Supply was one of the most successful pop groups of the 1980's, selling over fifteen million records. Their light pop-rock hits earned Air Supply several platinum albums and gold singles worldwide.

How It Started. In April, 1975, Russell Hitchcock from Australia and Graham Russell from England met in Sydney, Australia, as cast members in the stage production of *Jesus Christ Superstar*. Over the next year, a close friendship evolved between Hitchcock and Russell, and they began performing at local pubs in Sydney. With Russell writing the songs and playing guitar and Hitchcock singing lead, they released their first album, *Air Supply*, in 1976. In 1977, Frank Esler-Smith (keyboards), Ralph Cooper (drums), David Green (bass), and David Moyse (lead guitar) joined Hitchcock and Russell. Known as Air Supply, the sextet released *Love and Other Bruises* in 1977, and the title song became a big hit in Australia.

With increasing popularity, Air Supply was invited to tour the United States and Canada in 1977 as an opening act for Rod Stewart. This opportunity exposed them to a massive new audience who were very receptive to their style of soft rock. *Life Support*, recorded in 1978 and released in 1979, contained Air Supply's first big hit, "Lost in Love," which rose to the number 1 spot on the Australian pop charts.

Gold and Platinum. After Air Supply signed with Arista Records in 1980, their single "Lost in Love" rose to number 3 on U.S. charts. In 1981, "Every Woman in the World" reached number 5 and "All Out of Love" rose to number 2 in the United States, while *Lost in Love* became their first platinum album. In 1981, *The One That You Love* claimed the number 2 spot on the U.S. album charts, becoming certified platinum, and the title song became Air Supply's first number 1 hit in the United States.

In 1982, "Even the Nights Are Better" reached number 5 on the U.S. charts, and "Making Love Out of Nothing at All" peaked at number 2 in 1983. *Now and Forever* (1982) became Air Supply's third album to reach platinum sales, and the *Greatest Hits* album released in 1983 gained quadruple platinum status in the United States. Air Supply released *Making Love* (1983) in the United Kingdom, establishing a link with more fans throughout the world. However, the music industry reached a turning point in the mid-1980's when romantic love songs waned in popularity, and Air Supply's last Top-20 hit was "Power of Love" in 1985. In 1988, Air Supply disbanded. Hitchcock ventured out on his own but released only one single, "Swear to Your Heart" (1988).

Together Again. In 1991, Hitchcock, Russell, and Cooper reunited to re-form Air Supply. Although their album *The Earth Is* (1991) failed to make the U.S. charts, it went gold in more than twenty other countries, and the single "Without You" was an international hit. Concentrating their efforts outside the United States, Air Supply's popularity continued to increase overseas. In 1993, "It's Never Too Late" and "Goodbye" both became platinum sellers in international markets.

Air Supply's 1995 album *News from Nowhere* contained an international hit with "Someone," and *Now and Forever: Greatest Hits Live* (1995) yielded another hit with "The Way I Feel." In the late 1990's, Air Supply continued to conduct a demanding worldwide tour schedule. The album *The Book of Love* was released in late 1997.

—*Alvin K. Benson*

SELECT DISCOGRAPHY
■ SINGLES
"Lost in Love," 1979
"Every Woman in the World," 1980
"All Out of Love," 1981
"Sweet Dreams," 1982
"Even the Nights Are Better," 1982
"Young Love," 1982
"Two Less Lonely People in the World," 1983
"Making Love Out of Nothing at All," 1983
"Power of Love," 1985
■ ALBUMS
Air Supply, 1976
Love and Other Bruises, 1977
The One That You Love, 1981
Greatest Hits, 1983
The Earth Is, 1991
Vanishing Race, 1993
Now and Forever: Greatest Hits Live, 1995

SELECT AWARDS
Best International Music Award, for "The One That You Love," 1982
Best International Music Award, for "Making Love Out of Nothing at All," 1983

SEE ALSO: Newton-John, Olivia; Reddy, Helen; Stewart, Rod.

For the Record

A sixteen-piece string section accompanied Air Supply in making *Now and Forever: Greatest Hits Live*, and the entire album was recorded live at a concert in Taipei, Taiwan, on Air Supply's Asian tour in 1995.

Alabama

ORIGINAL MEMBERS: Randy Owen (b. 1949), Jeff
    Cook (b. 1949), Teddy Gentry (b. 1952)
OTHER MEMBERS: Mark Herndon (b. 1955), others
FIRST ALBUM RELEASE: *My Home's in Alabama*, 1980
MUSICAL STYLES: Country, pop

Very few bands, as opposed to solo performers, have been successful on the country charts, but in the early 1980's, Alabama had a string of big country hits and sold in excess of 45 million albums. They won the Academy of Country Music's Artist of the Decade title for the 1980's and became the first band to be named the Country Music Association's Entertainer of the Year, changing forever the way bands were accepted in the country format.

Cousins Band Together. Having played music together since they were children, cousins Randy Owen (vocals and guitar), Jeff Cook (vocals and guitar), and Teddy Gentry (bass, vocals, and drums) formed a group in their hometown of Fort Payne, Alabama, in 1969, calling themselves Young Country. Their first paid performance was at Canyonland amusement park in Alabama in July, 1972. Their first break came in 1973, when they began performing at the Bowery Club in Myrtle Beach, South Carolina. During the early 1970's, they recorded for several small record labels before changing their name to Alabama in 1977, when they recorded a moderately successful single, "I Want to Be with You." When they sought to sign with a major label in Nashville, Tennessee, everyone turned them down.

In 1979, "I Wanna Come Over" made the country singles Top 40, and Mark Herndon joined the group as the regular drummer. In early 1980, "My Home's in Alabama" reached the Top 20, and later that year, RCA Records signed them to a recording contract. *Cashbox* magazine named Alabama the New Vocal Group of the Year in 1980.

Twenty-one Straight, Then More. Alabama's first number 1 hit, "Tennessee River," was released

Alabama (Frank Driggs Collection/Archive Photos)

For the Record

Alabama's Owen, Cook, and Gentry were all born in Fort Payne, Alabama, the "sock capital of the world." During their early years, all three worked at one or more of the one hundred sock mills in their home county.

in May, 1980, and their next twenty singles each reached the number 1 spot on the country charts, making twenty-one in a row. Included in this series were "Old Flame" (1981), "Love in the First Degree" (1981), "Mountain Music" (1981), "Close Enough to Be Perfect" (1982), "Dixieland Delight" (1983), "The Closer You Get" (1983), "When We Make Love" (1984), and "Can't Keep a Good Man Down" (1985). After their Top-10 hit "Tar Top" (1987) broke the number 1 streak, twelve of Alabama's next thirteen singles again rose to the number 1 spot on the country charts.

Alabama's first album, *My Home's in Alabama* (1980), eventually went double platinum, and their second album, *Feels So Right* (1981), gained quadruple platinum sales, as did their third album, *Mountain Music* (1982). Beginning in 1982, Alabama won the Country Music Association's Entertainer of the Year Award for three consecutive years; in 1983, they won a Grammy Award for *Mountain Music*. In the mid-1980's, Alabama issued several albums that all became certified platinum, including *Roll On* (1984), *40 Hr. Week* (1985), *Alabama Christmas* (1985), *Alabama Greatest Hits* (1986), and *The Touch* (1986). In addition to producing hit after hit, Alabama toured extensively and gained a great deal of television exposure, including appearances on Johnny Carson's *The Tonight Show* and *The Merv Griffin Show*.

More Awards and Continued Popularity. During the last part of the 1980's, Alabama's sales began to decline, only achieving gold rather than platinum status. In 1990, "Juke Box" was number 1 for two weeks, and "Down Home," "Here We Are," and "Then Again" each topped the country charts during 1991. During 1992 and 1993, all six singles released made number 1 or number 2 on the major country charts. Through the late 1990's, Alabama had earned fourteen Academy of Country Music awards, seven Country Music Association awards, and fifteen American Music awards. Alabama also spent much time in humanitarian efforts, raising money for charities and promoting environmental issues. —*Alvin K. Benson*

SELECT DISCOGRAPHY
■ SINGLES
"Tennessee River," 1980
"If You're Gonna Play in Texas," 1984
"40 Hr. Week," 1985
"Forever's as Far as I'll Go," 1990
"Down Home," 1991
"Reckless," 1993
"Angels Among Us," 1994
■ ALBUMS
Feels So Right, 1981
Mountain Music, 1982
The Closer You Get, 1983
Alabama Greatest Hits, 1986
Alabama Greatest Hits II, 1991
Dancin' on the Boulevard, 1997
For the Record, 1998 (compilation)

SELECT AWARDS
Academy of Country Music Vocal Group of the Year Award, 1980, 1981, 1982, 1983, 1984, and 1985
Country Music Association Vocal Group of the Year Award, 1981, 1982, and 1983
Academy of Country Music Entertainer of the Year Award, 1981, 1982, 1983, 1984, and 1985
Grammy Award for Best Country Performance by a Duo or Group with Vocal, for *Mountain Music*, 1982
Country Music Association Entertainer of the Year Award, 1982, 1983, and 1984
Grammy Award for Best Country Performance by a Duo or Group with Vocal, for *The Closer You Get*, 1983
Academy of Country Music Artist of the Decade (1980's), 1989

SEE ALSO: Haggard, Merle; Jones, George.

Alice in Chains

ORIGINAL MEMBERS: Layne Staley (b. 1967), Jerry Cantrell (b. 1966), Sean Kinney (b. 1966), Mike Starr (b. 1966)
OTHER MEMBERS: Mike Inez (b. 1966)
FIRST ALBUM RELEASE: *Facelift*, 1990
MUSICAL STYLES: Alternative, grunge, hard rock, heavy metal

Although it was the first Seattle, Washington, band of the 1990's to achieve commercial success, Alice in Chains was at first rather detached from the Seattle grunge scene, initially seen as more of a heavy-metal band. In time, the band would become more closely aligned with the Seattle sound. Like other Seattle bands, it favored a dark, rich sound, creating music that seemed to revel in the seamier side of life. The band's dark image was compounded by lead singer Layne Staley's much publicized, prolonged bout with heroin addiction, which continually put the band's future in jeopardy.

Beginnings and Early Success. Staley began the band in the mid-1980's, while still in high school, as Alice 'n' Chains. In 1987, Staley met guitarist Jerry Cantrell, who eventually brought his friends Mike Starr (bass) and Sean Kinney (drums) into the band. Upon Cantrell's joining, the band changed its name to Alice in Chains and began playing Seattle clubs.

Commonly, the Seattle music experience involved a band releasing music on small, independent, often locally distributed labels before, if ever, moving to larger national labels. Alice in Chains challenged this practice when, in 1989, it signed its first record deal with the major label Columbia Records. A 1990 promotional extended-play single, *We Die Young*, yielded success, with the title track becoming a heavy-metal hit. That summer, the band released its debut album,

Alice in Chains: Mike Inez, Sean Kinney (rear), Layne Staley, Jerry Cantrell (Columbia/Danny Clinch)

Facelift, which went gold by the end of the year. A follow-up extended-play single, *Sap* (1991), was also well received.

The Age of Grunge. After Nirvana's single "Smells Like Teen Spirit" became a hit in late 1991, the Seattle music scene exploded into the mainstream. As a result, Alice in Chains was thought of as a Seattle grunge band. The band's second album, *Dirt* (1992), was released to positive reviews and commercial success. The album displayed the increasingly dark vision of the band, particularly of Staley, whose lyrics outlined his battles with heroin addiction. Shortly after the album's release, Starr left the band and was replaced by Mike Inez. In the summer of 1993, the band toured as part of the alternative music package tour Lollapalooza.

Near the Edge. The band's 1994 acoustic-flavored extended-play single *Jar of Flies* debuted at number 1, becoming the first extended-play single ever to reach the top of the charts, yielding the successful singles "No Excuses" and "I Stay Away." Despite its increasing success, these were troubled times for Alice in Chains. Staley was still battling his heroin problem, and his addiction was beginning to tear the band apart. Additionally, Kinney was dealing with an alcohol problem, and mediocre rehearsals for a 1994 tour with Metallica caused Alice in Chains to be dropped from the ticket, putting the band's future in question.

In January of 1995, Cantrell, Kinney, and Inez began working on material Cantrell had written for a solo project. Four months later, they decided to invite Staley to the sessions. The results were released later that year as *Alice in Chains*, as if to prove that the band was indeed alive and well. Despite another commercial success (the album debuted at number 1 on the charts), it soon became clear that the band was still plagued by troubles. A February, 1996, cover story on the band in *Rolling Stone* magazine hinted that Staley was still struggling with his drug addiction. As with *Jar of Flies*, the band did not tour to promote the new album, which led many to conclude that a band breakup was inevitable.

Alice in Chains did manage to tape an acoustic live performance for the successful MTV program *Unplugged* in 1996. Following in the tradition of Nirvana, Eric Clapton, and many others, the band released their *Unplugged* performance as an album in the summer of 1996. Despite its success, the rumors of the end of the band persisted. Cantrell's solo album *Boggy Depot* (1998), which featured Kinney and Inez, seemed to confirm Alice in Chains' seemingly inevitable demise.

—Michael Pelusi

SELECT DISCOGRAPHY
■ ALBUMS
Facelift, 1990
Dirt, 1992
Alice in Chains, 1995
Unplugged, 1996

SEE ALSO: Nirvana; Pearl Jam; Soundgarden.

The Allman Brothers Band

ORIGINAL MEMBERS: Duane Allman (1946-1971), Gregg Allman (b. 1947), Dickey Betts (b. 1943), Jai Johanny Johanson (b. 1944), Berry Oakley (1948-1972), Butch Trucks (b. 1947)
OTHER MEMBERS: Chuck Leavell (b. 1952), Lamar Williams (1947-1983), Warren Haynes, Allen Woody
FIRST ALBUM RELEASE: *The Allman Brothers Band*, 1969
MUSICAL STYLES: Southern rock, rock and roll, blues

The Allman Brothers Band was among the first American supergroups of the post-Beatles era. Formed in 1969 by guitarist Duane Allman, the original sextet became popular on the strength of albums and live concerts. With its jam-oriented melding of country, blues, soul, and jazz, and a distinctive sound resulting from the combination of two drumsets, twin lead guitars, and earthy vocals, the Allman Brothers Band established most of the standards of the southern-rock style. In 1973, following its first hit single, "Ramblin' Man," and a number 1 album, *Brothers and Sisters*, the Allman Brothers Band became one of the first American bands to make an outdoor-stadium tour of the United States. After experiencing dissension and a decline in popularity in the mid-1970's, the group disbanded for a time but enjoyed re-

For the Record

In addition to contributing to the sound track of the 1992 film set in Seattle, *Singles*, Alice in Chains performed in the film, as did the Seattle band Soundgarden. Members of Pearl Jam had acting roles in the film as Matt Dillon's band.

newed success with a reunion in 1989 and since has continued to tour and record together, developing new material of high quality.

Beginnings. Duane and Gregg Allman were the sons of a widowed mother who moved from Nashville to Daytona Beach, Florida, in 1959. Both took up the guitar, and in 1965 they formed a rhythm-and-blues quartet called the Allman Joys. The brothers made their first single with this group, a modest-selling cover of Willie Dixon's "Spoonful." Eventually the Allmans migrated to Los Angeles, where they recorded two albums with the studio group Hourglass, but a dispute over use of original material resulted in a return to Florida.

Occasional work with regional bands put the brothers in contact with drummer Butch Trucks, guitarist Dickey Betts, and bassist Berry Oakley. In 1968, Duane Allman was hired to play lead guitar for a Wilson Pickett recording session at Fame Studios in Muscle Shoals, Alabama. He quickly became Fame's primary guitarist, and over the next year he recorded with Percy Sledge, Aretha Franklin, and King Curtis. At Fame, Duane met Jai Johanny Johanson, a drummer with a strong rhythm-and-blues background and a taste for jazz.

The arresting quality of Duane Allman's session work secured for him a solo contract with Phil Walden's new company, Capricorn Records, and he and Johanson went to Florida to assemble a band. In March, 1969, Allman hired Trucks, Betts, and Oakley, and, with the vital addition on organ

For the Record

After overcoming a drinking problem during the mid-1980's, Greg Allman stated to *Los Angeles Times* writer Robert Hilburn that though he had gone through a difficult time, he preferred to look back on the good times. "There's a great comfort in the music itself," he added. "It helps you get through the darkest times. I hope on my death bed I'm learning a new chord or writing a new song."

and vocals of younger brother Gregg Allman (who had been pursuing a solo effort back in Los Angeles), the new Allman Brothers Band moved to Macon, Georgia, to record its debut album in Walden's studio.

Success. The self-titled first album won excellent reviews but sold well only in the South. Duane Allman continued his session work during this time, most notably appearing as a slide guitarist with Eric Clapton on the Derek and the Dominos classic, *Layla* (1970). The Allman Brothers Band meanwhile established itself as a popular live attraction, and its second album, *Idlewild South* (1970), became a hit. That was followed by a live double album, *At Fillmore East* (1971), a masterful concert recording that for the first time captured the depth of the group's ability and emotional power in a number of extended jams. Guitarists Betts and Duane Allman both reached exceptional heights in long improvisations on such cuts as "Whipping Post" and "In Memory of Elizabeth Reed." *At Fillmore East* made the *Billboard* Top 10 and compelled *Rolling Stone* to hail the Allmans as "America's best rock and roll group." Within months of this peak, however, the band suffered a serious setback when its musical leader, Duane Allman, was killed in a motorcycle accident in Macon.

The remaining quintet mixed new material with more Fillmore tapes to complete another excellent double album, *Eat a Peach* (1972). Pianist Chuck Leavell joined the band, adding a jazzy, mellower sound, and the Allman Brothers began work on a new album under the leadership of Betts. Momentum sagged in November, 1972, when Oakley, whose driving bass generated much of the group's energy, was killed in another motorcycle accident, a collision with a Macon city bus. He was soon replaced by Lamar Williams, a friend of Johanson.

Upheaval. On the strength of *Brothers and Sisters* (1973) and a rerelease of their first two albums under the title *Beginnings* (1974), the Allman Brothers Band spent 1973 on top of the pop music charts, but fortunes declined by 1975 as dissension developed and musical direction was lost. Betts and Gregg Allman pursued solo projects,

The Allman Brothers Band in 1981: Mike Lawler, Dave Goldflies, Greg Allman, Butch Trucks, Dickey Betts, Dan Toler, Dav Toler (AP/Wide World Photos)

and Leavell formed a jazz fusion group, Sea Level, with Johanson and Williams. In 1976 the band split following a notorious drug trial in which Allman, who was in the middle of a stormy marriage to Cher, testified against a former member of the band's road crew. There were several reunions and breakups over the next few years. Although new albums continued to appear, the quality of the music was decidedly uneven.

The high point of this period was the 1979 album *Enlightened Rogues*, the lineup for which included Allman, Betts, and Trucks. It went gold within weeks of release and made it to number 9 on the charts. Such moments of success were rare, however, and the group disbanded completely in 1982. The remainder of the 1980's saw the death

of Williams due to cancer (1983), the retirement of Trucks from music, a return to nightclub gigs for Johanson, separate recordings and tours for Allman and Betts, and the emergence of Leavell as keyboardist for the Rolling Stones.

Trouble No More. Following the lead of several classic bands, the four original members organized a successful comeback tour in 1989. With sympathetic newcomers Allen Woody (bass) and Warren Haynes (guitar and vocals), the Allman Brothers Band recovered the sound and emotional drive of its earliest days. Since 1990 the personnel have remained together and released a number of excellent albums, usually featuring the distinctive compositions of Betts. The virtuosic interplay of Haynes and Betts recalls and extends the foundations laid by Duane Allman, and the unique percussion combination is as supple as ever.

Over the course of its history the Allman Brothers Band has achieved legendary status among musicians and audiences interested in southern rock. Its legacy includes numerous successful acts, such as Lynyrd Skynyrd, the Dixie Dregs, and .38 Special, as well as countless regional bands. Moreover, the 1990's incarnation has introduced the classic Allman sound to a second generation, all the while maintaining a focus on the creation of innovative new music.   *—Charles Kinzer*

SELECT DISCOGRAPHY

■ ALBUMS

The Allman Brothers Band, 1969
Idlewild South, 1970
At Fillmore East, 1971
Eat a Peach, 1972
Brothers and Sisters, 1973
Enlightened Rogues, 1979
Seven Turns, 1990
Shades of Two Worlds, 1991

SELECT AWARDS

Billboard Trendsetter Award, 1973
Rolling Stone, named Band of the Year, 1973
Rock and Roll Hall of Fame, inducted 1995

SEE ALSO: Clapton, Eric; Daniels, Charlie; Dixon, Willie; Pickett, Wilson.

Herb Alpert

BORN: Los Angeles, California; March 31, 1935
FIRST ALBUM RELEASE: *The Lonely Bull*, 1962 (with the Tijuana Brass)
MUSICAL STYLES: Latin, jazz, easy listening

Herb Alpert has had one of the most productive, most successful, and longest careers in pop music. He cofounded a successful record label, made thirteen gold records with his band, the Tijuana Brass, and went on to release a number of solo albums.

The Tijuana Brass. Herb Alpert began writing songs and recording music in the late 1950's.

Looking for a musical outlet, he cofounded A&M Records with Jerry Moss in 1962. Alpert recorded the company's first single in his garage in 1962. The song was titled "The Lonely Bull," by the Tijuana Brass featuring Herb Alpert. From these modest beginnings, A&M would eventually become the largest independently owned record company in the world.

An even greater success story was beginning for the Tijuana Brass. "The Lonely Bull" was a hit, quickly selling more than 700,000 copies, and the album of the same name enjoyed brisk sales. Although the group of musicians backing up Alpert's trumpet were called the Tijuana Brass, they were primarily session musicians assembled in the recording studio. Still, the name had a certain prestige and an identifiable sound that took popular songs, arranged them as brassy instrumentals, and infused them with Latin musical flavor. The Tijuana Brass's next two albums (released in 1963 and 1964) did not sell especially well, but the Tijuana Brass sound was becoming noticeable in theme songs for television shows (including *The Dating Game*) and as background music on a television commercial.

With his own record company, Herb Alpert had a decided advantage over other new recording artists. Despite sluggish sales of his second and third albums, Alpert continued to work on new Tijuana Brass arrangements and recordings. Alpert did not write much of the music played by the Tijuana Brass. Instead, he was a consummate arranger who took contemporary pop songs, show tunes, old standards, and various other forms of music and arranged them as instrumentals for himself on trumpet, backed by the Tijuana Brass. With his fourth album, *Whipped Cream and Other Delights* (1965), this musical formula suddenly arrested the public's attention. All at once, Herb Alpert and the Tijuana Brass became the most popular act in pop music. They would remain preeminent for the rest of the decade.

The Tijuana Brass's popularity in the 1960's was staggering. *Whipped Cream and Other Delights* remained in the Top 10 from July, 1965, to March, 1967. With the release of *!!Going Places!!* in 1965, the Tijuana Brass had five albums in the Top 20

For the Record

"In my elementary school there was a music room loaded with different instruments. A student could just pick the instrument of his or her choice and try to make some noise with it. I picked up the trumpet—couldn't make a sound with it, but I liked the way it felt. I was kind of a shy person . . . and I liked the idea that you could make a lot of noise with the trumpet." —*Herb Alpert*

simultaneously. The next year the group had four albums in the Top 10 simultaneously—the first and only group to achieve this distinction. Herb Alpert and the Tijuana Brass not only dominated the radio but even appeared on their own television specials. For the rest of the decade they would release at least one, and sometimes two, albums each year.

Herb Alpert and the Tijuana Brass had attained celebrity status. Numerous touring engagements were booked, and Alpert hastily assembled a proper (though occasionally changing) band of musicians for live performances. The Tijuana Brass even performed for President Lyndon Johnson and Mexican President Gustavo Díaz Ordaz at the White House in 1967. "This Guy's in Love with You," a vocal arrangement, shot to number 1 in 1968, and the song became synonymous with Herb Alpert. Overall, Herb Alpert and the Tijuana Brass had the fourth largest album of the 1960's, surpassed only by Elvis Presley, the Beatles, and Frank Sinatra.

Dissolution and Reunions. The Tijuana Brass was a 1960's phenomenon. The group was disbanded in 1969 after the release of *The Brass Are Comin'* (although Brass compilation albums would continue to be released in the early 1970's). Alpert wanted to try other pursuits, and the public adoration of the Tijuana Brass was beginning to dissipate. Alpert concentrated on discovering and promoting new artists through A&M. Alpert

and Moss had some notable successes in this regard, including Joe Cocker, Carole King, Cat Stevens, the Carpenters, Rita Coolidge, the Police, Joe Jackson, Janet Jackson, and Suzanne Vega. In the mid-1970's Alpert assembled a new Tijuana Brass (with a few alumni) and released two albums, but these were not well received. The Tijuana Brass's magic was lacking, owing partly to Alpert's move toward jazz, partly to the band's new personnel, and partly to the passing of the era in which the Tijuana Brass had been rooted. The group was again disbanded, and aside from a second reunion in 1984 (which yielded the disappointing *Bullish*), Herb Alpert turned to solo efforts.

Later Recordings. Herb Alpert continued to perform, record music, and produce records after the Tijuana Brass had disbanded. He enjoyed some renewed public attention and a Grammy Award with his hit single "Rise" in 1979. That track, along with the others on his album of the same name, emphasized Alpert's newfound focus on jazz. The disco flavor of "Rise" was perhaps inevitable given the era, but this stylistic influence would diminish as the 1980's wore on. Alpert became increasingly involved in jazz in the late 1980's and the 1990's. He recorded *Midnight Sun* (1992) in memory of his late friend, jazz saxophonist Stan Getz. He also endowed three fellowships for jazz education in high schools. His 1997 release, *Passion Dance*, marked Alpert's return to Latin musical influences.

In 1990 Alpert and Jerry Moss sold A&M to Polygram for about one-half billion dollars. The two subsequently formed a new label called Almo Sounds. Once again Alpert had a guaranteed outlet for his music. He maintained a respectable presence on the contemporary jazz charts.

—*Steve D. Boilard*

SELECT DISCOGRAPHY
■ SINGLES
"The Lonely Bull," 1962
"A Taste of Honey," 1965
"Tijuana Taxi," 1966
"Spanish Flea," 1966
"The Work Song," 1966

■ ALBUMS

Herb Alpert and the Tijuana Brass

The Lonely Bull, 1962

Herb Alpert's Tijuana Brass, Volume 2, 1963

South of the Border, 1964

Whipped Cream and Other Delights, 1965

!!Going Places!!, 1965

What Now My Love, 1966

SRO, 1966

Sounds Like . . . , 1967

Herb Alpert's Ninth, 1967

The Beat of the Brass, 1968

The Herb Alpert and the Tijuana Brass Christmas Album, 1968

Warm, 1969

The Brass Are Comin', 1969

Summertime, 1971

You Smile—The Song Begins, 1974

Coney Island, 1975

Bullish, 1984

Classics Volume 1, 1987 (compilation)

Herb Alpert solo

Just You and Me, 1976

Rise, 1979

Midnight Sun, 1992

Passion Dance, 1997

SELECT AWARDS

Grammy Awards for Record of the Year, Best Instrumental Performance, Non-Jazz, and Best Instrumental Arrangement for "A Taste of Honey," 1965

Grammy Awards for Best Instrumental Performance, Non-Jazz, and Best Instrumental Arrangement for "What Now My Love," 1966

Grammy Award for Best Pop Instrumental Performance for "Rise," 1979

Billboard Lifetime Achievement Award for Latin Music, 1997

SEE ALSO: Captain and Tennille; Carpenters, The; Mendes, Sergio.

America

ORIGINAL MEMBERS: Dewey Bunnell (b. 1952), Dan Peek (b. 1950), Gerry Beckley (b. 1952)

FIRST ALBUM RELEASE: *America*, 1972

MUSICAL STYLES: Pop, rock

The sons of U.S. servicemen stationed in the United Kingdom, the members of America named themselves after their distant homeland. Inspired by the acoustic rock of Crosby, Stills, and Nash, the band went straight to the top of the charts with their debut single, "A Horse with No Name." More hits followed, among them "Ventura Highway," "Tin Man," and "Sister Golden Hair." The group continued as a duo after the departure of Dan Peek in 1976 but failed to achieve further success until the early 1980's, when "You Can Do Magic" and "The Border" hit the Top 40.

Made in England. Spending their high school years in England, where their fathers were stationed as U.S. Air Force officers, Dewey Bunnell, Dan Peek, and Gerry Beckley were drawn together by their love of music as well as a mutual longing for home. After high school they formed an acoustic folk-rock band called Daze in London, which toured small clubs in England under the promotion of Jeff Dexter. By 1971 the band had changed its name to America and won a recording contract with Warner Bros. Unable to decide which of the songs on the album to release as a single, however, the group returned to the studio and added one more: "A Horse with No Name."

The song, written by Bunnell in a style reminiscent of Neil Young, featured surrealistic lyrics with a fairly obscure environmentalist message. It was an immediate success in the United Kingdom, carrying America's self-titled album to number 14 on the British charts and paving the way for a U.S. release the following spring. The band was on a U.S. concert tour, opening for the Everly Brothers, when "A Horse with No Name" became a number 1 hit in the United States, knocking Neil Young's "Heart of Gold" off the top of the charts.

Best New Artist. The band quickly proved that they were not going to be a one-hit wonder when their next single, Beckley's more conventional love ballad, "I Need You," became a Top-10 hit later that summer. Beatles producer George Martin agreed to collaborate on their next album, appropriately titled *Homecoming* (1972), which led to their third straight Top-10 single, "Ventura Highway." It was no great surprise when America was awarded the Grammy Award for Best New Artist of 1972.

America named their next album *Hat Trick* (1973) but failed to score one after the success of their last two albums. *Holiday* (1974) returned them to the top of the charts, however, with the singles "Tin Man" and "Lonely People." In the former, Bunnell repeats the lyrical surrealism of the group's first hit, while in the latter, Peek addresses the theme of personal isolation in more straightforward language. In 1975 their fifth album, *Hearts*, produced the number 1 single "Sister Golden Hair." That same year America released their greatest-hits album, *History: America's Greatest Hits*, which eventually sold over four million copies.

Hideaway, featuring Beckley's "Watership Down" in honor of the 1972 Richard Adams novel, was one of the last albums America released as a trio. Peek left the group in 1977 to pursue a career as a contemporary Christian musician. Bunnell

For the Record

America's third album, *Hat Trick*, included the band's recording of "Muskrat Love"; with the addition of some animal sound effects, it was a big hit for the Captain and Tennille.

§

Several of America's album covers, including those for *Harbor*, *Hideaway*, and *Silent Letter*, were designed by future *Saturday Night Live* comic and *NewsRadio* star Phil Hartman.

and Beckley continued to record and perform as America, producing such listenable albums as *Silent Letter* (1979), with Beckley's enchanting love song "All My Life." They also recorded the sound track for the animated film *The Last Unicorn*, but it was not until the 1980's that the pair repeated the group's earlier success with the hits "You Can Do Magic" and "The Border." —*Ed McKnight*

America (Archive Photos)

SELECT DISCOGRAPHY
■ ALBUMS
America, 1972
Homecoming, 1972
Hat Trick, 1973
Hearts, 1975
History: America's Greatest Hits, 1975 (compilation)
America Live, 1977
Silent Letter, 1979
Alibi, 1980
Live at Central Park, 1981
Perspective, 1984
America in Concert, 1985
Encore: More Greatest Hits, 1991 (compilation)
Hourglass, 1994
Human Nature, 1998

SELECT AWARDS
Grammy Award for Best New Artist, 1972

SEE ALSO: Beatles, The; Captain and Tennille; Crosby, Stills, Nash, and Young; Young, Neil.

Tori Amos

(Myra Ellen Amos)

BORN: Newton, North Carolina; August 22, 1963
FIRST ALBUM RELEASE: *Little Earthquakes*, 1992
MUSICAL STYLES: Pop, alternative, grunge

Myra Ellen Amos grew up in the Baltimore, Maryland, area, the third child of Dr. Edison Amos, a Methodist minister, and Mary Ellen Amos. Her mother's father was a well-known Cherokee Indian singer who significantly influenced Amos's music. Both of her father's parents were Methodist ministers. This religious background had a great influence on Amos.

A Girl and Her Piano. At the age of two, Amos, called Ellen by her family, first began to play the piano. She learned to play music by ear while her brother and sister practiced the piano. Soon she was playing classical, pop, and many other musical pieces. She showed such promise that, at the age of five, her father had her audition for the prestigious Peabody Conservatory at the Johns Hopkins University in Baltimore.

In 1968, Amos was admitted to the Peabody Conservatory as the youngest student the institute had ever accepted. She attended Peabody every Saturday, on a scholarship, from 1968 to 1974. There she learned how to read music and play the classical repertoire. She showed an enthusiasm for interpreting the classics in her own style, much to her teacher's dismay. When she was eleven, her annual scholarship to Peabody was not renewed. The following years were hard for Amos, as she bore the burden of being a failed child prodigy. She continued playing the piano and even auditioned for Peabody again, only to be rejected. She gave up her ambition to be a concert pianist and decided to become a rock star.

Her father, interested in supporting Amos's talents, suggested that she take a job playing the piano. In the summer of 1977, Amos began playing at Mr. Henry's, a gay bar in Georgetown, Maryland. She played occasionally for tips while her father chaperoned. Later that year, she played at Mr. Smith's. She continued playing at bars throughout high school, as well as playing at weddings and banquets. During the summer of 1981, she was hired by the Hilton hotel of Myrtle Beach, South Carolina, as its main entertainer. From 1981 to 1983 she played in such places as the Cellar Door and the Lion's Gate Taverne in Washington, D.C. Amos mostly played cover songs at these clubs and practiced her original music when she had a chance. It was during these years that she adopted the name Tori.

For the Record

Tori Amos is considered a bit eccentric. She has said of herself, "I'm too wacky for most weirdos." About her song "Cornflake Girl," she has commented, "I would like to think that I'm a raisin girl, because in my mind they're more open-minded. Cornflake girls are totally self-centered." On music: "The music is the magic carpet that other things take naps on."

Tori Amos (Ken Settle)

Trying to Be a Rock Star. In September, 1984, Amos moved to Los Angeles to start a band and to seek stardom as a singer. She has affectionately called this period in her life the "rock-chick phase." Within three weeks of moving to Los Angeles she had assembled a three-piece band and had an engagement at the downtown Sheraton hotel. The experience of singing with a band was less than satisfying. Amos had always relied on herself to create music, and she found it difficult to coordinate a band. Band members came and went, but Amos remained dedicated.

Her hard work eventually paid off in 1987, when Atlantic Records signed her to a record deal. Amos's band, Y Kant Tori Read, recorded a self-titled album. It was released in May, 1988, to very few reviews and even less praise. *Billboard* magazine labeled Amos's album "bimbo music." Amos was crushed by the complete rejection of her first major effort. She returned to the consolation of

playing the piano. In the fall of 1989, Atlantic Records offered her another chance after hearing that she was writing music using a piano.

A Woman and Her Piano. Amos spent the next year and a half struggling with the record company to approve her work. In early 1991, with an album of ten songs, Atlantic Records decided to send Amos to their British counterpart, East West Records in London. She was well received by the president of East West, Max Hole, and it was decided that the album would be completed in London. Amos also had a chance to introduce herself to England by playing her music at selected local venues. The British press were very favorable and ultimately would become great supporters of her work.

Little Earthquakes was released in early 1992. It was composed of eleven songs. The first single, "Silent All These Years," is about a woman struggling to find the courage to speak out. One of the most compelling songs on the album, sung a capella, is "Me and a Gun." In this autobiographical song, Amos sings about being sexually assaulted. Critics loved the intimate, confessional quality of the album, although they had trouble placing Amos in a musical category and compared her to everyone from Kate Bush to Joni Mitchell. This album is generally considered Amos's best work.

In 1993 Amos settled down to work on her follow-up album, *Under the Pink*. She chose to build her own studio out of an old hacienda in Taos, New Mexico. Many of the songs on *Under the Pink* use unusual recording techniques, such as detuning and muting the piano strings for the song "Bells for Her." The first single released in the United States was "God," a satiric song that asks God, "Do you need a woman to look out for you?"

When *Under the Pink* was released in early 1994, it debuted at number 1 in the United Kingdom and went gold within one week. Critics were less enthusiastic about her sophomore effort, claiming that it was less intimate than her first album. Amos explained the difference: "*Under the Pink* was an impressionist painting, it wasn't supposed to be diary form like *Little Earthquakes*."

Amos recorded her third album, *Boys for Pele* (1996), on location in Ireland and New Orleans, Louisiana, and was the sole producer. One of the recording techniques used for this album was the construction of a large box to hold a harpsichord, a piano, and a microphone. Amos had to climb into the box for recording sessions. On this album she also played the harmonium and clavichord. Steve Caton played guitar for many of the songs and later accompanied her on the album tour. A local brass band and amateur bagpipe players also made an appearance on this album.

Mixed Reviews. *Boys for Pele* debuted at number 2 on the *Billboard* charts in the United States and number 1 in the United Kingdom. The album received mixed reviews; critics in the United States were far less accepting of Amos's brand of eccentricity than their U.K. counterparts. If Amos considered *Under the Pink* an impressionist painting, *Boys for Pele* could be considered a cubist sculpture. The songs are challenging and the lyrics are hard to comprehend, even for the avid Amos listener. The chorus of "Caught a Light Sneeze," the first single, offers these lyrics: "Caught a light sneeze/ dreamed a little dream/ made my own pretty hate machine." Abstract lyrics like these characterize the other songs on the album.

Amos recorded her next album, *from the choirgirl hotel*, in a converted farmhouse in Cornwall, England. Caton again supplied the guitars, and Matt Chamberlain played drums. George Porter, Jr., a well-known blues bassist, lent his talents for a few songs. This shift to playing with a band was welcomed by fans. The collaboration of artists on *from the choirgirl hotel* toned down the experimentation found on *Boys for Pele*, making it more approachable. In many ways the songwriting is similar to *Little Earthquakes*, with some biographical songs. *From the choirgirl hotel* was released in May, 1998, to mixed reviews, but went gold within a few weeks.   —*K. L. A. Hyatt*

SELECT DISCOGRAPHY
■ ALBUMS
Y Kant Tori Read, 1988
Little Earthquakes, 1992
Under the Pink, 1994
Boys for Pele, 1996
from the choirgirl hotel, 1998

SELECT AWARDS
Rolling Stone, named Best New Female Singer, 1993

SEE ALSO: McLachlan, Sarah; Madonna; Mitchell, Joni; Vega, Suzanne.

Laurie Anderson

BORN: Chicago, Illinois; June 5, 1947
FIRST SINGLE RELEASE: "It's Not the Bullet That Kills You—It's the Hole," 1977
MUSICAL STYLES: Performance art, pop, spoken word

Laurie Anderson is internationally recognized as a performance artist. Although her contribution as a musician is significant, she is also an important contributor to the visual arts community. Her work is multimedia, combining poetry, sculpture, videos, film, slide projectors, costumes, computers, and both electronic and acoustic instruments. The lyrics in her music are generally spoken narratives (although her releases since 1989 include singing), and they often relay some social commentary.

Her music incorporates numerous electronic devices that alter her voice (sometimes providing a chorus of voices, other times making her sound like a man) and the sounds of the acoustic instruments used. One of the most important aspects of her work is humor. Both her words and her speaking style—slow-paced and filled with small pauses for emphasis—display a droll sense of humor that humanizes her extensive use of technology. "Performance artist" is an odd term, and Anderson herself has said she finds it awkward and amusing. An article in *Rolling Stone* in the early 1980's once referred to her simply as a new kind of pop star.

Anderson began her musical training as a violinist, often spending her summers at the Interlochen National Music Camp in Michigan. Her professional education, however, was in the visual arts. She attended Mills College in Oakland, California (1965-1966), and graduated magna cum laude from Barnard College in New York City with a degree in art history in 1969. She enrolled in Columbia University and graduated with an MFA degree in sculpture in 1972. She taught art history from 1970 to 1974 at City College of New York, Staten Island College, and Pace University, and she wrote art reviews for various periodicals.

Early Performances. During the 1960's and 1970's New York City was a mecca for visual and performing artists, who often created radical and controversial works. Anderson's reputation as a visual artist grew, and she was invited to participate in art shows in both the United States and Europe. Her works were primarily multimedia installations that incorporated electronics and were intended to be interactive with the viewer. Her interest in the visual arts, combined with her musical experience, ultimately led Anderson to develop her personal style.

Her reputation as a performance artist began in 1974 with the work *Duets on Ice*, which was performed in the streets of both New York City and Genoa, Italy. Anderson would insert a small cassette player, playing a prerecorded tape, in her violin and would then perform duets with herself. During the performance Anderson stood in ice skates that were frozen in blocks of ice. According to Anderson, "When the ice melted and I lost my balance, the concert was over."

From 1974 to 1978 Anderson traveled, often relocating to areas such as Chiapas, Mexico, and Berlin, Germany. She received numerous grants for her work from the New York State Council for the Arts and the National Endowment for the Arts. She was invited to perform at New York's Museum of Modern Art, the Whitney Museum, colleges and universities, and numerous "alternative" performance spaces. By 1979 she had begun to gain a reputation as a musician and composer as well as a visual artist.

Recordings. A milestone for Anderson came with the 1981 release of the single "O Superman" by a very small New York record label, 110 Records. "O Superman" (inspired by Jules Massenet's operatic aria "O Souverain") did not sell well in the United States, but it reached number 2 on the British pop charts. With the popularity of "O Superman" Anderson signed with Warner Bros. Records, which released "O Superman" on her 1982 debut album *Big Science*. This release launched a European tour.

In 1984, Warner Bros. released the *Mister Heartbreak* album, and Anderson received a Grammy Award nomination for the single "Gravity's An-

Laurie Anderson (Deborah Feingold/Archive Photos)

gel." The album also included "Excellent Birds," a duet sung and cowritten with Peter Gabriel, and "Sharkey's Night," featuring a brief recitation by Beat writer William S. Burroughs. Also released that year was *United States Live*, a five-album or four-CD set of her work *United States I-IV*, which included new material as well as live versions of works from previous albums.

She also began other collaborations with musician Peter Gabriel (*Good Morning Mr. Orwell*) and Jean-Michel Jarre (*Zoolook*). In 1985 Anderson began shooting *Home of the Brave*, a concert film, which would be released in 1986. *Home of the Brave* was composed of many pieces that evolved from the *Mister Heartbreak* tour. If not praised by film critics, the film was enormously successful with Laurie Anderson fans. In 1986 Anderson also composed the number "Forgetting," which appears on minimalist composer Philip Glass's *Songs from Liquid Days*, and appeared on Peter Gabriel's *So* album. In 1987 Anderson was involved in several benefits for AIDS research and a concert with Paul Simon and Bruce Springsteen at Madison Square Garden for the New York Children's Health Project.

Anderson began recording *Strange Angels* in 1988 and presented an early version of the concert

For the Record

"In 1980 I released 'O Superman' on a small New York label, Bob George's 110 Records. The idea was that we would sell it mail order, and the initial pressing was 1,000 copies financed by a $500 grant from the National Endowment for the Arts. Then one day I got a call from London, an order for 20,000 copies of the 'single' immediately followed by another 20,000 by the end of the week. I looked around at the cardboard box of records and said, 'Listen, can I just call you back?'"

—*Laurie Anderson*, from *Stories from the Nerve Bible*, 1994

tour *Empty Places* in Rio de Janeiro in 1989. The premiere of *Empty Places* was at the Spoleto Festival in Charleston, South Carolina. It then ran for two weeks at the Brooklyn Academy of Music. In 1990 Anderson played 150 performances of *Empty Places* throughout the United States and Europe. She also began a series of meetings with musicians and composers Brian Eno and Peter Gabriel, planning a theme park to be called "Real World" and located in Barcelona, Spain. The park would celebrate technological achievements. As of 1997, no definite plans had been made in regard to "Real World."

In 1991 Anderson participated in the series "High Art Low Art," sponsored by the Museum of Modern Art. Anderson's contribution, "Voices from the Beyond," was a response to the media buildup surrounding the impending Gulf War. It included commentary on censorship, AIDS, women, and other topics. Her contributions in 1992 included the creation of a "Rock the Vote" public service announcement for the VH-1 music cable network and the premiere of *Stories from the Nerve Bible*, performed at Expo '92 in Seville, Spain. A dramatic personal experience occurred in 1993 when Anderson, while hiking in the Tibetan Himalayas, got lost and almost died from altitude sickness. This experience influenced her next projects, *Bright Red* (1994), produced by Brian Eno, and *The Ugly One with the Jewels and Other Stories* (1995).

Anderson published a number of books between 1971 and 1994, including *Empty Places, a performance* (1991) and *Stories from the Nerve Bible: A Retrospective 1972-1992* (1994). In 1995 Anderson's *The Puppet Motel*, an interactive CD-ROM music computer program, was made available in the Macintosh format.

Collaborations. Anderson has been a friend to many composers, such as John Cage, whom Anderson met in 1980, and Philip Glass. The talents of many well-known artists also appear on her albums. Included are Bobby McFerrin (*Strange Angels*), Phoebe Snow (*Mister Heartbreak*), Lou Reed (*Bright Red*), Peter Gabriel (*Mister Heartbreak*), the Roches (*Strange Angels*), and photographer Robert Mapplethorpe, who took the photograph used on the cover of *Strange Angels.* Anderson also cowrote, with John Cale and David Byrne, material for the sound track of Jonathan Demme's 1986 film *Something Wild.* In 1995 she appeared on Lou Reed's album *Set the Twilight Reeling.*   —*Brent Register*

SELECT DISCOGRAPHY
■ SINGLES
"It's Not the Bullet That Kills You—It's the Hole," 1977
"O Superman," 1981 (EP)
■ ALBUMS
Big Science, 1982
Mister Heartbreak, 1984
United States Live, 1984
Home of the Brave, 1986 (also on video and laser disc)
Strange Angels, 1989
Bright Red, 1994
The Ugly One with the Jewels and Other Stories, 1995
The Puppet Motel, 1995 (CD-ROM)

SEE ALSO: Eno, Brian; Gabriel, Peter; McFerrin, Bobby; Reed, Lou; Talking Heads / David Byrne.

The Animals

ORIGINAL MEMBERS: Eric Burdon (b. 1941), Alan Price (b. 1942), Hilton Valentine (b. 1943), John Steel (b. 1941), Chas Chandler (b. Bryan James Chandler, 1938-1996)
OTHER MEMBERS: Dave Rowberry (b. 1943), Barry Jenkins (b. 1944), John Weider (b. 1947), Vic Briggs (b. 1945), Danny McCulloch, Andy Summers (b. Andrew Somers, 1942), George "Zoot Money" Bruno
FIRST SINGLE RELEASE: "House of the Rising Sun," 1964
MUSICAL STYLES: Blues, psychedelic rock, rock and roll, rhythm and blues

In 1962, the Alan Price Combo was formed in Newcastle-upon-Tyne, England, consisting of Alan Price (keyboards), Chas Chandler (bass), Hilton Valentine (guitar), and John Steel (drums). Valentine had briefly been a member of a local band, the Gamblers, and Steel had played trumpet in college jazz bands with trombonist/vocalist Eric Burdon. When Burdon joined the group as lead singer in 1963, the band was renamed the Animals. The Animals then became fixtures at the legendary Newcastle club Cafe a-Go-Go before moving to London, where they briefly backed American blues legend Sonny Boy Williamson. There, rhythm-and-blues bandleader Graham Bond recommended them to Ronan O'Rahilly, who became their manager.

First Hits. In 1964, the group signed with producer Mickie Most and began recording their versions of rhythm-and-blues standards by Chuck Berry, Ray Charles, and Jimmy Reed. "Baby Let Me Take You Home," a remake of Eric von Schmidt's "Baby Let Me Follow You Down," became their first hit single. Other notable interpretations included their versions of John Lee Hooker's "Boom Boom" and Sam Cooke's gospel-flavored "Bring It on Home to Me."

In the summer of 1964, the Animals became an international sensation with the release of their adaptation of another blues standard, "The House of the Rising Sun." While previously covered by Bob Dylan, the Animals' version was immediately both historic and controversial. Four and a half minutes long, it was the first hit to break the three-minute barrier preferred by Top-10 radio stations. The earthy vocals, Valentine's guitar introduction, and Price's organ playing, however, were an irresistible mixture, and the song became an important benchmark in rock history. Reportedly, this song helped inspire Bob Dylan to move from acoustic to electric guitar, an important change in rock's mid-1960's direction. The Animals' appeal went beyond teenage fans, largely due to Burdon's vocals, which attracted a large number of black listeners. In 1964, *Ebony* magazine devoted five pages to Burdon's singing, comparing him to his acknowledged African American influences.

Under the direction of producer Most, a string of hit singles followed, demonstrating the group's movement from rhythm and blues to pop originals including "We Gotta Get Out of This Place" and "Don't Let Me Be Misunderstood." While the

The Animals (Archive Photos)

group still recorded covers of American blues tunes, Burdon became unhappy with the commercialization fostered by Most. Price and Burdon began feuding, and Burdon and his bandmates became upset after Price arranged for all royalties for "The House of the Rising Sun" to go only to him.

Winds of Change. In 1966, Price left the band, reportedly because of weariness on the road and his fear of flying, although Burdon later wrote he believed Price no longer needed the band. Dave Rowberry took his place, and other key changes quickly followed. The group relocated to New York, fired Most, and released their last single with him, "It's My Life." They left their British record label and began working with Bob Dylan's producer, Tom Wilson.

Their next single, "Inside Looking Out," a rewrite of blues singer Leadbelly's "Rosie," was an interesting lyrical and instrumental vision of prison life. Later, Michigan band Grand Funk Railroad successfully covered the song, and many fans erroneously believed that band had composed the hit. As group dissension continued, Steel departed and was replaced by Nashville Teens drummer Barry Jenkins, who had played with Carl Perkins, Bo Diddley, and Jerry Lee Lewis.

The Animals' next single, Carole King and Gerry Goffin's "Don't Bring Me Down," continued the organ-based soulful sound of the first lineup, but disintegration became imminent as the members discovered that their earnings had been siphoned off by their management. After Chandler's departure, Burdon disbanded the group and released the posthumous "See See Rider," a rock standard quickly covered by another Michigan band, Mitch Ryder and the Detroit Wheels.

Second Generation. Burdon began organizing Eric Burdon and the Animals, and with

Jenkins, he issued a primarily solo effort, "Help Me Girl," a Motown-influenced failure. It was followed by the album *Eric Is Here* (1967), an anomaly in the Animals' canon, again largely a Burdon solo project.

Moving to the West Coast, where he and Valentine had become immersed in the psychedelic sounds of San Francisco bands such as the Jefferson Airplane, Burdon hired keyboardist Vic Briggs, who had played with the Brian Auger Trinity and Steampacket. Guitarist Danny McCulloch from Lord Sutch and bassist John Weider completed the new Animals, who debuted with "When I Was Young" in April, 1967. The heavy fuzz-tone guitar sound continued in "A Girl Named Sandoz," a Briggs-arranged tribute to the drug LSD.

The Animals' next single, "San Franciscan Nights" (1967), became the new lineup's biggest-selling release despite British disc jockeys' fears that their listeners could not relate to the obviously topical and regional lyrics. Expanding the group's sounds to include sitar and electric violin, the band's next album, *Winds of Change* (1967), became perhaps their high-water mark. The diverse collection included philosophic lyrics and poetic narratives ("Winds of Change," "The Black Death") and personal confessions by Burdon ("Good Times"). In the album's title track, Burdon began his use of listing his influences from 1950's jazz singers to rock iconoclast Frank Zappa. (Previously, Burdon had recorded Zappa's "Another Side of This Life," one of the few covers of

For the Record

Contrary to myth, the Animals did not get their name from being called "animals" by their audiences. Around the time that Eric Burdon joined the Pagans in 1962, he and John Steel were spending time with a gang led by an army veteran known as "Animal Hog." The band took its name from him.

the Mothers of Invention's eccentric composer Zappa.) The 1967 single "Monterey" was another tribute to West Coast youth culture, praising the all-star Monterey International Pop Festival, at which the Animals, Jimi Hendrix, the Mamas and the Papas, and others reached high visibility.

The anti-Vietnam War song "Sky Pilot" was the Animals' last major hit. By 1968, Burdon had begun interpreting less raw, more orchestrated material, and the group's popularity waned. As a result, the group's personnel changed one last time, billed as Eric Burdon and the New Animals. George Bruno (known as "Zoot Money") temporarily became keyboardist, and Andy Summers took over guitars in time for the last, disastrous Japanese tour.

After *Every One of Us* (1968), a starker, bluesier effort featuring the group's last single, "White Houses," the Animals released their final record collection, *Love Is* (1968). Despite the extended jam on "River Deep, Mountain High," the rest of the 1968 material seemed far removed from what fans expected of Burdon. Complaints were particularly leveled at his versions of Johnny Cash, Traffic, and Bee Gees ballads such as "To Love Somebody," seemingly the embodiment of the commercialism Burdon had criticized under Most's direction. Finally disbanding the group at the end of 1968, Burdon proclaimed the album his farewell to rock.

Aftermath. In 1970, Burdon reappeared with his new band, Eric Burdon and War, which released one Top-10 single, "Spill the Wine." After two albums, *Eric Burdon Declares War* (1970) and *The Black Man's Burdon* (1971), War reorganized and had a successful career without Burdon. Other Burdon solo projects included a 1971 album, *Guilty*, with blues singer Jimmy Witherspoon. In 1974, Burdon released *Sun Secrets* with remakes of Animals tunes. In subsequent years, Burdon primarily remained a live performer singing his 1960's catalog with Brian Auger and former Doors guitarist Robby Krieger. In 1986, he published his autobiography and an album of the same name, *I Used to Be an Animal, but I'm All Right Now*.

After leaving the Animals, Chas Chandler contributed to rock history by discovering, managing, and producing the Jimi Hendrix Experience. After forming the Alan Price Set, Price briefly surfaced with his sound track for the 1973 film *O Lucky Man!* John Weider joined the British band Family, led by future Blind Faith bassist Rick Grech. A decade after the Animals' breakup, Andy Summers achieved stardom as a founding member of the Police.

The original Animals briefly reunited in 1968 and recorded an album in 1976. The public proved disinterested, as with the 1984 reunion tour in which Valentine was reportedly so out of practice, another player had to be used. After realizing the group could not last, the original Animals finally disbanded for good.

—*Wesley Britton*

SELECT DISCOGRAPHY
■ SINGLES
"The House of the Rising Sun," 1964
"Don't Let Me Be Misunderstood," 1965
"We Gotta Get Out of This Place," 1965
"It's My Life," 1965
"Don't Bring Me Down," 1966
"San Franciscan Nights," 1967
■ ALBUMS
The Animals, 1964
The Animals on Tour, 1965
Animal Tracks, 1965
The Most of the Animals, 1966 (compilation)
Animalization, 1966
Animalisms, 1966
Eric Is Here, 1967 (as Eric Burdon and the Animals)
Winds of Change, 1967 (as Eric Burdon and the Animals)
Every One of Us, 1968 (as Eric Burdon and the New Animals)
Before We Were So Rudely Interrupted, 1976
Ark, 1983
Rip It to Shreds: Greatest Hits Live! 1984 (compilation)

AWARDS AND ACHIVEMENTS
Rock and Roll Hall of Fame, inducted 1994

SEE ALSO: War.

Fiona Apple

BORN: New York, New York; September 13, 1977
FIRST ALBUM RELEASE: *Tidal*, 1996
MUSICAL STYLES: Rock and roll, pop

Fiona Apple quickly established herself as one of the leading female singer-songwriters of the 1990's, alongside such artists as Alanis Morissette and Tori Amos, and she is often compared with Kate Bush. Her initial rise to fame occurred while she was still a teenager, with the platinum album *Tidal* (1996). Despite her youth, Apple brought significant depth to her music. It has been said that she sounds twice as old and wise as she is. Her musical ability is paired with a waifish beauty that makes her look quite young.

Apple, born Fiona Apple Maggart, is the second child of singer-dancer turned nutritionist Diana McAfee and actor Brandon Maggart. Maggart and McAfee separated when Fiona was four and her sister, Amber, was six. While their father relocated to California, the sisters and their mother remained in New York, living on Manhattan's Upper West Side. This urban setting would help shape the sensibilities that later defined Apple's music.

Troubled Childhood. Apple endured an unhappy, traumatic childhood that seems to have left an indelible mark on her. The breakup of her parents served as an early source of anguish. Also, she has said, people found her "weird and ugly." At school, classmates called her "Dog" because of her long, unkempt hair. At home, she frequently got into fights with her family. An intruder broke into her family's Manhattan home when Apple was eleven and sexually assaulted her. As she became increasingly withdrawn, her mother started taking Apple to therapy sessions. They only aggravated her condition.

The poems of Maya Angelou provided her with a luminous ray of hope during her troubled adolescence. In the poems, Apple found both solace and a validation of her own sensitive nature. Angelou also served as something of a musical inspiration. As Apple recalls, "I would have trouble sleeping. So I would sing her poetry and then I'd

Fiona Apple (Paul Natkin)

Tidal Wave. Slater produced Apple's first release, *Tidal.* It was a remarkable work for such a young songwriter. Its sparse instrumentation and minimalist arrangements revealed an artist mature beyond her years. The album includes "Shadowboxer," "Criminal," and "Sullen Girl." In the last, Apple sings of her sexual assault as an eleven-year-old, "They don't know I used to sail the deep and tranquil sea/ But he washed me ashore and he took my pearl/ And left an empty shell of me." The song quickly led the press to label Apple a sullen, angry girl, but she was quick to dispute the characterization as being two-dimensional.

Most of the songs on *Tidal* are stark confessions brimming with emotional turmoil. In general, Apple comes across as a defiant victim, but "Criminal" also shows her as the wrongdoer. In the sultry alto voice that has inspired comparisons with Nina Simone, she declares, "I've been a bad, bad girl/ I've been careless with a sensitive man." For many, the sturm und drang of Apple's lyrics was too much. One reviewer called her "a hard-to-please emotional invalid." For others, her songs touch the heart. In particular, the singer-songwriter has spoken of the strong response she has received for "Sullen Girl" from other childhood victims of sexual assault.

Meteoric Rise. Success in the music industry is typically preceded by years of diligent career building. However, Apple's rise to stardom did indeed happen overnight. Before signing with Sony, she had never played with a band or even performed for an audience. Her first public performance was an August, 1996, concert in Paris. By the end of the same year, she had starred as the musical guest on television's *Saturday Night Live*, and the video of "Shadowboxer" was playing regu-

close the book when I got tired." This anecdote reflects the therapeutic role music played in her young life; she began lessons on the piano when she was eight as a way to relieve her aggression. Writing music soon became a form of self-help. Feeling misunderstood by parents and friends, she confided her feelings to a blank page, discovering not only an effective form of therapy but also a distinctive approach to lyric writing.

Apple attended a high school in New York for students with learning disabilities but moved to Los Angeles to be with her father when she was sixteen. Under his influence, she enrolled in acting classes and was even offered the lead role in a motion picture that was never released. Acting's loss became music's gain when Apple made a short demo tape of original songs that eventually found its way to veteran producer and manager Andrew Slater. Slater was not convinced that Apple, who was clearly only seventeen, had written those lyrics. After determining that the lyrics were in fact Apple's, Slater convinced Work Group, a Sony Music label, to offer her a contract.

For the Record

Concerning her appearance, Apple has said, "I spent so much of my life being called 'Dog.' Now I go to a photo shoot, and they're like, 'Oh, you're lovely!'"

larly on MTV. She then joined other top female singer-songwriters as part of the acclaimed "Lilith Fair" tour the following summer. Apple has likened her meteoric success to a fairy tale.

Apple's good looks have received almost as much media attention as her music. In particular, much attention has been given to the sort of beauty Apple possesses. The press has often referred to her as waifish and innocent looking and has made much of the incongruity between her youthful appearance and the grown-up music that she delivers. One need only compare Apple's lyrics and sultry voice with the cover photo for *Tidal* to appreciate this disparity.   —*David Lee Fish*

SELECT DISCOGRAPHY
■ ALBUMS
Tidal, 1996

SELECT AWARDS
Grammy Award for Best Female Rock Vocal Performance for "Criminal," 1998

SEE ALSO: Amos, Tori; Morissette, Alanis.

Louis Armstrong

BORN: New Orleans, Louisiana; August 4, 1901
DIED: New York, New York; July 6, 1971
FIRST RECORDINGS: "Just Gone" and "Canal Street Blues," 1923 (as sideman with Joe "King" Oliver)
FIRST RECORDING AS BANDLEADER: "My Heart," 1925 (with the Hot Fives)
MUSICAL STYLES: Jazz, blues, musical theater, pop

Louis Armstrong's long career produced one of the most varied and distinguished lists of accomplishments produced by any musician. He was a trumpet virtuoso, a superb vocal stylist, the chief inventor of scat singing, a superb blues musician, one of the most compelling improvisers in the history of jazz, a leader of innovative bands, a beloved performer who appeared in numerous films, and one of the first African American musicians to reach an interracial audience without emphasizing prevailing white stereotypes about African Americans.

Youth and Apprenticeship. Armstrong was born in a largely black slum in New Orleans, Louisiana. His father abandoned Armstrong and his mother soon after Armstrong's birth. His mother worked variously as a domestic and a prostitute. While growing up, Armstrong heard the emergence of the "hot" jazz style that evolved out of ragtime. This energetic new music was the creation of New Orleans' poorer African Americans and featured an ensemble usually made up of cornets, trombones, clarinets, saxophones, a tuba or string bass, a piano, a guitar or a banjo, and drums. The structure of this music was based on group improvisation on composed songs, often supported by blues harmonic patterns. While the musical landscape was rich, Armstrong grew up in a terrible environment in all other respects. His mother was certainly well intentioned, but her conduct was irresponsible and resulted in real hardship for her children. Neglected as a child, Armstrong carried a lifelong insecurity and a desire to please.

When Armstrong's delinquency led to a two-year sentence in the Home for Colored Waifs—a sort of reform school—Armstrong was allowed to sing in a barbershop quartet and given a cornet. Once released, Armstrong took his cornet to honky-tonks and played along with blues and ragtime favorites, which he picked up by ear. Progressing rapidly, Armstrong secured work with Joe "King" Oliver, a bandleader who was widely considered the finest cornet player in New Orleans. Oliver exercised a powerful influence over Armstrong in personal matters, but musically Armstrong owed Oliver very little. In 1918, Oliver left for Chicago, and Armstrong joined Kid Ory's band. Armstrong was no longer the second cornet player, and he began to win increasing recognition for his superb playing and profound musical imagination. Armstrong had a brief and unhappy marriage in 1919.

In 1922, Oliver invited Armstrong to join him in Chicago and play second cornet once again. Armstrong accepted the invitation. During this second stint with Oliver, Armstrong remarried. His second wife (Armstrong would marry four times), Lil Hardin, was Oliver's pianist. Hardin and Armstrong made their first recordings with Oliver's band in Chicago, after which, at Hardin's insistence, Armstrong left Oliver and moved to New York City, where he and his wife joined the Fletcher Henderson Orchestra. In New York, Armstrong quickly gained a reputation as the finest practitioner of the hot jazz style he had learned as a youth in New Orleans.

Transforming Jazz. In 1925, Armstrong returned to Chicago, where he and his band, first known as the Hot Fives and later the Hot Sevens, made roughly sixty recordings. This body of work transformed jazz from a genre anchored in group improvisation closely related to a composed melody into a vehicle for individual brilliance, placing a premium on imaginative rethinking of melodies and musical daring. During this time, Armstrong switched from the mellow cornet to the more brilliant trumpet. The style he cultivated during the mid- to late 1920's had a far-reaching impact on jazz. Important seeds of both swing and bebop (a style that did not emerge until the 1940's) were sewn by Armstrong during the 1920's. Among Armstrong's most delightful innovations was his invention of scat singing (first heard on the song "Heebie Jeebies" in 1926), which calls for the singer to improvise on nonsense syllables, thus allowing the voice to shed the function of delivering words and take on the characteristics of any other musical instrument within the jazz ensemble. Armstrong's work as a scat singer was invariably cheerful and managed to capture the imagination of his times.

Armstrong's solos were always the centerpiece of his recordings. His first recorded solo can be heard with King Oliver's band on "Chimes Blues" (1923).

On this recording, the youthful Armstrong never strayed from a composed melody. By the time that he was recording with the Hot Fives—Armstrong, Johnny Dodds (reed instruments), Kid Ory (trombone), Johnny St. Cyr (banjo), and Armstrong's wife Lil (piano)—his solo work afforded the listener fanciful departures from composed melodies. Rhythmic displacement of his melodies against the metric pulse of the rest of the ensemble was an Armstrong trademark. On "Potato Head Blues" (1927), Armstrong played entire phrases that placed strong melodic accents on weak beats while avoiding any changes in the melody on strong beats. While singing, Armstrong was just as adventuresome. On "Hotter than That" (1927), Armstrong sang long passages

A young and dapper Louis Armstrong (Columbia Legacy)

For the Record

Louis Armstrong had many nicknames during his long career, including Dippermouth, Pops, Satchelmouth, and, most famously, Satchmo. Satchelmouth and Satchmo both pay homage to Armstrong's large mouth, which he opened wide when he sang.

in a meter with two notes against every three played by the rest of the ensemble. The result offered the sort of metric energy that jolted America into the Jazz Age.

National Fame. During the 1930's, Armstrong was encouraged by a series of persuasive managers to devote himself more to becoming a popular figure and less to the serious pursuit of musical innovation. In 1929, he appeared in the Broadway show *Hot Chocolates*. Armstrong proved to be a compelling stage performer. Happy to let managers (Tommy Rockwell and, starting in 1935, Joe Glaser) chart the direction of his career and eager since childhood to please, Armstrong was steered into motion pictures. He appeared in nearly fifty feature-length films. Armstrong was the first African American to have his own sponsored radio program. Throughout the 1930's, he led a big band that until the mid-1930's was influential in codifying the swing sound. Later the group centered on supporting Armstrong in singing popular songs, and its influence declined while its popularity soared. In 1947, Armstrong returned to serious jazz and his hot New Orleans roots with the All Stars, a small ensemble that allowed him to reunite with one of his long-time collaborators, pianist Earl Hines. In 1959, Armstrong suffered a heart attack, which forced him to curtail his activities. However, he continued to play, sing, and act until shortly before his death.

Legacy. From 1925 to 1935, Armstrong was perhaps the most influential man in American music. He crafted the apex of the hot style of New Orleans jazz and pioneered the swing style that dominated the 1930's. His subsequent career and wild popularity, while less important in purely musical terms, was of tremendous social significance as he led the way for wider acceptance of African American entertainers. His 1964 All Stars hit "Hello Dolly!" knocked even the Beatles from the top of the charts. During the 1960's, some jazz musicians criticized Armstrong for failing to take a more emphatic stand against racial stereotypes. Time has dulled these criticisms, and Armstrong's positive influence both as a musician and as a man shape his legacy. It was therefore quite appropriate that the revival of Armstrong's "What a Wonderful World" on the sound track to the motion picture *Good Morning, Vietnam* in 1987 met with such resounding success. —*Michael Lee*

SELECT DISCOGRAPHY
with King Oliver's Creole Jazz Band
■ SINGLES
"Just Gone"/"Canal Street Blues," 1923
"Chimes Blues"/"Froggie Moore," 1923
with Fletcher Henderson's Orchestra
■ SINGLES
"Go 'Long Mule," 1924
with the Hot Fives and the Hot Sevens
■ SINGLES
"My Heart," 1925
"Heebie Jeebies," 1926
"S.O.L. Blues," 1927
"Hotter than That"/"Savoy Blues," 1927
■ ALBUMS
West End Blues, 1928
with his big bands
■ SINGLES
"Mahagony Hall Stomp," 1929 (with Louis Armstrong and His Savoy Ballroom Five)
"Ain't Misbehavin'," 1929 (with Louis Armstrong and His Orchestra)
"When You're Smilin'," 1929 (with Louis Armstrong and His Orchestra)
with the All Stars
■ SINGLES
"Rockin' Chair"/"Save It Pretty Mama," 1947
"Hello Dolly!" 1964

SEE ALSO: Davis, Miles; Fitzgerald, Ella; Parker, Charlie.

Eddy Arnold

BORN: Near Henderson, Tennessee; May 15, 1918
FIRST SINGLE RELEASE: "Each Minute Seems a Million Years," 1945
FIRST ALBUM RELEASE: *Anytime,* 1952
MUSICAL STYLES: Country, pop

Born Richard Edward Arnold, Eddy was taught by his mother to play the guitar when he was a young boy. His father died on his eleventh birthday, so Arnold left school to work on farms. His childhood was filled with memories of farm work, but his real love was music. As a teenager, he began playing his guitar at local square dances, earning about fifty cents per night.

While working on a cotton farm in Jackson, Tennessee, when he was eighteen years old, Arnold met a man who was selling the local newspaper. Knowing that the newspaper owned a radio station, Arnold played his guitar and sang for the newspaperman and earned an audition. He landed a job at WTJS-radio in Jackson, working with his fiddle-playing friend Speedy McNatt. For the next four years, Arnold performed on radio stations in Memphis, St. Louis, and Louisville. From 1940 to 1943, Arnold was a member of Pee Wee King's Golden West Cowboys, and he appeared with them on the radio program *Grand Ole Opry.* Arnold married Sally Gayhart in 1941, and in 1943 he signed a recording contract with RCA Victor and launched his solo career billed as "The Tennessee Plowboy." During the next five years, he became the most commercially successful singer in country music.

Country Music Giant. Arnold made his country chart debut in 1945 with "Each Minute Seems a Million Years," and with Colonel Tom Parker as his manager, Arnold soon became a nationally known star, replacing Roy Acuff as the most popular country music singer. Much of the distinctive instrumental flavor of his songs came from the melodious steel-guitar work of Roy Wiggins.

Arnold began his solo Grand Ole Opry career, between 1946 and 1948, as the host of the Ralston Purina segment. Wearing a tuxedo and a bow tie, Arnold became a genuine country crooner. His first number 1 hit, "What Is Life Without Love?," allowed him to dominate the country charts for nearly half of 1947. "Cattle Call," one of Arnold's best-remembered records, was also a number 1 hit in 1947.

During 1948, Arnold had nine Top-10 records. His first number 1 hit in 1948 was "Anytime," followed by a string of top hits, including "Bouquet of Roses," "Just a Little Lovin' Will Go a Long Way," "A Heart Full of Love," and "Texarkana Baby." With the exception of Jimmy Wakely's recording of "One Has My Heart," Arnold's records held the number 1 position on the country charts for all of 1948.

Between 1945 and 1955, Arnold had sixty-eight hits on the U.S. country charts, including twenty-one number 1 singles. From 1948 to 1963, he led all country performers with a total of fifty-three Top-10 songs. During the 1950's, he appeared on all the major radio shows, making guest appearances on *Western Theater, The RCA Victor Show, We the People, The Spike Jones Show, The Paul Whiteman Show,* and *Breakfast Club.* He was a regular performer on the *Grand Ole Opry* radio program and hosted his own radio show, *Checkerboard Square,* from 1947 to 1955. Arnold also appeared on many major television shows, including shows hosted by Ed Sullivan, Perry Como, Danny Kaye, Dinah Shore, Danny Thomas, Mike Douglas, Jackie Gleason, Johnny Carson, Dean Martin, and Red Skelton, and he was the first country singer to host his own network television program, *The Eddy Arnold Show* (1952-1956). Arnold also appeared in the motion pictures *Feudin' Rhythm* (1949) and *Hoedown* (1950).

Transition to Pop. In the early 1950's, Arnold adopted a more popular singing style. His choice of songs, the character of accompaniments, and his crooning vocal sound were all focused on making his music more appealing to a broader audience. His 1954 recording, "I Really Don't Want to Know," with background vocals and muted guitars, epitomizes the new style which suited him best. Many of Arnold's early fans disliked the change, but because his television and radio performances gained him numerous new fans, he easily maintained his popularity and success on the music charts. After 1954, his nickname "Tennessee Plowboy" no longer appeared on his records or albums, and because of his musical variety, Arnold began calling himself "Heinz 57."

In 1966, Arnold became one of the first country singers to appear at New York's Carnegie Hall, and in 1967, he made his debut at the Coconut Grove nightclub in Los Angeles. In addition, he appeared in numerous concerts with many major symphony orchestras during the 1960's. Between 1956 and 1983, he increased his number of U.S. country chart hits to 145, with ninety-two in the Top 10 and twenty-eight making it to the number 1 slot. Many of his recordings were both country and pop hits, including "Tennessee Stud," "What's He Doing in My World?," and "Make the World Go Away," which was his biggest U.S. pop hit, reaching number 6 in 1965. In 1980, he had another Top-10 hit, "Let's Get It While the Gettin's Good."

From 1952 to 1993, Arnold recorded eighty-three albums, several of which reached Top-10 status in the United States. Although he was no longer strictly a country singer, he was elected to the Country Music Hall of Fame in 1966. Arnold was one of the first country artists to cross over to pop. In 1967, he became the first recipient of the Country Music Association Entertainer of the Year Award. He has sold more than eighty-five million records and his record sales are surpassed only by Elvis Presley and the Beatles; his overall chart success eclipses all other recording artists.

Business Ventures. Arnold became very active in other areas besides music; he became a successful, respected businessman in real estate, land development, and music publishing. Arnold also served on the boards of several corporations and banks and became the owner of a car dealership, water utilities, music publishing, and record pressing companies. On several occasions, both Republicans and Democrats asked him to run for public office.
—*Alvin K. Benson*

SELECT DISCOGRAPHY
■ SINGLES
"Anytime," 1948
"Bouquet of Roses," 1948
"Cattle Call," 1955
"Make the World Go Away," 1965
■ ALBUMS
Anytime, 1952
All Time Favorites, 1953
Chapel on the Hill, 1954
A Dozen Hits, 1956
My Darling, My Darling, 1957
Eddy Arnold, 1959
Eddy Arnold Sings Them Again, 1960
Let's Make Memories Tonight, 1961
Cattle Call, 1963
Country Songs I Love to Sing, 1963
Pop Hits from the Country Side, 1964
Lonely Again, 1967
Turn the World Around, 1967
Welcome to My World, 1971
I Love How You Love Me, 1973
Country Gold, 1975
Eddy Arnold's World of Hits, 1976
Last of the Love Song Singers Then and Now, 1993

SELECT AWARDS
Country Music Hall of Fame, inducted 1966
Country Music Association Entertainer of the
    Year Award, 1967
Academy of Country Music Pioneer Award, 1983
Songwriter's Guild President's Award, 1987

SEE ALSO: Atkins, Chet; Cash, Johnny; Frizzell, Lefty; Jones, George; Perkins, Carl; Williams, Hank.

For the Record

In the late 1940's Eddy Arnold's manager, Colonel Tom Parker, had Arnold travel to a disc-jockey convention in Nashville astride an elephant. Wrapped around the elephant was a cloth saying "Never Forget Eddy Arnold."

Arrested Development

ORIGINAL MEMBERS: Speech (b. Todd Thomas, 1968), Headliner (b. Tim Barnwell, 1967),

Rasa Don (b. Donald Jones, 1968), Aerle Taree (b. 1973), Montsho Eshe (b. 1974), Baba Oje (b. 1932)

OTHER MEMBERS: Ajile, Kwesi, Nadirah

FIRST ALBUM RELEASE: *3 Years, 5 Months & 2 Days in the Life of . . .*, 1992

MUSICAL STYLES: Rap, hip-hop

Smoothly blending the "native tongues" school of hip-hop (featuring world music and light hip-hop) with southern folk and blues, Arrested Development became one of a handful of successful crossover rap acts in 1992 with a Top-10 single ("Tennessee," number 6) and Top-20 debut album (*3 Years, 5 Months & 2 Days in the Life of . . .*, number 13). They were successful, in part, because they abandoned their early experiments with "gangsta" rap and began to incorporate Christian values into their songs.

Arrested Development (Paul Natkin)

Getting Together. Todd Thomas and Tim Barnwell met at the Art Institute of Atlanta, Georgia, in 1987. After their initial foray into "gangsta" rap as Disciples of a Lyrical Rebellion, in 1988 they reexamined their art and took the names Speech (Thomas) and Headliner (Barnwell), suggesting a more politically conscious brand of rap. By the time they signed with Chrysalis Records in 1992, their music had become softer and more thoughtful, and the band had expanded into a multigenerational extended family, including Speech's cousin, Aerle Taree, and spiritual adviser Baba Oje. Though dismissed by many "gangsta" rappers as tame, Speech explained, "Our purpose was to make people want to live. How can anybody change the situation they're living in if they don't want to live?"

The album *3 Years, 5 Months & 2 Days in the Life of . . .* also featured the hit singles "People Everyday" (number 8), which incorporated the chorus to Sly and the Family Stone's "Everyday People," and "Mr. Wendal" (number 6). The single "Revolution," recorded for Spike Lee's 1992 film *Malcolm X,* failed to make the Top 40, but their follow-up album *Unplugged* (1993) reached number 38 on the rhythm-and-blues charts.

Coming to the End. After participating in the third annual "Lollapalooza" tour, Ajile, Kwesi, and Nadirah joined the band to record *Zingalamaduni* (1994), which means "beehive of culture" in the east African language of Swahili. The group took more musical chances on the album but still con-

For the Record

Dionne Farris, who sang on the hit "Tennessee," went on to have her own Top-10 single in 1995 with "I Know" (number 4).

veyed optimism in the midst of an ongoing struggle for African Americans around the world. "WMFW (We Must Fight and Win)" and "United Front" demonstrate their concern for the cause of racial justice, while "Praisin' U" and "Pride" provide clear reasons for hope. Most black critics dismissed *Zingalamaduni* as heavyhanded and self-righteous. Arrested Development disbanded in 1996.   —*John Powell*

SELECT DISCOGRAPHY
■ ALBUMS
3 Years, 5 Months & 2 Days in the Life of . . ., 1992
Unplugged, 1993
Zingalamaduni, 1994

SELECT AWARDS
Grammy Awards for Best New Artist and Best Rap Performance by a Duo or Group for "Tennessee," 1992

SEE ALSO: De La Soul; Sly and the Family Stone.

The Artist. *See* Prince

Asia

ORIGINAL MEMBERS: John Wetton (b. 1949), Steve Howe (b. 1947), Carl Palmer (b. 1947), Geoffrey Downes (b. 1952)
OTHER MEMBERS: Armand "Mandy" Meyer, Greg Lake (b. 1948), Pat Thrall, Vinnie Burns, Trevor Thornton, Michael Sturgis, John Payne, Aziz Ibrahim, Elliot Randall, Al Pitrelli
FIRST ALBUM RELEASE: *Asia*, 1982
MUSICAL STYLES: Rock and roll, pop

On paper, the emerging British supergroup Asia was a collection of artists who appeared destined to push progressive rock into the 1980's. Founding members John Wetton, Steve Howe, and Carl Palmer all had strong progressive rock roots—Wetton with King Crimson, Roxy Music, and Uriah Heep; Howe with Yes; and Palmer with Emerson, Lake, and Palmer. Leaving behind the eight-minute-long song format of Yes as well as other progressive rock tendencies, the Asia founders instead chose to apply their skills as musicians to a more modern pop format. After they added keyboard player Geoffrey Downes, the initial lineup was complete. The chemistry worked, and Asia recorded "Heat of the Moment," its first hit single.

Success from the Start. Asia released its self-titled debut album in 1982, which spent nine weeks atop the *Billboard* album chart. The lead single, "Heat of the Moment," reached number 4 on the singles chart. The album also included two other hits: "Only Time Will Tell" and "Sole Survivor." Asia toured the United States, Europe, and Japan, selling out many venues along the way. While the album was definitely pop-oriented, progressive rock fans could not help but notice the cover art imagery and band logo, designed by famed science-fiction illustrator and Yes cover artist Roger Dean.

Lineup Changes. In 1983, Asia released *Alpha*, which spent twenty-five weeks on the *Billboard* chart, peaking at number 6. Including the singles "Don't Cry" and "The Smile Has Left Your Eyes," the album failed to match the popularity of the band's debut. Later that year, as tension built within the band, Wetton left and was replaced by Greg Lake (formerly of Emerson, Lake, and Palmer). After a short stay, Lake left the band and Wetton returned. Soon after, Howe left and was replaced by guitarist Armand "Mandy" Meyer, who had played previously with Krokus.

In 1985, Asia released *Astra*, but the album was met with minimal interest and the band broke up. While band members continued to pursue other projects throughout the 1980's, various combinations of old and new members conducted short tours under the Asia name in the latter part of the decade. The band more firmly reunited in 1991 when Downes, Palmer, Howe, bassist-vocalist John Payne, and guitarist Al Pitrelli recorded *Aqua*, Asia's fourth studio album. Following the end of the Aqua tour in 1993, Howe left the band again to pursue solo projects. Asia continued playing and recording and released *Aria* in 1994 and *Arena* in 1996. Asia fans considered *Arena* to be a turning point, as the band tried for a new sound by putting Downes's keyboard at the center of the mix.   —*Harriet L. Schwartz*

SELECT DISCOGRAPHY
■ SINGLES
"Heat of the Moment," 1982
"Only Time Will Tell," 1982
"Sole Survivor," 1982
"Don't Cry," 1983
■ ALBUMS
Asia, 1982
Alpha, 1983
Astra, 1985
Then and Now, 1990
Live in Moscow, 1991
Aqua, 1992
Aria, 1994
Arena, 1996
Archiva 1, 1996 (previously released material)
Archiva 2, 1996 (previously released material)
Anthology, 1997 (previously released material)

SEE ALSO: Emerson, Lake, and Palmer; King Crimson; Roxy Music; Yes.

The Association

ORIGINAL MEMBERS: Terry Kirkman (b. 1941), Gary "Jules" Alexander (b. 1943), Ted Bluechel, Jr. (b. 1942), Russ Giguere (b. 1943), Brian Cole (1942-1972), Jim Yester (b. 1939)
OTHER MEMBERS: Larry Ramos, Jr. (b. 1942)
FIRST SINGLE RELEASE: "Babe I'm Gonna Leave You," 1965
MUSICAL STYLES: Easy listening, folk rock, pop rock

The Association was a six-man band that emerged from the California folk music scene in the mid-1960's to record some of the most popular pop-rock songs and ballads of the era. Five of their singles reached the Top 10 between 1966 and 1968, and four of those, particularly "Never My Love," went on to become classic songs, played on the radio millions of times since their inception.

The group walked a fine line between trying to appeal to the teenage fans of catchy pop songs and addressing a developing audience that preferred more progressive music. For example, while the band looked clean-cut and wrote well-crafted, short songs (attributes of pop bands), they were also invited to perform at the Monterey Pop Festival in 1967.

The Beginnings. The Association formed in 1965 in Los Angeles, when members of a large group called the Men pared down to a sextet. Terry Kirkman could play more than twenty wind, reed, and percussion instruments as well as keyboards. Guitars were handled by Jim Yester, Gary "Jules" Alexander, and Russ Giguere, bass by Brian Cole, and drums by Ted Bluechel, Jr.

The Association was discovered performing at the hot L.A. nightclub the Troubadour and, after releasing two unsuccessful singles, signed to Valiant Records in 1966. That summer they had their first major hit, the up-tempo folk-rock song "Along Comes Mary." It eventually hit number 7 despite charges by some conservative members of the radio establishment that Mary was actually a code word for marijuana, which the group denied. The group's first album, *And Then . . . Along Comes the Association* (1966), also did well, reaching number 5.

Softening Up. For their follow-up single, they chose "Cherish," a soft ballad written by Kirkman. At first the group did not believe the record would become a hit, but it ultimately stayed at number 1 for three weeks and has since gone on to become a classic love song of the 1960's. "Pandora's Golden Heebie Jeebies" was not a huge hit, nor was "No Fair at All," but the group soon made up for those setbacks as well as for the resignation of Alexander, who was replaced by Larry Ramos.

In mid-1967 the Association switched to Warner Bros. Records and delivered "Windy," a breezy light rock song. Written by the group's friend Ruthann Friedman, it rose to number 1. Like their other songs, "Windy" possessed an addictive melodic hook and a solid arrangement, its peppy vocal delivered by several members of the band, all of whom often shared vocals. Just as "Windy" reached the charts, the Association joined such music luminaries as Jimi Hendrix, the

Who, the Grateful Dead, Simon and Garfunkel, Otis Redding, and the Mamas and the Papas at the Monterey Pop Festival, one of rock's pivotal events.

Million-Airs. In only a few months, the group was back near the top of the charts with another ballad, "Never My Love," written by Don and Dick Addrisi. Although the record peaked at number 2, it would become such a consistent favorite over the years that it was certified as one of the four most-aired songs of all time on radio. (The group's other placements in Broadcast Music Incorporated's "Million-Airs Club"— records that have been played on the radio over a million times—are "Windy," "Cherish," and "Along Comes Mary.")

The Association had just one Top-10 single left, 1968's "Everything That Touches You," and a number 4 *Greatest Hits* album (1968). They also recorded a sound-track album, *Goodbye Columbus* (1969). The Association continued to record into the mid-1970's, but their time had clearly passed. Cole died of a drug overdose in 1972, but some of the other members continued to perform in various combinations. In 1981, most of the original members joined together again

The Association (Archive Photos/Frank Driggs Collection)

and signed with Elektra, managing to place one last single, "Dreamer," on the charts. In the late 1990's, a version of the Association that included Giguere and Ramos still continued to tour and record.
— *Jeff Tamarkin*

SELECT DISCOGRAPHY
■ SINGLES
"Along Comes Mary," 1966
"Cherish," 1966
"Windy," 1967
"Never My Love," 1967
■ ALBUMS
And Then . . . Along Comes the Association, 1966
Insight Out, 1967
Greatest Hits, 1968

SEE ALSO: Lovin' Spoonful, The; Mamas and the Papas, The; Simon and Garfunkel.

For the Record

Jim Yester's brother, Jerry, replaced Zal Yanovsky in the Lovin' Spoonful in the late 1960's. When that band partially re-formed in the 1990's, Jim Yester also briefly became a member of the reunited Spoonful.

Chet Atkins

BORN: Luttrell, Tennessee; June 20, 1924
FIRST ALBUM RELEASE: *Chet Atkins Plays Guitar*, 1951
MUSICAL STYLES: Country

A product of rural poverty, Chester Burton (Chet) Atkins was an accomplished musician at an early age. His father, an itinerant evangelist, encouraged all family members to pursue musical careers, and young Atkins learned the fiddle first and then his true musical love, the guitar. As an adult, Atkins gained fame not only as a vocalist and musician but also as a highly respected arranger, producer, and record company executive.

The Beginnings. Atkins decided at a young age to dedicate his life to music. While still a teenager, he was a professional fiddle player for Archie Campbell before switching over permanently to the guitar. His musical virtuosity was soon widely known, and he served as both a session and performance guitarist for such artists as the Carter family, Bill Carlisle, and Red Foley. Heavily influenced by Les Paul and Merle Travis, Atkins developed his own distinctive finger-picking style of playing. His fame continued to grow as a response to his frequent appearances on the long-running "Mid-Day-Merry-Go-Round" radio program broadcast over WNOX in Nashville.

In 1947, Atkins signed a recording contract offered to him by Steve Sholes of RCA Victor Records. Unfortunately, this partnership did not produce a series of big-selling hits for Atkins, yet it did open the door for a whole new career. Sholes noticed immediately that Atkins was kind, imaginative, and solicitous, qualities that could at least help produce hit records for others. The guitarist had fresh new ideas, many of which he learned through listening to and being a fan of different types of music such as jazz, blues, gospel, and classical. In addition to possessing a widespread knowledge of these various musical genres, Atkins was daring and creative in experimenting with different recording methods. One practice Atkins helped establish was the use of multiple microphones during recording sessions to produce a fuller, lusher sound. He also suggested that recording artists move closer to the microphones, a relatively simple idea that ended the long-running problem of largely incoherent-sounding vocals.

The Producer Years. As the 1950's progressed, Sholes became even more impressed by Atkins's vast array of musical skills. Atkins was in constant demand as the preeminent guitarist in Nashville and, increasingly, as a miracle worker in the control booth. In 1957, to no one's surprise, Sholes offered Atkins the coveted position of musical director for RCA's country recordings. Despite the offering of a bigger paycheck and an almost totally free hand in selecting artists and recording methods, Atkins hesitated before accepting. Only when Sholes reassured the artist that he could continue to make his own recordings did Atkins sign the contract and thus officially become what he had unofficially been for the past several years.

In his new position, Atkins continued his experimentation. For reasons largely unknown, the use of drums on country recordings had always been considered unacceptable. The Grand Ole Opry, for example, would not even allow them in its building, the Ryman Auditorium. Atkins had always considered this a curious practice, so he violated convention and began using them, going as far as attaching a microphone to the bass drum to make the sound even more pronounced. Despite screaming protests from traditionalists, the move was well received; eventually, it became rare to find a country band without drums.

Atkins's reputation for innovation and risk taking continued to grow. He was trying to create a musical structure for country music that would allow its artists to enjoy success on the pop charts as well, a feat accomplished at that time only by the late and mythic Hank Williams. Some of his new concepts included balancing the treble and bass, using new chords and bass lines, developing the use of echo and reverberation studio effects, and introducing the tremolo guitar.

As gifted as he was as a player and producer, Atkins's skills were not limited to those areas. He quickly proved that he was an outstanding judge of musical talent, and he was responsible for the birth or rebirth of several careers. One artist who benefited greatly from Atkins's support and encouragement was Don Gibson. Gibson was a talented songwriter, but earlier producers had mismanaged his recordings and, after being released from four previous record contracts (including an earlier RCA agreement), his career was apparently over. Atkins, though, had always been a fan, and he persuaded Sholes to re-sign Gibson for one more shot at stardom. Atkins eliminated the steel guitars and fiddle that had cluttered Gibson's earlier recordings and added a bass drum for rhythm. The results of the collaborative effort were the million-selling "Oh Lonesome Me" and a song that eventually emerged as a pop and country classic, "I Can't Stop Loving You." Atkins's reputation as a producer was so exalted that many of the top recording artists in the country, such as Perry Como, Eddy Arnold, Ray Charles, Elvis Presley, and Jim Reeves, sought him out for recording assistance. The fact that these artists embraced a variety of musical styles and yet were all aided by Atkins's ideas is a tribute to both his talent and versatility.

Music Man for All Seasons. In 1974, Atkins abruptly resigned from RCA Records. His executive career had been hugely successful, moving from the producer's position in 1957 to Nashville studio manager in 1960 to vice president of RCA Records in 1968. Feeling overwhelmed by paperwork and bureaucracy, he wanted to have the time and energy to pursue other musical interests. His subsequent accomplishments include performing with the Boston Pops Orchestra, and Atlanta Symphony Orchestra, Indian sitarist Ravi Shankar,

Chet Atkins (Archive Photos/Frank Driggs Collection)

For the Record

Although Chet Atkins's career spans seven decades, he was the youngest person (at age forty-nine) to be inducted into the Country Music Hall of Fame.

and jazz artist George Benson. Always fascinated by the mechanics of playing, Atkins designed a whole series of Chet Atkins Signature Guitars, and he also found time to write a well-received autobiography, *Country Gentleman* (1974). Always eager for something new, in the 1980's Atkins was joined by folk archivist and wit Garrison Keillor on a cross-country tour.

Although not primarily known as a performer, Atkins has released over one hundred albums, which have sold over thirty million copies. Many of these albums have been duets featuring artists such as Les Paul, Jerry Reed, and Doc Watson. There is no part of the recording industry left untouched by the talent of Chet Atkins. He nearly single-handedly created what later became known as the "Nashville Sound" while taking country music into new venues and introducing it to previously untouched markets. Few artists from any field have enjoyed such pervasive influence and respect. —*Thomas W. Buchanan*

SELECT DISCOGRAPHY
Chet Atkins Plays Guitar, 1951
Mister Guitar, 1960
Chet Atkins Picks on the Beatles, 1966
For the Good Times, 1971
The Atkins-Travis Travelin' Show, 1974 (with Merle Travis)
Chester and Lester, 1976 (with Les Paul)
Neck and Neck, 1990 (with Mark Knopfler)
Sneakin' Around, 1992 (with Jerry Reed)

SELECT AWARDS
Country Music Hall of Fame, inducted 1973

SEE ALSO: Arnold, Eddy; Orbison, Roy; Paul, Les.

Average White Band

ORIGINAL MEMBERS: Alan Gorrie (b. 1946), Onnie McIntyre (b. 1945), Roger Ball (b. 1944), Malcolm "Molly" Duncan (b. 1945), Robbie McIntosh (1950-1974), Hamish Stuart (b. 1949)
OTHER MEMBERS: Steve Ferrone (b. 1950), Alex Ligertwood
FIRST ALBUM RELEASE: *Show Your Hand*, 1973
MUSICAL STYLES: Funk, soul, disco

After years of playing the European club scene in other bands, the members of Average White Band (later shortened to AWB) joined forces in 1972 to create a dynamic, jazz-oriented sound. The Scottish band received their big break when they opened for Eric Clapton at his famous Rainbow Theatre comeback concert in 1973. Nevertheless, their first, self-produced album of that year, *Show Your Hand*, went almost unnoticed.

Attention. It took the number 1 single "Pick Up the Pieces" (1974) to finally lure the public's attention with their hard-driving sound. The hit featured a clever dual-guitar arrangement by Hamish Stuart and Onnie McIntyre and an outstanding saxophone solo by Molly Duncan. Their album *AWB* (1974), produced by Arif Mardin, also went to number 1 on the *Billboard* charts.

The follow-up album, *Cut the Cake* (1975), dedicated to drummer Robbie McIntosh, who had died of a drug overdose the previous year, peaked at number 4. It contains the band's only other Top-10 single, "Cut the Cake" (number 10). *Soul Searching* (number 9, 1976) was released at the peak of the funk era. Though it contained no hits, it was their biggest commercial success and became their only platinum album. With the advent of the disco sound, AWB's popularity began to decline. *Person to Person* (1976) and *Warmer Communications* (1978) both went to number 28 on the album charts and were certified gold.

With their mid-1970's success, the AWB determined to settle in the United States, which had produced the rhythm-and-blues and soul music so instrumental in the development of their sound. After 1975, band members increasingly played as sidemen with other groups, including doing

For the Record

The AWB embarked on their debut tour of the United States in 1973 with second-hand equipment borrowed from the Who.

backup work for Chaka Khan's debut album in 1978, also produced by Mardin. Steve Ferrone, who had replaced McIntosh, went on to play drums with Duran Duran, and Stuart played guitar with Paul McCartney (*Flowers in the Dirt*, 1989, and *Unplugged*, 1991).

No Stopping. Though AWB never regained the popularity attained in the mid-1970's, their solid talent has worn well. In 1989 bassist Alan Gorrie, McIntyre, and keyboardist Roger Ball reformed the band, releasing *Aftershock* that year. Bringing in session players such as Alex Ligertwood and friends with great funk credentials, including Chaka Khan and the Ohio Players, they produced a solid album which nevertheless broke no new ground. Though they enjoyed no chart action after 1979, AWB continued to tour into the 1990's.

—*John Powell*

SELECT DISCOGRAPHY
■ ALBUMS
Show Your Hand, 1973 (rereleased as *Put It Where You Want It*, 1975)
AWB, 1974
Soul Searching, 1976
Benny and Us, 1977 (with Ben E. King)
Feel No Fret, 1979
Volume VIII, 1980
Cupid's in Fashion, 1982
Best of Average White Band, 1984 (compilation)
Aftershock, 1989
Pickin' Up the Pieces: The Best of the Average White Band (1974-1980), 1992 (compilation)

SEE ALSO: Khan, Chaka.

B

The B-52's

ORIGINAL MEMBERS: Kate Pierson (b. 1948), Fred Schneider (b. 1951), Keith Strickland (b. 1953), Cindy Wilson (b. 1957), Ricky Wilson (1953-1986)
FIRST ALBUM RELEASE: *The B-52's*, 1979
MUSICAL STYLES: Rock and roll, new wave

The B-52's have described themselves as "a tacky little dance band." The characterization reveals more than a self-deprecating sense of humor; the B-52's certainly are a dance band, and they certainly managed to make tackiness chic. Founded in the late 1970's, the B-52's offered fun-loving theatrics and an optimistic tone as a striking alternative to the gloominess and self-importance of so many punk and new-wave bands popular at the end of that decade. Their strengths include fanciful lyrics, a spare and tight sound, a flair for reviving the worst (and therefore most amusing) aspects of 1960's culture, and an irreverent sense of humor about everything, including themselves. The name of the band refers to southern slang for bouffant hairstyles, a look popular in the late 1950's and early 1960's, which Kate Pierson and Cindy Wilson wore proudly.

From Athens to New York. The members of the band met in Athens, Georgia, site of the University of Georgia. Keith Strickland and the Wilson siblings, Cindy and Ricky, grew up in Athens, while the other members relocated there during the 1970's. The band started out as a lark. After eating and drinking at a Chinese restaurant in 1976, the members retired to a friend's house where they began jamming on various instruments. Fred Schneider, Cindy Wilson, and Kate Pierson improvised lyrics and vocals to a song about killer bees forcing a car into a lake where the occupants are devoured by piranhas. While this first effort was never recorded, the band's method of collaborative generation of songs with absurd themes vaguely recalling cheap horror and science-fiction films of the early 1960's was established. Pleased with what they created, the band wrote more songs, culminating in a performance at a Valentine's Day party in 1977. Although never in hot demand in Athens, the band did enjoy a small and devoted following.

At the suggestion of friends, the band went to New York City and played at Max's Kansas City. The audience scarcely knew what to make of a band dressed in thrift-store clothes salvaged from a bygone era delivering songs with unabashedly silly lyrics and a lean sound derived from a peculiar mixture of punk and 1960's girl groups, presented with considerable theatricality. Their performance drew return invitations to play at Max's Kansas City. Within a year, the B-52's were the most sought-after act at trendy New York dance clubs.

Their early success was in part dependent on their bizarre signature song, "Rock Lobster." Inspired by beach-party films and Roger Corman's

For the Record

The stage costumes of the B-52's were mostly purchased at thrift and secondhand stores. Typically appearing in outlandish color schemes and wearing fashions that had not been popular since before most of their fans were born, the band prided itself on its unorthodox look. Kate Pierson explained in *Rolling Stone*, "We always shopped at thrift stores; it was sort of a pastime. . . . It's actually good to think that you're recycling clothes like this, too. I mean look at this new stuff. So much of it is acrylic. I think this stuff will be around after the earth disintegrates."

low-budget monster films of the 1960's, "Rock Lobster" captures the essence of the band. The song begins with guitarist Ricky Wilson playing a memorable recurring figure. Wilson boasted an original guitar sound, owing in part to his removal of the middle two strings from his guitar. Strickland's precise and energetic drum lines made "Rock Lobster" an irresistible dance favorite. Pierson played organ on "Rock Lobster" and most of the band's subsequent songs. Pierson also sang, sometimes in tight harmony or unison with Cindy Wilson. Perhaps the most distinctive aspect of the song is Schneider's ironically animated yet monotone delivery of the lead vocals. The lyrics of "Rock Lobster" celebrate innocent fun through images of beach parties featuring by then out-of-fashion dances such as the twist.

In 1979, the extraordinary popularity of the band with club audiences prompted a flood of offers for recording contracts. The band signed with Chris Blackwell of Island Records, who produced their first album, *The B-52's*. The album won considerable critical success and sold reasonably well despite receiving almost no support through radio airplay. The album features a cover of Petula Clark's "Downtown" presented with loving irreverence. The song "Planet Claire" also proved to be a fan favorite with its unlikely instrumental solos evocative of 1950's science-fiction films. These outlandish lyrics demonstrate their ingenuity: "Planet Claire has pink air/ All the trees are red/ No one ever dies there/ No one has a head."

The 1980's and 1990's. *The B-52's* was followed by a second album, *Wild Planet* (1980). While containing no superb hit of the stature of "Rock Lobster," *Wild Planet* proved that the group could sustain the same energy that had made their de-

The B-52s (Archive Photos/Frank Driggs Collection)

but album such an unexpected hit. *Wild Planet* commercially outperformed the debut album by making the *Billboard* Top 20. If anything, *Wild Planet* was an amplification of the most singular elements found in the first effort. Moreover, the band sounded even tighter and the production values were greater. One of the stronger songs on the album, "Private Idaho," features Pierson and Cindy Wilson crooning in close harmony: "You're living in your own, private Idaho/ Underground like a wild potato." Other standout tracks include "Devil in My Car" and "Strobe Light."

Setbacks. The saddest moment in the band's history came with the untimely death of Ricky Wilson due to acquired immunodeficiency syndrome (AIDS) in 1986. He had been a crucial part of the band's success and was a coinventor of their sound, thanks to his limitless capacity for making inventive choices while generally playing only two chords and short riffs. After his death, the B-52's did not record any new songs for three years.

When the band returned to recording and performing, they scored a triumph with the extraordinarily popular "Love Shack," the first B-52's song to win extensive radio exposure. "Love Shack" was supported by a hilarious music video that enjoyed favor on MTV.

In 1992, Cindy Wilson left the band. Various singers, including Julie Cruise, would take her place when the band played its early material in concert. Some band members would pursue solo projects or work prominently with other bands. Fred Schneider undertook several solo projects, including two albums: *Fred Schneider and the Shake Society* (1991) and *Just Fred* (1996). Kate Pierson has been a guest vocalist with Iggy Pop and most successfully with R.E.M. on the hit "Shiny Happy People."

Impact. The B-52's established one of the most recognizable and enduring new-wave sounds. Their music anticipated the 1990's more than one decade prior, with a revival of interest in all things associated with the 1960's. Echoes of their first album can be heard in the music of many of the most popular bands of the 1980's through their introduction of a lean sound coupled with surgically precise rhythms.

Despite the B-52's' involvement in all manner of liberal political causes and environmental activities, their views scarcely had an impact on their music. At most, their songs could be said to convey a vaguely subversive message through their willful nonconformity.

—Michael Lee

SELECT DISCOGRAPHY
■ ALBUMS
The B-52's, 1979
Wild Planet, 1980
Party Mix! 1981 (remix, extended-play single)
Mesopotamia, 1982 (extended-play single)
Whammy! 1983
Bouncing Off the Satellites, 1986
Cosmic Thing, 1989
Good Stuff, 1992

SEE ALSO: Devo; R.E.M.

Babyface

(Kenneth Edmonds)

BORN: Indianapolis, Indiana; April 10, 1959
FIRST ALBUM RELEASE: *Lovers*, 1987
MUSICAL STYLES: Pop, soul

Kenneth Edmonds became, with production partner Antonio "L.A." Reid, one of the most prolific writers of number 1 rhythm-and-blues hits in the late 1980's and 1990's. A talented vocalist, he has also recorded a string of hit singles since "Two Occasions" raced to number 4 on the pop charts early in 1988. By 1998, he had had a hand in writing, producing, or performing 110 Top-40 rhythm-and-blues hits, 31 of which went to number 1.

The Writer and Producer. Edmonds broke into the recording industry in the late 1970's playing guitar and singing for local and area bands, including the Crowd Pleasers, a Michigan Top-40 cover band, and Manchild. After writing "Slow Jam" for Midnight Star, he was invited to the recording session, where he began working with Reid, who was part of Midnight Star's production team. Their close collaboration led Reid to invite Edmonds to join his Cincinnati, Ohio, rhythm-

and-blues and funk band the Deele. Together they began writing and producing their own material. Though none of the band's three albums made the Top 40, *Material Thangz* marked their first joint production, and their final album, *Eyes of a Stranger* (1987), included the hit "Two Occasions."

After an introduction to Dick Griffey of Solar Records, Reid and Babyface were soon producing other acts. They had an uncanny ability to produce number 1 rhythm-and-blues hits. The Whispers ("Rock Steady," 1987), Mac Band ("Roses Are Red," 1988), Bobby Brown ("Don't Be Cruel," 1988; "Every Little Step," 1989; "On Our Own," 1989), Karyn White ("The Way You Love Me," 1988; "Superwoman," 1989; "Love Saw It," 1989), and the Boys ("Dial My Heart," 1988; "Lucky Charm," 1989) all took songs produced by Reid and Babyface to the top at the end of the 1980's.

The Recording Artist. At the same time, Babyface pursued a solo recording career. Though his first album, *Lovers* (1987), went almost unnoticed, it did produce "I Love You Babe" (number 8, rhythm and blues) and suggested that he had an irresistible romantic touch, simultaneously vulnerable and experienced. His second album, the double-platinum *Tender Lover* (1989), left no doubt. With "It's No Crime" (number 7, pop; number 1, rhythm and blues), "Tender Lover" (number 14, pop; number 1, rhythm and blues), "My Kinda Girl" (number 30), and "Whip Appeal" (number 6) all crossing over to the pop charts, Babyface laid claim to the silky, romantic mantle of Sam Cooke and Luther Vandross.

Clearly established as a writer, producer, and singer, Babyface became famous in the 1990's. As a vocalist, he had the first number 1 rhythm-and-blues hit of the 1990's ("Tender Lover"). As a writer and producer, the Babyface/Reid duo gave Whitney Houston the number 1 pop hit "I'm Your Baby Tonight" (1990), lengthening her streak of consecutive number 1 singles to eight and helping her win back the African American audience she had been losing. By the end of 1990, Babyface had written and produced eighteen number 1 rhythm-and-blues hits, almost all in conjunction with Reid.

LaFace. In 1989, Babyface and Reid moved to Atlanta, Georgia, and formed the record com-

Babyface collecting his American Music Awards in 1998 (AP/Wide World Photos)

pany LaFace, whose stable in the 1990's included Toni Braxton, TLC, Damian Dame, and Az Yet. They continued to write for and produce stars such as Aretha Franklin, Paula Abdul, Pebbles, Johnny Gill, Sheena Easton, the Jacksons, and Boyz II Men. Reid and Babyface won Grammy Awards in 1992 as producers and songwriters for Boyz II Men's "End of the Road" and in 1993 for production of Whitney Houston's sound track for *The Bodyguard*.

From the early 1990's, creative differences with Reid led Babyface to seek more solo projects, though the two continued to produce together. *For the Cool in You* (1993) included the hit "When Can I See You" (number 4), which earned Babyface a 1994 Grammy Award for Best R&B Male Vocal Performance. In the same year he received the Grammy for Best R&B Song for "I'll Make Love to You," performed by Boyz II Men. Babyface launched his first tour as a solo artist in December, 1994, coheadlining with Boyz II Men.

He continued strong in 1995, as "Take a Bow," on which he sang backup for Madonna, spent seven weeks atop the pop charts. At the same time, he was at work on what he called a "once-in-a-life-time opportunity" for a songwriter-producer, writing or cowriting fifteen of the sixteen tracks for the *Waiting to Exhale* sound track and producing arrangements for an all-star cast of vocalists, including Whitney Houston, Toni Braxton, Aretha Franklin, Patti LaBelle, TLC, Brandy, and Mary J. Blige.

Grammy Fever. In 1996 Babyface tied a record for earning twelve Grammy nominations. He won awards for Record of the Year (as coproducer of Eric Clapton's "Change the World"), Best R&B Song for "Exhale (Shoop Shoop)," and Producer of the Year (for writing and producing most of the songs on the *Waiting to Exhale* sound track and production work on albums by Boyz II Men, Toni Braxton, Az Yet, and others). He (as producer) and Eric Clapton paired up to take "Change the World," from the film *Phenomenon*, to number 1. The double-platinum *Day* was also released to strong reviews in 1996 and produced the hits "This Is for the Lover in You," featuring L. L. Cool J (number 6), and "Every Time I Close My Eyes," with background vocals by Mariah Carey and a saxophone solo by Kenny G (number 6).

In the late 1990's Babyface continued his prolific output as both singer and producer. The live

---

For the Record

While still in his teens, Kenny Edmonds played with the legendary funk bassist Bootsy Collins, who gave him the nickname Babyface because of his youthful looks.

MTV Unplugged NYC 1997 featured fourteen songs written and sung by him, with guest appearances by Eric Clapton and Stevie Wonder. Also that year he became executive producer of his first feature film, *Soul Food*, whose sound track went platinum and helped earn him yet another Grammy Award for Producer of the Year, Non-Classical. In the following year he teamed up with Des'ree to sing and produce a cover of Bruce Springsteen's "Fire," one of the most memorable tracks from the sound track to *Hav Plenty*, which entered the Top 40 in the summer of 1998.
—John Powell

SELECT DISCOGRAPHY
■ ALBUMS
Lovers, 1987
Tender Lover, 1989
A Closer Look, 1991
For the Cool in You, 1993
Day, 1996
Kenny "Babyface" Edmonds & Manchild, 1997
MTV Unplugged NYC 1997, 1997

SELECT AWARDS
Grammy Awards for Best R&B Song for "End of the Road" (wr. with L.A. Reid and Daryl Simmons) and Producer of the Year, Non-Classical (with L.A. Reid, tie with Daniel Lanois and Brian Eno), 1992
Grammy Award for Album of the Year for *The Bodyguard*, 1993 (with others)
Soul Train Music Album of the Year Award for *For the Cool in You*, 1993
Grammy Awards for Best R&B Song for "I'll Make Love to You" and Best Male R&B Vocal Performance for "When Can I See You," 1994
Grammy Award for Producer of the Year, 1995
Grammy Awards for Record of the Year for "Change the World," Best R&B Song for "Exhale (Shoop Shoop)," and Producer of the Year, 1996
Grammy Award for Producer of the Year, Non-Classical, 1997
American Music Award for Favorite Male Pop Artist, 1997

SEE ALSO: Boyz II Men; Braxton, Toni; Houston, Whitney.

Bachman-Turner Overdrive. *See* **The Guess Who / Bachman-Turner Overdrive**

Bad Company

ORIGINAL MEMBERS: Paul Rodgers (b. 1949), Simon Kirke (b. 1949), Mick Ralphs (b. 1948), Raymond "Boz" Burrell (b. 1946)

OTHER MEMBERS: Brian Howe, Geoffrey Whitehorn, Paul Cullen, Rick Wills, David "Bucket" Colwell, Robert Hart, others

FIRST ALBUM RELEASE: *Bad Company*, 1974

MUSICAL STYLES: Blues, rock and roll

Bad Company combined the talents of four experienced British rock musicians to produce blues-influenced hard rock in the tradition of Led Zeppelin. After enjoying great success in the 1970's and early 1980's, the band went through numerous changes in its membership but survived to record albums well into the 1990's.

Coming Together. The roots of Bad Company go back to British rock and roll of the 1960's. Guitarist Paul Kossoff had played with drummer Simon Kirke in a band called Black Cat Bones. Kossoff and Kirke, together with vocalist Paul Rodgers and bassist Andy Fraser, formed the band Free in 1968. Free enjoyed critical acclaim and moderate success, particularly in the United Kingdom. From 1969 to 1973 they recorded half a dozen albums and had one hit single, "All Right Now." Rodgers's strong vocals on this song were a preview of the many hits he would record with Bad Company.

Free broke up in 1973. Kossoff went on to form the band Back Street Crawler. On March 19, 1976, Kossoff died of heart failure while aboard an airplane taking him from Los Angeles to New York. Rodgers and Kirke joined with guitarist

Bad Company in 1977: Mick Ralphs, Paul Rodgers, Simon Kirke, Boz Burrell (Archive Photos)

Mick Ralphs and bassist Raymond "Boz" Burrell to form Bad Company in 1974. Ralphs had been a member of Mott the Hoople and Burrell had been a member of King Crimson. Given the experience of all four band members, it was not surprising that Bad Company quickly signed a recording contract. They became the first band to join Swan Song Records, the company formed by Led Zeppelin.

Early Success. Bad Company's self-titled debut album was an immediate success, with popular songs such as "Bad Company," "Ready for Love," and "Movin' On." The album's biggest hit, "Can't Get Enough," reached number 1 in the United States and the United Kingdom.

The band spent the next five years touring and recording almost constantly. They released a new album nearly every year and were famous for their outstanding live shows. Bad Company remained best-selling musicians on both sides of the Atlantic throughout this period, releasing such hits as "Good Lovin' Gone Bad" (1975), "Feel Like Makin' Love" (1975), and "Rock and Roll Fantasy" (1979). The last album from this period, *Desolation Angels* (1979), included the use of strings and synthesizers, but Bad Company remained true to their roots in guitar-based blues rock.

After Rodgers. After a three-year rest, Bad Company released another successful album, *Rough Diamonds*, in 1982. The next year Rodgers left the group to release a solo album. He later went on to form two new bands: the Firm, with Led Zeppelin guitarist Jimmy Page in 1984, and the Law, with drummer Kenney Jones in 1991. In 1993, along with other well-known artists, he recorded tribute albums to blues musician Muddy Waters and rock musician Jimi Hendrix.

Meanwhile, vocalist Brian Howe, who had formerly worked with Ted Nugent, took the place of Rodgers in Bad Company. The new version of the band released approximately one album every two years and enjoyed moderate success in the late 1980's and early 1990's. The band added guitarist Geoffrey Whitehorn and bassist Paul Cullen in 1990. The same year, the album *Holy Water* yielded the hit singles "If You Needed Somebody" and "Walk Through Fire." In 1992 bassist Rick

For the Record

The album that Paul Rodgers recorded after leaving Bad Company (*Cut Loose*, 1983) was one of the few true solo albums in the history of rock and roll: Rodgers not only produced it, but also played all the instruments.

Wills, formerly a member of Foreigner, joined Bad Company. The band did not enjoy the same popularity in the 1990's as it had in the 1970's, but it was clear that there were still many fans of traditional hard rock who continued to enjoy their music.
—*Rose Secrest*

SELECT DISCOGRAPHY
■ ALBUMS
Bad Company, 1974
Straight Shooter, 1975
Run with the Pack, 1976
Burnin' Sky, 1977
Desolation Angels, 1979
Rough Diamonds, 1982
10 from 6, 1986 (previously released material)
Fame and Fortune, 1986
Dangerous Age, 1988
Holy Water, 1990
Here Comes Trouble, 1992
The Best of Bad Company Live: What You Hear Is What You Get, 1993 (live)
Company of Strangers, 1995

SEE ALSO: Foreigner; King Crimson; Led Zeppelin.

Erykah Badu

(Erica Wright)

BORN: Dallas, Texas; 1972
FIRST ALBUM RELEASE: *Baduizm*, 1997
MUSICAL STYLES: Jazz, rhythm and blues, hip-hop

Erykah Badu brought neosoul music into the spotlight in 1997, winning a Grammy Award and

Erykah Badu (Paul Natkin)

ing to New York City, in 1996. Though she had offers from other labels, she liked Massenburg and his personal approach. "He was young, black, very smart, and he had a vision," she said. He proved it by distributing ten thousand sampler cassettes at the 1996 Soul Train Awards ceremony and twenty-five hundred vinyl copies of "On and On" to radio stations and clubs.

The aggressive marketing paid off, and 1997 proved to be a year of great achievement. Badu recorded "Your Precious Love" with another Kedar Entertainment client, D'Angelo. Massenburg then invited legendary bassist Ron Carter and hip-hop innovators the Roots to work on her debut album, *Baduizm* (1997), which entered the pop charts at number 2 and went platinum in only two months. The hit single "On and On" went to number 1 on the rhythm-and-blues charts (number 12, pop). *Baduizm* had critics competing for superlatives to describe her fresh fusion of jazz and hip-hop, which helped earn for her a Grammy Award for Best Female R&B Vocal Performance. Late in the year she released her second album, *Live* (number 1, rhythm and blues), which contained live cuts from her first album and renditions of 1970's soul standards. In 1998 she further expanded her horizons, booking a four-night engagement at Manhattan's Soul Café and contributing what one reviewer called "a meditative, spiritual masterpiece" ("Ye Yo") to the Babyface-produced sound track for *Have Plenty*. She was also featured at the popular all-female Lilith Fair festivals.

Heritage. Race has been at the heart of Badu's musical vision. While in high school, she consciously embraced her African American heritage, rejecting Erica as a slave name. Though her mother was unpleased, they compromised with the new spelling, Erykah. She later changed her last name to Badu, which means "to manifest truth and light" in Arabic. In concert she wore traditional African fashions and symbols, including distinctive high headwraps. "I like adorning myself with my culture," she observed. Badu self-consciously avoided labels and tags. Believing that contemporary rhythm and blues had become too monotonous, she wanted "to be the midwife to a

attracting widespread attention from the mainstream press, who were quick to compare her to Billie Holiday. Though she listened to Holiday while growing up in Dallas, Texas, she has also credited Stevie Wonder, Chaka Khan, and James Brown for her early development.

Discovery. As a teenager, Badu attended the prestigious Dallas High School of Performing and Visual Arts, where she became deeply involved in hip-hop, taking the name MC Apple. She studied theater and dance at Grambling State University but dropped out in 1993 to pursue her music career. With her cousin, Robert "Free" Bradford, she formed the group Erykah Free, which opened shows for A Tribe Called Quest, Wu-Tang Clan, and Mobb Deep. She was discovered in 1995 by Kedar Massenburg and became the first artist to sign with the fledgling Kedar Entertainment, mov-

new sound," and early critics suggested that she may have been successful. —*John Powell*

SELECT DISCOGRAPHY

■ ALBUMS
Baduizm, 1997
Live, 1997

SELECT AWARDS

Grammy Award for Best Female R&B Vocal Performance for "On and On," 1997

Soul Train Awards for Best R&B/Soul Single, Female, for "On and On," Best R&B/Soul Album for *Baduizm*, Best R&B/Soul or Rap Album for *Baduizm*, Best R&B/Soul or Rap New Artist, 1997

SEE ALSO: Babyface; Holiday, Billie; Khan, Chaka.

Joan Baez

BORN: Staten Island, New York; January 9, 1941
FIRST ALBUM RELEASE: *Joan Baez*, 1960
MUSICAL STYLE: Folk

After teaching herself to play the guitar when she was in high school, Joan Baez had achieved celebrity status by the time she was twenty. She used her considerable influence to promote social causes from civil rights to global peace, and became an icon for the disaffected generation of the 1960's.

The Beginning. Baez, the second child of a physics professor and a homemaker, moved frequently as a child and was very influenced by the year her family spent in Iraq when she was ten. The poverty and brutality she saw on the streets probably triggered a strong social conscience which influenced her life and work. She had difficulty adjusting to private school and was permitted to study at home for the year, where she pursued biology and art.

Baez attended high school in Palo Alto, California, while her father was at Stanford University. When she was sixteen, she met an activist for Gandhian nonviolence, Ira Sandperl, at a Quaker meeting. He became a major influence in her life. After high school, Baez moved with her family to

Boston, where she briefly attended the Fine Arts School of Drama at Boston University. Coffeehouses with live entertainment were popular at that time, and she performed around Harvard Square, where her ethereal soprano and simple style attracted attention. She soon met Manny Greenfield, a Boston impresario who managed her career for many years. After a second appearance at the Newport Folk Festival in Rhode Island in 1960, she made her first recording for Vanguard Records, *Joan Baez*. The album was an immediate success, and her national concert tour in early 1961 drew capacity crowds and critical raves.

Doing It Her Way. Baez accepted fame on her own terms, as she had won it. During the 1960's she turned down offers for concert engagements, Broadway musicals, and Hollywood films. She knew she was at her best when she confronted the audiences with only a guitar and her haunted soprano, radiating both innocence and arrogance. Her material was made up of old ballads, spirituals, blues, and folk songs from around the world, as well as topical songs on brotherhood and disarmament.

Baez settled in California in 1961, first in Big Sur and then in Carmel. By the end of 1963, she had joined the protest movement and focused on civil rights issues, singing at black colleges in the South and at the Lincoln Memorial with Dr. Martin Luther King, Jr., during the March on Washington. She participated in the antiwar movement and went to jail with her mother for practicing civil disobedience at the Oakland Military Induction Center. She was active at the University of California at Berkeley in the fall of 1964, where she joined the free speech movement with Ira Sandperl. A few months later, Baez and Sandperl established the Institute for the Study of Nonviolence in an old schoolhouse near her home in Carmel. Her 1963 album, *In Concert, Pt. 2*, featured Bob Dylan's "Don't Think Twice, It's All Right" and led Baez to invite the emerging Dylan on tour, which fostered a well-documented romance. She interpreted many of his songs over the years. Baez gave about twenty concerts a year, many of them benefits for Quaker meetings or peace groups. She earned vast sums on record royalties and donated generously to nonviolent political activities.

In 1967, Baez met David Harris, a leader in the movement against the draft who shared Baez's commitment to nonviolence. She went on the road with Harris and Sandperl, singing and speaking against the Vietnam War to large audiences. In 1968 she married Harris, who was imprisoned the following year for refusing induction. Baez worked on a film, bore their son, and traveled, but when Harris was released she found that she was too independent to be his wife, and the couple divorced.

Joan Baez (National Archives)

Recording Landmarks. *The First Ten Years*, a landmark album released with Vanguard in 1970, was on the charts for months. "The Night They Drove Old Dixie Down" gave Baez a hit single in 1971, and that year she recorded *Blessed Are . . .* , the first album to include a number of her own songs. Shortly afterward, she parted company with Vanguard and signed with A&M Records, a larger and more prestigious company that allowed her a certain artistic license. The first two releases from A&M were political: *Come from the Shadows* (1972) and *Where Are You Now, My Son?* (1973), based on her controversial peace mission to Hanoi during the Christmas season of 1972. Although the albums sold fairly well, the political climate that responded to Baez was beginning to change. Although she was considered radical during the years of her greatest influence, she simply reflected the views with which she was brought up: a Quaker commitment to peace and a profound belief in the equality of all people.

Baez decided to record an album that was nonpolitical in 1975, and became involved with the music for its own sake for the first time. The album went gold, and Baez realized that *Diamonds and Rust* was one of the best albums she had ever made. The title track refers to her relationship with Dylan, and it presaged a musical reunion with him after ten years apart. She went on tour and released an album of that tour in 1976, titled *From Every Stage*.

Changing Times. At about this time, Baez realized she was having trouble with her voice and acquired a voice coach, Robert Bernard, for the first time. She left A&M and signed with Portrait, a move she later considered a mistake. Her first two albums with Portrait sold badly, and by the end of the decade Baez slowly and painfully realized she was no longer in tune with public taste.

As her musical career foundered during the 1980's, Baez seriously considered giving it up, but decided she needed change and sought help. Private therapy helped her through this trying period, and she divided her time between social activism, therapy, and singing. In 1989, she released an album celebrating thirty years of performing, titled *Speaking of Dreams*, which included duets with her old friends Paul Simon and Jackson Browne. She looked for a manager and settled on Mark Spector, who signed her with Virgin Records. Her 1992 release, *Play Me Backwards*, was her first album with a major label in more than ten years. The album was warmly greeted by critics and sold well. It was contemporary and sophisticated country rock, with acoustic guitar, electric bass, and percussion backing Baez on songs by Janis Ian, Mary Chapin Carpenter, and Baez herself. After the release she went on tour, singing new songs as well as familiar ones.

—*Sheila Golburgh Johnson*

SELECT DISCOGRAPHY

■ ALBUMS

Joan Baez, 1960
In Concert, 1962
Joan, 1967
The First Ten Years, 1970
Blessed Are . . ., 1971
Come from the Shadows, 1972

Diamonds and Rust, 1975
Speaking of Dreams, 1989
No Woman No Cry, 1989
Play Me Backwards, 1992

SELECT AWARDS

American Civil Liberties Union (ACLU) Earl Warren Civil Liberties Award, 1979
American Institute of Public Service Jefferson Award, 1980
Lennon Peace Tribute Award, 1982
Baez has received numerous other awards for her work in human rights, the primary area where she has directed her energies

SEE ALSO: Carpenter, Mary Chapin; Collins, Judy; Dylan, Bob; Seeger, Pete.

Anita Baker

BORN: Toledo, Ohio; January 26, 1958
FIRST ALBUM RELEASE: *The Songstress*, 1983
MUSICAL STYLES: Soul, pop

Anita Baker took the sultry rhythm-and-blues scene to new heights of sophistication in the late 1980's. Between 1986 and 1990, she had seven Top-5 rhythm-and-blues hits and earned a remarkable seven Grammy Awards with what she called her "fireside love songs."

Inspirations. Baker, the granddaughter of a barnstorming Christian minister, first began singing in an inner-city church in Detroit, Michigan. At the age of twelve she decided she wanted to be a singer. Already displaying a low and silken vocal timbre, she patterned herself after gospel singer Mahalia Jackson. According to Baker, "There was nobody else I could identify with except her, because her voice was heavy and kinda thick." At the age of sixteen she began challenging herself with jazz, especially the work of Sarah Vaughan and Nancy Wilson. About that time she also began to sing in local clubs and bars.

In 1978 Baker became lead singer for Chapter 8, a hard-core, ten-piece funk band. They had a minor regional hit with "I Just Want to Be Your Girl" (1980) but were soon dropped by the strug-

Anita Baker (Ken Settle)

the addition of former Chapter 8 friend Michael J. Powell to the production team. This winning combination produced Baker's *Rapture* (1986, number 11), which included four Top-10 rhythm-and-blues hits and established her as a star. The follow-up, *Giving You the Best That I've Got* (1988), was even bigger, spending four weeks at the top of the pop charts and producing the title track that went to number 3 on the pop charts and number 1 on rhythm-and-blues charts.

Baker continued to produce lush and well-crafted albums into the 1990's, though they failed to produce either the artistic or public sensation of *Rapture* and *Giving You the Best That I've Got*. *Compositions* (1990), full of jazz phrasing, failed to produce any hit singles but did go platinum and reached number 5 on the album charts. It also earned Baker a Grammy Award for Best R&B Vocal Performance, Female. *Rhythm of Love* (1994) rose to number 3 on the charts and went double platinum.

—*John Powell*

SELECT DISCOGRAPHY
■ ALBUMS
The Songstress, 1983
Rapture, 1986
Giving You the Best That I've Got, 1988
Compositions, 1990
Rhythm of Love, 1994

SELECT AWARDS
Grammy Awards for Best R&B Song for "Sweet Love" (with Gary Bias and Louis Johnson) and Best R&B Vocal Performance, Female, for *Rapture*, 1986
Grammy Award for Best Soul Gospel Performance by a Duo or Group, Choir or Chorus, for "Ain't No Need to Worry," 1987 (with the Winans)

gling Ariola Records for lacking star quality. After two years out of the music business, Baker, with great reluctance, accepted the offer of Otis Smith, a former Ariola executive, to come back to Los Angeles to record with his new label, Beverly Glen. The result, *The Songstress* (1983), was a radical departure from her recent funk background and one of the early examples of the coming "quiet-storm" style of smooth, romantic soul for adults. Though it went relatively unnoticed at the time, *The Songstress* was a harbinger of more elegant phrasing and sensual soul singing in the future.

Giving the Best. For two years Baker fought Smith in the courts for control of her career. In 1986 she finally won the right to leave Beverly Glen records. Elektra gave her the extensive authority in production she wanted, which led to

For the Record

Anita Baker, who is only four feet, eleven inches tall, has a vocal range of nearly four octaves.

Grammy Awards for Best R&B Song (wr. with Randy Holland and Skip Scarborough) and Best R&B Vocal Performance, Female, for "Giving You the Best That I've Got," 1988

Grammy Award for Best R&B Vocal Performance, Female, for *Giving You the Best That I've Got*, 1989

Grammy Award for Best R&B Vocal Performance, Female, for *Compositions*, 1990

Grammy Award for Best Female R&B Vocal Performance for "I Apologize," 1995

SEE ALSO: Jackson, Mahalia.

The Band

ORIGINAL MEMBERS: Rick Danko (b. 1943), Levon Helm (b. 1940), Garth Hudson (b. 1937), Richard Manuel (1943-1986), Robbie Robertson (b. 1943)

FIRST ALBUM RELEASE: *Music from Big Pink*, 1968

MUSICAL STYLES: Country rock, rock and roll

In January of 1970, the Band appeared on the cover of *Time* magazine. The accompanying story opened with a Mark Twain quote about the Mississippi River and called the group "five musical Huck Finns" who had absorbed, redefined, and transformed American rock music into "the new sound of country rock." The term "country rock" does not adequately define the fusion of musical influences—including rhythm and blues, gospel, folk, country, carnival, classical, and church music—that shaped the unique sound and mystique of one of the most influential rock bands of the late 1960's and 1970's.

The Beginnings. Formed in the late 1950's as the Hawks, the backup band of rockabilly artist Ronnie Hawkins, the group consisted of four Canadians and an American. The Canadians were guitarist Robbie Robertson, bass guitarist Rick Danko, pianist Richard Manuel, and organist Garth Hudson. Like Hawkins, drummer Levon Helm was from rural Arkansas. Touring on a circuit that ranged from its base in Canada to the southern United States, the young Canadians were profoundly influenced by the music, traditions, and folklore of the Deep South. The quintet left Hawkins in 1963, calling themselves Levon and the Hawks. Because they had three strong singers and each member played several instruments, the group did not have a "front man." They dedicated themselves to becoming one of the best bands in America.

Bob Dylan's Backup Band. While not widely known outside their club circuit, the Hawks were nevertheless highly regarded by other musicians, including John Hammond, Jr., a blues artist who invited them to play on his album. Hammond and others recommended the Hawks to Bob Dylan in 1965, when Dylan was looking for a band to support his "electric" tour. Dylan jolted the folk music world in July, 1965, when he appeared at the Newport Folk Festival accompanied by a rock band (not the Band, but members of the Paul Butterfield Blues Band). His performance was met with hostility by folk purists. Robbie Robertson and Levon Helm joined Dylan for a show at Forest Hills, New York, in August, 1965. They were later joined by the other Hawks, who backed Dylan on a world tour in 1965-1966. Frustrated by the constant booing of irate fans, Helm left the tour before it concluded.

Big Pink and Beyond. While Bob Dylan recovered from a 1966 motorcycle accident near his home in Woodstock, New York, the band took up residence nearby in a house they dubbed "Big Pink" (pictured on the back cover of their first album). Reunited with Helm and relieved of touring, the group thrived in the clubhouse atmosphere of the makeshift recording studio in the basement. Bob Dylan often joined the sessions, which were released years later as *The Basement Tapes*. The group signed a contract with Capitol Records and produced their debut album, *Music from Big Pink*, in 1968. The group was now officially called the Band, implying both anonymity of the individual players and consummate musicianship. The album contained eleven songs, three of which were written by or with Dylan, who also contributed the painting for the album's cover. Robertson's "The Weight," one of the group's best-known songs, was also included in the sound track of the 1969 film *Easy Rider*. The Band's intricate musical arrangements, mythical themes, and often cryptic lyrics, as well as their perceived aloofness, contributed to the aura of mystery that surrounded the group throughout its career.

The Band followed their successful debut album with the self-titled *The Band*, widely regarded as the group's masterpiece. The twelve original songs captured the essence of the rural South.

Among the best known are "The Night They Drove Old Dixie Down," and their first and only Top-40 hit, "Up on Cripple Creek." Helm never disguised his pronounced Arkansas accent and sang lead on most of the distinctively "southern" songs. Richard Manuel's singing ranged from a soulful timbre, often compared with Ray Charles, to a pure, ethereal falsetto that enabled him to perform ballads as well as hard-driving rock songs.

Rick Danko's voice was versatile, strong, and smooth. In many songs all three sang lead vocal in different parts, then blending together in the group's trademark harmonies. Although organist Garth Hudson never sang, he provided an additional "voice" by contributing intricate improvisations that helped shape the group's unique sound. *The Band*, well received by critics and fans, sold over one million copies and established the group as a major force in rock music.

The Band's subsequent albums did not achieve the success of their earlier efforts. *Stage Fright* included the semi-autobiographical title song, as well as "The Shape I'm In." *Cahoots* included a guest performance by Van Morrison on "4% Pantomime." *Rock of Ages*, recorded live, was well-received but included no new material. *Moondog Matinee* contained classic cover songs of the rock-and-roll legends who had influenced the Band. *Before the Flood* and *The Basement Tapes*, compilations of sessions with Bob Dylan and the Band, caused many to wonder if the group would ever again release new original material.

Retreating to Malibu, California, the Band built their own

The Band in 1969 (Archive Photos)

recording studio in an attempt to re-create the "clubhouse" atmosphere of their first albums. In 1975 they released *Northern Lights—Southern Cross*, consisting of eight new songs. Among them were "Ophelia," "It Makes No Difference," and "Acadian Driftwood." "Acadian Driftwood," the album's centerpiece, combined elements emblematic of the group: a historical theme, evocative lyrics, shared lead vocals, and tight harmonies, all enriched by Garth Hudson's beautiful keyboard playing. This was the Band's best effort since their second album, but it also marked a turning point because the group had decided to stop touring.

The Last Waltz. At the end of the summer of 1976, the Band announced that they would play their final show on Thanksgiving night in San Francisco (at the Winterland), where their concert career began in 1969. The farewell celebration featured an impressive array of guests who had worked with or influenced the Band, including Bob Dylan, Van Morrison, Joni Mitchell, Eric Clapton, and other rock, blues, and country superstars. A film of the concert, directed by Martin Scorsese, and a live album, both entitled *The Last Waltz*, were released in 1978. Although the Band at first planned to continue as a recording group, *Islands* was their last studio album. As the members of the Band became involved in individual projects and drifted further apart, it became clear that the quintet would never again perform as a unit.

Legacy. After the Band dissolved, Levon Helm, Rick Danko, and Robbie Robertson recorded solo albums. In spite of his limited singing abilities, Robertson's first solo album was particularly well received by critics, but his subsequent releases did not fare as well. Helm harbored bitter feelings toward Robertson for what he saw as Robertson's domination of the group, and he felt that Robertson had not properly credited others for their writing and arranging contributions. Garth Hudson, the most outstanding musician of the group, became a sought-after session player. Helm also pursued a film and television acting career, and Robertson worked on music scores for films and television. The Band reunited and toured without

For the Record

At the Band's first major concert appearance in San Francisco in 1969, Robbie Robertson, weakened by the flu and severe stage fright, had to be hypnotized in order to leave his bed. The group played a short set with the hypnotist strategically placed where he could give the distressed guitarist visual cues to reinforce the hypnotic suggestions. The incident inspired Robertson to write one of the Band's most popular concert songs, "Stage Fright."

Robertson in the 1980's. It was during a 1986 tour that Richard Manuel, who had suffered from depression, committed suicide in a motel room in Florida. Helm, Danko, and Hudson later reformed the Band, releasing albums in 1993 and 1996 and touring throughout the 1990's. The 1993 album *Jericho* included new original songs as well as a version of Bruce Springsteen's "Atlantic City."

The career of the original five-man group continued to capture the attention of rock aficionados and became the subject of video documentaries, numerous retrospective anthologies, and several books. The Band's music greatly influenced many musicians of the 1970's. What might simply be called the "American-ness" of their sound and subject matter, as well as their prominent use of keyboards—piano and organ, and sometimes accordion or synthesizer—undoubtedly influenced artists including Springsteen, Bob Seger, and John Mellencamp.

—*Kevin J. Bochynski*

SELECT DISCOGRAPHY
■ ALBUMS
Music from Big Pink, 1968
The Band, 1969
Stage Fright, 1970
Cahoots, 1971
Rock of Ages, 1972
Moondog Matinee, 1973

Before the Flood, 1974 (with Bob Dylan)
The Basement Tapes, 1975 (with Dylan)
Northern Lights—Southern Cross, 1975
Islands, 1977
The Last Waltz, 1978
Jericho, 1993
Live at Watkins Glen, 1995
High on the Hog, 1996

SELECT AWARDS
Canadian Music Hall of Fame, inducted 1989
Rock and Roll Hall of Fame, inducted 1994

SEE ALSO: Clapton, Eric; Dylan, Bob; Mitchell, Joni; Morrison, Van; Young, Neil.

The Beach Boys

ORIGINAL MEMBERS: Brian Wilson (b. 1942), Dennis Wilson (1944-1983), Carl Wilson (1946-1998), Mike Love (b. 1941), Al Jardine (b. 1942), Bruce Johnston (b. 1944)
FIRST ALBUM RELEASE: *Surfin' Safari*, 1962
MUSICAL STYLE: Rock and roll, pop

The Beach Boys did not invent surf music—there were many surf bands in Southern California at the time they first had a hit record, most notably Dick Dale and the Del-tones and the Ventures. Those bands played an energetic, distinctive style of guitar-driven instrumental rock that is still widely imitated. The Beach Boys did, however, bring a new vision to the early 1960's Southern California scene.

Southern California in 1963 was a place about which teenagers all across the United States dreamed. It conjured seductive images: two fast cars in every garage—one definitely a convertible—sun, sand, and surfing. The Beach Boys captured and reinforced these fantasies perfectly, projecting powerful images of teen utopia. They sang about two primary obsessions of teenage boys: girls and cars. "Surfer Girl" and "The Girls on the Beach" beautifully express longing for love, and the lyrics of "Little Deuce Coupe" and "409" accurately portray the world of hot rods and drag racing. "In My Room" may have hinted at the darker side of paradise, but for the most part the world of the early Beach Boys' music was "Fun, Fun, Fun."

Beginnings. The Beach Boys were a family band from Hawthorne, California, a suburb south of Los Angeles. The three Wilson brothers—Brian, Dennis, and Carl—formed the group in 1961 with their cousin Mike Love and Al Jardine, who was a neighbor. Bruce Johnston joined them in 1966. The Wilson household was full of music when the boys were growing up. The father, Murry Wilson, had been an aspiring songwriter in his younger days, but he was an abusive father, prone to violent outbursts, and he left all three boys with deep psychic wounds.

Brian, who was the oldest, seems to have been a lightning rod for his father's explosions. Brian was beaten several times and subjected to constant verbal abuse. The most damaging and bizarre incident occurred when Murry forced Brian to defecate on a newspaper on the kitchen floor of their home. Brian was humiliated and traumatized. He would later trace his severe emotional problems to that and other events involving his father. When the Beach Boys arrived at the top of the charts, Murry clearly resented their success, even though he had been their first manager and had negotiated their first record contract. He tried to keep hundreds of thousands of dollars that were owed to Brian after Brian fired him and took control of the group in early 1964.

Hit Records. The Beach Boys' first hit singles came in 1963. From 1963 to 1966 they had an impressive string of successes, including "Surfer Girl," "Little Deuce Coupe," "I Get Around," "Help Me Rhonda," "California Girls," and "Wouldn't It Be Nice."

The legendary Beach Boys sound flowed from a single source: Brian Wilson. Deaf in one ear, he overcame that disability to write, arrange, and record some of the most extraordinary songs in the history of rock music. The soaring vocal parts of "Surfer Girl," "God Only Knows," "Sloop John B," and every other Beach Boys song were arranged by Brian. He was influenced by the vocal groups of the late 1950's such as the Four Freshmen, and his songs are noted for their beautiful melodies and rich vocal harmonies. He also had the good luck to be in a band with a number of singers whose voices blended amazingly well. Highly regarded as a record producer, Wilson used innovative instrumentation. The french horn on "God Only Knows" and the harpsichord and percussion on "Caroline No" are good examples. Brian was influenced by early 1960's "girl-group" producer Phil Spector. Spector's "wall of sound" featured wonderful voices backed by large numbers of instruments and innovative percussion; the same attributes may be heard in much of Wilson's music.

Pet Sounds and "Good Vibrations." Brian Wilson reached a creative summit with the 1966 album *Pet Sounds* and the single "Good Vibrations." The arrangements are sophisticated, featuring strings, timpani, and other percussion. There are unusual instruments, such as the bass harmonica and banjo used on "I Know There's an Answer." The signature Beach Boys vocal harmonies are heard throughout the album. Brian's arrangement of the folk song "Sloop John B" is brilliantly performed. Lyrically, too, the album showed a maturing songwriter. *Pet Sounds* did not celebrate the nonstop good times of the early Beach Boys.

The Beach Boys in 1966 (AP/Wide World Photos)

These songs dealt with loneliness, isolation, and regret ("I Just Wasn't Made for These Times," "Caroline No"). *Pet Sounds* is often ranked by critics as one of the most innovative and influential albums of all time. Paul McCartney has remarked in interviews that *Pet Sounds* was the single biggest influence on the Beatles' *Sgt. Pepper's Lonely Hearts Club Band* (1967).

The song "Good Vibrations," a number 1 hit in 1966, is a singular achievement. The time it took (reportedly more than six months) and the large sum of money it cost to record were unheard of for a single song in the mid-1960's. The main parts of the song were written and recorded separately, in different studios, and then put together by Brian. The first section establishes the main verse; next is the chorus, with a pulsing cello and high notes played on a theremin, an early electronic instrument ("I'm pickin' up good vibrations/ She's giving me excitations"). Several other vocal and instrumental sections set off the repetitions of these two main ideas. "Good Vibrations" was hailed by some as a "perfect record" when it was released, and it is widely regarded as a pop masterpiece.

There would be only a few more great songs from Brian after *Pet Sounds* and "Good Vibrations." Notably, collaborations with Van Dyke Parks produced the 1967 single "Heroes and Villains" and parts of the later album *Surf's Up* (1971).

After the Hits. Unfortunately, a major part of the Brian Wilson story comprises his battles with drugs, mental illness, and obesity. Unable to cope with enormous wealth and fame in his twenties, and suffering the lingering psychological effects of his father's abuse, Wilson slowly sank into drugs, depression, and withdrawal. He had stopped touring with the band by 1965. He envisioned an ambitious album project entitled *Smile* and began working with Parks on the recording sessions. However, they were beset by problems—both within and without. There was a fire at the studio, and Wilson is said to have destroyed the tapes on which they were working.

The Beach Boys music seemed out of date to many by the late 1960's, with the country divided over the Vietnam War and torn by urban unrest, and their popularity faded in the 1970's. Brian Wilson's personal problems kept him out of action for much of the time. In the late 1970's clashes among other members of the band caused problems. The 1980's proved even more difficult, yet the Beach Boys persevered. Carl Wilson quit, then rejoined. In 1983 Dennis Wilson died by accidental drowning. The group's new recordings were met with little interest, and they came to be viewed as an oldies act. As such, they were still a successful performing group.

Brian Wilson, with severe mental and emotional problems, had been in therapy for some time with a controversial psychiatrist named Eugene Landy. With Landy's help he released a solo album, *Brian Wilson*, in 1988. Critics generally liked it, but the media and the public showed little interest. On the other hand, the Beach Boys, without Brian, had their biggest hit in years in 1988 with the number 1 song "Kokomo" from the film *Cocktail*. The 1990's brought more legal and personal problems, with Mike Love suing Brian Wilson, first for defamation, then to collect royalties due him.

Endless Summer. The Beach Boys continued to do concert performances through the 1990's with and without Brian Wilson and other key members of the band. They played several Fourth of July concerts in the 1970's and 1980's in Washington, D.C., and elsewhere that drew huge crowds. By 1997 several prolonged and bitter legal entanglements had caused tremendous acrimony among all concerned, with large sums of money at stake. Carl Wilson died early in 1998.

—*John W. Clark*

For the Record

The Beach Boys were adept at conjuring images of sun, sand, and surfers. However, only one of the original Beach Boys, Dennis Wilson, actually surfed.

The Beastie Boys

ORIGINAL MEMBERS: King Ad-Rock (b. Adam Horovitz, 1967), MCA (b. Adam Yauch, 1965), Mike D (b. Michael Diamond, 1966)

FIRST ALBUM RELEASE: *Polly Wog Stew*, 1982 (EP)

MUSICAL STYLE: Punk, rap, hip-hop

Originally a New York hardcore punk band, the Beastie Boys became the first significant white rap group. The Beasties Boys' blend of punk, hard rock, and rap produced the first number 1 album from the rap genre and made hip-hop accessible to a more diverse audience.

Cookie Puss. All three of the Beastie Boys came from privileged New York families and had become a part of the New York punk scene in the early 1980's. Adam Yauch and Michael Diamond decided to start their own hardcore punk band and formed the first incarnation of the Beastie Boys with drummer Kate Schellenbach and guitarist John Berry. The band recorded an eight-song EP for Rat Cage Records entitled *Polly Wog Stew* in 1982. Later that year, Yauch and Diamond met Adam Horovitz, who had been playing for a local hardcore group, the Young and the Useless, since he was fourteen. Schellenbach and Berry left the Beastie Boys, so Horovitz joined.

With the addition of Horovitz, the band continued to play punk but began to experiment with rap. In 1983, the Beastie Boys released their first rap single, "Cookie Puss," which was based on a crank telephone call the band had made to the Carvel ice cream company. "Cookie Puss" became an underground hit in New York, and the band turned their focus completely to rap, signing with Rick Rubin (DJ Double RR) as both producer and DJ, scratching records on turntables during the band's performances. Rubin and fellow New York University student Russell Simmons had recently formed Def Jam Records.

Licensed to Ill. In 1985, Def Jam Records officially signed the Beastie Boys to a recording contract. That year the Beastie Boys adopted the reversed baseball caps, gold chains, and hooded sweatshirts of New York street fashion. Rubin chose "Rock Hard" for the Beastie Boys' debut rap single. This was followed with the single "She's on It," which featured sampled guitar riffs from AC/DC's "Back in Black." "She's on It" was the hit single from the sound track of the seminal rap film *Krush Groove* in 1985. The Beastie Boys then took their new act on tour, opening for Madonna's Virgin tour only to be booed off the stage night after night.

The Beastie Boys then opened a series of concerts for Run-D.M.C.'s Raisin' Hell tour, which set the stage for the release of *Licensed to Ill* in 1986.

The Beastie Boys (Paul Natkin)

the Beastie Boys cultural pirates, while others charged that the band's lyrics were sexist and violent and that their stage show incited criminal behavior. By 1988 the band was also involved in a bitter fight with Def Jam Records over royalties. As a result of all the turmoil, the Beastie Boys decided to change direction musically and geographically. They signed with Capitol Records, moved to California, and began to work on their second album.

Paul's Boutique. The Beastie Boys' second album, *Paul's Boutique*, released in August of 1989, was a thickly layered, pseudopsychedelic funk effort that, at the time, garnered weak sales. Six years later, primarily because the record became a cult favorite, *Paul's Boutique* surpassed one million copies in sales.

The Beastie Boys went on to build their own studio and, in April of 1992, marked another change in their musical style by playing live instruments at an acquired immunodeficiency syndrome (AIDS) benefit concert in Los Angeles. This return to instrument playing apparently helped the Beastie Boys gain new fans: Their 1992 album release, *Check Your Head*, became a surprise Top-10 hit on college and alternative rock album charts. This was followed in 1994 by *Ill Communication*. The album debuted at number 1 on the album charts and included the hit singles "Sabotage" and "Sure Shot." That same year, the Beastie Boys were invited to join the Lollapalooza tour with the Smashing Pumpkins, the Breeders, and George Clinton. The 1996 album *The In Sound from Way Out!* collected the instrumentals from the previous two albums and also added a few new songs.

In the late 1990's, the Beastie Boys turned their attention to political causes, organizing and per-

Licensed to Ill, while critically derided as a mindless party album, became the first rap album to reach number 1. It stayed at the top spot for seven weeks, eventually sold over five million copies, and spawned the hit single "(You Gotta) Fight for Your Right (to Party)," which reached number 7 on the singles chart.

The success brought criticism. Rap fans called

For the Record

In 1992, the Beastie Boys' MCA married Ion Skye, daughter of 1960's folksinger Donovan.

forming in the Tibetan Freedom Concert and playing in benefits for the Leonard Peltier Defense Fund. —*B. Keith Murphy and Nyawi Willis*

SELECT DISCOGRAPHY
■ ALBUMS
Polly Wog Stew, 1982 (EP)
Licensed to Ill, 1986
Paul's Boutique, 1989
Check Your Head, 1992
Ill Communication, 1994
The In Sound from Way Out! 1996 (compilation)
Hello Nasty, 1998

SEE ALSO: Run-D.M.C.; Smashing Pumpkins.

The Beatles

MEMBERS: John Lennon (1940-1980), Paul McCartney (b. 1942), George Harrison (b. 1943), Ringo Starr (b. Richard Starkey, 1940)
FIRST SINGLE RELEASE: "Love Me Do," 1962
FIRST ALBUM RELEASE: *Please Please Me,* 1963
MUSICAL STYLES: Rock and roll, pop, psychedelic rock

Overstating the place of the Beatles not only in popular music but also in popular culture in the latter third of the twentieth century would be impossible. Capturing the scope and range of the group's impact and influence is difficult. Attempting to pinpoint the precise elements that combined to create the phenomenon known as Beatlemania is futile. Elvis Presley may have galvanized youth culture in the Eisenhower years, and Bob Dylan may have sparked its conscience on the New Frontier. The Beatles, however—John Lennon, Paul McCartney, George Harrison, and Ringo Starr—opened the gates and led a generation through to the Age of Aquarius. Long after that age has passed, the group's music and legacy endures as strong as ever.

This musical and cultural legacy is an impressive achievement for four working-class lads from the unlikely town of Liverpool, England. Yet it was the very nature of Liverpool that forged the ele-

ments that came to be the Beatles. Perched on the Mersey River about halfway up England's western shore, the town is a major port, a beehive of comings and goings from all points. In post-World War II England, Liverpool was a depressed and depressing place. For restless youths such as Lennon and McCartney, 45 rpm rock-and-roll records—brought in by such sailors as Lennon's merchant marine father—were sacred texts from America, the land of dreams. Elvis was the messiah, Buddy Holly, Gene Vincent, Eddie Cochran, Carl Perkins, Phil Spector, Chuck Berry, and Little Richard among the apostles.

Early Years. There was little reason to think that history was being made on July 6, 1957, the day Lennon and McCartney met at a church fete. Lennon, then sixteen, was fronting a fairly unskilled group called the Quarry Men, playing a rough version of skiffle, a British variant of American folk music, as typified by Lonnie Donegan and his hit version of "Rock Island Line." McCartney, just turned fifteen, was impressed not so much with the musicality but by the rock-and-roll swagger and intensity that radiated from Lennon's eyes (as can be seen in a famous picture of the young group from that day). When the two were formally introduced in the church hall later that day, Lennon (whose breath smelled of beer, McCartney noted) in turn was impressed that his new acquaintance knew the chords to Eddie Cochran's "Twenty Flight Rock"—which he and the Quarry Men did not, but had nonetheless attempted to play. In many ways, that contrast of raw passion and steady craft would define their relationship.

Lennon had not had an easy time of life. When he was very young, his father had essentially fled for the sea, unable to cope with family commitment. His mother, too, had difficulties, showing signs of mental illness. She turned young John over to his Aunt Mimi. A year after meeting McCartney, Lennon lost his mother entirely when she was struck and killed by a car. McCartney's youth had been easier only by comparison. His mother died of cancer when he was fourteen, and his father did his best to provide stability for Paul and his younger brother, Mike.

The lure of rock and roll drew Lennon and McCartney together, first in a reconstituted Quarry Men, and then with McCartney's young friend George Harrison, a talented guitarist, under the name Johnny and the Moondogs. In January, 1960, Stuart Sutcliffe, an art-school friend of Lennon, was persuaded to sign on as bassist. Sutcliffe could not play a note, but because he had sold a painting for a handsome sum, he could afford to help upgrade the group's equipment. Thus the Silver Beetles were born, the name in part a tribute to Buddy Holly's Crickets. Soon the name mutated to the Beatles, the spelling pun relating to the "beat group" style of music they were now playing. The group was now a going concern, playing occasional gigs and developing a small following around Liverpool; they even made a tour of Scotland. Soon they were offered a job as "house band" at a club in Hamburg, Germany.

As chronicled in the 1993 film *Back Beat*, the German stints were a trial by fire. The addition of drummer Pete Best rounded out the band's lineup, and grueling schedules of playing for drunken sailors and roughnecks in seedy clubs with squalid living conditions (when they were even allowed to take a break) forced the band to focus on its musicianship. In the process they realized that Sutcliffe was a liability. On the other hand, friendships with bohemian artists such as Astrid Kirchherr and Klaus Voormann opened the young Liverpudlians' eyes to new worlds—and in the process led to Sutcliffe's exit in order to follow his calling as an artist. (Sutcliffe died a year later of a brain hemorrhage.)

On return trips home, crowds at such local dives as the subterranean Cavern Club grew, and with them the group's confidence. The Beatles began to include more of their own material in their sets. Their first real professional recording, with McCartney now having switched to bass, came around this time, backing crooner Tony Sheridan on "My Bonnie." It was a rather inconsequential session, save for one thing: Young fans inquiring about it at a Liverpool shop made Brian Epstein, the son of the store's owners, curious enough to attend a Cavern Club show. While the music may not have been exactly to his taste, the musicians' bubbling charisma and the packed-in fans' boisterous enthusiasm won him over instantly—he approached the group about becoming its manager. It was the luckiest day in the Beatles' career.

Into the Studio. Whether Epstein had any idea of the musical talents of the group is uncertain, but he sensed immediately that he was seeing diamonds in the rough that only needed a bit of polish. He replaced their James Dean leather jackets with coats (eventually the trademark collarless style) and ties. When Epstein tried to get record companies interested in the group, however, he was roundly frustrated. In early 1962 Decca paid for a tryout recording session but passed on the group; the key executive dismissed guitar groups as on the way out. Finally, EMI's George Martin was persuaded to give them a try.

Martin was largely unimpressed by the musical aspects of the session. He was, however, completely taken by the personalities of Lennon, McCartney, and Harrison, whose interplay and directness could in part be traced to a zany radio program called *The Goon Show*. (Its humor sprang from the offbeat talents of Spike Milligan, Harry Secombe, and Peter Sellers, whose recordings Martin had produced.) The clincher was the fact that after Martin had repeatedly tried to explain problems with the performances and technical aspects of the recording, he finally shrugged and asked the Beatles if there was anything they did not like. Harrison, without hesitation, dryly replied, "Yeah, I don't like your tie." That was that.

For the Record

"He kept putting his arm around my shoulders. His breath smelt, but I showed him a few chords he didn't know. I left feeling I'd created an impression."

—*Paul McCartney*, recalling his first encounter with a somewhat inebriated John Lennon in 1957.

The Beatles at the height of Beatlemania: Paul McCartney, George Harrison, Ringo Starr, and John Lennon (Archive Photos/Popperfoto)

A deal was forthcoming, and a crucial relationship with Martin—one that would far transcend the standard artist-producer arrangement—was forged. Martin believed that, of the band's several musical deficiencies, one was insurmountable: drummer Best was not up to snuff. Lennon, McCartney, and Harrison did not disagree. Best was replaced by Richard Starkey, a.k.a. Ringo Starr, whom they had come to know well as the drummer in rival Liverpool band Rory Storm and the Hurricanes.

The band made one more trip to Hamburg. (An amateur tape from this period was released in the early 1980's as *Live at the Star Club.*) Then, on June 1, 1962, the Beatles officially made their recording debut in EMI's Abbey Road studios.

The album that resulted, *Please Please Me*, only hints at the greatness to come. Even the standout numbers—"I Saw Her Standing There," the title track, and "Do You Want to Know a Secret"—though exuberant, infectious performances and finely crafted tunes, are not advances of the form. More than half of the collection consisted of songs that they did not write—songs such as "Twist and Shout" and "A Taste of Honey," drawn from their Hamburg repertoire.

Yet there was an electricity in the blending of the voices and guitars and in the working-class accents in the singing. A new British generation, emerging from the gloom of World War II and inspired by America, was looking for its own voice. It found it. "Love Me Do," a trifle of a song despite Lennon's indelible harmonica lick, was an instant sensation in the United Kingdom when it was released in October, 1962. "Please Please Me," a somewhat more substantial song, released January 11, 1963, was an even bigger hit. The album, released on March 22, rapidly made the group the number 1 pop act in the country, even getting an unprecedented regular spot on BBC radio, recordings from which were released in 1994 on the *Beatles at the BBC* CD set.

Beatlemania Comes to America. America was a different story. There was so little interest in the Beatles that Capitol Records, the American arm of EMI, declined even to release their singles or album. Instead, a collection entitled *Introducing the Beatles: England's No. 1 Vocal Group* was released in 1963 by the independent company Vee Jay. The situation would soon change. A summer single that was not included on the album, "She Loves You," upped the ante. The lyrics were still basic teen-pop, but the musical sophistication was at a much higher level. The song's rhythmic accents and stunning shifts in the harmonies sounded a wake-up call that something truly special was happening.

A second album, *With the Beatles*, was released in Britain on November 22, 1963, raising both the clamor and the quality even more. The team of Lennon and McCartney—now having been writing songs together for seven years—were gaining in confidence and skills. "It Won't Be Long" opened the album with its churning chorus and crisp rhythm. "All My Loving" provided a mid-tempo sparkler, and even the relatively rudimentary "I Wanna Be Your Man" (sung by Ringo) showed them to be building on their rock heroes' work, not merely honoring it. The cover songs, too, were nearly all winners, in both choice and performance, with "Please Mister Postman" and the Motown-originated "Money (That's What I Want)" essential additions to their catalog—the latter in particular due to Lennon's raw-throated vocals.

The next single, not on either of these albums, established the group in America, where, in January of 1964, young people seemed crying for something to dispel the gloom of John F. Kennedy's assassination two months before. The number 1 single "I Want to Hold Your Hand" picked up where "She Loves You" left off—it is a distinctive rocker that transcends its simple sentiments. Capitol Records came to its senses and released the record in the United States to ecstatic response. "I Saw Her Standing There" and ten other songs were collected on an album entitled *Meet the Beatles* (1964), sporting the same trend-setting black-and-white cover photo as *With the Beatles*.

Before long, the ultimate U.S. endorsement came—an invitation to perform on *The Ed Sullivan Show*, a popular television variety show. After a warm-up performance in Washington, D.C., the Fab Four, as they had come to be called, landed in New York to a crowd of frantic, screaming teenagers. On February 9 they played five songs on the live telecast, with close-up shots accompanied by graphics of their first names—it was hard to tell the Mop Tops (another nickname) apart, after all. The event shattered U.S. prime-time television records, with more than 73 million people tuned in. During the week they played Carnegie Hall before making a second Sullivan appearance the following Sunday. (This phase of Beatlemania is nicely captured in the mid-1970's fiction film *I Want to Hold Your Hand*.)

In 1964 and 1965 the Beatles' rocketing popularity in the United States launched the "British invasion": Their success prompted a desire among the young record-buying public for almost anything by British rock-and-roll bands. Some bands were near-exact copies of the Beatles; others, notably the bad-boy Rolling Stones, brought a different slant to their music and presentation. Among the many British artists with hits during these years were the Dave Clark Five, the Hollies, the Kinks, the Animals, the Yardbirds, Gerry and the Pacemakers, Herman's Hermits, Peter and Gordon, and Manfred Mann. Young men in bands, and soon their male listeners, grew their hair long, adopting their own versions of the "Beatle haircut."

Onto the Screen. With hardly a break after their U.S. performances, the Beatles went back to London to make their first movie. It was first entitled *Eight Arms to Hold You*, then changed to *A Hard Day's Night*, the title of a song Lennon hastily wrote after a chance remark by Ringo concerning their frantic schedule. While such literati as conductor and composer Leonard Bernstein had already given approval to the Beatles' music, it was probably this film that did the most to open the doors to wide respect and create a sense that Beatlemania might be more than a passing fad. Parents, forced to take their children to see it, were in large numbers won over by the presentation of four likable, charming, witty, and gifted young men.

The film's story is simple: It depicts a day of Beatlemania from the objects' perspective. Writer Alun Owen added such fictional elements as Paul's "clean" grandfather, but the dialogue and situations are so natural that the film almost seems like a documentary. In a great stroke of luck for the Beatles, the director hired for the film, Richard Lester, had the perfect touch for the material. From the indelible opening scene of fans chasing the tripping and stumbling group, to a very realistic press reception (reporter: "What do you call that haircut?" George: "Arthur"), to a dejected, soul-searching interlude featuring Ringo, Lester maintained the perfect tone. *A Hard Day's Night* remains today not only the essential pop-music film—Elvis was never treated as well on celluloid—but also a classic, regardless of genre.

The songs, too, are uniformly superb, and for the first time an entire Beatles album was com-

posed of original material. The title song, with its harmonic shifts and self-reflexive lyrics, is only one of several standouts. "Things We Said Today," "Can't Buy Me Love," and "Tell Me Why" also see the Beatles growing both musically and thematically. The growth is especially amazing considering the pace at which the group was moving, with concerts (including a first full American tour) and another album scheduled before 1964 was done. That album, *Beatles for Sale*, suffered a bit from the rush, with only eight of fourteen songs being originals, but the best of them, "No Reply" and "Eight Days a Week" in particular, continued their creative growth.

Neither the pace nor the escalation of Beatlemania slowed in 1965, with another film and related album, another American tour (including the famous appearance at New York's Shea Stadium), and another nonfilm album. (The Beatles' concert experience of the time was captured in a 1976 album, *The Beatles at the Hollywood Bowl*, collected from 1964 and 1965 shows.) The film, *Help!*, shows the toll that the pace of the Beatles' rise was beginning to take. A silly, contrived farce concerning an Indian cult trying to repossess a gaudy ring from one of Ringo's bejewelled fingers, *Help!* had the Beatles globe-hopping from London to the Bahamas to the Alps for no apparent reason other than the scenery. Only the Beatles' own witty exchanges and director Lester's knack for slapstick carried over from the predecessor. For evidence of the band's own frustrations, one need only listen to the film's title song. It was an earnest plea from Lennon, who along with his mates was starting to lose his bearings: "Help me get my feet back on the ground," he sang.

Remarkably, not only did the music not suffer from all this, but it actually seemed to benefit, perhaps because of the very questions the Beatles had to ask themselves about their lives at the time. The *Help!* songs continued the increase of musical and lyrical sophistication ("Ticket to Ride," "You've Got to Hide Your Love Away" and McCartney's existential tour de force, "Yesterday"). The next album, *Rubber Soul*, released December 3, 1965, was full of monumental breakthroughs.

Rubber Soul and Revolver. It was at this point that the Beatles transcended being a pop phenomenon and became a force that would redefine the nature of pop music and youth culture. Spurred by Bob Dylan's lyrical daring and the sonic advances being realized by Brian Wilson with the Beach Boys, the Beatles had set about to make music that really *meant* something. George Martin's talents came fully into play; he evolved from producer to collaborator, helping the Fab Four realize their new ambitions. Their personal frustrations were manifest, cathartically, via "I'm Looking Through You," "You Won't See Me," and the menacing edge of "Run for Your Life." "In My Life" (with Martin's baroque harpsichord flourishes) and "Norwegian Wood (This Bird Has Flown)" further open Lennon's confessional side; the latter, with its sitar parts, shows Harrison's growing interest in Indian music and spirituality. "Nowhere Man" matches socially astute lyrics with rich harmonies and twelve-string guitar mosaics. "Michelle" marks the maturation of McCartney as a romantic balladeer. With Lennon's "The Word," the Beatles gave their fans their first true anthem and, arguably, unleashed the "flower-power" energy that was starting to grow from the antiwar and civil rights fights, especially in the United States. *Rubber Soul* was a true landmark album.

The Beatles topped it with their next one. *Revolver*, with its line-drawn cover by Klaus Voormann, spins off in dozens of new directions at once, each a fruitful exploration and advancement. Harrison's "Taxman"—petulant from a rich rock star, but still barbed rock and roll—led off, with McCartney's elegant "Eleanor Rigby" next, followed by Lennon's "I'm Only Sleeping," his first use of dream consciousness as song fodder. The songs range from wistful ("Here, There, and Everywhere") to silly ("Yellow Submarine") to buoyant ("Got to Get You into My Life"). Two Lennon songs stand out: "And Your Bird Can Sing" moves beyond even "Nowhere Man" in weaving harmonies and twelve-string cascades, while "Tomorrow Never Knows," with its stuttered quasi-Indian beat and hypnotic swirls of tape loops, may have been the first truly psychedelic pop song, and it still ranks among the best.

For the Record

"The Beatles are bigger than Jesus Christ."—*John Lennon*, 1966. Lennon's off-the-cuff remark sparked a boycott and record burnings in the United States. Lennon responded that he had been misunderstood, that he was decrying the fact that young people heeded the Beatles more than they did the words of Jesus.

Up through these albums, Capitol had released U.S. versions of Beatles albums that differed from the British collections, utilizing combinations of album tracks, EP tracks, and singles. *Rubber Soul* and *Revolver* in the United States were made into three albums, with *Yesterday . . . and Today* coming between them. *Yesterday . . . and Today* was most notable for the "butcher cover," picturing the Beatles wearing aprons, wielding cleavers, and holding bloody meat and dismembered baby dolls. The cover was, reasonably enough, rejected by Capitol and replaced by an innocuous photograph of the band sitting in and around steamer trunks. The first run of the album, with the new art merely pasted over the offending one, stands as one of the most sought-after collector's items of rock and roll. Musically, the U.K. versions of the albums are superior, and when the albums were issued on CD in the late 1980's, they were released in the original U.K. versions.

The Beatles again went on the road. Tired and cranky, they finished their third U.S. tour with a show at San Francisco's Candlestick Park and then declared that they would play no more concerts. The rift between what they were doing in the studio and what the fairly primitive conditions of live concerts at that time allowed was growing wider. The concerts were not fun or creative, and the madness of touring was grinding them down. In dire need of recharging, the Beatles took their first real break since the early Liverpool days—five months to deal with their outside lives. Lennon spent part of the time costarring in another Lester film, *How I Won the War*. Then, in early 1967, the Beatles convened again at Abbey Road to commence a new album.

Sgt. Pepper's Lonely Hearts Club Band. A preview single was released on February 17, indicating that new horizons were being approached. The pairing of "Strawberry Fields Forever" and "Penny Lane" ranks as one of the great singles in pop music. Both sides dealt with Liverpool nostalgia. Lennon's "Strawberry Fields" is a surreal dream of the hurt and abandonment of his young life. Strawberry Fields was the name of an orphanage, and it seems to provide an odd comfort. The arrangement wraps the melody in spectral Mellotron and cello and includes backward-tape experiments. It may be the greatest recording the Beatles ever made, and it was certainly a monumental studio achievement. McCartney's "Penny Lane" is literally the sunny flip side, a series of snapshots depicting lost innocence. It ends with a

trumpet obligato that Martin transcribed after McCartney hummed it to him. The single whetted the public appetite for what was to come.

The Beatles' status now was as much oracle as band, and in the summer of 1967—the "Summer of Love"—its vast following awaited its latest pronouncement. Whether *Sgt. Pepper's Lonely Hearts Club Band* is actually the Beatles' greatest album is open to debate, but the impact it had is undeniable. On June 1, 1967, it seemed as if a new color had been added to the sky. Top-40 radio stations, which usually played only an act's latest single, played the entire album straight through. In a few cases, they continued to do so for days; others treated each song as if it were a single. The album's elaborate cover photo depicted the band, now sporting mustaches, decked out in bright uniforms; they stood in front of a panel of cultural dignitaries at what appeared to be a funeral for the Beatles themselves (wax figures of their earlier incarnations stood in mourning). The cover be-

The Beatles in 1967 at the time of Sgt. Pepper's: *McCartney, Lennon, Starr, Harrison* (Archive Photos/Popperfoto)

came the subject of all-night discussions attempting to decode its messages. (Searching Beatles covers and songs for secret clues would escalate later to the "Paul is dead" hysteria, in which the "Cute Beatle's" demise was supposedly proven by a series of coded references. It was total foolishness.)

The album itself was based on a simple conceit: What if the Beatles could perform under another identity? That idle thought, which struck McCartney during a trans-Atlantic flight, was translated into a straightforward concept in which Sgt. Pepper and his ensemble, with guest singer Billy Shears, performed a series of songs in concert. The opening, with the "Sgt. Pepper's Lonely Hearts Club Band" theme segueing into "With a Little Help from My Friends" (with Ringo in the role of Shears), effectively established a distinct world in which this music existed. Next came "Lucy in the Sky with Diamonds." Lennon insisted that the song was inspired by a painting done by his young son Julian and that the fact that the first letters of the title's nouns spelled out LSD was pure coincidence. Nevertheless, the song's lyrics and sound indicated a clear chemical assistance in the project.

The album's concept breaks down after this song, returning only at the end with the punchy "Sgt. Pepper's" reprise and the vivid psychedelic dream sequence "A Day in the Life." There is hardly a dull moment in the album, however. "Getting Better," Harrison's Indian manifesto "Within You Without You," "For the Benefit of Mr. Kite," "She's Leaving Home," and even the fluffier "Lovely Rita" all seemed to have mystical qualities.

Part of the album's artistic success may be attributed to the astounding arrangements and production—still largely done by the four Beatles and Martin, using only a four-track tape machine. Inspired by the Beach Boys' *Pet Sounds* album, the Beatles used the studio environment itself as an instrument and orchestrator. (The farm-animal sounds on "Good Morning" are certainly a nod to the California competition.)

After *Sgt. Pepper's*. Only a month after the album's release, the band was already back with another anthem, "All You Need Is Love," which was debuted in an unprecedented live global satellite telecast from a set festooned with flowers and love-filled friends, including Mick Jagger. It was the pinnacle coup for Brian Epstein, who had plastered the Beatles' image and name on everything from lunch boxes to shampoo without costing them their dignity and had provided the right advice along every step of their five-year climb to world dominance. Yet it was also the point at which the Beatles began to grow away from his steadying hand. Not coincidentally—though much great music was still to come—it was the beginning of the end for the Beatles, the point at which everything would start to unravel.

On Harrison's lead, the Beatles went on retreat in Wales to study with transcendental meditation guru Maharishi Mahesh Yogi. While they were on the sojourn, the shocking news was delivered that Epstein, depressed and alone in London, had died of an overdose of prescription medication (deemed an accident), a shock that rended the very fabric of the group. Even apart from the deep grief they felt, without Epstein there was no one to tell them when they were going astray, and huge mistakes began to mount. Frustrated with the *Help!* experience, they set about making their own film, *Magical Mystery Tour*. Although such songs as the title number and Lennon's stunning stream-of-subconscious "I Am the Walrus" are arguably even better than most of the *Sgt. Pepper's Lonely Hearts Club Band* material, the film was a mess—a psychedelic bus trip with no discernible story, structure, or point, despite a few great moments.

Beginning of the End. A trip to India to study with the Maharishi was also less than a rousing success, as Lennon in particular became disillusioned with what he perceived to be the guru's greater interest in wealthy celebrities than spirituality. Next came the establishment of Apple Corps, a business venture including a new record label, a London boutique, and various other enterprises. Apple was designed to give the Beatles full artistic and financial independence, but in reality it became more a vehicle through which shiftless hangers-on could siphon money into their own pockets. It was a disaster. About this time Lennon (still married to art-school girlfriend Cynthia) met Japanese artist Yoko Ono at an exhibit of her Dada-esque work in a London gallery. McCartney, having broken off a relationship with Jane Asher, met Linda Eastman, a daughter of the group's American attorney. The new romances brought about new dynamics that ultimately were stronger than those within the group.

The public was little aware of the troubles brewing, especially with McCartney's "Hey Jude" single becoming the best-seller of the band's entire career. Given the circumstances behind the scenes, however, it is little surprise that the 1968 album *The Beatles*, known as "The White Album" due to its plain packaging (a stark contrast to *Sgt. Pepper's Lonely Heart's Club Band*), is more an album of solo ventures than a true group effort. Still, much of the double album is spectacular—including Lennon's aching paean to his late mother, "Julia," encoded swipe at the Maharishi, "Sexy Sadie," and disjointed word jumble "Happiness Is a Warm Gun," and McCartney's sentimental "Martha My Dear" and "I Will." Such rockers as "Back in the U.S.S.R." and the furious "Helter Skelter" are also essential Beatle songs. Harrison, whose writing contributions had largely been afterthoughts in the past, made a mark with three solid efforts, notably the enduring "While My Guitar Gently Weeps." Even Lennon's tape-collage "Revolution 9" (certainly showing Ono's influence) is impressive on its own terms.

The Last Albums. While the animated film *Yellow Submarine* returned the Beatles to cinematic respect (though they had little to do with it besides adding a few new songs), the group decided to try, in essence, going back to square one. The idea was to record an album more or less live in the studio—a basic group performance, with only American keyboardist Billy Preston sitting in, rather than the orchestras and session players that had augmented the last number of albums. It was a good idea, but as the eventual film of the project, *Let It Be*, shows clearly, it was too late. The tension in the studio is palpable, with Ono always at Lennon's side and McCartney's efforts to muster a unified effort both self-serving and futile. The songs are hit and miss, with the performances often sounding distracted. The *Let It Be* album was

shelved, only to be released in 1970 after American producer Phil Spector was called in to salvage it. Spector buried some of the songs, especially McCartney's "The Long and Winding Road," under layers of superfluous strings and other textures. A spontaneous performance of "Get Back" on the rooftop of the Apple offices, the last time the Beatles would perform in public together, was the one moment of true joy.

Amazingly, there was still a masterpiece to come. *Abbey Road* (1969), though again not really a group effort, as many of the tracks were recorded in separate sessions, is full of highlights, especially the side-two suite of fragments and snippets, woven into a dynamic pop sequence. McCartney's is the dominant presence, but all four contribute solidly (Harrison wrote the hit "Something") and with an aura of unity, manufactured or otherwise. By the time it was released, however, Lennon had already told his mates of his intention to leave the group. He was persuaded to keep his decision quiet while various business elements were ironed out. He did so, only to see McCartney announce that he was leaving and release a solo album. Before the close of 1969, the Beatles were no longer a group. The May, 1970, release of the revamped *Let It Be* album was extremely anticlimactic—a "cardboard tombstone," as one review put it, for the most significant act in pop history.

After the Beatles. The Beatles all launched solo careers that would prove only sporadically worthy of their legacy. They all appeared, though separately, on Starr's 1973 album *Ringo*, but constant rumors and requests for a reunion were unfulfilled. Lennon's "How Do You Sleep?"—a vicious attack on McCartney that provided a contrasting note of vitriol to his peace anthem "Imagine"—seemed to indicate that the differences would not be easily resolved. By 1980, however, Lennon and McCartney had patched up their feud and bygones were bygones. Any slim chance of the four Beatles working together again was snuffed out when a mentally disturbed fan shot and killed Lennon in 1980, only months after he had ended a five-year retirement with his and Ono's *Double Fantasy* album. The tragedy led the three surviving Beatles to team on Harrison's 1981 eulogy, "All Those Years Ago." In 1995 the three effected an electronic reunion with Lennon to complete "Free as a Bird," a partial song that Lennon had recorded (singing and playing piano) in his New York apartment before his death. The song was featured in the first volume of the Beatles *Anthology* series, archival collections of outtakes and unreleased songs that accompanied a long-planned documentary television series on the group. A second such effort, "Real Love," led off volume 2. These efforts may have come close, but they were not the Beatles. That, indeed, was yesterday.

—*Steve Hochman*

SELECT DISCOGRAPHY

■ SINGLES

"I Want to Hold Your Hand"/"I Saw Her Standing There," 1964
"She Loves You," 1964
"Please Please Me," 1964
"Can't Buy Me Love," 1964
"Love Me Do," 1964
"A Hard Day's Night," 1964
"I Feel Fine"/"She's a Woman," 1964
"Eight Days a Week," 1965
"Ticket to Ride," 1965
"Yesterday," 1965
"We Can Work It Out"/"Day Tripper," 1965
"Paperback Writer," 1966
"Penny Lane"/"Strawberry Fields Forever," 1967
"All You Need Is Love," 1967
"Hello Goodbye," 1967
"Hey Jude/Revolution," 1968
"Get Back"/"Don't Let Me Down," 1969
"Come Together"/"Something," 1969
"Let It Be," 1970
Note: Single release dates are American dates.

■ ALBUMS

Please Please Me, 1963
With the Beatles, 1963
Beatles for Sale, 1963
Meet the Beatles, 1964 (American release)
A Hard Day's Night, 1964
Help! 1965
Rubber Soul, 1965
Yesterday . . . and Today, 1966 (American release)
Revolver, 1966
Sgt. Pepper's Lonely Hearts Club Band, 1967
Magical Mystery Tour, 1967
The Beatles, 1968 ("The White Album")
Yellow Submarine, 1969
Abbey Road, 1969
Let It Be, 1970
Past Masters, Vol. 1, 1988
Past Masters, Vol. 2, 1988
Live at the BBC, 1994
Anthology 1, 1995
Anthology 2, 1996
Anthology 3, 1996

SELECT AWARDS

Grammy Awards for Best Performance by a Vocal Group for "A Hard Day's Night" and for Best New Artist, 1964
Grammy Awards for Album of the Year and Best Contemporary Album for *Sgt. Pepper's Lonely Hearts Club Band*, 1967
Rock and Roll Hall of Fame, inducted 1988
Grammy Award for Best Pop Performance by a Duo or Group with Vocal for "Free as a Bird," 1996

SEE ALSO: Berry, Chuck; Harrison, George; Hollies, The; Holly, Buddy; Kinks, The; Lennon, John; Little Richard; McCartney, Paul; Monkees, The; Perkins, Carl; Presley, Elvis; Rolling Stones, The.

Beck

(Bek David Campbell Hansen)

BORN: Los Angeles, California; July 8, 1970
FIRST RELEASE: *Golden Feelings*, 1993 (cassette)
MUSICAL STYLES: Rock and roll, alternative

Beck emerged as one of the most popular and critically acclaimed singer-songwriters of the 1990's. He was also one of the most eclectic, combining funk, hip-hop, Delta blues, folk, and a host of other musical influences to create his own distinctive brand of postmodern rock. Beck pairs this musical breadth with a lyrical gift that can serve up both direct utterances and opaque phrases worthy of Bob Dylan. His talents have won for him a number of awards, especially for his second major-label release, *Odelay* (1996).

Beck, born Bek David Campbell, grew up in an artistic family in Southern California. His mother, Bibbe Hansen, began frequenting Andy Warhol's Factory when she was only thirteen and went on to become part of Los Angeles's punk-rock scene. His father, David Campbell (Beck took his mother's maiden name, Hansen, when she and Campbell divorced), was a former bluegrass musician who, as an arranger, worked with such groups as Cracker, Aerosmith, and the Rolling Stones. Artistic talent spanned generations in Beck's family. His maternal grandfather, Al Hansen, was a founder of the pop-art movement FluXus, which Beck's older half-brother Channing Hansen would help perpetuate through his own works.

Antifolk Roots. In the late 1980's, Beck climbed on a Greyhound bus headed for New York to join the antifolk scene on Manhattan's Lower East Side. Before long, he was performing original material at open-microphone nights in clubs and associating with such figures as Paleface, Roger Manning, and Michelle Shocked. Beck may not have distinguished himself during this period, but he did learn much from his New York apprenticeship. After about one year, he returned to the West Coast with some of his first songs in and, including "Pay No Mind" and "Cut ½ Blues."

Back in Southern California, Beck began performing frequently, mainly in coffeehouses and as the opening act for other local artists. He also started recording demo tapes. By 1992, his music had caught the attention of the small independent label Flipside, which included two of Beck's songs on the *Beck/Bean* split single. The same year, Bong Load Records released a twelve-inch single of two other songs by Beck. The A-side, "Loser," propelled Beck into the musical limelight as the song's hip-hop groove and unusual folklike overtones caught on at dance clubs. "Loser" was soon playing on underground and alternative radio stations across the United States. *Newsweek* magazine called it "one of the great weird pop singles." The lyrics for "Loser" present a mishmash of references and images, including such

Beck in 1997 (Geffen Records)

gems as "beefcake pantyhose" and "wax fallin' on a termite."

First Albums. The success of "Loser" made Beck the object of an intense bidding war among major labels. He eventually signed with DGC, in large part because of a special contractual agreement that he could record projects for other labels. DGC released *Mellow Gold* in 1994, and the major-label debut quickly climbed the charts on the strength of "Loser." Both MTV and radio stations played the song extensively, helping *Mellow Gold* go platinum. At age twenty-four, Beck had already found significant commercial success.

However, the young singer-songwriter was looking for more than success. He was also experi-

For the Record

"The image of me as a workaholic hermit is all true. No, not really, but I do spend an inordinate amount of time writing and recording. It's just always been necessary to do that, to get deeper into it." —*Beck*

menting artistically. Accepting DGC's offer to let him work for other labels, Beck recorded two more albums in 1994, both for independent labels. Flipside Records released the experimental *Stereopathic Soul Manure* (1994). At nearly the same time, K Records released *One Foot in the Grave*, a folk-oriented work ringing with echoes of Bob Dylan, Woody Guthrie, and Mississippi Delta blues tunes. Beck had established himself as an extremely versatile artist.

Taken together, Beck's first three albums should have convinced the world of his artistic breadth and depth. Unfortunately, the success of "Loser" produced the opposite effect. Critics typecast Beck as a "dork-hop" club artist, and the song's lyrics made him an unwitting spokesman for the post-baby-boom generation, despite Beck's claim that "Loser" was a musical joke.

Odelay. In a way, the pigeonholing created by the success of "Loser" may have been to Beck's ultimate advantage. It left the world unprepared for the artistic surprise delivered by his second major release, *Odelay*. For production help, Beck turned to Dust Brothers Tom Rowlands and Ed Simmons, much respected for their work with Tone Loc, the Beastie Boys, and others. Together, the three produced a work that *Spin* and *Rolling Stone* magazines gave a perfect rating. Reviewers were particularly taken with Beck's masterful eclecticism. *Spin*, for example, praised his blend of "Muzak and Mattel, rare groove and old school, pedal steel and psychedelia."

Such rave reviews marked just the beginning of the acclaim Beck and *Odelay* were to receive in 1997. Critics from the aforementioned two magazines named him Artist of the Year while the

Village Voice joined *Spin* in honoring *Odelay* as Album of the Year. In addition, Beck brought home MTV video music awards and two Grammy Awards, for Best Alternative Performance and Best Male Rock Vocal Performance.

Other Interests. Beck also enjoyed extra–musical success during his career. He was named Most Stylish Pop Star at the 1997 *Elle* Style Awards and Most Fashionable Artist at VH1's Fashion Awards the same year. Also, the Santa Monica Museum of Art celebrated its 1998 reopening with an art exhibit featuring works by Beck and his late grandfather entitled "Beck and Al Hansen: Playing with Matches." Despite his achievements in and out of music, Beck has remained a remarkably down-to-earth individual. He has also become an accomplished and active live performer as well as a humanitarian, making appearances for such fund-raising concerts as Farm Aid and the Tibetan Freedom Concert.

One mark of an artist's ultimate success is his influence upon others. Beck's talent and clear musical vision certainly suggest that he will be important to peers and younger musicians. On the other hand, the eclecticism that makes Beck's music most distinctive may prove, by its very nature, difficult, if not impossible, to emulate.

—*David Lee Fish*

SELECT DISCOGRAPHY
■ ALBUMS
Mellow Gold, 1994
One Foot in the Grave, 1994
Stereopathetic Soul Manure, 1994
Odelay, 1996
Mutations, 1998

SELECT AWARDS
Spin, named Artist of the Year, 1996
Rolling Stone Critics Poll, named Artist of the Year, 1996
Grammy Awards for Best Male Rock Vocal Performance for "Where It's At" and Best Alternative Music Performance for *Odelay*, 1997
Rolling Stone Reader's Poll, named Best Male Performer, 1998

SEE ALSO: Beastie Boys, The; Dylan, Bob.

The Bee Gees

ORIGINAL MEMBERS: Barry Gibb (b. 1946), Robin
   Gibb (b. 1949), Maurice Gibb (b. 1949)
FIRST SINGLE RELEASE: "The Battle of the Blue and
   the Grey," 1963
MUSICAL STYLES: Soft rock, pop, easy listening,
   disco

The Bee Gees were one of the most successful pop
groups of the 1960's and 1970's. Composed of
Barry Gibb and his younger twin brothers Robin
and Maurice, they produced a string of melodic
pop-rock ballads during the late 1960's. They fell
from grace for a few years but then returned in
the mid-1970's with a new rhythm-and-blues-
based dance sound that boosted their popularity
to great heights, making them the best-selling
music group of the 1970's. The Bee Gees would
be permanently linked with the 1977 hit film
Saturday Night Fever and the disco style it popularized. The group had already been performing for
more than one decade by the time that sound
track brought them new attention, and they continued to make music in various styles during the
subsequent decades, long after their popularity
had settled.

The Beginnings. The Gibb family lived in Manchester, England, during the mid-1950's. The
boys' parents, Hugh and Barbara, were involved
with music as an orchestra leader and as a singer,
respectively. Barry, Robin, and Maurice first performed publicly at film theaters in late 1956 and
soon formed a group called the Rattlesnakes,
followed by another called Wee Johnny Hayes and
the Bluecats. During this period, Barry began
composing his own songs.

In 1958, the family relocated to Brisbane, Australia. By that time they had another child, Andy,
who would go on to have a brief but lucrative solo
vocal career concurrent with his brothers' disco
years. In 1959, Barry, Robin, and Maurice sang at
a racetrack, where they were introduced by one of
the drivers, Bill Goode, to a disc jockey named Bill
Gates. Gates recorded some songs by the boys that
were played on the radio.

By the following year, they had moved to television performances and had taken the name
B.G.'s. Although it was popularly assumed that the
name was an abbreviation for Brothers Gibb, the
group has said that it is actually a tribute to the
two men who discovered them and launched
them on their career, both of whom had the
initials B. G.

By 1961, the trio had found continuous work
as a musical group in hotels and lounges. An
Australian artist, Col Jaye, became the first to
record one of Barry's songs, "(Underneath the)
Starlight of Love." In 1963, the Gibb family moved
to Sydney, Australia, where Jaye placed them in a
concert. They were heard by an executive from a
local record label called Festival who signed the
Gibbs to a contract. They released their first single, "The Battle of the Blue and the Grey," backed
with "The Three Kisses of Love," that same year.
At this time they changed their name officially to
the Bee Gees.

Although they (and other artists) continued to
record their songs, the Bee Gees did not have any
great success. In 1965, they recorded their first
album, *The Bee Gees Sing and Play 14 Barry Gibb
Songs*, which was released only in Australia. A
second album, *Spicks and Specks*, was issued the
following year, and the title track was a big hit in
Australia.

International Success. By 1967, it was obvious
that if the Bee Gees were to expand their popularity, they would have to find mass audiences. The
Gibb family moved back to England, where they
quickly signed a management contract with
Robert Stigwood of NEMS, the same company
that managed the Beatles, who had greatly influenced the Bee Gees by this point. Stigwood had
the group signed to Polydor Records in the
United Kingdom and most of the world, and to
Atco (a division of Atlantic) in the United States.
The group recorded an album in 1967, titled *Bee
Gees' 1st* (although it actually was not). The trio
also took on two additional members, drummer
Colin Peterson and guitarist Vince Melouney,
both Australians.

International success came almost immediately. The single "New York Mining Disaster 1941"
was a Top-20 hit in both England and the United

States in 1967 and was followed before the end of the year by three other hit singles: "To Love Somebody," "Holiday," and "Massachusetts." All of these early Bee Gees songs were richly textured ballads stressing the boys' melodic songwriting and close vocal harmonies.

The hit streak continued into 1968 with such songs as "Words," "I've Got to Get a Message to You," and "I Started a Joke." Meanwhile, their albums, including *Horizontal* and *Idea* (both 1968), were well received by both critics and the public. By 1969, though, things began falling apart for the Bee Gees. Robin left the band, as did the two sidemen, Peterson and Melouney. Robin attempted to launch a solo career, but his album did not find success. Barry and Maurice carried on as the Bee Gees, but the fans were no longer interested. It seemed as if the brothers were going to go down in history as a short-lived phenomenon.

Resurgence. As the 1970's began, though, the group reconciled and found success. In late 1970,

Robin rejoined his brothers, and they immediately bounced back to popularity with a number 3 single, "Lonely Days," which was a little bouncier than their previous fare. Another sweet ballad, "How Can You Mend a Broken Heart," went all the way to number 1 in mid-1971.

Any optimism soon gave way, however, as the Bee Gees entered a four-year decline. Although they signed to a new label, RSO Records (run by manager Stigwood), the Bee Gees did not see the top of the charts again until 1975, when they reached number 1 with "Jive Talkin'." This was a new sound for them: Upbeat and danceable, it was taken from their album *Main Course*, produced by Arif Mardin.

Disco Fever. As the disco era began, the Bee Gees were happy leaders of the style. Their next single, "Nights on Broadway," was also a Top-10 hit in 1975 and was followed the next year by the frantic "You Should Be Dancing," which went to number 1, and "Love So Right," a number 3 hit.

By this time, the tempo of much of the Bee Gees' music had accelerated considerably. To accommodate the insistent dance rhythms, Barry adopted a falsetto vocal style. It was a winning formula, and the Bee Gees seemed like the natural choice to supply the music for a new film about the disco lifestyle in New York, *Saturday Night Fever*.

Starring John Travolta, the film was a massive hit, and the Bee Gees' music was an integral part of its success. The soundtrack album itself, including songs by the Bee Gees and others, was number 1 for nearly half a year, and three Bee Gees singles taken from the album also reached number 1: "How Deep Is Your Love," "Stayin' Alive," and "Night Fever," the latter two quintessential disco tunes. The Bee Gees were also involved in other hits from the film and

The Bee Gees in 1994 (Paul Natkin)

For the Record

Although *Saturday Night Fever* remained at number 1 on the *Billboard* album chart for twenty-four weeks, that is not a longevity record, even for a sound-track album. In 1961-1962, the sound track from the film *West Side Story* was at the top for a staggering fifty-four weeks—more than a year.

sound track, including Tavares' "More than a Woman" and Yvonne Elliman's number 1 hit "If I Can't Have You." Barry also wrote hits for Samantha Sang, Frankie Valli of the Four Seasons, and brother Andy Gibb (who died in 1988).

Endurance. For the duration of the 1970's, the Bee Gees remained a strong act, with three more consecutive number 1 hits, "Too Much Heaven," "Tragedy," and "Love You Inside Out," and a top-selling album, *Spirits Having Flown* (1979). By 1979, however, some rock fans had started a backlash against disco, and the Bee Gees were a prime target. Costarring (with Peter Frampton) in a 1978 film version of the Beatles' *Sgt. Pepper's Lonely Hearts Club Band*, which critics disliked and filmgoers ignored, did not help their careers. The group's popularity subsided again.

In the late 1980's, the Bee Gees signed with Warner Bros. Records and in the 1990's to Poly-Gram, and they managed one last number 1 single, 1989's "One." Although they continued to record and perform together (and work with other artists), the Bee Gees would primarily be remembered as a product of the 1960's and 1970's.

—*Jeff Tamarkin*

SELECT DISCOGRAPHY
■ SINGLES
"New York Mining Disaster 1941," 1967
"To Love Somebody," 1967
"I've Gotta Get a Message to You," 1968
"How Can You Mend a Broken Heart," 1971
"Jive Talkin'," 1975

"Love So Right," 1976
"You Should Be Dancing," 1976
"How Deep Is Your Love," 1977
"Stayin' Alive," 1977
"Night Fever," 1978
"Too Much Heaven," 1978
■ ALBUMS
Bee Gees' 1st, 1967
Saturday Night Fever, 1977 (sound track)
Spirits Having Flown, 1979

SELECT AWARDS
Grammy Award for Best Pop Vocal Performance, Group, for "How Deep Is Your Love," 1977
Grammy Awards for Album of the Year and Best Pop Vocal Performance by a Duo, Group, or Chorus for *Saturday Night Fever*, for Best Arrangement for Voices for "Stayin' Alive"; for Best Producer of 1978 (with Albhy Galuten and Karl Richardson); all 1978
Grammy Award for Best Pop Performance by a Duo or Group with Vocal for "Guilty," 1980 (Barry Gibb with Barbra Streisand)
Rock and Roll Hall of Fame, inducted 1997

SEE ALSO: Beatles, The; Four Seasons, The / Frankie Valli; Frampton, Peter.

Harry Belafonte

BORN: New York, New York; March 1, 1927
FIRST ALBUM RELEASE: *Mark Twain and Other Folk Songs*, 1955
MUSICAL STYLES: Folk, calypso, pop, blues, jazz

Harold George Belafonte, Jr.'s family moved from New York City to his mother's old home in Kingston, Jamaica, when he was eight years old. In 1940, the family returned to New York City, where Harry attended St. Thomas (parochial) School and later George Washington High School. Harry left school in 1944 and served in the United States Navy from 1944 to 1946. Returning to civilian life, Belafonte attended Erwin Piscator's Manhattan New School for Social Research Dramatic Workshop (1946-1948) and studied acting. He pursued a career in the theater, but work was very difficult to obtain.

In 1949, the owner of the Royal Roost, a Broadway jazz club, gave Belafonte an audition to sing, then signed him for a two-week engagement. Because his silky-smooth, gently relaxing singing voice became so popular with the clientele, his contract was extended to twenty weeks. Thereafter, Belafonte was booked for a national tour, and he spent two years singing popular songs in nightclubs throughout the United States. In late 1950, he rejected his popular song repertoire. He investigated folk music by searching the Archive of Folk Song at the Library of Congress and began singing his interpretations of traditional melodies from Jamaica, Africa, Asia, and America. In 1952, he secured a recording contract with RCA Victor, which launched him as a recording star.

King of Calypso. Belafonte's greatest fame is a result of his talent as a recording artist. In 1956, he was at the forefront of the calypso craze, which was a perfect vehicle for his happy-go-lucky folksongs. His interpretations of Trinidadian calypso music between 1956 and 1959 won him great success and marked the pinnacle of his career. Early hits (1956-1957) included "Jamaica Farewell," "Mary's Boy Child," and the classic transatlantic hit "Banana Boat Song" with its memorable refrain, "Day-oh, dayyy-oh, day light come and me wanna go home." He had incredible success during the 1950's because he was able to cross over into many different markets by appealing to pop, folk, blues, and jazz fans, as well as to the ethnic population with whom he became closely associated during the Civil Rights movement of the 1950's and 1960's. During this time, Belafonte became the most popular folksinger in the United States.

Belafonte's success as an album artist is considerable. He recorded thirty-one albums between 1955 and 1992. His album *Calypso* (1956) became the first album ever to sell one million copies, and it spent thirty-one weeks at the top of the music charts in the United States. Between 1956 and 1962, his music was almost never absent from the album chart. His appeal as a concert hall attraction was immense, with seven of his albums recorded live in concert. *Belafonte at Carnegie Hall*

For the Record

In order to earn a living while pursuing an acting career in the late 1940's, Harry Belafonte worked in New York's garment district pushing a dress cart.

(1959) spent over three years on the charts, with similar success for *Belafonte Returns to Carnegie Hall* (1960). Belafonte has performed in concerts in Cuba, Jamaica, Europe, Australia, New Zealand, and the United States.

During the late 1960's and the 1970's, Belafonte's popularity waned, but he continued to record and to perform in nightclubs and theaters. In 1976, 1979, and 1983, he made world tours, performing his folk-inspired songs for large crowds of devoted followers. In 1985, he produced and sang on the star-studded album and video *We Are the World* to raise funds for famine victims throughout central Africa and drought victims in Ethiopia, and his efforts earned him a Grammy Award.

Films, Broadway, and Television. Belafonte began his acting career with a role in *Bright Road* (1952). This film was followed by a starring role as Joe (Don José) in Oscar Hammerstein's *Carmen Jones* (1954), an adaptation of Georges Bizet's *Carmen*. Between these two films, he performed on Broadway in *John Murray Anderson's Almanac* in 1953, and this performance won for him the 1954 Tony Award for Best Featured Actor in a Musical. He also starred in the Broadway performance *Three for Tonight* in 1955.

In 1957, Belafonte sang the title song in the film *Island in the Sun*. Later that year, he formed his own motion-picture production firm, HarBel. Over the next twelve years, he starred in three of his own HarBel film productions: *The World, the Flesh, and the Devil* in 1958, *Odds Against Tomorrow* in 1959, and *The Angel Levine* in 1970. Belafonte costarred with Sidney Poitier in *Buck and the Preacher* in 1972 and acted in his last film, *Uptown Saturday Night* in 1974.

Belafonte frequently appeared on television and was a popular performer. Among his television successes, the 1959 special "Tonight with Belafonte" won for him an Emmy Award in 1960 for Outstanding Performance in a Musical Program. Belafonte produced the television specials "A Time for Laughter" (1967) and "Harry and Lena" (1969), in which he performed with Lena Horne. In 1984, he produced *Strolling Twenties TV* and coproduced *Bear Street.*

Human Rights Activist. In the 1960's, Belafonte became an ambassador of civil rights. President John F. Kennedy named him a cultural adviser to the Peace Corps, making Belafonte the first entertainer to hold that position. In 1965, he joined Martin Luther King, Jr., in the civil rights march from Selma, Alabama, to Montgomery, Alabama. Through his music, Belafonte was a major figure in achieving equal rights for African Americans.

During the 1980's and 1990's, Belafonte worked diligently for the United Nations International Children's Emergency Fund (UNICEF), serving as its goodwill ambassador. He became a figure of hope to children throughout the world, with a mission to mobilize world support for the plight of low child survival rates and to end world starvation and sickness. He was the mastermind for the United States of America for Africa movement, serving as its vice president and spokesperson. In 1990, TransAfrica Forum, a group that lobbies on behalf of Africa and the Caribbean, made Belafonte the recipient of the Nelson Mandela Courage Award for his valiant efforts as a champion of human rights.   —*Alvin K. Benson*

SELECT DISCOGRAPHY
■ ALBUMS
Mark Twain and Other Folk Favorites, 1955
Belafonte, 1956
Calypso, 1956
An Evening with Belafonte, 1957
Belafonte Sings of the Caribbean, 1957
Belafonte Sings the Blues, 1958
Love Is a Gentle Thing, 1959
Porgy and Bess, 1959
Belafonte at Carnegie Hall, 1959

Belafonte Returns to Carnegie Hall, 1960
Jump Up Calypso, 1961
The Midnight Special, 1962
The Many Moods of Belafonte, 1962
Streets I Have Walked, 1963
Ballads, Blues, and Boasters, 1964
In My Quiet Room, 1966
Calypso in Brass, 1966
Homeward Bound, 1970
Turn the World Around, 1977
Loving You Is Where I Belong, 1981
Paradise in Gazankulu, 1988
Banana Boat Song, 1988 (compilation)
The Very Best of Harry Belafonte, 1992 (compilation)

SELECT AWARDS
Tony Award for Supporting or Featured Actor, Musical, for *John Murray Anderson's Almanac,* 1954
Emmy Award for Outstanding Performance in a Variety or Musical Program or Series for *Tonight with Belafonte,* 1960
Grammy Award for Best Folk Recording for *An Evening with Belafonte/Makeba,* 1965 (with Miriam Makeba)
Martin Luther King, Jr., Nonviolent Peace Prize, 1982
Grammy Awards for Record of the Year, Best Pop Performance by a Duo or Group with Vocal, and Best Music Video, Short Form, for *We Are the World,* 1985 (with USA for Africa)
Nelson Mandela Courage Award, 1990
National Medal of Arts Award, 1994

SEE ALSO: Bennett, Tony; Cole, Nat "King"; Davis, Sammy, Jr.; Kingston Trio, The; Mathis, Johnny.

Pat Benatar

BORN: Brooklyn, New York; January 10, 1953
FIRST ALBUM RELEASE: *In the Heat of the Night,* 1979
MUSICAL STYLE: Rock and roll

Known for her powerful vocals and tough yet sultry image, the diminutive Pat Benatar (she is five feet tall) was one of the most successful female rockers of the early 1980's. Benatar earned an unprecedented four straight Grammy Awards for Rock Vocal Performance, Female, from 1980 to 1983 and was one of the early artists to bolster her image through the then-fledgling MTV channel. Her career slowed considerably in the 1990's, although she continued to record new material and perform live.

The Beginnings. Benatar, born Patricia Andrzejewski, grew up on Long Island. She planned to study opera at the Juilliard School of Music but decided the strict regimen was not for her. She married Dennis Benatar at age eighteen, living with him in Richmond, Virginia, and Worcester, Massachusetts, before returning to New York in 1975. That year she began appearing as a cabaret singer in clubs in New York.

Having evolved into a rock performer, Benatar was signed to Chrysalis Records in 1978 through her appearances at showcases at Catch a Rising Star. During this period she met guitarist Neil Giraldo, who became her cowriter and producer—and, later, her second husband. He assembled a backing band for the recording of her million-selling debut album, *In the Heat of the Night*. The 1979 album peaked at number 12 on the U.S. charts, with the first single, "Heartbreaker," reaching number 23.

The Hits Keep Coming. Capitalizing on her newfound success, Benatar released *Crimes of Passion* in 1980. The singles "Hit Me with Your Best Shot" and "Treat Me Right" went to number 9 and number 18, respectively. The album peaked at number 2 in early 1981. Benatar also earned the first of four Grammy Awards that year. Her next release, *Precious Time*, became her first album to

top the charts, and spawned it two successful singles, "Fire and Ice" and "Promises in the Dark." In 1982, Benatar (now divorced from Dennis Benatar) married Giraldo in Maui. Later that year she released her fourth album, *Get Nervous*.

Get Nervous became her fourth consecutive million seller, peaking at number 4 and featuring the number 15 single, "Shadows of the Night." Her next release, *Live from Earth*, hit number 13, spurred by the number 5 single, "Love Is a Battlefield," whose video became a mainstay on MTV. Benatar's last major album of this period, *Tropico*, was released in 1985. Peaking at number 14, the album featured the Top-5 single "We Belong."

Motherhood and a Career Break. Benatar gave birth to her first child, Haley, in February, 1985, and took some time off. She would never regain the career momentum she enjoyed in the first half of the decade, although her next few albums still went gold. *Seven the Hard Way*, released in December of 1985, reached number 26 on the charts and included the Top-10 single "Invincible," from the film *The Legend of Billie Jean*. Benatar was also among fifty artists to participate in the recording of "Sun City" for Artists Against Apartheid. Her 1988 release, *Wide Awake in Dreamland*, yielded the number 19 single, "All Fired Up." Frustrated with the state of her career, Benatar went in a blues direction for her 1991 release, *True Love*, which also went gold.

The Nineties: Back to Rock. In 1993, she returned to more familiar territory with the rock album *Gravity's Rainbow*. She gave birth to her second child, Hana, in 1994. That same year she released *All Fired Up: The Very Best of Pat Benatar*, a two-CD compilation. In 1995, Benatar returned to the road to tour with REO Speedwagon and Fleetwood Mac in Japan, Australia, and the United States. She toured again in 1996, and the following year she left her longtime recording company, Chrysalis, for CMC International, which released *Innamorata*.   —*Robert DiGiacomo*

For the Record

"Musically, we're still in touch with each other," Benatar once said of married life with her musical collaborator, Neil Giraldo. "We like to play together. It's who's cooking dinner tonight that's the problem."

SELECT DISCOGRAPHY
■ ALBUMS
In the Heat of the Night, 1979
Crimes of Passion, 1980

Precious Time, 1981
Get Nervous, 1982
Live from Earth, 1983
Tropico, 1984
Seven the Hard Way, 1985
Wide Awake in Dreamland, 1988
Best Shots, 1989
True Love, 1991
Gravity's Rainbow, 1993
All Fired Up: The Very Best of Pat Benatar, 1994
   (2-CD set)
Innamorata, 1997

SELECT AWARDS

Grammy Award for Best Rock Vocal Performance, Female, for *Crimes of Passion,* 1980
Grammy Award for Best Rock Vocal Performance, Female, for "Fire and Ice," 1981
Grammy Award for Best Rock Vocal Performance, Female, for "Shadows of the Night," 1982
Grammy Award for Best Rock Vocal Performance, Female, for "Love Is a Battlefield," 1983

SEE ALSO: Heart.

Tony Bennett

(Anthony Dominick Benedetto)

BORN: Queens, New York; August 13, 1926
FIRST SINGLE RELEASE: "Boulevard of Broken Dreams," 1950
MUSICAL STYLES: Pop, jazz

When Tony Bennett rose to stardom in the early 1950's, his repertoire consisted of classic American popular songs. Forty years later, when a younger generation joined with longtime fans and revitalized his career, he was still drawing from the classic popular song treasury. Perhaps more than any other singer, Bennett has embraced the wealth of great music produced by Cole Porter, Duke Ellington, Richard Rodgers and Lorenz Hart, George and Ira Gershwin, and other U.S. composers and lyricists. Bennett's masterful renditions of these songs have made him one of the most highly regarded American performers.

Becoming a Singer. Bennett was born in the Astoria section of Queens, New York. His father was a grocer who had emigrated to the United States from Italy in 1922. Bennett was only nine when his father died, but he kept memories of his father's love of singing. His mother found work as a dressmaker to support herself and three children.

Bennett studied music and painting in junior high school, and he began singing as an amateur for school functions and social gatherings in the community near his home. His first professional engagement occurred when he was thirteen, and other club dates followed. His love of painting remained part of his life; he would eventually become renowned for his work, exhibiting in galleries around the world.

After military service in Europe as World War II was ending, Bennett returned to New York and began studies with professional voice teachers. One of them, Miriam Speir, encouraged him to visit the many jazz clubs that were operating on New York's 52nd Street. She knew that Bennett could learn much about song interpretation from the great jazz instrumentalists and vocalists performing nightly along this famous thoroughfare. Thus, Bennett listened to and absorbed the influences that helped him shape his personal style. Without any steady singing work, however, he took jobs as an elevator operator, a grocer's assistant, and a singing waiter.

Breakthrough. In 1949, Bennett auditioned for a stage production which starred Pearl Bailey. Bailey was an established artist, having sung with big bands and in Broadway musicals. Bennett was given roles as a singer and master of ceremonies, and he began using the stage name Joe Bari.

During one performance, entertainer Bob Hope heard Bennett and asked if he would sing in Hope's show, which was in its final night at another theater. Bennett agreed; Hope, learning that his new singer's real name was Tony Benedetto, introduced him that night as Tony Bennett. Bennett then went on tour with Hope, which led to a 1950 audition for Columbia Re-

Tony Bennett (Columbia)

cords. After hearing Bennett's demo of "Boulevard of Broken Dreams," producer Mitch Miller signed him to the label and released the song. It was a minor hit, and Bennett became an attraction in big-city nightclubs.

Bennett's next single, "Because of You," was released in 1951. It was a number 1 hit and stayed on the charts for thirty-two weeks. That same year, Bennett had hits with "Cold, Cold Heart" and "Solitaire"; as a result, he was named the leading recording male vocalist for 1951 by *Cash Box* magazine.

Singles to Albums. Bennett released a series of hit singles throughout the 1950's and early 1960's. They included the number 1 "Rags to Riches" in 1953, "There'll Be No Teardrops Tonight" in 1954, and "Firefly" in 1958. In 1962, the single "I Left My Heart in San Francisco" won two

Grammy Awards and became forever identified as Bennett's theme song. Also in 1962, Bennett performed to a sold-out audience at New York's Carnegie Hall; the concert was recorded and produced a best-selling album.

By 1954, Bennett was looking to record a jazz-oriented album. The expectation at Columbia at that time, however, was that pop singers such as Bennett released only singles; albums were for classical music. Mitch Miller eventually allowed Bennett to proceed, and his first album, *Cloud 7*, was released in 1954. Bennett was backed by a jazz combo in songs that evoke a relaxed nightclub setting. His 1957 album, *The Beat of My Heart*, features top jazz drummers and Latin American percussionists. The two albums endeared Bennett to the jazz community and paved the way for his future jazz-influenced projects. Some of these include a recording with the Count Basie Orchestra in 1959 (*Basie Swings, Bennett Sings*), a tribute to Nat King Cole in 1964 (*When Lights Are Low*), and recordings with jazz pianist Bill Evans in 1975 and 1977 (*The Tony Bennett/Bill Evans Album* and *Together Again: Tony Bennett and Bill Evans*).

A Lull and a Comeback. Though he continued to perform concerts, Bennett made no recordings from 1978 to 1985. His dedication to the classic popular song literature was seen as old-fashioned when other stars of his generation were performing youth-oriented material. Bennett remained committed to his standards, to the point of starting his own label to record the songs he wanted to. His effort quickly failed, and his contract with Columbia expired.

The rift was mended, however, and Bennett returned to Columbia (CBS) in 1986. His next two albums were well received by audiences and critics, and a 1991 four-compact-disc anthology (*Forty Years: The Artistry of Tony Bennett*) reminded the public of the extent of his remarkable career. His 1992 tribute to Frank Sinatra, *Perfectly Frank*, won a Grammy Award, as did 1993's tribute to Fred Astaire, *Steppin' Out*. Bennett's popularity was surging. His older fans were thrilled to hear him doing the same kinds of songs he had always done. Younger fans became enamored of him through television appearances such as the 1993 MTV

Video Music Awards. His 1994 album, *Tony Bennett—MTV Unplugged*, won two more Grammy Awards.

In the liner notes to *Perfectly Frank*, Bennett recalled the time he heard Sinatra declare on television that Bennett was his favorite singer. Comparisons of their careers are perhaps inevitable; Bennett compares well, without all of the flamboyant extramusical trappings that attended Sinatra's professional and private life. Bennett's slightly raspy voice was full-bodied and resonant with a friendly, inviting quality; listeners could easily imagine Bennett singing directly to them with a smile on his face and a hand on their shoulder. His would be one of the most instantly recognizable and durable voices in American music.   —*Mark W. Bolton*

SELECT DISCOGRAPHY
■ SINGLES
"Because of You," 1951
"Cold, Cold Heart," 1951
"Rags to Riches," 1953
"I Left My Heart in San Francisco," 1962
■ ALBUMS
The Beat of My Heart, 1957
Basie Swings, Bennett Sings, 1959
Tony Bennett at Carnegie Hall, 1962
When Lights Are Low, 1964
The Movie Song Album, 1966
The Rodgers and Hart Songbook, 1973
The Art of Excellence, 1986

For the Record

Early in his career, Bennett's rather prominent nose was perhaps a liability, keeping him from winning auditions. At one point he was advised to have plastic surgery. He refused, knowing that one's vocal qualities are affected by such features. The voice of Tony Bennett, spared from alteration, became one of the great sounds in American popular music.

Bennett/Berlin, 1987
Forty Years: The Artistry of Tony Bennett, 1991
    (4-CD boxed set, compilation)
Perfectly Frank, 1992
Steppin' Out, 1993
Tony Bennett—MTV Unplugged, 1994
Here's to the Ladies, 1995
Tony Bennett on Holiday, 1997

SELECT AWARDS
Grammy Awards for Record of the Year and Best Solo Vocal Performance, Male, for "I Left My Heart in San Francisco," 1962
Grammy Award for Best Traditional Pop Vocal Performance for *Perfectly Frank*, 1992
Grammy Award for Best Traditional Pop Vocal Performance for *Steppin' Out*, 1993
Grammy Awards for Album of the Year and Best Traditional Pop Vocal Performance for *Tony Bennett—MTV Unplugged*, 1994
Grammy Award for Best Traditional Pop Vocal Performance for *Here's to the Ladies*, 1996
Grammy Award for Best Traditional Pop Vocal Performance for *Tony Bennett on Holiday*, 1997

SEE ALSO: Sinatra, Frank.

George Benson

BORN: Pittsburgh, Pennsylvania; March 22, 1943
FIRST ALBUM RELEASE: *The New Boss Guitar of George Benson with the Brother Jack McDuff Quartet*, 1964
MUSICAL STYLES: Rhythm and blues, jazz, pop

George Benson's artistry in crafting an appealing fusion of rhythm and blues, jazz, and pop has earned him immense international popularity. Benson is both a guitarist of dazzling technical fluency and a vocalist with a smooth, elegant quality perfectly suited to his material. His unprecedented chart-topping crossover successes in the 1970's came after he had established himself as an important jazz guitarist. As his hit albums continued into the 1980's, his stature enabled him to pick and choose his projects; he maintained his momentum in the 1990's with more number 1 albums and a busy touring schedule.

Early Career. Benson became involved in music at a young age, singing in amateur contests, on radio, and in clubs with his stepfather, who played guitar. Exposure to recordings of the great jazz guitarist Charlie Christian sparked his interest, and he began formal guitar study at age eleven. He sang and played with Pittsburgh-based rhythm-and-blues bands, eventually leading his own group by the time he was seventeen. Jazz guitarist Wes Montgomery was another important influence, as was legendary saxophonist Charlie "Bird" Parker.

Benson's break came when he joined the band of rhythm-and-blues organist Brother Jack McDuff. Through this group's recordings and his work backing other jazz musicians, Benson's reputation grew. Though he was a newcomer to the jazz scene, Benson became known as someone who made the other musicians, particularly the leader, sound good, whether live or in the recording studio. In 1965, Benson left McDuff, moved to New York, and assembled his own quartet. They signed with Columbia and began releasing a series of well-received albums. These recordings, along with subsequent efforts for the A&M and CTI labels, showcased Benson's guitar in a mainstream jazz setting. His vocal talent was virtually unknown outside his hometown.

Stardom. That changed when Benson signed with Warner Bros. Records in late 1975. His 1976 debut album for Warner, *Breezin'*, featured a mix of instrumentals and vocals, including his soulful cover of Leon Russell's bittersweet ballad "This Masquerade." This single became the first in history to reach number 1 on the pop, jazz, and rhythm-and-blues charts, and it was the Grammy Award winner for Record of the Year. The instrumental title track featured Benson's ringing, fluid guitar over a relaxed medium-tempo dance beat. This tune won the Grammy Award for Best Pop Instrumental Performance. Benson finished 1976 by receiving multiple honors from magazines such as *Billboard*, *Record World*, and *Rolling Stone*.

Breezin' is often cited as the best-selling jazz album of all time, and it is indicative of the changes jazz was undergoing in the 1970's. The style known as jazz fusion had started with the groups of Miles Davis and Weather Report at the end of the 1960's. At that time, fusion designated a mix of jazz with rock and dance rhythms and electric and electronic instruments. As more jazz musicians played fusion, it absorbed elements from soul, funk, Latin American, and other styles. By adding vocals, Benson brought jazz fusion to a more mainstream pop audience; his jazz-pop sound established a trend that defined the label "contemporary jazz." In the 1990's, featuring music by Kenny G, Sade, Al Jarreau, and others, contemporary jazz became a popular urban radio format.

George Benson (Paul Natkin)

For the Record

At age eighteen, George Benson auditioned for Brother Jack McDuff when the latter came through Pittsburgh. Benson impressed McDuff and joined the tour but was promptly fired the first night. The song arrangements proved too challenging for the young guitarist. McDuff, however, could not find a replacement, so he worked painstakingly with Benson on the arrangements. Benson's diligent rehearsal of his parts saved his place in McDuff's quartet. The resulting four-year stint gained Benson the recognition necessary to launch his solo career.

Benson's solos frequently featured a remarkable technique which combines an improvised vocal line using nonsense syllables, known as scat singing, with the same line played simultaneously on guitar. Heard initially on "This Masquerade," Benson used it to good effect on his remake of the Drifters' "On Broadway," a performance which won another Grammy in 1978. That year Benson toured Japan, Europe, and Australia and was invited by President Jimmy Carter to perform at the White House.

Continuation. Quincy Jones produced Benson's 1980 release, *Give Me the Night*. Cosponsored by Warner Bros., it was Jones's first album for his new Qwest label. The album won a Grammy in the rhythm-and-blues category, as did one of its tracks, the instrumental "Off Broadway." The album also contains a Grammy-winning performance in the jazz category, "Moody's Mood," with vocals by Benson and guest Patti Austin. It is based on a version of the standard "I'm in the Mood for Love," recorded by jazz saxophonist James Moody.

Benson won another Grammy in 1983, again in the pop category. A look at the different areas of his Grammy successes reveals what his fans would call his versatility; to his critics, it showed a lack of direction. Jazz critics, in what became standard procedure with many crossover jazz artists, criticized Benson for becoming commercial in their reviews of Benson's jazz-pop albums, starting with *Breezin'*. Benson asserted that he had recorded many mainstream jazz albums that his companies would not release. Many jazz artists, including Benson, felt that they needed to have sufficient clout and be financially secure to be able to devote time to the less popular, less lucrative mainstream jazz market. In the middle and late 1980's, Benson did return to his jazz roots, and in 1990, he recorded an outstanding album with one of the great jazz ensembles of all time, the Count Basie Orchestra. However, his number 1 albums of 1993 (*Love Remembers*) and 1996 (*That's Right*) were again in the contemporary jazz style.

Benson obviously had the talent to produce outstanding music in any musical category. His dilemma would perhaps be deciding which fan base to please with his next project. Though critics might be exasperated by the continuous alternations, his fans could be certain that Benson would give them the best that his multiple talents could provide.

—*Mark W. Bolton*

SELECT DISCOGRAPHY

■ ALBUMS

It's Uptown, 1965
The George Benson Cookbook, 1966
Shape of Things to Come, 1968
Beyond the Blue Horizon, 1971
White Rabbit, 1972
Breezin', 1976
Weekend in L.A., 1978
Livin' Inside Your Love, 1979
Give Me the Night, 1980
20/20, 1984
Collaboration, 1987 (with Earl Klugh)
Big Boss Band, 1990
Love Remembers, 1993
That's Right, 1996

SELECT AWARDS

Grammy Awards for Record of the Year for "This Masquerade," Best Pop Instrumental Performance for *Breezin'*, and Best R&B Instrumental Performance for "Theme from Good King Bad," 1976

Grammy Awards for Best R&B Vocal Performance, Male, for *Give Me the Night*, Best R&B Instrumental Performance for "Off Broadway," and Best Jazz Vocal Performance, Male, for "Moody's Mood," 1980
Grammy Award for Best Pop Instrumental Performance for "Being with You," 1983

SEE ALSO: Drifters, The; G, Kenny; Sade.

Chuck Berry

BORN: St. Louis, Missouri; October 18, 1926
FIRST SINGLE RELEASE: "Maybellene," 1955
MUSICAL STYLES: Rhythm and blues, rock and roll

Charles Edward Anderson (Chuck) Berry is one of the most legendary and enigmatic figures in the history of rock and roll. His evasive answers about his early life and his reluctance to grant interviews and participate in publicity campaigns have only contributed to his mystique. As one of the pioneers of rock and roll and one of the pivotal figures between rhythm and blues and the early rock styles, he had enormous influence on later rock performers. His energy and drive reached successive generations and have contributed to his popularity through the decades.

Early Years. As with several major rock-and-roll figures, there is some confusion about Berry's early years; he has misled writers and reporters about the specific year of his birth, which was long reported to have been 1931. He was raised in St. Louis and Wentzville, Missouri. Like those of many other rock-and-roll artists, his childhood was characterized by a strong influence from the church. Typically, this influence was tempered by worldly pursuits and became a marginal influence in his later years.

Unlike many black musicians of his era, however, Berry was raised in a comfortable middle-class environment and was not exposed to the poverty experienced by many other rockers of his generation. Berry's first brush with the law came during World War II, when he was sent to reform school for attempted robbery. After his release, he

obtained a job in a General Motors plant and studied cosmetology; he also formed a trio that played small club shows in St. Louis. During a trip to Chicago, Berry arranged to meet Muddy Waters, who encouraged him to audition for Leonard Chess of Chess Records. The first song Berry recorded for Chess was "Ida Red," the name of which was changed to "Maybellene" and became his first big hit (1955). Promoted by rock-and-roll disc jockey Alan Freed (who was also granted coauthor status), "Maybellene" was the first rock-and-roll single to move to a high place on the pop, country, and rhythm-and-blues charts.

Berry's subsequent hits became standards of the early rock movement. Among the songs from the latter part of the decade are "Roll Over Beethoven" and "Brown-Eyed Handsome Man" (both from 1956 and successful on the rhythm-and-blues charts), and "School Days," "Rock and Roll Music," "Sweet Little Sixteen," and "Johnny B. Goode" (from 1957 and 1958), which made it into the Top 10. Like many of the early rockers, Berry also appeared in several rock films; the best known of these was *Rock, Rock, Rock!* (1956) and *Go, Johnny, Go!* (1958).

Later Career. Berry's career came to a standstill in 1959 when he was arrested for violation of the Mann Act. An underage prostitute from El Paso, Texas, had joined the tour, and Berry later gave her a job in his St. Louis club. When he fired her a few months later, she reported him to the police and charges were filed against him for transporting a female across state lines for immoral purposes. His first conviction was overturned, but he was subsequently retried and served several years in a federal penitentiary. After his release from prison, he returned to concertizing and recording, scoring several hits, including "No Particular Place" (1964) and "My Ding-a-Ling" (1972). The latter became his only single to reach number 1 on the pop charts.

Berry would continue to perform through the 1990's, having made a significant comeback after a successful tour of England and Europe in the mid-1960's. He also benefited from the revival of late 1950's and early 1960's rock and roll that began in the 1970's and continued through the decades.

His performance practices have been unique and rather eccentric. Because of his various troubles with the law and the feeling that he has been mistreated by the media, he has rarely granted interviews or participated in preconcert publicity. Choosing not to travel with a band, he has relied instead on temporary bands hired for each specific occasion; little or no rehearsal would take place before performances. He has driven himself to the venue shortly before he is to take the stage and left immediately after his performance. Nonetheless, he has continued to draw crowds for summer concert series or oldies concerts, remaining popular with the general public.

Influence. Berry's importance in the history of rock and roll is multifaceted. Along with Little Richard, Fats Domino, and others, he was one of the artists who made the transition from rhythm and blues to rock and roll. He has used both the twelve-bar structure and harmonic progression of blues in his music. In pieces such as "Johnny B. Goode," this pattern forms the basis for both the verses and the chorus, with little deviation throughout the song. To this style he adds a heavy emphasis on the backbeat, a rhythmic characteristic that was to be the trademark of the new rock-and-roll style.

Berry was very aware of the culture around him. His songs were shorter and faster than the typical rhythm-and-blues pieces, making them ideal for airplay on the increasingly popular Top-40 radio stations in the 1950's. The fast tempi and rhythms of the songs were well suited to the fast-paced lifestyle experienced by the teenagers who were his typical audience. The songs were perfect for being played on the car radio or on a jukebox.

The lyrics of Berry's earlier songs are of a higher caliber than those of many of his contemporaries. They reflect the everyday trials and tribulations of the teenage class. His songs deal with high school, dancing, free time, and the relationships between boys and girls. In his music, he incorporated the prevailing fascination with cars, the fact that attendance at high school was mandatory, not vol-

Chuck Berry in the 1950's (Archive Photos/Frank Driggs Collection)

untary, and the overwhelming popularity of the new rock-and-roll style, all signs of the time. Teenagers felt they had discovered an ally who understood their feelings and translated those feelings into song lyrics. The pieces written after Berry's release from prison are less innocent and are often laced with metaphors or double entendres that make his songs highly suggestive (especially "No Particular Place" and "My Ding-a-Ling").

Berry's most important contribution, however, is in the area of instrumentation. He continued the tradition of bluesmen who used the electric guitar as a second voice rather than as an accompanying instrument. On each of his songs, he performed a duet with his guitar, alternating his voice and the instrument in a call-and-response style or treating it as an equal partner ("Johnny B. Goode," "No Particular Place," and "School Days"). He claimed Carl Hogan and T-Bone Walker as the major influences on his style; both of these bluesmen had adapted distinctive guitar techniques in their rhythm-and-blues songs. Berry's guitar introductions became a thumbprint of his style and now mark the songs as clearly as did the lyrics.

Berry's use of the electric guitar contributed to the increasing decline of the popularity of the acoustic guitar in rock and country music. Concert venues, as well as the nature of the music, were changing, leading artists to find ways to make their instruments heard above the rest of the band and the noise of the crowd. This problem was magnified with a performer who made the guitar

such an integral part of his compositions. Berry placed these instrumental parts in a higher register, using the electric guitar to generate the volume needed for the instrument to be heard in nightclubs and concert situations.

Chuck Berry's music was covered by a number of later rock artists who were influenced by his incorporation of the blues style and his treatment of the guitar lead. The Beatles recorded several of his songs ("Roll Over Beethoven," "Rock and Roll Music") and the Beach Boys indirectly acknowledged his influence when they modified the music of "Sweet Little Sixteen" for "Surfin' USA."

—*Karen M. Bryan*

SELECT DISCOGRAPHY
■ SINGLES
"Maybellene," 1955
"Brown-Eyed Handsome Man," 1956
"Havana Moon," 1956
"Roll Over Beethoven," 1956
"Rock and Roll Music," 1957
"School Days," 1957
"Johnny B. Goode," 1958
"Sweet Little Sixteen," 1958
"Back in the U.S.A.," 1959
"No Particular Place," 1964
"My Ding-a-Ling," 1972
■ ALBUMS
After School Session, 1958
Rockin' at the Hops, 1960
St. Louis to Liverpool, 1964
Chuck Berry in Memphis, 1967
The London Chuck Berry Sessions, 1972
Rockit, 1979

SELECT AWARDS
Grammy Award for Lifetime Achievement, 1984
Rock and Roll Hall of Fame, inducted 1986

SEE ALSO: Beatles, The; Little Richard; Presley, Elvis.

For the Record

"In 1971, the great John Lennon mentioned once that I was his hero. . . . On my forty-fifth birthday, the only time we stood side by side performing together the music we both loved so well, though sixteen years apart in age, we stood sixteen inches apart sharing the lyrics of 'Johnny B. Goode.'"
—*Chuck Berry*

Big Brother and the Holding Company. *See* **Janis Joplin**

Björk / The Sugarcubes

Sugarcubes

ORIGINAL MEMBERS: Björk Gudmundsdóttir, Einar Örn Benediktsson (b. 1962), Thór Eldon Jonsson (b. 1962), Einar Mellax, Bragi Ólafsson (b. 1962), Sigtryggur "Siggi" Baldursson (b. 1962)
OTHER MEMBERS: Margret "Magga" Ornolfsdottir
FIRST ALBUM RELEASE: *Life's Too Good*, 1988
MUSICAL STYLES: Pop, punk rock, alternative

Björk

BORN: Reykjavik, Iceland; November 21, 1965
FIRST ALBUM RELEASE: *Debut*, 1993
MUSICAL STYLES: Pop, punk rock, alternative

Björk combined a distinctive voice with a wide variety of musical styles ranging from classical, jazz, and big band to rock, punk, and electronic. Although Björk's music is difficult to classify, it bears some resemblance to alternative music by certain unique artists such as Beck.

A Child Prodigy. Björk Gudmundsdóttir began her musical career at a very early age. She studied classical flute and piano in her native Iceland and released an album of Icelandic folksongs at the age of eleven. At thirteen she began to play in a series of punk rock bands in Iceland. Two of these groups, Tappi Takarrass and KUKL, released two albums apiece. While in KUKL, Björk worked with Einar Örn Benediktsson and Sigtryggur "Siggi" Baldursson, who would later be members of the Sugarcubes. At this time Björk also met and married Thór Eldon and gave birth to their son Sindri.

The Sugarcubes. In 1986 the Sugarcubes were formed, with Björk on vocals and keyboards, Benediktsson on vocals and trumpet, Baldursson

Björk in 1997 (Popperfoto/Archive Photos)

on drums, Eldon on guitar, Bragi Ólafsson on bass, and Einar Mellax on keyboards. The band's first single, "Birthday" (1987), was a surprise hit in the United Kingdom, with critics giving particular praise for Björk's voice. Their first album, *Life's Too Good* (1988), featured a blend of pop and punk rock that also won critical acclaim. By the time the Sugarcubes released their second album in 1989, Björk was divorced from Eldon. He married Margret "Magga" Ornolfsdottir, who replaced Mellax as the band's keyboardist.

The second album by the Sugarcubes, *Here Today, Tomorrow, Next Week!* (1989), featured more elaborate production, including the use of brass and strings, but was not as popular as the first album. During this period the Sugarcubes also ran a company in Iceland known as Bad Taste, which included an art gallery, a poetry bookstore, a record company, a radio station, and a book publisher.

For the Record

Her American fans may be unaware that Björk's name does not rhyme with "pork," but with "work."

Solo Career. Björk began to experiment with various musical styles. In 1990 she appeared with an Icelandic pop/jazz trio on the album *Gling Glo.* Soon afterward, she appeared with the dance band 808 State on the album *Ex:el* (1991). Although the Sugarcubes continued to release albums until 1992, it was clear that Björk was heading for a successful career on her own.

Björk's first solo album, *Debut* (1993), included hit songs such as "Human Behaviour," "Venus as a Boy," "Play Dead," and "Big Time Sensuality." Her second album, *Post* (1995), included her most popular single in the United States, "Army of Me." The success of these songs was partly because of remixed dance versions that appeared on her third album, *Telegram* (1996). Her popularity was also aided by the regular appearance on the MTV of songs such as "It's Oh So Quiet."

The year 1996 was difficult for Björk. While on tour in Bangkok, Thailand, she attacked a reporter in an attempt to protect her son. Several months later, police intercepted a bomb sent to her home by a deranged fan who later killed himself. In an attempt to escape unwanted media attention, Björk recorded her next album in a small town in the south of Spain. *Homogenic* (1997) was Björk's most experimental album. The instruments used on the album ranged from synthesizers to classical string octets. *Homogenic* combined electronic music, often thought of as unemotional, with Björk's passionate vocals to produce music that could not fit easily into any established category. —*Rose Secrest*

SELECT DISCOGRAPHY
■ ALBUMS
Sugarcubes
Life's Too Good, 1988
Here Today, Tomorrow, Next Week!, 1989
Stick Around for Joy, 1991
Björk solo
Debut, 1993
Post, 1995
Telegram, 1996 (remixes of previously released material)
Homogenic, 1997

SEE ALSO: Beck.

Clint Black

BORN: Long Branch, New Jersey; February 4, 1962
FIRST ALBUM RELEASE: *Killin' Time,* 1989
MUSICAL STYLE: Country

Although born in New Jersey, where his father was working on a pipeline for an oil company, Clint Black moved to Houston, Texas, with his family when he was only six months old. Black loved athletics, but since he was physically too small to excel in sports, he learned to play a borrowed harmonica when he was thirteen years old. When he turned fifteen, he received a guitar as a Christmas gift and soon learned to play that as well. Playing in his older brother's band, Black performed at barbecues and chili cook-offs, and he began writing his own songs. At age seventeen, Black dropped out of high school, a decision that he would always regret.

His brother's band split up when Black was eighteen, and for the next seven years, he spent his time playing country music in Houston nightclubs. During this time, he supplemented his income as an ironworker and as a baitcutter and guide on a fishing boat. Black met Hayden Nicholas, his main songwriting collaborator, at a country-club performance in Houston in 1987. Nicholas joined Black's band, and the two soon developed some demos. In 1988, Black met Bill Ham, who was impressed with the demos and agreed to manage Black, getting him a contract with RCA Records.

A Strong Beginning. Black's debut album, *Killin' Time,* was released in May, 1989, and by October, it was certified double platinum. Black wrote four of the songs, and he and Nicholas cowrote the rest of the album. The album generated five number 1 country singles: "A Better Man," "Killin' Time," "Nobody's Home," "Walkin' Away," and "Nothing's News," and Black became the first artist in any music format to have that many number 1 hits from a debut album. In addition, Black's hit song "A Better Man," which Black had written about a broken romance he had experienced, marked the first time a new male performer had taken a debut single to the number 1 spot on the *Radio & Records* charts.

In October of 1989, Black garnered the Horizon Award from the Country Music Association (CMA), and in April, 1990, he won four trophies from the Academy of Country Music, for Album of the Year, Single Record of the Year, New Male Vocalist of the Year, and Male Vocalist of the Year. Other awards kept coming, as he was presented with the Star of Tomorrow and the Album of the Year Awards by The Nashville Network/Music City News in June, 1990, and he was named the Male Vocalist of the Year by the CMA in October, 1990.

The Hits Keep Coming. Black's second album, *Put Yourself in My Shoes*, was released in November, 1990, and became certified double platinum in October, 1991. Two number 1 singles were spawned from this album—"Loving Blind" and "Where Are You Now." Two other singles from the album were also very successful; "Put Yourself in My Shoes" peaked at number 4 on the country charts, while "One More Payment" rose to number 5. Black also hit the charts in 1991 with a duet titled "Hold On Partner," sung with the legendary "King of the Cowboys," Roy Rogers.

In October of 1991, Black married television's *Knots Landing* star Lisa Hartman, and many of his songs have since been dedicated to her. Managerial disputes with Bill Ham from 1991 to 1992 halted Black's recording career, and the two finally parted in February, 1992. Black's third album, *The Hard Way*, was released in July, 1992, and three number 1 hits resulted, "We Tell Ourselves," "Burn One Down," and "When My Ship Comes In." The album went platinum in September of 1992.

Black's fourth album, *No Time to Kill* (1993), was another big success, and the title song, "No Time to Kill," rose to number 1 on the country music charts. The album also contained a duet with Wynonna Judd, "A Bad Goodbye," which peaked at number 2 and was nominated for a Grammy Award in 1994. Other hit songs from the album included "State of Mind" and "Half the Man," which Black wrote for his wife.

One Emotion, released in 1994, yielded several more country Top-10 singles for Black, including the number 1 "A Good Run of Bad Luck." In June,

1995, "Summer's Comin'," written by Black and Nicholas, reached the number 1 position on the country charts, and another song they cowrote, "Life Gets Away," peaked at number 4 in the fall of 1995. Toward the end of 1995, Black released his holiday album, *Looking for Christmas*, and in the fall of 1996, Black's album *The Greatest Hits* was in the Top 10 on the hit lists. Black had another number 1 hit, "Like the Rain," in 1997, and again that year, with "Nothin' but the Taillights," the title song from his album of the same name.

Other Kudos. Unlike preceding country acts, Black toured with his studio band and became a major concert attraction. Black has made public appearances at New York's Carnegie Hall and

Clint Black at the Country Music Association Awards in 1994 (Archive Photos/Nashville Banner Publishing Co.)

Macy's Thanksgiving Day Parade, and he has appeared on nearly every national television show, including his first appearance on the *Grand Ole Opry* in April, 1989. His impressive achievements as a songwriter were highlighted when he received a CMA Triple Play Award, which was established to recognize member composers who had written three or more songs that had reached number 1 status on the country singles charts in *Billboard, Radio & Records*, and *The Gavin Report* over the previous twelve-month period. Black received the Triple Play Award in 1996 for "Wherever You Go," "Summer's Comin'," "One Emotion," "A Bad Goodbye," and "A Good Run of Bad Luck." Black acknowledges that his career began as a songwriter, and as a result, he donates money periodically to the Nashville Songwriters Association.

With his good looks, his husky, expressive voice, and his easygoing, charming charisma, Black appeals to all country music fans, young and old. He is often compared to Merle Haggard for both his vocal and his songwriting abilities. His trademarks are his black hat, his dimpled smile, his literary lyrics, and his wonderful voice.

—*Alvin K. Benson*

SELECT DISCOGRAPHY

■ ALBUMS
Killin' Time, 1989
Put Yourself in My Shoes, 1990
The Hard Way, 1992
No Time to Kill, 1993
One Emotion, 1994
Looking for Christmas, 1995
The Greatest Hits, 1996
Nothin' but the Taillights, 1997

For the Record

Of all his number 1 hits, Clint Black's favorite song to perform on stage is "Put Yourself in My Shoes," but the song he is most proud of as a songwriter is "A Bad Goodbye."

SELECT AWARDS
Academy of Country Music Album of the Year for *Killin' Time*, Single Record of the Year for "A Better Man," New Male Vocalist of the Year, and Male Vocalist of the Year Awards, 1989
Country Music Association Horizon Award, 1989
Country Music Association Male Vocalist of the Year, 1990
Country Music Association Triple Play Award, 1996

SEE ALSO: Buffett, Jimmy; Eagles, The; Haggard, Merle; Judds, The / Wynonna Judd; Loggins and Messina / Kenny Loggins; Strait, George.

Black Flag / Henry Rollins

Black Flag

ORIGINAL MEMBERS: Greg Ginn (b. 1954), Charles Dukowski, Keith Morris, Brian Migdol
OTHER MEMBERS: Chavo Pederast, Dez Cadena, Robo, Bill Stevenson, Henry Rollins, Kira Roessler
FIRST RELEASE: Nervous Breakdown, 1978 (EP)

Henry Rollins

BORN: Washington, D.C.; February 13, 1961
FIRST ALBUM RELEASE: *Hot Animal Machine*, 1987
MUSICAL STYLES: Punk rock, heavy metal, alternative

Black Flag was at the forefront of the hardcore punk-rock scene that arose from the Los Angeles suburbs in the late 1970's. Despite numerous lineup changes and legal problems, the band persevered for nearly a decade and became the model for countless postpunk and alternative bands throughout the world. After the band's breakup in 1986, vocalist Henry Rollins continued to record loud, high-intensity music with the Rollins Band.

The Birth of Hardcore Punk. Black Flag was formed in Hermosa Beach, California, in 1977 by Greg Ginn shortly after he graduated from the University of California at Los Angeles. The origi-

Henry Rollins (Ken Settle)

nal lineup of Ginn on guitar, Charles Dukowski on bass, Brian Migdol on drums, and Keith Morris on vocals recorded the *Nervous Breakdown* extended-play single in 1978 on SST Records, a label started by Ginn and Dukowski for the specific purpose of getting Black Flag's music to the public. (After signing such underground luminaries as Hüsker Dü, Sonic Youth, the Minutemen, and the Meat Puppets, SST Records became the largest independent label of the 1980's.) The four songs on the album were characterized by loud, distorted guitar playing, thudding bass lines, rapid drumbeats, and shouted lyrics about the pressures of society and the virtues of drunkenness. This angrier, louder, and more aggressive style of punk became known as hardcore and was widely imitated, first by local bands that sprang up in the suburban neighborhoods that surrounded Los Angeles and later by bands in other cities.

Shortly after the album was released, Morris quit Black Flag to form his own hardcore band, the Circle Jerks. He was replaced on vocals by Chavo Pederast, who stayed with the band long enough to record the extended-play single *Jealous Again* (1980) before quitting in the middle of a live performance at the Fleetwood, a Huntington Beach, California, club known for its violent crowds.

Legal Problems. In 1981, Black Flag settled on vocalist Dez Cadena, replaced Migdol with a drummer known as Robo, and began a series of low-budget U.S. tours that helped fuel the growing U.S. hardcore punk scene. During a show in New York City, a fan from Washington, D.C., named Henry Rollins (born Henry Garfield) jumped onstage to perform vocals on one song. Duly impressed, the band invited Rollins to be their permanent vocalist and moved Cadenza to guitars along with Ginn. Later that year, Black Flag was signed to Unicorn Records, a subsidiary of MCA Records, and recorded *Damaged*, their first full-length album. The record company, however, deemed the recording antiparent and refused to release it. Ginn and Dukowski decided to release the album on SST Records and were promptly sued for breach of contract, sparking a legal battle that crippled Black Flag until 1983, when Unicorn Records went bankrupt and all rights reverted to the band.

Now able to focus their energies on their music, Black Flag entered a period of unbelievably high productivity. With a new lineup (Rollins on vocals, Ginn on guitar, Bill Stevenson on drums, and Kira Roessler on bass), the band released three albums (*My War*, *Family Man*, and *Slip It In*) in 1984, followed by three more (*Loose Nut*, *The Process of Weeding Out*, and *In My Head*) in 1985. In addition, the band toured extensively during this period. This new version of Black Flag played music that was somewhat heavier and slower than their earlier songs, often coming close to crossing over from punk to heavy metal. This willingness to blur the boundaries between genres would become an important element in Seattle grunge and other 1990's alternative music. In 1986, Ginn, whose increasingly dynamic guitar playing

For the Record

After vocalist Chavo Pederast quit Black Flag in the middle of their performance at the Fleetwood, the band continued to play. A small-scale riot erupted as members of the audience began fighting over the microphone. Such brawls became a staple of Black Flag shows in the ensuing weeks, during which they played instrumental versions of their songs while they searched for a new vocalist.

seemed to be leaving the rest of the band behind, decided to disband Black Flag so he could concentrate on running SST Records and playing with his more experimental side band, Gone.

The Rollins Band. By 1987, Rollins had already recorded a solo album, *Hot Animal Machine*, with guitarist Chris Haskett. In the spring of 1987, the two musicians hired drummer Sim Cain and bassist Andrew Weiss and formed the Rollins Band; they managed to book a six-week U.S. tour before they had even rehearsed together. While playing in Europe later in the year, the band added sound man Theo Van Rock, who subsequently appeared on album credits as a full member of the band. The band released the album *Life Time* in 1988. After several years of extensive touring and recording, the Rollins Band began to expand their audience in 1991, when they signed to Imago Records, a label distributed by BMG Records, and played as the opening band of the inaugural Lollapalooza tour. In 1993, Weiss quit and was replaced by Melvin Gibbs, whose bass playing added a jazz-funk dimension to the band's intensely noisy hard-rock sound. The release of *Weight* (1994) led to a Grammy Award nomination for Best Metal Band and a chance to perform at the widely televised awards ceremony. In 1997, the Rollins Band signed to Dreamworks Records for the release of the album *Come in and Burn* (1997).

Throughout this period, Rollins's creative proliferation was not limited to his work with the

Rollins Band. In addition to publishing numerous books of essays and poetry (many of which were published by 2.13.61, Rollins's own vanity press and record label), he released several highly regarded spoken-word albums and promoted them with tours. One such recording, the audio version of his book *Get in the Van: On the Road with Black Flag*, won the 1994 Grammy Award for Best Spoken Word or Non-Musical Album. Rollins also embarked on a motion-picture acting career, making minor appearances in such films as *Heat* (1995), *Johnny Mnemonic* (1994), and David Lynch's *Lost Highways* (1996).   —*Douglas Long*

SELECT DISCOGRAPHY
Black Flag
■ SINGLES
Nervous Breakdown, 1978 (extended-play single)
Jealous Again, 1980 (extended-play single)
■ ALBUMS
Damaged, 1981
Family Man, 1984
My War, 1984
Slip It In, 1984
In My Head, 1985
Loose Nut, 1985
Rollins Band
■ ALBUMS
Life Time, 1988
Hard Volume, 1989
Turned On, 1990
The End of Silence, 1992
Weight, 1994
Come in and Burn, 1997
Henry Rollins solo
■ ALBUMS
Hot Animal Machine, 1987
Deep Throat, 1992 (spoken word, compilation)
Rollins: The Boxed Life, 1993 (spoken word)
Get in the Van: On the Road with Black Flag, 1994 (spoken word)

SELECT AWARDS
Grammy Award for Best Spoken Word or Non-Musical Album for *Get in the Van: On the Road with Black Flag*, 1994 (Rollins)

SEE ALSO: Sex Pistols, The; Sonic Youth.

Black Sabbath / Ozzy Osbourne

Black Sabbath

ORIGINAL MEMBERS: Tony Iommi (b. 1948), Terry "Geezer" Butler (b. 1949), Bill Ward (b. 1948), Ozzy Osbourne (b. 1948)

OTHER MEMBERS: Ronnie James Dio (b. c. 1950), Ian Gillan (b. 1945), Vinnie Appice, Bev Bevan (b. 1946)

FIRST ALBUM RELEASE: *Black Sabbath*, 1970

Ozzy Osbourne

BORN: Birmingham, England; December 3, 1948

FIRST ALBUM RELEASE: *Blizzard of Ozz*, 1980

MUSICAL STYLES: Heavy metal, hard rock, psychedelic rock

Black Sabbath was neither the first nor the most successful heavy-metal band; Iron Butterfly and Blue Öyster Cult predated them, and Van Halen and Def Leppard outsold them. Black Sabbath was, however, the quintessential heavy-metal band. From its bone-crunching sonic style to its occult imagery, from stories of fan suicides to rumors of backward masking of Satanic messages, Black Sabbath embodied the stereotypical parent-opposed, teenager-admired heavy metal.

The Beginning. Black Sabbath started innocently enough in a working-class section of Birmingham, England, in the late 1960's. Drummer Bill Ward and guitarist Tony Iommi were playing in a psychedelic rock band called Mythology. Down the street, bassist Terry "Geezer" Butler and singer John "Ozzy" Osbourne were in a blues band called Rare Breed. The foursome joined forces in a "hippie blues band," as Osbourne called it, named Earth. With its slow, oppressive guitar style (Iommi had lost the fingertips of his left hand in a childhood electrical accident) and Osbourne's eccentric vocal approach (melody was never Osbourne's strength), it was notoriously unsuccessful. Watching a 1964 Boris Karloff horror film titled *Black Sabbath* late one night, the group was inspired to change their name and image forever. Suddenly, Butler's dark lyrics, Iommi's throbbing lead lines, and Osbourne's moaning delivery worked.

Black Sabbath (1970), the band's debut album, was recorded in twelve hours on an eight-track tape machine for less than twelve hundred dollars. It sold more than one million copies. It also began the Black Sabbath controversy when a young British nurse was found dead by suicide, with a copy of the album still spinning on her turntable.

Two more platinum albums were released in less than one year, and Black Sabbath established themselves as the "Monsters of Heavy Metal." Their excessive lifestyle, though, took a heavy toll: Iommi collapsed onstage, Ward and Butler were both hospitalized, and Osbourne later claimed he was spending one thousand dollars per week for drugs.

The Beginning of the End. Black Sabbath split in 1976, only to reunite in 1978. However, internal squabbling, most notably the long-standing feud between Osbourne and Iommi, drove them apart again. Black Sabbath hired Rainbow vocalist Ronnie James Dio, and Ozzy Osbourne moved to Los Angeles to start a band of his own.

New Band. Osbourne's new band featured Uriah Heep drummer Lee Kerslake, Rainbow bassist Bob Daisley, and Quiet Riot guitarist Randy Rhodes. Osbourne hired Sharon Arden as his manager and signed to her father's record label, Jet Records; he later married her. He wrote and recorded the album *Blizzard of Ozz* (1980), featuring the signature tune "Crazy Train," in two months.

For the Record

Black Sabbath's second album, to be called *War Pigs*, was complete when the bandmates decided to use their last hour of recording studio time; it was, after all, already paid for. They hastily recorded a song called "Paranoid," writing it as they went along. "The song turned out so good," said Geezer Butler, "that we changed the name of the album from *War Pigs* to *Paranoid*."

Sharon Osbourne felt that Jet Records' parent company, CBS Records, was not giving the album the attention it deserved. She thought of a stunt that would give Osbourne publicity: He walked into a CBS Records marketing meeting and bit the head off a live dove, "so people would look at him," said Sharon Osbourne.

Whether because of or in spite of Osbourne's pulling a live animal out of his pocket and biting its head off, *Blizzard of Ozz* was a hit. He mounted an enormous tour that set the standard for on-stage overkill. However, at a performance in Des Moines, Iowa, in 1982, he lived to regret the bird-biting incident. Osbourne assumed that it was a novelty-store rubber bat that a fan had tossed on the stage. Obligingly, he bit its head off, much to the fans' amusement. It turned out to have been a live animal, and Osbourne was put through a series of rabies and tetanus shots which were not only painful but so weakened his hair that he had to shave his head.

In March of 1982, talented and popular guitarist Rhodes was killed in a plane accident when he and the tour driver went for a joyride in the driver's light plane. The plane crashed into the tour bus, killing all aboard the plane. Rhodes was twenty-five years old. Guitarist Brad Gillis, formerly of Night Ranger, appeared on Osbourne's next album, *Speak of the Devil* (1982). He was soon replaced with young newcomer Jake E. Lee.

By 1983, heavy metal was in the middle of a maelstrom. The concerts were enormous—200,000 fans watched Osbourne play the US Festival in Southern California—and so was the controversy. A California assemblyman had claimed that demonic messages were hidden in rock albums, messages that could be heard only when the album was played backward. Many Americans took the backward-masking hysteria seriously, and town councils frequently banned appearances by Osbourne. As late as 1997, Osbourne concerts were in danger of being canceled. As Osbourne

Ozzy Osbourne (Paul Natkin)

said, "These people, they forget how to have a good hearty laugh."

There was a dark side to Ozzy Osbourne, but it was not backward masking. It was his addiction to drugs and alcohol. He checked himself into the Betty Ford Clinic in 1984, which he said helped him moderate his drinking. This change in lifestyle may also have contributed to his willingness to join Black Sabbath for the 1985 Live Aid charity concert. The reunion of Black Sabbath, however, was overshadowed by simultaneous reunions of the Who and surviving members of Led Zeppelin.

The reunited Black Sabbath was not to last; the two factions went their separate ways. In 1987, Osbourne hired guitarist Zakk Wilde to replace Jake E. Lee. Black Sabbath replaced Ronnie James Dio with Ian Gillan of Deep Purple. Drummer Bill Ward was replaced by Vinnie Appice and Electric Light Orchestra's Bev Bevan. By 1990, only Iommi remained of the original band.

Life in the 1990's. Black Sabbath and Ozzy Osbourne struggled in the late 1980's and early 1990's. They had trouble getting radio airplay because programmers were afraid of protests by religious conservatives. The emergence of grunge rock chipped away at their core audience, even though Black Sabbath are considered an inspiration to popular grunge bands such as Soundgarden.

Ozzy Osbourne enjoyed a revival in 1995 with the album *Ozzmosis*. In the summer of 1997, his Ozzfest hard-rock tour was second only to the all-woman "Lilith Fair" tour in ticket sales. Admittedly, the tour's drawing power was due as much to new acts, such as the controversial Marilyn Manson, as to the final reunion of the original Black Sabbath. Black Sabbath and Ozzy Osbourne are proof that heavy metal will always enjoy some degree of popularity.   —*Ethlie Ann Vare*

SELECT DISCOGRAPHY
Black Sabbath
■ ALBUMS
Black Sabbath, 1970
Paranoid, 1971
Master of Reality, 1971

We Sold Our Soul for Rock 'n' Roll, 1976
Heaven and Hell, 1980
Reunion, 1998
Ozzy Osbourne
■ ALBUMS
Blizzard of Ozz, 1980
Diary of a Madman, 1981
Speak of the Devil, 1982
Bark at the Moon, 1983
The Ultimate Sin, 1986
No More Tears, 1991
Ozzmosis, 1995

SEE ALSO: Deep Purple; Manson, Marilyn; Soundgarden; Van Halen.

Rubén Blades

BORN: Panama City, Panama; July 16, 1948
FIRST ALBUM RELEASE: *Buscando América*, 1984
MUSICAL STYLES: Latin, pop

One of the most versatile musicians to come from Latin America, Rubén Blades is a Panamanian-born composer, singer, actor, lawyer, and politician. His most significant contribution to salsa music has been the quality of the content of his songs. He has described his lyrics as "musical journalism" and "an urban chronicle." During the 1970's, he supplied songs to a number of bands and artists, including Ismael Miranda, José Feliciano, and Tito Puente, and twelve original recordings of his compositions by other artists were collected on the album *Interpretan a Rubén Blades* in 1981.

Growing Up. Blades family roots extend throughout North and South America. His mother, Anoland, was a Cuban pianist, bolero singer, and actress; his father, Rubén Blades, Sr., was a police detective and bongo player from Panama. His grandparents came from the West Indies, the United States, Cuba, and Colombia. His maternal grandfather was an American who went to Cuba with Theodore Roosevelt during the Spanish-American War. However, it was his paternal grandmother, Emma Bosques Laurenza, who raised him, taught him how to read, and introduced him to modern art and American films.

Blades was musically self-taught. Growing up in the 1950's and 1960's, he admired rock-and-roll music. In 1963, his brother Luis recruited him as the lead singer of a band called the Saints. According to Blades, the Panama situation in 1964, following a massive riot in which U.S. troops killed twenty-one Panamanians and injured five hundred others, and other problems experienced throughout the world in the 1960's, forced many Latin Americans to become more aware of world issues and to examine their roots. He began reading more books on history and politics and stopped singing in English, turning to Latin musicians for inspiration. His role models became Benny Moré, Ismael Rivera, and others.

After graduating from high school, Blades began his law education at the University of Panama. Pancho Cristal, a New York producer who heard Blades sing, asked him to join Joe Cuba's band. Instead, Blades decided to continue his studies, but was interrupted when, one year later, government officials closed down the university after a confrontation with students.

First Trip to New York. In 1969, Blades traveled to New York and realized that Latin music was in need of more meaningful lyrics. Therefore, he began writing songs dealing with the social and political issues that affected Latinos. Many producers found these lyrics too long and too controversial, but musician Pete Rodríguez gave Blades a chance, and in 1970, they recorded *De Panama a Nueva York*.

After a few months, the University of Panama reopened, and Blades returned there. After earning his degree in law, he worked as an attorney for the National Bank of Panama. In 1974, while visiting his family, who had relocated to Miami, Florida, Blades took a second trip to New York.

Return to New York. Blades relocated to New York after securing a job in the mail room of Fania Records. He met Latin jazz instrumentalist Ray Barretto and auditioned for him there. He collaborated with Barretto on such albums as *Barretto* (1975) and *Barretto Live: Tomorrow* (1976).

In 1976, Blades joined Willie Colón's orchestra as a singer-songwriter. The association lasted six years, and together they produced some of the biggest-selling salsa records in history, beginning with *¡Metiendo Mano!* (1977) and ending with *Canciones del Solar de los Aburridos* (1981).

Their best-selling album, *Siembra* (1978), included several hit singles, such as "Pablo Navaja" ("Mack the Knife") based on an East Harlem, New York, criminal and the murder he commits. "Plástico," another song on this album, warns against sacrificing one's beliefs to materialism. In "Brother Latino, Friend," Blades sings, "Never sell your future for comfort or gold."

In 1980, Blades's song "Tiburón" was banned from radio stations in Miami. "Tiburón" depicted international interventionists (the United States and the U.S.S.R.) in the Caribbean as prowling, sleepless sharks. Even though it was aimed at both superpowers, the most popular radio stations issued an editorial accusing Blades of having Communist sympathies. His parents, who were living in Miami at the time, were sorely embarrassed, and Blades received various death threats. He then wrote *Maestra Vida*, a gold record with theatrical opera elements issued in two parts by Fania, before breaking with Colón.

Going Solo. In 1984, Blades switched to Elektra/Asylum Records when Jerry Masucci sold Fania. He decided to create a new group, Seis del Solar (Six from the Courtyard), and they debuted with the successful album Buscando América (1984). In 1986, Blades graduated with a law degree from Harvard University. In the British television documentary *The Return of Rubén Blades* (1986) he mentioned his intent to follow a possible political career. While in Massachusetts, Blades met actress Lisa Lebenson, whom he later married.

After renaming his band Son del Solar, Blades tried to cross over to American audiences with his album *Nothing but the Truth* (1988). It was not successful, but during that same year, *Antecedente* became a Grammy Award-winning album.

Other Interests. In 1991, Blades founded the Papa Egoro (Mother Earth) political party and ran for president of Panama. Possible reasons for not winning the presidency were that he lived

For the Record

In the early 1960's, Rubén Blades admired the band Frankie Lyman and the Teenagers. After seeing them in the 1956 film *Rock, Rock, Rock!* he wrote them a letter asking for a job as a singer. His mother threw out the letter instead of mailing it and bought him a plastic guitar.

outside his country and that he was accused of being arrogant and distant. However, after the elections, he became more involved with musicians in Panama and began spending more time there.

Blades developed a successful acting career. His more than thirty films include *Critical Condition* (1986), *The Milagro Beanfield War* (1988), *Mo' Better Blues* (1990), *The Two Jakes* (1990), and *The Devil's Own* (1996). Blades also conquered the theater as the star of *The Capeman* (1997), Paul Simon's first Broadway musical.   —*José A. Carmona*

SELECT DISCOGRAPHY

■ ALBUMS

De Panama a Nueva York, 1970 (with Pete Rodríguez)

The Good, the Bad, the Ugly, 1975 (with Willie Colón)

Canciones del Solar de los Aburridos, 1981 (with Willie Colón)

El que la Hace la Paga, 1982

Mucho Mejor, 1984

Escenas, 1985

Agua de Luna, 1987

Doble Filo, 1987

Poetry, 1994

Greatest Hits, 1996 (compilation)

La Rosa de los Vientos, 1997

SELECT AWARDS

Grammy Award for Best Tropical Latin Performance for *Escenas*, 1986

Grammy Award for Best Tropical Latin Performance for *Antecedente*, 1988

Grammy Award for Best Tropical Latin Performance for *La Rosa de los Vientos*, 1996

SEE ALSO: Miguel, Luis; Ronstadt, Linda.

Bobby "Blue" Bland

(Robert Calvin Bland)

BORN: Rosemark, Tennessee; January 27, 1930

FIRST ALBUM RELEASE: *Blues Consolidated*, 1958 (with Little Junior Parker)

MUSICAL STYLES: Blues, soul

Raised with gospel and the blues, Bobby Bland was a pioneer of the modern soul sound made famous in the 1960's. After working in the cotton fields of Tennessee as a young man, in 1947 Bland moved to Memphis, Tennessee, where he joined the gospel band the Miniatures. Three years later he began to play with the Beale Streeters, an informal group of uncommonly talented blues musicians including B. B. King, Willie Nix, Roscoe Gordon, and Johnny Ace.

Recording Contract. Bland first recorded for Sam Phillips at Chess Records in 1951, moving to Modern the following year, where he was backed by Ike Turner's band. Late in 1952 he began his association with Duke Records, which soon fell under the control of Don Robey. Robey and arranger and trumpeter Joe Scott helped shape a distinctive sound for Bland that moved away from the strict blues conventions of his mentor B. B. King. Throughout the late 1950's Bland toured the country as part of the "Blues Consolidated" tour, headlined by Little Junior Parker. Drawing upon blues and big-band jazz, Bland and his group anticipated many of the developments of 1960's soul music. Under the pseudonym Deadric Malone, members of his band wrote or cowrote much of the backing for Bland's piercing vocals.

With a string of rhythm-and-blues singles including "Farther up the Road" (number 1, 1957), "I'll Take Care of You" (number 2, 1959), "I Pity the Fool" (number 1, 1961), and "Don't Cry No More" (number 2, 1961), by the early 1960's Bland had eclipsed Parker's popularity. "Turn On

Your Love Light" crossed over to reach number 28 on the pop charts in 1962. Bland was at the peak of his popularity in the mid-1960's, singing both traditional blues and early soul. His *Call on Me* album went to number 11 on the pop charts in the summer of 1963. Though he never became a genuine crossover star, he was reaching a wider audience than ever when a falling out with Robey in 1968 nearly destroyed his career.

Popularity. When Duke Records was taken over by ABC-Dunhill in 1972, they assigned Four Tops producer Steve Barri to Bland's recordings. Barri guided him back to a bluesier style of music and gave him more contemporary songs, including material by Leon Russell, Luther Ingram, and Gladys Knight and the Pips. As a result, Bland

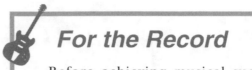

For the Record

Before achieving musical success, Bobby Bland was B. B. King's chauffeur.

produced *His California Album* (1973) and *Dreamer* (1974), which were among the most popular albums of his career.

In the 1990's, Bland continued to explore a wide variety of vocal styles, including soul, pop, gospel, country, and jazz, though always with a blues foundation. Bland's influence on modern soul music is widely recognized, and it led to his induction into the Rock and Roll Hall of Fame in 1992. He continued to tour and produce solid albums into the 1990's. —*John Powell*

SELECT DISCOGRAPHY
■ ALBUMS
Blues Consolidated, 1958 (with Little Junior Parker, rereleased in 1974 as *Barefoot Rock and You Got Me*)
Two Steps from the Blues, 1961
Call on Me, 1963
Ain't Nothing You Can Do, 1964
The Best of Bobby "Blue" Bland, 1967 (compilation)
His California Album, 1973
Dreamer, 1974
B. B. King and Bobby Bland/Together for the First Time . . . Live, 1974 (with B. B. King)
I Feel Good, I Feel Fine, 1979
Blues You Can Use, 1987
Portrait of the Blues, 1991
I Pity the Fool: The Duke Recordings, Vol. 1, 1992 (compilation)
Turn On Your Love Light: The Duke Recordings, Vol. 2, 1994 (compilation)

SELECT AWARDS
Rock and Roll Hall of Fame, inducted 1992
Rhythm and Blues Foundation Pioneer Award, 1992

Bobby "Blue" Bland (Freddie Patterson Collection/ Archive Photos)

SEE ALSO: King, B. B.

Mary J. Blige

BORN: Bronx, New York; January 11, 1971
FIRST ALBUM RELEASE: *What's the 411?* 1992
MUSICAL STYLES: Rhythm and blues, pop, blues, gospel, hip-hop

Mary J. Blige was born on January 11, 1971, to Cora Blige. Her father (whom she does not name) was a jazz musician. For the time that he was an active part of the family, Mary's father played an important part in the early stages of her musical development. She explains: "My father played the bass guitar, and he played in a band. He taught me how to sing my notes, and gospel gave me my depth."

For most of her life, Blige lived with her mother and older sister LaTonya in Yonkers's Schlobohm projects—appropriately renamed the "Slow Bomb" projects by its tenants. Later, the three were joined by two more children, Bruce and Jonquell. Cora, aware of the negative social forces that confronted her children on a daily basis, made church mandatory. They attended the Prayer Pentecostal Church, where, by age seven, Blige was singing in the choir.

Inspirations. Blige's musical foundations included not only jazz, learned from her father, and gospel, learned at church, but also the blues. In general, the blues focuses upon the hardship of individual experience and the belief that the act of singing and making one's voice heard enables one to survive.

Blige developed her blues sensibilities from everyday life. She explained that, while living in "Slow Bomb," "It seemed like I was always an older person. I was always worrying about stuff and I didn't have anything to worry about." This pressure to worry was most certainly augmented by the events happening every day outside her own window. Rather than rely upon television to understand life and its possibilities, Blige looked out her window at the reality of urban society. She developed a sense of the blues that arose more from her personal experiences than from anything else. Blige was also influenced by a wide range of African American musical artists, including Sam Cooke, Aretha Franklin, Stevie Wonder, Chaka Khan, and Gladys Knight.

As a child, Blige could often be found in front of a mirror, singing into a hairbrush. Over time, her talents grew. She moved from bedroom mirrors to local talent shows. Despite her talent and love of singing, Blige never really counted on music as a career. She opted instead for part-time jobs to earn money. Then, as a joke with friends at a local mall, she stepped up to a karaoke machine and sang Anita Baker's "Caught Up in the Rapture." Somehow, Blige's first "demo" found its way into the hands of Andre Harrell, an executive at Uptown Records.

Instant Success. Blige's first record on Uptown was *What's the 411?* (1992), a beat-driven, heavy-track-laden mix of hip-hop and rhythm and blues. By the time her record hit the stores, the "new jack swing" approach to rhythm and blues, used by groups such as Teddy Riley and Guy, had led to a rebirth of rhythm and blues. The public loved Blige's sultry contralto combined with a hip-hop quality and urban appeal. As her title suggests, *What's the 411?* is about Blige, the insecure, antagonistic, rap and rhythm-and-blues newcomer, as she searches for information about the music industry and herself. The most popular songs, "Real Love" and "You Remind Me," contain sentiments that she would refer to and expound upon in her second album, *My Life*.

Despite her achievements, Blige had deep problems; her success came much too fast. She soon became known as the "queen of mean," notorious for missing photo shoots and interviews. Aloof and moody, Blige failed to live up to the industry's codes of conduct for professional behavior, causing her to retreat further inward. Eventually, she relied upon the comfort of drugs and alcohol to help her cope with this difficult period of adjustment. With the help of the public-relations firm Double XXposure and its president Angelo Ellerbee, Blige's entire approach to the music business, and to her life, changed. She told *Vibe* magazine that Ellerbee "gave me a totally new kind of life. There was a time when I wouldn't read nothin'." With his help, Blige was introduced to the black literary classic by Zora Neale Hurston,

Mary J. Blige (MCA/Anthony Cujatar)

Their Eyes Were Watching God. Just as the main character, Janie, embarked upon a quest for self-discovery, leaving behind husband and friends, after the completion of her second album, *My Life* (1994), Blige left her producer Sean "Puffy" Combs and took up the reins of executive production herself.

Despite *My Life's* intense introspection, that project marked the point when Blige began to give herself room to grow and learn. In 1995, Blige collaborated with Wu-Tang Clan's Method Man on "I'll Be There for You/You're All I Need to Get By." This song features a sample from the original version by Marvin Gaye and Tammi Terrell and reverberates with the influence of an old soul cut mixed with a hip-hop sensibility. "Mary Jane" was

a collaborative effort between her and Rick James, and she also performed "I'm Goin' Down," written by Norman Whitfield.

Whereas Blige had done little writing on her first two albums, her next, *Share My World* (1997), was almost entirely her own. From writing to production, Blige had a hand in the project from start to finish. With her direct lyrical input in nine of the seventeen songs, *Share My World* invites the listener into Blige's consciousness. The audience feels the pain and experiences the fruits of Blige's labor, from songwriting to production. With the completion of this album, she had worked through her insecurities, emerging a more committed artist.

Legacy. Blige's transformation from album to album is similar to the change in the hip-hop world from "gangsta" rap in the early 1990's to the later eclectic music which emits healing energies. Each album marks a different stage in her personal development: With each, Blige embarked upon a quest for love, driven by a desire to heal the wounds, both personal and professional, accrued during the span of her life. Especially for young women in search of love and self-esteem, Blige's success shows that the best love emerges from self-love. Blige speaks to a generation of women, urban and otherwise, with the crossover appeal of Motown artists such as the Supremes and the soul-searching, gospel-inspired influence of artists such as Aretha Franklin.

—*Shanna D. Greene*

SELECT DISCOGRAPHY
■ SINGLES
"I'll Be There for You/You're All I Need to Get By," 1995 (with Method Man)
■ ALBUMS
What's the 411? 1992
What's the 411? Remix, 1993
My Life, 1994
Share My World, 1997

SELECT AWARDS
Soul Train Music Award, 1993

SEE ALSO: Baker, Anita; Cooke, Sam; Franklin, Aretha; Khan, Chaka; Wonder, Stevie.

Blondie

ORIGINAL MEMBERS: Debbie Harry (b. 1945), Chris Stein (b. 1950), Billy O'Connor, Fred Smith (b. 1948)

OTHER MEMBERS: Gary Valentine, Jimmy Destri (b. 1954), Clement Burke (b. 1955), Frank Infante, Nigel Harrison (b. 1951)

FIRST ALBUM RELEASE: *Blondie*, 1976

MUSICAL STYLES: Pop, glitter rock, art rock, punk rock, new wave, disco

Blondie began with a love story in New York in 1975, when a visual arts major and recreational guitarist, Chris Stein, first saw Debbie Harry singing in a girl rock group. The relationship between the two became the nucleus of Blondie. The group's commercial success resulted from its versatility and solid power-pop sound, as it became one of the few groups able to survive punk rock and move on to disco. Although the group broke up in 1982, compilations and rereleases would continue as other musicians measured their own successes by Blondie's achievements.

The Early Days. New York in the 1970's provided the setting and support for the new sounds evolving from 1960's rock. Offbeat styles from glamour and glitter rock to garage-band tough rock released the creative energy from which punk and power pop emerged. Debbie Harry had moved to New York after attending Centenary College in New Jersey for two years, planning a musical career. She gained experience and also supported herself by working as a waitress (at Max's Kansas City), a beautician, and a Playboy bunny. Her first release came with a folk-rock group, Wind in the Willows, but their album was unsuccessful and the group did not last. Harry's talents were better suited to her efforts with the Stilettoes, a three-girl rock group, where she at-

Blondie in 1977 (AP/Wide World Photos)

tracted the attention of a young graduate from New York's School of Visual Arts in Manhattan, Chris Stein. Stein was very impressed with Harry and began playing guitar for the Stilettoes. Stein and Harry, joined by two other members of the Stilletoes, Billy O'Connor (drums) and Fred Smith (bass), formed a new band in 1974, at first calling themselves Angel and the Snakes.

Within a year, Blondie emerged. Harry's bleached hair and her position as lead singer made the name seem natural, although it caused problems later when the group did not want to be known as a backup band for her. Stein and Harry, by now romantically involved, replaced Smith and O'Connor—Smith went to the group Television and O'Connor returned to school—with Clem Burke (drums) and a friend of Burke, Jimmy Valentine, who learned the bass in order to join. While looking for a pianist, Stein and Harry met Jimmy Destri, who played an old Farfisi organ. The unique sound of this organ became a signature for the group. Regular appearances at New York clubs Max's and CBGB followed.

Recording Artists. Blondie's first single, released in 1975, was "X Offender," a title toned

For the Record

Before their first album and without much money, Blondie performed using whatever equipment became available. Until the group made their first recording, Jimmy Destri claimed he was not sure that Debbie Harry could really sing, because he could never hear her on stage.

§

Blondie's 1970's hit "One Way or Another" with its refrain, "We're gonna get ya, get ya, get ya," became the theme of the New Jersey Division of Taxation's tax amnesty program in 1996. While some residents tired of the repeated commercials, others suggested that it would be a better state song than the official one.

down from the original "Sex Offender." Their first album, *Blondie*, was released in 1976, with four songs written by Stein and Harry and four songs from the rest of the band. *Blondie* was well received and soon the group began playing on the West Coast, opening for the Ramones at Los Angeles's Whisky-a-Go-Go and then for Iggy Pop on a national tour. Subsequently, Blondie signed with Chrysalis Records and went on tour in Australia and Japan. Gary Valentine, tired of playing bass in the background, left the group in 1977 to form his own band, but with Frank Infante (originally bass, then guitar) and Nigel Harrison (bass) the group achieved its most consistent lineup. With a new album, *Plastic Letters* (1977), and its popularity rising overseas, Blondie toured Great Britain and Europe in 1978.

Blondie as a Group. In the early stages, Blondie showed few signs of its musical history-making potential. Blondie's unique mix of talent and character often led to lackluster performances, as the group operated without adequate cohesiveness. However, three major features that were to determine Blondie's future existed from the beginning: Debbie Harry's beguiling yet satirical delivery, the songwriting talent of the band members, and the group's willingness to revise the sound of each song to fulfill its potential.

Debbie Harry. Throughout Blondie's short life, the purity of Harry's voice seemed mocked by her deadpan tones, inexpressive eyes, and tough lyrics, such as those in "Little Girl Lies" or "Rip Her to Shreds." Harry acted on her conviction that fans loved and deserved a performer with an image worthy of their wildest dreams, a "platinum blonde." She was compared to actresses Greta Garbo and Marilyn Monroe by the press, but Harry, who by now had married Stein, disliked being described as a sex symbol, and other band members resented the implication that Blondie's success depended on Harry.

Big Hits and Outside Activities. *Parallel Lines* (1978) was the album that brought Blondie fame in the United States. "Heart of Glass" was the biggest single on the album, and its European disco sound and biting lyrics proved typical of the group: "Once I had a love/ And it was a gas/ Soon turned out to be a pain in the ass." After the album went platinum, the group collaborated with European disco producer Georgio Moroder for the sound track to the 1980 film *American Gigolo*, which included "Call Me," the only Blondie single to go platinum. A reggae song, "The Tide Is High," also went to number 1 that year, and a rap number, "Rapture," achieved the number 1 spot the next year. After years of hard work, Blondie was making music history but could not continue its string of hits. Individual members became involved in other projects. Burke produced for a New York band named Colors, and Destri produced a solo album, as did Harry. Her 1981 album *KooKoo* went gold but received a mixed response.

Blondie's Last Tour. Blondie released its last album, *The Hunter*, and started an American tour in 1982, but Chris Stein had become gravely ill. The group disbanded and Harry, who had just won recognition for her acting role in the 1983 film *Videodrome*, left her career to nurse Stein while he regained his health. Burke worked in the Eurythmics and later the Romantics, Harrison supervised music for several films, and Stein and Destri continued producing.

Debbie Harry never achieved superstar status, but she continued to sing with various groups and was featured on the 1996 album *Individually Twisted* by Jazz Passengers. Harry also became increasingly popular as an actress, appearing in films such as *Hairspray* (1988) and *Copland* (1997). Blondie made many new appearances in remixed releases. The group reunited to try recording again in 1997. —*Margaret A. Dodson*

SELECT DISCOGRAPHY
■ SINGLES
"Rapture," 1994 (12-inch single; remix)
"Heart of Glass," 1995 (12-inch single; remix)
"Atomic," 1995 (12-inch dance remix)
■ ALBUMS
Blondie, 1976
Plastic Letters, 1977
Parallel Lines, 1978
Eat to the Beat, 1979
Autoamerican, 1980
The Best of Blondie, 1981
The Hunter, 1982
Blonde and Beyond, 1993 (compilation)
Blondie: The Platinum Collection, 1994
　(compilation)

SEE ALSO: Eurythmics, The / Annie Lennox; Talking Heads / David Byrne.

Blood, Sweat, and Tears

ORIGINAL MEMBERS: Al Kooper (b. 1944), Steve Katz (b. 1945), Fred Lipsius (b. 1944), Jim Fielder (b. 1947), Bobby Colomby (b. 1944), Dick Halligan (b. 1943), Randy Brecker (b. 1945), Jerry Weiss (b. 1946)
OTHER MEMBERS: Chuck Winfield (b. 1943), Lew Soloff (b. 1944), Jerry Hyman (b. 1947), David Clayton-Thomas (b. David Thomsett, 1941), Dave Bargeron (b. 1942), others
FIRST ALBUM RELEASE: *Child Is Father to the Man*, 1968
MUSICAL STYLES: Pop, jazz rock

Between 1969 and 1971, Blood, Sweat, and Tears offered the promise of a jazz-rock fusion unlike anything then found on the radio. After three number 2 hits in 1969 and three more Top-40 hits in 1970 and 1971, the band quickly faded from the pop scene.

Rise to Stardom. Blood, Sweat, and Tears was Al Kooper's experiment in expanding both the instrumentation and the scope of traditional rock bands. By 1967, when Blood, Sweat, and Tears was formed, Kooper had a solid reputation as a musician, songwriter, and producer. He helped write the number 1 hit "This Diamond Ring" for Gary Lewis and the Playboys; played organ and guitar for Bob Dylan on "Like a Rolling Stone," *Highway 61 Revisited* (1965), and *Blonde on Blonde* (1966); and had been a member of two successful groups, the Royal Teens and the Blues Project. Kooper and guitarist Steve Katz formed the original Blood, Sweat, and Tears with Jim Fielder on bass and Bobby Colomby on drums, but almost immediately added the four-piece horn section that set the early standard for the "jazz rock" style.

Blood, Sweat, and Tears (Archive Photos/John Platt Collection)

After the release of the ambitiously eclectic but commercially unsuccessful album *Child Is Father to the Man* (1968), Kooper and trumpeters Weiss and Brecker left the band. Incredibly, the replacements and producer James William Guercio immediately took the group to new heights. Behind sophisticated horn arrangements and the dominant voice of David Clayton-Thomas, *Blood, Sweat, and Tears* (1969) went double platinum in less than one year, spent seven weeks as the number 1 album in the United States, and earned a Grammy Award for Best Album of the Year. Three singles, "You've Made Me So Very Happy," "Spinning Wheel," and Laura Nyro's "And When I Die," all reached number 2 on the charts and kept the group constantly on the airwaves.

More Changes. Though Blood, Sweat, and Tears lost Guercio to the newly formed band Chicago, their next two albums were substantial hits. *Blood, Sweat, and Tears 3* spent two weeks at number 1 in 1970, with two Top-40 singles, "Hi-De-Ho" (number 14) and "Lucretia MacEvil" (number 29). *B, S, and T 4* hit number 10 in 1971 and produced "Go Down Gamblin'" (number 32). Clayton-Thomas's departure in 1972 marked the end of the band's Top-40 success, as more

For the Record

"I was playing in an all-night jam session, and I had cut my finger and I didn't know it. When they turned the lights on at the end, the organ keyboard was covered with blood. So I called everybody over and said, 'Wouldn't this make a great album cover for a band called Blood, Sweat, and Tears?' And so we called it that, except we didn't use that picture because no one had a camera."
—*Al Kooper*

accessible horn bands such as Chicago and the Ides of March took their place on the charts.

Clayton-Thomas's return in 1974 failed to revive Blood, Sweat, and Tears as a pop band. They nevertheless developed a popular Las Vegas act, recruiting regularly from the big bands of Maynard Ferguson, Woody Herman, Doc Severinsen, and others. The band continued to tour occasionally into the 1990's, billed as Blood, Sweat, and Tears Featuring David Clayton-Thomas.

—*John Powell*

SELECT DISCOGRAPHY

Child Is Father to the Man, 1968
Blood, Sweat, and Tears, 1969
Blood, Sweat, and Tears 3, 1970
B, S, and T 4, 1971
Blood, Sweat, and Tears' Greatest Hits, 1972
    (previously released material)
New Blood, 1972
No Sweat, 1973
Mirror Image, 1974
New City, 1975
More than Ever, 1976
Brand New Day, 1977
Nuclear Blues, 1980
Live and Improvised, 1991

SELECT AWARDS

Grammy Awards for Album of the Year for *Blood, Sweat, and Tears* and for Best Contemporary Instrumental Performance for "Variations on a Theme by Erik Satie," 1969

SEE ALSO: Chicago.

Blues Traveler

ORIGINAL MEMBERS: Chan Kinchla, Brendan Hill, John Popper (b. 1967), Bob Sheehan
FIRST ALBUM RELEASE: *Blues Traveler*, 1990
MUSICAL STYLE: Rock and roll, blues

First gaining attention on the New York City club scene, Blues Traveler suddenly attained international acclaim with the success of their 1994 album, *Four*. Seldom played on the radio during the early 1990's, Blues Traveler nonetheless built a faithful following by offering exciting and musical live performances. Blues Traveler built a reputation similar to those of other bands known for their onstage improvisations, such as the Grateful Dead and Phish. Beyond its onstage jam sessions, Blues Traveler has built a solid repertoire of material from their studio albums.

The Beginning. As far back as 1983, Brendan Hill and John Popper were jamming at home after school. Like many suburban teenage boys, the founding members of Blues Traveler congregated in the basement of a home to play music. Hill, Popper, and Bob Sheehan, all high school students in Princeton, New Jersey, began to play drums, guitar, and harmonica together in 1986. The three were soon joined by Chan Kinchla on bass guitar. Most of their time together was spent jamming. Popper moved to New York City and entered his freshman year of college. Hill, Sheehan, and Kinchla soon followed, after finishing high school in Princeton, New Jersey. At this early stage the band was known simply as the Blues Band. Understandably not satisfied with that name, the members tried various combinations of words until finally settling on Blues Traveler.

During Popper's first few months in New York City, he met Joan Osborne at an open-mike jam session at a local night spot, Abeline's Blues Bar. Popper rehearsed with Osborne's newly formed band, but little materialized for him except a growing familiarity with the New York music scene. (Osborne later recorded two songs with Blues Traveler for their first album, "Warmer Days" and "100 Years.") During this period Popper met Eric Schenkman in school, and they struck up a friendship that would last through the formation of the Spin Doctors (Schenkman became their bass player) and the success of Blues Traveler.

The Big Break. While attending Columbia University, David Graham, son of rock-concert promoter Bill Graham, heard Blues Traveler play a campus event in 1989. Blues Traveler first signed with Bill Graham and then, later that year, with A&M Records. Graham is credited with first recognizing that the song "But Anyway" could be successful as a single. For more than three years David

Graham took a leading role in planning the direction of the band. Later, he was replaced by Dave Frey, who started Silent Partner Management for the purpose of managing Blues Traveler after the death of Bill Graham and the closing of Bill Graham Management's New York office in 1992.

In the spring of 1992 Popper arranged for a meeting with representatives of a number of bands in New York City. Members of Widespread Panic, the Spin Doctors, Col. Bruce Hampton, and Phish met to talk with Popper about their similar problems—including having few outdoor facilities to play and the difficulty of drawing crowds to see small to mid-size bands. From that meeting the HORDE (Horizons of Rock Developing Everywhere) tours began.

Most of the bands involved with HORDE were bands that, like Blues Traveler, had developed a following by touring rather than through radio play. The first pair of HORDE tours in 1992 lasted one week each and featured Aquarium Rescue Unit, Blues Traveler, Phish, the Spin Doctors, and Widespread Panic. Popper suffered serious injuries in a motorcycle accident in October of 1992. His injuries to his hip relegated him to a wheelchair for three months, but he managed to tour with the band anyway.

In 1993 the HORDE tour played twenty-six shows in six weeks and included Aquarium Rescue Unit, Allgood, Big Head Todd and the Monsters, Blues Traveler, the Samples, and Widespread Panic. Over the years the HORDE tours continued to expand. Blues Traveler appeared on every HORDE tour until 1997, when the band (which was averaging over 250 shows a year) set out on a concert tour of Europe.

Blues Traveler's fourth album, simply titled *Four*, was released in 1994. Its sales were small at first, but in 1995 the song "Run-Around" became a tremendously successful single, and Blues Traveler was suddenly being played on the radio everywhere, making videos, and performing on television. The song showcased the most immediately distinctive feature of the band's sound, Popper's nimble, amazingly fast harmonica playing. "Hook" was another successful single from the *Four* album, which sold more than five million copies. After releasing a live album in 1996, the group released *Straight on Till Morning* in 1997; in that year they also opened for the Rolling Stones on a number of dates on the Stones' "Bridges to Babylon" tour.　　—*Donna Addkison Simmons*

Blues Traveler (Paul Natkin)

SELECT DISCOGRAPHY
■ ALBUMS
Blues Traveler, 1990
Travelers and Thieves, 1991
Save His Soul, 1993
Four, 1994
Runaround CD5, 1995 (EP)
Live from the Fall, 1996
Straight on Till Morning, 1997

SEE ALSO: Grateful Dead, The; Phish.

Blur

ORIGINAL MEMBERS: Alex James (b. 1968), Damon
    Albarn (b. 1968), Graham Coxon (b. 1969),
    Dave Rowntree (b. 1964)
FIRST ALBUM RELEASE: *Leisure*, 1991
MUSICAL STYLES: Alternative, rock and roll, pop

As latecomers to the largely successful British musical movement dubbed "baggy," Blur was initially seen as a group of upper-middle-class art students trying to profit from the current craze. That assessment was not far off the mark, as singer Damon Albarn, guitarist Graham Coxon, bassist Alex James, and drummer Dave Rowntree were certainly interested in becoming the newest stars of British pop. What the band probably did not realize is that their path to fame and artistic success would not be a straight one.

Leisure. Blur's first pair of singles—"She's So High" and "There's No Other Way"—came at a time when similarly styled psychedelic pop bands such as the Stone Roses and Inspiral Carpets were just becoming successful. By the time Blur's debut album, *Leisure*, was released in 1991, the baggy scene Blur aspired to be part of was nearly gone. The album cannot be completely dismissed, however, as it features a couple of classic tracks, but it proved ultimately to be a group of songs the band would rarely revisit.

The two years following *Leisure* saw a complete reinvention of Blur, but not without serious trials. Their British label, Food Records, rejected demo versions of the songs for their second album, and

their U.S. label, SBK, suggested that they record the album with popular grunge producer Butch Vig. Instead, Blur decided to record their second album with Andy Partridge, the pop genius behind XTC. Sessions with Partridge disintegrated quickly, and the band turned to the producer of *Leisure*, Stephen Street (best known for his work with the Smiths), for help.

The result, 1993's *Modern Life Is Rubbish*, was worth the trouble. It presented a completely new Blur, one with no interest in current trends but rather a deep interest in the history of British pop. Two working titles for the album exemplify this: *England Versus America* and *British Image 1*. The latter would have been the perfect title, because *Modern Life Is Rubbish* is quintessentially British, with musical references to classic British groups such as the Kinks, the Jam, the Who, and XTC. Although often considered their best album, *Modern Life Is Rubbish* was, by most accounts, commercially unsuccessful. The band was particularly unhappy with their record sales in America.

Success on Their Own Terms. If *Modern Life Is Rubbish* proved *Leisure* to be a false start for the group, 1994's *Parklife* proved that Blur had found itself. "Girls & Boys," the first track on *Parklife*, was a goofy send-up of 1980's European disco, complete with a funky bass line and catchy chorus. The song, with help from a club remix done by the Pet Shop Boys, was the band's biggest success yet in America. At home in England, it made them musical deities gracing the covers of all the music magazines and headlining the largest venues. Ironically, the remainder of *Parklife* was nothing at all like "Girls & Boys"; rather, it was a second installment of Blur's obsession with English life. The title track featured Cockney narration from Phil Daniels, who was famous for playing Jimmy the Mod in the Who's film version of *Quadrophenia*.

Britpop. Blur became the kings of another British press creation: "Britpop." This was a convenient label which ultimately signified nothing. Determined not to ride forever on the worldwide success of one single, Blur wrote a triumphant album almost immediately. *The Great Escape*, released in 1995, was a smash hit—in England. It entered the charts at number 1, selling more than

Blur's other albums combined. Although an excellent album, *The Great Escape* clearly lacked a U.S. radio hit, something the band had briefly experienced with "Girls & Boys." Europeans were quick to pick up on *The Great Escape*, though, with its combination of typical Blur pop songs such as "Country House" and more plaintive ballads such as "The Universal" and "Yuko & Hiro."

Modern Life Is Rubbish, Parklife, and *The Great Escape* can be viewed as Blur's great British trilogy. While not remaining musically stagnant, the albums are all clearly made by the same group working with similar ideals throughout the process. Each album certainly has its own personality: *Modern Life Is Rubbish* is cynical, *Parklife* is almost a novelty album, and *The Great Escape* shows the band having fun. Blur was ready to reinvent itself, this time with more of a logical extension than a huge stylistic jump.

The American Way. The first British single from Blur's fifth album, 1997's *Blur*, was not destined to find success in the United States—it was too British and too similar to the band's previous work. "Beetlebum" was another trip through British musical history, acknowledging Albarn's new friend Ray Davies of the Kinks. Surprisingly, the remainder of *Blur* was quite different from the Blur music to which the world had previously been exposed. The sound was, shockingly, quite American. The band acknowledged the difference, citing influential U.S. rockers Pavement as a source of inspiration.

Blur's new record label in America, Virgin, picked one of Blur's most straightforward and rocking songs as its first single, and "Song 2" became a radio and MTV staple. Blur found themselves suddenly filling much larger halls and selling more records in the United States than ever before. While still not as successful abroad as their British rivals Oasis (whose Noel Gallagher once publicly wished for Albarn's death), Blur had finally been noticed in the United States, a country that barely knew the band existed previously. In spite of the fact that it deserves credit for branching out musically, *Blur* was Blur's weakest musical moment since *Leisure*, forsaking some of the group's songwriting ability in favor of new sounds and textures. Also gone were the more elaborate

> ## For the Record
>
> When Blur covered Rod Stewart's "Maggie May" for a tribute compilation, bassist Alex James refused to participate because he disliked Rod Stewart. His parts were played on keyboards.
>
> §
>
> Blur was originally called Seymour, but one of the stipulations of their British record label was that they change the name.

productions and occasional string sections that made some of Blur's music so extraordinary.

The U.S. release of 1998's *Bustin' + Dronin'* album of remixes, which was originally released only in Japan, seemed to be a vote of confidence from Blur's U.S. record label, because the album had little commercial potential. A collection of lackluster remixes by underground stars such as Thurston Moore of Sonic Youth and John McEntire of Tortoise augmented by a second album of radio session tracks, *Bustin' + Dronin'* was destined for the collections of serious fans only. Blur's generally excellent track record has ensured that those fans exist.

—*Josh Modell*

SELECT DISCOGRAPHY
■ ALBUMS
Leisure, 1991
Modern Life Is Rubbish, 1993
Parklife, 1994
The Great Escape, 1995
Blur, 1997
Bustin' + Dronin', 1998 (remixes and radio sessions)

SEE ALSO: Kinks, The; Oasis; XTC.

Michael Bolton

BORN: New Haven, Connecticut; February 26, 1954
FIRST ALBUM RELEASE: *Michael Bolotin*, 1975
MUSICAL STYLES: Pop, soul

After more than two decades of relative obscurity in the music business, Michael Bolton emerged in the late 1980's as one of the most successful male vocalists in the pop music recording field. Epic Records released his first single in 1969, but his first number 1 hit did not materialize until twenty-one years later in early 1990.

Early Life. Michael Bolton was born Michael Bolotin in New Haven, Connecticut, the youngest of three children. His mother, Helen, encouraged Bolton to develop his interest in music at an early age. By the age of eight, he was playing a rented saxophone. At eleven, he had progressed enough to perform at the local Jewish community center. After his parents' divorce in the mid-1960's, Bolton used his music to escape the self-consciousness he felt about his parents' marital problems. He learned to play the guitar, wrote his first song when he was twelve, and formed his first band, the Nomads, when he was fourteen. The Nomads quickly became one of the most popular bands in that area of Connecticut and were signed to a singles contract by Epic Records in 1968. Their first single was released when Bolton was only fifteen. The two Nomads singles released by Epic were not particularly successful and the label dropped their contract.

With his parents' blessing, Bolton dropped out of school when he was sixteen to pursue his music career. Over the next several years, he fronted a succession of unsuccessful bands and tried several different performing styles, including heavy metal and southern rock. In 1975, RCA Records signed him to a two-album contract under his real name, Michael Bolotin. After two failed albums, he was again released from his contract. Next came a deal with Polydor, with Bolton as the lead singer for the heavy-metal band Blackjack. Two more albums produced the same unsuccessful results. After Bolton was dropped by Epic, RCA, and Polydor, most of the other record companies were skeptical about his potential for success, but his new manager, Louis Levin, convinced Columbia that Bolton's songwriting ability was worth a publishing deal with CBS Songs and a recording contract with Columbia Records. Still specializing in hard rock, he changed his name from Bolotin to Bolton (it was easier to pronounce) for his debut album with Columbia. "Fools Game" became his first single to crack *Billboard*'s Hot 100 singles chart at number 82 in May, 1983.

Man Behind the Music. His first major success was not as a singer but as a songwriter. Laura Branigan's recording of "How Am I Supposed to Live Without You," which Bolton had written with Doug James, went to number 12 on the Hot 100 and number 1 on the adult contemporary chart in the fall of 1983. He had written songs on albums by the Pointer Sisters, Kenny Rogers, Joe Cocker, Rex Smith, and Starship before Branigan's success. Over the next several years, he wrote songs for Barbra Streisand ("We're Not Making Love Anymore"), Kiss ("Forever"), Cher ("I Found Someone"), and Peabo Bryson ("By the Time This Night Is Over"). Other artists who have covered Bolton's songs include Patti LaBelle, Greg Allman, Lee Greenwood, and Conway Twitty.

Michael Bolton (Paul Natkin)

After his second Columbia album, *Everybody's Crazy*, was a failure, Bolton finally began to realize that hard rock might not be the musical style that suited him best. Almost twenty years after the release of his first single, Bolton had his first successful album with *The Hunger* in 1987. Bolton's first Top-40 chart single was "That's What Love Is All About," written by Bolton and Eric Kaz, which made it to number 19 in late 1987. His cover version of Otis Redding's "(Sittin' on) The Dock of the Bay" was his next chart single, and it climbed to number 11 in March, 1988.

Success in His Own Right. In June, 1989, Columbia released the album *Soul Provider*. That album provided the impetus Bolton needed to become one of the top male singers of the pop music world. Bolton's version of "How Am I Supposed to Live Without You" became his first number 1 hit and the first number 1 single of the 1990's. Bolton won his first Grammy Award as Best Male Pop Vocalist for his version of the song that he had cowritten in 1983. Other popular singles from this project were the title track and another cover, "Georgia on My Mind," the 1930 Hoagy Carmichael song that had been revived by Ray Charles in the early 1960's.

Bolton's fifth Columbia album, *Time, Love and Tenderness* (1991), sold eleven million copies. Its global success helped catapult him to the status of international superstar. The first single from the album was "Love Is a Wonderful Thing," which rose to number 4 in June, 1991. (A federal jury ordered that the Isley Brothers receive 66 percent of all profits from the song after determining that Bolton's version borrowed significantly from the Isleys' song of the same name.) The second single was the title track, which made it to number 7. Bolton's cover of Percy Sledge's 1966 number 1 hit, "When a Man Loves a Woman," was the third single from the album and became Bolton's second number 1 hit in November, 1991. That single also earned him his second Grammy Award for Best Male Pop Vocalist. The honors continued with 1992 American Music Awards for Favorite Male Vocalist and Favorite Album, Pop/Rock, Male, along with the Broadcast Music Incorporated (BMI) Award for Songwriter of the Year.

Bolton grew up idolizing the great writers and artists who produced pop music's classic recordings, particularly the pioneers of rhythm and blues. In 1992 he released *Timeless (the Classics)*, a collection of standards such as the Four Tops' "Reach Out I'll Be There," Sam Cooke's "You Send Me," and the Beatles' "Yesterday."

In 1993 the multiplatinum *The One Thing* was released, which included the single "Said I Loved You . . . but I Lied." The album and single garnered more awards, including the American Music Awards for Favorite Artist, Pop/Rock, Male, and Favorite Artist, Adult Contemporary, a feat he repeated in 1995.

Other Projects. Bolton has used his celebrity status to raise money for local charities during his tours by challenging local radio stations to games of baseball or basketball. In 1993, he established the Michael Bolton Foundation, which provides assistance to children and women. His other charitable activities have included raising money for the Harlem School of the Arts, the Starlight Foundation, the Pediatric AIDS Foundation, and the National Committee for the Prevention of Child Abuse.

He has authored a children's book, *The Secret of the Lost Kingdom*. He also joined tenor Luciano Pavarotti for the "Luciano & Friends Together for Children of Bosnia" benefit concert in Modena, Italy. The experience led Bolton to record an album of classical arias that was released in 1997. He also recorded "Go the Distance" for the animated film *Hercules* in 1997, which was nominated for an Academy Award for Best Song. *—Don Tyler*

SELECT DISCOGRAPHY
■ ALBUMS
Michael Bolton, 1983
The Hunger, 1987
Soul Provider, 1989
Time, Love and Tenderness, 1991
Timeless (the Classics), 1992
The One Thing, 1993

SELECT AWARDS
Grammy Award for Best Pop Vocal Performance, Male, for "How Am I Supposed to Live Without You," 1989

Grammy Award for Best Pop Vocal Performance, Male, for "When a Man Loves a Woman," 1991

SEE ALSO: Charles, Ray; Cooke, Sam; Four Tops, The; G, Kenny; Pointer Sisters, The; Rogers, Kenny; Sonny and Cher / Cher; Streisand, Barbra; Twitty, Conway.

Bon Jovi

MEMBERS: Jon Bon Jovi (b. John Bongiovi, 1962), David Bryan (b. David Bryan Rashbaum, 1962), Richie Sambora (b. 1959), Alec John Such (b. 1956), Tico Torres (b. Hector Torres, 1953)
FIRST ALBUM RELEASE: *Bon Jovi*, 1984
MUSICAL STYLES: Hard rock, heavy metal

Formed in 1983 in Sayreville, New Jersey, Bon Jovi combined hard rock and pop to become one of the leading U.S. mainstream rock bands by the end of the decade. After a brief hiatus during 1990, the group reunited, recording several successful albums during the 1990's. Vocalist Jon Bon Jovi and guitarist Richie Sambora have been responsible for most of the band's songs, sometimes in collaboration with writer Desmond Child.

The Beginnings. During the late 1970's, while a student at Sayreville High School, singer John Bongiovi appeared with bands in New York and New Jersey, the most successful of which was the Atlantic City Expressway, a rhythm-and-blues group that opened for Bruce Springsteen, Southside Johnny and the Asbury Jukes, and Squeeze. He later worked sweeping floors at New York's Power Station recording studio, where he also began to make demo tapes. In 1983, with his boyhood friend David Bryan, Bongiovi (then known as Jon Bon Jovi) organized his band, with Bryan on keyboards, Sambora on lead guitar, Alec John Such on bass guitar, and Tico Torres on drums. Among Bon Jovi's early concerts was an appearance with ZZ Top at Madison Square Garden.

While working at the recording studio, Jon Bon Jovi had recorded a demo tape, one track of which, his solo "Runaway," was chosen for a regional compilation album of new artists. This led to a contract with Mercury Records, which issued the band's first album, *Bon Jovi* (1984), from which "Runaway" and "She Don't Know Me" were moderate hits.

Recording Classics. Another album followed in 1985, *7800° Fahrenheit*, but it was not until an appearance in the United Kingdom with ZZ Top that year that Bon Jovi achieved major critical acclaim. By this time, Jon Bon Jovi and Sambora had teamed with songwriter Child. Their "You Give Love a Bad Name" became a British Top-20 hit and then a number 1 hit in the United States when it appeared on the album *Slippery When Wet* in 1986. "Livin' on a Prayer" from the same album also topped the U.S. charts and won the Best Stage Performance Award at the fourth annual MTV Video Music Awards.

The next album, *New Jersey* (1988), included two more number 1 hits, "Bad Medicine" and "Born to Be My Baby," as well as the ballad "Blood on Blood," a memoir of Jon Bon Jovi's adolescence. Both *Slippery When Wet* and *New Jersey* were huge sellers, establishing Bon Jovi as the premier hard-rock band of the day. The group continued to tour extensively, and in 1989 they appeared at Moscow's Music Peace Festival in Lenin Stadium.

Other Directions. For most of 1990 the band's members pursued solo projects. Jon Bon Jovi had a bit part in the 1990 film *Young Guns II*, for which he recorded the sound track, *Blaze of Glory*, with contributions by Jeff Beck, Elton John, Little Rich-

For the Record

"If you want to torture me, you'd tie me down and force me to watch our first five videos."
—*Jon Bon Jovi*

§

Bon Jovi drummer Tico Torres is an accomplished visual artist whose work has been exhibited in New York, New York; Miami, Florida; Cleveland, Ohio; and Las Vegas, Nevada.

ard, and others. Reunited in late December, 1990, Bon Jovi resumed touring. Their next album, *Keep the Faith*, appeared in 1992, followed by a greatest-hits collection, *Cross Roads* (1994), and an album of new songs, *These Days* (1995).

Style. Bon Jovi has combined hard rock and heavy metal with a catchy pop sound. Although sometimes criticized for their manicured image, the band found a formula that has continued to be commercially successful. In the 1990's the group maintained an extensive touring schedule and often performed for charitable causes.

—*Mary A. Wischusen*

SELECT DISCOGRAPHY

■ ALBUMS

Bon Jovi, 1984
7800° Fahrenheit, 1985
Slippery When Wet, 1986
New Jersey, 1988
Blaze of Glory, 1990 (Jon Bon Jovi solo)
Keep the Faith, 1992
Cross Roads, 1994 (compilation)
These Days, 1995

SEE ALSO: John, Elton; Little Richard; Springsteen, Bruce; ZZ Top.

Booker T. and the MG's

ORIGINAL MEMBERS: Booker T. Jones (b. 1944), Lewis Steinberg (b. 1933), Al Jackson (1935-1975), Steve Cropper (b. 1941)
OTHER MEMBERS: Donald "Duck" Dunn (b. 1941), Willie Hall (b. 1950), Steve Jordan, James Gadson, Steve Potts (b. 1953)

For the Record

Booker T. and the MG's recorded an instrumental version of the Beatles' entire 1969 *Abbey Road* album, entitled *McLemore Avenue* for the street on which the Stax studios were located in Memphis.

FIRST ALBUM RELEASE: *Green Onions*, 1962
MUSICAL STYLES: Soul, blues

Booker T. and the MG's were masters of the southern soul sound. As the house band for Stax Records, they invigorated the songs of Wilson Pickett, Otis Redding, and Sam and Dave, among others, with their crisp, funky instrumentation. The group would also find success on their own with their instrumental soul hits.

Formation. Booker T. Jones was originally a saxophonist who began session work for Stax in Memphis, Tennessee, in 1960. The organ soon became his main instrument, however. At Stax he met guitarist Steve Cropper of the Mar-Keys, who had set a standard for Memphis soul with their organ, saxophone, and guitar setup. They recruited drummer Al Jackson and bassist Lewis Steinberg and had an almost immediate number 3 hit with "Green Onions" (1962), a bluesy instrumental piece.

In the late 1960's, after Steinberg was replaced by Donald "Duck" Dunn, also of the Mar-Keys, the band scored more hits with "Hip Hug-Her," "Hang 'Em High," and "Time Is Tight." They also appeared on countless hit records as the backup band for Stax artists. Cropper cowrote, and the MG's appeared on, Wilson Pickett's "In the Midnight Hour," Eddie Floyd's "Knock on Wood," Sam and Dave's "Soul Man," and Otis Redding's "(Sittin' on) The Dock of the Bay."

Breakup and Reunion. The band decided to break up in 1971 because of the members' interests in outside projects. Jones was busy earning his music degree at Indiana University, while Cropper was playing sessions in Los Angeles, producing for Redding, and recording solo albums at his own Memphis studio. Jones and Jackson would go on with session work until 1975, when the group decided to reunite. However, Jackson was killed by an intruder in his home in that year. Booker T. and the MG's did release a few more albums in the mid-1970's, with Willie Hall on drums, but they were relatively unsuccessful.

During the 1980's, the band members successfully pursued other projects, with Dunn and Cropper appearing in the 1980 *Blues Brothers* film and

Cropper producing for Jeff Beck, John Prine, and José Feliciano, among others. The group got together again as the backup band for a Bob Dylan tribute concert in 1992 and a Neil Young tour in 1993. Finding success, they released another album in 1994, *That's the Way It Should Be*, with Steve Jordan on drums. The album yielded a Grammy Award for Best Pop Instrumental Performance for the single "Cruisin'."

"Mixed" Message. Booker T. and the MG's were instrumental in helping break the racial barriers of the 1960's. A band with two African Americans and two Caucasians, they proved that soul music was not just for African Americans and that race was unimportant when it came to producing hit records.

— *Lauren M. D'Andrea*

SELECT DISCOGRAPHY
"Green Onions," 1962
"Hip Hug-Her," 1967
"Hang 'Em High," 1968

■ ALBUMS
Green Onions, 1962
And Now, Booker T. and the MG's, 1966
The Best of Booker T. and the MG's, 1968
   (compilation)
Soul Limbo, 1968
Melting Pot, 1971
Memphis Sound, 1975
Universal Language, 1977
That's the Way It Should Be, 1994

SELECT AWARDS
Rock and Roll Hall of Fame, inducted 1992
Grammy Award for Best Pop Instrumental
   Performance for "Cruisin'," 1994

SEE ALSO: Pickett, Wilson; Redding, Otis; Sam and Dave.

Booker T and the MGs in the early 1960's (Frank Driggs/Archive Photos)

Boston

ORIGINAL MEMBERS: Tom Scholz (b. 1947), Brad Delp (b. 1951), Barry Goudreau (b. 1951), Fran Sheehan (b. 1949), Sib Hashian (b. 1949)
OTHER MEMBERS: Jim Masdea
FIRST ALBUM RELEASE: *Boston*, 1976
MUSICAL STYLES: Rock and roll, pop

Influenced by the guitar-dominated rock of groups such as Led Zeppelin and the harmony vocals of groups such as Yes, Boston's carefully engineered blend of hard rock and melodic pop pioneered the musical style known as adult-oriented rock (AOR). The phenomenal success of Boston's first album paved the way for other

Boston's Tom Scholz (Ken Settle)

worked in the regional warehouse of ABC Records. The tape eventually made its way to Charlie McKenzie, who worked for ABC Records in the Boston area. McKenzie was impressed with the professionalism of the tape and contacted Paul Ahern at Asylum Records in Los Angeles. McKenzie and Ahern had previously worked together for Warner-Elektra-Atlantic Records in the Boston area. In 1972 they had been successful in promoting Yes and the J. Geils Band.

Convinced that they could make Scholz and his partners into a successful band, McKenzie and Ahern formed a company called Pure Management to represent the group. They presented the tape to Epic Records, which was impressed with its quality. In November of 1975, the band, as yet unnamed, presented a live performance for Epic. Epic agreed to release their first album, and Ahern suggested that the band call itself Boston.

Boston. The group consisted of Scholz on guitars, bass, organ, and other instruments, along with lead vocalist and guitarist Brad Delp, guitarist Barry Goudreau, bassist Fran Sheehan, and drummer Sib Hashian. Drummer Jim Masdea appeared on the song "Rock and Roll Band" but did not continue as a member of the group. The various members of Boston had spent years playing in local bands such as Mother's Milk, Middle Earth, and the Revolting Tones Revue. These bands played in bars in the Boston area while members worked various day jobs.

After signing a contract with Epic, Scholz stayed in Boston to finish engineering his tapes, while the rest of the band traveled to Los Angeles to record new songs. Only one of these songs, "Let Me Take You Home Tonight," appeared on the group's self-titled first album. The rest of the album consisted of slightly altered versions of Scholz's original basement tapes.

A Classic First Album. *Boston*, released in August of 1976, was an unprecedented success for a band that had never played together in front of a live audience. The album reached number 1 in the United States and stayed on the charts for two years. It eventually sold more than ten million copies worldwide. The album's biggest hit single was "More than a Feeling," but almost every song

AOR groups such as Foreigner, Journey, Styx, and REO Speedwagon.

Out of the Basement. Tom Scholz, the founder of Boston, earned a master's degree in mechanical engineering from the Massachusetts Institute of Technology (MIT) in Cambridge, Massachusetts, in 1970. After graduation, he was employed as an engineer for the Polaroid corporation in Boston. In his spare time he played guitar and keyboards in local bands with musicians who would later become the other members of Boston.

Using his engineering expertise, Scholz spent the next six years making tapes in a homemade recording studio that he constructed in his basement. He sent copies of the tapes to anyone who might be able to help him launch his career. One copy went to a fellow engineer whose cousin

on the album received extensive radio play. As of the 1990's, *Boston* was still the fastest-selling debut album in history.

Many reasons have been suggested for Boston's sudden rise to fame in the mid-1970's. At a time when popular music was dominated by disco, many fans of hard rock were ready for a group like Boston to emerge. They combined the heavy guitars, bass, and drums of hard rock with memorable melodies and expertly harmonized vocals that appealed to fans of pop music. Scholz managed to blend his love of guitar-oriented rock with his technical skills to produce music which was meticulously engineered yet true to its roots as classic rock and roll.

Eventually McKenzie left the managerial partnership, leaving Ahern in charge of managing the band. Various reasons have been given for the loss of McKenzie, but most observers agree that neither the band nor their managers were quite ready for the enormous financial success they achieved so suddenly. Based on the success of their first album, Boston began playing concerts for huge, enthusiastic audiences. Fans eagerly anticipated the group's next album, but they would have to wait two years before the perfectionist Scholz was ready to release it.

Two More Hit Albums. In 1978 Boston's second album, *Don't Look Back*, reached number 1.

For the Record

Epic Records made much of Tom Scholz's engineering background in its publicity campaign for Boston's first album. It used the slogan Better Music Through Science to promote the band and ran ads showing Scholz in a spacesuit. Scholz was not entirely pleased with this approach: "They took a full-page ad in *Billboard* that more or less said I single-handedly built the SX-70 camera with paper clips and rubber bands on my lunch hour. I don't even know how to load one."

Although it did not sell quite as well as *Boston*, the album was highly successful and included the hit single "Don't Look Back" and other popular songs. In response to criticism that the band relied too much on technology to produce their music, *Don't Look Back*'s inside cover included the statement, "No Synthesizers Used. No Computers Used."

Fans of Boston had to wait even longer for the band's third album. During this time, Goudreau recorded a self-titled solo album in 1980 and eventually left Boston to form the group Orion. Scholz spent part of this time inventing a small guitar amplifier with headphones which was marketed as the Rockman.

The third Boston album, *Third Stage*, was finally released in 1986. It also reached number 1 in the United States. Included on the album were the hit singles "We're Ready" and "Amanda," which reached number 1. Together, the group's first three albums eventually sold more than twenty million copies. Many critics agree that the main reason *Don't Look Back* and *Third Stage* were not quite as popular as *Boston* is the similarity of all three albums. Superficially, the lack of distinction was obvious: all of Boston's album covers have featured spaceships shaped like guitars that carried cities in domes and were labeled Boston.

Into the 1990's. After another extended waiting period, Boston released its fourth album, *Walk On*, in 1994. The album was not particularly successful and produced no major hit singles. After nearly twenty years it seemed that Boston was at last losing its popularity. Despite this fact, Boston's classic songs, particularly those which appeared on the first album, continued to enjoy frequent airings by radio stations dedicated to classic rock and album-oriented rock. —*Rose Secrest*

SELECT DISCOGRAPHY
■ ALBUMS
Boston, 1976
Don't Look Back, 1978
Third Stage, 1986
Walk On, 1994

SEE ALSO: Foreigner; Journey; Led Zeppelin; REO Speedwagon; Styx; Yes.

David Bowie

BORN: London, England; January 8, 1947
FIRST ALBUM RELEASE: *The World of David Bowie*, 1967
MUSICAL STYLES: Rock and roll, funk, pop

After struggling through the 1960's, David Bowie achieved his first success in 1969 with "Space Oddity." A string of hits followed, and Bowie became as famous for his glamorous onstage Ziggy Stardust costumes as for his music. He dropped the Ziggy Stardust persona in 1973 and proceeded to remake himself several times over the next twenty-five years. His greatest commercial success came with his "Serious Moonlight" tour in 1983. He remained a creative and influential musician in the 1980's and 1990's.

The Beginnings. David Bowie was born David Robert Jones, and his youth was spent in a small suburban house in Brixton, England. It was clear in his early days that both David and his father hoped he would become an entertainer. In 1956, when David was nine, Elvis Presley took England by storm. Young David was inspired by the energetic rock-and-roll performer. In 1957 the family moved to Bromley, where David learned about jazz. Impressed by a local saxophonist, he began to take saxophone lessons.

When the Beatles released "Love Me Do," David Jones was the first in his class to buy it. He learned to play the harmonica by copying the solo in the song. At sixteen he joined George Underwood's band as a saxophone player; the group concentrated on jazz. Their next group, the Hooker Brothers, was named for African American bluesman John Lee Hooker and focused on blues. It was clear at this early point in David's career that he would never be tied to one musical style. Graduating from Bromley High in 1963, he moved to London. In 1964 his band, Davie Jones and the King Bees, passed an audition with Decca, the record label that had the Rolling Stones. They recorded a single, "Liza Jane," but it failed miserably. In 1965 David was invited to join a London rhythm-and-blues group called the Lower Thirds as the lead singer. For a while they imitated the newest phenomenon in England, the Who. Most of the little money they made came from radio commercials for American products.

Becoming David Bowie. The only lasting thing that David got from his period with the Lower Third was a new name. David wanted a moniker that would somehow combine his two greatest heroes—Mick Jagger and John Lennon. Jagger came from the old English word for knife, so David searched for a name that began with *B* for Beatles but also meant knife. He came up with Bowie, which had the added attraction of being American. In late 1965 Davie Jones became David Bowie. In 1967, still only twenty years old, Bowie tried going solo. A single, "The Laughing Gnome," failed. In mid-1967 Bowie's first album, *The World of David Bowie*, was released by Deram Records. It was not a hit. At this point Bowie became aware of the New York music and art scenes and such figures as artist Andy Warhol and Lou Reed of the Velvet Underground. Their creativity and success at manufacturing images made a major impression on him.

Commercial Success. In 1969 Bowie took dancing lessons, donned a wig, and had his teeth fixed. He was starring in a television film, *Love You Till Tuesday*, and his manager suggested that he write a hit song to make the movie successful. After seeing Stanley Kubrick's film *2001: A Space Odyssey*, Bowie began to conceive of a song about an astronaut named Major Tom, trapped in space. Bowie and his guitarist John Hutchinson produced Bowie's first breakthrough, "Space Oddity."

Coming out just as Americans landed on the moon, "Space Oddity" climbed into the Top 10 in England. In 1970 Bowie released an innovative album entitled *The Man Who Sold the World*, which had a cover featuring Bowie in a dress. The remarkable career of David Bowie had truly begun, and he was still only twenty-three. That year also saw major changes in Bowie's personal life: His father died, his brother entered a mental hospital, and Bowie married Angela Barnett (they divorced in 1980). In 1971 they had a son, Duncan Zowie Haywood, whom they preferred to call Zowie.

In 1971 Bowie signed a lucrative deal with RCA Records. He recorded *Hunky Dory*, which in-

David Bowie (Paul Natkin)

cluded the futuristic song "Life on Mars" and the hit "Changes." He embarked on a successful concert tour of the United Kingdom, featuring his new material and wild costumes. The big breakthrough, however, came in the summer of 1972 with the release of the album *The Rise and Fall of Ziggy Stardust and the Spiders from Mars.* On stage Bowie played Ziggy, a rock star clad in space-age costumes and sporting makeup and orange hair. A number of the new songs continued the space theme, with the best being "Starman." Bowie garnered attention for his androgenous sexuality; he had told a British reporter in 1972 that he was gay, and he seemed to enjoy being an ambiguous object of desire. Bowie's key musical collaborator at this point in his career was guitarist Mick Ron-

son, a member of his band and a very creative musician in his own right.

Bowie took his Ziggy Stardust show on the road in the United States and was met with media attention and tremendous fan support. At this point Bowie released "Space Oddity" in the United States, where it became a hit. His success rubbed off, and he produced big hits for Lou Reed ("Walk on the Wild Side") and Ian Hunter's band, Mott the Hoople ("All the Young Dudes"). In 1973 Bowie announced the retirement of Ziggy Stardust but was back with a new album, new stage persona, and major tour in 1974. *Diamond Dogs* did not live up to the success of Ziggy Stardust, but it cleverly adapted to music some ideas from George Orwell's dystopian novel *Nineteen Eighty-Four* (1949).

Ongoing Career. During his 1974 tour of the United States, Bowie began experimenting with the Philadelphia soul sound. The result was the 1975 *Young Americans* album and the number 1 single "Fame," which John Lennon helped write. Bowie stayed in the United States for another year, then moved to Berlin. He remained in Germany for three years, working closely with Brian Eno on several projects. The best work from this period was the single "Heroes" (from the album *Low*), which reached number 35 in 1977. During that year Bowie also produced two albums for Iggy Pop and backed Iggy on piano. After a major world tour in 1978, Bowie settled in New York City.

Bowie had done some acting in the 1970's, most notably in the film *The Man Who Fell to Earth*. In 1980 he devoted most of his energies to the stage, playing the main character in the Broadway production of *The Elephant Man*. He did release the album *Scary Monsters*. While it was not a huge hit, it was important because along with the album Bowie made some early and innovative music videos. In 1981 he worked with Queen to produce a fine pop song, "Under Pressure," and continued acting, including a role as a vampire in the movie *The Hunger* (1982).

In 1983 Bowie moved from RCA to EMI Records, which offered him money in the range of ten million dollars, and released the successful *Let's Dance* album. Produced by Nile Rodgers, it reached number 4, and three singles made the Top 20: "Let's Dance" (number 1), "China Girl," and "Modern Love." The songs were soulful and danceable, and the accompanying videos received considerable airplay on MTV. *Let's Dance* also benefited from the great guitar work of Stevie Ray Vaughan. As a result, Bowie's "Serious Moonlight" tour sold out across America. This was arguably the high point of Bowie's remarkable career, at least in terms of popularity and profits.

Bowie continued to tour and record throughout the 1980's, including the 1984 hit "Blue Jean" and a duet with Mick Jagger on "Dancing in the Streets" for the 1985 Live Aid benefit concert. He also continued acting, most notably in the 1986 movie *Labyrinth*. In 1989 Bowie formed a band, Tin Machine, which first played at clubs in New York and Los Angeles. The group released two albums, receiving some critical attention, but disbanded in the early 1990's. Bowie's love life made headlines in 1992 when he married Somalian supermodel Iman.

In 1994 Bowie rejoined his old partner, Brian Eno, and the two visited a psychiatric hospital in Austria in search of ideas for a new album. They released *Outside* in 1995 and toured the United States and Europe to promote it. As part of Bowie's efforts to stay in touch with cutting-edge music, he hired Nine Inch Nails as his opening act. He and Nine Inch Nails' Trent Reznor began discussing future projects together. As the 1995 tour wound down, it was announced that Bowie would be inducted into the Rock and Roll Hall of Fame in Cleveland.

This recognition was only one of many honors Bowie received in the 1990's. Not content to rest on his laurels, Bowie recorded *Earthling* in 1997, with some help from Reznor. While not nearly as popular as his material from the 1970's or 1980's, Bowie's work retained the originality that has marked his long career. In particular, the song "I'm Afraid of Americans" demonstrated that he still had original insights and things to say. As the 1990's came to an end David Bowie ranked among the most recognizable and influential musicians in the world.

—*Andy DeRoche*

SELECT DISCOGRAPHY

■ ALBUMS

The Man Who Sold the World, 1970
Hunky Dory, 1971
The Rise and Fall of Ziggy Stardust and the Spiders from Mars, 1972
Diamond Dogs, 1974
Young Americans, 1975
Let's Dance, 1983
Tin Machine, 1989 (with Tin Machine)
ChangesBowie, 1990 (greatest hits compilation)
Earthling, 1997

SELECT AWARDS

Rock and Roll Hall of Fame, inducted 1996

SEE ALSO: Beatles, The; Queen; Reed, Lou; Rolling Stones, The; Vaughan, Stevie Ray; Who, The.

Boy George. *See* **Culture Club / Boy George**

Boyz II Men

ORIGINAL MEMBERS: Wanya "Squirt" Morris
(b. 1974), Michael "Bass" McCary (b. 1972),
Shawn "Slim" Stockman (b. 1973), Nathan
"Alex Vanderpool" Morris (b. 1972)
FIRST ALBUM RELEASE: *Cooleyhighharmony*, 1991
MUSICAL STYLES: Pop, soul

The nostalgic, close harmonies of Boyz II Men catapulted this Philadelphia, Pennsylvania, teen-age group to stardom in 1991 with the release of their first album, *Cooleyhighharmony*. The album produced two Top-10 hits, sold more than five million copies, and earned a Grammy Award for Best R&B Vocal Performance by a Duo or Group with Vocal.

Getting Started. The band members met at the Philadelphia High School for the Creative and Performing Arts in 1988. Inspired by the jazz fusion and gospel sounds of the a cappella group Take 6, they formed Boyz II Men late in 1988. After sneaking backstage at a New Edition concert in March, 1989, they performed an impromptu a cappella audition for group member Michael Bivins. When Bivins formed his own management and production company, he signed the group and helped them get a record deal with Motown.

Cooleyhighharmony was an astounding debut for a young group. The title was derived from *Cooley High*, a 1975 film that featured a sound track of classic Motown hits. Boyz II Men had been inspired by both the Motown classics and the Philadelphia sound of the O'Jays and the Blue Notes. Together, these styles contributed to the "new jack swing" sound of the first single, "Mo-townphilly," which went to number 3 on the pop charts. "It's So Hard to Say Goodbye to Yesterday," the second single, was a ballad first performed by former Spinner G. C. Cameron for the *Cooley High* sound track. While Cameron only took it to number 38 on the rhythm-and-blues charts in

1975, Boyz II Men topped the same charts in 1992 and came in at number 2 on the pop list. "Uhh Ahh," the third single, also made the Top 20.

Breaking Records. Boyz II Men spent the first half of 1992 as the opening act for Hammer, but with the release of their fifth single, "End of the Road" (from the sound track to 1992's *Boomerang*), they became superstars in their own right. Written by Babyface and L.A. Reid, "End of the Road" spent thirteen weeks at the top of the pop charts, breaking Elvis Presley's 1956 record of eleven weeks with "Hound Dog"/"Don't Be Cruel." It also earned Boyz II Men their second Grammy Award for Best R&B Performance by a Duo or Group with Vocal. They followed "End of the Road" in early 1993 with the single "In the Still of the Night (I'll Remember)," from the television miniseries *The Jacksons: An American Dream*, which went to number 3.

After the release of a successful holiday album, *Christmas Interpretations* (1993), Boyz II Men produced an even bigger hit album than their debut. *II* hit the charts in September, 1994, spent four weeks at number 1, and in less than a year sold more than seven million copies. The first single from the album, "I'll Make Love to You," spent an incredible fourteen weeks at number 1, breaking their own record. It was succeeded at the top by their second release from *II*, "On Bended Knee," which spent six weeks at number 1. Only Elvis Presley and the Beatles had previously succeeded themselves in the top spot. "Thank You" (number 21) and "Water Runs Dry" (number 2) were both hits from the same album.

Full Steam Ahead. When it seemed that there was nowhere to go but down, Boyz II Men had another coup, teaming with Mariah Carey for the

For the Record

Two of Boyz II Men's Top-10 hits were performed a cappella: "It's So Hard to Say Goodbye to Yesterday" and "In the Still of the Night (I'll Remember)."

number 1 pop single of all time, "One Sweet Day."
It stayed at the top for sixteen weeks, dominating
the charts from December, 1995, through March,
1996. Though the group consistently included
both ballads and dance tracks in their repertoire,
the ballads proved to be the hook that simultaneously attracted the pop, rhythm-and-blues, and
adult-contemporary audiences. Their third studio
album, *Evolution* (1997), proved that Boyz II Men
had not lost their touch, going double platinum
in less than one year and rising to number 1 on
the rhythm-and-blues charts. The full-length
Spanish version, *Evolucion*, spent seventeen weeks
on the *Billboard* Latin Top 50 and was the first
Motown record to earn that distinction.

—*John Powell*

SELECT DISCOGRAPHY

■ ALBUMS
Cooleyhighharmony, 1991
Christmas Interpretations, 1993
II, 1994
Evolution, 1997

SELECT AWARDS
Grammy Award for Best R&B Performance by a
    Duo or Group with Vocal for *Cooleyhighhar-
    mony*, 1991
Grammy Award for Best R&B Performance by a
    Duo or Group with Vocal for "End of the
    Road," 1992
Grammy Awards for Best R&B Album for *II* and
    Best R&B Performance by a Duo or Group
    with Vocal for "I'll Make Love to You," 1994

SEE ALSO: Babyface; New Edition / Bobby Brown;
Spinners, The.

Toni Braxton

BORN: Severn, Maryland; October 7, 1968
FIRST ALBUM RELEASE: *Toni Braxton*, 1993
MUSICAL STYLES: Pop, rhythm and blues

Before becoming one of the premier divas of the
1990's, Toni Braxton sang with her four younger
sisters as the Braxtons in her father's Pentecostal
church. Strictly raised, the girls were not allowed
to watch cartoons or films until Braxton was
eleven, and they were forbidden to listen to secular music. Braxton nevertheless caught glimpses
of *Soul Train* and other popular television shows
when her parents were away, and she has counted
Dionne Warwick and young Janet Jackson as early
influences. The Braxtons continued to sing but
were strictly a local act, while Toni worked at odd
jobs and attended several schools and colleges
trying to find direction in her life.

New Face at LaFace. Through a chance meeting with songwriter Bill Pettaway, who heard Braxton singing while filling her car at an Annapolis,
Maryland, gas station, the Braxtons were introduced to executives at Arista Records, who signed
the group. Though their 1990 single "The Good
Life" fared poorly, producers Babyface and L.A.
Reid liked Braxton's voice. In 1991 they offered
her a solo recording deal with LaFace, the new
Atlanta, Georgia-based record label they were establishing, and Braxton was soon being touted as
"the First Lady of LaFace."

Before recording an album for her new label,
Braxton became lucky when newly pregnant Anita
Baker was unable to fulfill her agreement to sing
two songs for the sound track to the 1992 film
Boomerang. As a result, Braxton was given the opportunity to sing the songs in her place, a duet
with Babyface on "Give U My Heart" (number 29)
and the torch song "Love Shoulda Brought You
Home" (number 33). Braxton created a sensation. In addition to her obvious vocal talent, she
had a sultry voice and winning personality that
made her a popular guest on the talk-show circuit,
leading to appearances on *The Tonight Show, Good
Morning America, Today*, and *Entertainment Tonight*.

Success. Braxton established herself as a star
with her much-anticipated self-titled first album,
which produced three Top-10 hits. "Another Sad
Love Song" hit the charts in August, 1993, to
much critical and public acclaim. It peaked at
number 7 and earned Braxton a Grammy Award
for Best Female R&B Vocal Performance.
"Breathe Again," her biggest hit, spent thirty-
three weeks on the charts and rose to number 3,
while "You Mean the World to Me" went to

Toni Braxton in 1996 (Popperfoto/Archive Photos)

Toni Braxton, 1993
Secrets, 1996

Soul Train R&B Album of the Year Award for
    Toni Braxton, 1993
Grammy Awards for Best New Artist and Best
    R&B Vocal Performance, Female, for "An-
    other Sad Love Song," 1993
Grammy Award for Best Female R&B Vocal
    Performance for "Breathe Again," 1994
Grammy Awards for Best Female Pop Vocal
    Performance for "Un-Break My Heart" and
    Best Female R&B Vocal Performance for
    "You're Makin' Me High," 1996

SEE ALSO: Babyface; Baker, Anita.

Bread

ORIGINAL MEMBERS: David Gates (b. 1940), James
    Griffin, Robb Royer, Mike Botts (b. 1944)
OTHER MEMBERS: Larry Knechtel
FIRST ALBUM RELEASE: *Bread*, 1969
MUSICAL STYLES: Pop

number 7. In a masterpiece of production and performance, the LaFace team of Braxton, Babyface, and Reid utilized the singer's husky voice in a range of emotional moods to attract both male and female listeners across the adult-contemporary spectrum. By the end of 1994, *Toni Braxton* had sold more than nine million copies.

Braxton stayed in the public eye in 1995 as the opening act for Maze, with her sisters singing backup. She also toured Europe, made guest television appearances on *Roc* and *Living Single*, and contributed to the Grammy Award-winning sound track to 1995's *Waiting to Exhale*. Her follow-up album, *Secrets* (1996), was more ambitious than her debut, featuring Braxton in more sensuous moods. It entered the charts at number 2 and produced the number 1 single "You're Makin' Me High." *Secrets* also marked a new stage in Braxton's professional development, as she coproduced the album and cowrote four of its songs. —*John Powell*

The diversity of the music recorded by Bread in the early 1970's was overshadowed by the apparent uniformity of their half-dozen or so hit love songs, among which were "Make It with You," "If," and "Lost Without Your Love." The collaboration between David Gates and James Griffin also produced songs ranging from the infectious "London Bridge" to the sweetly melancholy "Aubrey." However, their work was always characterized by catchy melodies, lush harmonies, and Gates's smooth tenor voice. The group disbanded in 1973, only to get back together three years later to record the hit album *Lost Without Your Love* (1977).

Early Career. At the age of twenty-one, David Gates left Tulsa, Oklahoma, where his father was the musical director of the public school system, and headed for Los Angeles to make a name for himself in the music business. He soon established himself as an arranger and songwriter, writing the Murmaids' 1963 hit "Popsicles and Icicles"; he eventually composed or arranged songs for the Monkees, Bobby Darin, and Frank Sinatra. He also worked as a producer and studio musician for such performers as Pat Boone, Duane Eddy, Captain Beefheart, and Merle Haggard.

Gates became associated with Robb Royer and James Griffin in 1968, when the three of them worked on an album for the group Pleasure Faire. Royer and Griffin were gifted songwriters who collaborated on the Oscar-winning song "For All We Know." The three decided to form their own band and soon released their first album, *Bread*, which featured the smooth tenor vocals and melodic soft rock that were to become the band's trademark.

The album was not an immediate commercial success, but at least one song, "London Bridge," demonstrated the striking originality that the group was capable of achieving but that ultimately became obscured by their phenomenal success with more formulaic love songs. Another track from the album, "It Don't Matter to Me," eventually became a Top-10 hit for the band, but not until after the release of their second album, *On the Waters* (1970), and its number-1 single, "Make It with You."

Cast Thy Bread. The title of *On the Waters* was a subtle play on the group's name. In the eleventh chapter of Ecclesiastes in the Bible, the first verse reads: "Cast thy bread upon the waters: for thou shalt find it after many days." The passage is a meditation on the impossibility of controlling or predicting the future and the need to hazard the risk of commitment in spite of it. The group's acknowledgment of the mercurial quality of fame and the uncertainty of success was a rare display of humility in the entertainment world.

With the success of *On the Waters*, the group added a fourth member, drummer Mike Botts, and went on tour. In 1971 the band released its third album, *Manna*, a title with yet another biblical reference to the band's name. While not as successful as the gold-selling *On the Waters*, it produced what is now perhaps Bread's most famous single, the Top-10 "If." Gates frustrated the many performers who would eventually record their

For the Record

Of all Bread's songs, "If" is the one most frequently recorded by other musical groups. In 1975, a spoken version of the song became a surprise international hit for *Kojak*'s Telly Savalas.

own versions of the song by including more strings in the orchestration than any subsequent arrangement could possibly equal. Less noticed at the time was "He's a Good Lad," a lively song that displayed a broader musical range than most of the group's hit singles.

Royer left the group the same year that *Manna* was released and was replaced by Larry Knechtel, a Los Angeles session musician unknown to most listeners but regarded as a superstar within the industry. Knechtel had played on some of the most famous recordings of the 1960's, including the Byrds' "Mr. Tambourine Man," Mason Williams's "Classical Gas," and Simon and Garfunkel's "Bridge over Troubled Water." The group's first single with Knechtel, "Mother Freedom," barely scraped the bottom of the Top 40, but it was soon followed by "Baby I'm-a Want You," which became the new lineup's first Top-10 hit. The album of the same name, released the following year, was the group's most successful ever, thanks to a boost from yet another Top-10 hit, "Everything I Own." Other noteworthy songs from the album were the wistful "Diary," in which a would-be lover makes the painful mistake of misinterpreting his beloved's secret thoughts, and the more rollicking but still touching "Daughter," in which a father offers some sound romantic advice to his child.

Bread's next album, *Guitar Man* (1972), displayed an even greater diversity of musical styles than previous albums from the group. Songs on the album ranged from the sadly reflective title number to the engaging "Yours for Life" and the bittersweet "Aubrey." Unfortunately, it was to be the band's last album for several years; the conflicts that inevitably arise between even the closest of colleagues had finally torn the group apart. Griffin objected to the fact that Gates, who had written most of the group's hits, had reneged on an alleged promise to split the singles evenly between them. The two pursued somewhat lackluster solo careers, while Botts joined Linda Ronstadt's band.

Second Rising. In 1976, the group reconvened to record a new album, *Lost Without Your Love*, the title track of which became another huge hit for the group in 1977. Success was not enough to hold the group together, however, and Griffin soon went his own way once again. Gates formed a new band, which toured under the name Bread until ordered to stop because of a legal dispute over ownership of the name. The case was finally settled in 1984, paving the way for the release of *Anthology* in 1985.

Gates struck gold once more in his solo career with the title theme to *The Goodbye Girl* (1977), a Neil Simon comedy starring Richard Dreyfuss and Marsha Mason. The song became a Top-20 hit in 1978. After this success, Gates became more interested in ranching than performing. Griffin relocated to Nashville and formed the group Black Tie with Billy Swan; the duo had a country hit with a version of Buddy Holly's "Learning the Game."

—*Ed McKnight*

SELECT DISCOGRAPHY
Bread, 1969
On the Waters, 1970
Manna, 1971
Baby I'm-a Want You, 1972
Guitar Man, 1972
The Best of Bread, 1973 (previously released material)
The Best of Bread, Volume Two, 1974 (previously released material)
Lost Without Your Love, 1977
Anthology, 1985 (previously released material)
Retrospective, 1996 (previously released material)
Essentials, 1996 (previously released material)

SEE ALSO: Byrds, The; Eddy, Duane; Haggard, Merle; Holly, Buddy / The Crickets; Monkees, The; Ronstadt, Linda; Simon and Garfunkel; Sinatra, Frank.

Garth Brooks

BORN: Tulsa, Oklahoma; February 7, 1962
FIRST SINGLE RELEASE: "Much Too Young (to Feel This Damn Old)," 1989
MUSICAL STYLES: Country, country rock, pop

Garth Brooks revolutionized country music in 1989 by bringing it to a mass audience for the first time. Without sacrificing basic country music themes and styles, he brought to his live performances the theatrics of 1970's arena rock shows. He shattered country record sales expectations with his several multiple-million-selling albums. He has crossed over into the pop music charts time after time and become both the best-selling artist and the largest audience draw in the United States.

Oklahoma Days. Troyal Garth Brooks's parents played and sang country music; in fact, his mother had a brief career as a professional singer. His parents' favorite singers were Merle Haggard and George Jones, whose styles impressed Brooks, as did the music of George Strait. In the 1960's and 1970's, Brooks listened to many other styles of music that would influence his later style, songwriting, and performances. Singer-songwriters James Taylor, Dan Fogelberg, and Billy Joel were favorites, and Brooks became encouraged to start writing songs that expressed inner feelings and conflicts.

Growing up in the town of Yukon, Oklahoma, near Tulsa, Brooks became a good athlete and won a scholarship to Oklahoma State University, where he majored in advertising and marketing. While in college he sang in local clubs and put together a band. He learned to develop a wide repertoire for his young audiences: some country, some rock, and some introspective material. He went to Nashville in 1985 to try to break into country music but within a day returned to Oklahoma, having quickly been rejected.

Back to Nashville. Brooks married and remained determined to succeed in Nashville, the center of modern country music. He went back in 1987 and persevered. He worked in a footwear store while writing songs, meeting other young writers trying to enter the business, and going to studios making demonstration tapes. Singing his own "If Tomorrow Never Comes" in a songwriter's club, he helped convince executives at Capitol Records to sign him to the label in 1988.

Brooks arrived in Nashville at a fortunate time. Since the mid-1980's, country music had started to move back to some of its roots, after a decade when the music had become diluted by a tendency to copy the mannerisms of pop music (with lush strings, overproduced songs, and a move away from country's more serious themes). Performers such as George Strait, Ricky Skaggs, Randy Travis, Dwight Yoakam, the Judds, and Reba McEntire had started to return to basics in instrumentation (such as bringing back steel guitars and fiddles) and in hard-edged songs. These artists were called new traditionalists. In 1989, these types of singers began to win attention in the industry, namely Brooks, Clint Black, Alan Jackson, and Travis Tritt. Several of them decided to wear cowboy hats as they performed. This style had not been common in recent decades, but Strait and Yoakam started a trend. The singers who broke out around 1989 were labeled the "Class of '89," and their penchant for wearing hats led to them being termed "hat acts."

Brooks Expands Country Music. Brooks's first single, "Much Too Young (to Feel This Damn Old)," which he cowrote, was a classic rodeo type of song common in the Southwest. It did well on the country charts, but it was his second single of 1989, "If Tomorrow Never Comes," another song he cowrote, that was his first number 1 country hit. His 1989 album (featuring these two songs) was called simply *Garth Brooks* and became a top seller that crossed over to the pop charts, making the Top 20. It has since sold in the multiple millions. Of all the singles released from this first album, the blockbuster song was "The Dance." It became Brooks's "career" song. One line captures the song's essence: "I could have missed the pain, but I'd have had to miss the dance." The country music industry had just started to sense the value of music videos (long after rock acts had), especially with the new cable channel The Nashville Network (TNN) airing by the mid-1980's. Brooks, trained in marketing, eagerly used videos to his advantage. "If Tomorrow Never Comes" had been a successful debut, but the video for "The Dance" stunned, expanding the meaning of the song beyond the idea of taking a chance on love to offer glimpses of national heroes who had died, making the theme of the song universal and profound.

Brooks's second album, *No Fences*, was released in 1990 and peaked at number 1 on the country charts and number 3 on the pop charts. Four number 1 country hits came from it, the most notable of which were the rocking "Friends in Low Places," about a man driven by an un-

Garth Brooks (Paul Natkin)

happy relationship to go carousing, and "The Thunder Rolls," a story song about a cheating husband who has to face his wife after being with another woman. The atmosphere of a storm and the sound effects on the recording increase the doom-laden feeling. The video, however, was banned on country channels because it added a graphic depiction of a verse Brooks (who cowrote the song) had omitted from the recording, in which the wronged wife shoots her returning husband while their daughter looks on. The video also indicated that the wife was abused by her husband. This music video raised Brooks's national profile higher than ever and showed him to be an outspoken figure. Accused of sensationalism, he forthrightly said that the song was a message about the dangers of adultery and the horrors of wife beating. Indeed, country music had entered a new era of explicit social and moral commentary in the hands of a superstar who had crossed over musically into the pop charts and who was quickly becoming a cross-cultural force as well.

Making History. With his third album, *Ropin' the Wind* in 1991, and his fourth, *The Chase* in 1992, Brooks made more country music history. These albums debuted at number 1 on both the country and pop charts. Both sold in the multiple millions. These albums continued the pattern for several singles to reach number 1 on the country charts. Brooks's music videos were packaged and sold as a home video that became a best-seller, quickly exceeding half a million sales. In early 1992 he had his own television special that was one of the top ten programs of the week, with twenty-eight million viewers. His album *In Pieces* (1993) and his collection of best-sellers, *The Hits* (1994), became number 1 sellers on both charts. Clearly, Brooks was the crossover artist of his time. He had become in a few short years the most popular singer in American music. Even if his fifth album, *Fresh Horses* (1995), did not sell quite as well as the previous ones, it still went to number 1 (country) and number 2 (pop).

As a live performer, Brooks was a sensation. Wearing a cordless headset microphone, he was able to move all over the stage without being

---

For the Record

In May, 1998, Brooks's boxed set of his first six albums (with six new songs) debuted at number 1 (country and pop). By this time, he had sold in excess of seventy million albums, making him one of the three all-time top sellers of records, along with the Beatles and Elvis Presley.

---

hampered by microphone stands or extended cords. His stage show was modeled on the arena rock shows of the 1970's and 1980's—a new dimension for country acts. Flashing lights, smoke, and Brooks held by wires rising onto the stage from an elevator and catapulting over the audience made his road shows spectacular sold-out events. By 1997, he was the U.S. top grossing act in show business. His tours outside the United States were equally successful, particularly in Ireland. This excitement was captured on the home video of his massive New York's Central Park show in August, 1997.

Brooks's Music. Brooks's success was attributable to a variety of factors. Country acts were successful on the pop music charts in the 1990's partly because *Billboard*, the leading magazine of the music business, changed its rating methods by using a more accurate system based on actual bar-code data on albums sold. Country music proved more popular across the nation than had been noticed before, when more casual data-gathering methods focused on a limited number of record stores and not on popular retail chains, such as Wal-Mart, where the bulk of country music sales are made. Brooks himself was the main reason country music became popular. His savvy business sense and demand for almost complete control over his music was unique. His outgoing and warm, outspoken personality made him a media favorite.

The heart of his success really lay in his voice, the instrumentation and production of his sound and records, and his song selection. His voice revealed his Oklahoma heritage. Like many other singers with roots in that state or in Texas, he had little of the twang or nasal tones found in singers from the southeastern United States, qualities which are often unpopular with audiences unfamiliar with country singing. His drawling, warm, light baritone voice could be intimate and relaxed. Varying the register and timbre of his voice to suit the lyrics, he could sing meditative or introspective songs just as well as rocking and raucous tunes.

His instrumental sound would rely mostly on traditional country lineups. His band could accompany his voice without overpowering it. Although the production of his records reflects all the modern conveniences of multiple-track processes and refinements, the soundscape featured steel guitar, electric guitar, fiddle, piano, and harmony singing in the choruses (sometimes with fellow country star Trisha Yearwood, sometimes with his own overdubbed voice), as well as the occasional Dobro, mandolin, or acoustic guitar solo.

In his choice of songs, Brooks was a master of country traditions and at the same time embodied the changes in American music since the rise of rock and roll, the 1960's folk revival, and the advent of the singer-songwriter. Brooks has written or cowritten most of his songs, using many of the same writers and cowriters for all of his albums. He has recorded several rodeo songs, such as "Rodeo," "Wild Horses," and "The Beaches of Cheyenne." Some of these are also story songs or have a strongly implied narrative—a characteristic of many country songs that are not full or detailed narratives. For story songs as such, Brooks has recorded "The Thunder Rolls," "The Cowboy Song," and "That Ol' Wind." His rocking fast songs are justly live favorites: "Friends in Low Places," "Dixie Chicken," and "Rollin'." Several of these use a style called western swing, derived from Bob Wills and his jazz, big-band, and blues style.

Brooks can very effectively sing slow, quiet, and contemplative songs of lost love and tension between sweethearts: "Unanswered Prayer," "Same Old Story," and "That Ol' Wind." A few of these feature some harder honky-tonk stylings as Brooks builds a song's intensity to the end; others remain wistful throughout with delicate instrumental work. He has also performed inspirational songs such as "We Shall Be Free," "If Tomorrow Never Comes," and "The River." Brooks has remained inside country music's traditional themes with finely crafted songs and a voice that can attract the widest audience. Not since Johnny Cash was at his peak in the late 1960's has country music seen such an artist who can cross over to a mass general audience.

A Superstar Endures. In 1997 Brooks played to more than half a million people in New York's Central Park at no charge. Broadcast on cable television, the show reached millions more and has since become a top-selling home video. In 1997 every one of his ninety-eight shows sold out, making him the top country act. His 1997 album *Sevens* sold in the millions and produced hit singles such as "She's Gonna Make It" and "Two Piña Coladas." In 1998, Brooks sold out concerts again with crowds ranging from forty to fifty thousand at each show, continuing his stature as a country phenomenon.

—*Frederick E. Danker*

SELECT DISCOGRAPHY

■ ALBUMS
Garth Brooks, 1989
No Fences, 1990
Ropin' the Wind, 1991
The Chase, 1992
In Pieces, 1993
Fresh Horses, 1995
Sevens, 1997
Double Live, 1998

SELECT AWARDS
Country Music Association Music Video of the Year for "The Dance" and Horizon Awards, 1990
Grammy Award for Best Country Vocal Performance, Male, for *Ropin' the Wind,* 1991
Country Music Association Album of the Year for *No Fences,* Single of the Year for "Friends in Low Places," Music Video of the Year for "The Thunder Rolls," and Entertainer of the Year Awards, 1991

Country Music Association Album of the Year for *Ropin' the Wind* and Entertainer of the Year Awards, 1992

Grammy Award for Best Country Collaboration with Vocals for "In Another's Eyes," 1997 (with Trisha Yearwood)

SEE ALSO: Haggard, Merle; Joel, Billy; Jones, George; Strait, George; Taylor, James; Wills, Bob, and His Texas Playboys; Yearwood, Trisha.

Brooks and Dunn

ORIGINAL MEMBERS: Leon Eric "Kix" Brooks III (b. 1955), Ronnie Gene Dunn (b. 1953)
FIRST SINGLE RELEASE: "Brand New Man," 1990
MUSICAL STYLES: Country, country rock, progressive country

Former solo acts Ronnie Dunn and Kix Brooks spent twenty years entertaining in clubs and bars before being teamed up by Tim DuBois, the head of Arista Records. Previously performing as opening acts for such music greats as Reba McEntire and Alabama, their own career began to take off in 1990. Brooks and Dunn's dynamic success has been compared to a musical rocket ride. After just seven years together, their five albums had sold more than fourteen million copies, thirteen of their singles had risen to number 1 on the music charts, and they had been presented with more than twenty major music industry awards.

Early Years. Kix Brooks was born and raised in Shreveport, Louisiana, and made his musical debut at the age of twelve, singing with Johnny Horton's daughter. He continued singing and songwriting throughout high school. After graduating, he worked on the Alaska pipeline, which was completed in 1977. However, his desire for success in the music business eventually led him to Nashville, Tennessee, where he joined Tree Publishing. Many of the songs he cowrote proved successful for artists such as John Conlee ("I'm Only in It for the Love," 1983) and Highway 101 ("Who's Lonely Now?" 1990); some even reached number 1 on the country charts. Brooks's first

solo recording experience was in 1983 with "Baby, When Your Heart Breaks Down," which made the Top 75. His second solo release, *Kix Brooks*, was in 1989. That same year his single "Sacred Ground" made the Top 90.

Ronnie Dunn was born in Coleman, Texas, but his family later moved to Tulsa, Oklahoma. He learned to play bass in high school and later studied psychiatry and religion in college, with intentions of becoming a Baptist preacher. Instead, his love of music led him to a recording contract with the Churchill label, where he had two Top-60 solo hits, "It's Written All Over Your Face" in 1983 and "She Put the Sad in All Her Songs" in 1984. Dunn won a regional Marlboro talent contest in Tulsa because one of his friends secretly entered a tape of his music. He eventually went to the finals in Nashville, where he won thirty thousand dollars and a recording session with Scott Hendricks, one of Music City's biggest producers. Hendricks provided Tim DuBois of Arista with Dunn's new material. When Dunn returned to Nashville, he joined Tree Publishing, where he met Kix Brooks. They not only wrote songs together, but they began singing as a duo as well. Impressed by their sound and their approach to music, DuBois offered them a recording contract.

The Legend Begins. Brooks and Dunn's first single, "Brand New Man," released in 1990, rapidly rose to number 1 on the country music charts. Their follow-up number 1 country single, "My Next Broken Heart," is the first song the duo wrote together. In 1991, their debut album, *Brand New Man*, was an instant success. Their single "Neon Moon" skyrocketed to country's number 1 spot in 1992. The flip side, "Boot Scootin' Boogie," which won the 1992 Single Record of the Year Award from the Academy of Country Music (ACM) and launched a dance by the same name, has been their best-selling single to date. The duo's second album, *Hard Workin' Man*, released in 1993, received the Album of the Year Award from the ACM. Certified triple platinum, their third album, *Waitin' on Sundown*, was released in 1994. Feeling comfortable with their careers, they decided to depart slightly from their traditional country and country-rock sound and head into progressive country on their fourth album, *Border-line* (1996). When Brooks and producer Don Cook suggested they include a remake of the B. W. Stevenson hit "My Maria" on the album, Dunn was somewhat hesitant. He felt that doing covers is an indication one's career has peaked and is on a downhill slide. With strong encouragement by Brooks and Cook, the song was recorded and included on the album. Although it took tremendous concentration for Dunn, he successfully slid his rich voice into the falsetto-heavy chorus of "My Maria," which was released in 1997. Their fifth album, *The Greatest Hits Collection*, released in 1997, contains sixteen hits from their first four albums, plus three new songs: "Honky Tonk Truth," "He's Got You," and "Days of Thunder." As a rule, most of the songs on Brooks and Dunn's albums were written by one or both of them.

Although the blending of their vocal and instrumental talents contributes largely to their success, the parity seems to end with their love of music. On stage their individual personalities shine through. Just as Dunn positions himself in one spot and rarely moves, Brooks rambles energetically across the stage and rarely stays in one spot. After a couple of falls during performances, Brooks needed stitches, not realizing he was injured until the show was over. The two credit their individual styles in part to the influence of artists Johnny Horton, Bruce Springsteen, and Dwight Yoakam.

For a period of time, it seemed as if the continued success of Brooks and Dunn was in jeopardy. In 1995, Dunn was plagued by a sinus condition that affected his singing and threatened to worsen, thereby ending his career as a vocal artist. Fortunately, his problems were corrected by surgery. This experience reinforced the duo's belief that success cannot be taken for granted.

Extended Creativity. Not only are Brooks and Dunn outstanding performers and talented singer-songwriters; they are also fashion design-

Brooks and Dunn in 1996 (Archive Photos/Scott Harrison)

ers, car dealers, and writers. They designed the trademark flame shirt for manufacturer Panhandle Slim, which has become one of the best-selling styles in western wear.

Their attention to style and detail extends to their business and leisure interest in Legends race cars. Brooks and Dunn own the Tennessee sales rights for these $^5/8$-scale fiberglass full-fendered versions of the famed National Association for Stock Car Auto Racing (NASCAR) modifieds.

Their talent as writers is evident in the Howdy and Slim saga, which they began including in the liner notes of their first album. The two hard-riding cowboys represent Brooks's and Dunn's alter egos. In the *Brand New Man* album, Slim (Dunn) asks Howdy (Brooks), "What say we ride together for a piece . . . see what we turn up?" Judging from all of their awards and multi-platinum albums, Brooks and Dunn turned up "another day ridin' the trail of dreams."

—*Elizabeth B. Graham*

SELECT DISCOGRAPHY
■ ALBUMS
Brand New Man, 1991
Hard Workin' Man, 1993
Waitin' on Sundown, 1994
Borderline, 1996
The Greatest Hits Collection, 1997 (compilation)
If You See Her, 1998

SELECT AWARDS
Academy of Country Music New Vocal Duet or Group of the Year and Vocal Duet of the Year Awards, 1991
Academy of Country Music Album of the Year for *Brand New Man*, Single Record of the

---

🎸 **For the Record**

As a part of the Kellogg's cereal company's promotion of the Legends race cars in 1996, Brooks's and Dunn's image appeared on twenty million boxes of Kellogg's Corn Flakes.

Year for "Boot Scootin' Boogie," and Best Vocal Duet Awards, 1992
Country Music Association Vocal Duo of the Year Award, 1992, 1993, 1995, 1997
Grammy Award for Best Country Performance by a Duo or Group with Vocal for "Hard Workin' Man," 1993
Academy of Country Music Best Vocal Duet Award, 1993, 1994, 1995
Country Music Association Album of the Year for *Common Thread: The Songs of the Eagles* (with others) and Vocal Duo of the Year Awards, 1994
Country Music Association Entertainer of the Year and Vocal Duo of the Year Awards, 1996
Grammy Award for Best Country Performance by a Duo or Group with Vocal for "My Maria," 1996
Academy of Country Music Entertainer of the Year and Best Vocal Duet Awards, 1996, 1997

SEE ALSO: Alabama; McEntire, Reba; Springsteen, Bruce; Yoakam, Dwight.

Bobby Brown. *See* New Edition / Bobby Brown

James Brown

BORN: Barnwell, South Carolina; May 3, 1933
FIRST SINGLE RELEASE: "Please, Please, Please," 1956 (with the Flames)
FIRST ALBUM RELEASE: *Please, Please, Please*, 1959 (with the Flames)
MUSICAL STYLES: Soul, funk, rhythm and blues, rock, disco, pop, rap

James Brown combined pop, rhythm and blues, and traditional gospel music to produce his distinctive musical style, a style which was to earn him the title "Godfather of Soul." Although his first single release was followed by nine less spectacular releases, Brown's 1962 live album, *The James Brown Show Live at the Apollo*, would become one of the most successful and influential albums of the twentieth century. Indeed, by 1964, Brown had become one of the most popular musicians in the world. Although his popularity waned in the 1970's, he was to stage an important comeback in the 1980's.

The Beginnings. James Joe Brown, Jr., was born in a one-room cabin near Barnwell, South Carolina, on May 3, 1933. His parents separated when he was four years old, his mother leaving him in the care of his father. Because his father worked in the turpentine camps, Brown spent much of his early childhood alone. Shortly after his separation, Brown's father was forced to move to Augusta, Georgia, to look for employment. He left his son in the care of two aunts, Minnie Walker and Hansome (Honey) Washington, who lived on Twiggs Street in Augusta. Brown's Aunt Honey ran a house that specialized in moonshine, gambling, and prostitution. When Brown was seven years old, his Aunt Honey told him that someday the world would hear about him. She undoubtedly recognized the talent and determination to succeed which would carry Brown to wealth and fame.

Although Joe Brown did not live with his son, he maintained close contact and profoundly influenced James's life. James learned to play the harmonica and the guitar at an early age. Then Joe Brown bought him an old, battered organ which he propped up on fruit crates in the front yard. Brown learned to play the organ in one day, entertaining the whole neighborhood with his apparent musical talent. Unfortunately, Brown's childhood was marred by poverty. He was often sent home from school because he did not have shoes or proper clothing. In order to survive, he shined shoes, picked cotton, washed cars, and sang and danced for troops arriving at nearby Camp Gordon. After Brown's father entered the service during World War II, the allotment check sent to his family enabled them to survive. When he was eleven years old, Brown performed at Augusta's Lenox Theater's Amateur Night, winning first prize.

As an adolescent, Brown delivered bootleg liquor, stole car parts, and committed other petty crimes. He was apprehended and jailed, and soon after he turned sixteen, he was tried and given an extremely harsh prison sentence of eight to sixteen years. Consequently, he was taken to the Georgia Juvenile Training Institute in Rome, Georgia. Brown's life in prison was not entirely unhappy. He served as a pitcher for the inmates' baseball team, and he sang and formed several bands in which he played the piano, earning the nickname "Music Box." After two years, the prison relocated to Toccoa, Georgia, where Brown met and befriended a local athlete and musician, Bobby Byrd. At the age of nineteen, with the support of the Byrd family, Brown was paroled and given a job at Lawson's Motor Company. While living in Toccoa, Brown played in a local band and sang in the church choir. On June 19, 1953, he married Velma Warren. The couple were to have three sons, Teddy, Terry, and Larry.

Prior to his marriage, Brown and Byrd formed a band, the Flames, which included Sylvester Keels, Doyle Oglesby, Fred Pulliam, Nash Knox, and Roy Scott. Over the next few years, Brown and the Flames began a series of one-night engagements throughout Georgia and neighboring states, playing at a number of southern colleges and universities. In 1955, Brown and the Flames even upstaged Little Richard, who was playing an engagement at Bill's Rendezvous Club in Toccoa. They made such an impression that Clint Brantley, Little Richard's agent, helped Brown and the Flames relocate to Macon, Georgia, where they played a number of Little Richard's former nightclubs. Ralph Bass saw one of Brown's performances near Milledgeville, Georgia, and offered the group a recording contract with King Records.

Recording Career. In 1956, Brown and the Flames drove to Cincinnati to record "Please, Please, Please," their first single release, a record which eventually sold one million copies. Syd Nathan, owner of the recording company, did not like Brown's style and sound. At first, Nathan refused to release "Please, Please, Please," but Brown finally persuaded him to take a chance on the record. It was finally released by a subsidiary of King known as Federal Records. Nine other singles, such as "Why Do You Do Me?," "I Feel That

Old Feeling Coming On," and "No, No, No," followed in rapid succession, but none was a chart-topping hit. Nevertheless, Brown continued touring in the late 1950's, developing and refining his act. In 1957, Ben Bart, founder of Universal Attractions, brought Brown and the Flames to the New York area for a series of performances. Bart was to become Brown's manager and promoter, billing the group as James Brown and his Famous Flames. The original Flames disbanded, in part because of this billing decision, but Brown had really been the star of the show from the beginning. Brown recorded "Try Me" (1958), a single which combined rhythm and blues with a gospel-edged plea and which was to become Brown's first immediate hit. As Syd Nathan was reluctant to record and release this new single, Brown and Brantley agreed to underwrite the recording them-

James Brown (Library of Congress)

selves. By December, 1958, "Try Me" was number 1 on the rhythm-and-blues chart and was in the Top 50 on the pop chart.

In January of 1959, King released the *Please, Please, Please* album and Brown signed new contracts with both King Records and Universal Attractions. Brown and the Flames, members of which often changed, played a number of one-night performances which ended with a series at New York's Apollo Theatre. During his series of appearances at the Apollo, Brown's performing routine reached its final form, including his encore appearance in a cape, a routine borrowed from the wrestler known as Gorgeous George. He also reestablished his relationship with his mother, who now lived in New York, and he visited her whenever he performed in New York City. Between 1959 and 1962, Brown continued to record both singles and albums while touring the

United States and often performing at the Apollo. In late 1962, Brown suggested recording a live album of one of his performances at the Apollo Theatre. Nathan opposed the idea, but Brown finally persuaded him to record and release *The James Brown Show Live at the Apollo* (1963), an album which quickly topped the charts and made recording history by remaining on the best-seller charts for sixty-six weeks. Brown's band became a full-fledged orchestra, appearing with Brown on the Teen-Age Music International (TAMI) show as Brown upstaged the Rolling Stones. During this appearance, in 1964, Brown announced the arrival of funk, a revolutionary and decisive shift in musical rhythm. In 1964, Brown also made his film debut, appearing in Frankie Avalon's *Ski Party*. By 1965, Brown had become one of the most popular musicians in the United States, adding songs such as "I Got You," "Out of Sight," and "Papa's Got a

Brand New Bag," his first international hit, to his long list of chart-topping singles.

During the 1960's, Brown became involved in public issues, specifically in support of the Civil Rights movement. He integrated concerts in Macon and Augusta, Georgia, and took a lifetime membership in the National Association for the Advancement of Colored People (NAACP), becoming a personal friend and supporter of civil rights leader Roy Wilkins. On April 5, 1968, Brown agreed to perform a concert which was televised in Boston and Washington, D.C., in an attempt to stem the threat of violence in the wake of Martin Luther King, Jr.'s assassination. In the latter part of the 1960's, Brown worked with Vice President Hubert Humphrey in a campaign which urged students to stay in school and encouraged others to return to school for equivalency diplomas. In addition to writing and recording "Don't Be a Drop-Out," he personally visited schools and talked with young students. In early 1968, Brown visited the Ivory Coast for a brief performing tour (a visit to Africa which he was to repeat in the following years). Upon his return, President Lyndon Johnson invited Brown to dinner at the White House, an event which was soon followed by Brown's tour of Vietnam.

The Godfather of Soul. The evolution of Brown's music into funk coupled with his political activities earned him several titles: "Soul Brother Number One," "Grand Minister of Funk," and "Godfather of Soul." In 1968, Brown released two important and controversial singles. Many African Americans criticized his recording "America Is My Home" for what they considered Brown's unqualified support of the United States government during an era when many American citizens were protesting the Vietnam War. Brown recorded "America Is My Home" in May, 1968, followed by "Say It Loud, I'm Black and I'm Proud" in August of that year. Another storm of criticism followed the August release, as white Americans labeled it militant and angry; nevertheless, "Say It Loud" was number 1 on the rhythm-and-blues charts by October.

Brown became one of the most successful black entrepreneurs in the United States. In 1968,

For the Record

"When I do music, I include a lot of people, but nobody's really involved except myself. Just God and me. I guess I'm like Einstein—let 'em worry about my theory after I'm dead."

§

"What you should do is give people more than their money's worth. Make them tired 'cause that's what they came for. Anytime you can go out and work for an hour and make $10, $15, $40, $100,000 as opposed to a man workin' 13 hours, 10 hours a day and makin' $75, you've been blessed. You owe those people something. And I wear uniforms so that you know you came to see a show—not to see somebody look like you look on the street."

—*James Brown*

Brown bought three radio stations (within a few years he was to own five). The following year he purchased a franchise and opened two Gold Platter restaurants in Macon, Georgia. By this time, he owned a fleet of cars, a huge home in Queens, New York, and a $713,000 Lear jet. He recorded a number of singles, half of another live album, *Sex Machine* (1970), and ended the year with a concert at the Apollo. He divorced his first wife, and in October of 1969 he married Dierdre Jenkins. The couple had two daughters, Deanna and Yamma.

The Internal Revenue Service began investigating Brown's income in the 1970's, specifically targeting the cash payments he received for his live concerts. The investigation of Brown's tax obligations became a nagging problem that was to follow the entertainer for the next two decades. Added to Brown's troubles was the death of Ben Bart, his friend and business associate. In 1970, Brown toured parts of Europe and Africa once again, being especially warmly received in the Ivory Coast, Zambia, and Congo (Zaire). In the early 1970's, Brown's recording success continued with the release of the *Sex Machine* album and singles such as "Hot Pants" (1971) and "Talking Loud and Saying Nothing" (1972). Unfortunately, this success was short-lived as Brown faced conflict with his new recording company, Polydor. Polydor expected Brown to sound like a disco artist, a style to which he did not relate. He began a television series, *Future Shock*, which aired from 1974 to 1976, but his record sales declined, and there were lawsuits against his radio stations. He was also hurt by the untimely death of his oldest son, Teddy, in an automobile accident in 1973.

The Comeback. Brown began a comeback in the 1980's. He appeared on television variety shows such as *Saturday Night Live, Solid Gold*, and *American Bandstand*, but his role as the preacher in the film *The Blues Brothers* in 1980 really brought him before the American public once more. He recorded "Rapp Payback (Where Iz Moses?)," a record which mixed rap and funk in 1980. In February, 1982, he met Adrienne Rodriguez, the woman who was to become his third wife. In 1986, Brown appeared in the film *Rocky IV*. The music video which appeared in the film contained a new song, "Living in America," which catapulted Brown to the forefront of the music scene once again.

Brown's fame and good fortune were not to continue, however, for he was arrested on September 24, 1988. According to police reports, Brown had entered an insurance seminar in an office adjacent to his own in Augusta, Georgia. Upon entering the office, Brown brandished a shotgun and accused the audience of using his restroom without permission. Brown then resisted arrest by trying to escape in his pickup, crossing the state line from Georgia into South Carolina, where his sixty-two-acre homesite was located. He was apprehended and brought to trial on seven misdemeanor charges. He was sentenced to serve two concurrent six-year terms in a South Carolina prison. There were also allegations of illegal drug use, but Brown denied that he had used PCP or any other illegal drug. On February 27, 1991, he was paroled after twenty-six months and staged a very successful pay-per-view cable special. Brown

was welcomed home by his wife, Adrienne, but his personal life remained stormy, with continuing allegations of domestic abuse and illegal drug use. A final tragedy occurred on January 6, 1996, when Brown's wife, Adrienne, died of an accidental drug overdose following liposuction surgery.

Legacy. James Brown created an artistic legacy that is unparalleled in American music history. With his mid-1960's hits "Out of Sight" and "Papa's Got a Brand New Bag," Brown introduced totally new rhythmic conceptions to the American music scene. His creative rhythmic shifts provided the foundation not only for funk but also for disco and rap. In addition, his vocal and dance innovations have influenced performers such as Mick Jagger and Michael Jackson. From 1960 to 1977, each of his records reached the music charts. He has written and composed most of his one hundred hits. His recordings and his dynamic performances made him the number 1 rhythm-and-blues box-office attraction in the country for two decades. In 1986, he was inducted into the Rock and Roll Hall of Fame, and in 1992 he received the Grammy Award for Lifetime Achievement for his contributions to the field of music. In 1993, a street in Augusta, Georgia, was named in his honor. Brown would remain active on the music scene into his sixties, being a motivated performer who provides inspiration and encouragement for younger musicians.   —*Yvonne Johnson*

SELECT DISCOGRAPHY
■ SINGLES
"Please, Please, Please," 1956 (with the Flames)
"Try Me," 1958
"You've Got the Power," 1960
"Out of Sight," 1964
"Papa's Got a Brand New Bag," 1965
"I Got You (I Feel Good)," 1965
"Cold Sweat," 1967
"Say It Loud, I'm Black and I'm Proud," 1968
"Hot Pants," 1971
"Talking Loud and Saying Nothing," 1972
"Living in America," 1986
■ ALBUMS
The James Brown Show Live at the Apollo, 1963
Papa's Got a Brand New Bag, 1965

I Got You (I Feel Good), 1966
Say It Loud, I'm Black and I'm Proud, 1969
Sex Machine, 1970
Hot Pants, 1971
The Payback, 1974
Body Heat, 1976
The Original Disco Man, 1979
Bring It On! 1983
Roots of a Revolution, 1989
The Greatest Hits of the Fourth Decade, 1992
    (compilation)
Soul Pride: The Instrumentals (1960-1969), 1993
    (compilation)

SELECT AWARDS
Grammy Award for Best R&B Recording for
    "Papa's Got a Brand New Bag," 1965
Grammy Award for Best R&B Recording, Male,
    for "Living in America," 1986
Grammy Award for Lifetime Achievement, 1992

SEE ALSO: Clinton, George / Parliament / Funkadelic; Franklin, Aretha; Redding, Otis; Wilson, Jackie.

Jackson Browne

BORN: Heidelberg, West Germany; October, 9 1948
FIRST ALBUM RELEASE: *Jackson Browne,* 1972
MUSICAL STYLES: Folk, rock and roll

Clyde Jackson Browne was born in Heidelberg, Germany, where his father was stationed as an Army journalist. When he was around the age of three the family relocated to Southern California. In time, Browne's songs would help form the core of the "L.A. sound" that dominated radio and the music business in the early 1970's. A proficient pianist and guitarist by his late teens, Browne found himself in demand as a backup player after moving to New York. He accompanied Tim Buckley and the Velvet Underground's Nico before returning to Los Angeles. Nico recorded several of his tunes on her 1968 album *Chelsea Girl.*

Browne concentrated on writing rather than performing. His songs were soon being recorded by Tom Rush (who also figured in boosting the early careers of Joni Mitchell and James Taylor), Johnny Rivers, and the Nitty Gritty Dirt Band. He did not begin recording until the 1970's, when he became the first artist signed by the newly formed Asylum label run by David Geffen. "Singer-songwriters" were very much in vogue at the time, in the wake of Bob Dylan's combining the lyrical complexity of folk music with rock sounds and styles in the late 1960's. Browne's first album, *Jackson Browne* (often referred to as "Saturate Before Using," as this phrase appears on the cover), was released in 1972.

Unlike many of his peers, Jackson Browne enjoyed chart success right away. "Doctor My Eyes" from his first album was a Top-10 hit. "Rock Me on the Water," with vocal harmonies by David Crosby, also received significant airplay. Also in 1972 Geffen labelmates the Eagles released a version of his "Take It Easy" (cowritten with Eagle Glenn Frey) that landed in the Top 20. These early successes, as well as versions of his tunes recorded by artists including the Byrds, Bonnie Raitt, Linda Ronstadt, and Richie Havens, took the pressure of creating follow-up hits off Browne.

Browne's songs use nature imagery and metaphoric constructions to make their points. Singing frequently of water, wind, earth, and sky, Browne seemed to be in touch with the natural world. Also appropriating "the road" as a symbol in numerous tunes, he never fully let go of his connections with the everyday world of being a working musician.

The Archetypal Singer-Songwriter. In creating songs for his subsequent releases, Browne was never rushed. As a result, he always recorded well-crafted, lyrically expressive songs. Until the late 1970's Browne's chief strengths lay in songs describing his emotional experiences, relationships with women, and the natural world. On the 1973 album *For Everyman,* the title track ponders both apocalypse and utopia in the possibility of withdrawing from the rigors of everyday life. *Late for the Sky* (1974) included "Before the Deluge," about trying to protect the earth from ecological disaster and about the earth's revenge against her abusers. *Late for the Sky* is often cited as Browne's

Jackson Browne in the mid-1970's (Archive Photos/John Platt Collection)

best album. Though considered a solo artist, Browne enjoyed important support from multi-instrumentalist David Lindley in the mid-1970's. On his recordings and on tour, Lindley's lap-steel guitar in particular did much to create the sound that was unmistakably Browne's. They went their separate ways after a while but reunited for benefit shows in the 1980's and at least one acoustic tour in the 1990's.

A number of songs from this time document the unfolding intimacy of a love relationship in full bloom. It was in these songs that Browne most plainly bared his soul. Browne's partner at the time, Phyllis Major, no doubt taught him many of the lessons he shared in song. Their relationship produced Browne's first son, Ethan (born in 1973), and then a life-defining tragedy: Major committed suicide when Ethan was three. The impact of this event showed clearly in his next release, *The Pretender*, produced in 1976 by Jon Landau. Much of this album was downbeat, introspective, and understandably depressing, which earned him the nickname "Jackson Bummer" in some circles. However, he shook off the doldrums in 1978 with a live album, *Running on Empty*, which charted two Top-20 tunes, the title track and "The

Load Out/Stay." The album was recorded at shows, in hotel rooms on the road, and even on the tour bus while traveling between shows.

Browne closed out the decade playing an instrumental role in the activist organization Musicians United for Safe Energy (MUSE). This group staged a series of "No Nukes" benefit concerts at New York's Madison Square Garden and a rally in the city's Battery Park to raise funds and awareness for the crusade against nuclear power. Other participants included Bonnie Raitt, Bruce Springsteen, James Taylor, Carly Simon, Gil Scott-Heron, and Crosby, Stills, and Nash. The multirecord album and film of these shows document the music onstage, the organization backstage, and the situation that prompted the artists' concern. After making a career of looking inward, Browne found himself possessed of a more global vision and the luxury of following up his convictions with action. The 1980's would be a more activist decade.

The 1980's and 1990's. The activism did not take anything away from his popular momentum. Browne's 1980 album *Hold Out* went to number 1 on the strength of the single "Boulevard," about life on L.A.'s Sunset Boulevard and other city streets. The album was followed by the inclusion of his pop song "Somebody's Baby" on the sound track of the film *Fast Times at Ridgemont High*, which peaked at number 7 on the charts. About this time Browne married again, but the relationship did not last. It did, however, produce his second son, Ryan (born in 1982). Now a concerned father, Browne became more involved in seeking a secure future for the next generation. In addition to his antinuclear work, Browne assisted Amnesty International on its 1986 Conspiracy of Hope tour. His records in this period directly expressed his political and social concerns, and they did not sell as well as his earlier records had. *Lawyers in Love* (1983) brought Browne into the music-video era. Songs on *Lives in the Balance* (1986) and *World in Motion* (1989) began to express his concern for the poor and oppressed in Central America as well as at home.

Browne's next album, *I'm Alive*, was released after a very messy and public breakup with his longtime companion, actress Daryl Hannah. The couple's relationship had long been a stormy one. The songs and his performances on tour supporting the record overtly celebrated his newfound sense of independence and liberty. Browne appeared at the Concert for the Rock and Roll Hall of Fame and Museum in Cleveland, performing Bob Marley's "Redemption Song." In 1996 *Looking East* struck an easy balance between personal and global concerns. In 1997 a "best-of" collection featuring two new songs and the first inclusion of "Somebody's Baby" on a Browne disc was released to celebrate twenty-five years of recording. In the 1980's and 1990's Browne's songs were covered by Joan Baez, Natalie Merchant, and Third World. Through the years Browne has also served as a producer, most notably producing records for David Lindley and Warren Zevon.

—*Paul D. Fischer*

SELECT DISCOGRAPHY
■ ALBUMS
Jackson Browne, 1972
For Everyman, 1973
Late for the Sky, 1974
The Pretender, 1976
Running on Empty, 1978
No Nukes, 1979 (with others)
Hold Out, 1980
Lawyers in Love, 1983
Lives in the Balance, 1986
World in Motion, 1989
I'm Alive, 1993
Looking East, 1996
The Next Voice You Hear: The Best of Jackson Browne, 1997

SELECT AWARDS
Amnesty International Spotlight Award, 1997

SEE ALSO: Eagles, The; Ronstadt, Linda.

Dave Brubeck

BORN: Concord, California; December 6, 1920
FIRST ALBUM RELEASE: *Distinctive Rhythm Instrumentals*, 1951 (with the Dave Brubeck Trio)
MUSICAL STYLES: Jazz, classical

Composer-pianist Dave Brubeck's emergence in the late 1940's helped revitalize jazz at a time when its popularity had dwindled following World War II. Brubeck's rhythmic and harmonic innovations and classically influenced improvisations brought an invigorating freshness to jazz. His style, despite protracted media criticism, captivated worldwide audiences in clubs, concert halls, and college campuses. The Dave Brubeck Quartet was one of the most popular of all musical groups in the 1950's and 1960's, producing the first million-selling instrumental jazz recording. That single, "Take Five," is but one highlight in a monumental career that would span more than half a century.

California. Brubeck's father was a ranch worker, his mother a piano teacher. When he was twelve, Brubeck and his parents moved from Concord, California, to a ranch near Ione, California. His two older brothers were at this time establishing themselves as music educators, but his father hoped at least one son would continue ranching. During his high school years, Brubeck was a ranch hand who found frequent opportunities to play piano professionally after the day's chores. Upon entering the College (now University) of the Pacific in Stockton, California, still torn between ranching and music, he began pursuing a veterinary degree. Steady piano work interfered with his studies, however, and he was advised to transfer to the conservatory of music. Despite being unable to read music, he graduated in June, 1942.

Brubeck then joined the army and was assigned to a band at a base in Riverside, California. Shortly after enlisting, he married Iola Whitlock, who became his lifelong partner. In 1944 Brubeck arrived in Europe under General George Patton's command. His musical ability spared him from imminent combat, as he was given leadership of a band that entertained battle-weary troops. He was discharged in 1946.

Octet, Trio, Quartet. Returning to California, Brubeck began studies in composition with French composer Darius Milhaud at Mills College in Oakland. Milhaud encouraged Brubeck to apply his experiments in rhythm and harmony to jazz. Brubeck had developed an aggressive, percussive technique, and he used combinations of chords from different keys and unusual time signatures, such as $5/4$, $7/4$, and $11/4$. Group composition lessons led to the formation of an octet, an early vehicle for Brubeck's creative expressions. The octet had few professional opportunities; Brubeck found solo and trio engagements, but his young family was struggling with little income.

Fortunately, San Francisco's entertainment industry was entering a postwar boom. The city was attracting a large share of the newcomers flocking to California, and live music and comedy were in great demand. In 1949, Brubeck's trio (piano, bass, drums) was booked into a club called the Blackhawk. The trio soon developed a large following, especially among college students, and the club became a magnet for them as well as musicians and celebrities. Nationwide recognition came in 1950, when the trio was named Best New Combo of the Year by both *Down Beat* and *Metronome* magazines. The Fantasy record label began at this time; its first recordings were of Brubeck's trio and octet.

In 1951, the trio broke up after Brubeck was seriously injured in a swimming accident that sidelined him for months. After recovering, he formed a new group, one that included alto saxophonist Paul Desmond. Desmond's smooth, lyrical style was a perfect complement to Brubeck, and the Dave Brubeck Quartet became an immediate success through its recordings and tours. It was a frequent first-place finisher in national polls.

In 1954, Brubeck appeared on the cover of *Time*, only the second jazz artist to be so honored. That same year he signed with Columbia Records, and the quartet recorded *Brubeck Time*, the first of fifty albums for Columbia. It sold 100,000 copies, unprecedented for a jazz release.

Many critics who had earlier been supporters of Brubeck then turned against him. His music was characterized as too intellectual and outside the jazz tradition. His piano playing was nothing like that of other pianists who were followers of the jazz style known as bebop. In comparison to other saxophonists, Desmond's unique sound was deemed too soft and polite. The quartet, however, continued to reap popular acclaim with every album and tour. Brubeck contended that he had not changed his artistic approach from previous years, during which he was not widely known but had been critically admired.

***Time Out* and Beyond.** In 1959, despite Columbia's objections to its all-original content, the album *Time Out* was released. It sold so well that two tracks, "Take Five" and "Blue Rondo à la Turk," were issued on a record in 1962. The single sold more than one million copies. Written in $5/4$ time, "Take Five" featured Brubeck's repetitive,

Dave Brubeck in 1959 (Columbia Legacy)

hypnotic piano and Desmond's minor-key, blues-inflected melody; "Blue Rondo à la Turk" is in $^9/_8$ time with a rhythm that Brubeck recalled hearing while touring in Turkey.

Drummer Joe Morello had become the quartet's drummer in 1956, and bassist Eugene Wright joined in 1958. With Brubeck and Desmond, this foursome, regarded as the classic Dave Brubeck Quartet, was intact until November of 1967, when they presented a farewell concert in Paris.

As Wright was African American, the group often encountered segregationist policies in its travels. Brubeck was often told that Wright could not perform with the quartet or be shown on camera during a telecast. Brubeck, who was himself about one-quarter Native American, had no tolerance for racism; the quartet would not perform unless such terms were revoked.

After the November, 1967, disbanding of the quartet, Brubeck returned home to rest and compose. His rest did not last long; early in 1968 he returned, leading a new quartet. With some lessening of activity, Brubeck would remain involved with a trio or quartet from then on. On several occasions in the 1970's, three of his sons, pianist Darius, bassist Chris, and drummer Danny, toured and recorded with him. A reduced schedule gave Brubeck the opportunity to compose large-scale classical works for orchestras and choirs; many of these works feature one version or another of the Dave Brubeck Quartet, one of music's most durable and influential ensembles. —*Mark W. Bolton*

SELECT DISCOGRAPHY
■ ALBUMS
Jazz at Oberlin, 1953
Brubeck Time, 1954
Dave Digs Disney, 1957
Dave Brubeck Plays and Plays and Plays, 1957
Jazz Impressions of Eurasia, 1958
Time Out, 1959
Time Further Out: Miro Reflections, 1961
The Real Ambassadors, 1961
Time In, 1966
Last Set at Newport, 1972
Two Generations of Brubeck, 1973
Dave Brubeck Quartet 25th Anniversary Reunion, 1976
Concord on a Summer's Night, 1982
Reflections, 1986
Time Signatures: A Career Retrospective, 1992 (4-CD boxed set)
Trio Brubeck, 1993
Young Lions and Old Tigers, 1995 (with others)

SELECT AWARDS
National Medal of Arts Award, 1994
Down Beat Hall of Fame, inducted 1994
Grammy Award for Lifetime Achievement, 1996In 1988, the Dave Brubeck Quartet, fresh from a tour of the Soviet Union in 1987, was invited to join the U.S. delegation attending a Moscow summit between President Ronald Reagan and Soviet leader Mikhail Gorbachev. The palpable tension between the two sides was broken by the quartet's spirited performance. Both American and Soviet diplomats cheered and tapped their feet to the beat. The shared appreciation of Brubeck's music helped make friends out of political enemies and may have helped saved the summit.

SEE ALSO: Cole, Nat "King"; Crusaders, The.

For the Record

In 1988, the Dave Brubeck Quartet, fresh from a tour of the Soviet Union in 1987, was invited to join the U.S. delegation attending a Moscow summit between President Ronald Reagan and Soviet leader Mikhail Gorbachev. The palpable tension between the two sides was broken by the quartet's spirited performance. Both American and Soviet diplomats cheered and tapped their feet to the beat. The shared appreciation of Brubeck's music helped make friends out of political enemies and may have helped save the summit.

Buffalo Springfield

ORIGINAL MEMBERS: Stephen Stills (b. 1945), Neil
   Young (b. 1948), Richie Furay (b. 1949), Bruce
   Palmer (b. 1947), Dewey Martin (b. 1950)
OTHER MEMBERS: Jim Fielder (b. 1947), Jim Mess-
   ina (b. 1949), others
FIRST ALBUM RELEASE: *Buffalo Springfield*, 1966
MUSICAL STYLES: Rock and roll, pop, folk rock,
   country rock

Formed in Los Angeles in 1966, Buffalo Springfield contained two strong songwriters and performers, Neil Young and Stephen Stills, who went
on to very successful group and solo ventures. Two
other singer-songwriters, Richie Furay and (later)
Jim Messina, also had successful careers—if less so
than those of Stills and Young—after the band
dissolved. Buffalo Springfield itself lasted only
from 1966 to 1968 and was marked by considerable turmoil and squabbling among its members.
Nonetheless, it was deeply influential on many
rock and country-rock musicians.

The Beginnings. Los Angeles in the mid-
1960's was home to a creative and growing music
scene. It was a magnet that drew musicians from
all over North America. The Byrds, pioneers of
folk rock, were probably the most successful
group that could be called a local Los Angeles
band. One musician who responded to the lure of
Southern California was Texas-born Stephen
Stills. Stills moved to Los Angeles after a time in
New York, where he had played in a folk group
with Richie Furay. Another was Neil Young, who,
along with fellow Canadian Bruce Palmer, drove
out from Toronto in Young's old hearse.

The band was formed early in 1966 shortly after
Stills and Furay, driving on Los Angeles's Sunset
Boulevard, spotted Neil Young behind the wheel
of his hearse. Furay had met Young before and
recognized him. Young had apparently been looking for Stills and Furay but had been unable to
find them. The four decided to start a band, and
they added drummer and singer Dewey Martin.
The band's name was taken from the name of a
steamroller manufacturer.

The band began to play regularly at the Whisky-
a-Go-Go and other Los Angeles clubs around the
same time as groups such as the Doors, Love, and
Spirit. They rapidly gained a reputation as a
strong live act and did short tours as the opening
act for the Byrds and the Beach Boys. From the
beginning, Buffalo Springfield's music was hard
to classify, containing elements of folk, country,
pop, and driving rock and roll. Its diversity reflected the differing styles of Stills, Young, and
Furay. The group soon signed a recording contract with Atlantic Records and was in the recording studio almost immediately. Their first album,
however, did not capture the sound of the band
well. Before its release, the band wanted to shelve
it and start again, but their manager-producers
refused to let them. The album was unsuccessful,
and internal tensions and lack of money were
threatening to destroy the group. Then, in November of 1966, came the "riots" on the Sunset
Strip.

"Battle Lines" on the Strip. The Sunset Strip
(a section of Sunset Boulevard in Hollywood
noted for its nightlife) had long been a place
where young people congregated, and by the middle of 1966 it had become the scene of clashes
between teenagers and older store owners, nightclub operators, and their patrons. A 10:00 P.M.
curfew was put in place for anyone under eighteen. In November a demonstration against the
curfew was violently put down by the Los Angeles
police and sheriff's departments, and the media
called the event a riot.

Buffalo Springfield was playing in San Francisco that weekend, notes Fred Goodman in *The
Mansion on the Hill* (1997), and they saw the violence on television. A few days later Stills wrote,
and the band recorded, "For What It's Worth." Its
chorus, "Stop, hey, what's that sound/ Everybody
look what's going down," and lines such as
"There's battle lines being drawn" and "There's a
man with a gun over there," referring to the L.A.
police, identified it as a protest song. It was a new
type of protest song, however, both because it
admitted that "Nobody's right if everybody's
wrong" and because it was an expression of what
had become known as the generation gap between long-haired young people and American

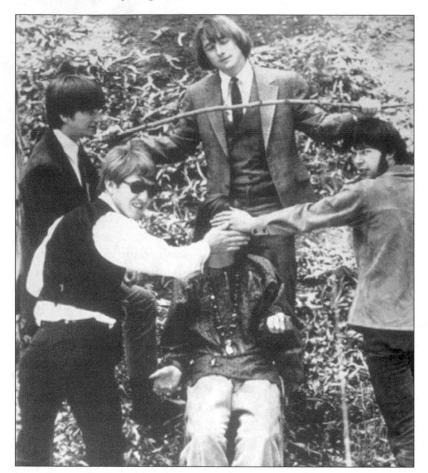

Buffalo Springfield in 1967 (Archive Photos)

tion, Bruce Palmer had trouble with U.S. immigration authorities and was deported to Canada because of a drug conviction. After some temporary fill-in bass players, Jim Messina replaced him before the band's last album.

Recording Classics. Work on the second album, *Buffalo Springfield Again*, proved difficult. Recording generally involved each member's supervising the recording of his own material, and some of the tracks were augmented by session musicians. Yet the sessions produced songs that became classics. Young's "Mr. Soul" and "Expecting to Fly" and Stills's "Bluebird" and "Rock and Roll Woman" were among the highlights. *Buffalo Springfield Again* is regarded as the best of the group's three albums of original material.

By this time the differences in the songwriters' styles were clearly apparent: Young's narrative sense and eye for surreal details, Stills's folk-pop sensibility, Furay's country leanings. The group's vocal harmonies, however, were a unifying element. Though Furay was not the songwriter that Stills and Young proved to be, his voice was strong and smooth and blended beautifully with those of the other singers. Buffalo Springfield, along with the Beatles, the Byrds, and the late 1960's version of the Beach Boys, combined strong harmonies, intelligent and sometimes offbeat lyrics, and powerful rock-and-roll instrumentation and soloing.

Between completion of the second album and the release of the group's third, *Last Time Around*, Buffalo Springfield broke up for good. The newest member and producer, Jim Messina, assembled the album. Highlights include Stills's "Pretty Girl Why," Young's "I Am a Child," and Furay's

society at large. The song was quickly played by Los Angeles radio stations and soon rose to number 7 on the national *Billboard* singles charts, saving Buffalo Springfield from obscurity. In 1967 a Top-10 single was tremendously significant, even for an album-oriented artist's career, since the FM rock market had not yet developed. The band now had a nationwide audience and could appear on television shows such as *The Smothers Brothers Comedy Hour*. The band's album was re-pressed and re-released with "For What It's Worth" on it. The song was their only hit single.

Despite this burst of success, the wealth of talent and ambition in the band continued to cause clashes between members. Stills and Young, in particular, were strong personalities driven to compete against each other. In 1967 Young quit, then rejoined, the band more than once. In addi-

"Kind Woman." The Stills song "Questions" was later reworked as part of "Carry On" on the Crosby, Stills, Nash, and Young album *Déjà vu*.

Legacy. After the breakup of Buffalo Springfield, Neil Young began a solo career. Stills joined with David Crosby of the Byrds, and they recruited English singer Graham Nash from the Hollies to form Crosby, Stills, and Nash. Young joined that group as well and for a time juggled a solo career with his involvement in Crosby, Stills, Nash, and Young. Furay and Messina founded the country rock group Poco, and Messina then went on to form Loggins and Messina with Kenny Loggins. Beyond this direct lineage, it could also reasonably be argued that Buffalo Springfield pioneered country rock. (The Byrds were also early converts, notably on their 1968 album *Sweetheart of the Rodeo*.) From this perspective, Buffalo Springfield's descendants include artists ranging from the Flying Burrito Brothers to Linda Ronstadt to the hugely successful Eagles.   *—McCrea Adams*

SELECT DISCOGRAPHY
■ ALBUMS
Buffalo Springfield, 1966, re-released 1967
Buffalo Springfield Again, 1967
Last Time Around, 1968
Retrospective, 1969 (compilation)

SELECT AWARDS
Rock and Roll Hall of Fame, inducted 1997

SEE ALSO: Byrds, The; Crosby, Stills, Nash, and Young; Loggins and Messina; Young, Neil.

Jimmy Buffett

BORN: Pascagoula, Mississippi; December 25, 1946
FIRST ALBUM RELEASE: *Down to Earth*, 1970
MUSICAL STYLES: Country rock, folk

Jimmy Buffett achieved success with several hit songs in the 1970's, most notably "Margaritaville," which went to number 8 on the charts in 1977. Celebrating escapism and fun in his music, which often relates tales of life in the Caribbean, Buffett has built a large and loyal legion of fans known as Parrot Heads. In the early 1990's, his fortune was estimated at twenty million dollars, based on profits from his music, writing, and restaurants.

The Beginnings. Buffett grew up in Mobile, Alabama, in a middle-class home. His father, who enjoyed boating, was a naval architect in the shipyards, and his mother was a writer. Despite their comfortable existence, young Buffett started shining shoes at the age of thirteen out of a desire for independence. His imagination was fueled by tales from his grandfather, who had made a living as a sea captain shipping lumber, sugar, and salt out of New Orleans. Grandpa Buffett frequented places such as Havana, Cuba, at the height of its glamour, and would bring Buffett mysterious presents.

In addition to the influence of his grandfather, Buffett's philosophy of escapism was boosted by frequent high school visits to New Orleans during the fantastic Mardi Gras celebration, with their amazing parades. As he turned his creative instincts toward music, his parents were supportive. His mother and her friends attended his earliest shows in small clubs in Biloxi, Mississippi.

School and Music. Buffett attended the University of Southern Mississippi in Hattiesburg. He attended school primarily so he could get a deferment from the military draft and not have to fight in the Vietnam War. He chose Southern Mississippi because Hattiesburg was only about seventy miles from New Orleans. He worked day shifts in New Orleans' French Quarter, then commuted to his night classes. He spent much more time playing in his band and meeting girls than he did studying but nonetheless managed to earn his degree.

After graduation, most of his friends settled down and took office jobs. He opted to keep playing music. He bought a Volkswagen and toured the Midwest, playing in steak houses and similar small venues. He was traveling endlessly and barely earning enough money to live, but he enjoyed his lifestyle. He was certain that he wanted to be an entertainer. In the late 1960's he migrated to Nashville to try to break into the world of country music. He released his first album in 1970, but it sold only 324 copies.

Florida and Success. Life in Tennessee did not go well. His first marriage failed, and the cloudy winter drove him to shoot six holes in his freezer. Hiding the expiration date on his defunct credit card, he purchased a plane ticket to Miami, Florida. The job he had arranged at a coffeehouse near the University of Miami fell through, but he found another at a club for folksingers called Bubbah's. He opened for comedians, including Robin Williams and Steve Martin, and worked his way from fifth billing to first.

In November of 1971, he borrowed a friend's car and drove down to Key West, where he found employment playing during the happy hour at Howie's Lounge. After a few more years of barely making a living, he was offered a recording contract by ABC records. He went to Nashville and recorded *A White Sport Coat and a Pink Crustacean* (1973), which included several semiautobiographical fables such as "He Went to Paris," the type of song that would become his trademark. He received twenty-five thousand dollars for the effort and immediately bought a boat.

Buffett had found a lucrative formula with his mix of Caribbean and Nashville sounds. In 1974 he released *Living and Dying in 3/4 Time*, which included "Come Monday," his first Top-30 hit. Buffett knew he was really breaking through when he heard a Muzak version in a London department store. In 1975 Buffett organized his Coral Reefer Band, and they recorded *Havana Day-Dreamin'* in 1976. It was during the following year that they made it to the top, however, with the release of *Changes in Latitudes, Changes in Attitudes*. This would become his most popular album, and it included his only Top-10 hit, "Margaritaville." The song was released just a few years after the Watergate affair and the end of U.S. fighting in Vietnam, during a mounting recession. It featured a down-on-his-luck former hippie, with whom many Americans in their late twenties and thirties could easily identify.

In 1978 Buffett and the Coral Reefers scored another success with *Son of a Son of a Sailor*, which included the pop hit "Cheeseburger in Paradise." In 1979, while spending most of his time on his yacht, Buffett stopped in the Carribean island of Montserrat long enough to record *Volcano*. A single by the same name from that album quickly became a favorite at his concerts, which were attracting large crowds of colorfully clad fans who called themselves Parrot Heads.

The "Margaritaville" Empire. During the 1980's, Buffett worked to make much new music, but little of it was as popular as the hits he wrote in the 1970's. Nevertheless, his fame continued to expand; in 1985 he released a compilation of his best tunes called *Songs You Know by Heart—Jimmy Buffett's Greatest Hit(s)*, which sold more than two million copies. Furthermore, although he wrote and recorded new music, he never tired of playing the old favorites that crowds wanted to hear.

The 1990's. Heading into the 1990's, Buffett continued to labor diligently as a musician but also expanded into other creative arenas. His first book, *Tales from Margaritaville*, was published in 1989. It consisted of several autobiographical essays and several fictional short stories and sold more than one million copies. His second book, a novel called *Where Is Joe Merchant?*, also became

Jimmy Buffett (Paul Natkin)

For the Record

"I never did think I'd become family entertainment."
—*Jimmy Buffett*

§

In the mid-1990's, when Jimmy Buffett first contacted renowned author Herman Wouk about turning one of Wouk's books into a musical, Wouk had no idea who Buffett was. After checking up a bit, he agreed to go ahead with the project. The elderly Wouk, an orthodox Jewish man from New York, eventually could be seen wearing a straw hat and dancing the merengue.

a best-seller. The 1990's, moreover, saw Buffett succeed as an entrepreneur. He opened two Margaritaville cafés, one in Key West and one in New Orleans. These ventures—combined with the ongoing popularity of his albums, books, and concerts—made Buffett a regular on the *Forbes* magazine list of wealthiest entertainers.

In the late 1990's, Buffett continued to try new things. He and his oldest daughter, Savannah Jane, coauthored two children's books. He recorded a Christmas album in 1996 that was typically Buffett in style but also included a version of John Lennon's "Happy Xmas (War Is Over)." He collaborated with Pulitzer Prize-winning author Herman Wouk on a musical, which opened in Miami in 1997. He also became involved in a number of environmental causes. He played benefit concerts to raise money for a group trying to preserve the coast of Long Island, New York, and for another attempting to save the manatees in Florida. Buffett even became a family man, living in Palm Beach with his second wife and their three children.

It is somewhat ironic that a performer whose most popular songs celebrate relaxing in the Caribbean achieved such incredible commercial success. This was because the growing numbers of Parrot Heads loved his philosophy of escapism.

Parrot Heads included all types, from suburban mothers to fraternity boys to businessmen, all those who long for the idyllic lifestyle of Buffett's songs. They all voraciously bought Buffett products, whether in the form of books, compact discs, or food from his restaurants. As a result, the musician who once toured the Midwest in an old Volkswagen patrolled his Margaritaville empire in the late 1990's in a red Porsche and his own airplane. Buffett's career represents one long and enjoyable ride, both for him and for his fans.
—*Andy DeRoche*

SELECT DISCOGRAPHY
■ ALBUMS
Down to Earth, 1970
A White Sport Coat and a Pink Crustacean, 1973
Living and Dying in 3/4 Time, 1974
Rancho Deluxe, 1975
Havana Day-Dreamin', 1976
High Cumberland Jubilee, 1976
Changes in Latitudes, Changes in Attitudes, 1977
Son of a Son of a Sailor, 1978
Volcano, 1979
Coconut Telegraph, 1981
One Particular Harbour, 1983
Riddles in the Sand, 1984
Songs You Know by Heart—Jimmy Buffett's Greatest Hit(s), 1985
Floridays, 1986
Off to See the Lizard, 1989
Boats Beaches Bars and Ballads, 1992
Margaritaville Cafe Late Night Menu, 1993
Fruitcakes, 1994
Banana Wind, 1996
Christmas Island, 1996

SEE ALSO: Grateful Dead, The; Marley, Bob.

Bush

ORIGINAL MEMBERS: Gavin McGregor Rossdale (b. 1967), Nigel Kenneth Pulsford (b. 1963), Robin Goodridge (b. 1963), David Parsons (b. 1964)
FIRST ALBUM RELEASE: *Sixteen Stone*, 1994
MUSICAL STYLES: Rock and roll, heavy metal

Bush (Paul Natkin)

class Kilburn section of northern London. As a teenager, he was part of the same London underground party scene that had, years before, helped launch Boy George. Rossdale became the singer for a band called Midnight, which released one single but had no success.

From Rivals to Riches. Rossdale and Nigel Pulsford were in rival pub bands when they discovered they had similar musical tastes, with a preference for reggae, English punk rock, and avant-garde experimentation. Bassist David Parsons had already made a name for himself in a popular cult band called Transvision Vamp. Introduced by a mutual friend, he joined Bush and, with a pick-up drummer, the band began to tour the English pub circuit. At one gig, a drummer in the audience came backstage and told Rossdale that the group would be great if they had a better drummer. Robin Goodridge became a member of the group that night.

The quartet continued to play in pubs for years, with little interest from English record companies. In 1993, they were signed by a small American label called Trauma Records, a division of Interscope Records, which is known for its risk-taking, ground-breaking roster.

Sixteen Stone. Bush's first album, *Sixteen Stone*, released in 1994, was a huge success in the United States. The album title is a reference to an English measure of weight. Because interest in England was relatively small, the label immediately arranged a U.S. club tour, during which the band played small venues and travelled in the cramped confines of a van. Turning down a support slot on a Jimmy Page/Robert Plant tour, Bush continued on their own. *Sixteen Stone* eventually yielded five

While Bush has a legion of fans in the United States, they are relatively unknown in their native England. The band is not a favorite with critics on either side of the ocean and are often accused of sounding too much like Nirvana. In addition, lead singer Gavin Rossdale is often not taken seriously because he has the sculpted good looks of a model. On the other hand, the band has consistently released resoundingly guitar-heavy multi-platinum albums that contain lyrics that deal with weighty subject matter.

Each member of Bush developed his taste for music from older siblings, who listened to records of diverse genres. Rossdale grew up in the middle-

singles that were helped along by radio and MTV airplay. One year later, Bush was still touring the United States when its album went double platinum (eventually selling over eight million copies) and the single "Glycerine" went to number 5 on the *Billboard* Hot 100 chart. Bush, along with Oasis and the Stone Roses, was heralded in a cover story in *Billboard* magazine as being frontrunners of a new "British invasion."

Making Some Noise. In 1996, Bush released its second album, *Razorblade Suitcase.* Thumbing its nose at the already prevalent Nirvana comparisons, the band hired producer Steve Albini, who had produced Nirvana's *In Utero* album, and artist Vaughn Oliver, who had designed *In Utero*'s cover. The album revealed the band's wide dynamic range and utilized extensive feedback and dissonance. Albini added studio noise to further distort the overall sound. The result was infectious and positive, perhaps despite the wishes of Rossdale, the sole songwriter, who claimed to tap his negative side when writing. *Deconstructed*, an album of Bush songs remixed by some of the world's top club DJs, was released in 1997.

—*Deirdre Rockmaker*

SELECT DISCOGRAPHY
■ ALBUMS
Sixteen Stone, 1994
Razorblade Suitcase, 1996
Deconstructed, 1997 (remixes)

For the Record

Bush's Gavin Rossdale is so devoted to his dog, a black Hungarian Sheepdog with dreadlocks named Winston, that he has featured the dog on the inside cover of the booklet for the *Sixteen Stone* compact disc release and in two videos. Rossdale has named his independent record label Mad Dog Winston and has even had the prestigious Lloyd's of London insure the dog for approximately two million dollars.

SELECT AWARDS
American Music Award for Best Alternative Group, 1997

SEE ALSO: Clash, The; Nirvana; Pearl Jam.

The Byrds

ORIGINAL MEMBERS: Roger McGuinn (b. James Joseph McGuinn III, 1942), David Crosby (b. David Van Cortland, 1941), Gene Clark (1941-1991), Chris Hillman (b. 1944), Michael Clarke (Michael Dick, 1944-1993)
OTHER MEMBERS: Gram Parsons (Ingram Cecil Conner III, 1946-1973), Clarence White (b. 1944), Gene Parsons (b. 1944), Skip Battin (b. 1934), Kevin Kelley, John York
FIRST ALBUM RELEASE: *Mr. Tambourine Man*, 1965
MUSICAL STYLES: Folk rock, pop, rock and roll, psychedelic rock, country rock, country

The Byrds' fusion of folk music with rock and roll established them as the first and foremost of the American bands to respond to the musical "British invasion" of 1964. Their increasingly eclectic albums explored pop, psychedelic, electronic, and country music, while their numerous personnel changes delivered key players to Crosby, Stills, Nash, and Young and to the Flying Burrito Brothers. Their influence is clearly audible in the sound of such later bands as Tom Petty and the Heartbreakers and R.E.M.

The Band. The Byrds' first single, which topped both the American and British charts within weeks of its release, built a bridge between a centrally important American folksinger and songwriter, Bob Dylan, and a centrally important British pop group, the Beatles. "Mr. Tambourine Man," a Dylan song arranged in a rock-and-roll style, introduced the instantly recognizable trademarks of the Byrds' sound: Roger McGuinn's lead vocal (which consciously blended elements of Dylan's and John Lennon's voices), the distinctive ring of his electric twelve-string Rickenbacker guitar (which he had bought after seeing George Harrison play one in the Beatles' 1964 film *A Hard*

Day's Night), and the rich harmonies of Gene Clark and David Crosby on backup vocals. Their first two albums, *Mr. Tambourine Man* (1965) and *Turn! Turn! Turn!* (1966), defined the parameters of folk-rock music and turned out to be reciprocal influences on both Dylan (who moved toward rock after hearing the Byrds play his songs) and the Beatles (avowed Byrds fan George Harrison would even steal the guitar part for his "If I Needed Someone" from McGuinn's work on "The Bells of Rhymney"). While these albums featured several other Dylan songs, including the Byrds' second single, "All I Really Wanna Do" (eclipsed on the charts, however, by Cher's cover version), they also showcased a number of remarkable originals, especially those written and sung by Clark, who contributed the B sides to their first three singles and the A side to their fourth, "Set You Free This Time." However, Clark, who had established himself as the strongest writer in the group, suddenly left the band in 1966 due to a combination of his fear of flying, personal problems, and friction within the group, especially with the notoriously difficult Crosby, who had previously ousted Clark as rhythm guitar player (leaving him to play tambourine).

Something Lost, Something Gained. Despite, or perhaps because of, Clark's departure, the band turned even more to original material on their next two albums, *Fifth Dimension* (1966) and *Younger than Yesterday* (1967). Their next four singles all credited McGuinn, Crosby, or both as writers, with occasional coauthor credit given to Chris Hillman, a renowned bluegrass mandolin player who took up bass guitar for the Byrds, and

For the Record

Despite the role that the Byrds played in inspiring the term "raga rock" and introducing their peers to sitar music, there is no sitar on any of the Byrds' recordings; McGuinn always imitated the sounds on his twelve-string guitar.

to Michael Clarke, who had been hired on the basis of his good looks but had become a solid drummer. Underscoring the band's new direction, *Fifth Dimension* included no Dylan songs, and the first single mapped out the new genre of psychedelic music. "Eight Miles High," widely (though unfairly) perceived as a song about drugs, reflected the band's interest in jazz musician John Coltrane, whose innovative saxophone work McGuinn consciously tried to emulate with his guitar. Its B-side, "Why," showed their peers, particularly the Beatles' Harrison, how to blend the sounds of Ravi Shankar's Indian sitar music with rock (to produce "raga rock"). *Younger than Yesterday* confirmed Hillman's arrival as the third strong writer in the group with his contribution of four original songs in addition to cowriting the hit single "So You Want to Be a Rock 'n' Roll Star," a sharp satire on the commercialization of popular music as exemplified by the recent rise of the Monkees (the song also featured South African trumpeter Hugh Masakela, another marker of the Byrds' range of influences). The B side, the meditative ballad "Everybody's Been Burned," also established a new high-water mark for Crosby as a serious songwriter. The Byrds appeared to have hit their creative peak.

More Changes. The Byrds began work on their fifth album, *The Notorious Byrd Brothers* (1968), as a quartet but finished it as a duo, with Crosby being fired and Clarke quitting during the sessions. Despite the personal tensions fragmenting the band, this album, with the Beatles' 1967 *Sgt. Pepper's Lonely Hearts Club Band* and the Beach Boys' 1966 *Pet Sounds*, remains one of the masterpieces of Baroque art-pop. McGuinn, Crosby, and Hillman had become such accomplished and prolific songwriters that there seemed to be no room on the album to keep everyone happy; Crosby's firing was largely due to his refusal to play when it became clear that a version of "Goin' Back," a song by Carole King and Gerry Goffin (whose two songs on the album played the key role of the Dylan material on earlier albums), would appear in place of his own "Triad." (He instead gave the song to the Jefferson Airplane.) The Byrds replaced Clarke on drums with Hillman's cousin

Kevin Kelley and brought in friend Gram Parsons to play jazz piano, in line with McGuinn's idea for a concept album covering the history of American popular music. To the utter astonishment of fans and peers alike, however, the Byrds instead released *Sweetheart of the Rodeo* (1968), a straight country music album. This innovative and influential move, especially when followed by Dylan's 1969 *Nashville Skyline*, finally helped to lift the pop music taboo on country influences. Parsons shortly quit the band in a dispute over a concert tour of South Africa, and Hillman soon joined him to form the seminal country-rock group the Flying Burrito Brothers (which eventually included Michael Clarke on drums).

McGuinn. McGuinn, the only remaining original member of the Byrds, brought in Clarence White, a brilliant guitarist who had played on several cuts on earlier Byrds albums, with Gene Parsons on drums and John York on bass for the next two somewhat uneven albums, *Dr. Byrds and Mr. Hyde* and *Ballad of Easy Rider* (both 1969). The Byrds were now overshadowed by Crosby's work with Crosby, Stills, Nash, and Young and Hillman's with the Flying Burrito Brothers, but their next release, the double-album set *(Untitled)* (1970), with Skip Battin replacing John York, is ranked by most critics as one of the band's best. The studio album evidenced a resurgence of McGuinn's songwriting, especially on the quasi-allegorical "Chestnut Mare," and the concert album documented their inspired live performances. Two more solid if unspectacular albums, *Byrdmaniax* (1971) and *Farther Along* (1972), were followed by the forgettable *The Byrds* (1973), reuniting the original lineup, and a series of McGuinn/ Clark/Hillman, McGuinn/Hillman, and even

McGuinn/Crosby/Hillman collaborations, but the band had clearly lost their spark and would not again reach the level of their best work.

—*William Nelles*

SELECT DISCOGRAPHY
"Mr. Tambourine Man," 1965
"Turn! Turn! Turn! (To Everything There Is a Season)," 1965
"Eight Miles High," 1966

■ ALBUMS
Mr. Tambourine Man, 1965
Turn! Turn! Turn! 1966
Fifth Dimension, 1966
Younger than Yesterday, 1967
The Notorious Byrd Brothers, 1968
Sweetheart of the Rodeo, 1968
Dr. Byrds and Mr. Hyde, 1969
Ballad of Easy Rider, 1969
(Untitled), 1970
Byrdmaniax, 1971
Farther Along, 1972
The Byrds, 1973

SELECT AWARDS
Rock and Roll Hall of Fame, inducted 1991

SEE ALSO: Beatles, The; Buffalo Springfield; Crosby, Stills, Nash, and Young; Dylan, Bob; Jefferson Airplane / Jefferson Starship; Monkees, The; Parsons, Gram; Petty, Tom, and the Heartbreakers; R.E.M.; Sonny and Cher / Cher; Young, Neil.

David Byrne. *See* **Talking Heads / David Byrne**

C

Glen Campbell

BORN: Billstown, Arkansas; April 22, 1936
FIRST SINGLE RELEASE: "Turn Around, Look at Me," 1961
FIRST ALBUM RELEASE: *Big Bluegrass Special*, 1962 (with the Green River Boys)
MUSICAL STYLES: Country, country rock, pop

Glen Campbell is best known today for his country-pop hits covering a span of twenty years, from the John Hartford bluegrass classic "Gentle on My Mind" (1967) to the Jimmy Webb country ballad "Still Within the Sound of My Voice" (1987). Yet Campbell was already a well-known and respected session musician long before he found success as a solo act.

Master of All Trades. Taught to play a five–dollar Sears & Roebuck guitar by his Uncle Boo, Glen Campbell had become well known among local musicians by the time he was eight years old. He became adept at playing everything from jazz standards to country and pop tunes. Never the most dedicated student, Campbell dropped out of school at the age of fourteen to travel with two of his uncles and their band of musicians.

Campbell eventually outgrew the circuit of proms, weddings, dance halls, and local radio shows and moved to California in the late 1950's. By 1960 he had joined Dash Crofts and Jimmy Seals to form the newest lineup of the revamped pop band the Champs. The group had already hit its peak with the Top-40 instrumental single "Tequila." One year later Campbell became a staff writer for American Music and cowrote, with Jerry Capehart, "Turn Around, Look at Me." Campbell recorded and released this song as his first solo effort on Capehart's Crest label, but it would be a vocal group called the Vogues, fashioned after the Lettermen, who would turn the song into a smash hit seven years later in 1968.

While he continued writing songs and playing in a variety of bands, Campbell supplemented his income by becoming an in-demand session guitarist and vocalist. He played guitar and occasional bass and supplied background vocals on hundreds of studio recording sessions for some of the most important pop stars of the 1950's and 1960's, including Jan and Dean, the Crystals, Rick Nelson, Bobby Darin, Wayne Newton, the Kingston Trio, Elvis Presley, Dean Martin, Nat King Cole, Jack Jones, and Frank Sinatra.

Glen Campbell in 1970 (AP/Wide World Photos)

Campbell's most productive early association, however, was with the Beach Boys. Having already played and sung on several Beach Boys recordings, Campbell was asked to fill in for Brian Wilson in 1964 when the increasingly reclusive pop songwriter refused to tour with the group. In 1965 the group asked Campbell to become a permanent member, but he declined. He was ready to devote all his energy to his fledgling solo career.

The Webb Years. Although Campbell's first hit single was the John Hartford song "Gentle on My Mind" (1967), his recordings of three classics by songwriter Jimmy Webb (who also had his first hit in 1967 with the Fifth Dimension's "Up, Up, and Away") cemented the connection between the two. In 1968 Campbell's recordings of "By the Time I Get to Phoenix" and "Wichita Lineman" made the singer an instant crossover success as both songs dominated the pop, country, and easy-listening charts. Webb's unique blend of down-home lyricism, urbane melodies, and slightly psychedelic arrangements (as in the organ part at the end of "Wichita Lineman") satisfied the upscale inclinations of Campbell's traditional country audience while attracting new recruits from both the pop and rock audiences. In 1969 Campbell hit it big again with two more Webb songs, "Galveston" and "Where's the Playground, Susie?" In 1970 he recorded Webb's "Honey Come Back," a song that had only moderate success on the country charts. Campbell, who once called Webb the "best songwriter ever born in America," would eventually record more than thirty Jimmy Webb songs over the course of his career.

Later Recordings. Campbell's biggest-selling single and album are 1976's "Rhinestone Cowboy" and the album of the same name. The song and its follow-up hit, "Country Boy (You've Got Your Feet in L.A.)," also from the album *Rhinestone Cowboy*, successfully played off Campbell's image as a slick pop singer who had abandoned his country roots. "Rhinestone Cowboy" tells the tale of a country singer resigned to acting out a role to make a living ("There's been a load of compromisin'/ on the road to my horizon") while "Country Boy (You've Got Your Feet in L.A.)" is more critical of that same role. Both songs were

smash hits, selling millions of copies, making them Campbell's biggest-selling records.

Yet these are essentially novelty records. Campbell will more likely be remembered as the singer of the Jimmy Webb classics "By the Time I Get to Phoenix," "Wichita Lineman," and "Galveston." His 1987 hit single "Still Within the Sound of My Voice," was also a Webb composition.

The Legacy. Glen Campbell continued to record albums but his more noteworthy activities in his later career were his conversion to Christianity and the publication of his ghostwritten autobiography, *Rhinestone Cowboy* (1994). Campbell divulges all in rich detail, including his infamous drug-ridden affair with Tanya Tucker in the late 1970's and early 1980's. Campbell opened the Glen Campbell Goodtime Theatre in Branson, Missouri, and performs there about six months per year. He was honored at a surprise sixtieth birthday party in Branson in April, 1996. Among the many guests, Jimmy Webb and Larry Weiss (the composer of "Rhinestone Cowboy") staged an impromptu performance of their songs

---

For the Record

Glen Campbell may have been robbed of yet another Jimmy Webb hit when Capitol refused to release the title cut from his 1979 album, *Highwayman*. Webb's version had appeared on his own *El Mirage* album two years before, and Atlantic had also refused to release it as a single. Six years later Campbell showed the song to Johnny Cash, who decided to put it on his next album. However, when his friends Kris Kristofferson, Waylon Jennings, and Willie Nelson heard Cash's demo version, they convinced Cash to do it as a quartet. "Highwayman" by the Highwaymen was a Top-10 country hit in 1985 and led to several years of Nelson, Jennings, Cash, and Krisofferson touring and recording as the Highwaymen.

with the man who made them hits. In the fall of 1996, Campbell was the featured subject of The Nashville Network's *Life and Times* biography series.

Glen Campbell was an important contributor to country music. He was one of the first major country artists to successfully cross over and dominate the country and pop charts. More significant, he introduced many country artists of the late 1960's to a general television audience by insisting to CBS that they be regular guests on his successful 1968 television variety show, *The Glen Campbell Goodtime Hour*. Unbeknownst to all, Campbell's music and promotion of country music performers paved the way for the new country explosion of the 1980's and 1990's. One could argue that without him there would be no future country superstars such as Vince Gill or Garth Brooks.

—*Tyrone Williams*

SELECT DISCOGRAPHY

■ ALBUMS

Gentle on My Mind, 1967
By the Time I Get to Phoenix, 1967
Wichita Lineman, 1968
Galveston, 1969
Reunion—The Songs of Jimmy Webb, 1974
Still Within the Sound of My Voice, 1987
The Essential Glen Campbell Volumes I, II, and III, 1995 (compilation)

SELECT AWARDS

Grammy Awards for Best Country & Western Recording (with Al De Lory) and Best Country & Western Solo Vocal Performance, Male, for "Gentle on My Mind"; for Best Vocal Performance, Male, and Best Contemporary Male Solo Vocal Performance for "By the Time I Get to Phoenix," all 1967
Grammy Award for Album of the Year for *By the Time I Get to Phoenix*, 1968 (with Al De Lory)
Country Music Association Entertainer of the Year and Male Vocalist of the Year Awards, 1968

SEE ALSO: Beach Boys, The; Cash, Johnny; Jennings, Waylon; Kristofferson, Kris; Nelson, Willie; Tucker, Tanya.

Captain and Tennille

ORIGINAL MEMBERS: Toni Tennille (b. Catheryn Antoinette Tennille, 1943), Daryl Dragon (b. 1942)
FIRST ALBUM RELEASE: *Love Will Keep Us Together*, 1975
MUSICAL STYLE: Pop

With their most famous hit single, "Love Will Keep Us Together," the Captain and Tennille stood apart from the 1970's rock scene by introducing a cheerful, upbeat pop sound. Fans also believed that Daryl "the Captain" Dragon and Toni Tennille's marriage made their love ballads especially romantic.

Origins. Born in Alabama to a big-band singer, Toni Tennille became involved in theater and music at an early age. She dreamed of a career in show business and joined a acting repertory company in California while working secretarial jobs to earn money.

Music was also a part of native Californian Daryl Dragon's life from the early days. The son of symphony conductor Carmen Dragon, he formed a band with his brothers during school and even put together a homemade record. Dragon turned professional when he joined the Beach Boys as keyboardist, and it was during a

For the Record

Daryl Dragon acquired the nickname "the Captain" while with the Beach Boys. He was performing a keyboard solo and wearing a captain's hat when Beach Boy Mike Love spontaneously called him "Captain Keyboard." Somehow, the "Captain" part of the nickname stuck and lent Dragon an air of quiet mystery. The Captain reinforced this image by rarely speaking a single word during the Captain and Tennille variety show, allowing his wife to do all the talking.

The Captain and Tennille in 1977 (Archive Photos)

break from the group's tour schedule that he met Tennille. She had cowritten an ecological rock musical called *Mother Earth*, in which Dragon filled in for the regular keyboardist. The two became close immediately, and Dragon brought Tennille back to the Beach Boys, where she spent a brief time as the only woman ever to sing with the group.

On Their Own. When the Beach Boys' 1971 tour ended, Dragon and Tennille continued to work together, originally calling themselves the Dragons. Before releasing their first, self-financed single, "The Way That I Want to Touch You," they changed their name to the Captain and Tennille and gathered a small but dedicated following in Los Angeles nightclubs. The single earned them the attention of A&M Records, with whom they recorded *Love Will Keep Us Together* in 1975; the title song of the album, written by Neil Sedaka, was their first major hit and won a Grammy Award.

Only a few weeks before the album's release, the Captain and Tennille were married, in part due to pressure from Tennille's mother. They had a quick Las Vegas, Nevada, wedding, but in 1995, they returned to Las Vegas, renewing their wedding vows in a more traditional ceremony, and celebrated the release of a new album, *Twenty Years of Romance*. In the interim, the Captain and Tennille enjoyed ample success, with several albums and hit singles including "Muskrat Love," "Shop Around," and "Do That to Me One More Time." In 1976 and 1977, during the height of their popularity, the duo hosted a variety television show in the vein of *Donny and Marie* and *The Sonny and Cher Comedy Hour*. Tennille also hosted a short-lived daytime talk show in 1980.

Settling Down. In 1984, with their popularity waning, the Captain and Tennille moved from California to Carson City, Nevada, and slowed down their pace. While still performing occasionally as the Captain and Tennille on cruise ships and in Las Vegas, the couple would pursue other projects such as building their own recording studio (in which the Beach Boys would eventually record). Tennille also recorded two albums of old standard ballads such as "Let's Do It" and "But Not for Me."
—*Amy Sisson*

SELECT DISCOGRAPHY
■ ALBUMS
Love Will Keep Us Together, 1975
Song of Joy, 1976
Come in from the Rain, 1977
The Captain & Tennille Greatest Hits, 1977
   (compilation)
Make Your Move, 1979
Keeping Our Love Warm, 1980
All of Me, 1987 (Toni Tennille solo)
Things Are Swingin', 1994 (Toni Tennille and the
   Matt Catingub Big Band)
Twenty Years of Romance, 1995 (compilation)

SELECT AWARDS
Grammy Award for Record of the Year for "Love
   Will Keep Us Together," 1975

SEE ALSO: Beach Boys, The; Osmonds, The; Sedaka, Neil; Sonny and Cher / Cher.

Captain Beefheart and the Magic Band

ORIGINAL MEMBERS: Captain Beefheart (b. Don Van Vliet, 1941), Alex St. Clair (b. Alex Snouffer), Jerry Handley, Antennae Jimmy Semens (b. Jeff Cotton), Drumbo (b. John French), Ry Cooder (b. 1947)

OTHER MEMBERS: Zoot Horn Rollo (b. Bill Harkleroad), Rockette Morton (b. Mark Boston), the Mascara Snake (b. Victor Hayden), Ed Marimba (b. Art Tripp III), Roy Estrada, Bruce Fowler, Jeff Morris Tepper, Gary Lucas, Cliff Martinez, Richard "Midnight Hatsize" Snyder (b. 1958), Denny Walley, Robert Williams, Black Jewel Kitabu (Eric Feldman), others

FIRST ALBUM RELEASE: *Safe as Milk*, 1967

MUSICAL STYLES: Blues, avant-garde jazz rock, rock and roll, spoken word

Captain Beefheart (born Don Van Vliet on January 15, 1941, in Glendale, California) never sold large amounts of records, but his wonderfully eccentric music has been influential to other musicians. Some critics go so far as to include his 1969 album *Trout Mask Replica* on their lists of the most significant rock albums of all time. His music is characterized by polyrhythmic drumming, unusual instrumentation and arrangements, and discordant and inventive guitar work.

Although by the end of his recording career (in 1982) Captain Beefheart's own instrumental contributions to his albums had ranged from jingle bells to saxophone to bass clarinet, his intense harmonica compositions and his wide-ranging and eccentric vocal style—growling, gravelly, and warm but intense—became the distinctive features of his albums with the Magic Band, a name almost synonymous with Van Vliet's stage name. Beefheart's unique, improvisational-sounding lyrics sound sometimes like Beat poetry and sometimes like weird postmodern blues. They contain unexpected insights and flashes of wry humor.

Early Years. Don Van Vliet's artistic talent was recognized when he was a child, and he was considered a child-prodigy sculptor. When he was thirteen, his family moved from Glendale to Lancaster, California, where he met Frank Zappa, forming a friendship that would develop into an intense professional relationship in the years to come. In these early days, Van Vliet took up the harmonica and the saxophone and began playing locally with rock-and-roll and rhythm-and-blues groups.

Van Vliet adopted the name Captain Beefheart and formed the first version of the Magic Band in 1964. They recorded a regional-hit version of Bo Diddley's "Diddy Wah Diddy" for A&M Records. After the modest success of this single, the group hurried forward to gather material for their first album. A&M rejected the album, however, claiming that it was too negative, a remark which probably means that the album too vigorously denied conventional, and therefore positive, rock-and-roll expectations. Beefheart then went to Buddah Records, which released his first album as *Safe as Milk*. One can hear the distinctive guitar stylings of a very young Ry Cooder on "Sure 'Nuff 'N Yes, I Do" and "Grown So Ugly." Cooder, who also arranged these two cuts, left the group after this album and embarked on his own solo career. After *Safe as Milk*, Beefheart asserted even greater artistic control, writing all music and lyrics, and never completely giving control over the musical arrangements to others.

Recording Career. The stylistic range of *Safe as Milk* set the precedent for subsequent albums. From the romantic "I'm Glad" to the almost heavy-metal sounds of "Dropout Boogie," the album reaches back into the lyrical 1950's, anticipates the heavy metal of the 1980's, touches a few folk nerves, and generally begins what became Beefheart's relentless assault on the limits of rock and roll.

Some critics point to Captain Beefheart's free-form lyrics and his abandonment of rock and blues conventions as a result of Frank Zappa's influence. Zappa undeniably influenced Beefheart, but their musical relationship might well have been more mutual than is generally assumed. The two musicians certainly shared a common concern for breaking the rules. In 1969, after the release of the poorly mixed *Strictly Per-*

sonal, an album over which Van Vliet had little production control, Zappa offered Beefheart a chance to record for his new Bizarre/Straight record label. He gave Beefheart and his band complete artistic control over their next album. The double album *Trout Mask Replica*, produced by Zappa, is acknowledged by many critics as the most forward-looking rock album of its time. No artist had previously blended singing, spoken poetry, seriousness, satire, and whimsy with music that was by turns bluesy and jarringly improvisational. The songs had titles such as "Frownland," "Pachuco Cadaver," "Neon Meate Dream of an Octafish," "Old Fart at Play," and "Orange Claw Hammer."

The record-buying public did not agree with favorable critical views of *Trout Mask Replica*, and Captain Beefheart struggled on with intermittent success until the production of *Unconditionally Guaranteed* (1974). This album, gentler and more uniform than any previous album, became Beefheart's best seller. Never one to settle for uniformity—or popularity it seems—Beefheart almost immediately recorded *Blue Jeans and Moonbeams* (1974), described by one critic as "demented." Apart from his work with the Magic Band, Beefheart collaborated with Zappa and the Mothers of Invention on *Bongo Fury* (1975) and attempted recording as a solo act as Mallard (*In a Different Climate*, 1977), but nothing else was as successful a vehicle for his music as the Magic Band was.

The Magic Band. While the composition of the Magic Band changed over the years, some names appear as core members of the band until 1975, when various members moved on to other groups or individual careers. Some of the regular members of the earlier days were drummer John French ("Drumbo"), guitarist-flutist Bill Harkleroad ("Zoot Horn Rollo"), guitarist Jeff Cotton ("Antennae Jimmy Semens"), bass player Mark Boston ("Rockette Morton"), and bass clarinetist and vocalist "Mascara Snake" (Victor Hayden). Later, Art Tripp ("Ed Marimba") played drums and marimba on *The Spotlight Kid* and *Clear Spot*. For various nightclub and concert appearances after the breakup of the original core group, Beefheart called upon Jeff Tepper and Denny Walley (guitars), Bruce Fowler (trombone), Robert Williams (drums), and Eric Feldman (bass and keyboards). When Captain Beefheart and the Magic Band put their name to the 1980 release *Doc at the Radar Station*, the group contained Tepper, Feldman, Williams, and "Drumbo," who reappeared to play slide guitar, guitar, marimba, bass, and drums.

Style and Range. The album *Doc at the Radar Station* is representative of the essential force of Captain Beefheart and the Magic Band, no matter what the career stage or composition of the group. The musical style in its twelve cuts ranges from the instrumental "A Carrot Is as Close as a Rabbit Gets to a Diamond," with an almost childlike simplicity, to the complex and savage imagery of lyrics spoken over a dissonant and uneven instrumental background of

Captain Beefheart in 1980 (Deborah Feingold/Archive Photos)

"Making Love to a Vampire with a Monkey on My Knee." In this song, Beefheart's artistic association with Frank Zappa appears clearly; the language borders on what some might call the indecent, although it clearly applies to the message of transgression that the song contains. Lyrics aside, this album reflects clearly the eclecticism that marks Beefheart's work from the very beginning. One hears not only the extensive range of Beefheart's vocal stylings but also Chinese gongs, harmonica, soprano saxophone, and bass clarinet (by Beefheart as well), slide guitar, guitar, nerve guitar, synthesizer, bass, mellotron, grand piano, electric piano, trombone, marimba, french horn, and drums. *Doc at the Radar Station* caught the attention of new-wave musicians as well as the new avant-garde, and many critics call it Beefheart's best.

Retiring from music after recording *Ice Cream for Crow* in 1982, Don Van Vliet turned his attention to poetry, contemplation, and primarily, painting. He and his wife lived in a trailer in California's Mojave Desert. The visual arts had always been a part of his world; his own sketches and drawings adorn his album covers and liner notes. The fact that he has turned from music to poetry is not surprising when one considers the unorthodox and unconventional lyrics which accompany his avant-garde musical explorations.

The Legacy. Beefheart takes a place in music history more as an influence, a sign of change, than as a popular musician in his own right.

For the Record

Not even Frankie Valli at the peak of his singing voice could match Captain Beefheart's four-and-a-half-octave vocal range. Beefheart reached such a high note while recording *Safe as Milk* in 1965 that his voice destroyed the internal workings of an expensive microphone. In those days his range was often outside the recording capability of the equipment used.

Among his musical offspring can be counted several innovative groups such as Devo, Pere Ubu, Talking Heads, and many lesser-known "alternative" bands of the 1980's and 1990's.

—*D. M. Frances Batycki*

SELECT DISCOGRAPHY
■ ALBUMS
Safe as Milk, 1967
Trout Mask Replica, 1969
The Spotlight Kid, 1972
Clear Spot, 1972
Unconditionally Guaranteed, 1974
Doc at the Radar Station, 1980
Ice Cream for Crow, 1982

SEE ALSO: Devo; Talking Heads / David Byrne; Zappa, Frank / The Mothers of Invention.

Mariah Carey

BORN: New York, New York; March 27, 1970
FIRST SINGLE RELEASE: "Vision of Love," 1990
FIRST ALBUM RELEASE: *Mariah Carey*, 1990
MUSICAL STYLES: Pop, rhythm and blues, soul

Mariah Carey's name is taken from the song "They Call the Wind Mariah" from the 1951 musical *Paint Your Wagon*. She was born to a half-Venezuelan, half-African American father and an Irish American mother, and the family faced much prejudice due to their mixed heritage. Carey's mother, Patricia, an opera singer and vocal coach, was disowned by her family when she married Alfred Carey, an aeronautical engineer, and over the years, the couple faced many challenges from bigots, including having their car blown up and their dogs poisoned. Under such strain, the couple divorced when Mariah was three years old. Mariah remained with her mother, who struggled to make ends meet, as they moved to a succession of different towns in Long Island, New York. Carey's mother often worked at three jobs to put food on the table, and Carey recalls those very poor days when she had a few worn-out clothes and one pair of shoes with holes in them.

Because of her background in music, Patricia

Mariah Carey in 1997 (AP/Wide World Photos)

the rent for her small, barren apartment, Carey worked as a waitress, coat checker, beauty salon janitor, and part-time backup singer. While looking for her big break in music, she often referred to herself as the "world's worst waitress," claiming to have been fired from twenty restaurants because of her bad attitude.

While working in New York City, Carey met and befriended keyboardist and songwriter Ben Margulies, who became her songwriting partner. With Carey writing the melodies and most of the lyrics and Margulies arranging the songs, they developed a simple blend of soul, gospel, and pop that demonstrated Carey's amazing voice. Based on varying reports, Carey has a vocal range of between five and seven octaves, and the demos that her and Margulies put together began drawing attention and helped her land several backup singing jobs.

While working as a backup singer for rhythm-and-blues singer Brenda K. Starr, Carey received a very important break. At a party Starr and Carey were attending, Starr met Tommy Mottola, the president of Sony Music in the United States, and she gave him a demo tape of Carey's songs. While driving back home, Mottola listened to the tape in his car and was so impressed that he turned around, went back to the party, and found Carey. He signed her to a singing contract with Sony in late 1988 and made her career development a top priority.

Hits Galore. Carey's debut album, *Mariah Carey* (1990), stayed on top of the album charts in the United States for twenty-two weeks. Her debut single from the album, "Vision of Love," was a smash hit, putting Carey on top of the pop charts. It spawned four number 1 singles, "Vision of Love," "Love Takes Time," "Someday," and "I Don't Wanna Cry." In 1991, Carey won Grammy Awards for Best Female Pop Vocal Performance and Best New Artist.

Carey's success continued when her second hit album, *Emotions*, was released in 1991, yielding three more top singles, "Emotions," "Can't Let Go," and "Make It Happen," and in 1992, *MTV Unplugged* sold millions of copies. After a three-year love affair with Mottola, who was more than

quickly recognized her daughter's musical talents when Carey was a tiny girl, and the proud mother helped develop Carey's musical abilities by coaching her at home. As a young girl, Carey sang for friends, and she made her first public performances in talent shows and at folk music festivals when she was only six years old. Until the age of twelve, Carey sang and performed in a number of school plays but then concentrated on music. By the time she was in junior high school, Carey was writing her own songs.

The World's Worst Waitress. In order to study music with professionals, Carey commuted daily to Manhattan during her high school years, and at the age of seventeen, she moved to New York City to pursue her musical career. In order to pay

For the Record

In 1995 Mariah Carey donated one million dollars to a New York camp that provides summer vacations for disadvantaged inner-city children. The camp has subsequently been named Camp Mariah.

twenty years older than Carey, she married him in June of 1993. It was an extremely lavish wedding, costing more than half a million dollars, with fifty flower girls, an eight-piece orchestra, a boys choir, and three hundred famous celebrities in attendance.

After her marriage, Carey's success continued to rise, and her *Music Box* album (1993) sold more than twenty-four million copies and produced the number 1 hits "Dreamlover" and "Hero." In the fall of 1993, Carey made her first musical tour, which received mixed reviews. In 1994, her Christmas album, *Merry Christmas*, yielded the hit "All I Want for Christmas Is You." The generally well-regarded album *Daydream* (1995) pushed Carey's career sales past the eighty-million mark and earned her six Grammy Award nominations, including Album of the Year and Best Pop Album. Carey cowrote all the songs but one on that album, which spawned three big hits, "One Sweet Day," "Fantasy," and "Always Be My Baby."

The year 1997 led to more top hits, but also saw the separation of Carey and Mottola. *Butterfly* (1997) reflects Carey's mixed emotions, being full of hopeful, uplifting songs, but also infused with songs expressing a sense of sadness and loss, most notably "Breakdown." Carey's more modern, hip-hop style of singing on this album also removed her from earlier comparisons that were made between her and Whitney Houston. Hit singles produced from *Butterfly* included the title single, "Honey," "My All," and "Breakdown." In early 1998, Carey had a successful tour in Australia, being well received by large audiences.

Other Dimensions. After becoming a multimillionaire, Carey has generously helped to support her family financially and emotionally. She dedicated her first album to her sister Alison, and Carey has spent much time trying to help Alison overcome a drug addiction problem. Carey donated money from her best-selling album *Emotions* for research on acquired immunodeficiency syndrome (AIDS), and she often donates money to help disadvantaged children.

Having studied acting for more than a year, Carey's future aspirations include acting as well as continuing her music career. She has made three musical videos, *The First Vision*, *MTV Unplugged*, and *Daydream*, at Madison Square Garden.

—*Alvin K. Benson*

SELECT DISCOGRAPHY
■ SINGLES
MTV Unplugged, 1992 (extended-play single)
■ ALBUMS
Mariah Carey, 1990
Emotions, 1991
Music Box, 1993
Merry Christmas, 1994
Daydream, 1995
Butterfly, 1997
#1's, 1998 (compilation)

SELECT AWARDS
Grammy Awards for Best New Artist and Best Pop Vocal Performance, Female, for "Vision of Love," 1990
Soul Train Best New Artist Award, 1990
Soul Train Best Album Award for *Daydream*, 1995

SEE ALSO: Bon Jovi; Dion, Celine; Grant, Amy; Houston, Whitney; Jackson 5; Streisand, Barbra.

Mary Chapin Carpenter

BORN: Princeton, New Jersey; February 21, 1958
FIRST ALBUM RELEASE: *Hometown Girl*, 1987
MUSICAL STYLES: Country, folk, rock, blues

Mary Chapin Carpenter rose to the heights of popularity in country music because of her exceptional abilities to capture in song moments from life and present them in a universal way.

The Beginnings. Carpenter, an accomplished singer-songwriter, was born February 21, 1958, in Princeton, New Jersey, the third of four daughters. Her father, Chapin Carpenter, was an executive with *Life* magazine, and her mother, Bowie Carpenter, worked at a private school. As a child, Mary's first love was ice skating. She was also exposed to all kinds of music at a very young age, learning to strum chords on a guitar as a second-grader.

Mary's family members represented great diversity in their musical interests. Her oldest sister liked classical music while her middle sister liked musical comedy and her younger sister liked rock and roll. Added to that mix were her father's taste for jazz and her mother's preference for opera.

The Carpenter family moved to Tokyo in 1969, when Mary's father was named publishing director of *Life's* Asian edition. In 1971 they returned to New Jersey. Mary's father accepted a job in Washington, D.C., in 1974, forcing the family to relocate again. A short time thereafter, her parents divorced, and Mary left home to finish high school at the Taft School in Watertown, Connecticut. Partly due to the instability of her childhood, she became a loner. Writing music was her way of coping with her insecurities. Mary told Karen Schoemer for a *New York Times Magazine* profile (August 1, 1993): "In high school . . . I just wasn't cool enough, I wasn't pretty enough, I wasn't savvy enough. . . . And I was so convinced of all these feelings that that's when I really retreated into playing music, being by myself, scribbling my thoughts on paper."

Carpenter deferred college for a year after her high school graduation in order to travel, even though she had been accepted by Brown University. As a freshman in 1976 at Brown University, she began performing in Washington-area clubs at the urging of her father. She described her first public performance as an uncomfortable experience because she felt she was going to vomit. Despite her stage fright, she performed at Brown campus's coffeehouse during the school year and in Washington, D.C during summer vacations.

In 1981 Carpenter graduated from Brown University with a B.A. in American Civilization. She returned to Washington, D.C., where she became a popular regular on the bar circuit, doing songs by such well-known performers as Bonnie Raitt, Billie Holiday, and James Taylor. Late nights and hard drinking soon wore her down, but she made the necessary change in 1983 when she accepted a job in Washington as an administrative assistant with the R. J. Reynolds philanthropic organization, dealing with human rights issues in Central America and South Africa. The steady paycheck allowed her to take better care of herself, so that she was able to concentrate on her writing. Eventually, she began to include some of her own numbers among the popular cover songs she sang in her shows.

Mary Chapin Carpenter at the 1992 Country Music Association Awards (AP/Wide World Photos)

Talented Musician and Songwriter. Mary Chapin Carpenter quickly gained a reputation as a talented songwriter. At the 1986 Washington Area Music Awards (known as the Wammies), she won five Wammies, including Best New Artist and Best Songwriter. The awards convinced her that she could be successful in the music business. In November, 1986, Carpenter was about to sign a record deal with Rounder Records, an independent folk-music label, when Gary Oelze, the owner of the Birchmere Club, Carpenter's musical home, told Larry Hamby, an executive with Columbia Records, about Carpenter's likely deal with Rounder Records. Hamby flew to Washington the same day, attended Carpenter's show, and listened to a tape she was selling at her concerts. The next day, he offered her a contract with Columbia Nashville, the label's country music division.

The tape that had caught Hamby's attention became Carpenter's first album, *Hometown Girl* (1987). This debut album announced the arrival of a striking new voice in music. Carpenter also took home five Wammies in 1987, including Artist of the Year, Best Vocalist (Country and Folk), and Best Songwriter. She continued to work at R. J. Reynolds until May, 1989, at which time she decided to devote herself to music full time. In 1989 she again dominated the Wammies, receiving eight awards.

While her first album marked a professional breakthrough, it was her second album, *State of the Heart* (1989), that launched Carpenter into the public eye for good. The album generated four successful singles and paved the way for Carpenter to receive the Academy of Country Music (ACM) Award for New Female Vocalist of the Year in 1989.

For the Record

"My work helps me have an identity, which helps me feel like I have a place, which makes me feel like I have a purpose."
—*Mary Chapin Carpenter* in 1996

In the same year, she was again the star of the Wammies, walking away with nine awards.

Any doubts about Carpenter's credentials were erased in October of 1990, with the release of her third album, *Shooting Straight in the Dark,* a collection of songs about coming to terms with aging and dealing with relationships. The album contains some of her most personal lyrics; it became her first-ever platinum record.

Carpenter's career reached a milestone when she was invited to perform at the 1990 Country Music Association (CMA) Award show. Another highlight of her career was her first Grammy Award, for Best Country Vocal Performance, Female, in February, 1991.

Carpenter's strength as a songwriter was fully evident with the release of her fourth album, *Come On Come On* (1992). The triple-platinum album generated a remarkable seven hit singles. It ultimately scored five Top-10 hits, two number 1 singles, six Grammy Award nominations, and three Grammy Awards.

Carpenter's next album, *Stones in the Road* (1994), debuted at number 1 on the *Billboard* country album chart and held that position for five consecutive weeks. The first single, "Shut Up and Kiss Me," was a number 1 country hit, and Carpenter collected her fourth consecutive Grammy Award for Best Country Vocal Performance, Female. The album went on to win the Grammy Award for Best Country Album, the first award given in this new Grammy category. This clearly validated Carpenter's identity as a major force in American music.

With her sixth album, *A Place in the World* (1996), Carpenter created a multilayered look at an independent woman who measures her life and realizes that what she wants, more than anything, is a love that is magical and real. Through each of the album's twelve songs, she repeats her central point: She is a fool for love, and she would like to prove that her past foolishness will be erased when she makes a lasting connection that transcends all previous heartbreaks and mistakes. In doing so, Carpenter helps her listeners in their own quest to carve "a place in the world."

—*Inoke F. Funaki*

SELECT AWARDS

Academy of Country Music New Female Vocalist of the Year Award, 1989
Country Music Association Female Vocalist of the Year Award, 1991
Grammy Award for Best Country Vocal Performance, Female, for "Down at the Twist and Shout," 1991
Academy of Country Music Female Vocalist of the Year Award, 1992
Country Music Association Female Vocalist of the Year Award, 1992
Grammy Award for Best Country Vocal Performance, Female, for "I Feel Lucky," 1992
Grammy Award for Best Country Vocal Performance, Female, for "Passionate Kisses," 1993
Grammy Awards for Best Country Album for *Stones in the Road* and Best Country Vocal Performance, Female, for "Shut Up and Kiss Me," 1994

SEE ALSO: Cash, Rosanne; Griffith, Nanci; Indigo Girls, The; Raitt, Bonnie.

The Carpenters

MEMBERS: Richard Carpenter (b. 1946), Karen Carpenter (1950-1983)
FIRST ALBUM RELEASE: *Ticket to Ride*, 1969
MUSICAL STYLES: Soft rock, pop

Richard and Karen Carpenter were born in New Haven, Connecticut, but their family moved to Southern California in 1963 (to Downey, a Los Angeles suburb). At Downey High School, Karen took up drums and joined the choir, and Richard entered California State University as a music major in 1964. After Richard became friends with bassist Wes Jacobs, he formed the Richard Carpenter Trio with himself on keyboards, Karen on drums, and Jacobs on bass. After winning a Battle of the Bands talent contest at the Hollywood Bowl, RCA approached the trio with a recording contract. Although the trio did record for RCA, no records were released by the label.

Karen then subtly moved from drums to singing. In 1966 she signed with Magic Lamp Records, an independent label owned by Joe Osborn, and recorded several songs (with Richard on keyboards). One single was released, but only five hundred records were even made. After singing in a couple of vocal groups, including Spectrum, Karen and Richard eventually became a duet, recording all vocal parts via multitrack dubbing. Herb Alpert, after listening to a demo tape, signed the Carpenters to A&M Records, the label that he and Jerry Moss owned.

Offering, the Carpenter's first album (later renamed *Ticket to Ride*) was released late in 1969, which included a slow, ballad version of the Beatles' "Ticket to Ride." Since the first album was not a large commercial success, A&M decided to release only a single next, rather than another album. The single, "Close to You," reached number 1 in just six weeks and lifted the Carpenters to international fame. "Close to You" was the first of a string of hits for the group: sixteen consecutive Top-20 hits with ten gold singles, eight gold albums, and five platinum albums.

Formula for 1970's Success. One of the primary ingredients for the Carpenters' success was Karen's beautiful voice. Tom Nolan, in a 1974 *Rolling Stone* article, described her voice as having "fascinating contrasts: youth with wisdom, chilling perfection with much warmth." In a 1991 article for *Goldmine* magazine, Paul Grein related the Carpenters' success to "Karen's extraordinary voice, which radiated humanity and hope, warmth and wisdom. No female singer of the modern pop era commands greater control or technical skill."

Another key element to the Carpenters' sound was Richard's ability as an arranger. Richard had a flare for finding relatively unknown songs and arranging them into hits (such as "Close to You,"

The Carpenters (Fotos International/Archive Photos)

ard favored woodwind solos (such as clarinet and oboe) to give their music a sense of the richness of nineteenth century Romanticism. Veteran session musicians Joe Osborn, Hal Blaine, and Bob Messenger were some of the artists who also contributed to the duo's sound.

Richard also wrote many of their hits with lyricist John Bettis, including the singles "Goodbye to Love" and "Yesterday Once More." In the 1972 single "Goodbye to Love," Richard uses a rock-guitar solo by new lead guitarist Tony Peluso during the instrumental break (and at the end), which was unique to the soft-rock and pop sounds of the time. The *Now and Then* album (1973) was organized as a concept album, the first side containing new songs, and the second side having a medley of early rock hits, complete with disc-jockey dialogue to give the impression of listening to an oldies radio station.

Another ingredient to the Carpenter success was their clean image. In an era of ear-shattering rock associated with sex, drugs, and anti-establishment sentiment, the Carpenters were portrayed as wholesome and polite—wholesome enough for President Richard Nixon to invite them to the White House and call them "young America at its very best."

Later Experiments. The Carpenters' sound began to evolve in the second half of the 1970's. *Horizon* (1975) includes a remake of a 1937 song, "I Can Dream Can't I" (by Irving Kahal and Sammy Fain), and *Passage* (1977) includes the songs "Calling Occupants of Interplanetary Craft" and "Don't Cry for Me Argentina," which in-

by Burt Bacharach and Hal David, and "We've Only Just Begun," by Paul Williams and Roger Nichols). With Karen's voice in the spotlight, Richard filled in the background with thick vocal harmony, creating a choral sound with only the voices of himself and Karen and the benefit of multitrack dubbing. The chords were often more complex than typical rock harmony (using five-note chords rather than simple triads), and Rich-

cluded a non-Carpenter chorus (Gregg Smith Singers). However, their hits began to decline during this period.

In 1979, while Richard took time off to battle a quaalude dependency, Karen went to New York City to work on a solo album with Grammy Award-winning producer Phil Ramone. Both worked on selecting material that would portray Karen in a more mature light (such as "Remember When Lovin' Took All Night"). Although Karen and Ramone were happy with the results of the 1980 project, Richard and the record executives were skeptical and the project was never released.

An Early End. With Karen's marriage falling apart and her solo project put on the shelf, she teamed with Richard again to make another traditional Carpenters album, *Made in America* (1981). The album include the song that was the only Top-40 hit in the last five years of Karen's life, "Touch Me When We're Dancing." Karen, suffering for years from anorexia nervosa, died unexpectedly of heart failure in 1983, one month away from her thirty-third birthday.

After Karen's death, several albums were released using previously recorded material. *Lovelines* (1989) included four cuts from the Ramone album; the song "If I Had You" was released as a single and made the Top 20 on the adult contemporary chart. Richard also released a solo album, *Time* (1987), and served as the executive producer for the television film *The Karen Carpenter Story* (1989). He has also remixed some of the duo's old hits for rerelease, such as *From the Top*, a boxed set released in 1991.

Other Carpenters-related projects include *The Carpenters: The Untold Story* (1994), a biography by Ray Coleman, and *If I Were a Carpenter*, an album of Carpenters hits recorded by other pop musicians. —*Mark J. Spicer*

SELECT DISCOGRAPHY
■ ALBUMS
Ticket to Ride, 1969
Close to You, 1970
Carpenters, 1971
A Song for You, 1972
Now and Then, 1973

For the Record

Between 1970 and 1980 the Carpenters were the best-selling American group. They also rank second in the amount of number 2 hits, with five (Elvis Presley had six).

The Singles: 1969-1973, 1973
Horizon, 1975
A Kind of Hush, 1976
Passage, 1977
Christmas Portrait, 1978
Made in America, 1981
Voice of the Heart, 1983
An Old-Fashioned Christmas, 1984
Lovelines, 1989
From the Top, 1991
Interpretations: A 25th Anniversary Celebration, 1995

SELECT AWARDS
Grammy Awards for Best New Artist and Best Contemporary Vocal Performance by a Group for "Close to You," 1970
Grammy Award for Best Pop Vocal Performance by a Group for *Carpenters,* 1971
Academy Award for Best Original Song for "For All We Know," from *Lovers and Other Strangers,* 1970

SEE ALSO: Alpert, Herb; Beatles, The; Bread; Captain and Tennille.

The Cars

ORIGINAL MEMBERS: Ric Ocasek (b. Richard Otcasek, 1949), Benjamin Orr (b. Benjamin Orzechowski, 1955), Elliot Easton (b. Elliott Steinberg, 1953), Greg Hawkes, David Robinson (b. 1953)
FIRST ALBUM RELEASE: *The Cars,* 1978
MUSICAL STYLES: New wave, pop, rock and roll

Originating in Boston in 1977, the Cars used flat and detached vocals and tight repetitive rhythms to create a sound that proved to be popular with fans of traditional pop music as well as fans of more avant-garde sounds. The Cars were one of the most commercially successful new-wave bands of the late 1970's and early 1980's.

Milkwood. After dropping out of Antioch College and Bowling Green State University, Ric Ocasek met Ben Orr at a party in Cleveland, Ohio. The pair formed the folk band Milkwood, which, including Greg Hawkes, released two albums, *Milkwood* and *How's the Weather,* on the Paramount label. Settling in the Boston area, the band added guitarist Elliot Easton and renamed themselves Cap'n Swing. The addition of former Modern Lovers drummer David Robinson appears to have been the catalyst that led to the final name change, the adoption of the minimalist red, white, and black color schemes for their stage ensembles, and the circulation of demo tapes in 1976. The Cars' first live concert was at a New Year's Eve show at Pease Air Force Base in New Hampshire.

The Cars, as they were now called, were playing at Boston's Rat Club in 1977 when they attracted the attention of Fred Lewis, who was to become their manager. Lewis arranged for the Cars to open for Bob Seger at Boston's Music Hall. At the same time, the demo tape of "Just What I Needed" became a huge hit on Boston-area radio stations. Soon they were opening for the likes of the J. Geils Band and Foreigner. In November of 1977, after signing a recording contract with Elektra, the Cars were paired with Queen's producer, Roy Thomas Baker, to record their debut album.

"Just What I Needed." The Cars took only two weeks to record their self-titled first album. The crisp, punchy pop sound pushed *The Cars* (1978) to instant success. The debut single, "Just What I Needed," peaked at number 27 on the singles charts. The album jumped to number 18 on the charts. It would stay on the charts for 139 weeks and sell more than two million copies. The Cars stayed on the album chart so long that the follow-up album, *Candy-O,* which was recorded in early

The Cars in 1981 (Deborah Feingold/Archive Photos)

1979, was delayed until July of that year. In January of 1979, the Cars were voted Best New Band of the Year by the readers of *Rolling Stone* magazine.

"Let's Go." In July of 1979, aided by a cover painted by famous pinup artist Alberto Vargas, the band's second album, *Candy-O*, was released. Within a month, *Candy-O* reached number 3 on the album' charts. At the same time, the single "Let's Go" reached number 14 on the singles charts. In 1980, the band's third Baker-produced album, *Panorama*, was released, peaking at number 5 on the charts.

In 1981, the Cars' fourth album, *Shake It Up*, reached number 9 on the charts. In the meantime, Ocasek began to pursue solo ventures (*Beatitude*, 1983) and produce albums for such acts as Suicide, Romeo Void, and Bad Brains at the Cars' studio, Intermedia. The other band members followed in Ocasek's footsteps, engaging in both solo projects and production of other acts.

In 1984, the single "You Might Think" reached number 7 on the singles chart. The computer-generated video for "You Might Think," featuring Ocasek's romantic partner, model Paulina Porizkova, won first prize in the first International Music Video Festival in Saint Tropez, France, and would be named Video of the Year at the inaugural MTV Video Music Awards.

Lost Albums. For their fifth studio album, the Cars employed Robert "Mutt" Lange, who had worked with AC/DC, as producer. The result, *Heartbeat City* (1984), reached number 3 on the album charts. The single "Drive" went to number 3 on the singles charts and became a million seller. In 1985, "Drive" was repromoted at the Live Aid benefit concert. The Cars performed "Drive" while a film was shown documenting the results of a crippling famine in Ethiopia; the lyric "Who's gonna plug their ears when you scream" gained a powerful new meaning. As a result "Drive" made it back to the charts, peaking at number 4. Ocasek donated all subsequent royalties from "Drive" to the Band Aid Trust to fight world hunger.

In 1987, the Cars' final studio album, *Door to Door*, peaked at number 26 on the album charts. In February of 1988, the Cars announced that they had disbanded. Their final single, "Coming

up You," failed to reach the American Top 40. Of all the Cars' original studio albums, only *Door to Door* failed to generate enough sales to be certified platinum. Their debut album, *The Cars*, has sold more than six million copies.

—*B. Keith Murphy*

SELECT DISCOGRAPHY
■ ALBUMS
The Cars, 1978
Candy-O, 1979
Panorama, 1980
Shake It Up, 1981
Heartbeat City, 1984
Door to Door, 1987

Johnny Cash

BORN: Kingsland, Arkansas; February 26, 1932
FIRST SINGLE RELEASE: "Cry, Cry, Cry"/"Hey Porter," 1955 (with the Tennessee Two)
MUSICAL STYLES: Country, rockabilly, rock and roll

Johnny Cash has become an international symbol of American country and roots music over a career of more than forty years. Cash achieved superstar status in the late 1960's and 1970's. With his success on both the country and pop charts he has helped make country music accessible to new, vast audiences. His exploration of a wide variety of song styles and themes, including folk, has helped to expand the scope of country music, often bringing it back to its roots. As a songwriter and a careful selector of songs by others, Cash has not been reluctant to sponsor and encourage new young songwriters, even in the rock medium. As an actor, he has starred in films and television shows over many years and thus reached even more diverse audiences. With his 1996 acceptance of a Kennedy Center Honor, his status as a living legend and cultural icon has been cemented further.

The Beginnings. Cash grew up in the Dyess resettlement community organized under the New Deal in the 1930's. Located in the flat Delta cotton lands of northeast Arkansas, the Dyess colony was a cooperative where poor farmers were given housing and undeveloped land so that they might live independently. Cash worked in the fields picking cotton, along with his father, sisters, and brothers, and he served as a water boy for the levee camp gangs along the nearby Mississippi River.

Cash absorbed country and gospel music from such sources as his mother, older brother, and radio shows beamed from nearby Memphis and stations on the Texas-Mexico border. Groups such as the original Carter Family and the Louvin Brothers were radio favorites for Cash, and later he enjoyed the wide-ranging repertoire of Hank Snow, a particularly versatile singer of old folk songs and ballads and the writer of the uptempo hit "I'm Moving On." In the early 1950's, Cash tried work in the auto plants of Detroit, but he then decided to enlist in the U.S. Air Force. Serving in Germany for four years, he and some friends had a country band and played the current hits. On returning home in 1954, he decided to settle in Memphis, get married, and become an appliance salesman. Music, though, was always on his mind, and he teamed up with two local musicians, Marshall Grant and Luther Perkins, to form the Tennesse Two, which performed on gospel radio shows.

Like other local musicians who aspired to make music a professional career, Cash and his band auditioned for Sam Phillips' Sun Records after the label's success with Elvis Presley's 1954 recording "That's All Right." By 1955 Presley was a regional sensation, and anyone with talent was knocking on Phillips' door. He was not willing to record Cash's gospel songs but told him to use secular songs he could more easily market. Cash had already been writing songs and came forward with what would be his first single release: "Cry, Cry, Cry" backed with "Hey Porter." These were distinctly original efforts and brought Cash and the Tennessee Two to the notice of country music fans and the industry powers. His 1956 "I Walk the Line" (another original song) became a huge hit on both the country charts (number 1) and the pop charts (number 17). A number 4 country hit

For the Record

In 1956 Johnny Cash participated in one of the most legendary jam sessions in music history. On December 4, he and Elvis Presley happened to visit Sun Records in Memphis, Tennessee, at the same moment, while Jerry Lee Lewis was playing piano as a guest during a Carl Perkins recording session. Cash and Presley joined the other two for some impromptu jamming in what has been called the "Million Dollar Quartet."

in the same year was his own classic "Folsom Prison Blues."

The style he developed with Grant and Perkins, and later with the addition of drummer W. S. Holland, would serve him throughout his career. It was a new style in country music at the time: Instead of having his singing backed by such instruments as steel guitar, fiddle, and even another acoustic rhythm guitar (common in the 1940's and 1950's hard honky-tonk style favored by Hank Williams), Cash elected to work out a very spare sound that would let him highlight his singing and lyrics over a simple accompaniment of Perkins's electric guitar and Grant's upright bass. In other words, he sang with a minimal rhythm backing, with Perkins playing a simple bluesy solo break. Cash believed that less was more, and fans were quickly captivated by this approach. This style was not much different from that of the other artists at Sun who used small bands: Presley, Carl Perkins, and Jerry Lee Lewis. These young artists developed a fast rhythmic music blending country and uptempo blues, creating a style called rockabilly, one of the major substyles within the new rock-and-roll music of the mid-1950's.

Cash was more deeply country than the other Sun artists, and he was a major songwriter as well. Although "I Walk the Line" became his signature song, he saw pop music chart success with songs such as "Ballad of a Teenage Queen" (a number

1 country hit and a number 14 pop hit) and "Guess Things Happen That Way" (number 1, country; number 11, pop). These were written for Cash and produced on Sun Records and used a fuller instrumentation and chorus. His own "Big River" and "Give My Love to Rose" indicated his ability to craft folklike narrative songs.

Stardom in the 1960's. Cash's success in crossing over onto the pop charts led him to a label larger than Sun. In 1958 he began a long tenure with Columbia Records. There he had immediate success with "Don't Take Your Guns to Town" in 1958 (another Cash original which was a number 1 country hit as well as a pop hit). On Columbia he was able to record a more varied repertory and to create concept albums. Even though he had single hits such as "Ring of Fire" in 1963, his major interest was in exploring folk and roots music themes tied to American history. Albums such as *Ride This Train* (1960), *Blood, Sweat, and Tears* (1963), *Bitter Tears: Ballads of the American Indian* (1964), and *Ballads of the True West* (1965) illustrate the originality of Cash's approach to American music. Songs of the cowboy, the lumberjack, and the miner (often of his own composition) were added to old spirituals and gospel songs in his expanded repertoire. He adapted the folk ballad "John Henry" into an eight-minute saga called "The Legend of John Henry's Hammer" which he featured on his first-rate traveling show of the time.

Cash appeared at the 1964 Newport Folk Festival in Rhode Island and became friends with Bob Dylan, recording some songs with him. In the 1960's

Cash developed drug problems with amphetamines, and his marriage to Vivian Liberto ended in divorce. In 1968 he married June Carter, daughter of Maybelle Carter of the Carter Family. That same year he recorded a live album at Folsom Prison in California, producing an enormously popular hit in country and pop music. Indeed, his old cut of "Folsom Prison Blues" from that album became a number 1 country hit and reached number 32 on the pop charts. His career was then at a peak, with a follow-up live album at

Johnny Cash (Archive Photos)

San Quentin prison also hitting number 1 (country) and selling broadly across the musical spectrum. The novelty song "A Boy Named Sue" (written by Shel Silverstein) from the album went on to reach number 1 (country) and number 2 (pop) in 1969. Cash carried this new success with the general public into a network television show (*The Johnny Cash Show)* between 1969 and 1971, which featured country, folk, rock, and pop singers. His outspoken sympathy with prisoners and the plight of U.S. soldiers in Vietnam made him popular with a younger generation of protesters and concerned citizens. He encouraged the songwriters coming into country music who wrote more socially conscious songs, particularly championing the work of Kris Kristofferson whose "Sunday Morning Coming Down" was another crossover hit for Cash.

The 1970's and Later. In the 1970's and 1980's Cash went on to consolidate and expand his career. His biggest albums sold to a national audience, not just to country fans. Among his single hits were: "Jackson" and "If I Were a Carpenter" (duets with June Carter), "A Thing Called Love," "Oney," "One Piece at a Time," and "Ghost Riders in the Sky." His touring troupe included Maybelle Carter and her daughters Helen, Anita, and June, along with the four Statler Brothers. The Carters did old-time songs and with the Statlers provided backing for Cash's favorite religious songs. His troupe was the most elaborate at the time in country music, with concerts featuring film clips to illustrate songs and an expanded backup band. Cash also acted in several well-received productions: the feature film *A Gunfight* (1971) with Kirk Douglas, starring roles in television films *Thaddeus Rose and Eddie* (1978, with June Carter) and *The Pride of Jesse Hallam* (1981). He also produced his own religious film, *Gospel Road*, and has been a guest on the weekly television series *Dr. Quinn, Medicine Woman.*

Teaming up with his friends Waylon Jennings, Willie Nelson, and Kris Kristofferson to become the Highwaymen, Cash did a series of concert tours and recorded three albums: *Highwayman* (1985), *Highwayman 2* (1990), and *The Road Goes on Forever* (1995). Leaving Columbia Records in 1986, he recorded for Mercury, then American Recordings to put out two successful, very personal albums: *American Recordings* (1994) and *Unchained* (1996).

Legacy. Tall, charismatic, and dramatic, Cash helped make country a national music as well as an international favorite for millions. His openness to new songwriters and artists such as Kris Kristofferson, Bob Dylan, and Bruce Springsteen expanded the styles of country artists from the 1960's to the present. His interest in folk material and other roots music and his attention to traditions indicate his unique position as an American singer. His focus in song on the poor and the working class and his concern for the dispossessed is echoed in all his work, making him a true spokesman for the people.   —*Frederick E. Danker*

SELECT DISCOGRAPHY

■ SINGLES

"I Walk the Line," 1956

"Ring of Fire," 1963

"Folsom Prison Blues," 1968

"A Boy Named Sue," 1969

■ ALBUMS

Johnny Cash with His Hot and Blue Guitar, 1957

The Fabulous Johnny Cash, 1958

Ride This Train, 1960

Blood, Sweat, and Tears, 1963

Bitter Tears: Ballads of the American Indian, 1964

Johnny Cash at Folsom Prison, 1968

Johnny Cash at San Quentin, 1969

The Essential Johnny Cash, 1955-1983, 1992 (compilation)

Unchained, 1996

SELECT AWARDS

Grammy Award for Best Country & Western Performance, Duet, Trio, or Group (Vocal or Instrumental), for "Jackson," 1967 (with June Carter Cash)

Grammy Award for Best Country Vocal Performance, Male, for "Folsom Prison Blues," 1968

Country Music Association Album of the Year Award for *Johnny Cash at Folsom Prison*, 1968

Country Music Association Single of the Year for "A Boy Named Sue," Album of the Year for *Johnny Cash at San Quentin Prison*, Entertainer of the Year, Male Vocalist of the Year, and Vocal Group of the Year (with June Carter Cash) Awards, 1969

Grammy Award for Best Country Vocal Performance, Male, for "A Boy Named Sue," 1969

Grammy Award for Best Country Vocal Performance by a Duo or Group for "If I Were a Carpenter," 1970 (with June Carter Cash)

Country Music Hall of Fame, inducted 1980

Grammy Legend Award, 1991

Rock and Roll Hall of Fame, inducted 1992

Grammy Award for Best Contemporary Folk Album for *American Recordings*, 1994

Kennedy Center Honors, 1996

SEE ALSO: Dylan, Bob; Kristofferson, Kris; Orbison, Roy; Perkins, Carl; Presley, Elvis.

Rosanne Cash

BORN: Memphis, Tennessee; May 24, 1955
FIRST ALBUM RELEASE: *Rosanne Cash*, 1978
MUSICAL STYLES: Country, country rock, rock and roll, pop, folk

Rosanne Cash was a country music hit machine in the 1980's, a superb interpretive singer and excellent songwriter whose sultry vocals contrasted beautifully with the creative, glossy production of Nashville's best session musicians. Cash's mature commentary on relationships combined honest emotional vulnerability and open sexual desire, and her hits brought an important strong female voice to the rigidly controlled realm of country radio. In 1991, she moved to New York City, and left both country music and her first husband (producer and singer-songwriter Rodney Crowell) behind. Her 1990's albums were stark personal confessions in the singer-songwriter mode and retained only the soft rhythmic pulse and sharp turn of phrase suggestive of country ballads. The move from country music star to literary folksinger is an unusual one in American popular music, but Cash's music has always defied easy categorization.

The Cash Legacy. Cash was born in Memphis to country and rock-and-roll legend Johnny Cash

and his first wife, Vivian Liberto, just as rock and roll was being born in that city. When Cash was three, her family moved from Memphis to Southern California amid rumors of marital strife and the senior Cash's taste for wild living. Raised by her mother, Rosanne grew into a sullen, moody adolescent and rebelled against her parents and teachers. She experimented with marijuana and LSD and listened often to Joni Mitchell and the Beatles (two major influences). In 1973, she joined her father's road show as a laundress. Johnny Cash gave her a list of one hundred country songs she had to learn "if she was going to be his daughter," and she soon worked her way to being a backup singer for him.

Cash traveled extensively in the 1970's. She worked for Columbia Records in London for one year, attended Nashville's Vanderbilt University, and tried acting at the Lee Strasberg Institute in Los Angeles. In 1978, an obscure German record label offered her a record contract after hearing a demo tape. She recruited rising singer-songwriter and producer Rodney Crowell, whom she met at a party of country legend Waylon Jennings. Never released in the United States, the album forged a partnership that dominated the next ten years of her life. Cash and Crowell married in 1979, the year her second album, *Right or Wrong*, was released. Influenced by the studio-based Los Angeles country rock of the 1970's, the album (made with Crowell's rockabilly band) yielded two moderate hits and established her reputation as a member of the "young country" movement.

Three Country Classics. Cash broke through commercially and critically with *Seven-Year Ache* (1981). The album went gold, yielded three number 1 country hits (two of them written by Cash), and was nominated for a Grammy Award for Best Country Album. Cash imbued this eclectic batch of songs (from songwriters such as Tom Petty and Steve Forbert) with a unified mood of defiant yearning, yet each song told a story of its own. For example, the three number 1 hits all revolve around the classic country theme of adultery. Leroy Preston's "My Baby Thinks He's a Train" is a playful country-rock number about

For the Record

Rosanne Cash was nominated for five Grammy Awards in the 1980's, and she is number fifteen on the all-time list of female country hit makers.

cheating in the early stages of a relationship. Cash's "Seven-Year Ache" is also uptempo musically, but the driving beat is offset by a wife's late-night impatience with her husband's roving. "Blue Moon with Heartache" is a lover's lament that ponders the end of a fading relationship. All three songs seem to come from the same pen and the same heart.

Cash and Crowell had struck upon a fresh synthesis of country, rock, folk, and pop music. Using Nashville session musicians and state of the art rock-and-roll production values, they combined pop music hooks with country's traditional values and Cash's naked emotional honesty. Crowell set off Cash's cool, rhythmically-balanced vocal delivery either against a driving country beat with guitar solos (on uptempo songs) or paired with swirling keyboard accompaniment (on ballads).

This formula worked because each of the 1980's albums featured a distinctive set of themes. On *Rhythm and Romance* (1985), Cash used a rock-and-roll drive to give vent to her quiet anguish. Cash's success was belied by a turbulent personal life that included marital problems and a cocaine habit. She did not enjoy being part of one of Nashville's first families; she never toured much and preferred to spend time with her three daughters. Rock songs such as "Halfway House" openly discussed issues of addiction and recovery, and the album's two huge country hits (both written by Cash), "Hold On" and "I Don't Know Why You Don't Want Me," were testaments to both her loneliness and growing female strength. Cash used writing and singing for therapy and admitted she looked back on certain songs with relief: "I don't feel that way anymore, thank God," she once said to an interviewer.

King's Record Shop (1987) featured hard-driving stripped-down rock songs and acoustic country classics. The album yielded four number 1 country hits, including the Tex-Mex-flavored "The Way We Mend a Broken Heart" by John Hiatt and a remake of her father's 1955 hit, "Tennessee Flat-Top Box." In "Rosie Strike Back," she advises a battered woman to leave home, and in Crowell's "I Don't Have to Crawl," she sings about her leaving home rather than apologizing to her husband. In "The Real Me," Cash seems to ache for transformation, musically and emotionally: "This is the real me/ breaking down at last/ This is the real me/ crawling out of my past/ And the real me/ wants the real you/ so bad."

New Urban Folk. In 1990, Cash produced and wrote all the material for an intimate and revealing song cycle of acoustic songs, *Interiors*. The critically-acclaimed album represented a break from country music, from Crowell's control (the couple would divorce in 1992), and from her country-star days as captured in *Hits 1979-1989* (1989). In 1993, she released *The Wheel*, a story of emotional rejuvenation that featured her most relaxed singing and some lush production. Songs such as the title track and "Sleeping in Paris" showed Cash aspiring toward poetic models and the European art-song tradition. After marrying producer John Leventhal, she compiled an alternative musical autobiography entitled *Retrospective* (1995). Composed of mostly 1990's material and outtakes from Cash's 1980's albums, the album ignored hits and told a more compelling story of her learning process.

The country audience rejected Cash after *Interiors*, but she became a fixture on the folk and college circuits, often playing with her friends Lucinda Williams and Mary Chapin Carpenter. In *10-Song Demo* (1996), Cash attempted to meld folk simplicity, confessional poetry, and chamber music. Songs such as "If I Were a Man" provided a fresh take on relationships, but the songs lacked the flow of her country story songs and their defiant yearning. Cash focused more on the lyrics than on the rhythmic drive, and continued to bare her feelings as completely as possible.

—Joel Dinerstein

SELECT DISCOGRAPHY

■ ALBUMS

Right or Wrong, 1979
Seven-Year Ache, 1981
Rhythm & Romance, 1985
King's Record Shop, 1987
Hits 1979-1989, 1989 (compilation)
Interiors, 1990
The Wheel, 1993
Retrospective, 1995

SELECT AWARDS

Grammy Award for Best Country Vocal Performance, Female, for "I Don't Know Why You Don't Want Me," 1985
Billboard, named Top Singles Artist, 1988

SEE ALSO: Carpenter, Mary Chapin; Cash, Johnny; Mitchell, Joni; Petty, Tom, and the Heartbreakers.

The Chambers Brothers

MEMBERS: George E. Chambers (b. 1931), Willie Chambers (b. 1938), Lester Chambers (b. 1940), Joe Chambers (b. 1942), Brian Keenan (1944-mid-1980's)
FIRST ALBUM RELEASE: *People Get Ready*, 1965
MUSICAL STYLES: Rock and roll, rhythm and blues, psychedelic rock

Composed of five African American brothers from a Mississippi sharecropping family and an unlikely white man from New York City (on drums, no less), the Chambers Brothers represent one of the most unique and inspiring bands of the late 1960's. With roots in black gospel, the four brothers combined their interests in country, folk, blues, rhythm and blues, rock and roll, and psychedelia to create a sound appealing to both black and white audiences during a time when crossover artists were virtually unheard of.

The Beginnings. Spending their formative years doing intensive manual labor on various sharecropping farms outside Forest, Mississippi, the Chambers family endured through a shared love of music. As a nightly routine they would sing together, and, not surprisingly, the boys

formed their own gospel group as teenagers. In 1954 the family moved to Los Angeles in search of a better life.

During the Civil Rights movement of the 1950's-1970's, gospel music gained social importance for African Americans, and Los Angeles was home to a thriving gospel community. There, the brothers contributed to the struggle for equal rights while managing to make a living from their music. They joined the Interdenominational Singers Alliance, performed regularly at Brother Henderson's Gospel Corner and recorded two gospel songs, "I Trust in God" and "Just a Little More Faith." Sensing the vibrant energies of the area's folk scene, however, the Chamberses began performing in folk venues and even added folk songs to their gospel sets.

Newport News. By 1965 their act had gained enough attention to be booked into that year's Newport Folk Festival, a landmark event that featured Bob Dylan's crowd-stunning first electric-instrument performance, but the Chambers Brothers were no less memorable. They played the song that would later become their biggest hit, "Time Has Come Today," a poignant choice because of the song's sensitivity to civil rights activism and its understanding of the younger generation's discontentment with older conservatism in the folk scene and American culture in general. Their raucous performance caused a near riot and helped usher in a new movement that combined the energy of rock and roll with the social conscience of folk and gospel.

With new recognition the group signed to Vault Records and recorded *People Get Ready* in 1965, an album combining soul, blues, and gospel sensibilities. Written by soul performer Curtis Mayfield, the title track addresses civil rights themes of freedom for black Americans and shows the group's race pride and commitment to social change. In 1966 the band released their second album, *The Chambers Brothers Now*, with George on bass, Willie and Joe on guitars, and Lester on harmonica, while all shared vocal duties. Rounding out their lineup was drummer Brian Keenan, former member of the British rock band Manfred Mann. The Chambers were now an interracial band working within a primarily white music scene, a scene they were simultaneously working to make interracial.

A year later the band signed with Columbia Records after scoring a regional hit with the rhythm-and-blues song "All Strung Out over You." Columbia gave them a chance to rerecord "Time Has Come Today." Given the song's rock-and-roll feel, the label was apprehensive of letting a black group perform it: With the exception of Motown artists, most black soul and rhythm-and-blues acts did not garner much of a cross-over audience (the same was true for white pop groups crossing over to black audiences). Adding to the uncertainty, the Civil Rights movement's gospel vision of faith in positive change was beginning to sour. After major riots in the Watts neighborhood of Los Angeles and the assassination of black leader Malcolm X in 1965, the Student Nonviolent Coordinating Committee, a leading civil rights group, adopted a Black Power agenda that tended to alienate whites. These events precipitated increased racial tensions on a national level.

Sonic Revolution. As a primarily black interracial band playing a style that could certainly be called interracial itself, the Chambers Brothers were in a problematic position. Not compromising their vision, the band insisted on recording "Time Has Come Today" with their old producer, David Rubinson, who understood their ideas of transferring their psychedelic live performances onto records. Trust in their project paid off.

Released in December of 1967, by February the album *The Time Has Come* reached number 4, and by August "Time Has Come Today" had reached number 11 on the singles charts. The song's revolutionary plea linked the common struggles of blacks and whites through the mind-expanding ethic of psychedelia. Finding a common bond in the nation's youth, they sang "Young hearts can go their way/ they think we don't listen anyway." Speaking of the alienation shared by both blacks and the white counterculture, the Chamberses testified to the healing powers of the youth movement: "Now the time has come. . . . my soul has been psychedelicized!"

That year, their cross-cultural appeal would also be reflected in their live appearances. From performing at black clubs such as the Apollo Theatre in Harlem, New York, and hippie ballrooms on the West Coast just a year before, the group began playing venues such as the Fillmore West in San Francisco, sharing the stage with white subculture icons such as the Doors, the Byrds, and Jefferson Airplane. Branded a "psychedelic soul" group, they made the charts with two other songs that year, both hallucinogenic versions of popular soul hits "I Can't Turn You Loose" and "Shout." Their subsequent 1968 album, *A New Time—A New Day*, made it to number 16, but the band's popularity soon waned, and by 1972 they had officially disbanded. A short-lived reunion in 1974 produced two more albums before they disbanded once more.

Legacy. The Chambers Brothers' short-lived glory marks more than a notch on the historical timeline of rock history. As crossover innovators, they belong in the same category with such musical giants as Sly and the Family Stone and the Jimi Hendrix Experience. Columbia's 1996 compilation of their works attests to the band's enduring contribution to psychedelic soul (as evidenced by their experimental ten-minute version of the gospel standard "Wade in the Water"). Intermittently pursuing solo careers, the group would continue performing together for special events such as the 1989 Earthquake Relief benefit concert in San Francisco, though Keenan had recently died of a heart attack. The brothers continue to sing in a family-based gospel choir, the Chambers Family Singers.

—*Dave Junker*

For the Record

In 1965 the Chambers Brothers recruited drummer Brian Keenan after he performed with the group during an improvised appearance at a small club in New York that was secretly set up by Bob Dylan.

SELECT DISCOGRAPHY

■ ALBUMS

People Get Ready, 1965

The Chambers Brothers Now, 1966

The Time Has Come, 1967

A New Time—A New Day, 1968

Love, Peace and Happiness, 1969

The Chambers Brothers Greatest Hits, 1970
    (compilation)

New Generation, 1971

The Chambers Brothers Greatest Hits, 1971
    (compilation)

Oh My God! 1972

Unbonded, 1974

Right Move, 1975

Time Has Come: The Best of the Chambers Brothers,
    1996

SEE ALSO: Dylan, Bob; Redding, Otis; Sly and the Family Stone.

Harry Chapin

BORN: Greenwich Village, New York; December 7, 1942

DIED: Jericho, New York; July 16, 1981

FIRST ALBUM RELEASE: *Heads and Tales*, 1972

MUSICAL STYLE: Folk rock

A popular singer-songwriter of the 1970's, Harry Chapin is remembered as the creator of numerous story songs. "Taxi," the hit that first brought him national attention, and "Cat's in the Cradle" are the best known of these. Fans also remember Chapin as a tireless champion for social and artistic causes. An automobile accident on the Long Island Expressway cut short his life at the age of thirty-eight.

Early Years. Chapin came from an accomplished family. He was the second son of Jim Chapin, a drummer for musicians Tommy Dorsey and Woody Herman, and the maternal grandson of literary critic Kenneth Burke. Harry and his three brothers each took up music early, Harry beginning with the trumpet before switching to banjo and then guitar. As a boy, Harry also sang in the Brooklyn Heights Boys Choir and formed assorted bands with his younger siblings.

After high school, Chapin entered and quickly left the Air Force Academy. He then attended Cornell University but dropped out. In 1964, he reunited with his brothers Tom and Steve to form the Chapin Brothers. The ensemble, with their father on drums, performed at New York folk clubs and released an album on an independent label before disbanding. Chapin began work in films during the same period. He started as a crate packer and went on to produce airline commercials and boxing films. One of his documentaries, 1967's "Legendary Champions," garnered an Academy Award nomination.

"Taxi." Chapin returned to music in 1971. He assembled a new band, still with a familial core, and rented New York's Village Gate for a summer of performances. A local following developed and Chapin soon signed with Elektra Records. The company released his national debut, *Heads and Tales*, the following year. The album included Chapin's first hit, "Taxi." Partly autobiographical, it tells of a chance encounter between a taxi driver and his old high school sweetheart. Each learns that the other has abandoned youthful dreams to live out a life of quiet desperation.

Six other albums and a few more singles followed in subsequent years. Among Chapin's hit songs, "Cat's in the Cradle," with lyrics by his wife, Sandy, has proved the most enduring. Like many of his numbers, it tells a melancholy tale about the trials and tribulations of an everyday person, a businessman too busy to be a true father to his growing son. The characters in Chapin's other story songs are equally ordinary: a lonely night watchman, a singing dry cleaner, a washed-up deejay, a dirt farmer meeting his mail-order bride for the first time. Chapin's fans heard echoes of their own lives in the sentiments of these tales. They also heard sincerity in his leathery baritone voice and down-to-earth yet passionate delivery. To fans, Chapin offered succor from the glibness of most Top-40 songs.

Chapin's most profound statements tended to be the most directly autobiographical. The self-portrait that emerges from songs such as "There

Harry Chapin (Archive Photos)

Was Only One Choice" and "Story of a Life" is of an all-too-human individual plagued by but resigned to personal shortcomings and the passage of time. These personal statements reveal Chapin's deep devotion to his wife and family as well as a prophetic sense of his own early passage from this world. Chapin also penned a number of folk anthems, including "All My Life's a Circle" and "Remember When the Music," and saw himself as a politically active urban folksinger in the tradition of Pete Seeger and Phil Ochs.

Chapin also wrote for the stage. His 1975 Broadway musical, *The Night That Made America Famous*, received two Tony nominations, and his revue *Chapin* enjoyed runs in several cities during 1977. At the time of his death, *Cabbage Patch Gospel*, a musical retelling the Gospels of Matthew and John translated into southern vernacular, was playing Off-Broadway.

Chapin and His Critics. Reviewers dogged Chapin with unflattering remarks throughout his career. They accused him of being didactic, moralistic, unctuous, maudlin, banal, fatuous, and cloying. An unspoken subtext to much criticism seemed to be that Chapin just was not "cool." Some countered that the standard used to judge him was misapplied. He was not a composer of lyrically opaque songs, nor did he want to be. Chapin himself argued, "Art, schmart. I'm not trying to do art; art will take care of itself. I'm trying to communicate some basic truths." He did so through musical narratives that expressed meaning with utmost clarity. As Tony Kornheiser wrote in the New York Times, "Interpreting Chapin's songs is redundant; they are self-explanatory."

To give Chapin his full due, he did write his fair share of memorable melodies and finely wrought lyrics. Moreover, his use of longer musical forms, ones going beyond the standard alternation of verse and chorus, is noteworthy. More than anything, however, Chapin was without peer as a composer of story songs, a medium requiring skill in plot development, scene setting, and character portrayal in addition to ability in creating melody and verse. In fact, it is probably better to compare Chapin to Charles Dickens or O. Henry than to other singer-songwriters, "A Better Place to Be" and "Mail Order Annie" being no more banal, fatuous, or cloying than *A Christmas Carol* or "The Gift of the Magi."

Nothing Less than a Hero. In "The Parade's Still Passing By," Chapin sings, "But it's more than the words/ It's the deeds that are heard/ When all is said and done." He lived out this creed perhaps more than any other popular artist active during the 1970's. Chapin gave lavishly of his time, energy, and money to a long list of social and artistic causes. Statistics help tell the story. Of the more than two hundred concerts he performed each year at the height of his career, more than half were for charity. In 1977 alone, Chapin earned two million dollars and gave $700,000 of it to charity. First among his philanthropic interests was the fight against world hunger. With friend Bill Ayers, Chapin founded the nonprofit World Hunger Year and lobbied the United States Congress to address systemic problems that perpetuate hunger around the world. His Washington efforts culminated in President Jimmy Carter's establishment of the President's Committee on International, Domestic, and World Hunger.

Many fans remain loyal to Chapin years after his death. Such devotion stems from the lasting appeal of Chapin's music, the close bond he forged with live audiences, and the belief, held by many, that he was nothing less than a hero. Indeed, the United States Congress posthumously awarded him a Gold Medal in 1986 for his work toward ending world hunger. Pat Benatar, Graham Nash, the Smothers Brothers, Bruce Springsteen, Judy Collins, and others paid musical tribute to Chapin in a Carnegie Hall concert later the same year. As for the future, the popularity of Websites dedicated to Chapin and the continued release of posthumous albums suggest that the singer-songwriter's legacy will continue for many years.　　　　　　　　　　　　　*—David Lee Fish*

SELECT DISCOGRAPHY
■ ALBUMS
Heads and Tales, 1972
Short Stories, 1973
Greatest Stories, Live, 1976
Dance Band on the Titanic, 1977
Sequel, 1980

SELECT AWARDS
Special Congressional Gold Medal, 1986 (posthumous)

SEE ALSO: Chapman, Tracy; Croce, Jim; Dylan, Bob; Seeger, Pete.

For the Record

"Being a rock star is pointless. It's garbage. It's the most self-indulgent thing I can think of. I've got nothing against selling out. But let me sell out for something that counts. Not so Harry Chapin can be number 1 with a bullet, but so I can leave here thinking I mattered."*—Harry Chapin*

Tracy Chapman

BORN: Cleveland, Ohio; March 20, 1964
FIRST ALBUM RELEASE: *Tracy Chapman,* 1988
MUSICAL STYLES: Folk, blues

Tracy Chapman credits her mother and sister for her early interest in music. Coming of age in Cleveland, Ohio, in the 1970's, Chapman learned to play ukulele, piano, and clarinet and taught herself to play the guitar. Most important, perhaps, she was writing original songs by the time she was ten years old.

Youth and Education. Chapman's parents divorced when she was four, leaving her mother alone to raise two girls in a largely black middle-class neighborhood. Often there was not enough money to care for the three of them; sometimes they were on welfare. The impressions left on Chapman by early encounters with poverty and social injustice in an urban environment outfitted her to become a successful folksinger in a field where most do not meet with success. Excelling at high school academics, Chapman worked to win an A Better Chance (ABC) minority placement scholarship and transferred to the progressive Episcopalian preparatory Wooster School in Danbury, Connecticut. Wooster School provided an intellectual haven which encouraged social and political discussion and was a welcome relief to Chapman after the metal-detector protection of her public high school in Cleveland. Speaking of her Wooster experience in *Time* magazine, she said that some "students there just said very stupid things. They had never met a poor person before. In some ways they were curious, but in ways that were just insulting." The school also proved to be a haven for musicians. While in Connecticut, Chapman met other guitar players who introduced her to music she had never heard, including Bob Dylan's early protest music. The people at Wooster School were so supportive of Chapman's music that they took up a collection among the faculty and students to replace Chapman's battered old guitar with a new one.

Though she loved music and met with strong support, Chapman did not seriously consider a career in music after high school. When she enrolled at Tufts University near Boston, she planned to study veterinary medicine. Early in her college career, however, Chapman changed her major to anthropology with an emphasis in West African culture and eventually got her B.A. in that field. Throughout college, she continued to write and play her own music informally in coffeehouses and on the streets of Harvard Square. She impressed her listeners with her ability to speak with honesty and insight about all people's experiences. At one point, she was offered a recording contract with an independent label, but, uncomfortable with interrupting her studies, Chapman turned it down. Later, Brian Koppelman, one of Chapman's classmates, suggested that his father could help Chapman's singing career. Brian's father was Charles Koppelman, the "K" in SBK, a leading music publishing company. Chapman was considering a master's program in ethnomusicology, the branch of musicology dealing with native or folk music in relation to the culture that produces it. After graduating from Tufts in 1986, however, she signed with SBK, agreeing to representation by manager Elliot Roberts. A demonstration tape Chapman recorded at SBK studios led to a recording contract with Elektra Records in 1987.

Musical Career Begins. A prolific songwriter, Chapman had a plethora of material from which to choose the songs for her self-titled debut album. *Tracy Chapman* (1988) follows none of the standard rules for popular music marketing. It consisted of a variety of songs that she had written in previous years, as early as 1982. The melodies meander and the lyrics are oddly phrased; many of the songs discuss serious political issues—apartheid, domestic violence, racism, and poverty in the world's wealthiest nation. In defiance of all trends, Chapman's album rose to the top of the American charts and sold ten million copies worldwide. The singles "Fast Car" and "Talkin' 'Bout a Revolution" met with amazing success. Chapman emerged at a time when there was a demand for a sincere and humble cry against social problems at the end of the selfish and materialistic 1980's. The image of Chapman, dreadlocked and clad in blue jeans, taking the stage alone except for her acoustic guitar appealed to far more people than the marketing department at Elektra Records could have anticipated. At the 1988 Grammy Awards, Tracy Chapman came away with the awards for Best Contemporary Folk Album, Best New Artist, and Best Pop Vocal Performance, Female. Despite those reviewers who described her music as downbeat, Chapman hoped that her music could reach a wide audience and deliver a positive message. Certainly, her performance schedule was influenced by her social consciousness. Chapman joined the Sisterfire festival in Washington, D.C.; Amnesty International's worldwide "Human Rights Now!" tour; a march to commemorate Dr. Martin Luther King; Freedomfest, honoring Nelson Mandela; the concert honoring Bob Dylan's thirtieth anniversary; and the successful Lilith Fair tour celebrating women artists.

Tracy Chapman in 1992 (AP/Wide World Photos)

After the Debut. Her second album, *Crossroads* (1989), was very popular, selling four million copies in the first five months of its release, but it was considered too political to be successful on the radio. Because of her repeat success, many critics believed that Chapman would spark a resurgence in protest music. Not altogether comfortable with her celebrity, she admitted to McKenna of *Musician* magazine: "The idea of being famous doesn't appeal to me because I hate parties and it seems like it might be one big party. I value my privacy and I'm not used to dealing with lots of people. The prospect of wealth is scary too. When you're poor your first responsibility is to yourself, but when you have money you have to think about other people—and other people are definitely thinking about you!" This discomfort with publicity is evident in Chapman's adamant refusal to discuss her personal life.

In 1992, Chapman released *Matters of the Heart*, which was not very successful commercially. Critics had mixed reactions to the album, though almost all agreed that the song "Bang Bang Bang" was excellent. Chapman returned to the spotlight (and the good graces of audiences and critics alike) with the release of *New Beginnings* in 1995. The songs on this album are about personal change, growth, and renewal, and they return with startling sincerity to the stirring arrangements and powerful wordplay found on her debut album. With *New Beginnings*, Chapman puts forth the idea that "we're at a place right now, approaching the new century where we could find new solutions to old problems that are still plaguing society." The successful album boosted Chapman's musical career. The single "Give Me One Reason" became a number 1 pop hit and the album sold more than five million copies. Furthermore, Chapman won her fourth Grammy Award in 1997—Best Song for "Give Me One Reason"—and continued promoting her album with a successful tour. —*Melissa R. Grimm*

SELECT DISCOGRAPHY

■ ALBUMS
Tracy Chapman, 1988
Crossroads, 1989
Matters of the Heart, 1992
New Beginnings, 1995

SELECT AWARDS
Grammy Awards for Best New Artist, Best Contemporary Folk Recording for *Tracy Chapman*, and Best Pop Vocal Performance, Female, for "Fast Car," 1988
Grammy Award for Best Song for "Give Me One Reason," 1996

SEE ALSO: Dylan, Bob.

Ray Charles

BORN: Albany, Georgia; September 23, 1930
FIRST SINGLE RELEASE: "St. Pete's Blues," 1949
MUSICAL STYLES: Blues, country, gospel, jazz, rhythm and blues, soul

Ray Charles has been called "The Genius of Soul." From very difficult beginnings he went on to become one of the most successful and influential singers in U.S. history. Originating in blues and gospel, his style branches out into many musical genres and blurs the division of popular music into separate categories. Charles is credited for placing the blues tradition into a broader musical context and exposing it to larger audiences. He also helped create soul music by merging blues with gospel and expanded the scope of country and western music. Charles sings a country song, a jazz ballad, or a blues tune with the same naturalness and heartfelt sincerity. With his lush, inimitable voice he can recast into a unique and personal rendition any song he loves to sing, whether a traditional hymn or a pop tune. His musical talent is not limited to his singing and can be equally appreciated in his piano, clarinet, and saxophone playing; arranging; songwriting, and bandleading. His career spans more than fifty years of performing and recording, with many songs becoming lasting hits and selling more than one million copies.

The Beginnings. Ray Charles (born Ray Charles Robinson) grew up in extreme poverty in Greenville, a small rural town in northern Florida,

Ray Charles (Archive Photos/Fotos International)

difficulty of adapting to the new environment, while also coping with the loss of sight, he slowly started to feel more confident and his life appeared to have some semblance of stability. His father passed away when Charles was ten, then his mother died suddenly when he was fifteen. This was, of all the tragedies that had occurred to him, the most painful. Charles, only a teenager, but an aged man due to the harsh circumstances of his early life, decided to leave school. In his pursuit of music and of better life conditions, he moved often, finally winding up in Los Angeles.

Charles's emotional survival of this early part of his life is remarkable. It is partly to be credited to his strength of character, absence of self-pity, and immense love of music. His relentless ability to transform curiosity, joy, and pain into beautiful singing is a wonderful gift.

Musical Influences. The biggest early musical influence on Charles was Mr. Wylie Pitman. "Mr. Pit" owned a store in Greenville and played wonderful boogie-woogie piano. He patiently allowed Charles to sit at the piano and taught him some rudiments of music. Charles listened enthusiastically to the jukebox. Among the great artists featured at the time were pianists Pete Johnson and Meade Lux Lewis and bluesmen Blind Boy Phillips and Washboard Sam. At St. Augustine, Charles had formal piano lessons and studied the music of Bach, Chopin, and Strauss. He also listened intensely to jazz on the radio.

Among his jazz influences were clarinetist Artie Shaw, pianists Art Tatum and Earl Hines, and the big bands of Tommy Dorsey, Duke Ellington, and Count Basie. In school, Charles sang in the choir and was influenced by gospel groups such as the

close to the Georgia border. His father, Bailey Robinson, worked for the railroad and was absent most of the time. He died when Ray was ten. Ray was educated by his mother Aretha, who taught him respect, discipline, and commonsense life values. His early life, despite stringent poverty, was a happy one.

An appalling sequence of tragedies took place within the span of a few years. While playing outside the house, Charles witnessed the tragic death of his brother George, who drowned in a tub. Ray was five, George four. Shortly thereafter the first signs of blindness began to manifest themselves. By age seven Charles's sight was completely lost to what was later thought to be glaucoma. Charles attended St. Augustine's School for the Deaf and Blind in Orlando. After the initial

Golden Gate Quartet, country musicians such as Grandpa Jones, and vocalists such as Jo Stafford. His main idol, though, was Nat "King" Cole. Charles greatly admired his beautiful singing, piano accompaniment, and proficiency in all styles of music from blues to bop, and Charles learned to perform many of his songs.

During a summer in Tallahassee, a family friend donated a clarinet to Charles. Thus began his clarinet and, later, saxophone playing. Charles was fascinated by the harmony parts he heard in big-band music and learned to arrange by dictating the various melodic lines to someone who would write them down, a method he would use throughout his career.

Career. Charles began singing and playing the piano for tea parties and private functions while still a teenager. He also sat in with bands in the Florida area and joined the local Musicians Union in Jacksonville. His first songs were recorded, according to David Ritz who coauthored his autobiography *Brother Charles*, at age seventeen on a primitive recording device. Many of his early songs were released as singles between 1949 and 1951. In 1940 Charles moved to Seattle and worked with his own trio at the Elks Club and at the Rocking Chair. During this time he met arranger Quincy Jones, who was to remain a close friend of his.

Atlantic Records gave him a contract in 1952, after Charles had moved permanently to Los Angeles. Charles's music at this time had a strong blues and rhythm-and-blues feel to it. His group used piano, bass, drums, two trumpets, and two reeds. This band played many of Charles's ar-

For the Record

"I wasn't all that aware of the race thing. Going blind made me even less conscious of it. But imagine the nonsense of segregating *blind* kids. I mean, they can't even see!"
—From *Brother Ray*,
Ray Charles's autobiography

rangements and was equally adept at playing jazz. Notable during these years is Charles's participation in the Newport Jazz Festival and his recordings with the Count Basie band (without Count Basie himself) and with vibraphonist Milt Jackson, where he is featured on alto saxophone. Also recorded in the early 1950's was the arrangement of the song "Things That I Used to Do" for the blues musician Guitar Slim. It sold in the millions, and Charles went on to successfully blend blues and gospel in songs such as "I Got a Woman" (1954).

The year 1959 was eventful for Ray Charles: He had his first success with "What I Say," he recorded songs with string arrangements by Ralph Burns, and he recorded with his own big band. Charles also left the Atlantic label and signed up with ABC records, releasing huge hits, including his world-famous interpretation of "Georgia on My Mind" (1960) and other successes "Unchain My Heart" (1961) and "Hit the Road Jack" (1961). Continuous experimentation brought him to his first country-influenced album, *Modern Sounds in Country and Western Music* (1962), in two volumes. "I Can't Stop Loving You" from this collection became his all-time best-seller, topping both pop and country charts. Charles's band at this time was an octet, with the remarkable Leroy Cooper on baritone saxophone. During these years Charles also included pop songs in his repertoire: "Eleanor Rigby" and "Yesterday" by the Beatles are well-known examples.

Beginning in the late 1960's, Charles's activities included worldwide touring and such business ventures as running his own studio and record company. In the 1970's he released three albums with Tangerine and four with Crossover (his own labels) before signing up again with Atlantic (from 1977 to 1980) and finally with CBS in 1983. His recordings from this period continued to encompass various genres, ranging from jazz to pop and rock: "Porgy and Bess" (1976) with singer Cleo Laine, "Living for the City" by singer-songwriter Stevie Wonder, and "We Are the World" (1985) with USA for Africa. Charles has sung on many motion picture sound tracks, including *Cincinnati Kid* (1965), with music by Lalo

Schifrin, and has appeared in the films *Ballad in Blue* (1966) and *The Blues Brothers* (1980).

Legacy. Charles's influence is far reaching and has touched such artists as Stevie Wonder, Steve Winwood, Joe Cocker, Van Morrison, and Sly and the Family Stone. Charles's rhythm-and-blues band has been a model for James Brown and Tower of Power. His many songs with the female vocal quartet the "Raelettes" have set the standard for soul groups.

Charles's intense, smoky voice, which is able to leap suddenly into falsetto range, is familiar to many, if not through his music, then through his popular "you got the right one, baby" commercials for Diet Pepsi cola. Charles often intersperses his singing with spoken commentary that is usually charged with a sense of urgency. His piano playing is soulful and rhythmical, with Charles often stomping both feet while performing. Ray Charles is a truly talented artist who has made coherent musical choices following his quest for self-expression. He has given his fans a legacy of wonderful songs from all genres of popular music.

—*Michele Caniato*

SELECT DISCOGRAPHY

■ SINGLES
"What'd I Say," 1959
"Georgia on My Mind," 1960
"Hit the Road Jack," 1961
"Unchain My Heart," 1961
"I Can't Stop Loving You," 1962
"Crying Time," 1966

■ ALBUMS
The Great Ray Charles, 1956
Soul Brothers, 1958
The Genius of Ray Charles, 1959
Crying Time, 1966
A Message from the People, 1972
Renaissance, 1975
Just Between Us, 1988
My World, 1993

SELECT AWARDS
Grammy Awards for Best Vocal Performance, Album, Male, for *The Genius of Ray Charles*; for Best R&B Performance for "Let the Good Times Roll"; for Best Performance by a Pop Single Artist and Best Vocal Performance, Single Record or Track, Male, for "Georgia on My Mind," all 1960
Grammy Award for Best R&B Recording for "Hit the Road Jack," 1961
Grammy Award for Best R&B Recording for "I Can't Stop Loving You," 1962
Grammy Award for Best R&B Recording for "Busted," 1963
Grammy Awards for Best R&B Recording and Best R&B Solo Vocal Performance, Male or Female, for "Crying Time," 1966
Grammy Award for Lifetime Achievement, 1987
Grammy Award for Best R&B Performance by a Duo or Group with Vocal for "I'll Be Good to You," 1990 (with Chaka Khan)
National Medal of the Arts, 1993
Kennedy Center Award for Contributions to American Music, 1986

SEE ALSO: Cole, Nat "King"; Franklin, Aretha; Khan, Chaka; Kirk, Rahsaan Roland; Wonder, Stevie.

Cheap Trick

ORIGINAL MEMBERS: Rick Nielsen (b. 1946), Tom Petersson (b. 1950), Robin Zander (b. 1953), Bun E. Carlos (b. Brad Carlson, 1951)
OTHER MEMBERS: John Brandt
FIRST ALBUM RELEASE: *Cheap Trick*, 1977
MUSICAL STYLES: Pop, rock

Cheap Trick was "big in Japan" long before the phrase had become a cliché for aging rock bands that no longer had a following in the United States. After years of journeyman work opening for major groups such as Boston, Journey, and Kiss, Cheap Trick took advantage of their sudden popularity in Japan to achieve similar success in the United States with the platinum hit recording of their Japanese concert tour, *Live at Budokan* (1979). Consistently better onstage than in the studio, however, the band struggled in the 1980's after the departure of cofounder Tom Petersson but went platinum upon his return with *Lap of*

Cheap Trick: Tom Petersson, Robin Zander, Rick Nielsen, Bun E. Carlos (Epic/Legacy/Mark Seliger)

Luxury (1988) and its hit single "The Flame." Cheap Trick remains a powerful influence on popular music, evidenced by such groups as the Gin Blossoms, Soul Asylum, and Smashing Pumpkins.

Born in Rockford. Cheap Trick had its roots in Rockford, Illinois, where the musicians who would eventually form the group first played in several short-lived bands. Guitarist Rick Nielsen and bass player Tom Petersson first began performing together as members of Fuse, a band that folded after its debut album in 1969. After an encounter with Todd Rundgren at London's Marquee Club, Nielsen and Petersson recruited a pair of Rundgren's former colleagues, drummer Thom Mooney and vocalist Robert "Stewkey" Antoni, to form a new band called Sick Man of Europe.

Meanwhile, drummer Bun E. Carlos and vocalist Robin Zander were already performing together as members of the Toons. After the departure of Mooney and Antoni from Sick Man of Europe and the breakup of the Toons, Carlos teamed up with Nielsen and Petersson. After a brief period during which Randy "Xeno" Hogan

performed lead vocals for the group, Zander also came aboard, forming the quartet that for most of its existence would constitute the band Cheap Trick.

The group cultivated a striking visual appearance, deliberately contrasting the long-haired good looks of Zander and Petersson with the overweight Carlos's seedy attire and Nielsen's oddball ensemble: baseball cap, bow tie, and monogrammed sweater. If it was an unusual image for a rock band, it was nevertheless an appropriate accompaniment to their music, which combined the polished pop sound of the Beatles with the power of heavy metal, while infusing the blend with a sense of humor and eclecticism reminiscent of such British bands as the Move.

In 1976, after a grueling period on the barband circuit that culminated in a successful series of demo tapes, the group secured a recording deal with Epic Records, the label with which they would stay for most of their career. Nielsen and Petersson, who had spent years opening for such groups as Kiss, Queen, Journey, Boston, and the Kinks, had a generous supply of strong material to draw from, and the group produced three albums in rapid succession. Their self-titled debut, released in 1977, was followed later the same year by their more polished second album, *In Color,* featuring the group's first hit, "I Want You to Want Me." The following year's *Heaven Tonight* included what was to become the band's trademark song, "Surrender," with its familiar chorus, "Mommy's all right, Daddy's all right, they just seem a little weird/ Surrender, surrender, but don't give yourself away."

Live at Budokan. None of the group's first three albums was particularly successful in the United States, but they went gold in Japan. A live recording from the ensuing tour of Japan that was not originally intended for release in the United States succeeded in capturing the musical exuberance and vitality that the band could never quite duplicate in the studio; the phenomenal success of the triple-platinum hit *Live at Budokan* (1979) finally made Cheap Trick stars in their native land.

The band quickly released their now eagerly anticipated fifth album, *Dream Police* (1979), but failed to achieve in the studio what seemed to come so effortlessly onstage. They turned to Beatles producer George Martin for help with their next album, 1980's *All Shook Up,* but the band seemed to have lost some of its vitality. The replacement of cofounder Petersson with bass player John Brandt in 1981 was followed by a gradual slide in the quality of their finished work. This was caused as much by studio interference with the artistic process as by a diminishment in the band's creative powers. The commercial success of 1982's platinum-selling *One on One,* which included the singles "If You Want My Love" and "She's Tight," was followed by the less successful *Next Position Please* (1983), produced by Todd Rundgren. "We were told to make cuts that Todd refused to do," says Nielsen. "They took things off the record that were better than what we had to put on it. We caved in because we had to, and Todd didn't cave in because he thought it was wrong."

Return to the Top. The mid-1980's saw the group hit bottom with a pair of creative and commercial failures, *Standing on the Edge* (1985) and *The Doctor* (1986). After a promising start, Cheap Trick seemed headed for rock and roll oblivion.

For the Record

Rick Nielsen and Tom Petersson's first band, Fuse, changed its name from Grim Reaper after it had the misfortune of opening for Otis Redding on the night of his death.

The group bounced back in 1988, however, with the return of Petersson and the commercial hit *Lap of Luxury.* The album included the number-1 hit "The Flame," a soaring rock ballad penned by writers from outside the group. This song has been called "a woeful piece of power schmaltz" and "a treacly power ballad by a pair of song-mill hacks." Nevertheless, it put Cheap Trick back at the top of the charts for the first time in years.

Cheap Trick's reputation continued to grow throughout the 1990's, partly because of praise from younger musicians who were inspired by the group's early work. Billy Corgan of Smashing Pumpkins is a notable fan of the group, and Cheap Trick's blend of strong melody and powerful guitar-driven rock infected many in the new generation, including the Gin Blossoms, Soul Asylum, Nirvana, and Soundgarden. In response to this contemporary reappraisal of their music, the group released two new sets of recordings from the Japanese tour that made them famous, *Budokan II* (1994) and *At Budokan: The Complete Concert* (1998). They also released a collection of rarities and outtakes entitled *Sex, America, Cheap Trick* (1996).
—*Ed McKnight*

SELECT DISCOGRAPHY
■ ALBUMS
Cheap Trick, 1977
In Color, 1977
Heaven Tonight, 1978
Live at Budokan, 1979
Dream Police, 1979
All Shook Up, 1980
One on One, 1982
Next Position Please, 1983

The Chemical Brothers — 189

Standing on the Edge, 1985
The Doctor, 1986
Lap of Luxury, 1988
Busted, 1990
Woke up with a Monster, 1994
Budokan II, 1994 (live)
Sex, America, Cheap Trick, 1996 (compilation with
    previously released material)
At Budokan: The Complete Concert, 1998 (live)

SEE ALSO: Boston; Gin Blossoms, The; Journey;
Kinks; Kiss; Nirvana; Queen; Otis Redding; Todd
Rundgren; Smashing Pumpkins; Soundgarden.

The Chemical Brothers

ORIGINAL MEMBERS: Thomas Rowlands (b. 1971),
    Edmund Simons (b. 1970)
FIRST ALBUM RELEASE: *Exit Planet Dust,* 1995
MUSICAL STYLES: Dance, hip-hop, pop, techno,
    house, psychedelic rock

The Chemical Brothers have worked with electronics to sample (take a short clip of music and/or voice from a longer piece) a wide variety of sounds and distort them in many different ways. Whole compositions of these sounds are then marketed as songs, usually as instrumental dance pieces.

Digging Up from Dust. Chemical Brothers Tom Rowlands and Ed Simons met at Manchester University in 1991. Rowlands became interested in writing music at an early age. He began playing the piano around the age of eight; by the time he was twelve, he was composing songs on guitar. A drum machine followed at age fourteen, and he was given a sampler at seventeen. His older brother introduced him to imported hip-hop records from the United States. As a teenager, he carefully went through and listened to every single recording available at his local public library. While in college, he played in the band Ariel, which combined techno music and funk to produce danceable music. With the band, Rowlands put out many records.

The Chemical Brothers in 1997 (Scott Harrison/Archive Photos)

For the Record

"This idea of having to replicate the sound of a great piano or whatever. I mean, if you want that, get the real thing. For us, synthesizers are for making sounds that no other machines can make—not for copying other sounds." —*Tom Rowlands*

Ed Simons was working as a disc jockey while in college. He brought knowledge about musical systems and techniques for mixing sounds to the duo. Together Rowlands and Simons worked as disc jockeys at a Manchester dance club called Naked Under Leather. It was not long before they were working in London at the club Heavenly Sunday Social. Their new style of presenting music that brought in hip-hop to the then-popular house music caused a minor sensation. As local, obscure disc jockeys, they called themselves the Dust Brothers after a Los Angeles-based production team that had worked with the Beastie Boys. Once they received attention as a hot new act, it became necessary to change their name to the Chemical Brothers in 1995 to avoid legal conflict. The name was derived from "Chemical Beats," (1995) their third single.

Cult Choice. The Chemical Brothers produced their own single in 1992. "Song to the Siren" sold about five hundred copies. Junior Boy's Own gave them a recording contract, followed by Virgin Records, and they were on their way to success on both sides of the Atlantic Ocean. Their first hit single, "Setting Sun," (1996) featured Oasis singer Noel Gallagher and helped the Chemical Brothers' first album, *Exit Planet Dust* (1995), sell more than 100,000 copies in the United States. (The single sold more than 300,000 copies in Great Britain.) "Setting Sun" received plenty of airtime when MTV designated it a "buzz clip," or a song that was granted more airtime because of its popularity or new sound. It was followed by "Block Rockin' Beats," (1997) a tune that garnered them a Grammy Award

for Best Rock Instrumental Performance.

The Chemical Brothers suffered a minor setback in 1996 when representatives of the Beatles accused them of sampling from the Beatles' song "Tomorrow Never Knows" to produce "Setting Sun." A musicologist stated that the sounds of the two songs are similar, but no sampling had taken place, and the suit was dropped. With a second album that was favorably received, the Chemical Brothers continued to break ground in a new age of sampled music. —*Rose Secrest*

SELECT DISCOGRAPHY
■ SINGLES
"Leave Home," 1995
"Life Is Sweet," 1995
"Setting Sun," 1996
"Block Rockin' Beats," 1997
"Elektrobank," 1997
"The Private Psychedelic Reel," 1997
■ ALBUMS
Exit Planet Dust, 1995
Dig Your Own Hole, 1997
Brothers Gonna Work It Out, 1998

SELECT AWARDS
Grammy Award for Best Rock Instrumental Performance for "Block Rockin' Beats," 1997

SEE ALSO: Beastie Boys, The; Beck; De La Soul; Public Enemy; Rage Against the Machine.

Cher. *See* Sonny and Cher / Cher

Chic

ORIGINAL MEMBERS: Bernard Edwards (1952-1996), Nile Rodgers (b. 1952), Norma Jean Wright, Tony Thompson, Alfa Anderson (b. 1946)
OTHER MEMBERS: Luci Martin (b. 1955), Sterling Campbell, Sylver Logan Sharp, Jenn Thomas
FIRST ALBUM RELEASE: *Chic*, 1977
MUSICAL STYLE: Disco

Bernard Edwards and Nile Rodgers met just out of high school in 1970 and began playing at clubs and bars in New York. After ventures into power-fusion and new wave, they followed the disco craze of the 1970's to commercial success. Inspired by the theatrical rock group Roxy Music, they developed a clear concept for the band they wanted to create. The music itself was secondary to the creation of a marketing scheme that would tap into mainstream demand. As Rodgers said, "We wanted millions of dollars, Ferraris, and planes." Disco was, in his words, "like a gift from heaven."

Chic's Nile Rodgers and Bernard Edwards in 1983 (Deborah Feingold/Archive Photos)

Recording Contract. After years of frustration, Chic finally landed a deal with Atlantic Records in 1977, which resulted in the release of their first album the following year. The number 6 pop hit "Dance, Dance, Dance (Yowsah, Yowsah, Yowsah)" powered the debut album to number 27 on the charts. Just before their big break, Wright left and was replaced by vocalist Luci Martin. Riding the crest of the disco craze, *C'est Chic* (number 4, 1978) and *Risque* (number 5, 1979) both went platinum, and each produced a number 1 hit, "Le Freak" and "Good Times," respectively. Having produced the best-selling single of all time on Atlantic Records ("Le Freak"), Edwards and Rodgers were among the hottest writers and producers in the business.

Dissolution. As the disco wave began to subside, Chic failed to find a new audience. *Real People*

(1980) reached number 30, but the next three albums failed to make the charts. After Chic disbanded in 1983, Tony Thompson joined Robert Palmer, John Taylor, and Andy Taylor in the successful *The Power Station* album (1985), which produced two Top-10 hits. Solo albums by Edwards and Rodgers were unsuccessful.

Branching Out. However, Edwards and Rodgers became hugely successful as writers and producers for other artists. Between 1980 and 1986, they had a hand in five number 1 hits (Diana Ross, "Upside Down"; David Bowie, "Let's Dance"; Duran Duran, "The Reflex"; Madonna, "Like a Virgin"; Robert Palmer, "Addicted to Love"). Either individually or collectively, they produced hits for Sister Sledge, the Honeydrippers, Power Station, Jody Watley, Rod Stewart, Deborah Harry, Peter Gabriel, the Thompson Twins, Eric Clapton, Mick Jagger, the B-52's, Kim Carnes, the Stray Cats, David Lee Roth, and original Chic vocalist Norma Jean Wright.

Edwards and Rodgers reformed Chic in 1991 with Sylver Logan Sharp and Jenn Thomas as vocalists, but their *Chic-ism* (1992) was a commercial failure. Though many critics condemned Chic as a mindless party band, Rodgers and Edwards proved themselves to be master producers.

For the Record

Before making it big, Nile Rodgers and Bernard Edwards formed the punk band Allah and the Knife-Wielding Punks.

Other musicians were paying close attention to Edwards's innovative bass patterns, especially in "Good Times," which served as the foundation for the Sugar Hill Gang's seminal "Rapper's Delight" (1979) and Queen's big hit, "Another One Bites the Dust" (1980).   —*John Powell*

SELECT DISCOGRAPHY
■ ALBUMS
Chic, 1977
C'est Chic, 1978
Risque, 1979
Greatest Hits, 1979 (compilation)
Real People, 1980
Take It Off, 1981
Tongue in Chic, 1982
Believer, 1983
Dance, Dance, Dance: The Best of Chic, 1991
    (compilation)
Chic-ism, 1992

SEE ALSO: Duran Duran; Madonna; Palmer, Robert; Roxy Music / Bryan Ferry.

Chicago

ORIGINAL MEMBERS: Robert Lamm (b. 1944), James Pankow (b. 1947), Walter Parazaider (b. 1945), Lee Loughnane (b. 1946), Terry Kath (1946-1978), Peter Cetera (b. 1944), Danny Seraphine (b. 1948)
OTHER MEMBERS: Bill Champlin, Jason Scheff, Tris Imboden, Keith Howland
FIRST ALBUM RELEASE: *Chicago Transit Authority*, 1969
MUSICAL STYLES: Rock, pop

The late 1960's and early 1970's were a period of unparalleled diversity and creativity in the field of rock-oriented popular music. During the first half of the twentieth century, it was often jazz instrumentalists who were headliners in the popular music field. With a new generation came new ideas and ideals. The raw power of the amplified lead guitar and of the megastar vocalist grew to dominate and define the sound of rock. However, some musicians chose to expand the boundaries of rock by weaving other musical styles and instrumental colors into rock's basic fabric. The inclusion of brass, woodwinds, and additional percussion instruments interacting with the rhythm, bass, and drum nucleus of the prototypical four-member rock band added a new dimension to the music.

Skilled instrumentalists of an earlier era (such as drummer Buddy Rich, trumpeter Maynard Ferguson, and saxophonist/clarinetist Woody Herman) reinvented their careers by arranging and performing rock-oriented tunes with their big bands. Trumpeter Miles Davis and pianist Herbie Hancock stayed closer to the improvisational roots of jazz, but electrified their traditionally acoustic sound. James Brown and others on the rhythm-and-blues circuit continued to carry a contingent of backup instrumentalists that added tight punctuation to the music. Other instrumentally oriented groups that successfully fused the jazz, pop, and rock idioms include Blood, Sweat and Tears, Chase, and Tower of Power. At a point where these diverse stylistic influences intersect, the music of Chicago can be put into perspective.

Beginnings. Thousands of teenagers growing up in Chicago during the 1950's and 1960's had accordion lessons and a guitar from Sears, listened to their parents' record collections, played in the high school band, watched jazz legends on *The Ed Sullivan Show*, and organized garage bands. For a select few with the requisite talent, desire, musical training, and good fortune, there were opportunities for success in the music business.

Seven young Chicagoans pooled their talents in 1967, with the goal of forming a rock-and-roll band with a brass section. Initially called the Big Thing, the group played local and regional clubs. After attracting attention, the band became known as the Chicago Transit Authority (CTA) and began featuring original tunes written by band members. In 1968, on the advice of James Guercio, a producer for Columbia Records and friend of saxophonist Walt Parazaider, the band moved to Los Angeles to develop more original material and establish a reputation on the West Coast, playing club dates and opening for established headliners. CTA made a demo recording that led to a contract with Columbia, and in January, 1969, they went to New York City to record a double album released in April of that year as *Chicago Transit Authority*. As the album and several singles received airplay and began selling well, success for CTA soon followed. A heavy touring schedule, concert dates at New York's Carnegie Hall, and a studio recording pace that produced new albums on an annual basis developed a large and loyal audience. In 1969, the group changed their identity one final time, becoming simply Chicago.

Changing Direction. The band's quality of musicianship, songwriting, and arranging has remained consistent. The horn section, especially on early recordings, was prominently featured on introductions, transitions between verses, improvised solos, and alternations with lead vocals. The band's characteristically bright sound featured precise octave playing among trumpet and trombone as well as skillfully crafted open voice scoring and judicious overdubbing which allowed trumpet, sax, and trombone to give the music a jazz flavor.

From its inception, the band was an outlet for the songwriting talents of the membership, with many tunes created by Robert Lamm, James Pankow, Peter Cetera, and Terry Kath. The lyrics cover a wide variety of topics: observations of everyday life in "Saturday in the Park," political angst in "Harry Truman," nostalgia in "Take Me Back to Chicago," personal relationships in "If You Leave Me Now." Similarly, the music has been influenced by a variety of styles, including rhythm and blues in "Dialogue Part II," straight rock with "25 or 6 to 4" and "Alive Again," a relaxed mix of Latin and disco with "No Tell Lover," and light-rock balladry with "Wishing You Were Here."

The direction of the band shifted in the late 1970's and 1980's, as the musical product became more soft-rock oriented. The sound was dominated by Peter Cetera's (and later Jason Scheff's) lead tenor, close harmony background vocals, thickly synthesized accompaniment, love-song lyrics, and a predictable beat pattern. Even in the early days, Chicago had released ballads ("Beginnings," "Just You and Me") in which the individual components of the group (voice, rhythm, horns) performed as an integrated unit. However, in later efforts, the horns were either omitted, homogenized into the background, or spliced onto the end of a tune.

Chicago (Archive Photos/Frank Driggs Collection)

Take Me Back to Chicago. In 1997, the group celebrated its thirtieth anniversary. Continued success was due to the determination of the founding members to keep the band going and to supportive fans. The group would continue to perform perennial favorites for audiences, both internationally and in the United States, for more than thirty years. To date, Chicago has released twenty-three albums; most are titled chronologically (*Chicago II*, 1970, through *Twenty 1*, 1991), and are identified by the band's distinctive logo on each album cover. Total record sales are in excess of $120 million worldwide.

Through the years, Chicago experienced loss with the 1978 accidental death of lead guitarist Terry Kath, personnel changes with the departure of songwriter/lead vocalist/bass guitarist Peter Cetera and drummer Danny Seraphine, a difficult breakup with longtime manager and producer James Guercio, and artistic differences with recording industry decision makers. Chicago has also received much unfavorable press from music critics who suggested that the group had sacrificed their artistic integrity in order to become a more marketable, pop-oriented commodity.

Individual band members have become more assertive about the musical direction of the group. According to Robert Lamm, "We considered the possibility that perhaps it was better to succeed or fail on our own merits." And Walt Parazaider continued, "This band had to go back into doing a band approach . . . where the band lives with the music from the get-go . . . from the writing, to throwing out suggestions, to rehearsing. We were frustrated that we weren't doing what we wanted . . . just cranking out things that sold. You can't look a gift horse in the mouth, a hit is a hit is a hit. But there was other stuff for us to say."

Toward the goal of exerting additional control of their musical destiny, band members founded the Chicago Records label in 1995 and secured the rights to the recordings made between 1969 and 1980 with Columbia. The venture was established as an outlet for reissues and solo efforts by group members and as a means for signing new talent.

Peter Cetera embarked on a solo career after he left the group in 1985. His first release after departing was *Solitude/Solitaire* (1986). His album sales were more modest, but he had a string of Top-10 singles in the late 1980's, including "Next Time I Fall," a duet with Amy Grant.

—*William M. Camphouse*

SELECT DISCOGRAPHY
■ ALBUMS
Chicago Transit Authority, 1969
Chicago II, 1970
Chicago III, 1971
Chicago VI, 1973
Chicago IX, 1975 (compilation)
Chicago X, 1976
Chicago 16, 1982
Chicago 17, 1984
Group Portrait, 1991 (boxed set compilation)

SELECT AWARDS
Grammy Awards for Best Pop Vocal Performance by a Duo, Group, or Chorus for "If You Leave Me Now" and Best Album Package for *Chicago X*, 1976

SEE ALSO: Blood, Sweat, and Tears; Doobie Brothers, The

For the Record

Officials with the Chicago Transit Authority (the Windy City's mass transit system) were not amused at the idea of sharing their corporate name with a rock band. Hence, the group had to shorten their name to Chicago.

The Chieftains

ORIGINAL MEMBERS: Paddy Moloney (b. 1938), Martin Fay (b. 1936), Sean Potts (b. 1930), Michael Tubridy (b.1935), David Fallon
OTHER MEMBERS: Peadar Mercier (b. 1914), Sean Keane (b. 1946), Derek Bell (b. 1935), Kevin Conneff

The Chieftains in 1979 (AP/Wide World Photos)

FIRST ALBUM RELEASE: *The Chieftains*, 1963
MUSICAL STYLES: Celtic, folk, Irish traditional

The Chieftains, an Irish traditional music group, are the leading exponents of Celtic music and have been responsible for its revival worldwide. Using traditional instruments that are rarely heard outside small cult venues, they have widened their appeal by introducing them into new musical arenas, including orchestral and film settings. The Chieftains tour constantly, with more than two hundred dates per year scheduled throughout the world. Among their most prominent performances were the first Western concert on the Great Wall while touring China and playing for Pope John Paul's Mass during his visit to Ireland, with an audience of more than one million. John Glatt published The *Chieftains: The Authorized Biography*, the leading history of the group, in 1997.

The Beginnings. The Chieftains originated in 1963, when a group of friends who had played together in several informal groups around Dublin gathered to make a record. They took their name from a line of traditional Irish poetry. The members had all known one another while playing with Ceoltóirí, which was formed in 1961. The folk revival of the 1960's concentrated on vocal music, its most prominent exponents being Peter, Paul, and Mary and the Clancy Brothers with Tommy Makem. At first, the Chieftains played when they could and worked at non-musical jobs by day. Their first album, *The Chieftains* (1963) was an experiment to see if traditional music would appeal to more than a few cultists.

The music was classically arranged, largely by Moloney, who has been the group's musical genius. The uniqueness of the group lay in having the arrangements performed only with traditional instruments. All of the members, however, have been noted for their technically elegant professionalism. Celtic music has often suffered from an amateur approach that uses more charm than competence. The Chieftains insisted from the start on a high level of skills; Keane, for example, was an all-Ireland fiddle champion. To their skill they added a virtuoso style which was energetic and highly entertaining.

Traditional Irish music in the 1960's was regarded as rural and the music of the elderly, as rock and other imported popular strains swept the cities, especially Dublin. By forming an ensemble, bringing together the pipes and harp with the bodhran drum and tin whistle, a new sound emerged. Previous Irish music was often performed solo and seldom used more than two artists. The Chieftains, melding traditional instruments, created a new sound that ignited a spark and drew increasing numbers of fans, mostly people who had previously ignored traditional music.

The Chieftains were transformed in 1975, when they all became full-time musicians and signed a new managing contract. By this time they had produced four *Chieftains* albums (*Chieftains 4*, 1973, is considered outstanding). In 1975 *Chieftains 5* was released in the United States and was followed by an American tour which was highly successful. *Melody Maker*, the British pop journal, named them Group of the Year "for making unfashionable music fashionable," and on their return to Britain, the Chieftains sold out London's Royal Albert Hall twice. The commercial appeal was not only to expatriate Irish communities, however, as the music began to find favor beyond its cultural roots. The group's sound track for Stanley Kubrick's 1975 film, *Barry Lyndon*, was widely acclaimed that year, and they became an international phenomenon.

There were changes in the band's lineup throughout the 1970's, which they capped with a 1979 performance before Pope John Paul II in Dublin: 1.35 million people attended (and an estimated 800 million watched on television). That year the Chieftains also released their ninth album, *Boil the Breakfast Early*, their first to use vocals. Kevin Conneff, who first joined the group on bodhran in 1976, provided the lead vocals.

By 1980 the Chieftains were accepted as the leading exponents of Irish traditional music, and their accomplishments had begun to inspire the formation of other traditional groups. The best known of these are Clannad and Altan, which uses mainly Gaelic vocals. An important element in the Chieftains' success was the rising popularity of world music, which in turn brought a renewed interest in folk music of all kinds. In 1987, the Chieftains expanded their Celtic horizons in the album *Celtic Wedding*, which was devoted to Breton music. Their 1996 album, *Santiago*, which won a Grammy Award for Best World Music Album, presented the music of Galicia in northern Spain.

In 1983 the group moved beyond its cultural

For the Record

Irish musicians say that the uilleann pipes—played by the Chieftains' Paddy Moloney—are so difficult that they take seven years learning, seven years practicing, and seven years playing before a performer is competent.

heritage and toured China, playing with a traditional Chinese folk orchestra. The two types of traditional instruments blended perfectly, and the result was the first concert on the Great Wall and an album, *The Chieftains in China* (1987). The Chieftains have also played with a wide variety of popular performers, such as Van Morrison, Marianne Faithfull, Willie Nelson, and Paul McCartney.

Varieties of Performances. The Chieftains are noted for introducing Irish instruments into musical settings where they had never been used before. Their score for the film *Tristan and Isolde* (1979) was the first known incorporation of uilleann pipes into orchestral settings. They have integrated traditional music with a famous Irish play, John Millington Synge's *Playboy of the Western World* (1907). In the 1980's the Chieftains were among the first groups to incorporate Irish step dancing into their performances. They also provided the 1986 soundtrack for a National Geographic special, *Ballad of the Irish Horse*, and have appeared in twelve music videos.

Irish Instruments. A unique feature of the Chieftains' music is their use of traditional Irish instruments. The bodhran is a frame drum with a head made of goat skin. It looks like an oversized tambourine, and it can be played with the hand or a single drumstick. Animal bones are played like castanets. The tin whistle, seemingly unimpressive, can produce lovely flute sounds in the hands of a master. The Irish harp, a national symbol, is much smaller than the classical harp, and produces a narrower range of sound. The court instrument of the ancient Irish aristocracy, it can be traced to the eighth century. The fiddle is the same type of instrument used in American country music, and creates a similar sound.

Uilleann pipes are bellows-blown, like Scottish bagpipes, except the bellows are held under the arms and are not breath-blown. The pipes are extremely difficult to master. Moloney's work in reviving uilleann pipes was considered so historically important that Trinity University in Dublin awarded him an honorary doctorate in music.

—*Norbert Brockman*

SELECT DISCOGRAPHY

■ ALBUMS

The Chieftains, 1963
Chieftains 2, 1969
Chieftains 4, 1973
Barry Lyndon, 1975 (sound track)
Bonaparte's Retreat, 1976
The Chieftains 9: Boil the Breakfast Early, 1979
The Chieftains in China, 1987
Celtic Wedding, 1987
Irish Heartbeat, 1988 (with Van Morrison)
The Bells of Dublin, 1991
The Celtic Harp, 1993 (with the Belfast Harp Orchestra)
The Long Black Veil, 1995
Santiago, 1996

SELECT AWARDS

Melody Maker, named Group of the Year, 1975
Genie Award for Best Score for *The Grey Fox*, 1983
Grammy Awards for Best Contemporary Folk Album for *Another Country* and Best Traditional Folk Album for *An Irish Evening Live at the Grand Opera House, Belfast*, 1992
Grammy Award for Best Traditional Folk Album for *The Celtic Harp*, 1993
Grammy Award for Best Pop Collaboration with Vocals for "Have I Told You Lately That I Love You," 1995 (with Van Morrison)
Grammy Award for Best World Music Album for *Santiago*, 1996

SEE ALSO: McCartney, Paul; Morrison, Van; Nelson, Willie; Peter, Paul, and Mary.

Eric Clapton

BORN: Ripley, England; March 30, 1945
FIRST ALBUM RELEASE: *Five Live Yardbirds*, 1964 (with the Yardbirds)
FIRST SOLO ALBUM RELEASE: *Eric Clapton*, 1970
MUSICAL STYLES: Blues, rock and roll

Eric Clapton (born Eric Patrick Clapp) got his first electric guitar at the age of eighteen, and quickly joined a band called Rhode Island Red and the Roosters. The Roosters were a blues and rock-and-roll band, covering the material of Muddy Waters, Freddie King, Howlin' Wolf, Chuck Berry, Little Richard, and others. The experience in this band and others gave Clapton some seasoning as a player and performer, providing the platform for his move into a more established band, the Yardbirds.

The Birth of "Slowhand." Clapton and Keith Relf of the Yardbirds both had the musical ability to play engaging solos, so extended improvisations quickly became a staple of their repertoire. They ended 1964 by backing up American blues great Sonny Boy Williamson on a number of dates in England. Soon, the owner of the Crawdaddy Club, Giorgio Gomelsky, gave Clapton the long-lived nickname "Slowhand," a joke about his speed on the lead guitar. Clapton was also receiving calls for session work and played lead guitar on two tracks by Otis Spann alongside one of his early influences, Muddy Waters. By March, 1965, when the Yardbirds' single "For Your Love" climbed the charts in England and America, Clapton had formally left the group.

Clapton was soon offered a spot playing in John Mayall's Bluesbreakers, one of the most influential blues bands in England at that time. Clapton moved into Mayall's house and, with access to Mayall's extensive record collection, quickly moved his study of the blues to a new level. During this time, London's subways came to be graced with ubiquitous graffiti proclaiming, "Clapton Is God." In a few short years, Eric Clapton had become the preeminent blues guitarist in England.

Cream Rises. In June of 1966, drummer Ginger Baker sat in with the Bluesbreakers at one of their live shows. He and Clapton soon formed a new group with Baker's then-bandmate Jack Bruce. Baker and Bruce's dislike of each other caused tension in the new group, but by June of 1966, they were officially playing as a band.

The new trio, called Cream, consisted of Baker on drums, Bruce on bass and lead vocals, and Clapton on guitar. They recorded their first album, *Fresh Cream*, in the summer of 1966 and it was released that December. It included a few unforgettable tunes, such as "Sunshine of Your Love" and "Strange Brew." The band spent 1967 touring the United States, playing to enthusiastic crowds. Their improvisational style, stretching the songs they played to nearly thirty minutes in length, broke new ground. The tensions within the band, however, particularly between Baker and Bruce, were worsening. *Disraeli Gears* was released in November, 1967, and Cream returned to the United States in February of 1968. They began recording instrumental tracks for their

next album, *Wheels of Fire* (1968), which included the important tracks "Politician" and "White Room." Even as they gained new levels of fame and critical acclaim, the band veered closer to breaking up. As professionals, Cream honored its contractual commitments but reached no new creative peaks and broke up in November, 1968.

After Cream. Over the next several months, Clapton began jamming privately with Steve Winwood, formerly of Traffic, and Ginger Baker joined in on drums after a while. When word got out, they started recording and playing live. Adding Rick Grech, formerly of Family, on bass, the new "supergroup," called Blind Faith, made its public debut in front of more than 100,000 fans on June 7, 1969, in London. When the group's U.S. tour ended in Hawaii, however, so did the band.

Next, Clapton toured as lead guitarist for Delaney and Bonnie and Friends, fronted by Delaney and Bonnie Bramlett. Their British tour included a string of guest appearances by Clapton's friend George Harrison. After the tour, work began on Clapton's first solo album, with Bramlett producing. Released in August, 1970, *Eric Clapton* included J. J. Cale's "After Midnight," "Let It Rain," and "Blues Power," which have become standards in his repertoire. Returning to England after a U.S. tour with Delaney and Bonnie, Clapton returned to session work, notably on Howlin' Wolf's *The London Sessions* (1971), which paired him with another of his earliest American blues influences.

Derek and the Dominos. As time went on, another band formed around Clapton; it included Bobby Whitlock on piano, Jim Gordon on drums, and Carl Radle on bass. Their first major endeavor was backing George Harrison on his solo ef-

Eric Clapton at the 1992 Bob Dylan tribute concert at Madison Square Garden (AP/Wide World Photos)

fort *All Things Must Pass* (1970). They played their first concert in London during June of 1970. The show was booked as an Eric Clapton appearance, but the band played under the name of Derek and the Dominos.

While recording in Miami, Clapton became acquainted with slide guitarist Duane Allman and invited him to join the band's sessions. With Allman in the lineup, the excitement level went up a notch in the recordings of "Why Does Love Got to Be So Sad" and "Layla." The sessions yielded the double album *Layla and Assorted Love Songs* (1970), and the band toured in England and the United States, then disintegrated. Clapton next appeared at George Harrison's benefit concert for Bangladesh in August of 1971 with Ringo Starr, Billy Preston, Bob Dylan, Harrison, and others. The next time he played publicly on his own was in January of 1973 at London's Rainbow Theater. He then began the arduous, but ultimately successful, process of withdrawing from his drug dependency.

Solo Career. Clapton's next career move, in the spring of 1974, was to return to the studio in Miami. The album he released in August, 1974, was called *461 Ocean Boulevard* after the house that Clapton and the band lived in. The album contains some of Clapton's most popular tracks, including Bob Marley's "I Shot the Sheriff," which became a hit single. Above all, with this project Clapton emerged a confident and engaging vocalist. He participated in the Band's "Last Waltz" concert, album, and film in 1976. His next solo success was with the *Slowhand* album (1977), which earned extensive radio play with the "Wonderful Tonight" and "Lay Down Sally" singles. Clapton's 1979 tour supporting the album *Backless* (1978) featured Muddy Waters as the opening act, exposing the Chicago blues great to hundreds of thousands of new listeners.

After a period of seclusion which included time in alcohol rehabilitation, Clapton released *Money and Cigarettes* (1983), recorded with session players rather than his touring band. The single "I've Got a Rock 'n' Roll Heart" boosted the album's profile. The next album was a major departure from his typical sound. *Behind the Sun*

(1985), produced by Phil Collins, included Clapton's first use of guitar synthesizers. Clapton also made his first music video, supporting the single "Forever Man."

The next highlight in Clapton's career was playing at the Live Aid charity concert in Philadelphia on July 13, 1985. November, 1986, saw the release of *August*, named after the birth month of his son Conor. The years 1987 and 1988 were largely spent working on other artists' projects, notably Sting's *Nothing Like the Sun* and George Harrison's *Cloud Nine*. Also in 1988 PolyGram put together the six-compact-disc career retrospective *Crossroads*. That year, Clapton concentrated on sound-track work, for which he was in demand since his successful involvement on the *Lethal Weapon* sound track. His next studio work was *Journeyman*, released in November, 1989.

Clapton began the 1990's well, with an ambitious series of performances at London's Royal Albert Hall. He then embarked on a U.S. tour which included two August dates in East Troy, Wisconsin, with Robert Cray and Stevie Ray Vaughan sharing the bill. It was after the second of these shows that the lives of Vaughan, Clapton's agent, and road crew members were claimed in a helicopter crash. To begin 1991, Clapton played another series of shows at the Royal Albert Hall, which resulted in the album *24 Nights*. It was in March of 1991, however, that Clapton's four-year-old son Conor fell out of an apartment window and was killed. Again, Clapton went into seclusion.

The musical result of this family tragedy was the ballad "Tears in Heaven," which became the centerpiece of the sound track of the 1991 film *Rush* and appeared on Clapton's 1992 *Unplugged* release. His acoustic performance on MTV reconfirmed Clapton's abilities and introduced him to many new fans. The performance also included a reworked version of "Layla," which raised his visibility to its highest point in years. He soon solidified his place as a bluesman with *From the Cradle* (1994), a collection of blues standards and his personal favorites. As Clapton pursues a lifelong career in music, he continues to pay homage to the blues, the American music that most inspired him and provided his most important role models. —*Paul D. Fischer*

SELECT DISCOGRAPHY

■ ALBUMS

For Your Love, 1965 (with the Yardbirds)

John Mayall and the Blues Breakers with Eric Clapton, 1966

Disraeli Gears, 1967 (with Cream)

Blind Faith, 1969 (with Blind Faith)

Layla and Assorted Love Songs, 1970 (with Derek and the Dominos)

Eric Clapton, 1970

The History of Eric Clapton, 1972

461 Ocean Boulevard, 1974

E. C. Was Here, 1975 (live album)

Slowhand, 1977

Just One Night, 1980 (live album)

Money and Cigarettes, 1983

Crossroads, 1988 (boxed set)

Unplugged, 1992 (live album)

From the Cradle, 1994

Pilgrim, 1998

SELECT AWARDS

Rock and Roll Hall of Fame, inducted 1993 (with Cream)

Grammy Award for Best Rock Vocal Performance, Male, for "Bad Love," 1990

Grammy Awards for Record of the Year, Song of the Year (wr. with Will Jennings), and Best Pop Vocal Performance, Male, for "Tears in Heaven"; for Album of the Year and Best Rock Vocal Performance, Male, for *Unplugged*; for Best Rock Song (wr. with Jim Gordon) for "Layla," all 1992

Grammy Award for Best Traditional Blues Album for *From the Cradle*, 1994

Grammy Awards for Record of the Year, Song of the Year (wr. with Gordon Kennedy, Wayne Kirkpatrick, and Tommy Sims), and Best Pop Vocal Performance, Male, for "Change the World," 1996

SEE ALSO: Allman Brothers Band, The; Cream; Guy, Buddy; Hendrix, Jimi; Waters, Muddy; Yardbirds, The.

Roy Clark

BORN: Meherrin, Virginia; April 15, 1933

FIRST ALBUM RELEASE: *The Lightning Fingers of Roy Clark*, 1962

MUSICAL STYLES: Country, pop, gospel

Widely regarded as a musician's musician, Roy Linwood Clark combined outstanding playing ability on guitar, banjo, mandolin, and fiddle with a distinctive vocal style and an engaging personality to become one of country music's best-loved and most enduring stars. Early hits on both country and pop charts, such as "The Tip of My Fingers" (1963) and "Yesterday When I Was Young" (1969), established him as one of the first country crossover stars and led to national television exposure. In 1983, after achieving celebrity status as cohost of the long-running television series *Hee Haw*, Clark opened a theater in Branson, Missouri, and continued, through the 1990's, to be an influential force in the country music industry.

A Musician's Musician. Roy Clark was born during the Depression in a small Virginia town southwest of Richmond. His father, Hester, a sawmill worker, played traditional mountain music on the banjo, guitar, and mandolin. The elder Clark played for dances after work, and his young son often borrowed his instruments to pick out melodies and chords. A quick learner in any pursuit, Roy later recalled that music seemed to come to him "as natural as walking." In 1942 the Clarks moved to Washington, D.C., where Roy's father worked for the Navy, making telescope lenses. Hester remained active in music and formed connections among bluegrass musicians in the district. Meanwhile, Roy's own musical interests deepened, and his parents eventually gave him a guitar as a Christmas gift. After just two weeks of practice with a method book, the excited thirteen-year-old played at a dance with his father's band.

Clark soon gained local prominence as a virtuoso guitarist. In the 1940's, Washington became a hub for country music, sometimes supporting up to thirty-five square dances on a single night. It was also a center for television production, and several of the live shows involved local musicians.

For the Record

In his 1994 autobiography, *My Life in Spite of Myself*, Roy Clark recalls the moment he realized his stardom extended beyond the typical bounds of country music. One evening, after several years as a regular on television, he took his manager to dinner at a fashionable French restaurant in Manhattan: "We were standing there when the maître d' came up and in very broken English said, 'Your table is rehdee, and as they say in my countree, Monsieur Clark, "*Hee Haw.*" That's when I knew I had really arrived!"

Before he could finish high school, Clark began playing for dances every night of the week and appeared regularly on radio and television, often with his father. He spent the next decade on the D.C. club circuit, gaining valuable experience as a singer, bandleader, and multi-instrumentalist.

At age seventeen, Clark won the USA Country Banjo Contest and was awarded an opportunity to perform at the Grand Ole Opry. A six-month stay in Nashville made him a star when he returned to Washington, and helped gain the attention of such notables as Grandpa Jones and Hank Williams. In 1954, Clark joined Jimmy Dean for a two-year stint on Dean's nightly television show, *Country Style*. During this period Clark married twice (he remains married to his second wife, Barbara) and briefly considered athletic careers in baseball and boxing. A national television appearance on Arthur Godfrey's *Talent Scouts*, however, brought a recommitment to music and a desire to expand his horizons beyond Washington. In 1960, Clark jumped at an offer to tour the Midwest as bandleader for the popular country singer Wanda Jackson.

Crossover Stardom. Clark's recording career began in earnest when he played lead guitar on Jackson's hit single "Let's Have a Party." In Las Vegas, he signed with her manager, Jim Halsey, as

a solo act, and in 1961, Halsey landed him a contract with Capitol Records. His all-instrumental first album, *The Lightning Fingers of Roy Clark* (1962), produced material that received play on country, pop, and soul radio stations. The following year Clark broke from touring to appear as a guest on NBC's *The Tonight Show*, where he sang "The Great Pretender," a 1950's hit for the black vocal quartet the Platters. He was developing a solid national image as a mainstream pop artist, and he soon scored a significant crossover hit with a single release of Bill Anderson's sentimental song, "The Tip of My Fingers." It made both the country and pop charts and led to further national exposure, including an appearance on Dick Clark's *American Bandstand*.

As the 1960's progressed, Roy Clark's natural comedic talent helped make him a true television star. He guest-hosted several talk shows, including *The Tonight Show* and *The Joey Bishop Show*, and landed a regular cameo role on the popular comedy series *The Beverly Hillbillies*. In 1969, he established himself as a leader in the crossover market with two double-charting singles, "Yesterday When I Was Young" and "September Song." Both were country adaptations of pop material, and their success helped paved the way for other country-pop singers, such as Glen Campbell, Kris Kristofferson, and Kenny Rogers.

Television Country Style: *Hee Haw*. Just as he gained new success on the charts, Clark was invited to cohost the new country comedy show *Hee Haw* with Buck Owens. Already popular on television, Clark helped generate interest among urban audiences. Although *Hee Haw* drew excellent ratings, CBS canceled the show after two seasons because they felt its rural, slapstick comedy did not suit their national image. Syndicated immediately, *Hee Haw* actually grew in popularity and remained in production until 1991. Clark stayed with the show throughout its entire run. Because its production schedule occupied only a few weeks each year he was able to maintain a rigorous concert schedule and in the mid-1970's began a residency in Las Vegas. During this period he had numerous country hits, including "Come Live with Me" (1973), his only single to reach number 1. In addition, in 1976, Clark took his band on a twenty-one-day State Department tour of the Soviet Union, opening the door for other American musicians and marking the first of many foreign concert tours for him.

Country Eminence. By the early 1980's, Roy Clark had achieved a position of eminence rivaled by few in country music. In August, 1983, he led in developing what has since become the dominant way to market "classic" country music when he opened a celebrity theater in the obscure Ozark Mountain town of Branson, Missouri. As of 1994, he was playing as many as two hundred concerts per year in Branson—the town had by then been transformed into a community of showplaces serving as a major entertainment center for country music fans. As a universally loved statesman of the country mainstream, Clark has helped numerous others become established in Branson, including Glen Campbell and Ray Stevens. Throughout his distinguished career he has remained a personable and humble man, a master musician dedicated to people and to the art of entertainment. —*Charles Kinzer*

SELECT DISCOGRAPHY
■ ALBUMS
The Lightning Fingers of Roy Clark, 1962
The Tip of My Fingers, 1963
Urban, Suburban, 1968
Yesterday When I Was Young, 1969
I Never Picked Cotton, 1970
Superpicker, 1973
Come Live with Me, 1973
The Hee Haw Gospel Quartet, 1981
Live from Austin City Limits, 1982

SELECT AWARDS
Country Music Association Entertainer of the Year Award, 1973
Country Music Association Instrumental Group of the Year Award, 1975 (with Buck Trent)
Country Music Association Instrumental Group of the Year Award, 1976 (with Buck Trent)
Guitar Player, named Best Country Artist, 1976, 1977, 1978, 1979, 1980, 1981
Country Music Association Musician of the Year Award, 1977
Country Music Association Musician of the Year Award, 1978
Country Music Association Musician of the Year Award, 1980
Grand Ole Opry, became member 1987

SEE ALSO: Campbell, Glen; Owens, Buck.

The Clash

ORIGINAL MEMBERS: Mick Jones (b. 1955), Joe Strummer (b. John Graham Mellor, 1952), Paul Simonon (b. 1955), Tory Crimes (b. Terry Chimes)
OTHER MEMBERS: Nicky "Topper" Headon (b. 1955), Vince White (b. 1961), Pete Howard (b. 1960), Nick Shephard (b. 1961)
FIRST ALBUM RELEASE: *The Clash*, 1977
MUSICAL STYLES: Punk rock, reggae, pop, funk, rap, rock and roll

Formed in London in 1976, the Clash was led by Joe Strummer and Mick (Michael Geoffrey) Jones, both of whom wrote, sang, and played guitar. Along with the Sex Pistols, the group was among the earliest and most influential punk rockers. They outlasted most of their punk colleagues and achieved considerable commercial success in the early 1980's by branching out into other styles. Jones left the band in 1983 and formed Big Audio Dynamite. Without Jones, the Clash recorded one more album in 1985, but after it flopped they disbanded. In addition to helping make punk famous, the Clash encouraged other groups to include political or social commentary in their lyrics and to work constructively with black reggae artists.

The Beginnings. In London in 1976, young people were flocking to see the Sex Pistols. Their frantic music and wild antics spoke to the frustration that many youth felt, struggling to find jobs in a weak British economy and frustrated by the traditional ways of British society. Paul Simonon, inspired by the Sex Pistols, bought a bass guitar and joined Mick Jones's band, the London SS, which also included Tory Crimes (real name

Terry Chimes) and Nicky Headon. Joe Strummer, while playing with a rock band called the 101ers, was also impressed by the Sex Pistols. In the summer of 1976 he left the 101ers. He, Jones, Simonon, and Crimes formed a punk band. Jones named it the Clash, since headlines in British papers frequently described clashes between police and rioters.

The Clash opened for the Sex Pistols that summer in their first public performance, then toured with them. In February of 1977 CBS Records signed the Clash to a hefty contract. Their first album, *The Clash*, did very well in Britain. At this point, Topper Headon replaced Crimes as the drummer. The lineup of Jones, Strummer, Simonon, and Headon would remain intact for the next five years. They toured Britain as headliners in spring, 1977, but several dates were cancelled after fans severely damaged the Rainbow Theatre during a May concert. Not only were their fans

rowdy, but also the Clash themselves had trouble with police for several incidents, including petty theft and shooting some pigeons.

Young working-class fans in England identified with the Clash. With the exception of Strummer, whose father was a British diplomat, the Clash came from blue-collar backgrounds. In the early days, the band developed a strong bond with their crowds. In one instance in 1977, after security roughed up a young man who had tried to get on stage, Jones pulled the fan up and let him sing along for the last two songs. Their dress during the first years, which consisted mainly of jeans and t-shirts, also appealed to working-class youth. The group and their fans perfected the art of writing outrageous graffiti on their clothes.

Success in the United States. Meanwhile, their music was beginning to have an impact in the United States, where youth also identified with the sounds of punk rock. Although CBS did

The Clash: Mick Jones, Paul Simonon, Joe Strummer, Nicky "Topper" Headon (Archive Photos/Jon Hammer)

not release *The Clash* in the United States in 1977, over 100,000 copies were purchased as expensive imports, a remarkable figure. The single "I Fought the Law" and the Clash's second album, *Give 'Em Enough Rope*, were released in the United States in 1978. Although the album failed to break into the Billboard 200 chart, the Clash decided to play American cities in 1979. American fans received them enthusiastically. A slightly different version of *The Clash*, which went on sale in the United States during their tour, became a gold record.

During these first three years, both the live and recorded music of the Clash was primarily hard-driving punk. They incorporated some reggae from the start, but guitars and frantic lyrics dominated. As the 1970's drew to a close, the group expanded their musical tastes. They experimented with new instruments and rhythms, and they crafted clever, sometimes humorous lyrics. Their creativity paid off in 1979 and 1980. They continued to draw large audiences across America and in 1979 released the extremely successful album *London Calling*, which went to number 23. *London Calling* included some straightforward punk and rock tunes, but it also featured mellower songs that benefited from a horn section. Many of the tunes blended memorable lyrics with danceable beats. The hit single "Train in Vain" (with its chorus, "Did you stand by me?/ No not at all"), in particular, boosted the album's sales in Britain and America. Their following project, the three-record-set *Sandinista!* (1980), did not sell very well in Britain. It did well in the United States, selling better than *London Calling*, and a critics' poll by the New York weekly *Village Voice* named it album of the year.

After *Sandinista!* the Clash once again achieved commercial success in 1982 with *Combat Rock* (number 7). Headon left the band in 1982, but before leaving he wrote "Rock the Casbah," which became a Top-10 hit in both England and the United States. With Crimes back on drums, the Clash opened for the Who in huge stadiums across the United States. Sales of *Combat Rock* skyrocketed, and the album went platinum. It included another pop hit, "Should I Stay or Should I Go," but also branched out into funk and rap.

The poet Allen Ginsberg even appeared on one of the songs. Furthermore, the popularity of "Rock the Casbah" reflected the emergence of a new medium—the music video. The video for "Rock the Casbah" was among the early mainstays on Music Television (MTV) and greatly helped increase the success of the Clash in the United States.

The Band Disintegrates. Early in 1983, Pete Howard replaced Crimes as drummer. The more serious blow to the group occurred in the fall of 1983, when Strummer and Simonon removed Jones from the band. Strummer would later regret the move. The Clash limped through 1984 and 1985, but without Jones they did not please fans or critics as they had before. Their final album, *Cut the Crap*, was far inferior to their earlier work. In 1986 Strummer broke up the band.

Jones formed Big Audio Dynamite and produced some hit songs, notably the lively dance song "Globe." Strummer played guitar briefly for the Pogues (also producing their 1990 album *Hell's Ditch*), then was in charge of producing the sound track for the 1986 film *Sid and Nancy*, about the lives and deaths of Sid Vicious of the Sex Pistols and his girlfriend. Strummer released a solo album, *Earthquake Weather*, in 1989. The original work of the Clash remained popular long after they broke up. For example, a rereleased "Should I Stay or Should I Go" made it to number 1 in England in 1991 after being featured in a Levi's commercial.

For the Record

After the Clash released their album *London Calling*, some critics charged that they had "sold out" by using more varied and melodic musical forms in their album. Joe Strummer responded, "When I read that, the notion was so new to me I just laughed. In that dirty room in Pimlico, with one light and filthy carpet on the walls for soundproofing, that had been the furthest thought from our minds."

Legacy. The Clash rank second only to the Sex Pistols among the bands who established punk rock in the 1970's. Their fast-paced sounds of anger and frustration directly influenced innumerable groups throughout the 1980's around the world. In the 1990's the sound of the early Clash lived on, most notably in the popular American group Green Day.

In addition to helping found punk, the Clash contributed to other important trends in the music industry. Their songs often contained a strong element of social or political commentary. "White Riot" praised young Jamaican immigrants who stood up to the London police in 1976. "Career Opportunities" lamented the lack of power among people working menial jobs. They named *Sandinista!* in honor of the revolutionaries in Nicaragua and modeled their dress in the early 1980's after that of guerrilla soldiers. Their broad spectrum of targets thus included the foreign policy of the United States, the capitalist economic system, and police brutality.

In particular, the Clash fought against racism. In April, 1978, they played along with black reggae artists Steel Pulse at an anti-Nazi League rally in East London before twenty thousand people. The respect that the Clash had for black musicians also showed in their music; they recorded several reggae numbers, including "Police and Thieves" and "Pressure Drop." In recognition, they were inducted into the Reggae Hall of Fame in Jamaica. Their blending of reggae and rock was carried on successfully in the 1980's by groups such as the Specials and UB40. The Specials also carried on the fight against racism, particularly against apartheid in South Africa. The social consciousness displayed by the Specials and others in the 1980's was attributable in part to the precedent set by the Clash.   —*Andy DeRoche*

SELECT DISCOGRAPHY
■ ALBUMS
The Clash, 1977
Give 'Em Enough Rope, 1978
London Calling, 1979
Sandinista! 1980
Combat Rock, 1982

Cut the Crap, 1985
The Story of the Clash, 1988
The Singles Collection, 1991

SEE ALSO: Green Day; Ramones, The; Sex Pistols, The; Specials, The.

Jimmy Cliff
(James Chambers)

BORN: St. Catherine area of St. James Parish, Jamaica; April 1, 1948
FIRST SINGLE RELEASE: "Daisy Got Me Crazy," 1962
MUSICAL STYLES: Reggae

Reggae songwriter, singer, and actor Jimmy Cliff was born in 1948 in the Maroon country of Jamaica. His early years were taken up with listening to his father sing island songs while working as a laborer. Cliff attended school until the age of thirteen, when he decided to leave and go to Kingston, the largest urban center in Jamaica. There he was taken in by the city environment with its rich culture and vibrant lifestyle. The ska-based homespun rhythms, the imported rhythm-and-blues music of African Americans in the 1960's, along with calypso and reggae sounds, created a backdrop for the crucial stages of Jimmy Cliff's musical career.

Inspirational Beginnings. The social and political backdrop of the Rastafarian movement and the economic decay experienced in the shanty-towns of the city proved to be the source material for the lyrics of Cliff's songs. Having come from an impoverished background, Cliff was able to invent his songs from the harshness of reality. Immersed in the raw competition of reggae-inspired music, Cliff and many young musicians struggled to get their music heard in the recording world. Working at odd jobs and near death, poverty-stricken Cliff soon learned how to deal with the thriving but treacherous producers who would take his songs for little or no money.

When he was fourteen, his first recording was released: "Daisy Got Me Crazy." His first hit, "Dearest Beverly" in 1962, enabled him to record more songs for producers the Kong Brothers. Such songs as "Hurricane Hattie," "Miss Jamaica," and "Rudie in the Court" set in motion an opportunity to tour England, along with other musicians, for the Jamaican government, as a kind of recruiter for tourism in Jamaica. From 1961 to 1963 Cliff was signed with Island Records, which enabled him to attract larger audiences. However, interest in his music was sparse. Despite growing public awareness after a move to England, Cliff's living standard did not change very much, as he faced discrimination in many facets of his life.

Experimentation. Cliff's seach for a musical identity resulted from a hesitancy on the part of record buyers to purchase Jamaican pop music in Europe. He thus began experimenting with musical hybrids such as soul and reggae. Working the European club circuit, Cliff traveled through Europe, finding a sympathetic audience in France. He received a credible amount of success in Brazil in 1968, where he stayed briefly to write and perform.

His album in 1970, *Wonderful World, Beautiful People*, contained his most popular song, "Many Rivers to Cross," one of the first reggae songs to find popularity outside Jamaica. Cliff's ambiguity on his records was responsible for peaks and valleys in his musical career. His often eclectic style elicited mixed response, thereby raising and lowering his success ratio far too often for any sustainable presence on the charts. Cliff's hit "Vietnam" expressed his musical talents for social protest at a time when audiences were looking for changes in the conditions of American and global society.

Film and Fame. In 1972 Cliff had a startling rise in fortune when Perry Henzell, a Jamaican filmmaker, summoned him to make a film. It was an important move for Cliff, as it became a major cult film of the 1970's. *The Harder They Come* (1973) was based loosely on experiences of the music business in Jamaica and on Cliff's own past. This film took on fantasy proportions, in that Cliff became a kind of folk hero for the underclass. The sound track from the film, which includes "You Can Get It If You Really Want" and "Many Rivers to Cross," caused a brief resurgence in Cliff's

Jimmy Cliff (Paul Natkin)

aspirations of superstardom, but several albums that followed failed to make it big.

Since the 1980's Cliff has found some notoriety with another film, *Bongo Man* (1980), and his 1990 album release, *Images*. After forming his own company in 1990, Cliff Sounds and Films, Cliff continued to find ways in which to bring about a balance in his musical selections. "Break Out, Pulse" a 1992 release, summed up his contributions to the international movement.

Forging His Own Path. Cliff's musical efforts have won him audiences in Africa, South America, and Europe. Being truly independent, Cliff's career has been sporadic and unconventional. His interest in his African roots and his switch from Rastafarianism to Islam have caused much of his Jamaican audience to denounce him. Cliff has chosen to focus on his religious beliefs and an independent working ethic, paths which have also tended to alienate him from the mainstream. However, Jimmy Cliff will be best known as a reggae star of the caliber of Bob Marley and Peter Tosh.   —*James G. Pappas*

SELECT DISCOGRAPHY
■ ALBUMS
Hard Road to Travel, 1967
Wonderful World, Beautiful People, 1970
The Harder They Come, 1972 (sound track, with others)
Follow My Mind, 1975
Special, 1982
Cliff Hanger, 1985
Images, 1990

SELECT AWARDS
Grammy Award for Best Reggae Recording for *Cliff Hanger*, 1985

SEE ALSO: Marley, Bob; Tosh, Peter.

Patsy Cline

(Virginia Patterson Hensley)
BORN: Winchester, Virginia; September 8, 1932
DIED: Camden, Tennessee; March 5, 1963
FIRST SINGLE RELEASE: "A Church, a Courtroom, and Then Goodbye"/"Honky Tonk Merry-Go-Round," 1955
MUSICAL STYLES: Country, pop

As a teenager, Patsy Cline began her musical career singing in talent contests and with a swing band in and around Winchester, Virginia. Although she died at the age of thirty, Cline managed, through her sophisticated and passionate renditions of songs that presented the pain of loving and losing, to establish an eminent position in the world of country and pop music. Decades after her death she was still being emulated and was still receiving awards for her music and her performances.

The Beginnings. Born to a middle-aged blacksmith and his teenage wife, Virginia Patterson Hensley (later Patsy Cline) was a sixteen-year-old high school sophomore when her father Sam Hensley deserted his wife and three children. Working as a seamstress, Virginia Hensley, Cline's mother, was unable to support the family of four, so Cline quit school and began a series of jobs to help support herself, her brother Sam, and her sister Sylvia Mae. She had a variety of jobs: working in a poultry plant (cutting off chicken heads); working at the Greyhound bus station; and serving sodas at Hunter Gaunt's drugstore in Winchester. After work, Cline often sang in talent shows, at fairs, in supper clubs, and at honkytonks. By the time she went to work to help support her family, Cline had already begun her musical career; at the age of thirteen she started sitting in and singing with Bud Armel's Kountry Krackers, a Winchester swing band.

In 1954, at the age of twenty-two, Cline signed an exclusive two-year contract with Bill McCall, the manager of a small California record label (Coral Records). On the advice of her first manager, Bill Peer, Cline used the name Patsy as her recording name, rather than Virginia or Ginny. On July 1, 1955, Cline made her debut on the Ralston-Purina segment of the Grand Ole Opry, hosted by Ernest Tubb. There she sang "A Church, a Courtroom, and Then Goodbye." This song was released later that month as a single by Coral Records; on the flip side was "Honky Tonk Merry-Go-Round."

In 1956, Cline moved to the Decca label, and in July, 1956, she recorded the single "I Loved and Lost Again" with "Stop, Look, and Listen" on the flip side. In November, 1957, she recorded "Walkin' After Midnight." However, the label did not immediately release it. After Cline appeared on the television show *Arthur Godfrey's Talent Scouts* and sang the song, it was released in February, 1957. "Walkin' After Midnight" became Cline's first genuine hit, reaching number 3 on the *Billboard* country chart and number 15 on the *Billboard* pop chart.

Early in her singing career Cline stuck very closely to her country roots and often yodeled and growled as she sang; as her career developed Cline was more likely to sing ballads, particularly torch songs which detailed the pains of loving and losing. Cline's rendition of these songs became very sophisticated. She knew how to achieve a range of keys and sounds as she sang. She was admired by songwriters because she knew how to use phrasing to get the most from a song, and she knew which syllables to emphasize to achieve exactly the right shade of meaning from a line.

1957 and After. In 1957, after obtaining a divorce from her first husband, Gerald Cline, a Winchester businessman whom she had married in 1953, Cline married Charles Dick, a Linotype operator at *The Winchester Star*. In 1959, they moved to Nashville, where Cline began to record hit after hit. In the summer of 1961, Cline's recording "I Fall to Pieces" became number 1 on the *Billboard* country chart and number 12 on the pop chart. In June, 1961, Cline and her brother Sam Hensley were involved in a head-on car collision in Nashville. The crash sent Cline through the windshield and nearly to her death. Yet only weeks after this accident (August 21, 1961), Cline recorded Willie Nelson's song "Crazy." By 1962, when, according to *Cash Box* magazine, "Crazy" was the number 1 country song, Patsy Cline had replaced Kitty Wells as the biggest female star in country music. "She's Got You," released on January 10, 1962, was also a number 1 hit on the *Billboard* country chart and number 14 on the pop chart.

Legacy. In 1961, when Patsy Cline was in a Nashville hospital recovering from her car accident, she heard a young singer named Loretta Lynn live on the radio dedicating her rendition of "I Fall to Pieces" to the recuperating Cline. Cline was so impressed with Lynn's concern that she sent her husband Charles Dick to Ernest Tubb's record shop to get Lynn to come to the hospital. Cline befriended Lynn and helped Lynn with her career. Lynn tells about her relationship with Cline in Lynn's 1976 autobiography *Coal Miner's Daughter*.

Lynn was not the only country star who was helped by Cline. Cline's personal style and her singing style were very different from the styles of female country singers who had appeared before the early 1960's. Patsy Cline, through her lifestyle and her performing style, projected the image of a woman making it in a man's world. She was brassy and unconventional; these qualities helped her to succeed. Her success made it possible for less conventional female singers, such as Emmylou Harris, who came after her, to succeed as well.

It is also true that, while Cline loved country music, her smooth and sophisticated rendition of such songs as "Crazy" and "I Can't Help It (If I'm Still in Love with You)" made her successful as a pop singer and as a country singer. Thus, Cline's ability to use her voice as a sophisticated musical instrument of wide range and virtuosity, her ability to tell a story in a controlled three-minute song, and her appeal as a torch singer contributed to country music's ability to attract a wider audience than it had prior to her popularity. This increased appeal helped country musicians who performed in the decades after Cline's death.

Patsy Cline (Archive Photos)

For the Record

Since its release in 1962, no other song has been played as much on jukeboxes as has Patsy Cline's recording of "Crazy."

§

"I sing just like I hurt inside."

—*Patsy Cline*

Posthumous Fame. Cline's popularity and fame only grew after her death. More than thirty years after Cline's death, her albums were being released, she was receiving awards, plays were being written about her, and her fans were constructing Websites on the Internet to immortalize her.

In 1982, Owen Bradley, who had produced Cline's records, combined one of her vocal tracks with a Jim Reeves track to create the duet "Have You Ever Been Lonely?" It went to number 7 on the country charts. By 1997, *Patsy Cline's Greatest Hits,* released in 1967, had been certified platinum seven times. In 1997 MCA Nashville released *Live at the Cimarron Ballroom,* a live Cline performance taped at the Cimarron Ballroom in Tulsa, Oklahoma, on July 29, 1961. In this release Cline not only performs, but also talks with her audience about topics such as her car accident.

In 1985, the motion picture *Sweet Dreams,* starring Jessica Lange, was released. The film was highlighted by recordings of Patsy Cline singing her own songs. Beginning in 1988, the two-woman musical "Always . . . Patsy Cline," about the relationship between Cline and a female fan, has been performed in various places including Nashville and Off-Broadway. In 1993, the United States Postal Service issued a Patsy Cline stamp.

Since Cline's death in 1963, various female artists have been identified as her successor or as having her sound, including Mandy Barnett and LeAnn Rimes. Barnett portrayed Cline in the Nashville production of "Always . . . Patsy Cline." Grammy Award-winning Rimes has also been identified as a successor to Cline, and, in fact, Rimes's hit "Blue," written by Bill Mack in 1962,

was presented to Cline as a possible recording, but she died before she could record it.

—*Annita Marie Ward*

SELECT DISCOGRAPHY

■ SINGLES

"A Church, a Courtroom, and Then Goodbye"/"Honky Tonk Merry-Go-Round," 1955

"I Loved and Lost Again"/"Stop, Look, and Listen," 1956

"Walkin' After Midnight," 1957

"I Fall to Pieces," 1961

"Crazy," 1961

"She's Got You," 1962

■ ALBUMS

Patsy Cline, 1957

Patsy Cline's Greatest Hits, 1967

Live at the Cimarron Ballroom, 1997

SELECT AWARDS

Country Music Hall of Fame, inducted 1973

Grammy Award for Lifetime Achievement, 1995

SEE ALSO: lang, k. d.; Lynn, Loretta; Nelson, Willie; Rimes, LeAnn.

George Clinton / Parliament / Funkadelic

George Clinton

BORN: Kannapolis, North Carolina; July 22, 1940

FIRST ALBUM RELEASE: *Computer Games,* 1982

Parliament / Funkadelic

ORIGINAL MEMBERS: George Clinton, Eddie Hazel (b. 1950), Raymond "Tiki" Fulwood (b. 1944), Billy Nelson, Lucius "Tawl" Ross

OTHER MEMBERS: Bernie Worrell (b. 1944), William "Bootsy" Collins (b. 1951), Gary Shider, "Junie" Morrison

MUSICAL STYLES: funk, rhythm and blues

With the help of his bands Parliament, Funkadelic, and the hybrid P-Funk, George Clinton combined the funk of James Brown and Sly Stone with the psychedelic sensibilities of Jimi Hendrix

George Clinton (Paul Natkin)

to emerge as one of the most influential black artists of the 1970's. He and his groups reached the top of rhythm and blues (R&B) charts with numerous albums and singles until he turned to a solo career in the early 1980's. A few more hits followed, but Clinton's popularity faded as newer forms of black music developed. He made somewhat of a comeback in the 1990's and received long-overdue recognition for his innovative efforts.

Doo-Wop Roots. Clinton was born in Kannapolis, North Carolina, and then moved with his family to Plainfield, New Jersey, during the early 1950's. There, the teenage Clinton fell in love with doo-wop music, which was very popular at the time. He also found work in the back room of a barbershop straightening hair. "Everybody who sang doo-wop back in the 1950's had their hair

done, all those little guys that sang like Frankie Lymon had the 'do," recalls Clinton. "So we got into the barbershop business ourselves while we were waiting for our chance to become rock stars before the world."

It was a long wait. Clinton started his own vocal ensemble, the Parliaments, in 1955, but they did not record a hit until 1967's "(I Wanna) Testify." In 1964, Clinton formed an instrumental ensemble to back the Parliaments. The original lineup changed completely in 1967 when the founding members all enlisted in the U.S. Army. After some shuffling of personnel over the next year or so, the ensemble took semipermanent shape with Billy Nelson on bass, Eddie Hazel and Lucius "Tawl" Ross on guitars, and Raymond "Tiki" Fulwood on drums.

Nelson suggested the name Funkadelic for the new band. It reflected the group's enthusiasm for two trends then current: funk music and psychedelic culture. It also seemed to signal a change in Clinton's own musical tastes, so much so that he formed his own recording label bearing the same name in 1968. He seems to have been most inspired by Sly Stone during this period in his career, a fact that would become clear as the musical "tribe" called Funkadelic evolved.

Getting Funky with Funkadelic. In the late 1960's, Clinton wanted to record his vocal ensemble, now simply called Parliament, but the group was contractually bound to Revilot Records. His solution was to record Funkadelic's debut, *Funkadelic* (1970), for Westbound Records with Parliament's singers but without listing the group or its members among the album's credits. Clinton's deception succeeded, but it also sowed a seed of head-scratching confusion over the difference between Parliament and Funkadelic. Matters became more confused as Clinton released other albums during the 1970's, some bearing the Parliament name, some with Funkadelic. Clinton even starting using the name P-Funk for the combined group.

The difference between Parliament and Funkadelic became increasingly irrelevant as Clinton's touring ensemble grew to include some fifty performers. On stage, Clinton's ensemble looked more like a funky remake of Exodus than a band. Keyboardist and arranger Bernie Worrell, who studied classical music at both the New England Conservatory and Juilliard, became a key musical member of the assemblage, as did bassist William "Bootsy" Collins, a veteran from the James Brown band, who joined in 1972. More than anyone, it was Clinton, Worrell, and Collins who defined the Parliament/Funkadelic/P-Funk sound. Collins, in his own right, would go on to inspire a generation of bass players, including Flea of the Red Hot Chili Peppers.

Clinton and his groups churned out chart-placing albums and singles, one after the other, throughout the 1970's. In doing so, they gave black listeners a potent antidote to the slick Philadelphia sound that dominated the airwaves. Clinton's music even came with its own ethos that evolved into an all-embracing attitude toward life. As one album title seemed to proclaim, Clinton was the funky president of "one nation under a groove."

Clinton's live shows became legendary, not only for the multitude of performers involved but also for their pageantry. He and his musicians wore outfits that made the psychedelic clothing of the early 1960's look tame in comparison. As outrageous as they were, the costumes could not outdo the music. Theaters throbbed to the ferocious groove that would go for hours. In 1976, Clinton began descending onto the stage in a flashing model of a spaceship (it was the era of theater rock as made famous by such acts as David Bowie and Kiss). Taking a cue from jazz artist Sun Ra, Clinton went on to make the "mothership" a central part of the group's mythology.

The 1980's and 1990's. Clinton continued to record successful albums and tour during the remainder of the 1970's. However, he was beset with problems not long into the 1980's, including financial difficulties, unhappy band members, and personal difficulties with drugs. In addition, several former members of Funkadelic reemerged with a 1981 album using the band's name, and legal hassles erupted when Polygram Label Group acquired Parliament's label Casablanca in 1980.

Clinton responded to these collective woes by striking out as a solo artist. He heralded his new start with the album *Computer Games* in 1982. It sold reasonably well, and he continued to tour with veterans of P-Funk as the P-Funk All Stars, but the 1980's were definitely not the 1970's. Musical tastes were changing among black listeners, and almost everything connected with the earlier decade had become a bad joke. Dressed-down rappers were starting to make dressed-up funkers look silly. Clinton kept churning out the funk with near-religious zeal in smaller and smaller venues, ones that could not even accommodate the spaceship stage set.

Clinton fared somewhat better during the 1990's. Prince signed him to his own Paisley Park label for 1989's the *Cinderella Theory*, and a younger generation of musicians seemed to hold him in high esteem: His songs have been covered or sampled by the Red Hot Chili Peppers, Public Enemy, and Dr. Dre. In 1996, Clinton signed with Sony Records and released a new album, *The Awesome Power of a Fully Operational Mothership (TAPOAFOM)* and continued to tour widely with the P-Funk All Stars. As a further sign of his importance, Clinton was inducted into the Rock and Roll Hall of Fame in 1997.   —*David Lee Fish*

For the Record

George Clinton's wardrobe, stage antics, and "belief" in the mothership led one interviewer to ask if the artist minds people not taking him seriously. Clinton responded, "No, because I do that on purpose. That's my own protection for taking myself too serious."

SELECT DISCOGRAPHY
■ ALBUMS
Funkadelic
Funkadelic, 1970
Maggot Brain, 1971
Hardcore Jollies, 1976
Tales of Kidd Funkadelic, 1976

One Nation Under a Groove, 1978
The Electric Spanking of War Babies, 1980
Parliament
Mothership Connection, 1975
Trombipulation, 1980
George Clinton and the P-Funk All-Stars
*The Awesome Power of a Fully Operational
    Mothership (TAPOAFOM)*, 1996
George Clinton solo
Computer Games, 1982
The Cinderella Theory, 1989

SELECT AWARDS
Rock and Roll Hall of Fame, inducted 1996

SEE ALSO: Brown, James; James, Rick; Sly and the Family Stone.

The Coasters

ORIGINAL MEMBERS: Carl Gardner (b. 1928), Billy Guy (b. 1936), Leon Hughes, Bobby Nunn (1925-1986), Adolph Jacobs
OTHER MEMBERS: Earl "Speedoo" Carroll (b. 1937), Will "Dub" Jones (b. 1939), Ronnie Bright (b. 1939)
FIRST SINGLE RELEASE: "Down in Mexico," 1956
MUSICAL STYLES: Rock and roll, rhythm and blues, novelty

Under the direction of Jerry Leiber and Mike Stoller, who wrote their songs and produced their records, the Coasters were the great rock-and-roll novelty act of the 1950's, with humorous songs about everything from unrequited love ("Young Blood") to television Westerns ("Along Came Jones"). Their songs enriched the national vocabulary with such phrases as "Yakety yak—don't talk back" and "Why's everybody always picking on me?"

The Beginnings. In 1955 Jerry Leiber and Mike Stoller were writing songs and producing records for black musicians. (Their "Hound Dog" had been recorded by Big Mama Thornton and would soon be recorded by Elvis Presley.) They owned a small California record label, Spark Records, on which a group called the Robins re-

corded Leiber and Stoller's "Smoky Joe's Cafe." Atlantic Records offered the songwriters a contract to produce records for its new subsidiary, Atco. There was dissension among the Robins, but Leiber and Stoller persuaded two of its members, lead singer Carl Gardner and bass Bobby Nunn, to leave the Robins and become the nucleus of a new group, to which they added Billy Guy, Leon Hughes, and guitarist Adolph Jacobs. The group was called the Coasters because of their West Coast location.

Their first record, "Down in Mexico," may have sounded too much like "Smokey Joe's Cafe." Their second, "One Kiss Led to Another," may have been too lubricious. They found two-sided success with their third outing, however: "Searchin'," backed with "Young Blood." "Searchin'" seems to have been the first of many songs to blur the distinction between romantic pursuit and stalking. With copious references to famous detectives (Charlie Chan, Bulldog Drummond), the singer makes clear that he will not rest until he has found his woman. The other side, "Young Blood," a tale of lost love, offers three voices echoing the lead singer's lament, while bass Bobby Nunn represents the girl's father: "You better leave my daughter alone." Both sides were hits, but the follow-up, an oddity called "Idol with the Golden Head" about a magical object that enables the singer to find out what his girlfriend is doing, sold disappointingly.

The Bad Boys. In 1958 Leiber and Stoller reinvented the group to give them the image for which they became known. As perhaps never before in American culture, popular music had become a teenage market. The love songs seemed to have more adolescent imagery, and there was a niche for images of teen rebellion. The Coasters exploited that. On "Yakety Yak" the group repeated some standard parental commands, then followed them with a loud "Yakety Yak" and the reply (by new bass singer Will "Dub" Jones), "Don't talk back." The song also introduced a saxophone sound by King Curtis, sometimes called "Yakety Sax" because of both the original song's name and the way it sounded. Parents complained; kids loved it.

The Coasters (Archive Photos/Frank Driggs Collection)

a country-born piano man/ Playing in between the cracks." Their next record, "Poison Ivy," reached the charts in spite of, or because, some listeners considered it a thinly veiled reference to venereal disease. Its flip side, a jolly love song called "I'm a Hog for You," also made the Top 40.

After the Big Hits. The group's next song, "Run, Red, Run," may have been the Coasters' funniest. To the accompaniment of Mike Stoller's honky-tonk piano playing, it tells of a man who taught a monkey to play poker, only to learn that he had achieved his mission too well when the monkey caught him cheating and robbed him at gunpoint. "Run, Red, Run" was a minor hit. The flip side, "What About Us?" is a song in which the group complains that an unidentified "he" is getting a generally better deal than they are. The song's racial implications make it an early protest song.

The next year the group recorded "Snake and the Bookworm," a lively return to the "bad boy" theme in which the "snake" attempts to distract the "bookworm" from her studies. Sales were low.

Two new members joined the group. Earl "Speedoo" Carroll had sung lead with another popular novelty group, the Cadillacs; his nickname had given that group its biggest hit. Ronnie Bright replaced bass Dub Jones. (In 1963 Bright would represent all basses, singing the featured bass part on Johnny Cymbal's doo-wop tribute, "Mr. Bass Man.") At this point the group was sliding in popularity. "Little Egypt," a song about a sideshow stripper, was a moderate hit in 1961, but it gained more notice when performed in a film by Elvis Presley. In 1963 the Coasters recorded "Ain't Nothin' to Me," a story of a violent

Again, the Coasters followed a smash hit with a record that sold poorly: "The Shadow Knows," a reprise of the "Searchin'" theme, backed with "Sorry, but I'm Gonna Have to Pass," a cynical tale of an adventurer with a wife and children at home. The Coasters returned to the top, however, with "Charlie Brown," the tale of a teen troublemaker who writes on the walls, shoots dice in the gym, and keeps wondering why everyone picks on him.

The group stayed in the Top 10 with "Along Came Jones," which satirized television Westerns by presenting an image of seeing the same show whatever channel one turned to. Its flip side, "That Is Rock and Roll," attained little notice, but it offered a witty description and defense of its subject: "That ain't no freight train that you hear/ Rollin' down the railroad tracks./ That's

and perhaps fatal barroom confrontation narrated in action by a participant-observer, live on-stage at the Apollo Theater. Record listeners tended to wonder just what the Apollo audience had seen. The group then left Atlantic and Leiber and Stoller to seek success with other labels. They never had another Top-40 hit.

The Memories. The Coasters remain in the public memory for their comic portrayals of 1950's life. As with many 1950's groups, there have been at least three acts on the oldies circuit using the Coasters' name, sometimes with only one actual member of the original group. Coasters' songs are periodically covered by other artists; in the 1971 Bangladesh concert, an all-star cast led by Leon Russell performed "Young Blood." Warren Zevon's song "Gorilla, You're a Desperado" (1980) may well have been influenced by the similar tale in "Run, Red, Run."

There have been retroactive complaints about two white men (Leiber and Stoller) having written songs alleged to portray black stereotypes of violence, laziness, and insolence to be performed by a black group. Most listeners, however, find the Coasters' work a delightful presentation of universal human experiences to which pigmentation is irrelevant. The Coasters themselves, when first hearing Leiber and Stoller's material, were impressed at how effectively the writers managed to capture the feeling and attitude of young black life in the late 1950's.

Both the Coasters and Leiber and Stoller were inducted into the Rock and Roll Hall of Fame in 1987, the second year of its operation. In the 1990's a Broadway revue of Leiber-Stoller songs called *Smokey Joe's Cafe: The Songs of Leiber and Stoller* was well received, and the sound-track album won a Grammy Award for Best Musical Show Album in 1995.

—*Arthur D. Hlavaty*

SELECT DISCOGRAPHY
■ SINGLES
"One Kiss Led to Another," 1956
"Searchin'"/"Young Blood," 1957
"Yakety Yak," 1958
"The Shadow Knows," 1958
"Charlie Brown," 1959

> ## For the Record
>
> Singer-songwriter Curtis Mayfield once saluted the Coasters as "my biggest inspiration."

"Along Came Jones," 1959
"That Is Rock & Roll," 1959
"Poison Ivy"/"I'm a Hog for You," 1959
"Bad Blood," 1959
"Run, Red, Run," 1959
"What about Us?" 1959
"Little Egypt (Ying Yang)," 1961
"Ain't Nothin' to Me," 1963
■ ALBUMS
The Coasters' Greatest Hits, 1958
Fifty Coastin' Classics: The Coasters Anthology, 1992
The Very Best of the Coasters, 1994

SELECT AWARDS
Rock and Roll Hall of Fame, inducted 1987

SEE ALSO: Drifters, The.

Eddie Cochran

BORN: Albert Lea, Minnesota; October 3, 1938
DIED: Chippenham, Wiltshire, England; April 17, 1960
FIRST HIT SINGLE RELEASE: "Sittin' in the Balcony," 1957
MUSICAL STYLES: Country, rock and roll, rockabilly

Eddie Cochran had a developing songwriting career that was augmented by his good looks, trademark moves, and great guitar skills. Before he was twenty-two years old, he had released several hit singles and been in two films. An untimely car accident would deny the rock world the chance to see him grow and develop, yet his small body of work would influence generations of rock guitarists and songwriters.

Humble Beginnings. Eddie Cochran was born in Albert Lea, Minnesota, to parents who had just moved from Oklahoma. The youngest of five children, Cochran grew up with the country-and-western music popular at that time. Cochran begged his parents for a guitar of his own and received it when he was twelve. In 1951, the family migrated to the Los Angeles area. Cochran was already a good guitarist and was then playing the electric Gretsch 6120 hollow-body guitar, the thick guitar that would be a part of his trademark rockabilly sound.

The Big Break. In 1954, Cochran met country songwriter Hank Cochran (no relation). They performed as the Cochran Brothers, as country brother groups were popular at the time. In 1955 they began recording singles. "Tired and Sleepy" featured hints of Cochran's half-speaking, half-singing style, but it drew little radio attention. They went to Nashville, where they recorded "Skinny Jim," a Little Richard-influenced song. That single also failed, and the duo broke up. (Hank Cochran stayed in Nashville and became successful writing songs for others, including Patsy Cline's "I Fall to Pieces.")

Eddie Cochran returned to Los Angeles in 1956 and signed with the Liberty label, which procured him an appearance in the 1956 teenage rock-and-roll film *The Girl Can't Help It*, starring Jayne Mansfield. Just after the film was released, Cochran had his first hit, "Sittin' in the Balcony." Although he was criticized for trying too hard to sound like Elvis Presley, the song nonetheless went to number 18 on the charts. It also earned Cochran another film role (*Flaming Youth*) and more recording sessions, but none of these songs made the Top 100.

In 1958 Cochran recorded "Summertime Blues," which he had written with Jerry Capehart. It would be the most popular song of the summer and the song that made Cochran a star. His half-singing, half-speaking vocal style was augmented by the "King Fish" growl he used in some of the vocal lines typically found in rhythm-and-blues records of the time. The somewhat humorous lyrics spoke of teenage boredom and frustration caused by the adult oppressions of the day. The song was Cochran's biggest hit and reached number 8 on the pop charts. It would be rerecorded by many, including the Who and Bruce Springsteen, and would be a staple of summertime rock and roll on most U.S. radio stations for decades to come.

Untimely Death. Later in 1958, Cochran had another hit with "C'mon Everybody," which reached number 35 on the charts. He then had a very successful tour in Europe with friend Gene Vincent. The tour was continually extended, until finally the homesick Cochran got in a taxi on

Eddie Cochran (Freddie Patterson Collection/Archive Photos)

April 17, 1960, with Vincent and his girlfriend, songwriter Sharon Sheeley, and headed to the London airport. Cochran was said to be looking forward to getting back to Los Angeles and doing more recording, and he had told a reporter that he wanted to make a record where he played all the instruments. Cochran never made it to the airport. The taxi crashed, and while Vincent and Sheeley were only injured and would recover, the accident was fatal for Cochran.

Legacy. While Cochran was a rising star extinguished before his time, his influence was heard not only in the other early rock artists of his generation but also in artists from later decades. His blend of country and rock would be revived with groups such as the Stray Cats, who had a hit with one of Cochran's tunes, "Jeanie Jeanie Jeanie." His "Summertime Blues" has also gone down in history as one of the ultimate songs of summer.

—Kevin M. Mitchell

SELECT DISCOGRAPHY
■ SINGLES
"Sittin' in the Balcony," 1957
"Summertime Blues," 1958
■ ALBUMS
Eddie Cochran, 1960
Cherished Memories, 1961
Somethin' Else: The Fine Lookin' Hits of Eddie Cochran, 1998

SEE ALSO: Presley, Elvis; Stray Cats, The.

For the Record

He is better known in Europe than in the United States, and there is still an Eddie Cochran Memorial Society in England.

§

Cochran was supposed to have toured with his friends Buddy Holly, Richie Valens, and the Big Bopper (J. P. Richardson) on the 1959 tour on which all three died in a plane crash.

Joe Cocker

BORN: John Robert Cocker, Sheffield, England, May 20, 1944
FIRST ALBUM RELEASE: *With a Little Help from My Friends*, 1969
MUSICAL STYLES: Rock and roll

White-soul singer Joe Cocker's gravelly voice and inimitable stage antics made him one of the top performers of the early 1970's before drugs and alcohol almost destroyed him. Cocker endured, however, and weathered well to become one of the most respected vocalists of the 1990's.

The Beginnings. In 1959 Cocker joined his first band, the Cavaliers, as drummer and harmonica player. By 1961 he had become lead vocalist of the newly christened Vance Arnold and the Avengers, who were gaining regional notice through the release of singles and local tours with such bands the Hollies and the Rolling Stones. A brief contract with Decca Records produced no success.

In 1965 Cocker and Avengers keyboardist Chris Stainton formed the Grease Band and began performing covers of Motown songs in local pubs. While still working day jobs, Cocker and Stainton sent a demo tape of "Marjorine" to Denny Cordell (producer of Procol Harum and the Move), who convinced Deram Records to release the single and agreed to manage Cocker. "Marjorine" hit the British Top 50 in 1967, leading Cocker and the Grease Band to move to London. There they recorded their first album, *With a Little Help from My Friends* (1969). The title track, his version of the Beatles song, reached the top of the British charts (and number 68 in the United States) and was a massive European hit. With the help of friends such as Jimmy Page and Steve Winwood, who played on several tracks, Cocker's first album broke into the Top 40, peaking at number 35 in the summer of 1969.

Still relatively unknown in the United States, Cocker became a counterculture celebrity in 1969 with his performance of Traffic's "Feelin' Alright" on the Ed Sullivan show and his rendition of "With a Little Help from My Friends" at the Woodstock music festival. His supercharged, spastic

For the Record

Joe Cocker and Jennifer Warnes had never met before the evening they recorded the award-winning "Up Where We Belong." Cocker, on tour in the Pacific Northwest, flew to Los Angeles in the afternoon. He and Warnes recorded the song in the evening, then he hopped a plane to rejoin his tour.

stage performances and a musical partnership with Leon Russell led Cocker to the peak of his popular career between 1970 and 1972. Cocker's second album, *Joe Cocker!* (1969), with Leon Russell and the Grease Band, was arguably his best, yielding Cocker's classic cover of John Lennon and Paul McCartney's "She Came in Through the Bathroom Window."

Mad Dogs and Englishmen. Russell was one of the top session men of the rock era, having played with a who's who of rock superstars and on many of the biggest hits of the late 1950's and early 1960's. As a teenager he played with Ronnie Hawkins and the Hawks (later the Band), went to Los Angeles to work with Glen Campbell, Gary Lewis and the Playboys, and played on most of producer Phil Spector's West Coast hit sessions. After highly acclaimed but commercially unsuccessful solo efforts, Russell, along with Cordell, began Shelter Records and was primarily responsible for organizing the forty-person entourage of musicians and hangers-on that developed into Cocker's trademark Mad Dogs and Englishman tour (1970).

The Mad Dogs and Englishmen tour was a huge commercial success, yielding a film, a number 2 live album, and two hit singles ("The Letter" and "Cry Me a River"). However, the excesses of road life left Cocker broke, sick, and discouraged and led to a life of seclusion. Throughout the remainder of the 1970's, frequent bouts with drugs and alcohol limited his production, though at his best (1975's "You Are

So Beautiful," for example), Cocker was still sensational.

Cocker's career turned around in 1982 when his duet with Jennifer Warnes, "Up Where We Belong," went to number 1. The song, the theme from the hit film *An Officer and a Gentleman*, also earned a Grammy Award for Best Pop Vocal Performance by a Duo or Group with Vocal. Though Cocker only hit the Top 40 once after this ("When the Night Comes," number 11, 1990), he continued to chart into the 1990's and was in high demand for special projects and movie scores. Having survived both success and self-destruction, Cocker's impassioned voice was still crackling with sincerity.

—*John Powell*

SELECT DISCOGRAPHY
■ ALBUMS
With a Little Help from My Friends, 1969
Joe Cocker!, 1969
Mad Dogs and Englishmen, 1970
Joe Cocker, 1972
I Can Stand a Little Rain, 1974
Stingray, 1976
Joe Cocker's Greatest Hits, 1977 (previously released material)
Sheffield Steel, 1982
Civilized Man, 1984
Unchain My Heart, 1987
Classics, Volume 4, 1987
One Night of Sin, 1989
Joe Cocker Live, 1990 (live)
Night Calls, 1992
The Best of Joe Cocker, 1993 (previously released material)
Have a Little Faith, 1994
The Long Voyage Home, 1995 (box set)
Organic, 1996
Across from Midnight, 1997
On Air—Live at the BBC, 1997 (live)

SELECT AWARDS
Grammy Award for Best Pop Vocal Performance by a Duo or Group with Vocal for "Up Where We Belong," 1982 (with Jennifer Warnes)

SEE ALSO: Beatles, The; Traffic / Steve Winwood / Dave Mason.

Leonard Cohen

BORN: Montreal, Canada; September 21, 1934
FIRST ALBUM RELEASE: *Songs of Leonard Cohen*, 1968
MUSICAL STYLES: Folk, folk rock, pop

Leonard Cohen is a genuine poet. Having published two novels and four volumes of poetry before recording his first song, Cohen brought literary experimentation, artful sexual longing, and a sense of spiritual journey to the folk music boom of the 1960's.

Musical Poet. During this traditional folk phase, Cohen created powerful, intimate songs that focused on the desire for some kind of communion, be it sexual, spiritual, or political; this phase is best represented on *The Best of Leonard Cohen* (1975). He later gained control over his voice as an instrument and began to set his songs to livelier rhythms, discovering a new folk-pop synthesis—especially on *I'm Your Man* (1988) and *The Future* (1992)—that merged his personal and social concerns. His appeal to a new generation of listeners was cemented when "Everybody Knows" (1988), a cynical dirge of low expectations, played over the opening credits of the teen film *Pump Up the Volume* (1990): "Everybody knows/ the boat is leaking/ Everybody knows the captain lied/ Everybody's got this broken feeling/ that their father or their dog just died." With the exception of Bob Dylan's work, Cohen's body of work best illustrates the path literature has taken into popular music.

Early Years. The son of middle-class Jewish immigrants in Montreal, Canada, Cohen was Canada's most promising young writer when folksinger Judy Collins recorded his classic ballads "Suzanne" and "Dress Rehearsal Rag" in 1966. Collins encouraged Cohen to begin performing his own songs, and his set at the Newport Folk Festival in 1967 impressed legendary musical scout and impresario John Hammond. *Songs of Leonard Cohen* (1968) features all of Cohen's now-famous trademarks: a grave, low monotone that carries the hypnotic appeal of chanting and prayer; themes of wandering and self-discovery; and a hostility toward all pretense, including his

Leonard Cohen (Chester Higgins Jr./New York Times Co./Archive Photos)

own. Four of the album's songs later provided background narrative for Robert Altman's classic film *McCabe and Mrs. Miller* (1971).

Throughout the 1960's and 1970's, Cohen experimented with religion, drugs, and sex. His stark, guitar-only meditations are those of an exile searching for spiritual tranquility without traditional religion. For example, "Story of Isaac" (from 1969's *Songs from a Room*) tells the biblical tale of Abraham's near-sacrifice of his only son from the boy's point of view. Part short story, part epic ballad, and part biblical commentary, it is also an anti-Vietnam War song that indicts war enthusiasts for sacrificing young boys without spiritual purpose. More often, Cohen maps his own inner terrain of pain, as in "Avalanche" from 1971's *Songs of Love and Hate*. He once said, "A poet is deeply conflicted and it's in his work that he reconciles those deep conflicts."

Balladeer. In the 1970's, Cohen began to develop both his voice and the ballad form into a musical format that would complement his literary skills. "Is This What You Wanted" and "There Is a War" (from 1974's *New Skin for the Old Ceremony*) are examples of his attempts to use livelier rhythms and to treat the folk refrain more as a pop chorus. His attempts to be more vocally expressive, however, resulted only in yells and screams. For *Death of a Ladies Man* (1977), he looked for outside help, but legendary producer Phil Spector's dense soundscapes overmatched Cohen's voice. On *Recent Songs* (1979), Cohen returned to the troubadour ballads, but with a newly calm, almost dispassionate vocal style. Songs such as "The Guests" and "The Traitor" are minor classics in which Cohen infused gypsy fiddles and modernist irony into medieval tales of pilgrimage, intrigue, and romance.

Cohen did not release an album for the next five years, but in that time he fastened onto the two musical elements that have become essential to his folk-pop synthesis: female backup singers and solid rhythmic grooves. *Various Positions* (1984) is a set of new-age parables mixing Cohen's ancient chanting cadences with slow, languorous grooves. He used simple, potent, universal images—the dance, the law, the idea of personal will, the requirements of leadership—to launch into spiritual commentary. For example, "Dance Me to the End of Love" uses the folk-dance rhythms of

For the Record

Leonard Cohen's albums consistently reach the Top 10 in many European countries, and *I'm Your Man* (1988) was a number 1 album throughout the Continent.

§

"I'm the only guy around who has some jokes in his songs, and I take the rap as this suicidemeister." —*Leonard Cohen*

an ethnic wedding to meditate on the possibility of any lifelong communion. "If It Be Your Will" is a prayer disguised as a song, a grave, stunning pledge of loyalty sung in hushed reverence to a great love. Cool, beautiful female voices mediate Cohen's rough voice and grave mesages, while the deep, relaxed background rhythms provide a new sense of musical depth.

I'm Your Man (1988) was Cohen's comeback record, a critically acclaimed set of songs that announced a renewed sense of social engagement. In the first song, "First We Take Manhattan," Cohen nearly predicts the fall of the Berlin Wall: "I'm coming back/ I'm coming back/ to haunt you," he sings, "First we take Manhattan/ then we take Berlin." A tinny drum machine dominates the song and seems to reflect the superficial values and rampant consumerism Cohen despises. Still, his jazzy phrasing lends humor and style to the prophet's rage—especially on "Tower of Song," in which Cohen mocks his own "golden voice"—while Jennifer Warnes's backing vocals help soothe the angry vision.

1990's Folk Rock. *The Future* (1992) is a folk-rock masterpiece: the album is deep and light, cool and passionate, perceptive and playful. Cohen was sympathetic to the losers who drown their lives at "Closing Time" and cautiously hopeful in contemplating the risk of new love ("Be for Real"). He's reverent and humble while he meditates on the imperfect nature of the universe in "Anthem": "There is a crack/ in everything/ that's how the night gets in." In "Always," he turns an old Irving Berlin song about pledging eternal love into a gospel-influenced meditation on the hard work required of any intimate relationship. Yet this is not a mellow album: the title track is full of apocalyptic warnings, calling for Americans (in particular) to fill the "hole in their culture" and quench their "spiritual thirst."

Cohen Live! (1994) reveals the extent of the poet's musical retooling. The dark, heavy tone of his voice now bespeaks gravity and authority, yet he wears this mantle lightly. His vocals are spare and relaxed, and they blend with the colorful musical textures of his eight-piece band. His vocal delivery is so original and his use of language so compelling that he no longer needs to slam the songs against the walls of the listeners' ears; his style is almost slick in an old-fashioned sense. Cohen has often stated that he has been looking for "the harbor," a calm zone where he can still watch the business of the marketplace of life. He must be at least halfway there, having turned his early documents of pain into songs of relaxed intensity and tough humanism.   —*Joel Dinerstein*

SELECT DISCOGRAPHY

■ ALBUMS

Songs of Leonard Cohen, 1968
Songs from a Room, 1969
Songs of Love and Hate, 1971
Live Songs, 1973
New Skin for the Old Ceremony, 1974
The Best of Leonard Cohen, 1975 (compilation)
Death of a Ladies' Man, 1977
Recent Songs, 1979
Various Positions, 1984
I'm Your Man, 1988
The Future, 1992
Cohen Live! 1994
More Best of Leonard Cohen, 1997 (compilation)

SELECT AWARDS

Juno Awards' Canadian Music Hall of Fame, inducted 1991
Officer of the Order of Canada, 1991
Governor General's Performing Arts Award, 1993

SEE ALSO: Collins, Judy; Dylan, Bob.

Nat "King" Cole

BORN: Montgomery, Alabama; March 17, 1917
DIED: Santa Monica, California; February 15, 1965
FIRST SINGLE RELEASE: "Straighten Up and Fly Right," 1943
MUSICAL STYLES: Jazz, rhythm and blues, pop

As a vocalist, Nat "King" Cole enjoyed one of the most phenomenally successful careers in pop music history. His string of hits, many of them million-selling singles, stretches from the mid-1940's to the mid-1960's. His luxuriant baritone voice was particularly effective on sentimental ballads that remain his most popular recordings. Prior to and overlapping this period of pop supremacy, however, were the years he spent establishing himself as a jazz pianist. To jazz performers and fans, Cole's style and influence as a pianist are as important as the standards he set as a pop vocalist.

Chicago to Los Angeles. When he was four, Nathaniel Adams Cole's family moved to Chicago, which, in the 1920's, was a fast-growing metropolis and jazz center. Its bustling, nonstop musical atmosphere captivated the adolescent Cole, who'd been studying piano, and his older brother Eddie, who took to sneaking out to play bass in South Side nightspots. Nat also began sneaking out, absorbing the sounds from alleys, too young to gain admittance. Later, when allowed in, Nat showed he had developed as a pianist to the point that he could compete for engagements.

By high school, Nat had gained a considerable reputation. Eddie was impressed enough to include him in his sextet, Eddie Cole and His Solid Swingers. With this group, Nat Cole the pianist first appeared on records, with four sides made for Decca in 1936.

Cole split with his brother later that year when a stage production the sextet was accompanying began touring. Soon after leaving Chicago, Cole married Nadine Robinson, a dancer with the show. When the company reached Southern California, it ran out of money and broke up. Cole scrounged for whatever low-paying engagements he could find, a difficult task in Los Angeles. Its musical climate was not as active as Chicago's, and prejudice against African Americans was pervasive.

The King Cole Trio. Cole's perseverance and Nadine's help eventually led to better musical jobs. An offer from a popular club needing a small group for an extended run prompted Cole to contact guitarist Oscar Moore and bassist Wesley Prince, highly respected musicians working as Cole was. At some point during the engagement, Cole acquired the nickname "King," and the King Cole Trio was born.

Nat "King" Cole (Archive Photos)

The trio cultivated a style that featured deft instrumental interplay, propulsive swing, and innovative harmonies. Each member sang, and many of their numbers featured humorous, wisecracking lyrics rattled off in unison. Their success with critics and the public was immediate. In 1943, fledgling Capitol Records signed the trio to a seven-year contract; sales of its singles launched Capitol into major-label status. In spring of 1944, Capitol's rerelease of "Straighten Up and Fly Right" reached number 9 on the *Billboard* charts for seven weeks, selling a half million copies. With national and overseas tours, long-term engagements, first-place magazine poll finishes, and records in every store, the King Cole Trio was famous worldwide during the 1940's.

Cole the Singer. Because "Straighten Up and Fly Right" had featured Cole as the lone vocalist, his associates began suggesting he record more as a solo singer. Though the trio kept up its success

in the commercial market with uptempo novelty songs featuring his vocals, Cole hesitated, unsure how he would be received in a different setting.

"The Christmas Song" erased any doubt. Accompanied for the first time by a string-heavy studio orchestra, Cole's clear diction and mellow yet penetrating tone brought the heartwarming holiday imagery vividly to life. The recording soared to number 3 on the charts in November, 1946, and stayed in the Top 10 well into the next year.

Cole maintained appearances with the trio, but emphasis was steadily shifting toward selections on which only he sang. In 1948, Cole divorced Nadine and married Marie Ellington; her influential voice was added to those urging him to concentrate on singing solo. The stunning success that year of Cole's rendition of "Nature Boy"—number 1 for eight weeks, more than 1.5 million copies sold—proved that his voice could capture the poignancy and sincerity hidden in lyrics that on paper appeared simplistic or unmarketable. Cole's warmth and jazz-inflected phrasing elevated "Mona Lisa" to number 1 and a six-month stay on the charts in 1950. With Cole convinced of his future, the King Cole Trio dissolved in 1951.

The 1950's and early 1960's were golden years for Cole. His live appearances commanded top dollar. Songwriters approached him first with their best efforts. He toured frequently and recorded constantly. He was one of the first African Americans to star in his own weekly television series (it ran from 1956 to 1957). He appeared in a handful of films, mostly in supporting roles that called for singing. From "Too Young," the number 1 song of 1951 based on sales and radio play, to "Those Lazy-Hazy-Crazy Days of Summer" a million-seller in 1963, Cole churned out a steady stream of hit singles. In 1957, he was one of the founders of the National Academy of Recording Arts and Sciences, the organization that administers the Grammy Awards.

Struggle and Triumph. In the segregated America of the mid-twentieth century, African American celebrities found that popularity brought no immunity from racist conditions and

For the Record

The man who presented Nat "King" Cole with the lyrics for Cole's 1948 hit "Nature Boy" was an eccentric recluse named Eden Ahbez. He dressed in rags, ate only fruits and nuts, and claimed to live under one of the *L*'s in Hollywood's large hillside sign. Ahbez was likely not the actual writer, however; when "Nature Boy" was credited to him, he was sued for plagiarism by another songwriter and settled out of court.

actions encountered by most other African Americans. For Cole, the most serious episode of this nature occurred on April 10, 1956, in Birmingham, Alabama. Just after his trio opened the evening's first show, five white thugs rushed the stage. They managed to reach Cole and slightly injure him before being beaten back by police and taken away. Cole was subsequently urged by some African American civil rights leaders to boycott southern states. Cole refused, choosing to demonstrate that, in a free society, entertainers of any race should be able to perform wherever audiences welcomed them.

Cole countered other humiliations and outrages with dignity and calm determination. In his gentle, peace-loving way, Cole managed to change attitudes and remove racially demeaning policies at home and abroad.

Since his death from lung cancer in 1965, appreciation for Cole's professional achievements and personal struggles has greatly expanded. Cole's daughter, singer Natalie Cole, introduced her generation to her father's music with performances and recordings in the 1980's and 1990's, even singing with him in an electronically arranged "duet" of the hit "Unforgettable." Contemporary performers and audiences alike continue to find that there is much to be admired about this legendary "King" of American music.

—*Mark W. Bolton*

SELECT DISCOGRAPHY

■ SINGLES

"Sweet Lorraine," 1940
"Straighten Up and Fly Right," 1943
"The Christmas Song," 1946
"Nature Boy," 1948
"Mona Lisa," 1950
"Too Young," 1951
"Unforgettable," 1951
"Pretend," 1953
"Answer Me, My Love," 1954
"A Blossom Fell," 1955
"Send for Me," 1957
"Looking Back," 1958
"Ramblin' Rose," 1962

■ ALBUMS

King Cole for Kids, 1948
Nat King Cole Sings for Two in Love, 1954
Love Is the Thing, 1957
Nat King Cole at the Sands, 1960
The Complete Capitol Recordings of the Nat King Cole Trio, 1993 (18 compact-disc set)

SELECT AWARDS

Academy Award for Best Song for "Mona Lisa," from *Captain Carey, U.S.A.*, 1950
Grammy Award for Best Performance by "Top 40" Artist for "Midnight Flyer," 1959
Grammy Award for Lifetime Achievement, 1990 (posthumous)

SEE ALSO: Cole, Natalie.

Natalie Cole

BORN: Los Angeles, California; February 6, 1950
FIRST ALBUM RELEASE: *Inseparable*, 1975
MUSICAL STYLES: Jazz, pop, soul, rhythm and blues

Natalie Cole, one of five children of the late vocalist Nat "King" Cole, is a gifted performer who achieved a success equal to that of her father by singing heartfelt songs that captured the imagination of her audiences. One of the most successful artists of the late 1980's and early 1990's, many of her biggest hits were reminiscent of the style of her father.

Daddy's Little Girl. Cole grew up in a spacious home in Hancock Park, an affluent section of Los Angeles, where, as a child, she was introduced to some of the biggest names in show business. Her first exposure to performing came in 1962 when Cole, age six at the time, and her sister Carole joined their father on stage for one song during a performance. Cole also did her first recording with her father as part of a Christmas album. As a young child, she was trained in classical piano but preferred singing. At age eleven, she acted and performed vocal arrangements with her father in *I'm with You*, a stage play at the Los Angeles Greek Theater. By age twelve, she was performing with Daryl Dragon (later the Captain in the Captain and Tennille) and Skip Riddle.

Cole attended several private schools while in her teens, choosing to focus on preparation for a career in medicine or psychology rather than music. When her father died of cancer in 1965, she experienced a period of profound emotional instability. At that time, she was attending a private high school on the East Coast and went through what, in retrospect, she referred to as "a nervous breakdown."

After finishing high school, Cole enrolled at the University of Massachusetts at Amherst. She transferred during her junior year to the University of Southern California but, unhappy with the move, returned to the University of Massachusetts the following year. Still unsure of her career path, she began performing regularly at a local club and began to reconsider her decision to forego music as a profession. Upon completion of an undergraduate degree in child psychology, Cole decided to try to follow in her father's footsteps by pursuing a career in music. Initially, she began as a solo artist on the club circuit.

Recording Classics. Cole's big break came in early 1973, when she signed with manager-agent Kevin Hunter of Montreal, Canada. Convinced that Hunter would help her career, she took his advice and changed her musical style. The goal was to gain more appeal from younger audiences. Hunter also introduced Cole to Chuck Jackson and Marvin Yancy (whom she married in 1976). They provided her with the new material that became the basis for her mid-1970's chart-topping hits. Hunter also negotiated a recording agreement with Capitol Records, her late father's label.

Her debut album, called *Inseparable* and released in 1975, produced the Top-10 single "This Will Be." The album made the rhythm and blues (R&B) and general pop charts, eventually earning for Cole her first gold record. *Natalie*, her second album, contained two songs coauthored with Jackson and Yancy, "Sophisticated Lady" and "Not Like Mine." That album was also certified gold, and Cole received two Grammy Awards in 1975. The following year she won a third Grammy.

"I've Got Love on My Mind," from her 1977 album, *Unpredictable*, made number 1 on the soul charts and number 5 on the pop charts, earning her another gold record. The album, which included two songs she wrote herself, became her biggest-selling to that point and was eventually certified platinum. Her fourth album, *Thankful*, also went on to be certified platinum. It contained

Natalie Cole (Paul Natkin)

her second gold single, "Our Love." In 1978, she was selected Female Vocalist of the Year at the eleventh annual Image Awards.

Cole's first network television special, *The Natalie Cole Special*, which premiered on April 27, 1978, featured Earth, Wind, and Fire; Stephen Bishop; and Johnny Mathis. That same year Capitol Records released her first live album, *Natalie . . . Live!*, which soared to the top of the soul and pop charts. She also cohosted *Uptown: A Musical Comedy History of Harlem's Apollo Theater*, a two-hour television special. In February of 1979, she was presented with her own star on the famous Hollywood Walk of Fame. Continuing to record, Cole released her sixth album, *I Love You So*, in 1979. It would prove to be her sixth record to be certified gold. Also during that year, she recorded a duet album, *We're the Best of Friends*, with Capitol Records artist Peabo Bryson.

The 1980's and 1990's. Cole opened the 1980's with the album *Don't Look Back*, which contained material written by herself and Yancy. It was not as well received as her earlier work. *Happy Love*, released in 1981, also performed poorly on the charts despite input from a new producer, George Tobin. Drugs were beginning to interfere with Cole's career, and she spent six months at the Hazelden Clinic for drug rehabilitation, hoping to turn her life and career around. Cole's personal life was no better than her professional career during that period. Her marriage to Yancy ended in 1983. She did record *Unforgettable: A Tribute to Nat "King" Cole*, but its commercial success was not what had been anticipated.

In an effort to revive her career following a four-year lull, Cole signed with EMI Records' Manhattan label and released a new album, *Everlasting*, in 1987. *Everlasting* produced three hit singles: "Jump Start," "I Live for Your Love," and "Pink Cadillac." It was to be the beginning of her successful comeback and also began a string of successful albums, which included *Good to Be Back* (1989), *Unforgettable with Love* (1991), and *Take a Look* (1993). *Unforgettable with Love*, her most successful album, boasted sales in excess of five million copies. She won a Grammy for Best Jazz Vocal Performance in 1993 for *Take a Look*. Her 1997

album, *Stardust*, received mixed reviews. As in previous albums, advanced studio technology allowed her to sing with her father in some of the recordings. One reviewer called her efforts to continue to sing love songs with her father "creepy," but others gave the album rave reviews.

—*Donald C. Simmons, Jr.*

SELECT DISCOGRAPHY
■ ALBUMS
Inseparable, 1975
Don't Look Back, 1980
Everlasting, 1987
Unforgettable with Love, 1991
Take a Look, 1993
Stardust, 1996

SELECT AWARDS
Grammy Awards for Best New Artist and for Best R&B Vocal Performance, Female, for "This Will Be," 1975
Grammy Award for Best R&B Vocal Performance, Female, for "Sophisticated Lady," 1976
Grammy Awards for Record of the Year (with David Foster) and Best Traditional Pop Performance, both for "Unforgettable"; for Album of the Year for *Unforgettable with Love* (with Andre Fischer, David Foster, and Tommy LiPuma), all 1991
Grammy Award for Best Jazz Vocal Performance for "Take a Look," 1993

SEE ALSO: Cole, Nat "King"; Mathis, Johnny.

For the Record

During the 1990's, Natalie Cole made numerous appearances on television and in films. In March of 1998, she appeared in the highly touted Home Box Office (HBO) motion picture *Always Outnumbered*, in which she played a restaurant owner named Iula who falls for a tough convict played by Laurence Fishburne.

Paula Cole

BORN: Rockport, Massachusetts; April 5, 1968
FIRST ALBUM RELEASE: *Harbinger*, 1994
MUSICAL STYLES: Pop, rock and roll

A former high school prom queen and three-time class president, Paula Cole first made a mark on the music scene in the early 1990's as Peter Gabriel's onstage backup singer. Soon after, she became one of a new breed of women pop singers known as much for their strong, clear voices as for their thought-provoking lyrics.

The Beginnings. One of two daughters born to a college biology professor and his artist wife, Paula Cole once described herself as a "little canary," able to sing before she knew how to talk.

A self-confessed "repressed" perfect child, Cole grew up in the small New England community of Rockport, Massachusetts, where she was an academic overachiever: a perfect student, cheerleader, prom queen, and class president. From a young age, her musical talent was evident.

Music as Salvation. Cole was still a teenager when she began taking voice and piano lessons at Boston's prestigious Berklee College of Music, from where she graduated in 1990 with a degree in music. Shortly after completing her musical studies, Cole suffered an emotional collapse. She spent half a year in therapy, finding her greatest salvation in her music. She moved briefly to San Francisco and later to New York, writing the confessional, dark songs that would make their way on to her 1994 debut album, *Harbinger.*

Climb to Stardom. *Harbinger*'s standout single, "Bethlehem," was a jarring, tortured, musical self-portrait of her teen years. The song, Cole later said, resulted in a major fight with her father, who did not want her to include it on the album. While its thinly veiled story line made Cole anxious about attending her ten-year high school reunion, she was warmly welcomed by her peers, dispelling her fears of rejection. A prerelease copy of the *Harbinger* album, released on the small Imago label, made its way to Peter Gabriel, who recruited Cole to join his 1993-1994 *Secret World* tour after Sinéad O'Connor withdrew. The tour's visibility

Paula Cole (Ken Settle)

was a major boost for Cole's career, and it bolstered her musical confidence. She signed with Warner Bros. Records and began recording her second album with a producer whose work she admired.

This Fire. Eight songs and eighty thousand dollars into the effort, Cole decided the recording was imperfect and started over—with herself as the producer. The result, 1996's *This Fire*, was a passionate, fully realized recording that earned Cole seven Grammy Award nominations, including one for Producer of the Year, making her the first woman ever nominated in that category.

This Fire was a confident, more joyful record than *Harbinger*, and it revealed not only Cole's gift for melodies, but also the raw emotional force of her voice. Sweet and soaring in some songs, her voice could be shrill in others. Cole also played an array of instruments on the album, including piano, clarinet, and harmonium. The album's first single, "Where Have All the Cowboys Gone?," was a catchy tongue-in-cheek feminist lament that quickly climbed the charts, with its meaning debated by fans of both genders.

Just as *This Fire* was beginning its ascent, Cole was recruited by Sarah McLachlan—who said she "fell in love with that beautiful voice" the first time she heard a Cole song—to take part in the 1997 all-female Lilith Fair tour. Cole's stint with the festival, the most successful tour of the 1997 summer season, raised her profile even further, and she had two more Top-10 hits from *This Fire*, "I Don't Want to Wait" and "Me."

Grammy Award Fever. In all, the platinum-selling *This Fire* brought Cole seven Grammy Award nominations, including those for Record, Album, and Song of the Year. She won the Best New Artist Grammy. A prolific songwriter, she has already earned, with few albums to her name, a devoted legion of fans, and her place in pop music seems secure.   —*Nicole Pensiero*

SELECT DISCOGRAPHY
■ ALBUMS
Harbinger, 1994
This Fire, 1996

SELECT AWARDS
Grammy Award for Best New Artist, 1997

SEE ALSO: Gabriel, Peter; McLachlan, Sarah; O'Connor, Sinéad.

Judy Collins

BORN: Seattle, Washington; May 1, 1939
FIRST ALBUM RELEASE: *A Maid of Constant Sorrow*, 1961
MUSICAL STYLES: Folk, pop, musical theater, folk rock

In the early 1960's Greenwich Village in New York City was the center of a folk-music revival. Many artists, such as Bob Dylan, John Sebastian, Cass Elliot, Richie Havens, and Paul Stookey were attracted to clubs such as Gerde's Folk City and Art

D'Lugoff's Village Gate, where the careers of many musicians were launched. Among those who came to New York was Judy Collins, a young woman from Denver, Colorado, with a clear, pure voice and an ear for good songs.

The Beginnings. Judy Marjorie Collins was born in 1939 in Seattle, Washington, where her father, a professional singer, hosted a radio show. The family moved to Boulder, Colorado, and then to Los Angeles, where, at the age of five, Judy began to study piano. Her teachers considered her a prodigy and predicted a concert career. The plan was interrupted, however, when Judy contracted polio at the age of ten, soon after the family had settled permanently in Denver. After her recovery, Judy continued her piano studies and made her public debut at the age of thirteen with the Denver Businessman's Symphony (conducted by her teacher, Antonia Brico) in a performance of Mozart's Concerto for Two Pianos.

As a young teenager, Judy continued to study classical piano, but at the age of sixteen she turned more seriously to folk music and took up the guitar. She went to college for one year, but dropped out in 1958 to marry Peter Taylor; the following year their son, Clark, was born. Collins's interest in folk music intensified during these years, and in 1959 she made her professional debut in a Boulder club. After singing in coffeehouses and clubs in other cities, such as Chicago and Boston, she was eventually attracted to New York, where in 1961 she signed her first recording contract, with Elektra Records. Her debut album, *A Maid of Constant Sorrow* (1961), was praised by critics and folk-music audiences alike. Her personal life was less successful; she divorced in 1962 and lost a long, bitter custody battle for her son.

Recording Career. During the 1960's Collins was a major figure in the Greenwich Village folk scene, working in a genre sometimes called "urban folk." Her second album, *The Golden Apples of the Sun*, was released in 1962 and *Judy Collins #3* in 1964. Later the same year her first live album, *The Judy Collins Concert*, taken from her debut at New York's Town Hall, was released. During the mid-1960's many of her concerts across the United

States and Canada drew standing-room-only crowds.

Like many folk artists of the day, Collins became involved in the Civil Rights and antiwar movements. Not as outspoken as some of her contemporaries, she was nevertheless proud of her efforts: "I don't have the young rebel image," she said in 1967. "I'm trying to make statements as a woman. My message is in my music—what one woman is doing." She contributed her services to fund-raising events and participated in marches on behalf of these causes.

In the late 1960's Collins diversified her repertoire to include cabaret songs by Jacques Brel, theater songs by Kurt Weill, and contemporary ballads by Leonard Cohen. The album *In My Life* (1966) was her first to be certified gold (in December, 1970). It included the first recordings of Leonard Cohen songs, "Dress Rehearsal Rag" and "Suzanne"; on the latter, she gently sings its mysterious lyric about a "half crazy" woman over a hypnotic, cyclical acoustic guitar line. Collins was important in gaining attention for Cohen's—as well as Joni Mitchell's and Randy Newman's—early songwriting.

She was sometimes criticized for being an interpreter rather than a composer, and Collins soon attempted songwriting. Her first songs to be recorded, "Since You've Asked," "Sky Fell," and "Albatross," were included on *Wildflowers* (1967). The album's version of Joni Mitchell's "Both Sides Now" became a Top-10 hit for which Collins won a Grammy Award in 1968 for Best Folk Performance. *Wildflowers* also contained another Mitchell song, three by Cohen, and a fourteenth century Italian ballad. *Wildflowers* went to number 5 on *Billboard*'s album chart. Both *In My Life* and *Wildflowers* benefited from distinctive and perfectly suited orchestral arrangements by Joshua Rifkin.

For Collins's next album, *Who Knows Where the Time Goes* (1968), she turned to recording with electric instruments, and the record is an amalgam of folk and country rock. Songs include Collins's own "My Father," Ian Tyson's "Someday Soon," and two more Cohen songs. (Improbably, the first song on the album, Rolf Kempf's "Hello, Hooray," was later recorded—quite differently—by Alice Cooper.) Among the instrumental highlights is Steven Stills's guitar work. Stills and Collins were romantically involved for a time; the "Judy" in the Crosby, Stills, and Nash song "Suite: Judy Blue Eyes" is Collins.

Judy Collins became active in the feminist movement in the early 1970's, and in 1973 recorded *True Stories and Other Dreams*, which reflects her feminist views. While planning an interview of her former piano teacher, Antonia Brico, for *Ms.* magazine, Collins decided instead to do a documentary film. With Jill Godmilow, she directed *Antonia: A Portrait of the Woman*, about a female conductor in a male-dominated profession. This award-winning film opened the American Film-

Judy Collins (Archive Photos/Fotos International)

makers Series at the Whitney Museum in New York City, was named by *Time* magazine as one of the ten best films of 1974, and was nominated for an Academy Award in the Best Documentary category.

Personal problems, including battles with alcoholism, during the later 1970's limited the number of new albums that Collins released, but only rarely did they affect the quality of her work. *Judith*, issued in March, 1975, and certified gold before the end of the year, contains what is often considered the classic version of Stephen Sondheim's "Send in the Clowns." Released also as a single, this song has become one of her best-known works.

During the 1980's Collins wrote an autobiography, *Trust Your Heart* (1987), and chronicled a personal and spiritual renewal in such albums as *Home Again* (1984) and *Sanity and Grace* (1989). In the 1990's she focused on songs about family life and relationships. She performed children's songs and lullabies on *Baby's Bedtime* and *Baby's Morningtime*, two collections of poems by such writers as Robert Browning and Emily Dickinson, set to music by Ernest Troost. In 1992 she narrated and sang *The Angel Book: A Handbook for Aspiring Angels*, by Karen Goldman, and recorded duets with Tom Chapin for an album of children's songs.

Judy Collins became a UNICEF spokesperson in 1994 and has since visited several countries for UNICEF, including Bosnia and Vietnam. Her first novel, a mystery entitled *Shameless*, whose heroine is a photojournalist covering the music business, was published in 1995, accompanied by an album of original songs. In 1997 Elektra issued a two-CD collection, *Forever . . . An Anthology*, which contains many of her most famous songs plus a few new ones. In addition to her autobiography and novel, Collins has published songbooks that include well-written commentaries on the music and her life, including *The Judy Collins Songbook* (1969), and *My Father* (1989).

Legacy. Although Judy Collins was at the forefront of the urban folk revival during the 1960's, she is known for a wide variety of musical styles. Her repertoire is broad, ranging from the Anglo-American folk songs that began her career to cabaret songs, show tunes, contemporary ballads, children's songs, and soft rock. Many of her own compositions attest her ability as a songwriter. Her voice has been described as "liquid silver" and is characterized by clarity, purity, coolness, and sweetness, if sometimes lacking in emotional depth. Her range is wide, her intonation nearly perfect, and her articulation of lyrics flawless.

—*Mary A. Wischusen*

SELECT DISCOGRAPHY

■ ALBUMS

A Maid of Constant Sorrow, 1961
The Golden Apples of the Sun, 1962
Judy Collins #3, 1964
The Judy Collins Concert, 1964
In My Life, 1966
Wildflowers, 1967
Who Knows Where the Time Goes, 1968
Living, 1971
True Stories and Other Dreams, 1973
Judith, 1975
Running for My Life, 1980
Times of Our Lives, 1982
Home Again, 1984
Trust Your Heart, 1987
Sanity and Grace, 1989
Shameless, 1995
Forever . . . An Anthology, 1997

SELECT AWARDS

Grammy Award for Best Folk Performance for "Both Sides Now," 1968

For the Record

Antonia: A Portrait of a Woman, a film produced and codirected by Judy Collins, was named by *Time* magazine as one of the ten best films of 1974 and was nominated for an Academy Award for Best Documentary. It also received the Independent Film Critics Award, the Christopher Award, a Silver Medal at the Atlanta Film Festival, and the Blue Ribbon Award at the American Film Festival.

SEE ALSO: Baez, Joan; Cohen, Leonard; Crosby, Stills, Nash, and Young; Dylan, Bob; Mitchell, Joni.

Phil Collins

BORN: Chiswick, London, England; January 31, 1951

FIRST ALBUM RELEASE: Face Value, 1981 (first solo release)

MUSICAL STYLES: Rock and roll, pop, R&B, adult contemporary

One of the most successful artists of the 1980's, Phil Collins (born Phillip David Charles Collins) entered the spotlight while leading a dual career: He was lead singer and drummer for the group Genesis as well as a solo artist. Over the course of a musical career that began in the late 1960's Collins evolved from drummer to singer to talented songwriter and producer. Balding and diminutive, he seems an unlikely pop star, but his wit and easygoing stage presence made him the Everyman who had made it big. (Collins made it so big, in fact, that between 1984 and 1990 he had thirteen straight Top-10 hits in the U.S. alone.) Even more rare, Collins seemed content to remain with the group Genesis, writing songs collectively (and sharing the wealth and fame) for more than a decade after his solo career became successful.

Beginnings. As a child Collins acted on television, film, and the stage, and by the age of fourteen was playing the Artful Dodger in London's 1964 West End production of *Oliver!* However, presented with the possibility of pursuing more acting roles, he instead turned his energy to his first love, drumming. He liked the freedom and spontaneity that performing music for a live audience gave him. Through his teens, Collins worked with a number of groups, but his big break came at the age of nineteen. Answering an ad for a drummer who was "sensitive to 12-string guitar," he found himself hired as the drummer for the art-rock group Genesis. It was a good match, for Collins's drumming—both powerful and me-

lodic—helped energize the group, and his down-to-earth manner and good humor helped them relax, finding new enjoyment in their performances.

With Genesis, Collins sang backup vocals to singer Peter Gabriel's lead both on albums and during live performances. He sang the lead on the 1973 song "More Fool Me," an acoustic number written by him and bandmate Michael Rutherford. Even so, when Gabriel left Genesis in 1975 Genesis auditioned more than four hundred singers, but it was Collins who stepped in to fill Gabriel's shoes. With Collins singing lead the band developed a more straightforward approach to their music, gaining greater and greater popular acceptance as a result.

The Dual Career. In 1978, after an extensive world tour with Genesis, Collins returned home to find that his wife had taken their children and left him. In the emotional aftermath, Collins secluded himself in his home studio and poured his feelings of love and loss into recordings that became the basis for his first solo album, *Face Value* (1981). The album was coproduced and engineered by Hugh Padgham, who went on to coproduce and engineer all but one of Collins's albums as well as the next three Genesis albums. *Face Value*'s haunting drums, piano, and vocal style were quite a change from his work with Genesis, but the personal exploration of his feelings in the wake of his wife's departure resounded strongly with listeners. Driven by the singles "I Missed Again" (#19, 1981) and the powerful "In the Air Tonight" (#19, 1981) *Face Value* surprised Collins and the rest of the music world by selling more copies than any Genesis album to date; it went to number 7.

Collins's next album with Genesis, *ABACAB* (1981), saw the band's post-Gabriel sound solidify into a style that combined the musicianship and diverse themes of their earlier work with the compactness and pop sensibilities that seemed to stem from Collins's lead. With sales of over two million, the album did better than any previous Genesis album and brought both the band and Collins's voice further into the public consciousness.

In 1983 Collins released his second solo album,

Phil Collins (Paul Natkin)

his feelings struck a chord with his audience, and the album made it to the Top 10, securing Collins's status as a talented songwriter and solo artist.

Breakthrough. After another popular album with Genesis plus three hit singles ("Easy Lover," with Philip Bailey, "Separate Lives," with Marilyn Martin), and the Grammy Award-winning "Against All Odds"), Collins released his 1985 breakthrough album, *No Jacket Required*. With the amount of airplay he had received the preceding year, the market was primed for Collins, and the album shot to number 1 in only four weeks, faster even than Michael Jackson's *Thriller*. Collins had a new marriage and a happier outlook on life, and *No Jacket Required*'s strong pop songs generated five Top-5 singles. They ranged from energetic dance songs such as "Sussudio" to soft ballads such as "One More Night." Though Collins had moved on from his reflections on his first marriage, the songs remained rooted in their subject matter to relationships. However, the loss, bitterness, and anger that lay beneath his first two solo endeavors (and gave them some of their distinctive character) seemed to have been left in the wake of his new, healthier emotional life.

In 1986 another successful Genesis album, *Invisible Touch*, was released. Feeling that the airwaves were a bit oversaturated with his voice and songs, Collins took a break after the Genesis tour to act in *Buster*, a film about England's great train robbery. One thing led to another, and Collins found himself releasing two more hit singles from the soundtrack: "Two Hearts" and a cover of "Groovy Kind of Love."

In 1989 Collins released . . . *But Seriously* in response to critics who felt that his previous albums dealt with relationships to the point of the exclusion of larger issues that other, more "serious" artists often examined. In fact, Collins had been actively involved over the years with charities that ranged from Band Aid in the United States to the Prince's Trust in England. His first three albums had simply found him writing from the heart about the subject most on his mind—his estrangement from his wife—a subject to which audiences responded. Even so, . . . *But Seriously* was his most mature and sophisticated work to

Hello, I Must Be Going, an endeavor still motivated by his lingering feelings toward his wife. Though songs such as "Don't Let Him Steal Your Heart Away" and "Why Can't It Wait 'til Morning" still show his loss, most of the tone and subject matter of the album reflect his anger and bitterness over the separation, as in the song "I Don't Care Anymore." The album also clearly revealed Collins's love of classic rhythm and blues; the style was incorporated into many of his songs (Collins even used the horn section from Earth, Wind, and Fire), and he recorded a note-for-note cover of the Supremes' "Can't Hurry Love." The candidness and heartfelt energy with which Collins speaks of

date. It generated four more Top-5 hits with "Another Day in Paradise," "Do You Remember?" "Something Happened on the Way to Heaven," and "I Wish It Would Rain Down." The next year saw Collins release his last album with Genesis, *We Can't Dance* (1991). The album contained a number of hit singles, including "I Can't Dance," but for the first time the album sold fewer copies for the group than its predecessor.

In 1993 Collins's solo album *Both Sides*, which he produced and on which he played all the instruments, came out to mediocre reviews and falling sales. On the album he further explored the social issues as well as relationships, but the energy and pop-driven sensibilities from his earlier work felt stale and rather unoriginal after his fourteen-year reign of the airwaves. In 1995 Collins announced his departure from Genesis. The following year found him releasing a new solo album, *Dance into the Light*, working once more with Hugh Padgham. The album saw a return to the upbeat energy of *No Jacket Required*. Even with some adventuresome new inclusions of world-music elements into his songs, for the most part the album retraced familiar ground and failed to chart well.

Drummer and Producer. Aside from his popular image as a singer and songwriter, Collins is known and respected in the music industry for his talents as a producer and, even more so, his ability

as a drummer. As a producer in the 1980's he helped artists such as Philip Bailey and Eric Clapton bring new energy to their solo careers. Starting in the 1970's with Genesis and moving into his creative explosion in the 1980's, Collins evolved a style of drumming that was extremely musical, putting the importance of the drums within the arrangement equal to that of the keyboards, guitar, and bass. While working on Peter Gabriel's third solo album, Collins and engineer Hugh Padgham developed the cavernous gated-reverb drum sound that Collins later popularized on his own albums and with Genesis. Collins has also worked extensively as a session drummer, playing for artists ranging from Brian Eno to Thin Lizzy to Tears for Fears. In addition, he found room in his busy schedule to work with the fusion group Brand X, with which he played drums from 1974 through the early 1980's.

Though Collins has fallen away from the top of the charts, his reputation remains intact as a masterful drummer and innovator whose music moved a generation of listeners. Even as his work became more pop-oriented, his down-to-earth approach gained him an acceptance that almost seemed out of place in the glamorous era of Michael Jackson, Van Halen, Madonna, and Prince. At his best Collins was an artist whose honest and deeply personal songs have an almost universal appeal. As he once said in an interview comparing his songwriting philosophy to that of the other members of Genesis:

> The basic difference between me and Pete and Tony and Mike is that lyrically they're a bit emotionally screwed up. They went to boarding schools all their lives, only saw their families on holidays, while I went to a regular school, went home every day. They would never put 'I love you' in a lyric, whereas I think nothing of it.

—*Todd A. Elhart*

SELECT DISCOGRAPHY
■ SINGLES
"Against All Odds," 1984
"Separate Lives," 1985 (with Marilyn Martin)
"Easy Lover," 1985 (with Philip Bailey)

For the Record

When Phil Collins auditioned to join Genesis he arrived early and took advantage of their invitation to wait by swimming in the estate's pool. Hearing the other drummers audition, by the time his turn came he had memorized the songs. "When it was my turn and they asked me to play the same arrangements, I said, 'well . . . um,' and I paused to make it seem as though I was trying very hard. Then I went straight into it and got it."

■ ALBUMS

Face Value, 1981
Hello, I Must Be Going, 1982
No Jacket Required, 1985
. . . But Seriously, 1989
Serious Hits . . . Live! 1990
Both Sides, 1993
Dance into the Light, 1996
Hits, 1998

SELECT AWARDS

Grammy Award for Best Pop Vocal Performance, Male, for "Against All Odds," 1984
Grammy Awards for Album of the Year and Best Pop Vocal Performance, Male, for *No Jacket Required*, 1985

SEE ALSO: Eno, Brian; Gabriel, Peter; Genesis.

John Coltrane

BORN: Hamlet, North Carolina; September 23, 1926
DIED: Huntington (Long Island), New York; July 17, 1967
FIRST ALBUM RELEASE: *Dee Gee Days*, 1951 (with Dizzy Gillespie)
MUSICAL STYLE: Jazz

Brilliant improviser, creative composer, innovative leader, flawless technician, gentle and modest soul, deeply spiritual man: These are some of the many labels that have been aptly applied to John William Coltrane. "Trane," as he is often known, is one of the most respected and revered of all jazz musicians. The subject of numerous biographies, Coltrane has been an important influence on the world of jazz, and through jazz on other forms of music.

Beginnings. John Coltrane was born in 1926 in a small town in North Carolina, the son of a tailor and grandson of ministers. Scholars discussing Coltrane's formative influences emphasize the church, his mother's operatic aspirations, his father's untimely death, and the oppression of black Americans during this period. John began his musical career as a clarinetist but later switched to alto saxophone, developing a sound and style influenced by Lester Young and Johnny Hodges. In 1943 Coltrane moved to Philadelphia and took advantage of the well-developed musical life there by studying the saxophone at the Ornstein School of Music.

In 1945 Coltrane began his professional career, playing saxophone in the Jimmy Johnson Big Band. World War II interrupted, sending him to Hawaii with the Navy, where he played clarinet in a band called the Melody Masters. After being discharged from the Navy, Coltrane resumed his saxophone work in Philadelphia. Playing with the band of Eddie "Cleanhead" Vinson, Coltrane found the instrument that was to become his voice and his trademark, the tenor saxophone. Also, while on tour with Vinson's band, he met and jammed with the great alto saxophone innovator of bebop, Charlie Parker.

By 1948 Coltrane had established a regular routine of study and practice that was helping him mature as a musician. He moved to Jimmy Heath's band, returning to the alto saxophone. It was about this time that, unfortunately, Coltrane was introduced to drug use. In 1949, along with Jimmy Heath, Coltrane joined the band of the great trumpeter Dizzy Gillespie, with whom he eventually made his first professional recordings. When Dizzy had to dissolve the big band, he retained Coltrane as the tenor and alto saxophonist in his new, smaller group.

After leaving Gillespie in 1951, Coltrane returned to Philadelphia, where he played with several bands, including the rhythm-and-blues band of alto saxophonist Earl Bostic. In 1953 Coltrane joined a band led by one of his early influences, alto saxophonist Johnny Hodges. Coltrane's devotion to the tenor saxophone solidified while he was with Hodges, but drug and alcohol problems plagued Coltrane to the extent that they made it difficult for him to keep the job.

"Workin'" with Miles. In 1955 Coltrane's career took on a new direction when he joined the band of Miles Davis. Up to this point, much of Coltrane's playing had been in big bands or traditional swing or bebop combos. The Miles Davis Quintet was different. Davis was an innovator in

John Coltrane, with Miles Davis playing trumpet behind him (Library of Congress)

ously experiencing a spiritual rebirth. Following this transformation, Coltrane became even more intensely focused on and devoted to his art. His recordings and performances became increasingly prolific. He worked with many well-known artists, including Art Blakey, Red Garland, Cannonball Adderley, Milt Jackson, Thelonius Monk, and Cecil Taylor. He also did another stint with Davis. In 1957 Coltrane released his first recordings as a leader rather than as a sideman. It was also during this period that critic Ira Gitler invented the phrase "sheets of sound" to describe the incredible flurries of notes that Coltrane could produce while improvising.

Coltrane's devotion to the development of his harmonic sense culminated in the 1959 release of his own composition, "Giant Steps," considered by many to provide one of the most difficult frameworks for improvisation in jazz. Coltrane's masterpiece was the pinnacle of his achievement as both a technically proficient virtuoso performer and as a manipulator of harmonic relationships. "Giant Steps" became the touchstone by which all tenor saxophone players were measured. None could stand up to the original when it came to navigating the tricky waters of Coltrane's harmonic framework. Trane was not satisfied with technical mastery and harmonic brilliance, however. He had become so technically proficient that simply coming up with notes to fit a tricky harmonic framework was no longer a challenge to him. He sought, instead, to make his music more expressive.

Trane was absolutely in the right place at the right time when he joined Miles Davis in the studio to record "So What" for Davis's *Kind of Blue* album

the forefront of his profession, and this influence was part of what shaped Coltrane's quest for the ultimate expression in music. Despite continuing problems with substance abuse, 1956 was a banner year for Coltrane. He played several important dates with Miles (including the Prestige session at which they recorded the album *Workin'*). The association with Davis led to collaborations with Sonny Rollins, Tadd Dameron, and Paul Chambers. Coltrane also met innovative pianist McCoy Tyner, who would later figure prominently in Trane's recording career.

Coltrane's heroin problems finally prompted Miles Davis to fire him. Perhaps this incident was the wake up call that Coltrane needed. He sequestered himself in his mother's home in Philadelphia until he overcame his addictions, simultane-

(1959). This piece, which also featured Cannonball Adderley, Paul Chambers, Jimmy Cobb, and Bill Evans, minimized the importance of harmony and chords and emphasized the importance of melody and expression. It was the perfect catalyst for the next stage in Coltrane's development, as he sought to move in a new direction. It was also a fitting end to his career as a sideman for Davis, since Coltrane began leading his own groups in the recording studio and on the road.

The Quest. In the late 1950's, American blacks began seeking their freedom through the Civil Rights movement. At the same time, trumpeter Don Cherry and sax man Ornette Coleman sought musical freedom with their recordings, heralding the birth of the free-jazz movement. In 1960 Cherry became part of the Coltrane entourage, making it clear that Trane's path was diverging from that of the mainstream jazz musicians with whom he had worked in the preceding decade.

Despite starting in a new direction, Coltrane maintained a devoted following. In 1960 he won top honors among tenor saxophonists in both the readers' and critics' polls of *Down Beat* magazine. He also won in the "miscellaneous instrument" category for his soprano saxophone version of Richard Rodgers's "My Favorite Things" from *The Sound of Music*.

In September of 1963, racists bombed a Baptist church in Birmingham, Alabama, killing four young black girls. Coltrane's musical elegy "Alabama" was one of the high points of his career. Combining the modalism of Davis with the use of a drone or pedal tone influenced by the music of India, Coltrane and his friend McCoy Tyner wove a tapestry of sorrow and grace as they interacted with Jimmy Garrison on bass and Elvin Jones on drums. Coltrane had internalized the influences of Davis and Coleman and had created a new, expressive type of jazz.

Coltrane's studies of world religions and of the music of different cultures intertwined, allowing him to bring new flavors to jazz. Like the Beatles, Coltrane was among the first Western musicians to recognize and to study the genius of Indian sitar master Ravi Shankar. In fact, Coltrane named one of his children after the famous musician. The

For the Record

A California church has declared John Coltrane a saint and is dedicated to the man and his music: Saint John Coltrane African Orthodox Church in San Francisco.

hallmark of Coltrane's late career was an amalgam of free jazz, the influences of Indian and African music, the modalism of Davis, extended forms, and increasing emphasis on spiritualism. Most critics agree that Coltrane's 1964 release, *A Love Supreme*, is the quintessential example of this trend and the last major development in jazz before Coltrane's cultivation of avant-garde techniques.

The tumultuous mid-1960's provided the perfect setting for the final experimental chapter of Coltrane's opus, music so aggressive that some critics labeled it "anti-jazz." With his 1965 release, *Ascension*, Coltrane reached the summit of his musical mountain, a plateau to which there was no logical successor. Musicians can only imagine to what new heights Coltrane might have taken jazz had he outlived the decade. In May of 1967, he began experiencing severe abdominal pain. After only a few medical tests, Coltrane discharged himself from the hospital. Within two months he died of liver cancer, just short of his forty-first birthday.

Decades later, Coltrane's music lives on through his legacy of more than a hundred recordings and reissues with Prestige, Blue Note, Atlantic, Impulse! and other labels. The power and strength that were John Coltrane cast a long shadow. Although he remains one of the most imitated saxophonists and composers in jazz history. Coltrane's technique, tone, style, and power are truly inimitable.   *—William S. Carson*

SELECT DISCOGRAPHY
■ ALBUMS
'Round About Midnight, 1956 (with Miles Davis)
Workin', 1956 (with Davis)

Blue Train, 1957
Kind of Blue, 1959 (with Davis)
Giant Steps, 1959
My Favorite Things, 1960
Live at the Village Vanguard, 1961
Impressions, 1963
Live at Birdland, 1963
A Love Supreme, 1964
Meditations, 1965
Ascension, 1965

SELECT AWARDS

Grammy Award for Best Jazz Instrumental
    Performance, Soloist, for *Bye Bye Blackbird*,
    1981

SEE ALSO: Adderley, Julian "Cannonball"; Davis,
Miles; Parker, Charlie.

Shawn Colvin

BORN: Vermillion, South Dakota; January 10, 1958
FIRST ALBUM RELEASE: *Steady On*, 1989
MUSICAL STYLES: Folk, pop

Shawn Colvin began playing guitar at age ten.
Music became an important constant in her life
as her family moved frequently, leaving their
home in South Dakota to live in various towns in
the Midwest and Canada. Upon graduating from
high school, Colvin began college but then left to
devote more time to composing.

Folk Hits. While spending time in Texas, San
Francisco, New York, and Boston, Colvin played
in a variety of bands and experimented with a wide
range of musical styles. At the same time, she
began building a solo career. Colvin's 1989 solo
debut, *Steady On*, earned her a Grammy Award for
Best Contemporary Folk Recording and included
songs such as "Shotgun Down the Avalanche" and
"Diamond in the Rough." The album's success led
to a string of important opportunities, including
guest spots on albums by Suzanne Vega and Mary
Chapin Carpenter and tours with Neil Young,
Richard Thompson, and Lyle Lovett.

In 1992, Colvin released *Fat City*, which earned
two Grammy nominations and offered the power-

ful single "Polaroids." In 1994, Colvin interpreted
a collection of songs by her favorite songwriters
on the album *Cover Girl*. She also developed a
presence in the world of sound track recordings,
contributing songs to several motion pictures.
Colvin also continued to join friends and colleagues on their albums. She worked with Carpenter again and then with Lovett on *The Road to
Ensenada* (1996).

A Few Small Repairs. Through the years,
Colvin earned the respect of her peers in the
music business as well as the devotion of loyal fans
as she wrote thoughtful and emotional lyrics and
well-crafted songs. However, it was her fifth album,
A Few Small Repairs, that moved her from the status
of respected singer-songwriter to mainstream pop
star.

Colvin's album would no doubt have stood on
its own, yet it seems likely that she was helped by

Shawn Colvin (Columbia/Allison Dyer)

a renewed interest in singer-songwriters and female artists in particular. Ironically, the over-the-top success of artists such as Alanis Morissette and Jewel was made possible by the perseverance of Colvin and others. Yet it was the sales and MTV presence of Morissette, Jewel, and others, as well as the debut of Sarah McLachlan's all-female-fronted Lilith Fair tour that had the media claiming in 1997 that women had finally taken over the reigns of popular music. Colvin was writing thoughtful songs and singing them to enthusiastic crowds before Jewel saw her first video, yet Jewel's success in an odd way may have brought added recognition to Colvin, McLachlan, and others.

Back to the Grammys. Colvin's soon-to–become-signature single "Sunny Came Home" garnered 1997 Grammys for Record of the Year and Song of the Year. The single combined an almost gentle yet rolling musicality with a much more harsh lyric about a woman who returns home to set the place on fire: "Sunny came home with a list of names/ She didn't believe in transcendence/ It's time for a few small repairs she said/ Sunny came home with a vengeance." The album's other standout single, "Get out of This House," hit a bit harder musically while still offering nice instrumental depth as guitars, drums, and bass were joined by harmonica, keyboards, and strings.

For the Record

As a teenager, Shawn Colvin worked at a Baskin-Robbins in Carbondale, Illinois. Writer Stokes Howell notes, "Stints of scooping out frozen ice cream at Baskin-Robbins gave Colvin amazing strength in her hands and arms and perhaps contribute even now to her distinctive guitar playing. . . . When you hear her play you can't believe that one single person is creating all the intricate finger-picking and percussiveness that comes cascading out of her instrument."

A Few Small Repairs also marked a renewed collaboration between Colvin and John Leventhal, who was her writing partner and coproducer on *Steady On.* Along with the Grammy recognition, Colvin was named Songwriter of the Year at the Austin Music Awards.   —*Harriet L. Schwartz*

SELECT DISCOGRAPHY
■ ALBUMS
Steady On, 1989
Fat City, 1992
Cover Girl, 1994
A Few Small Repairs, 1996

SELECT AWARDS
Grammy Award for Best Contemporary Folk Recording for *Steady On*, 1990
Grammy Awards for Record of the Year and Song of the Year (with John Leventhal) for "Sunny Came Home," 1997

SEE ALSO: Cole, Paula; McLachlan, Sarah.

The Commodores

ORIGINAL MEMBERS: Lionel Richie, Jr. (b. 1950), Milan Williams (b. 1949), William King, Jr. (b. 1949), Thomas McClary (b. 1950)
OTHER MEMBERS: Walter "Clyde" Orange (b. 1946), Ronald LaPread (b. 1950), James Dean "J. D." Nicholas (b. 1952)
FIRST ALBUM RELEASE: *Machine Gun*, 1974
MUSICAL STYLES: Funk, soul, pop

The Commodores went through three incarnations. In the early 1970's they were a hard-funk party band. Under singer-songwriter Lionel Richie's direction, they achieved their greatest popular success as a ballad-oriented pop group between 1976 and 1985. Since the late 1980's they have had less success as a rhythm-and-blues trio.

Origins. Meeting as freshmen at the Tuskegee Institute in Alabama in 1967, a group including vocalist Lionel Richie and guitarist Thomas McClary entered the freshman talent show as the Mighty Mystics. Keyboardist Milan Williams and trumpet player William King were already part of

The Commodores (Archive Photos)

the top group on campus, the Jays. By the summer of 1968, Richie, McClary, Williams, and King joined forces and became the Commodores. Traveling to Harlem, New York, in the summer of 1969, they landed local jobs with the help of businessman Benny Ashburn, who became their manager. They briefly signed with Atlantic and recorded for them, but they never made the charts.

At one New York show they were spotted by Motown vice president Suzanne DePasse, who signed them in 1971 as the opening act for the Jackson Five's tour. By 1972, drummer Clyde Orange and bassist and trumpeter Ronald LaPread joined the band. Because the Commodores did not fit neatly into the polished Motown style, they were not signed to a recording contract until 1973. Their early work nevertheless made an impact on the soul market.

Their early, hard funk style was described by one critic as black music's response to heavy met-

al. The Commodores scored minor hits with "Machine Gun" (number 22, 1974) and "Slippery When Wet" (number 19, 1975). Their first Top-10 single, "Sweet Love" (number 5, 1975), marked a departure for the group, which would increasingly rely upon Richie's ballad writing and smooth vocal style. With a string of Top-10 hits, including "Just to Be Close to You" (number 7, 1976), "Easy" (number 4, 1977), "Three Times a Lady" (number 1, 1978), "Sail On" (number 4, 1979), "Still" (number 1, 1979), "Lady (You Bring Me Up)" (number 8, 1981), and "Oh No" (number 4, 1981), the Commodores established themselves as the premier black pop group. *Natural High* (number 3, 1978), *Heroes* (number 7, 1980), and *In the Pocket* (number 13, 1981) all went platinum.

Changes. Richie's high-profile success with the Commodores led to numerous outside collaborations, including number 1 hits with Kenny Rogers ("Lady," 1980) and Diana Ross ("Endless

For the Record

"Three Times a Lady," the all-time biggest Motown hit in the United Kingdom, was inspired by the thirty-seventh wedding anniversary of Lionel Richie's parents.

Love," 1981). The group's Lionel Richie era was already coming to an end when their manager, Benny Ashburn, died early in 1982. Richie left later that year, taking longtime producer James Anthony Carmichael with him.

McClary left in 1983, but the next year keyboardist J. D. Nicholas was recruited to share vocal duties with Orange. Though the Commodores never regained their phenomenal hold on the black pop charts, they scored a major hit with "Nightshift," which peaked at number 3 in both the United States and the United Kingdom, won a Grammy Award for Best R&B Performance, and was the third leading Commodore hit of all time. The album *Nightshift* peaked at number 12 in 1985.   —*John Powell*

SELECT DISCOGRAPHY

■ ALBUMS
Caught in the Act, 1975
Hot on the Tracks, 1976
Commodores Live, 1977
Greatest Hits, 1978 (compilation)
Heroes, 1980
In the Pocket, 1981
All the Greatest Hits, 1982 (compilation)
Nightshift, 1985
United, 1986
Rock Solid, 1988
Anthology: The Best of the Commodores, 1995
   (compilation)

SELECT AWARDS
Grammy Award for Best R&B Performance by a
   Duo or Group with Vocal for "Nightshift,"
   1985

SEE ALSO: Jackson Five, The; Richie, Lionel.

Harry Connick, Jr.

BORN: New Orleans, Louisiana; September 11, 1967
FIRST ALBUM RELEASE: *Harry Connick, Jr.*, 1987
MUSICAL STYLES: Jazz, jazz pop, big band, swing, blues

Born in New Orleans in 1967, Harry Connick, Jr., grew up surrounded by the sights and sounds of that city's famous jazz and blues music scene. His parents were both prominent members of the New Orleans legal community, but they were also known in music circles because they had managed a record store to put themselves through law school. They often took Harry Jr. and his older sister, Suzanne, to the French Quarter to listen to Dixieland and bebop bands on famous Bourbon Street.

A Child Prodigy. At three years old, the young Connick was beginning to pick out notes on the piano. By the time he was seven, he had played "The Star-Spangled Banner" at his father's inauguration as New Orleans District Attorney and was regularly sitting in with Dixieland groups on Saturday afternoons at the Maison Bourbon Club. Many of these moments are captured in childhood photographs of Connick with classic jazz artists, which he proudly displays as an adult. On one particularly memorable occasion when Connick was nine years old, he performed a duet of "I'm Just Wild About Harry" with the song's composer, then ninety-six-year-old Eubie Blake, as part of a documentary about Blake.

Shortly thereafter, Connick began a more formal music education by taking lessons at home with James Booker, a well-known rhythm-and-blues pianist. Connick looked up to Booker as a musical genius, and was strongly affected by the pianist's early death from drug and alcohol abuse when Connick was an impressionable thirteen years old. Connick has attributed his own drug-and alcohol-free existence in large part to that traumatic experience. Connick's mother, Anita, who was a small-claims court judge, also died in that year.

At age fourteen, Connick won a national jazz piano competition for teenagers. He also participated five days per week in a jazz course at the New Orleans Center for the Creative Arts, where he expanded his musical knowledge from Dixieland and classical to pure jazz and improvisational harmonies. This course was taught by Ellis Marsalis, the father of jazz trumpeter Wynton Marsalis and saxophonist Branford Marsalis. The Marsalis family, who helped bring instrumental jazz to a wider popular audience, strongly influenced Connick, who would ultimately use piano and vocals to bring his own accessible form of jazz to that same wider audience.

At age eighteen, after a single semester at Loyola University, Connick moved to New York City to try to break into the jazz industry. His father agreed to support him if he would continue his education, so Connick studied briefly at Hunter College and the Manhattan School of Music, although he did not complete a degree. He eventually began playing at the trendy Empire Diner in Manhattan on Saturday nights and worked as a church music director on Sunday mornings. Connick's first major breakthrough came when Wynton Marsalis introduced him to George Butler, a jazz producer at Columbia Records; this meeting led to the release of Connick's jazz trio album, *Harry Connick, Jr.*, in 1987. That album and its successor, *20* (1988), which included vocals as well

For the Record

Criticized by jazz purists for his showmanship, Harry Connick, Jr., does not apologize for his style: "I think that back when jazz music and dance music were the same thing, back in the big-band era, I mean, *that* was a wonderful time. Today it's the rock musicians who love to perform. They're always wearing wild clothes, they're trendsetters, they love the camera, the spotlight. And look at the guys back in the big-band era, man—Duke Ellington . . . Louis Armstrong—they would get out there and give the people a good time."

as instrumentals, did not receive a great deal of attention at first, although they did lead to a ten-city concert tour and a cable television performance with Herbie Hancock. However, in 1989, the release of the film sound track *When Harry Met Sally*, to which Connick contributed several tracks, pushed him to the forefront of popular music, an unusual position for a largely jazz musician. In 1991, four of Connick's albums, including the two-year-old *When Harry Met Sally*, simultaneously appeared on *Billboard*'s Top-200 chart.

Critical Reception. Throughout Connick's career, critics have found it difficult to neatly categorize his work. Jazz purists have long been annoyed by Connick's showmanship and his tendency to experiment with a wide variety of musical styles. Connick himself does not like to be referred to as a jazz musician, a label he finds too confining. He is often compared, both positively and negatively, to many other artists, from jazz great Thelonious Monk to Frank Sinatra. At age twenty-three, Connick was asked to sing at a tribute to Sinatra, and he was so nervous performing for the celebrated singer that he forgot the words to the song and was forced to start over.

Connick has complained that those who criticize his particular form of entertainment—which sometimes includes a softshoe routine, a turn playing the drums, and even comic impersonations of other performers—have forgotten that the original big-band jazz greats, such as Duke Ellington and Louis Armstrong, also took pleasure in putting on an entertaining show rather than playing in the darker, moody style that became the fashion in jazz circles in the latter half of the twentieth century. Other critics, however, have welcomed Connick's ability to entertain and to make an older style of music appealing to younger generations. While Connick does sing torch song classics such as "It Had to Be You" and "It's All Right with Me," he also writes original songs that are so reminiscent of the big-band era that listeners find it hard to believe the songs are contemporary.

New Directions. Connick continues to experiment musically and take on ever larger roles in the production of his work. For his 1991 album *Blue*

Light, Red Light, Connick not only wrote and sang most of the songs but also instrumentally arranged the pieces for the first time. He began expanding into yet another medium, film. Connick made his feature film debut in 1990 in *Memphis Belle* as the tailgunner of a World War II bomber crew. The role was a natural transition for Connick from musician to actor, as he played a soft-spoken dreamer who occasionally sang for his friends. Connick has since expanded his acting range to purely dramatic parts by appearing in a number of films, including *Little Man Tate* (1991), *Copycat* (1995), *Independence Day* (1996), and *Hope Floats* (1998).

Connick also expanded his horizons in his personal life when he married model and photographer Jill Goodacre in 1994. By 1997, the couple had two children. He continues to widen both his musical and acting ranges without letting either area overshadow the other, although it is clear that music is his first love. —*Amy Sisson*

SELECT DISCOGRAPHY

■ ALBUMS
Harry Connick, Jr., 1987
20, 1988
When Harry Met Sally, 1989 (sound-track album)
We Are in Love, 1990
Lofty's Roach Souffle, 1990
Blue Light, Red Light, 1991
Eleven, 1992
25, 1992
When My Heart Finds Christmas, 1993
She, 1994

SELECT AWARDS
Grammy Award for Best Jazz Vocal Performance, Male, for *When Harry Met Sally,* 1989
Grammy Award for Best Jazz Vocal Performance, Male, for *We Are in Love,* 1990

SEE ALSO: Armstrong, Louis; Sinatra, Frank.

Sam Cooke

BORN: Clarksdale, Mississippi; January 22, 1931
DIED: Los Angeles, California; December 11, 1964

FIRST SINGLE RELEASE: "Lovable," 1957 (as Dale Cook)
MUSICAL STYLES: Soul, gospel

Sam Cooke, gospel star, pop star, and songwriter, was one of the earliest soul singers to "cross over" to the pop charts. He was probably the first to make the transition from gospel star to pop star. Cooke took vocal techniques from the stylish gospel quartets of the 1940's and 1950's and applied them to popular music. Gospel-styled singers had previously applied those techniques to rhythm and blues, but Cooke directed his efforts at the pop audience. His success prepared European Americans for later gospel-inspired black artists.

Early Years. Sam Cooke (he changed the spelling from Cook to Cooke when he became a pop singer) was born in 1931 to Reverend Charles and Annie May Cook in the Mississippi Delta town of Clarksdale. The family later moved to Chicago. When Sam was ten years old the family children formed the Singing Children, a gospel group that participated in their father's ministry. In the mid-1940's, Reverend Cook became a traveling evangelist. The Singing Children toured with him, giving Sam valuable performing experience.

After the Singing Children disbanded, when Sam was a sophomore at Wendell Phillips High School in Chicago, he joined another gospel group called the Teenage Highway QCs. It was from this group that Sam made the big step into the Soul Stirrers. The Soul Stirrers, formed in 1933 in Texas—they relocated to Chicago in 1937—were one of the top gospel quartets of the era. While Sam was a member of the Teenage Highway QCs, the National Quartets Union, a gospel quartet organization, opened a meeting hall at 3838 South State Street, thereby exposing young Sam to the most important gospel artists in the nation. At the union's weekly "Battle of the Quartets," Sam came to the attention of the Soul Stirrers. When their lead singer retired, Cooke, then nineteen, was chosen as his replacement.

Gospel Star. Cooke further developed his ability to win and control audiences while touring with the Soul Stirrers and gained valuable experience in the recording studio. The Soul Stirrers

Sam Cooke (AP/Wide World Photos)

signed with Art Rupe's Specialty Records in 1950, and Sam's first recording session with them was March 1, 1951. At that first session Sam began his career as a professional songwriter when they recorded his "Until Jesus Calls Me Home." Cooke's recordings with the Soul Stirrers include "Peace in the Valley"/"Jesus Gave Me Water" (1951), "How Far Am I from Canaan?" (1952), "Jesus Paid the Debt" (1953), "One More River" (1955), and "Touch the Hem of His Garment" (1956).

During Cooke's years with the Soul Stirrers (1950-1957), European American teenagers began discovering rhythm and blues and steadily increased their spending in record stores special-izing in African American music. Previously, only relatively sedate black artists such as the Mills Brothers, Ink Spots, Billy Eckstine, and Nat "King" Cole had appeared on the pop charts, but now rhythm-and-blues singers were beginning to cross over. They were reaping financial rewards greater than those available on the gospel circuit.

Specialty's producer, Bumps Blackwell, was impressed by Sam's talent and believed that he could be very successful in popular music. Specialty already had experienced success on the rhythm-and-blues charts with performers such as Little Richard, Lloyd Price, Percy Mayfield, Roy Milton, and Joe Liggins, so Cooke asked Art Rupe to let him record in a secular format. Rupe was reluctant because he did not want to jeopardize the Soul Stirrers' loyal audience; at the time, popular music was considered the devil's music by devout gospel audiences.

Pop Star. On December 12, 1956, Cooke went into Cosimo Matassa's J&M Studio in New Orleans with producer Bumps Blackwell to record "Lovable"/"Forever" using the same backup band as Fats Domino, Little Richard, and Lloyd Price. Specialty Records released the recording under the pseudonym Dale Cook in an effort to hide Cooke's identity. The plan failed, however, and Rupe claimed that Cooke's move into secular music hurt the Soul Stirrers' sales. Although "Lovable" sold well enough to encourage another try, it was not a hit. On June 1, 1957, Sam went into Radio Recorders in Hollywood and recorded "You Send Me," this time using the Pied Pipers, a swing-era vocal group, as background singers. When Art Rupe arrived he was angered by the use of European American singers: Specialty was not a pop music label. As a result of that session, Cooke and Blackwell negotiated a separation from Rupe that freed Cooke to pursue a career in popular music.

Blackwell took Sam to Keen Records, a new label, and released "Summertime"/"You Send Me." Although they believed that "Summertime" would be the hit, it was "You Send Me" that impressed disc jockeys and audiences alike. The recording was popular with both black and white record buyers, finishing the year at number 3 on the rhythm-and-blues chart and number 20 on the

For the Record

Sam Cooke's songs have been recorded by an amazing range of later artists, including Otis Redding, Herman's Hermits, Paul Simon, the Animals, Cat Stevens, and Dr. Hook.

pop chart, eventually selling 1.7 million copies. Sam continued to have great success recording music designed for a multiracial audience; he averaged two hits per year until his death in 1964.

In 1959 he formed SAR Records, and later Derby Records, to produce other artists, usually helping gospel singers—such as the Womack Brothers, Mel Carter, and Johnnie Taylor—cross over into secular music. He also formed his own publishing company, KAGS, to better control the earnings from his compositions. In 1960 Cooke signed with RCA, where his recording sessions were produced by the team of Hugo and Luigi, although he eventually won the right to produce his own recordings.

The details of Sam Cooke's death are lurid and unseemly. He was shot to death by Bertha Franklin, a motel clerk at the Hacienda Motel in the Watts section of Los Angeles. She claimed that she shot him in self-defense after Cooke, partially clothed, had broken through the office door while looking for his female companion, Lisa Boyer. Franklin shot him at close range with a .22-caliber handgun. The death was ruled a justifiable homicide. Many of Cooke's fans did not believe the story, and some thought that he had been set up. Certainly his death at the age of thirty-three was a tragic incident, and the full story of what happened may never be known.

The Music. Sam Cooke had a clear vision of the sound required to reach the pop charts, although some have criticized his recordings as being too "light" and not containing rhythm-and-blues characteristics. His recording of "You Send Me," is a perfect example of the style he used on most of his early recordings. The arrangement was standard for pop singers of the era: The bass line is a polite two-beat pattern rather than a walking four-beat style; the drummer lightly taps the snare drum with brushes on the second and fourth beats; the singers "ooh" in the background without a hint of gospel-style call and response. Cooke's voice lightly soars above this simple accompaniment, lazily delivering the lyrics. As the melody descends, he elongates the syllable "yo-oo-oo-ou" with the same melismatic techniques he used in the Soul Stirrers. On later recordings after his career was firmly established, Cooke added instruments such as organ and horns that were more typical of rhythm-and-blues recordings. Cooke had a tremendous impact on the music industry, and his approach to singing was an important model for soul singers such as Smokey Robinson, Eddie Kendricks, and Marvin Gaye.

—*G. W. Sandy Schaefer*

SELECT DISCOGRAPHY

■ SINGLES

"You Send Me," 1957
"Everybody Likes to Cha Cha Cha," 1959
"Only Sixteen," 1959
"Wonderful World," 1960
"Chain Gang," 1960
"Cupid," 1961
"Twistin' the Night Away," 1962
"Bring It on Home to Me," 1962
"Somebody Have Mercy," 1962
"Another Saturday Night," 1963
"Ain't That Good News," 1964
"Shake"/"A Change Is Gonna Come," 1964

SELECT AWARDS
Rock and Roll Hall of Fame, inducted 1986

SEE ALSO: Gaye, Marvin; Redding, Otis; Robinson, Smokey; Wilson, Jackie.

Coolio

(Artis Leon Ivey, Jr.)

BORN: Los Angeles, California; August 1, 1963
FIRST ALBUM RELEASE: *It Takes a Thief*, 1994
MUSICAL STYLES: Hip-hop, rap

Coolio came to prominence in the mid-1990's, but he had been rapping since he was a teenager in the late 1970's. From the same district in Los Angeles as Dr. Dre and N.W.A., Coolio formed World Class Wreckin' Cru with Dr. Dre in the early 1980's, releasing a few singles that did not sell well. Also briefly a member of the Brothers Bass Crew, Coolio released a few solo songs under Eazy-E's Ruthless Records label, but he could only claim distinction as one of the first Los Angeles-based rappers to do so.

Crack and Rehabilitation. As a youth, Coolio committed robbery, joined a gang, served time in jail over a friend's larceny, and did drugs. When the record deal did not turn his life around, Coolio admitted an addiction to crack cocaine and left Los Angeles. He headed to Northern California and worked as a firefighter. Overcoming his addiction, he returned to rapping and recorded with such groups as Soundmaster Crew, NuSkool, Low Profile, and W. C. and the MAAD Circle. In the early 1990's he was still financially insolvent and had to resort to going on welfare,

Coolio (Paul Natkin)

an experience he revealed on "County Line," a single on his first album, *It Takes a Thief* (1994).

In 1993, Coolio signed a contract with Tommy Boy Records. Originally the label only wanted to risk putting out an extended-play single, but, after hearing Coolio's demo tape, they decided to release an album. *It Takes a Thief* sold 994,000 copies, and the hit single "Fantastic Voyage" reached number 3 on the rap charts, selling over two million copies.

Gangsta Business. In 1995, Coolio released *Gangsta's Paradise*. The title track was featured in the film *Dangerous Minds*, in which Coolio played a streetwise junkie. The chorus, sung by guest L. V., was a takeoff of Stevie Wonder's 1976 "Pastime Paradise." The single went to number 1 on the rap charts and sold over three million copies. Coolio was suddenly famous, doing special performances on Black Entertainment Television (BET) and MTV, hosting MTV specials, and appearing on major talk shows. He even had the dubious honor of being parodied by "Weird Al" Yankovic, whose "Amish Paradise" (1996) became popular in its own right. Yankovic even sported Coolio's distinctive dreadlocks on the cover of his album *Bad Hair Day* (1996).

Outside Interests. Coolio formed his own promotion company, Crowbar Management, in order to take care of all his commitments. In acknow-

For the Record

Originally known as rapper "Boo Daddy," thanks to a homemade tattoo that sported the Playboy bunny logo and the word "Boo," Coolio received his current nickname in the 1980's. "It was a snapping session," he explains. "We were biting, capping, ranking, talking about each other, playing the dozens. I had on this western shirt and was playing some goofy song with a little guitar, and my homeboy asked me, 'Who do you think you are, Coolio Iglesias?' They called me that and it stuck."

ledgment of his hairstyle, he helped finance a Long Beach, California, hair salon called Whoop Dee Doo and opened a Whoop Dee Doo Two in Los Angeles soon after. Coolio also planned to break into the soul-food restaurant business in the late 1990's. He has participated in the International AIDS Day CounterAID benefit in New York and expressed concern for his six children and one stepchild growing up in a world with so much violence.

Despite all of his business ventures, Coolio found time to release another album, *My Soul*, in 1997. Featuring the single "C U When U Get There" from the film *Nothing to Lose*, which reached number 16 on the rap charts and sold almost 500,000 copies its first month, *My Soul* made Coolio an international star, with tours in Europe and releases in Japan and Brazil.

—*Rose Secrest*

SELECT DISCOGRAPHY
■ ALBUMS
It Takes a Thief, 1994
Gangsta's Paradise, 1995
My Soul, 1997

SELECT AWARDS
Grammy Award for Best Rap Solo Performance
    for *Gangsta's Paradise*, 1995

SEE ALSO: Dr. Dre; N.W.A.

Alice Cooper

(Vincent Damon Furnier)

BORN: Detroit, Michigan; February 4, 1948
ORIGINAL BAND MEMBERS: Mike Bruce (b. 1948),
    Dennis Dunaway (b. 1948), Glen Buxton
    (1947-1997), Neal Smith (b. 1947)
FIRST ALBUM RELEASE: *Pretties for You*, 1969
MUSICAL STYLE: Hard rock

In 1968, Vincent Furnier changed the name of his band from the Nazz (no relation to Todd Rundgren's band of the same name) to Alice Cooper, reportedly because Furnier felt he was the reincarnated soul of a seventeenth-century witch. Furnier invented a character to fit the name and pioneered new ground in "shock rock."

Alice Is Born. The son of a preacher, Vince Furnier formed his first band, the Earwigs, with friends from his Phoenix, Arizona, high school. By 1965, with Buxton, Bruce, Dunaway, and Smith, the band, then known as the Spiders, had a local hit with "Don't Blow Your Mind." The Spiders soon relocated to Los Angeles and became the Nazz, and by 1968, the band had changed its name to Alice Cooper. The name Alice Cooper also became attached to Furnier, who created an androgynous, cadaverous stage persona to match the name. The band played music designed to shock and outrage and soon had gained the reputation as the worst band in Los Angeles. This notoriety attracted the attention of musician Frank Zappa, who signed them to a contract with his record label, Straight Records. In 1969 *Pretties for You* was released, but saw

Alice Cooper (Archive Photos)

only minor success. The follow-up album, *Easy Action* (1970), was equally unsuccessful. In 1970, after making a cameo appearance in the film *Diary of a Mad Housewife*, Alice Cooper left California for Detroit, Michigan.

"No More Mr. Nice Guy." In July of 1971, Alice Cooper released their first album with Warner Bros., *Love It to Death*. The album and its single "Eighteen" had moderate commercial success. In the meantime, the band's stage show became larger and more bizarre. The theatric performances featured a guillotine, an electric chair, and several large snakes. Cooper himself adopted a demonic visual appearance. The theatrics pushed the 1971 album *Killer* to number 21 on the U.S. album charts. This was followed by the teen-anthem single "School's Out" and its parent album, *School's Out* (1972), which reached number 2 in the United States.

Alice Cooper continued their successes with *Billion Dollar Babies* in 1973, which featured guest contributions from Marc Bolan, Donovan, and Harry Nilsson. Each of the next four years saw a new Alice Cooper album going gold, the last being *Alice Cooper Goes to Hell*, in 1976. Despite this, Cooper fired his original band in February of 1974, replacing them with former members of Lou Reed's band. A 1975 prime-time television special, *Alice Cooper—The Nightmare*, marked Cooper's sacrifice of unique artistry for commercial gain. He began regular performances in Las Vegas nightclubs. Cooper also became a frequent member of the celebrity panel on the television game show *Hollywood Squares*.

From the Inside. In 1977, everything began to unravel. The album *Lace and Whiskey* achieved only lackluster sales. Chronic alcoholism led to Cooper's hospitalization. The 1978 album *From the Inside* is based on Cooper's experiences while hospitalized and spawned the hit single "How Are You Gonna See Me Now?"

Over the next decade, Cooper continued to rapidly release solo albums that achieved only minor commercial success. In the late 1980's, Alice Cooper found himself in the midst of a revival. *Trash* (1989), which featured guest appearances by Jon Bon Jovi and Aerosmith, put

For the Record

Alice Cooper has been the star of a Marvel comic book on two occasions. The first was in the 1970's, and the second was in 1994, when Alice was the main character of *The Last Temptation*, a three-issue series written by Neil Gaiman of *Sandman* fame.

Cooper at number 2 on the British album charts and number 20 in the United States. Two years later, in 1991, *Hey Stoopid*, featuring Slash and Ozzy Osbourne, debuted at number 4 in Britain, peaking at number 47 in the United States.

Also in 1991, Cooper's status as a pop-culture icon was cemented when he appeared as Freddy Kreuger's father in the final *Nightmare on Elm Street* film. This status was echoed with Cooper's cameo appearance, as himself, in 1992's *Wayne's World*. The strength of Alice Cooper as a larger-than-life character would continue to grow. In 1994, Cooper linked his new album, *The Last Temptation*, to a commercially successful three-part comic book series written by Neil Gaiman and published by Marvel Comics.

—*B. Keith Murphy*

SELECT DISCOGRAPHY
■ ALBUMS
Pretties for You, 1969
Easy Action, 1970
Love It to Death, 1971
Killer, 1971
School's Out, 1972
Billion Dollar Babies, 1973
Muscle of Love, 1973
Welcome to My Nightmare, 1975
Alice Cooper Goes to Hell, 1976
Lace and Whiskey, 1977
The Alice Cooper Show, 1977
From the Inside, 1978
Flush the Fashion, 1980
Special Forces, 1981
Zipper Catches Skin, 1982
Da Da, 1983

Constrictor, 1986
Raise Your Fist and Yell, 1987
Trash, 1989
Hey Stoopid, 1991
The Last Temptation, 1994
A Fistful of Alice, 1997

SEE ALSO: Black Sabbath; Kiss; Manson, Marilyn.

Elvis Costello

(Declan Patrick MacManus)

BORN: London, England; August 25, 1955
FIRST ALBUM RELEASE: *My Aim Is True*, 1977
MUSICAL STYLES: Rock and roll, pop, country, classical, new wave

Since his debut in 1977, Elvis Costello has written more than three hundred songs and played in more musical styles than most record stores have categories for. Defined by his trademark eyeglasses and a razor-sharp lyrical ability, Costello brings to his craft an energy and originality that few musicians can equal, and in turn he has become one of music's most respected songwriters.

Beginnings. Born Declan MacManus on August 25, 1955, in London, England, Costello spent his early years after graduating from secondary school working at whatever jobs he could find, eventually becoming a computer operator for the Elizabeth Arden cosmetic company. In 1974 he met musician Nick Lowe, who would later become his producer. Married and with a child on the way, Costello began pursuing his future music career in earnest but had no success. Finally, in 1976 he sent a demo record to the newly formed Stiff Records, which was looking for artists who were not necessarily interested in becoming commercial stars. Costello was looking for a record label that would let him record songs as he saw fit; the two quickly signed a deal.

This Year's Model. Recording tracks during sick leave from work, Costello eventually amassed enough material to release an album. *My Aim Is True* (1977) quickly established him as a force to be reckoned with. Recorded as the punk scene was unfolding around him, *My Aim Is True* embraced music's new-wave movement and took Costello to the forefront of the movement with his edgy pop writing style.

Costello had been backed on his first album by the U.S. group Clover (notable for having Huey Lewis as a member), but he quickly hired the musicians who would form the Attractions. With Steve "Nieve" Nason on keyboard, Bruce Thomas on bass, and Pete Thomas (no relation to Bruce) on drums, Costello recorded *This Year's Model* in 1978. Working in the same studio that Chrissie Hynde's band, the Pretenders, was using to record "Stop Your Sobbing," Costello contributed the phrase "Gotta stop sobbing, oh-oh" to the Pretenders' track. Costello was becoming an active participant in shaping the music around him before he had even released his second album. *This Year's Model* was harder hitting than *My Aim Is True* and laid the groundwork for his third album, *Armed Forces* (1979), which brutally attacked Great Britain's colonialism and military politics. *Armed Forces* featured the hit singles "Oliver's Army" and "(What's So Funny 'Bout) Peace, Love and Understanding."

A Poor Choice of Words. After producing the 1979 debut album of the Specials (who led the ska-revival movement in England), Costello and the Attractions released *Get Happy!* in 1980. The title was somewhat ironic, since the band had just ended a difficult, if not disastrous, U.S. tour. Among other events, Costello aimed a racial slur against Ray Charles in a drunken barroom incident in Columbus, Ohio. (Charles was not present; Costello was arguing with Bonnie Bramlett and Stephen Stills.) Costello vehemently denied that he was a racist (he had often participated in antiracism benefit concerts), saying that he had made the remark to so shock the other party that it would quiet them down. He spent many years trying to live down the comment and even wondered if he would ever be able to tour the United States again.

Costello recorded *Almost Blue*, a collection of country blues standards that was the first album to show his widening musical diversity, in Nashville in 1981. Costello would also appear with

George Jones on a television special and would meet Johnny Cash; both Jones and Cash would later record Costello songs. Costello and the Attractions kept a low profile, touring mainly in Europe.

Imperial Bedroom (1982) is often cited as one of Costello's masterpieces. The first of Costello's albums to be recorded without Nick Lowe at the helm, it was produced by Geoff Emerick, whose credits included the Beatles' "Strawberry Fields Forever" and *Revolver* (1966). Costello followed this album with *Punch the Clock* in 1983, the most commercial album he ever released, which featured "Everyday I Write the Book."

Perpetual Reinvention. After the critical failure of *Goodbye Cruel World* (1984), Costello embarked on a solo tour, working with T-Bone Burnett and

Elvis Costello (Ken Settle)

producing the Pogues' second album (divorced from his first wife, he would eventually marry Caitlin O'Riordan, the Pogues' bass player.) In 1986 he released *King of America* to critical acclaim. A country-rock album with a decidedly American feel (i.e. songs such as "Eisenhower Blues" and "American Without Tears"), it featured the hit single "Brilliant Mistake" and a cover of the Animals' "Don't Let Me Be Misunderstood."

In 1986 Costello would reunite with both the Attractions (after using backup band the Confederates for *King of America*) and Nick Lowe on *Blood and Chocolate*. The reunion would last for one album. By 1989 Costello had signed a worldwide deal with Warner Bros. and had begun collaborating with Paul McCartney on several songs. *Spike* (1989) featured a varied backing band including Caitlin O'Riordan, T-Bone Burnett, Paul McCartney, Chrissie Hynde, and the Dirty Dozen Brass Band, again showcasing Costello's refusal to write in a musical box.

Costello's most daring project would come in 1993 when he collaborated with classical musicians the Brodsky Quartet. Taking the dual themes of Romeo and Juliet and communication through letters, *The Juliet Letters* featured Costello as co-lyricist and vocalist on what was essentially an album of chamber music, and his voice was more powerful than it had ever been. Costello's intelligent lyrics and vocal abilities pushed the album from an oddity to a masterpiece.

Brutal Youth (1994) featured the return of the Attractions, who had not played backup for Costello in eight years. This album was received with relief by many fans, who thought Costello had lost the ability to make a commercial album. *Kojak Variety* (1995) was a collection of covers Costello had assembled and had been wanting to record for a long time. The album was deliberately composed of obscure material by people such as Peggy Lee and Screaming Jay Hawkins, ensuring that fans would recognize very little of it.

Parting Songs. The last album Costello would record with the Attractions, 1996's *All This Useless Beauty*, was also a collection of covers, but of songs Costello had written for other musicians and never recorded himself. This would be his most critically acclaimed album in years, but Costello was nonetheless unhappy with Warner Bros.' promotion of it. In 1997 he would release a greatest hits album, *Extreme Honey,* and sever his ties with Warner Bros., signing a multilabel contract with PolyGram that would market Costello under the different music labels encompassed by his work. He would also disband the Attractions by the end of 1997, this time forever.

Despite Costello's prolific output, he still found time to perform on tribute albums, score music for television, and even write an entire album for singer Wendy James in a single weekend (Chrissie Hynde once described Costello as always finishing one project and beginning another). He was recording an album with pop composer Burt Bacharach in 1998. Costello is the rarest of musicians, capable of working in all styles with equal adeptness.

—*Kelly Rothenberg*

SELECT DISCOGRAPHY

■ ALBUMS

My Aim Is True, 1977
This Year's Model, 1978
Armed Forces, 1979
Almost Blue, 1981
Imperial Bedroom, 1982
Blood and Chocolate, 1986
King of America, 1986
The Juliet Letters, 1993
Kojak Variety, 1995
All This Useless Beauty, 1996
Painted from Memory, 1998 (with Burt Bacharach)

For the Record

Known for his sense of humor in his songs, one track on *The Juliet Letters* is especially revealing. A careful listen of "I Almost Had a Weakness," a song about a crazy but crafty old woman, reveals the main violin sequence to be the *Looney Tunes* cartoon theme, which is rather appropriate.

SEE ALSO: Cash, Johnny; McCartney, Paul; Pretenders, The; Squeeze.

Counting Crows

ORIGINAL MEMBERS: Adam Duritz (b. 1964), David Bryson (b. 1961), Steve Bowman (b. 1967), Charlie Gillingham (b. 1960), Matt Malley (b. 1963)
OTHER MEMBERS: Ben Mize (b. 1971), Dan Vickrey (b. 1966)
FIRST ALBUM RELEASE: *August and Everything After,* 1993
MUSICAL STYLES: Rock and roll, pop, alternative

San Francisco band Counting Crows became an overnight sensation when their debut album sold more than seven million copies and its hit single, "Mr. Jones," reached number 1 on the charts. On the strength of lead singer-songwriter Adam Duritz's expressive and angst-laden vocals and the band's rhythmic drive, Counting Crows struck an emotional chord of cautious yearning. In the tradition of great rock vocalists such as Van Morrison and Bruce Springsteen, Duritz can raise listeners' spirits with an open-throated cry of joy and release. On the other hand, like his peers Eddie Vedder (Pearl Jam) and the late Kurt Cobain, he is more often introspective and sometimes ponderous, shredding his emotions in songs filled with expressions of self-doubt. The band's hit videos enhanced their rocking confessionalism—Duritz standing and bouncing to the music, brown dreadlocks flying, singing with his eyes closed, radiating a blend of still-hopeful American spirit and stylistic rebellion.

Starting at the Top. In 1989, after a few years of depression, travel, and substance abuse, Duritz began to work with guitarist David Bryson. They composed songs together and played acoustic shows at local coffeehouses. Counting Crows assembled in 1991 and recorded a professional-quality demo tape that impressed a number of record executives. They were soon being compared to every great rock band in history, but especially to Van Morrison and the Band. Duritz's soulful, explosive vocals play off a number of Van Morrison's techniques: scatting and repeating words for effect ("I want to be someone who believes/ who believes/ who believes," he sings in "Mr. Jones"); shouting, moaning, muttering, and crying out—often all in the same song; peppering moments of joy with "sha-la-la-la-la"s. Duritz's musical model for a rock band is the Band, whose intuitive musical exchanges were recorded in the 1978 concert film *The Last Waltz.* As musical destiny would have it, Duritz met the Band's songwriter and guitarist Robbie Robertson before recording the first Counting Crows album. Robertson advised him to move the band into a big house to increase their ability to "think" together musically. Duritz was justly proud of the band's intuitive interplay on the first album's delicately textured ballads, "Perfect Blue Buildings," "Sullivan Street," and "Anna Begins." The playing on the songs was like "five musicians thinking as one," Duritz said.

The musical power of *August and Everything After* (1993) was the result of contrasts set up by Duritz's angst-laden tales, drummer Steve Bowman's crisp backbeat, and the band's classic sound of jangling guitars supported by subtle organ textures. Just as important, veteran producer T-Bone Burnett (Burnett has worked with Los Lobos and the Wallflowers) elicited a relaxed rhythmic drive from the band that reflects the new sophistication of post-grunge rock-and-roll rhythm sections. In many of the best songs on the album, the band downshifts in midstream from headlong drive to a confessional half-singing, half-talking mode without the song losing its focus. With Bowman able to switch easily from a country shuffle to more sophisticated syncopation, the band seamlessly shifts moods and energy levels.

The potent tension of upbeat music and downbeat lyrics can be seen in the hit ballad "Round Here," which seems to concern self-absorbed slackers in their late twenties beginning to face the idea of being losers. "Round here we talk just like lions," Duritz moans, "but we sacrifice like lambs." Yet the ringing guitars on the chorus, the funky bridge, and Bowman's precise playing keep the music driving relentlessly forward until

Counting Crows' Adam Duritz (Ken Settle)

Duritz's spirited outburst at the end subverts the inertia of these characters. In one sense, Counting Crows' rocking confessionalism shows how much rock and roll still owes to the original functions of old-time blues and jazz: to transform emotional pain into good-time music. As the great jazz clarinetist Sidney Bechet once described good New Orleans music, "Keep a lively tempo but get that crying tone in there."

Changes and Perseverance. Between the first and second albums, drummer Steve Bowman left the band after a dispute with Duritz; he went on to form the band Third Eye Blind. Bowman was replaced by Ben Mize. The band also added a lead guitarist, Dan Vickrey.

For the band's second album, *Recovering the Satellites* (1996), producer Gil Norton (who had worked with the Pixies and Echo and the Bunnymen) allowed Duritz's raw emotionalism full range without insisting on tight melodies. At times Duritz's vocals sound maudlin; he seems to be muttering in doorways about a woman—often only called "she"—who is trying to hold him back. Vickrey's solos lend a flashy arena-rock sound to the mix. Yet whatever the albums's shortcomings compared with the band's first release, it was a commercial success, entering the *Billboard* album charts at number 1 and selling more than two million copies. The mournful "A Long December" received considerable airplay. A standout is "Goodnight Elisabeth," a haunting, poignant lullaby sung from the road to a love left behind. Where the first album transformed Duritz's personal concoction of hope and self-doubt into a larger catharsis, the songs on *Recovering the Satellites* revolve about the less-pressing problems of lost innocence and newfound fame. Fame has undoubtedly shaken Duritz's perspective; he pleads, "Could you tell me/ the things you remember about me/ and have you seen me lately?"

The band released a live album, *Across a Wire: Live in New York*, in 1998. Counting Crows shows were being widely recorded and bootlegged by fans, so the band decided to release its own live album. They nicknamed it their "official bootleg."

One of Duritz's favorite images—that of himself as the "rain king"—appears on both records. "The Rain King," from the first album is an up-tempo rocking blast about joining a cause larger than oneself. "I belong in the service of the queen," he sings, "I belong anywhere but in between." At the time of the first album, Duritz was indeed stuck in-between—ready for big things yet plagued by doubts. By the second album, he is more wary, even frightened, than hopeful, and he scales down his expectations. In "Goodnight Elisabeth," he refers to himself quietly as "the king of the rain." It is a beautiful image of the archetypal troubadour as a passing storm front that fertilizes the emotional soil of his listeners and then moves on.

Duritz's confrontation with fame embodies one of rock and roll's great paradoxes: that in a music based on rebellion, unrestricted self-

For the Record

By a quirk of fate, Counting Crows played at the Rock and Roll Hall of Fame Awards before their first album was even released (in January 1993). They were a last-minute replacement for an ailing Van Morrison, and they played his song "Caravan."

expression, and the potential creativity of the average person, becoming famous instantly launches one into a rarefied world.

Ironically, the song that secured Counting Crows' fame, "Mr. Jones," is a commentary on the desire for fame and celebrity: "We all want to be big stars/ but we don't know why/ and we don't know how." Duritz does know at least one reason why, however: "When everybody loves me/ I'm going to be/ just about/ as happy as I can be." Duritz—or at least the persona singing the song—wants to become famous in order to feel loved, yet he also knows that being famous will not make him feel loved at all.

In "Mr. Jones," when Duritz sings the line "I want to be Bob Dylan," one senses that it is a job he both wants and fears. —*Joel Dinerstein*

SELECT DISCOGRAPHY
- SINGLE
"Going Back to Georgia," 1994 (Duritz duet with Nanci Griffith on *Flyer*)
- ALBUMS
August and Everything After, 1993
Recovering the Satellites, 1996
Across a Wire: Live in New York, 1998

SEE ALSO: Band, The; Dylan, Bob; Morrison, Van.

The Cowboy Junkies

ORIGINAL MEMBERS: Alan Anton (b. Alan Alizojvodic, 1959), Margo Timmins (b. 1961), Michael Timmins (b. 1959), Peter Timmins (b. 1965)

FIRST ALBUM RELEASE: *Whites off Earth Now!* 1986
MUSICAL STYLES: Blues, country rock, folk, pop

The Cowboy Junkies' mantra could be, "A whisper can convey more than a scream," and their music is best described as languid. When the Canadian band arrived on the music scene in the mid-1980's, their original songs and stripped-down versions of country, folk, and blues classics were like nothing critics or fans had ever heard before.

The Beginning. In 1979, Toronto natives Alan Anton and Michael Timmins formed an English-influenced band called Hunger Project, which they took to New York the following year. Still unknown and deciding that the United Kingdom was the right place for their music, Hunger Project once again relocated in 1981. When success still eluded them, Anton and Timmins disbanded the group and formed an experimental, instrumental-noise band called Germinal. Like its predecessor, Germinal did not succeed, but Timmins later told an interviewer that it allowed him to get a lot of noise out of his system in preparation for things to come.

By 1985, they were back in Toronto, playing in a rented garage with Michael's brother Pete on drums and sister Margo on vocals. The Cowboy Junkies were born. At first, the unusual name was strictly an attention-getter, but they found that it conjured up a slow, easy, western image that suited their distinctive sound. The new band recorded their first album in 1986, *Whites off Earth Now!* in that same rented garage and released it on their own label, Latent Records. The album consisted mainly of blues covers: "Shining Moon" by Lightning Hopkins, "Me and the Devil" and "Cross-

The Cowboy Junkies in 1989: Michael Timmins, Margo Timmins, Pete Timmins, Alan Anton (AP/Wide World Photos)

roads" from Robert Johnson, and three penned by John Lee Hooker, "Decoration Day," "I'll Never Get out of These Blues Alive," and "Forgive Me." In many cases, the music and melody had been stripped away, leaving only the original lyric amidst the Cowboy Junkies' languid groove. Though the initial release sold only four thousand copies, the band remained undaunted and soon went on tour.

The Trinity Session. The Cowboy Junkies discovered country music during the southern leg of the U.S. tour in support of *Whites off Earth Now!* Their next album, *The Trinity Session*, reflected these country music influences, covering artists such as Patsy Cline, Waylon Jennings, and Hank Williams. Reviewers noted the album for its stark beauty and simplicity, and it was unlike anything else on the airwaves. The tour and subsequent airplay earned the band a contract with RCA, who promptly rereleased *The Trinity Session* nationwide.

The Trinity Session also contained what would become the Cowboy Junkies' breakout song, a cover of the Lou Reed classic "Sweet Jane." Reed loved it, saying that this was the way the song was supposed to be played. This was not surprising; Michael cited Reed's former band, Velvet Underground, as one of his primary influences. "Sweet Jane" found another fan in director Oliver Stone, who used the version on the sound track to his controversial 1994 film *Natural Born Killers*. The song spent seventeen weeks on *Billboard*'s chart, cracking the Top 10 in December, 1994.

Into the Studio. The unexpected success of *The Trinity Session* raised expectations with the record label, the critics, and the fans. Keeping with tradition, the original follow-up album was recorded in a Quaker meetinghouse in northern Ontario, Canada. The results were moody and somber, and reactions were mixed—both from the band and from RCA. Ultimately, the effort (called *Sharon* after the meetinghouse where it was recorded) was shelved, and six months later the Cowboy Junkies found themselves in an actual recording studio.

Their third album, 1990's *The Caution Horses*, retained the live-recording approach but used more than one microphone to emphasize individual performers. Michael wrote all but two of the

songs, many of which were to have appeared on the ill-fated *Sharon*. *The Caution Horses* did not match the success of its predecessor, but it did not disappoint the faithful. The next release, *Black-Eyed Man* in 1992, was also a moderate success. Folk-country artist John Prine appeared on a duet, "If You Were the Woman, and I Was the Man." *Black-Eyed Man* also featured two effective numbers by country songwriter Townes Van Zandt: "Cowboy Junkies Lament," and "To Live Is to Fly."

While no one could complain about musicianship, critics had begun to grow weary of the same sound they had raved about back in 1988. *Pale Sun, Crescent Moon* in 1993 did nothing to change their tune. The Cowboy Junkies left RCA in 1994 under amicable conditions, and their final release on that label was *200 More Miles: Live Performances 1985-1994*. RCA released another compilation in 1996, *Studio: Selected Studio Recordings, 1986-95*, though as previously noted, most of the Cowboy Junkies' earlier work was not actually recorded in a studio.

A New Beginning. Their first album for Geffen, 1996's *Lay It Down*, was recorded in Athens, Georgia, and produced by John Keane, who had previously worked with R.E.M. and the Indigo Girls. *Lay It Down* produced the Top-20 single "A Common Disaster" and relied heavily on Michael's distinctive lead guitar as the band returned to basics. The howling guitars and feed-

For the Record

When it came time to record the Cowboy Junkies' second album, producer Peter Moore knew just the place: Toronto's Church of the Holy Trinity, where he had previously recorded orchestras and soundtrack scores. In November, 1987, the Cowboy Junkies, augmented by local folk musicians, spent fourteen hours singing into a single microphone, recording the entire album live to tape, with no overdubs. The entire session cost less than 250 dollars.

back contrasted with Margo's soft vocals, giving the music a new edge. Margo's voice grew stronger as she grew more comfortable with the spotlight, and she imbued the songs with her personal, female perspective.

The Cowboy Junkies' seventh album, *Miles from Our Home*, was scheduled for release in the summer of 1998 and promised a more layered sound, more instruments, and different tempos. The producer, John Leckie, had previously worked with such disparate acts as the Verve, Radiohead, and Stone Roses. —*P. S. Ramsey*

SELECT DISCOGRAPHY

■ ALBUMS

Whites off Earth Now! 1986
The Trinity Session, 1988
The Caution Horses, 1990
Black-Eyed Man, 1992
Pale Sun, Crescent Moon, 1993
Lay It Down, 1996

SELECT AWARDS

Los Angeles Times Critics Poll, named *The Trinity Session* Best Album, 1988

SEE ALSO: Reed, Lou; Velvet Underground.

The Cranberries

ORIGINAL MEMBERS: Dolores O'Riordan (b. 1971), Noel Hogan (b. 1971), Mike Hogan (b. 1973), Fergal Lawler (1971)
FIRST ALBUM RELEASE: *Everybody Else Is Doing It, So Why Can't We?* 1993
MUSICAL STYLES: Pop, rock and roll

The Cranberries burst onto the pop music scene in 1993 when their first album, *Everybody Else Is Doing It, So Why Can't We?*, went platinum. The band's music was labeled by some as "dream pop," an easy-listening variety of contemporary music with an occasional hint of brilliance. What set the band apart from others, however, was the main vocalist, Dolores O'Riordan. Her voice was similar to Irish singer Sinéad O'Connor's, but it also had an individualized power, moving easily between

For the Record

All four members of the Cranberries were born in the same hospital: Limerick's Maternity Hospital.

the yearning tenderness of quiet love songs and the husky bravado of more adamant, driven songs.

Origins. The last addition to the band, O'Riordan would also be its power. The Cranberries, in their first incarnation, were called the Cranberry Saw Us and were made up of four young men from Limerick, Ireland. When the lead singer and songwriter left the band in 1990, the three remaining members—brothers Mike and Noel Hogan on bass and guitar, respectively, and Fergal Lawler on drums—went in search of a vocalist. The Irish band found her just outside of Limerick, a nineteen-year-old who had won competitions for her singing in her church and school choirs.

The band polished their skills while O'Riordan and Noel Hogan worked together on writing the words and music for some new songs. When the band recorded a five-track demo and sent it to record companies, they were surprised to be involved in a bidding war that was eventually won by Island Records. When Stephen Street, the producer of one of their idols, the Smiths, offered to work with them, they agreed and were able to release, in 1993, after a skirmish with their manager, the impressive *Everybody Else Is Doing It, So Why Can't We?*

Transition. The album included the hits "Dreams" and "Linger," which climbed the charts as singles, and the album reached number 1 on the U.K. charts in June, 1994. Some music critics believe it was the tour the band made of the United States in the summer and fall of 1993 that ensured the Cranberries' success. U.S. audiences reacted with enthusiasm (and purchasing power) to the Cranberries' sound.

The band also used whatever time was available to them between concerts to work on new material for a second album. *No Need to Argue*, recorded in

The Cranberries' Dolores O'Riordan (Popperfoto/ Archive Photos)

the spring of 1994 with Stephen Street again as producer, appeared to great critical acclaim. The single "Zombie" marked a new development in the Cranberries' music. Instead of only creating songs about love and love's disappointments, the Cranberries made a direct, hard-hitting, guitar-driven political song in which the strife in Northern Ireland is addressed and those involved in the violence are labeled zombies. O'Riordan's voice reached a new level of power and intensity on this chilling song.

Things Change, Things Remain the Same. The Irish quartet was quick to build on their success from *No Need to Argue* and recorded a new album in November and December of 1995 in Dublin, releasing *To the Faithful Departed* in 1996. The album was dedicated to those who "have gone before us" into death, including President John F.

Kennedy, singer John Lennon, and the civil war victims in Sarajevo, Yugoslavia, but it also marked new beginnings. The band replaced their producer, Stephen Street, with Bruce Fairbairn, and in July, 1994, O'Riordan married the band's tour manager, Don Burton (becoming Dolores O'Riordan Burton), and many of the songs on the album reflect her love for Burton and her appreciation of her new life.

Even though *To the Faithful Departed* was not as successful as the two previous albums, it had the same power and drive that came from the songwriting team of O'Riordan Burton and Noel Hogan. The singles "Salvation" (with the new addition of a horn section), "Free to Decide," and "Forever Yellow Skies" are incredibly strong reminders of the rocking areas beyond dream-pop that the band is able to move in quite comfortably. A Website has been formed for all fans, and the information available is required reading for all those tracking the meteoric success of this band from Limerick.

—*Kevin Boyle*

SELECT DISCOGRAPHY

■ ALBUMS
Everybody Else Is Doing It, So Why Can't We? 1993
No Need to Argue, 1994
To the Faithful Departed, 1996

SEE ALSO: O'Connor, Sinéad; U2.

Robert Cray

BORN: Columbus, Georgia; August 1, 1953
FIRST ALBUM RELEASE: *Who's Been Talkin',* 1980
MUSICAL STYLES: Blues, rhythm and blues, rock and roll

One of the most important and successful of the 1970's generation of young African American blues artists, Robert Cray is considered by many to be the spiritual heir to the legacy forged by such blues elders as B. B. King, Aaron "T-Bone" Walker, and Muddy Waters. Working through a variety of musical genres, Cray has fashioned a role for himself in the music world rarely reserved for blues and blues-based artists.

The Beginnings. Robert Cray was born in Columbus, Georgia, in 1953 to a military family whose nearly constant travels took them from California to Virginia to Germany before they finally settled in Tacoma, Washington, in 1968. As a young man in Germany, Cray took an early interest in the piano, but during the early 1960's, perhaps spurred on by the "British invasion" of that decade, he switched to the guitar. Though he would grow to become an exceptional guitarist, he was always quick to point to pianist Ray Charles, another Georgia-born Washington transplant who found fame as a blues-based artist, among his major musical influences. Other early influences in Cray's life include Stax Records session guitarist Steve Cropper, Seattle's inimitable Jimi Hendrix, singer Sam Cooke, and Texas-born Chicago blues legend and noted "Master of the Telecaster," guitarist Albert Collins.

Robert Cray in 1997 (AP/Wide World Photos)

In 1974, Cray, along with bass player Richard Cousins, formed the first Robert Cray Band and developed a local following in and around Washington and parts of northern Oregon. A chance meeting with actor-comedian John Belushi during this period resulted in Cray's cameo appearance in the film *Animal House* (1978), playing a bass player in the film's fictional musical act Otis Day and the Knights.

Earliest Recordings. In 1978 the Robert Cray Band signed with Tomato Records. Their first album, entitled *Who's Been Talkin'* (1980), was recorded in only two sessions. The album gave every indication that Cray was indeed a rising star. In this release Cray paid homage to many of his musical influences, smoothly and adroitly handling everything from blues ballads, such as "The Welfare," to more traditional material, such as blues songwriting legend Willie Dixon's "Too Many Cooks." The label was struggling, however, and once it folded, the band's future was in serious doubt. It would be three years before Cray and the band would sign another record deal.

By 1982 the band was back in the recording studio for Hightone Records. Two Hightone releases, *Bad Influence* in 1983 and *False Accusations* in 1985, demonstrated the maturity of both Cray and the band as they distanced themselves from the more traditional Delta-based blues of their first album and delved more deeply into a soul-based blues sound, a common musical theme in the years to come. Later that year Cray recorded a critically acclaimed collaboration album alongside his idol Albert Collins and Texas bluesman Johnny Copeland. The album, on Chicago's Alligator Records, was called *Showdown!*, and it served as a major breakthrough in his career. In addition to introducing to Cray and his innovative and sophisticated guitar and vocal styles to a wider blues audience, it sold more than a quarter of a million copies and garnered Grammy Awards for all three artists.

Stardom. Following the group's move to the more visible Mercury label, the Robert Cray Band released its most important album, *Strong Persuader* in 1986, the first blues album in thirty years to reach the Top 20 on the album charts. In addition to Cray's increasingly familiar guitar work, he would also gain fame as a gifted and sensitive songwriter. This million-selling album is filled with narratives relating tales of lost loves and sorrows over misdeeds and included his first smash single, "Smoking Gun." Further adding to the crossover success of this Grammy Award-winning album was the first appearance in Cray's recorded legacy of Wayne Jackson and Andrew Love, the vaunted Memphis Horns, whose previous credits included the Stax recordings of Sam and Dave, Otis Redding, and others from the influential Memphis, Tennessee, label.

The commercial success of *Strong Persuader*, which landed Cray's face on the cover of virtually every music and entertainment-related magazine throughout the year, catapulted him into pop stardom and thrust him into the musical spotlight. In addition to recording other million-selling, Grammy Award-winning albums, such as his 1988 follow-up *Don't Be Afraid of the Dark*, and 1990's *Midnight Stroll*, which also featured the Memphis Horns and further reflected Cray's interest in soul, Cray was becoming a fixture in the increasingly popular celebrity jam sessions and collaborative efforts so prominent throughout the late 1980's and early 1990's. All five of his releases following *Strong Persuader* would either win or be nominated for a Grammy Award, an unprecedented feat for a blues artist.

In the late 1980's Cray toured Canada, Europe, and the Far East with rock-and-roll legend Chuck Berry and Keith Richards of the Rolling Stones, and in 1987 he appeared in Richards's film tribute to Chuck Berry, *Hail! Hail! Rock 'n' Roll*. He also toured with blues-rock guitarist Eric Clapton, and in 1991 he performed alongside Clapton, Collins, Jimmie Vaughan of the then-Fabulous Thunderbirds, Chicago blues legend Buddy Guy, and original Chuck Berry Trio pianist Johnnie Johnson at London's Royal Albert Hall, a performance immortalized in Clapton's *24 Nights*, released later that year.

Cray was also part of the celebrity concert on August 26, 1990 at Alpine Valley, just outside of East Troy, Wisconsin, which will forever be marred by tragedy after the helicopter carrying members of the concert's backing musicians and Texas guitarist Stevie Ray Vaughan crashed en route to the airport, killing all on board. Cray, like many of the others in attendance at the concert, would pay lasting tributes to Vaughan, participating in a number of celebrity and charitable concerts in Vaughan's memory.

Legacy. In a rather ironic twist, it has become Cray's legacy to older and newcoming generations of musicians to champion their causes for critical and commercial success. In addition to those listed above, Cray has appeared on countless tribute and collaborative success albums with musicians such as blues legend John Lee Hooker and rock-and-roll diva Tina Turner. He also co-starred in B. B. King's 1993 *Blues Summit*. Additionally, Eric Clapton recorded a version of Cray's "Bad Influence" on his 1987 album *Journeyman*, and the two coauthored "Old Love," which Clapton eventually recorded for his Grammy-winning 1992 album *Unplugged*.

With each new release, Cray has demonstrated a willingness to explore further any and all avenues of musical expression. His 1995 release, *Some Rainy Morning*, and 1997's *Sweet Potato Pie*, both on Mercury, suggest as well that he has begun to strike a balance between the blues traditions of the past and the future of the genre as a whole.

—*Joel Nathan Rosen*

SELECT DISCOGRAPHY
■ ALBUMS
Who's Been Talkin', 1980
Showdown! 1985 (with Albert Collins and Johnny Copeland)
Strong Persuader, 1986
I Was Warned, 1992
Some Rainy Morning, 1995

SELECT AWARDS
Grammy Award for Best Traditional Blues Recording for *Showdown!* 1986 (with Albert Collins and Johnny Copeland)
Grammy Award for Best Contemporary Blues Recording for *Strong Persuader*, 1987 (with the Robert Cray Band)
Grammy Award for Best Contemporary Blues Recording for "Don't Be Afraid of the Dark," 1988 (with the Robert Cray Band)

Grammy Award for Best Rock Instrumental Performance for "SRV Shuffle," 1996

SEE ALSO: Clapton, Eric; Hooker, John Lee; King, B. B.; Vaughan, Stevie Ray.

Cream

MEMBERS: Eric Clapton (b. 1945), Jack Bruce (b. 1943), Ginger Baker (b. 1939)
FIRST ALBUM RELEASE: *Fresh Cream*, 1966
MUSICAL STYLES: Rock, blues, psychedelic rock

In spite of its short-lived career as a band, Cream had a major impact on rock in the late 1960's. All the members in the group shared common backgrounds in playing jazz and blues, which would prove to be a driving force behind their blues-inspired songs. With their experimental tendencies, they also made significant contributions to psychedelic rock. Cream, along with Jimi Hendrix and a handful of others, laid the groundwork for the hard rock and heavy metal of the 1970's.

Cream was the original "power trio." The three members were highly regarded musicians in London before uniting as Cream, and together they greatly expanded the roll of the instrumentalist in rock music. Jack Bruce's bass lines were sometimes as rapid and as prominent as Eric Clapton's guitar work, and Ginger Baker's long drum solos set a precedent that would be adopted in concert by such bands as Led Zeppelin and Emerson, Lake, and Palmer. Clapton, however, was the standout, and some fans' appreciation of his guitar playing bordered on worship—"Clapton is God" became a common expression. At the end of Cream songs in concert, Bruce frequently said, "Eric Clapton, please," urging the audience to applaud his soloing. Clapton himself became uncomfortable being a guitar hero and object of extreme adulation. Finally, it should be noted that in Bruce and Clapton, the band had two songwriters and strong singers whose styles complemented each other.

Formation. The three members destined to become Cream were all active on London's jazz and blues scene in the early to mid-1960's. Baker was one of the most respected jazz drummers at that time, and he was a founding member of an influential blues band, the Graham Bond Organisation. Bruce, a classically trained cellist and bassist, also joined the group. After a falling out between him and Baker, he left to play with the Bluesbreakers, another popular London-based blues band. Bruce joined the Bluesbreakers just before their guitarist, Clapton, left to tour on his own. In the brief period they overlapped in the band, a close bond was established between Clapton and Bruce because of the musical interaction that occurred in their jam sessions.

In 1966 Baker wanted to form a new ensemble. In particular he wanted to work with Clapton, who by this time had established himself as one of the finest guitarists in the business. Baker proposed the idea to Clapton that the two form the core of a new band. While Clapton agreed, he also insisted that Jack Bruce join them on bass. This presented somewhat of a problem for Baker, since he and Bruce had been on bad terms for some time. The two reconciled their problems, however, and the group made their first appearance in July, 1966, at the Windsor Jazz and Blues Festival.

The Cream "Personality." Cream's first recorded efforts were two single releases in 1966, "Wrapping Paper" and "I Feel Free." "I Feel Free" had been a collaborative effort with the poet Pete Brown, who was brought in by Ginger Baker to write lyrics for the band. This marked the beginning of a long-standing relationship Brown had with Cream and particularly with Jack Bruce, his main collaborator. Brown's psychedelic lyrics for many Cream songs became a trademark for the group. After the group's breakup, Brown continued to collaborate with Bruce.

From the start, Cream established itself as a band with two identities. One personality of the band was influenced by the members' collective interest in the blues, which resulted in their transformation of traditional blues tunes into hard-driving rock-and-roll songs. The other side came in the band's original material, which, influenced by Brown's lyrics, took on a more free and psychedelic nature. The band maintained this dual per-

Cream in 1966: Eric Clapton, Jack Bruce, Ginger Baker (Popperfoto/Archive Photos)

sonality throughout its existence. Predominantly, band members tended toward their blues side as a live band and toward their psychedelic side in the studio.

In the Studio and on the Road. Cream released their first album, *Fresh Cream*, in December of 1966. Contained on the album are blues standards such as "I'm So Glad," "Rollin' and Tumblin'," and "Spoonful." Original compositions in a more free style include "N.S.U." and "Sweet Wine." The album had respectable sales in the United Kingdom, but the group had yet to be discovered in America.

In 1967 Cream went to New York to record their second album, *Disraeli Gears*, in the Atlantic studios. This album was the key to their estab-

lishing their success both in Britain and in the United States. From this album came many of the group's best efforts, including "Strange Brew," "Tales of Brave Ulysses," "SWLABR" (an acronym for "she was like a bearded rainbow"), and probably their best-known hit, "Sunshine of Your Love." As can be heard in "Sunshine of Your Love," Cream's sound was becoming heavily influenced by Jimi Hendrix. This song contains a driving, repeated bass line (one of the most familiar in all of rock history), maximum distortion on the guitar, and a wailing guitar solo by Clapton. "Sunshine of Your Love" rose to number 5 on the U.S. charts in 1968 and went on to become a standard of hard rock. Even Jimi Hendrix performed it several times in his own concerts.

Cream's next project would prove to be their most ambitious: *Wheels of Fire* (1968), a double-disc album that displayed their talents both in the studio and as a live band. This album, Cream's biggest commercial success, held the number 1 spot on the charts for four weeks in the summer of 1968. Among the singles that helped its sales were "White Room," "Politician," and "Born Under a Bad Sign." This album shows Cream at the height of both their popularity and their creativity.

The group's live work, captured at its best on the live disc of *Wheels of Fire*, is the consummate transformation of the blues idiom into improvisational rock. "Crossroads," a tune originally recorded by blues legend Robert Johnson in 1937 (titled "Crossroad Blues" by Johnson), was one of their most successful transformations. Cream's version of this song is at a much faster tempo than Johnson's original, which gives it the solid drive needed for its conversion into rock. Their performance is most certainly influenced by Hendrix in its distortion and free improvisation sections. The song's unique contribution to blues rock lies particularly in Clapton's soulful vocals and the strident rhythm put together by Bruce and Baker.

Goodbye. As *Wheels of Fire* hit its peak of popularity, rumors began to surface of internal strife among the members of Cream. The troubles between Bruce and Baker, which had initially been resolved, had resurfaced and resulted in tension among the three. Their troubles, it seems, had come to an unbearable point during the recording sessions for *Wheels of Fire*, and when they continued into their live shows, the situation proved to be the demise of the group.

Once the group had announced that they would disband at the end of their scheduled tour, two final concerts were scheduled in London's Royal Albert Hall to give fans one last chance to hear the famed live jam sessions for which the band had become so well-known. Cream also made it back into the recording studio to compile their last efforts. The result was their final album, *Goodbye*. This album compiled some previously released material and three new songs, one written by each member of the group, to commemo-rate the end. For *Goodbye*, Clapton produced "Badge," written with Beatle George Harrison, another song that was still being played on rock radio stations thirty years later. (The title, which has nothing to do with the song's lyrics, came from Clapton's misreading of Harrison's scrawled note, "bridge," at the top of the page on which he had written the chords for the song's middle section.) Baker wrote the aptly titled "What a Bringdown," and Bruce collaborated with Brown on "Doin' That Scrapyard Thing."

After Cream's breakup, Jack Bruce embarked on a solo career, keeping Pete Brown as lyricist. Bruce's first two releases, *Songs for a Tailor* (1969) and *Harmony Row* (1971), were quirky amalgams of folk and art rock and were too esoteric to be commercially successful. Bruce also performed with former members of Mountain (itself a band that owed a great debt to Cream) in the trio West, Bruce, and Laing in the early 1970's. He has also played jazz.

Clapton and Baker regrouped, joined by Steve Winwood (formerly of Traffic) and bassist Rick Grech, as Blind Faith. Blind Faith was the first band to be touted as a "supergroup." It put out one album (*Blind Faith*, 1969), which included "Can't Find My Way Home" and "Presence of the Lord," did one tour, and disbanded. Afterward, Baker released *Ginger Baker's Air Force* (1970), then became interested in African music, and occasionally put out more jazz-oriented material into the

For the Record

As Cream continued to tour, Clapton and Bruce added to their supply of amplifiers and speakers, striving to be louder. Ginger Baker once recalled: "There was, in fact, one gig where Eric and I stopped playing for two choruses. Jack didn't even know. Standing in front of his triple stack of Marshalls [amplifiers], he was making so much noise that he couldn't tell if we were playing or not."

1990's. Clapton went on to his own hugely successful solo career, releasing his first albums, *Eric Clapton* and *Layla and Other Assorted Love Songs*, in 1970. In 1993 Cream reunited for the first time in over twenty years to play at their induction into the Rock and Roll Hall of Fame.   —*Andrew Cook*

SELECT DISCOGRAPHY

■ ALBUMS
Fresh Cream, 1966
Disraeli Gears, 1967
Wheels of Fire, 1968
Goodbye, 1969
Live Cream, 1970
Live Cream, Vol. 2, 1972
The Best of Cream Live, 1975
Strange Brew: The Very Best of Cream, 1983
The Very Best of Cream, 1995

SELECT AWARDS
Rock and Roll Hall of Fame, inducted 1993

SEE ALSO: Clapton, Eric; Hendrix, Jimi; Johnson, Robert; Yardbirds, The.

Creedence Clearwater Revival / John Fogerty

Creedence Clearwater Revival
ORIGINAL MEMBERS: John Fogerty (b. 1945), Thomas Fogerty (b. 1941-1990), Stuart Cook (b. 1945), Douglas Clifford (b. 1945)
FIRST ALBUM RELEASE: *Creedence Clearwater Revival*, 1968

John Fogerty
BORN: Berkeley, California; May 24, 1945
FIRST ALBUM RELEASE: *The Blue Ridge Rangers*, 1973
MUSICAL STYLES: Rock and roll, country rock, pop

Creedence Clearwater Revival was an unusual band in its place and time. It was composed of four San Francisco Bay-area Californians playing songs that sounded as though they had been written in Louisiana. The band was also out of step with much rock music of the late 1960's: Whereas many bands were experimenting with psychedelic sounds and long solos and playing songs that went on for ten minutes or more, Creedence emphasized traditional song structure. Leader and songwriter John Fogerty became a master at writing three-minute songs that told a story or evoked a mood. In this sense, although Creedence Clearwater Revival sold huge numbers of albums, they could be considered a "singles band." Fogerty is also a powerful, intense singer, which adds urgency both to his work with Creedence and to his later solo work. Finally, his driving but often understated guitar work, drawing on country, rockabilly, and rock and roll, perfectly suits his material. Fogerty's songs represent a piece of American culture that will influence musicians for generations to come.

The Beginnings. In 1959 John Fogerty, who was only fourteen at the time, formed a mostly instrumental group with two of his schoolmates, Doug Clifford and Stuart Cook. They named themselves the Blue Velvets. They played at school functions, and even managed to make one recording on the tiny Orchestra label. In 1964 John's older brother, Tom Fogerty, joined the group. The group had changed their name several times and had managed to acquire a following in the region. They finally signed a contract with Fantasy Records, where a company executive renamed them the Golliwogs. Their few releases were not successful, and Fantasy dropped their contract. Then, in 1968, a former employee of Fantasy Records named Saul Zaentz bought the company and invited the Golliwogs back to try again. The band was still searching for a unique sound, and in 1967 the name was changed once again, this time to Creedence Clearwater Revival. Their first modest hit was a remake of Dale Hawkins's "Suzie Q," from their first album, *Creedence Clearwater Revival* (1968), but their real success came in 1969 with Fogerty's composition "Proud Mary," from the *Bayou Country* album. This huge hit propelled them forward (*Bayou Country* netted the band its first platinum record), and they continued with more than a dozen hit recordings composed by Fogerty.

Success. From their first hit single in 1968 until the band's breakup in 1972, Creedence

Creedence Clearwater Revival: Doug Clifford, Tom Fogerty, John Fogerty, Stu Cook (Archive Photos)

Clearwater Revival experienced huge successes in the music industry. In only four years they released six studio albums and were acclaimed by many in the industry to embody the quintessential characteristics of rock and roll. Their songs were innovative and earthy, combining the best of rock and roll and country. Without the aid of gimmicks or complicated studio productions, the band became known for rock and roll that was alive and straight from the soul. Amazingly, they released three hit albums in one year alone: *Bayou Country, Green River*, and *Willy and the Poorboys* all came out in 1969. The band played at the Woodstock festival that same year.

In addition to their albums, they had eight gold singles, including "Proud Mary"/"Born on the Bayou," "Bad Moon Rising"/"Lodi," "Green River"/"Commotion," "Down on the Corner"/"Fortunate Son," "Travelin' Band"/"Who'll Stop the Rain," "Up Around the Bend"/"Run Through the Jungle," "Lookin' out My Back Door"/"Long as I Can See the Light," and "Have You Ever Seen the Rain"/"Hey Tonight."

The Breakup. Since the beginning, there had been some dissatisfaction among the others in the band about John Fogerty's domination of the group. Besides writing all the original music for the band, John Fogerty was lead singer, lead guitarist, producer, and arranger of nearly everything Creedence Clearwater Revival released. After the success of their first album, other band members began to express an interest in writing, arranging, and singing. Fogerty, exuberant over the success of their first album after ten years of

For the Record

Creedence Clearwater Revival had two songs that made *Rolling Stone*'s list of the 100 best singles from 1968 to 1988: "Proud Mary," rated number 52, and "Who'll Stop the Rain," number 59. An odder statistic is the fact that in 1969 and 1970 they had five number 2 hit singles but never managed to capture the number 1 chart position.

§

Though Creedence Clearwater Revival was closely associated with the Louisiana bayou and the southern sound that they helped popularize, all four band members were from California.

struggling, refused to accept the contributions of the other band members. His philosophy—that what they had done on the first album worked, so they should stay with it—convinced the other members to go along with him. They allowed him to remain the driving force behind the band. However, this early rift between the members over controlling the material to be produced never completely healed, and it eventually led to the breakup of the band.

In 1971, after much wrangling between the members about being allowed more artistic freedom, Tom Fogerty left the band. The remaining members continued to tour and record for about another eighteen months. For the last studio album, *Mardi Gras*, Fogerty finally allowed Clifford and Cook to contribute songs and vocals, and the album was not nearly as successful (artistically or financially) as the previous ones. By July of 1972 Creedence Clearwater Revival had officially disbanded.

John Fogerty Solo. After four years of nearly nonstop writing, arranging, and performing, Fogerty seemed to drop from sight for a time after Creedence Clearwater Revival's breakup in 1972. He released an album in 1973 under a fictitious band name, *The Blue Ridge Rangers*, on which he

sang and played every instrument. "Jambalaya (on the Bayou)," a Hank Williams song, was a single from this album. Fogerty's excellent yet unsuccessful solo album *John Fogerty* came out in 1975. Fogerty essentially retired for the next many years, then released *Centerfield*, containing "The Old Man down the Road" and "Rock and Roll Girls," in 1985. The album was well received, going to number 1, but legal problems arose.

There were already bitter feelings between Fogerty and Saul Zaentz, the head of Fantasy Records; for one thing, Fogerty had had to relinquish some of the royalties to his Creedence songs in order to buy his way out of his contract in the early 1970's. On *Centerfield*'s "Zanz Kan't Danz," he sang, "Zanz can't dance/ But he'll steal your money/ Watch him or he'll rob you blind." Zaentz sued for libel and slander, and he added a charge of self-plagiarism, claiming that the album's "Old Man down the Road" was stolen from Creedence Clearwater Revival music—and that therefore Fogerty owed him money.

After years of legal problems and the breakup of his first marriage in 1987, Fogerty seemed to be at an all-time low. He had started working on a new album but was having great difficulties with it. He needed a change. Fogerty made one change in July of that year when, for the first time in years, he performed some Creedence Clearwater Revival songs at a concert for Vietnam War veterans. He had long refused to play any Creedence songs because of their connection with Zaentz. In 1988 the Zaentz suit was finally resolved in Fogerty's favor. Finally, with his legal problems settled, and having remarried, Fogerty began making what he called "pilgrimages" to the South to try to get back in touch with the man who in the past had written so many successful songs in a style nicknamed "bayou rock."

Fogerty released *Blue Moon Swamp* in 1997, to much acclaim. He had spent five years on the album, and the sound was reminiscent of the Fogerty that audiences had come to love with Creedence Clearwater Revival. Fogerty went on tour, and fans eagerly went to see him perform his new material as well as Creedence classics.

—*Lula Mae Martin*

SEE ALSO: Grateful Dead, The; Springsteen, Bruce.

The Crickets. *See* Buddy Holly / The Crickets

Jim Croce

BORN: Philadelphia, Pennsylvania; January 10, 1943
DIED: Natchitoches, Louisiana; September 20, 1973
FIRST ALBUM RELEASE: *Croce,* 1969
MUSICAL STYLES: Folk, pop, country rock

Born and raised in Philadelphia, Pennsylvania, Jim Croce was exposed to a wide variety of music and learned to play accordion as a child. He did not become intensely involved in music until his days as a college student at Villanova University, where he ran a radio program and began to put together his own bands, playing an eclectic mixture of American traditional and popular music. During his junior year, one of these bands was selected by the U.S. government to do a goodwill tour of the Balkans, the Middle East, and Africa. Also at this time, he became friends with classmate Tommy West, who also continued in music and later was able to help Croce at several points in his career.

Detours. After graduating, Croce returned to Philadelphia and worked as a salesman and producer of advertising jingles at a rhythm-and-blues radio station. After that, he worked at various manual labor jobs, and enlisted in the National Guard. He continued to play guitar and sing. In 1966 he married Ingrid Jacobson. That summer, he and Ingrid taught guitar and ceramics, respectively, at a children's camp in Pine Grove, Pennsylvania. In 1967, Croce found another teaching position at Pulasky Junior High in Chester, Pennsylvania, where he experimented with using music as a learning tool in special education classes.

Croce then accompanied his wife to Mexico so that she could study traditional pottery techniques. This was followed by a period of musical activity centered in New York City. The folk music revival of the 1960's had given rise to performance opportunities in Greenwich Village coffeehouses and on college campuses nationwide. Ingrid Croce often joined her husband on stage. Their recording, *Croce* (later released as *Jim & Ingrid Croce*) on Capitol Records in 1969 was not financially successful, however, and they returned to Pennsylvania to live on a farm. During this period, Jim worked as a truck driver, and the couple's child Adrian James (A. J.) was born on September 28, 1971. When work was unavailable, Croce sold some of his guitars to pay the bills.

Success. Undaunted by earlier setbacks, Croce continued his musical efforts as time permitted, and he eventually sent a tape of his songs to Tommy West, the former classmate who had originally encouraged him to come to New York City. With West's help, connections were made, and in the fall of 1971, Croce and guitarist Maury Muehleisen recorded the album *You Don't Mess Around with Jim* at the Hit Factory in New York. The title song from this record became Croce's first hit single, and "Operator," another of its tracks, was almost equally successful. A very busy schedule of tours, recording sessions, interviews, and television appearances ensued.

Just as he was reaching the pinnacle of professional success, his life ended. On September 20, 1973, only two months after "Bad, Bad Leroy Brown" became the number 1 record on the U.S. sales charts, he was killed in a plane crash, along with his guitarist Maury Muehleisen and four others. He had just performed at Northwestern State University in Louisiana and was on his way to another concert when his plane hit a tree.

Style. Several critics have pointed out that Jim Croce infused his music with characters who were inspired by actual people he had encountered in the course of his various occupations and adventures. The most popular examples of this are "Bad, Bad Leroy Brown," based on a man Croce met in Fort Dix, New Jersey, and Croce's first hit single, "You Don't Mess Around with Jim," based on Croce's experiences in poolhalls. Familiar urban scenes and environments appeared as backdrops, as in another hit single, "Workin' at the Car Wash Blues."

These often playful "character sketches" contrasted with Croce's wistful, innocent-sounding love songs, which often used softer textures. His lyrics were very direct: He tended to avoid obscure words, and even his use of slang was generally restricted to common expressions. His colorful, earthy phrases, such as "meaner than a junkyard dog," were easily remembered. His most popular songs avoided the generation-gap issues and social messages of the 1960's, and in some ways they were more reminiscent of earlier periods.

Musically, Croce's work stayed well within mainstream popular styles and American folk traditions, but these were integrated and blended in a very natural way that revealed his deep familiarity with all styles. Acoustic guitar was prominent in most of his songs, with Muehleisen's harmonized lines often weaving around Croce's arpeggios. His vocal tone was a bit nasal, but pleasant and relaxed-sounding, with its conversational tone complementing the narrative elements in his lyrics.

In addition to his own performances, many of Croce's songs have become "standards," recorded and rerecorded by other famous musicians, including three tribute albums (recorded by the Ventures, Jerry Reed, and one recorded by a group of artists), and individual covers by Bobby Vinton, Frank Sinatra, Charlie Daniels, Andy Williams, Melanie, Garth Brooks, Roger Whitaker, Crystal Gayle, and many others.

Posthumous Recognition. Ironically, much of Croce's music was released posthumously. Two of his songs were included in films. "I Got a Name" was featured in *The Last American Hero* (1973). Its energetic chorus, with the repeating phrase "rollin' me down the highway," could have referred to Croce's days as a truck driver. Particularly poignant was the delicate, waltz-flavored "Time in a Bottle," which was written for a television film, *She Lives* (1973), featuring Desi Arnaz, Jr. The film's plot centered on a woman's death from cancer. This song became the number 1 record in the United States just two months after Croce's death, and it was followed in popularity by "I Got a Name," which reached number 2 on the charts.

Jim Croce (AP/Wide World Photos)

For the Record

Jim Croce was a serious guitarist. He once broke his finger with a sledgehammer at a construction job, but he adjusted his technique and continued playing. Croce listened carefully to instrumentalists in styles ranging from blues and country to classical guitar. He and his partner Maury Muehleisen often exchanged melodic passages, and he accompanied Muehleisen on Muehleisen's *Gingerbread* album.

On May 30, 1990, Jim Croce was posthumously inducted into the Nashville Songwriters Hall of Fame. To many listeners, the lyrics to "Time in a Bottle," with its references to the quick passage of time, became even more meaningful in the context of Croce's own untimely death. —*Alice Myers*

SELECT DISCOGRAPHY

■ SINGLES
"Operator (That's Not the Way It Feels)," 1972
"You Don't Mess Around with Jim," 1972
"Bad, Bad Leroy Brown," 1973
"I Got a Name," 1973
"Time in a Bottle," 1973
"I'll Have to Say I Love You in a Song," 1974
"Workin' at the Car Wash Blues," 1974

■ ALBUMS
Croce, 1969
You Don't Mess Around with Jim, 1972
Life and Times, 1973
The Faces I've Been, 1975
His Greatest Hits, 1977
His Greatest Songs, 1980

SELECT AWARDS
American Music Award for Favorite Pop/Rock Artist, Male, 1974
Nashville Songwriters Hall of Fame, inducted 1990

SEE ALSO: Brooks, Garth; Daniels, Charlie; Gayle, Crystal; Sinatra, Frank.

Crosby, Stills, Nash, and Young

MEMBERS: David Crosby (b. David Van Cortland, 1941), Stephen Stills (b. 1945), Graham Nash (b. 1942), Neil Young (b. 1945)
FIRST ALBUM RELEASE: *Crosby, Stills, & Nash*, 1969
MUSICAL STYLES: Rock and roll, folk rock

Renowned for the remarkably precise harmonies they crafted in the studio, Crosby, Stills, Nash, and Young often had trouble harmonizing well on stage or getting along with one another in private. In truth, the four were less a group than an ephemeral collection of volatile artistic temperaments. Yet during their brief time in the sun from 1969 to 1971 they and their music encapsulated a moment in history when, during the Nixon presidency and the ongoing Vietnam War, a generation raised on the idealism of John Kennedy was facing disillusionment and escaping into self-absorption.

The Beginnings. Crosby, Stills, and Nash may have first sung together in Los Angeles in the summer of 1968 at the home of Joni Mitchell or John Sebastian, although perhaps it occurred at Stills's house in Laurel Canyon. Because each had been a member of other respected bands (David Crosby of the Byrds, Stephen Stills of Buffalo Springfield, and Graham Nash of the Hollies), critics referred to them as one of the first "supergroups" (the short-lived Blind Faith was another) even before they had released a record. Once they were freed from their contractual obligations to other record companies, they signed with Atlantic Records in January, 1969, and in June released *Crosby, Stills, & Nash*.

Their first album, famed for its impressive harmony singing, acoustic instrumentation, and engaging lyrics, sold two million copies in its first year, rose to number 6 on the *Billboard* charts, and made the group an immediate sensation. They then asked Neil Young, with whom Stills had worked (and squabbled) in Buffalo Springfield, to join to help Stills with the musical accompaniments and to add more variety to the vocals and songwriting. At the Woodstock festival in August, Crosby, Stills, Nash, and Young sang together live

Crosby, Stills, and Nash in 1977: Stephen Stills, David Crosby, Graham Nash (Andrew Sacks/New York Times Co./Archive Photos)

for only the second time, sounding somewhat ragged and out of tune, and in December they preceded the Rolling Stones at the infamous Altamont festival, at which an audience member was murdered by a member of Hells Angels.

In May, 1970, Crosby, Stills, Nash, and Young (CSNY) released one of the most eagerly anticipated albums since the Beatles' *Abbey Road. Déjà vu* charted at number 1 after only a week, a payoff for the reported eight hundred hours the band had spent in the studio recording it. A few days later, National Guardsmen fired on students protesting the Vietnam War at Kent State University in Ohio, killing four. The incident enraged Neil Young, among millions of others. In one evening he wrote the acerbic "Ohio." Emblematic of the artistic differences among the members of Crosby, Stills, Nash, and Young—and of the centrifugal forces beginning to pull them apart—in August, Nash's naïvely upbeat "Teach Your Children"

from *Déjà vu* was ranked sixteenth in singles sales, and Young's "Ohio" was seventeenth.

The Albums. Difficult as it is to believe that a song beginning "It's getting to the point where I'm no fun anymore" could have sold well in an era when hedonism was practically a sacrament, Stills's "Suite: Judy Blue Eyes," from *Crosby, Stills, & Nash* rose to number 21 on the charts. The song was actually four short song fragments full of appealing poetry, catchy alliteration ("Lacy lilting lady, losing love lamenting"), and shifting moods. Unlike its gloomy opening stanzas, its cadenza was an unforgettably joyous outburst—probably to the relief of Stills's girlfriend, singer Judy Collins, for whom the song was written. Later in the album Stills returned to the theme of heartache in the cleverly written "Helplessly Hoping." Crosby's despairing "Long Time Gone," a memoriam to Robert Kennedy, helped balance Stills's introspective romanticism with political concerns, but it maintained the album's air of self-indulgent melancholy. Nash's popular "Marrakesh Express" added some uptempo sunshine. Crosby's "Wooden Ships" (also recorded by the Jefferson Airplane on *Volunteers*) was a postnuclear-war survival fantasy.

Déjà vu was better balanced and less morose than the first album. If Steven Stills' gravity gave *Crosby, Stills, & Nash* its personality, then Neil Young's ardor gave *Déjà vu* its soul. Young's electric guitar and impassioned singing contributed a tone color and gutsiness to this album that the monochromatic and largely bloodless first album lacked. Additionally, the distinctive character of each member of the group stood out in sharper relief: Crosby's "Almost Cut My Hair" was a defiant counterculture anthem, Stills's "4 + 20" was a dark, self-pitying dirge, Nash's "Our House" a snapshot of cheerful hippie domesticity, and Young's "Country Girl" a poetically elusive waltz.

On the first album Stills had overdubbed all the bass parts, but on *Déjà vu* there was a full-fledged rhythm section, Dallas Taylor on drums and Greg Reeves on bass. Also contributing to the album's success were Jerry Garcia of the Grateful Dead on steel guitar and John Sebastian, formerly of the Lovin' Spoonful, on harmonica. Moreover, the album's cover, with its ersatz leather texture and sepia-tone photograph of the group depicted as Wild West outlaws, was among the most recognizable of the period.

The Breakup. By the summer of 1970, some in the music press were hailing CSNY as the successors to the Beatles, just then dissolving. However, their tremendous popularity could not erase the fault lines running through their ranks. At the height of their commercial success and after only two years together, they were splitting apart. In September, Young's third album under his own name, *After the Gold Rush*, appeared (see separate entry on Neil Young). In December, not long after being arrested for drug possession, Stills put out a solo album (*Stephen Stills*) that contained the hit "Love the One You're With." In May, 1971, Crosby, also drug dependent, recorded an album with the sadly appropriate title *If I Could Only Remember My Name*. In July, Nash delivered his own solo album,

Songs for Beginners. Also in July, Atlantic released the group's two-record live album, *Four Way Street*, which was first on the charts thanks to two million advance orders. The album highlighted the members' solo numbers. To the consternation of their fans, by the time *Four Way Street* was in stores, the members of CSNY had ended their collaboration.

Two years later CSNY tried to reunite to cut a new album but could not get along. Somehow they managed to tour together a year later, and in September, 1974, they played before eighty thousand fans at Wembley Stadium in England. They reassembled in January, 1975, but Nash and Crosby clashed during a recording session over a single note of harmony, and Young stalked off in frustration. Not until August, 1977, did they (minus Neil Young) put together an album of new material, *CSN*. They performed in 1979 at the Musicians United for Safe Energy (MUSE) No Nukes concert. *Daylight Again* was released in 1982; its best cut, "Wasted Along the Way," said volumes about the fate of the group that some had thought would become the American Beatles.

The Fall of David Crosby. The greatest waste was David Crosby. In March, 1982, police arrested him for drug possession and carrying a concealed weapon. Out on bail, he was arrested again for the same offenses. In August, 1983, he slept through most of the trial that ended with his being sentenced to five years in prison. Let off with compulsory drug rehabilitation, he bolted from a treatment center in March, 1985. Jailed again, he jumped bail and landed in jail in Florida. In 1986 he was finally imprisoned in Texas, a confinement

For the Record

Comedian Robin Williams once observed that if you can remember the 1960's you were not really there. By this standard, Crosby, Stills, and Nash were quintessential 1960's musicians. None of the original members of the group can remember exactly when or where they first sang together.

that his friends believe spared him from imminent self-destruction. Crosby continued to dodge bullets. Although finally free of narcotics, in November, 1990, he wrecked his motorcycle and was seriously injured. Worse still, alcohol and drug abuse had broken his health. It took a liver transplant to save his life in 1994.

Legacy. Except for occasional numbers such as "Ohio," CSNY represented a cooling-off phase, a thermidorean reaction to the intense rock revolution of the late 1960's. Some critics despised them for it. Although CSNY themselves would wince at the label, they were among the pioneers of "soft rock," the model for groups such as America, Bread, and, later, Fleetwood Mac in the 1970's. Their tight harmonies and "California country" sound (appropriated from the Byrds and Buffalo Springfield) also influenced Poco and led directly to the sound of the Eagles and Linda Ronstadt's 1970's albums.

After the group's breakup, Stills released two albums with his band Manassas. In addition to everyone's solo albums, various permutations of CSNY put out albums and toured, notably Crosby and Nash as a duo. Stills and Young even put out an album together in 1976. As noted previously, CSNY occasionally performed together and released new albums, although usually without Neil Young. Whereas early in their career the group had enormous difficulties duplicating the high, clean harmonies produced by numerous studio takes, in later years they developed into remarkably polished concert performers. Especially in the 1980's and 1990's, the appreciative crowds of middle-age fans who attended their concerts could not help noticing that CSNY were grayer and heavier but were obviously having fun again.

—*David Allen Duncan*

SELECT DISCOGRAPHY
■ ALBUMS
Crosby, Stills, and Nash
Crosby, Stills, & Nash, 1969
CSN, 1977
Daylight Again, 1982
Allies, 1983
Live It Up, 1990

Crosby, Stills, and Nash, 1991 (four-CD compilation with remixes and alternate versions)
After the Storm, 1994
Crosby, Stills, Nash, and Young
Déjà vu, 1970
Four Way Street, 1971
American Dream, 1988

SELECT AWARDS
Grammy Award for Best New Artist, 1970
National Academy of Songwriters Lifetime Achievement Award, 1994
Rock and Roll Hall of Fame, inducted 1997

SEE ALSO: America; Buffalo Springfield; Byrds, The; Eagles, The; Fleetwood Mac; Hollies, The; Neil Young.

Sheryl Crow

BORN: Kennett, Missouri; February 11, 1962
FIRST ALBUM RELEASE: *Tuesday Night Music Club*, 1993
MUSICAL STYLES: Rock, country rock, pop, folk

Sheryl Crow was born in 1962 in a small Missouri town as the third of four children. Crow, her two older sisters, and her younger brother received most of their musical training at home, where their mother, Bernice, taught each of them to play the piano beginning when they were five or six years old. Bernice Crow also played piano in swing bands on the weekends, along with her husband, Wendell, who played the trumpet when he was not practicing law. Crow has described her parents' home as one with a "freewheeling artistic climate," filled with live music, books, and many guests coming and going.

Crow, whose vocal style has been compared to Bonnie Raitt's and whose gritty lyrics are reminiscent of Alanis Morrisette's, formally continued her musical education by earning a degree in classical piano and voice from the University of Missouri in 1984. Upon graduation, she became engaged to a fellow member of the college band in which she played. They moved to St. Louis,

Sheryl Crow (Ken Settle)

move to Los Angeles in 1986, so that she could try to make a full-time living as a musician.

Breaking In. Once in Los Angeles, Crow made the rounds of studios, leaving audition tapes she had recorded on her own, but she was unsuccessful in attracting the attention of record producers. In later interviews, Crow attributed her struggle in part to the difficulty potential producers had in classifying her style of music. The 1980's, she asserts, were friendly to female pop musicians such as Madonna and Cyndi Lauper, but her lower-pitched voice and bluesy lyrics did not fit into that category and record producers did not believe her records would sell.

In order to make ends meet, Crow spent several years as a backup singer, but even those jobs were initially difficult to obtain. Finally, in 1987, Crow attended—uninvited—a closed audition to sing with Michael Jackson's "Bad" tour. She won the job, which lasted eighteen months, and found the experience simultaneously valuable and frustrating. She later sang backup for Don Henley, Foreigner, Sinéad O'Connor, and others and wrote songs that were eventually recorded by Eric Clapton and Wynonna Judd. Following advice from Henley, she then took time off to concentrate solely on her own music, but several months of self-induced isolation led to a period of severe depression, which ultimately required therapy treatment and antidepressant medication. Although Crow conquered the chronic depression, she would continue to experience anxiety and insecurity due to the pressures of performing.

Tuesday Night Music Club. In 1992, Crow was invited by record producer Bill Bottrell to participate in a weekly Tuesday night songwriting group. This seemed to provide the needed spark for Crow's enthusiasm and creativity, and led directly to the production of her first album in 1993, *Tuesday Night Music Club*, which was aptly named after the songwriting group. The album contained the single "All I Wanna Do," which rapidly climbed the charts and which Crow was invited to perform in front of 400,000 people at the Woodstock '94 music festival. The album won three Grammy Awards and has sold more than eight million copies. Crow's father, Wendell Crow,

where Crow worked as an elementary school music teacher and formed a new band in her spare time. A producer who ran an advertising studio out of his home saw Crow perform and signed her to sing for a McDonald's commercial. The advertisement, originally intended only for regional distribution, was distributed to the national market, earning Crow $42,000 for an hour's work, as compared to her $17,000 annual teaching salary. Around this time, Crow broke off her engagement, in part because her fiance, a devout Christian, insisted that she only sing religious songs. The broken engagement and her financial success from the commercial provided Crow with the incentive she needed to quit her teaching job and

For the Record

The lyrics of Sheryl Crow's hit "All I Wanna Do" had an unusual source. In 1987 a literature professor named Wyn Cooper published five hundred copies of a small collection of poetry. Crow's producer later came across a copy of the book and brought it to her attention. Crow incorporated many lines of a poem entitled "Fun" into her song, which eventually earned at least $50,000 in royalties for Cooper, as well as an opportunity to meet the musician who helped make him famous.

§

"Some of the best shows I've given . . . have been when I've been tired or my personal life has been getting me down. You bring it all out and people connect with whatever that energy is."   —*Sheryl Crow*

played trumpet on one of the album's songs.

Crow's second album, the self-titled *Sheryl Crow*, did not appear until 1996, in part because Crow spent two and a half years touring to promote her first album. Her second effort, which contains the singles "If It Makes You Happy" and "Every Day Is a Winding Road," was well received by critics and the public, and garnered two more Grammy Awards. Crow describes the album as a "trailer-park sounding record," with "swamp rhythms and Voodoo vibes of the South," and claims that her main inspiration was folk-pop singer Bobbie Gentry.

Sheryl Crow, however, was the subject of much controversy when it was banned by Walmart, the largest retail chain in the United States, shortly after its release. One of its songs, "Love Is a Good Thing," contains the lyrics: "Watch out sister, watch out brother, watch our children as they kill each other, with a gun they bought at Walmart discount stores." Walmart executives requested that these lines be deleted from or changed on every copy of the album. When Crow refused, the chain banned the album from their stores, and opinions differed as to whether the incident hurt Crow's sales or helped them by focusing the media's attention on the album.

Overnight Success. Although Sheryl Crow has often been called an overnight success due to her rapid rise in popularity in the 1990's, her success came about only after a decade of disappointing rejections and frustrating jobs singing other people's music. However, Crow, along with other young female musicians such as Alanis Morrisette and Tori Amos, was able to persevere until the music industry and the public were ready to make room for a new style of music, and she, along with these women, has made a valuable contribution to the rock music tradition.   —*Amy Sisson*

SELECT DISCOGRAPHY

■ ALBUMS
Tuesday Night Music Club, 1993
Sheryl Crow, 1996
The Globe Sessions, 1998

SELECT AWARDS
Grammy Award for Best New Artist, 1994
Grammy Awards for Record of the Year and Best Female Pop Vocal Performance for "All I Wanna Do"; for Best New Artist, all 1994
Grammy Awards for Best Rock Album for *Sheryl Crow* and Best Female Rock Vocal Performance for "If It Makes You Happy," 1996

SEE ALSO: Colvin, Shawn; Jones, Rickie Lee; Mitchell, Joni; Morissette, Alanis; Raitt, Bonnie.

The Crusaders

ORIGINAL MEMBERS: Nesbert "Stix" Hooper (b. 1938), Joe Sample (b. 1939), Wayne Henderson (b. 1939), Wilton Felder (b. 1940), Hubert Laws (b. 1939), Henry Wilson
OTHER MEMBERS: Max Bennett (b. 1928), Larry Carlton (b. 1948), Leon "Ndugu" Chancler (b. 1952), Robert "Pops" Popwell, Billy Rogers (d. 1987)
FIRST ALBUM RELEASE: *Freedom Sound*, 1961
MUSICAL STYLES: Jazz, jazz rock

The Crusaders originated in Houston, Texas, in 1953 through the leadership of drummer Stix Hooper, who, at age fifteen, joined forces with three of his fellow schoolmates—pianist Joe Sample, trombonist Wayne Henderson, and tenor saxophonist and electric bassist Wilton Felder—to form the Swingsters. Vernon Chambers's one-hour jazz radio program introduced the group to major East and West Coast jazz artists. The ensemble remained intact while its members attended Wheatley High School and Texas Southern University. Other early members were reed player Hubert Laws and bassist Henry Wilson. Acknowledged influences were Frank Butler for Hooper, Phineas Newborn and Oscar Peterson for Sample, J. J. Johnson for Henderson, and John Coltrane and Oliver Nelson for Felder.

As the Modern Jazz Sextet, the group established itself in Los Angeles in 1958. Though they had not yet recorded and were experiencing hard times, they did perform at Hollywood nightspots as part of Howard Lucraft's Jazz International project. The group played at the Sirocco and the Tailspin during a period when the jazz scene in Los Angeles was declining and rock and roll was becoming more popular. As the Nite Hawks, which included singer Micki Lynn, the group achieved some success playing rock and roll.

The Jazz Crusaders. In 1961, renamed the Jazz Crusaders—the new appellation contributed by Hooper's wife, Ramona—the group worked at the New Frontier in Los Angeles. The Jazz Crusaders were among the few California groups to develop a national reputation. Their first recording from the early 1960's was *Freedom Sound* (1961) for Dick Bock's Pacific Jazz label, the title composition written by Joe Sample. The album received a four-and-a-half-stars rating in *Down Beat*. During the period of 1961 to 1969, more than twenty albums were released under the name Jazz Crusaders. In 1962, their single "The Young Rabbits" was widely received. Another of their early recordings included a jazz-funk treatment of composer Johannes Brahms's piece known as "Lullaby."

Felder began playing electric bass with the group in 1968, and, one year later, the group took a one-year sabbatical followed by a 1970 name change to simply the Crusaders; certain critics thought this was done for commercial purposes. However, during this transitional period for jazz as a whole, in which the jazz designation suggested certain stylistic expectations, the members wanted to broaden their audience appeal by playing jazz-rock. This name change resulted in a wider presentation of the group on radio stations.

The Crusaders' Sound. The group's early sound was a blend of Texas country blues, gospel, rhythm and blues, funk, and contemporary jazz. The Crusaders were influenced by hard bop as well as by such blues artists as Bobby "Blue" Bland, B. B. King, and Lightnin' Hopkins, whom they heard on the local black radio station in Houston, Texas. The Crusaders' musical development paralleled the changes in lifestyles from the 1960's onward. Although the actual term funk became popular in the mid-1970's, the group had been associated with the style from the mid-1950's. Their unique sound was identified by Sample as Gulf Coast jazz, neither as laid back as the West Coast sound nor as slick as the East Coast style, but rather an aggressive and full-bodied sound, a swinging Texas funk. The group was known for their unison front line of tenor and trombone, and, in certain respects, the group's sound was a challenge to the jazz establishment because of its rhythm-and-blues elements. The Crusaders' overall musical intention was to make the audience feel good rather than to project individual virtuosity. Their sound was used as the background music for the television program *Wide World of*

For the Record

In the June 17, 1976, *Down Beat*, Stix Hooper commented, "A lot of people said we changed just to make our music commercial. No. What we really did was become more natural with ourselves. When we took 'Jazz' off our name, we took the shackles off of what was hanging us up."

Sports as well as other locally and nationally broadcasted programs.

Popular Success. After the name change in 1970, the signing with Chisa records, and the addition of guitarist Larry Carlton in 1971, the Crusaders' five successive albums made the Top 40 on the pop charts and reached number 1 on the soul and jazz charts. Although they had toured nationally by 1973, they had not secured an engagement in a New York club. Furthermore, the group's commercial success led to criticism by commentators who accused them of using a superficial, repetitious, formula approach. Also during this period, certain group members had become involved in separate ventures; Hooper played with George Shearing, and Wayne Henderson produced with South African trumpeter Hugh Masekela. Because of the opportunities for studio work in California, Felder, Sample, and Hooper developed that area of their careers in the 1970's. With other ensembles, the four original group stalwarts were part of some two hundred albums that achieved gold status, making the members among the world's most successful session musicians.

For the Crusaders, the decade of the 1970's was a productive period marked by numerous Grammy Award nominations, beginning with the 1972 nomination of *Crusaders I* (1971), a Blue Thumb release, for Best R&B Instrumental Performance. In 1973, *The 2nd Crusade* received the Best R&B Instrumental Performance nomination as did *Scratch* the following year. *Crusaders I* featured a Felder original, "That's How I Feel," which was a hit in its own right. As they rose in the charts, the Crusaders underwent further transitions involving the inclusion of Sample's electric piano as well as the continued use of electric guitar and electric bass, the latter played by Max Bennett and Robert Popwell, respectively, additions to the group in the mid-1970's. *Chain Reaction* (1975) was ranked number 26 on the pop charts. One of the group's most important changes occurred in 1975, when Henderson, who had been active as a record producer, departed the organization. By 1976, the group had made some thirty recordings, including *Those Southern*

Knights (1976), which displayed their electric sound. Having survived the critical attack by jazz purists, the Crusaders were a clear popular success. *Free as the Wind* (1977) sold among the best jazz albums and was given a five-stars rating by *Down Beat* magazine. Guitarist Billy Rogers joined the group in the late 1970's. The Crusaders' major commercial recording of this era was the album *Street Life* (1979).

Hooper's departure from the group in 1983 signaled the most dramatic transition, inasmuch as he had been the group's leader since its inception. With the addition of Ndugu (Leon Chancler) on drums, the group, whose remaining original members were now only Felder and Sample, continued to perform through the 1980's. The ultimate disbanding occurred in the late 1980's, though in the mid-1990's there was a reunion of the Crusaders in a seven-piece group that included Felder and Henderson. —*Joseph McLaren*

SELECT DISCOGRAPHY
■ ALBUMS
Freedom Sound, 1961
Lookin' Ahead, 1962
At the Lighthouse, 1962
Tough Talk, 1963
Chile con Soul, 1965
The Festival Album, 1966
Lighthouse, 1969
Crusaders I, 1971
The 2nd Crusade, 1973
Unsung Heroes, 1973
Scratch, 1974
Southern Comfort, 1974
Those Southern Knights, 1976
Free as the Wind, 1977
Images, 1978
Street Life, 1979
Standing Tall, 1981
Live in Japan, 1981
Royal Jam, 1982
Ghetto Blaster, 1984
The Good and Bad Times, 1986
Healing the Wounds, 1991

SEE ALSO: Bland, Bobby "Blue"; Brubeck, Dave; King, B. B.

Culture Club / Boy George

Culture Club

ORIGINAL MEMBERS: Boy George (b. 1961), Jon Moss (b. 1957), Michael Craig (b. 1960), Roy Hay (b. 1961)

FIRST ALBUM RELEASE: *Kissing to Be Clever*, 1982

Boy George
(George O'Dowd)

BORN: Eltham, Kent, England; June 14, 1961

FIRST ALBUM RELEASE: *Sold*, 1987

MUSICAL STYLE: Pop

Culture Club was one of the most popular musical groups of the early 1980's and brought international fame to singer Boy George. The group was part of the new pop movement in the United Kingdom, along with other popular performers such as Adam Ant and Duran Duran. Culture Club's best-selling blend of soft ballads and dance music influenced the style of pop music in the 1980's and 1990's. After the group broke up, Boy George began a successful solo career.

Before Culture Club. During the late 1970's and early 1980's, a new style of fashion and music appeared in the nightclubs of London. In sharp contrast to the simple, often ragged clothing and loud, harsh music associated with the punk-rock movement, the "new romantics" preferred elaborate, colorful costumes and upbeat dance music.

Boy George was born George O'Dowd on June 14, 1961. He was a familiar figure in London nightclubs before he began his musical career. His flamboyant hairstyles, makeup, and clothing led him to be frequently photographed by publications that reported on the new romantic movement. He caught the attention of Malcolm McLaren, who had previously brought together the members of the pioneering punk-rock group the Sex Pistols.

McLaren arranged for George to perform with the group Bow Wow Wow under the name Lieutenant Lush. George quickly left this position to appear with bass player Michael Craig in the group Sex Gang Children. George and Craig then formed the group In Praise of Lemmings. After adding Jon Moss on drums and Roy Hay on guitar and keyboards, the group was renamed Culture Club in 1981.

Fame and Fortune. Jon Moss was the most experienced musician in Culture Club, having already served as the drummer for artists Bow Wow Wow, London, the Damned, and Adam Ant. His knowledge of the music business helped Culture Club obtain a contract with Virgin Records in 1982. That year, Culture Club released its first two singles, "White Boy" and "I'm Afraid of Me." Neither song was a hit. The group's first album, *Kissing to Be Clever*, released later the same year, was much more successful.

The first hit from *Kissing to Be Clever* was "Do You Really Want to Hurt Me?" This soft, slow ballad emphasized George's rich vocals and Culture Club's ability to create memorable melodies. The song reached number 1 in the United Kingdom and number 2 in the United States. Culture Club followed up this international success with "Time (Clock of the Heart)," another soft love song from the same album. This song reached number 3 in the United Kingdom and number 2 in the United States. Although slightly less popular than these two ballads, the more upbeat dance tune "I'll Tumble 4 Ya" also reached the Top 10 in both countries.

Culture Club's second album, *Colour by Numbers*, released the next year, was even more successful. "Church of the Poison Mind" featured powerful vocals by George and guest singer Helen Terry and reached number 2 in the United Kingdom. The group's biggest hit, "Karma Chameleon," reached number 1 in the United Kingdom and the United States and sold more than one million copies. Other songs from the album which reached the Top 10 were "Victims," "It's a Miracle," and "Miss Me Blind." *Colour by Numbers* was the best-selling album of 1983 in the United Kingdom and was the second best-selling album in the United States.

During the early 1980's Boy George was the subject of a great deal of media attention. His colorful, androgynous appearance led to rumors about his sexuality. George frequently made provocative remarks to the press, as when he jokingly referred to himself as a "drag queen" when he accepted Culture Club's Grammy Award for Best New Artist in 1983.

Decline and Fall. None of the later albums released by Culture Club had as much success as the first two. The single "The War Song" from *Waking Up to the House on Fire* (1984) reached number 2 in the United Kingdom but was widely criticized for its simplistic political lyrics. The group's only other Top-10 hit was "Move Away" from the album *From Luxury to Heartache* (1986).

By this time media attention had turned to rumors of drug abuse within the group. In 1986, not long after referring to himself as "your favorite junkie," it was revealed that Boy George was addicted to heroin. Michael Rudetski, a visiting American keyboard player, died of a heroin over-dose while staying in George's London home. George was arrested for possession of marijuana and began treatment for his addiction. In early 1987 George announced that he had been cured. By this time Culture Club no longer existed.

Solo Career. Despite his drug problems and the demise of Culture Club, George quickly began to rebuild his career. In 1987 he had a number 1 hit in the United Kingdom with "Everything I Own," a remake of a song by the group Bread. After two solo albums for Virgin Records, he formed his own record company, More Protein Records, in 1989. He recorded an album for this company in 1991 as part of the group Jesus Loves You. In 1992 film director Neil Jordan chose Boy George to record a remake of the 1965 Dave Berry song "The Crying Game" for the film of the same name. The

Culture Club, 1982 (AP/Wide World Photos)

For the Record

Few debut albums have produced as many hit songs as Culture Club's first album, *Kissing to Be Clever* (1982). The album had three Top-10 hits, "I'll Tumble 4 Ya," "Do You Really Want to Hurt Me?" and "Time (Clock of the Heart)." Theirs was the first debut album to produce so many Top-10 hits since the Beatles' first album.

success of the film made the song a hit in 1993 and brought media attention back to George.

In 1995 he released *Cheapness and Beauty*, an album which marked a departure from his previous musical style. The album gave a more important role to the guitar player than previous albums and included punk rock influences. The lyrics dealt more openly with homosexuality than earlier, more ambiguous songs. The year 1995 also saw the publication of George's autobiography, *Take It Like a Man*, which discussed his homosexuality and drug addiction.

During the 1990's George also served as a disc jockey in British nightclubs, produced songs for other artists, wrote a newspaper column, and hosted a weekly radio show. Although he was no longer a superstar, he promised to remain an important voice in pop music well into the twenty-first century.

—*Rose Secrest*

SELECT DISCOGRAPHY
Culture Club
■ ALBUMS
Kissing to Be Clever, 1982
Colour by Numbers, 1983
Waking Up to the House on Fire, 1984
From Luxury to Heartache, 1986
Boy George
■ SINGLES
"The Crying Game," 1993
■ ALBUMS
Sold, 1987
Tense Nervous Headache, 1988

The Martyr Mantras, 1991 (with Jesus Loves You)
Cheapness and Beauty, 1995

SELECT AWARDS
Grammy Award for Best New Artist, 1983

SEE ALSO: Duran Duran; Michael, George / Wham!.

The Cure

ORIGINAL MEMBERS: Michael Dempsey (b. 1958), Robert Smith (b. 1959), Laurence "Lol" Tolhurst (b. 1959)
OTHER MEMBERS: Andy Anderson (b. 1951), Perry Bamonte (b. 1960), Jason Cooper (b. 1967), Simon Gallup (b. 1960), Matthieu Hartley (b. 1960), Roger O'Donnell, Porl Thompson (b. 1957), Phil Thornally (b. 1960), Boris Williams (b. 1957)
FIRST ALBUM RELEASE: *Three Imaginary Boys*, 1979
MUSICAL STYLES: Pop, rock and roll, alternative, grunge

The British rock band the Cure has achieved a degree of success and much credibility without much notoriety. Robert Smith, a founding member, lead guitarist, and singer, has been the main influence on the Cure since its inception. He has been the songwriter and the only permanent member in the band's ever revolving lineup of members.

Style. The Cure's music has been labeled gothic, trendy, and pure rock and roll. They have released songs that can be fit into certain genres, but as the band has grown, so has their ability to creatively try new music. The Cure has always been an experimental band, ruled by the intense Smith, who has provided interesting melodies for his lyrics and vocals. Especially in his early years, he tended to write very dark, depressing songs, but many times the songs were made more accessible after being reworked by the band. More than two decades after the band was first formed, they would continue to gather a following of loyal fans. As one critic has said about them, they have been "the biggest cult band in the world."

The Easycure. Robert Smith began playing guitar at age six, and by the time he was eighteen he had formed the Easycure with some school friends from Crawley, England. Lol Tolhurst played the drums, with Michael Dempsey on bass. Chris Parry, the founder of Fiction Records, noticed the Easycure and released their first single in 1979. The single, "Killing an Arab," was a notable success. Smith had been inspired to write the song after reading Albert Camus's 1942 novel *The Stranger.* "Killing an Arab" is an unusual song, especially for the early postpunk era, in that it uses a strong rhythmic beat covered by light, twangy guitars in minor chords. Smith's wavering, unsure vocals were perfect for the lyrics, "Standing on the beach with a gun in my hand/ staring at the sea, staring at the sand/ Staring down the barrel at the Arab on the ground." The meaning of this song has long been misconstrued, but it is by no means a racial epithet. Not all of the songs on their first album, *Three Imaginary Boys* (1979), were quite so intelligent, but all exhibited a strong melody and interesting lyrics.

The Cure, as they were then called, received a lucky break soon after their album release, earning the chance to open for the well-known Siouxie and the Banshees on their summer tour in 1980. This turned into a beneficial relationship for both bands. Siouxie's backup guitarist left the group early in the tour, so Smith played with both bands every night. In the fall, the Cure released an extended-play single. "Boys Don't Cry," the title song, is an early example of the pop music that Smith is capable of writing.

The Gloomy Period. After the Cure's initial success with their first album, they seemed fated to fade to the bottom of the charts. While their commercial success dwindled with their next three albums, their cult status skyrocketed. *Seventeen Seconds* (1980), *Faith* (1981), and *Pornography* (1982) were descending steps into dark, introspective music. One critic has described these albums as claustrophobic; Smith's music was clearly a reflection of the depression he was going through at the time. It was during this period that the band members started to come and go. Dempsey was the first to leave, but he was replaced

> ## For the Record
>
> Robert Smith hates to fly and will only do so on occasions when there is no other option. Since the tour for *Disintegration*, in 1989, the Cure has taken the Queen Elizabeth 2 ocean liner to get to the United States and will usually travel only by train or bus.

by a longtime friend of Smith's, Simon Gallup. The group also added a keyboardist in the early 1980's. This lineup did not last long, though, and other members also came and went.

Most songs from these albums can be described as having minimal arrangements, distorted guitars, unenthusiastic vocals, and depressing lyrics. Only "Charlotte Sometimes," from *Faith*, is unique, being more of a ballad. The band was extremely productive during this time; they released a new album every year for the better part of a decade. Smith simultaneously played with the Cure and Siouxie and the Banshees while working on independent projects.

End of the Gloom. The Cure's gloomy period ended with the extended-play single *Japanese Whispers* (1983), which showcased the single "Let's Go to Bed," an almost lighthearted ditty. "Love Cats," another single, is a completely carefree song, and it hit number 7 on the British charts. *Japanese Whispers* and their next full album, *The Top* (1984), paved the way for the wonderful turnaround that came with their following albums.

The Head on the Door, released in 1985, established the sound for which the Cure would become best known. One of the most popular Cure songs, "Close to Me," was the first single from this album. *The Head on the Door* was followed by the singles compilation album *Standing on a Beach: The Singles*. This album was cited by *Rolling Stone* magazine as one of the top albums of all time. It is a great introduction to early Cure music that saves the listener from having to trudge through some of their more bleak work.

Successful and Happy. The album *Kiss Me, Kiss Me, Kiss Me* (1987) ushered in the modern era of the Cure. Their music no longer wallowed in dark self-examination, although it did not lose that element entirely. They added a more self-assured, humoresque aspect that widened their fan base and made them a big draw at concert venues. The *Kiss Me* album spawned such recognizable hits as "Why Can't I Be You" and "Just Like Heaven," which reached the Top 20 in the United States. "Just Like Heaven" showcases Smith's romantic songwriting at its best. It features a catchy pop beat layered with instruments, supported by Smith's pleading voice singing about an intense relationship. All of the songs on *Kiss Me* are not easygoing, however; there is also the interminable "The Snakepit," which shows the Cure at their most dismal. Overall, its diversity makes *Kiss Me, Kiss Me, Kiss Me* a great album.

The Cure returned very strong in 1989 with the release of *Disintegration* . They found their largest American following with this album, selling out arenas on their U.S. tour. With *Disintegration*, the Cure reached the U.S. Top 10 with the wonderful ode "Lovesong," a glowing tribute to Smith's new wife, Mary. "Fascination Street" is a song that mimics the Cure's early gloom, but touches it up with a quick melody pleasing to both devoted fans and new listeners. "Lullaby," another single from the album, reveals the same take on paranoia that is found on their earlier songs "Hot, Hot, Hot" and "The Forest." *Disintegration* reveals the Cure in their prime, with the perfect mixture of talent and tension intoned in the album to give it a diverse personality.

The Cure made their next appearance in 1992 with the more balanced *Wish*. It reached number 1 on the U.K. charts and number 2 in the United States. The Cure's sense of humor has never been more evident than on the 1992 single "Friday I'm in Love." Of writing this song, Smith said that it was much harder to write a carefree pop song than the more serious material for which he is known. Many critics labeled *Wish* the group's best album. It is very approachable, but it does not push the musical limits of the band.

Different Path. They took an extensive break after touring for *Wish*, releasing only live material and playing in festivals for the next few years. Their next album of new material, *Wild Mood*

The Cure in 1989: Robert Smith, Boris Williams, Roger O'Donnell, Porl Thompson, Simon Gallup (AP/Wide World Photos)

Swings (1996), was similar sounding to *Wish* in terms of its carefree nature, but it paid more attention to different styles of music: Some songs on this album could alienate a longtime Cure fan. If it were not for the steel drums and quirky guitar harmony on the single "Strange Attraction," it could pass for a pop song from the 1970's. "Club America" is a digression into heavy metal, with screeching guitars and Smith singing in the lowest octave of which he is capable.

In 1998 the Cure released *Galore*, the follow-up singles compilation album to *Standing on a Beach*. The single release, "Wrong Number," is a return to the dark fun of "Let's Go to Bed" and "Why Can't I Be You." —*K. L. A. Hyatt*

SELECT DISCOGRAPHY
■ ALBUMS
Three Imaginary Boys, 1979
Boys Don't Cry, 1980 (EP)
Seventeen Seconds, 1980
Faith, 1981
Pornography, 1982
Japanese Whispers, 1983 (EP)
The Top, 1984
Concert, 1984
The Head on the Door, 1985
Standing on a Beach: The Singles, 1986 (compact disc release titled *Staring at the Sea*)
Kiss Me, Kiss Me, Kiss Me, 1987
Disintegration, 1989
Entreat, 1990
Mixed-Up, 1990
Wish, 1992
Paris, 1993
Show, 1993
Wild Mood Swings, 1996
Galore, 1997

SEE ALSO: Depeche Mode; Radiohead; Smashing Pumpkins; Smiths, The / Morrissey.

Cypress Hill

ORIGINAL MEMBERS: B-Real (b. Louis Freese, 1970), Sen Dog (b. Senen Reyes, 1965), DJ Muggs (b. Lawrence Muggerud, 1968)
OTHER MEMBER: Bobo
FIRST ALBUM RELEASE: *Cypress Hill*, 1991
MUSICAL STYLES: Rap, hip-hop

Cypress Hill became the first Latino hip-hop superstars, notorious as much for their controversial politics as for their music. Their rolling bass-and-drum loops were at the heart of a new musical sound—termed "stoned funk"—which widely influenced hip-hop music in the 1990's.

Beginnings. Formed in southeastern Los Angeles in 1986 as DVX, this group became one of the pioneers of Latin rap and urban culture, employing a streetwise combination of English and Spanish in their songs. DJ Muggs was a New York native of Italian American background, B-Real was a Californian of Mexican Cuban descent, and Sen Dog a native Cuban. When Sen Dog's brother, Mellow Man Ace, left DVX for a solo career in 1988, the group became Cypress Hill, named for a street in their neighborhood. Mixing bass-heavy rhythms with samples incorporating sirens and other street noises, the group became notorious for their open support of the legalization of marijuana. Their songs contain frequent references to marijuana and guns.

Early versions of "Real Estate," "Light Another," and "How I Could Just Kill a Man" led to a record deal with Philadelphia's RuffHouse label in 1990. Their platinum, self-titled debut album (1991) was on the charts for eighty-eight weeks, in part because of controversial songs such as "How I Could Just Kill a Man" (number 77) and "Hand on the Pump." It became a landmark hip-hop album of the early 1990's, reflecting an urban culture bathed in marijuana funk. Cypress Hill became official spokesmen for the National Organization to Reform Marijuana Laws (NORML).

Successful Second Album. By 1993, Muggs had refined his production techniques, producing and remixing material for House of Pain, Funkdoobiest, and the Beastie Boys. Cypress Hill's follow-up, *Black Sunday*, revealed this new mastery, debuting at number 1 on both the pop and rhythm-and-blues charts in the summer of 1993 and going double platinum. *Black Sunday* included their first Top-20 single, "Insane in the

Brain" (number 19). Cypress Hill continued to elicit controversy later that year when Muggs smoked a joint of marijuana on television's *Saturday Night Live* before performing "Insane in the Brain" and then trashed their equipment.

After performing on the Lollapalooza tours of 1992, 1994, and 1995 and collaborating with Pearl Jam and Sonic Youth on the *Judgment Night* film sound track (1993), Cypress Hill developed a huge crossover audience. *Cypress Hill III: Temples of Boom* (1995) was their third consecutive platinum album and featured rappers U-God and the RZA. In 1996 they released a critically acclaimed nine-song extended-play single, *Unreleased & Revamped*, which included creative mixes not previously available.

Outside Projects. After the "Smokin' Grooves" tour of 1996, group members took time to work on a variety of solo projects. Muggs recorded *Muggs Presents . . . The Soul Assassins* (1997), recruiting Wu-Tang Clan, KRS-One, Dr. Dre, Mobb Deep, and others to rap over some of his best and most innovative grooves. B-Real worked with Busta Rhymes, Coolio, L. L. Cool J, Dr. Dre, Nas, KRS-One, and Latino rappers Duke and Jacken on various album tracks. —*John Powell*

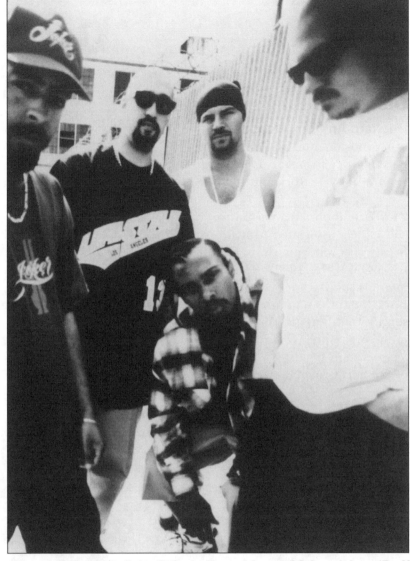

Cypress Hill, 1997: Bobo, B-Real, Shag, Muggs, DJ Scandalous (Ruff House/Columbia/Annalisa)

SELECT DISCOGRAPHY
■ SINGLES
Unreleased & Revamped, 1996 (extended-play single)
■ ALBUMS
Cypress Hill, 1991
Black Sunday, 1993
Cypress Hill III: Temples of Boom, 1995
IV, 1998

SEE ALSO: Coolio; Dr. Dre.

For the Record

Cypress Hill appeared in the 1993 film *Meteor Man.*

D

Dick Dale

(Richard Anthony Monsour)

BORN: Boston, Massachusetts; May 4, 1937
FIRST SINGLE RELEASE: "Ooh-Whee-Marie," 1958
MUSICAL STYLE: Rock and roll

Dick Dale founded a persuasive style of rock and roll closely associated with the surfing scene in Southern California during the late 1950's and throughout the 1960's. His style of surf instrumentals should not be confused with the Beach Boys' peppy songs on surfing themes. Dale's sound was always less refined and placed a premium on his precise and volcanic guitar solos. For a generation of surfers, Dick Dale was the "King of the Surf Guitar."

Eclectic Training. Dale's life as a musician began at age nine. He was classically trained on piano. He also studied a variety of classical and traditional instruments including trumpet, trombone, harmonica, and accordion. His family's roots in Eastern Europe and the Middle East led to an early interest in the folk music of those regions. Later in life, he would record blistering versions of a Greek folk song, "Misirlou," and a traditional Middle Eastern tune, "Hava Nagila."

In 1954, his family relocated to Southern California. There he adopted his new name and took up surfing as a very serious hobby. A photograph of Dale surfing graced the cover of his debut album. A member of the Surfing Hall of Fame in San Diego, California, Dale used his experiences with surfing in his aggressive, youth-oriented music.

Dick Dale (in the dark suit) and the Del-Tones in 1961 (AP/Wide World Photos)

During the late 1950's, Dale formed an association with Leo Fender of Fender Guitars. Through this association, Dale was given an early model of the now-famous Fender Stratocaster electric guitar. Dale's scintillating solo work on albums of the early 1960's drew considerable interest in the instrument. Dale was also instrumental in popularizing the Fender reverb and the Fender Showman amplifier. Along with the Stratocaster, these implements became stock tools for the electric guitarists of the 1960's.

King of the Surf Guitar. Dale's earliest recordings reveal a county-rock influence; his single "Let's Go Trippin'" (1961) was his first to reveal his surf-guitar style. This style is characterized by extremely fast tempos, rapid double attacks, the use of staccato and reverb, melodies using the harmonic minor scale or related modes with raised seventh scale degrees, and rare use of vocals.

Dale's initial popularity was established among surfers. He performed regularly at the Rendezvous Ballroom in Balboa, California, where crowds grew enormously until finally numbering in the thousands. Recordings on Del-Tone Records (Del-Tones being the name of Dale's backup band) helped to secure a geographically broader audience.

Dale released a series of singles with considerable appeal in the Southern California market. Eventually he released an album, *Surfer's Choice* (1962), which sold eighty-eight thousand copies in California alone. This proved sufficient sales for the album to reach number 60 on the national charts. His popularity, while localized, was massive within his region.

Capitol Years. Dale's growing notoriety in California led to a brief but interesting film career in which he generally played himself in beach-party films. He was a featured attraction in both *Beach Party* (1963) and *Muscle Beach Party* (1964) starring Annette Funicello and Frankie Avalon. Coupled with his recording success, Dale's popularity led to a seven-album deal with Capitol Records. Only five albums were made. After two years, the "British invasion" led to shifting priorities at Capitol and the termination of Dale's contract. During the next decades, Dale continued to entertain

For the Record

Leo Fender of Fender Guitars was amused when he first saw Dick Dale play one of his legendary Stratocasters. Dale, who is left-handed, was playing a right-handed model upside down without having restrung the strings. Throughout his career, Dale has played guitar with the strings in the reverse order of a normal guitar.

with an aggressive schedule of live appearances supported by some recording. A bout with cancer, from which Dale emerged completely cured, curtailed his activities for a time.

The 1994 film *Pulp Fiction* featured two Dale songs, "Misirlou" and "Bustin' Surf Boards." The film's popularity and top-selling sound track have served to introduce Dale to a new audience. Dick Dale surely stands as one of the outstanding and most innovative guitarists in the history of rock and roll. His influence on later rock guitar virtuosos was formidable.

—Michael Lee

SELECT DISCOGRAPHY
■ ALBUMS
Surfer's Choice, 1962
King of the Surf Guitar, 1963
Better Shred than Dead, 1997 (compilation)

SEE ALSO: Ventures, The.

Charlie Daniels

BORN: Wilmington, North Carolina; October 28, 1937
FIRST ALBUM RELEASE: *Charlie Daniels*, 1970
MUSICAL STYLES: Bluegrass, country, country rock, gospel

Charlie Daniels has had a long career in music that began when he was twenty-one years old. Always hard to classify, Daniels began in bluegrass,

Charlie Daniels in 1979 (Paul Natkin)

country-rock band the Charlie Daniels Band, which had two drummers and twin lead guitars and was modeled after the successful southern rock group the Allman Brothers Band. Again, as with his earlier group, Daniels toured constantly, playing between 200 and 250 shows a year. The band's first hit made the Top 10 on both the country and rock charts in 1973. "Uneasy Rider" was a novelty talking-bluegrass song that appealed to the rock audience by using a young hippie as narrator.

The mid-1970's saw Daniels and his band feature a southern rock style, with a minor hit in 1974, "The South's Gonna Do It Again," advising southerners to "be proud you're a rebel." Daniels also played at three fund-raising concerts for President Jimmy Carter's election, his inaugural ball, and at the Grand Ole Opry, apparently leaving behind any connection with rock music.

That changed for a brief time in 1979, when Daniels's smash hit "The Devil Went Down to Georgia" was number 1 on country charts, number 3 on the pop charts, and even in the Top 20 in the United Kingdom. The album it was from, *Million Mile Reflections* (1979), went double platinum. An odd twist on the classic "deal with the devil" story, the song pits a country fiddler's tune against the devil's screeching fiddle melody accompanied by a bass rhythm. The fiddler wins a golden fiddle and saves his soul from the devil's clutches. Daniels used the song's title for a short story collection in 1986, which features narratives based on Daniels's most popular songs.

switched to southern rock in the 1970's, veered into country by the 1980's, and ventured into gospel in the 1990's. Known only for a few hits and a succession of annual Volunteer Jams that have taken place in Nashville since 1974, Daniels has maintained a steady popularity and earned the respect of critics for his crossover hits and fiddle playing.

To the Devil. A member of the little-known bluegrass band the Jaguars for a decade, Daniels stopped playing in bars and accepted a job as session player in Nashville in 1967, playing guitar, fiddle, bass, and banjo on rock, country, and folk albums by such musicians as Ringo Starr, Marty Robbins, and Bob Dylan. He also had a minor songwriting hit in 1964 with "It Hurts Me," a B-side ballad sung by Elvis Presley, and wrote songs for country singers such as Tammy Wynette. While in Nashville, he gained experience as a record producer, producing a number of albums, including four for the group the Youngbloods.

It was not long before Daniels yearned to play live shows again, so in 1971 he started the

Politics and Religion. Daniels continued to be popular among country music listeners in the 1980's. A minor hit, "In America," (1980) was written in response to the 1979 Iranian hostage crisis, and "Still in Saigon" (1982) portrayed the traumas of a Vietnam War veteran. The title song from *Simple Man* (1990) detailed Daniels's anger against drug dealers, rapists, and child abusers. Another song, "America, I Believe in You," (1993) was a patriotic anthem that appeared to be a complete reversal from the satiric intent of "Uneasy Rider," which lampooned political conservatives.

After going solo in 1991, Daniels dabbled briefly in gospel music, recording the album *The Door* (1994) with Christian music songwriter Steven Curtis Chapman. He also released two greatest hits albums, a blues album, and an album featuring his fiddle music.   *—Rose Secrest*

SELECT DISCOGRAPHY

■ ALBUMS

Honey in the Rock, 1974
High Lonesome, 1977
Full Moon, 1980
Homesick Heroes, 1988
America, I Believe in You, 1993

SELECT AWARDS

Grammy Award for Best Country Vocal Performance by a Duo or Group for "The Devil Went Down to Georgia," 1979
Country Music Association Single of the Year for "The Devil Went Down to Georgia" and Instrumental Group of the Year Awards, 1979
Country Music Association Instrumental Group of the Year Award, 1980

SEE ALSO: Allman Brothers Band, The.

For the Record

Charlie Daniels is a superb guitarist and fiddle player, but he was no virtuoso as a child. He taught himself how to play both instruments by ear when he was fifteen.

§

To get the sound just right for the fiddle solo in the smash hit "The Devil Went Down to Georgia," Charlie Daniels overdubbed his fiddle playing seven times.

Mac Davis

BORN: Lubbock, Texas; January 21, 1942
FIRST ALBUM RELEASE: *Song Painter,* 1971
MUSICAL STYLES: Country, country pop, country rock

A true country boy weaned on country-and-western music, Mac Davis was drawn into rock and roll by the emergence of Buddy Holly and Elvis Presley. After beginning his career as a record company representative and songwriter, he found success as a recording artist, concert and nightclub performer, television host, film actor, and Broadway actor. His proudest achievement, however, has been writing songs recorded by himself and hundreds of other artists.

Early Life. Like Buddy Holly, Davis was born and raised in the dusty west Texas town of Lubbock, where the only music he heard outside of his Protestant church was pure country. Although no one in his family played an instrument, he grew up inventing melodies, which he whistled. When he was ten, his father ignored his son's fear of being considered a "sissy" by making him join a church choir. The experience taught Davis that he had a good voice and fostered his love for music.

In the mid-1950's, rock and roll penetrated the countrified airwaves of west Texas radio stations, and Davis's musical world suddenly expanded. In 1955 he saw Holly and Elvis Presley in the same show (an event to which his song "Texas in My Rearview Mirror" alluded twenty-five years later). Adopting Presley's dress and hairstyle, he acquired his first guitar and taught himself to play blues strains. Although Davis became an avid follower of pioneer rock performers such as the Coasters and Holly, Presley remained his primary inspiration, and he dreamed of writing songs for him.

After graduating from high school at only fifteen, Davis left his father's home for Atlanta, Georgia, where his mother was living. There he enrolled in Emory University, only to drop out after two years. (Later he claimed to have "majored in beer and rock and roll.") Meanwhile, he formed his first band, Zots (which took its name from the sound made by the anteater in the comic strip "B.C."), in which played high school and college parties, as well as redneck bars. By imitating black performers and using risque material, his band won a large and rowdy following.

While still in his late teens, Davis began working as a state probation officer. He resumed his education in night classes and occasionally performed with his band in local clubs. Meanwhile, he hung out around recording studios and made contacts in the music industry. In 1962 he became Chicago-based Vee-Jay Records' regional manager in Atlanta. Three years later he switched to Liberty Records to do similar work, but when his new company recognized that his strength lay in creative work, it sent him to manage Metric Music, its publishing subsidiary in Los Angeles.

Though Davis was not performing regularly through these years, he continued to write songs. His first professional sale came when he cornered Sam the Sham of the Pharaohs in a restroom and persuaded him to record "The Phantom Strikes Again." Davis's country-flavored tunes gradually caught on with other performers, including Bobby Goldsboro, Kenny Rogers, and Glen Campbell. His first chart success came in 1967, when Lou Rawls recorded his composition "You're Good for Me."

Eventually, Davis connected with Presley through Billy Strange, who was scoring a Presley motion picture. At Strange's suggestion, Davis wrote some songs for Presley, including "A Little Less Conversation," which Presley put on the charts in 1968. After Presley asked Davis to write more songs for him, Presley returned to the charts with such Davis compositions as "Don't Cry, Daddy," which sold 1,500,000 singles. Even more successful was Davis's gospel composition about

For the Record

Mac Davis prepared the music for Elvis Presley's first television special and two Presley films and wrote five songs for Glen Campbell's film *Norwood* (1970).

growing up black, "In the Ghetto," which returned Presley to the Top 10 in 1969. This song also earned Davis two Grammy Award nominations and became a permanent part of his own repertoire.

Performing Career. With many of his songwriting goals accomplished, Davis left Metric Music to devote himself to songwriting and singing full time. In 1970 he signed a recording contract with Columbia Records, which the following year released his first album, *Song Painter* (its title came from Glen Campbell's description of Davis). That same year two Davis singles made the charts: "Beginning to Feel the Pain" and "I Believe in Music." The latter—one of his biggest hits—was eventually covered by more than fifty other artists. In 1972 Davis's "Baby, Don't Get Hooked on Me" reached number 1 on the pop charts and made the Top 20 on the country charts—aided by publicity generated by angry feminists protesting against its apparently male chauvinist theme (which Davis disavowed as the song's intent). His next two albums, *I Believe in Music* (1972) and *Mac Davis* (1973), also made the pop and country charts. Throughout the 1970's Davis continued to enjoy crossover successes with songs such as "Stop and Smell the Roses" (1974) and "Forever Lovers" (1975).

By this time Davis was appearing regularly on television talk and variety shows and in Las Vegas nightclubs and was performing as many as 250 nights a year. His shows typically covered 1950's rock-and-roll hits, reprised his own current songs, and offered song and dance numbers by his stage troupe, Strutt. His diverse material and engaging personality attracted a cross-section of fans. From mid-1974 through early 1976 he hosted three different television variety shows. These shows earned good ratings but failed to catch on permanently; however, Davis continued to appear in television specials through the late 1970's.

In 1979 Davis made his dramatic acting debut when he costarred with Nick Nolte in *North Dallas Forty*—a film about professional football in which he did no singing. His performance as a tough quarterback was critically well received, and he was offered more film roles than his musical commitments allowed him to accept. However, his Hollywood film career was derailed in 1983 when he costarred with Jackie Gleason in *The Sting II*. This sequel to a hit Paul Newman-Robert Redford film bombed so badly that Davis was left out of Hollywood films until 1997, when he had a featured role as a high school football coach in *Possums*.

Meanwhile, "It's Hard to Be Humble," the ironic title song of Davis's 1980 album, launched a string of four consecutive Top-10 country songs, including his biggest country hit, "Hooked on Music" (1981). After "I Never Made Love (Till I Made Love with You)" made the Top 10 in 1985, he concentrated on performing in Las Vegas.

During the 1990's Davis's career took a new upward turn. He cowrote Dolly Parton's hit song "White Limozeen" in 1990. Two years later he made his Broadway debut in the title role of *The Will Rogers Follies*, in which he replaced actor Keith Carradine. In 1994 he signed a new recording contract with Columbia Nashville and released his first album in almost a decade, *Will Write Songs for Food*. It included ten new compositions, as well as new versions of three of his earlier hits, including "In the Ghetto" and "Texas in My Rearview Mirror."   —*R. Kent Rasmussen*

SELECT DISCOGRAPHY

■ ALBUMS

Song Painter, 1971
Baby Don't Get Hooked on Me, 1972
I Believe in Music, 1972
Mac Davis, 1973
Stop and Smell the Roses, 1974
All the Love in the World, 1975
It's Hard to Be Humble, 1980
Texas in My Rear View Mirror, 1980
Till I Made It with You, 1985
Will Write Songs for Food, 1994
I Sing the Hits, 1995

SELECT AWARDS

Academy of Country Music Entertainer of the Year, 1974
Georgia Music Hall of Fame, inducted 1996

SEE ALSO: Brown, James; Campbell, Glen; Coasters, The; Holly, Buddy; Parton, Dolly; Presley, Elvis; Rawls, Lou; Rogers, Kenny.

Miles Davis

BORN: Alton, Illinois; May 26, 1926
DIED: Santa Monica, California; September 28, 1991
FIRST ALBUM RELEASE: *Birth of the Cool*, 1950
MUSICAL STYLES: Jazz, blues

Miles Davis is recognized as one of the most innovative and influential musicians in the history of jazz. As a trumpet player, he was loved by audiences all over the world, especially in Europe, the United States, Canada, the Middle East, South America, and Asia. During his more than forty years in the front ranks of this American art form he collaborated with some of the greatest names in the genre, including Billy Eckstine, Charlie "Bird" Parker, Dizzy Gillespie, Sonny Rollins, Thelonious Monk, Art Blakey, John Coltrane, Cannonball Adderley, Wayne Shorter, and Herbie Hancock.

What Is Jazz? A display at the New Orleans Jazz Museum contains these words: "It is difficult to give a definition of jazz. Those offered are as varied and numerous as those who have played or listened to it." While there is no definitive definition of jazz, it is clear that West African rhythms, European harmonic structures, and American folk melodies are principal components of this musical form. Although the rural South and American ghettos have served as prime incubators for the development of this music, and despite the association of many African Americans with this eclectic art form, jazz is not "race" music. Musicians from many ethnic groups have been involved in the creation and promulgation of jazz.

While jazz is similar to many other forms of music, it is unusual in its use of improvisation, rhythm, and syncopation. Playing in a style known as free improvisation, jazz artists might, for example, depart from the standard approach to invent a new melodic line, or artists might freely compose lines only related to the sounds played by the other musicians. Rhythmically, the jazz artist might play slightly ahead of or behind the beat and, regarding syncopation, the jazz musician will often shift the melody in an intricate and natural way so that it does not always align itself with the beat.

The Early Years. The life of poverty and deprivation that characterizes the childhoods of many famed jazz performers was alien to Miles Davis, named after his father, a relatively affluent dentist, and his grandfather, a prosperous landowner. Young Davis loved to swim, box, and play football and baseball. Davis's real love for music began with a radio show, *Harlem Rhythms*, which he listened to when he was seven or eight. The show featured such luminaries as Louis Armstrong, Count Basie, Duke Ellington, and Bessie Smith. As youngsters, Davis and his brother Vernon, along with sister Dorothy, frequently staged talent shows. Davis accompanied his siblings' piano and dancing with his trumpet given to him by an uncle. Soon music became the most important element in the life of young Davis.

Miles Davis (Columbia Legacy/Jan Persson)

In September of 1944, at the age of eighteen, Davis arrived in New York, ostensibly to study music at the renowned Juilliard School of Music. He later admitted that he was more interested in the jazz scene, it being the real reason to come to New York. Initially, Davis spent his days in class at Juilliard but his nights in clubs such as the Three Deuces, the Onyx, Kelly's Stable, the Spotlite, and Minton's, any place where he thought Charlie Parker, Dizzy Gillespie, Coleman Hawkins, or any of the other musical greats might show up. A lively form of jazz, bebop, was very popular in the black clubs of New York City. To his delight, impressionable Davis, always with his trumpet at the ready, often was invited to sit in with his idols at various jam sessions.

After a few exasperating months of dividing his time between Juilliard and the clubs, Davis became increasingly disenchanted with academics, charging that he could learn more about the music of his interest frequenting clubs than he could at school. Furthermore, Juilliard, he felt, did not properly respect the musical accomplishments of black artists, and the instructors' knowledge of black performers was superficial.

The realization that his instructor was unfamiliar with names such as Fletcher Henderson and Duke Ellington was disconcerting to Davis. He stopped paying attention during his classes, spending most of his time thinking about the jam sessions and the various clubs he would be visiting that evening. Soon thereafter Davis left Juilliard, and his musical education in the crowded and frenzied clubs of New York City began in earnest. He never looked back.

The Artistry of Miles Davis. Davis acknowledged that many performers from Billy Eckstine and Nat "King" Cole to Frank Sinatra, owing to their inventive techniques in their singing or playing, exerted a significant influence on his style. Gillespie and Parker, early on, were the most influential. Charlie "Bird" Parker harbored disdain for written music; he merely played a melody of his creation and challenged the talented musicians in his band to remember what he had played. Eschewing Western concepts, Bird was spontaneous, giving every member of his band the freedom to play, adapting to the chords laid down by the leader. Davis was profoundly impressed by Bird's creative genius.

Bebop was at its zenith in New York in the mid-1940's. Gillespie and Parker were the pioneers of this musical craze. Davis, while not at the forefront of the bebop movement, did make a lasting impression on the art form. Experimenting with melody and its accompanying structure, while making liberal use of space, he evolved a method of playing bebop that departed from the more established approach and won a devoted following.

In 1950, Davis explored his emerging concept in a breakthrough album, *Birth of the Cool*. The album grew out of a number of sessions where Davis surrounded himself with a group of skillful musicians who understood his basic concepts. He gave them the freedom to go in various musical directions and then masterfully brought the results together in the end. Always experimenting, Davis in 1959 set out in a new direction. He sought to produce an album that would re-create some of the great gospel sounds he had heard as a youngster visiting his grandfather in Arkansas. *Kind of Blue* was the result. One year later, he used Spanish compositions and folk tunes as the base for his spectacular *Sketches of Spain*.

Davis exhibited a keen sensitivity to the many changes in the world of popular music and, to the dismay of some of his loyal fans, artfully incorporated the changes in his own music. *Bitches Brew* reflects his growing interest in the rock and funk phenomenon of the 1960's. Not only did the album sell more quickly than any work produced by Davis, it outsold all other albums in the history of jazz.

For the Record

On Thanksgiving day in 1981, Miles Davis and acclaimed actress Cicely Tyson were married in the home of Bill Cosby by former ambassador and mayor of Atlanta Andrew Young.

During that same decade, when the musical spotlight had turned to the Beatles, Little Richard, Elvis Presley, and Motown artists, Davis teamed with the incomparable Ron Carter, Tony Williams, Herbie Hancock, and Wayne Shorter to produce an impressive body of works: *E. S. P.* (1965), *Miles Smiles* (1966), *Sorcerer* (1967), *Nefertiti* (1967), *Miles in the Sky* (1968), and *Filles de Kilimanjaro* (1968). Davis explored different styles in the 1970's and 1980's, ranging from jazz-rock to funk and pop. In 1986, after severing ties with Columbia, Davis recorded his first album for his new label, Warner Bros. The album, *Tutu*, was named for Bishop Desmond Tutu, the 1984 Nobel Peace Prize winner. *Tutu* won a Grammy Award for Best Jazz Instrumental Performance.

Legacy. As a personality, Miles Davis was pensive, melancholy, and sometimes explosive. Married and divorced three times, the last to actress Cicely Tyson, he had difficulty trusting people and sustaining relationships. He was often a bitter and outspoken critic of the United States' social and racial practices. Musically, Davis was a trendsetter. Able to sense changing musical tastes and styles, he expertly fused them into his seminal art.

—*James E. Walton*

SELECT DISCOGRAPHY

■ ALBUMS

Birth of the Cool, 1950
Kind of Blue, 1959
Sketches of Spain, 1960
Bitches Brew, 1969
On the Corner, 1972
Tutu, 1986

SELECT AWARDS

Grammy Award for Best Jazz Composition of More than Five Minutes for "Sketches of Spain," 1960 (with Gil Evans)

Grammy Award for Best Jazz Performance, Large Group or Soloist with Large Group, for *Bitches Brew,* 1970

Grammy Award for Best Jazz Instrumental Performance, Big Band, for *Aura,* 1989

Grammy Award for Lifetime Achievement, 1990

Grammy Award for Best R&B Instrumental Performance for *Doo-Bop,* 1992

SEE ALSO: Adderley, Julian "Cannonball"; Benson, George; Coltrane, John; Hancock, Herbie; Mangione, Chuck.

Sammy Davis, Jr.

BORN: Harlem, New York; December 8, 1925
DIED: Beverly Hills, California; May 16, 1990
FIRST ALBUM RELEASE: *Starring Sammy Davis Jr.*, 1954
MUSICAL STYLE: Pop

Though primarily neither a singer, dancer, actor, nor impressionist, Sammy Davis, Jr., managed to tackle all those roles. He was an African American entertainer who recorded number 1 songs, won critical praise on the stage, and became a television and film star. He called himself a "variety artist," but whatever the medium in which he performed, he was known for his energy and unique rapport with his audiences. His exuberance frequently won over even hostile listeners and led to his being warmly embraced by both black and white audiences, thereby paving the way for later African American performers to achieve mainstream success. At the same time, however, his close identification with white artists, his conversion to Judaism, his marriage to the Swedish actress May Britt (1960-1968), and his shift from the Democratic to the Republican Party in the 1970's drew venomous criticism from many sources, but he never lost his ability to appeal to audiences through his exceptionally long career.

Early Life. Davis was born in New York City's largely black Harlem district, the only child of a show business couple who performed in a vaudeville song-and-dance troupe run by an adopted "uncle," Will Mastin. When Davis was two and a half, his parents separated, and his father, Sam Davis, Sr., took him on the road with Mastin's troupe. Davis made his professional debut on the stage at the age of three, when he was dubbed Silent Sam, the Dancing Midget. At seven he starred in a two-reel film, *Rufus Jones for President* (1933), playing a boy who dreams that he becomes president of the United States. As vaude-

ville faded, the twelve-member Mastin troupe shrank until only Davis, his father, and Mastin remained. By the late 1930's Davis's importance in the troupe was such that his own name was featured in its title.

In 1943 Davis went into the U.S. Army, where he encountered severe racial prejudice for the first time. He initially responded to taunts violently, but after being transferred to Special Services to entertain at military bases, he used his talent to convert his enemies to fans. The experience left him with a lifelong drive to make every audience love him.

After World War II Davis returned to the family trio, which struggled to secure nightclub bookings throughout the United States. Already an accomplished singer and dancer, Davis expanded his repertoire with new dance steps, impressions of popular film stars and singers, and musical instruments. Eventually, he mastered the trumpet, drums, piano, and vibraphone and grew even more important as the act's main draw.

Recording Career. While still working with the trio, Davis spent time with singers such as Mel Tormé and Billy Eckstine, through whom he arranged a recording session at Capitol Records. *Metronome* magazine designated one of his first recordings, "The Way You Look Tonight," Record of the Year and named him Most Outstanding New Personality of 1946. Meanwhile, the trio's bookings improved dramatically, and the group

For the Record

Through the second half of his life Sammy Davis wore an artificial eye. He lost his left eye in an automobile accident that occurred when he drove to Los Angeles from a nightclub engagement in Las Vegas on November 19, 1954. In later years, he credited his conversion to Judaism to the time he spent reflecting on his personal faults while recuperating from his accident in a hospital.

did a summer replacement show on television. By 1950, the trio was headlining in top clubs in New York and Hollywood, and Davis was constantly receiving standing ovations from audiences who appreciated the talent and pure energy that he poured into his singing, dancing, drumming, and impersonations. During this period he began his long career as a headliner in Las Vegas, Nevada, where he later became a part owner of a casino.

After the trio had a successful engagement at New York's Copacabana Club, Decca Records signed Davis to a recording contract. His first album, *Starring Sammy Davis Jr.* (1954), contained impressions of entertainers such as Dean Martin, Jerry Lewis, Jimmy Durante, and Bing Crosby; it rose to number 1 on the charts. On his second album, *Just for Lovers* (1955), he sang in his own voice. The wide radio play songs from that album received advanced his reputation as a pop singer in his own right, and a single from that album, "Hey There," made the charts.

Davis's career soon received a boost from an unexpected source. After losing his left eye in an automobile accident in late 1954, he received so much sympathetic publicity that clubs offered him and the Mastin Trio large fees to appear. He returned to performing in early 1955 more popular than ever and made the charts with "Something's Gotta Give," "Love Me or Leave Me," and "That Old Black Magic." The attention he received because of his accident increased his appreciation of the importance of keeping his name in the news, and he became noted for going out of his way to attract attention.

Jule Styne and George Gilbert produced a musical comedy, *Mr. Wonderful*, especially for Davis, who made his debut on Broadway in early 1956. Written by Joseph Stein and Will Glickman, the semibiographical show was about a young African American who overcame racial prejudice to succeed as a nightclub entertainer. Although the show earned tepid reviews, it lasted for 383 performances, thanks largely to Davis's charismatic performance. By this time, he ranked as the first African American performer widely popular among both black and white audiences.

After *Mr. Wonderful* closed in 1957, the Mastin

Sammy Davis, Jr. (AP/Wide World Photos)

Trio slowly dissolved. Nevertheless, Davis continued to share his own performing income with his father and uncle. During the late 1950's and into the 1960's he appeared frequently on television variety and dramatic shows. Meanwhile, he recorded dozens of albums and had several hit singles, including Anthony Newly and Leslie Bricusse's song "Candy Man," which held the number 1 position on the charts for three weeks in 1972 and became his biggest seller ever. Other hits included "Birth of the Blues," "Gonna Build a Mountain," and "Who Can I Turn To?"

Multimedia Star. Davis soon began appearing regularly in films. He scored a popular and critical success as Sportin' Life in the 1959 adaptation of George Gershwin's folk opera *Porgy and Bess*. He matched this screen success in 1963, when he played the Street Singer in Kurt Weill's *The Three Penny Opera*. Meanwhile, he was becoming known as a member of the so-called rat pack, an otherwise all-white, fast-living collection of friends that included singers Frank Sinatra and Dean Martin, comedian Joey Bishop, and actor Peter Lawford.

He appeared with other members of the group in such films as *Ocean's Eleven* (1960), *Sergeants 3* (1962), and *Robin and the Seven Hoods* (1964). In 1966 he produced *A Man Called Adam*, in which he played a bitter jazz musician. Two years later he played one of his strongest roles as the singing and dancing revivalist Big Daddy in *Sweet Charity*.

Meanwhile, Davis returned to Broadway. In 1964 he starred in an updated musical adaptation of Clifford Odets's 1930's play *Golden Boy*, in which he played an African American boxer trying to escape the ghetto. After an exhausting series of preview runs, during which the play's script was constantly revised, Davis expected the play to fail on Broadway. However, it earned strong reviews and ran for 568 performances, from October, 1964, into March, 1966. *Cue* magazine named Davis Entertainer of the Year.

In early 1965 Davis starred in several television specials built around his singing and dancing, then had a short-lived series, *The Sammy Davis Jr. Show* in 1966. The first variety show with a black host since a Nat King Cole show in the 1950's, it was critically well received but failed in the ratings war, matched against the popular sitcoms *Gomer Pyle* and *Hogan's Heroes*. Davis later hosted a syndicated variety show, *Sammy and Company* (1975-1977), made at least sixty guest appearances in both comedy and dramatic television series and soap operas, and occasionally hosted *The Tonight Show Starring Johnny Carson*. In recurrent appearances on television's popular *Rowan and Martin's Laugh-In* in 1969-1970, he contributed to American speech the expression "Here come da judge," which he took from an old vaudeville routine of Pigmeat Markham.

In late 1973 Davis scored a big hit on network television with a one-hour special reprising his show-business career; however, his second regular television variety show, *NBC Follies*, made it only halfway through the 1973-1974 season. After recovering from liver and kidney problems, attributed to heavy smoking and drinking, in early 1974, he returned to the New York stage in a revue titled *Davis on Broadway*. Four years later he starred in a new adaptation of Anthony Newley's musical *Stop the World—I Want to Get Off*.

After health problems slowed Davis down during the late 1970's and 1980's, he made an exhausting comeback tour in 1988, performing throughout Canada and the United States with Frank Sinatra and Dean Martin. The following year he toured Europe with Sinatra and Liza Minelli, but by then his health was nearly broken.

When Davis died in May, 1990, marquee lights on the Las Vegas strip were dimmed for ten minutes in recognition of his contributions to show business. Afterward, a plaza in the city's Lorenzi Park was renamed in his honor.

—*R. Kent Rasmussen*

SELECT DISCOGRAPHY

■ ALBUMS
Starring Sammy Davis Jr., 1954
Just for Lovers, 1955
Sammy Davis, Jr. at Town Hall, 1958
Mr. Entertainment, 1961
The Shelter of Your Arms, 1964
If I Ruled the World, 1965
Hey There! It's Sammy Davis Jr., 1977
Closest of Friends, 1984

SELECT AWARDS
Metronome, named Most Outstanding New Personality, 1946
Cue, named Entertainer of the Year, 1965

SEE ALSO: Cole, Nat "King"; Sinatra, Frank.

De La Soul

ORIGINAL MEMBERS: Posdnous (b. Kelvin Mercer, 1969), Trugoy the Dove (b. David Jude Jolicoeur, 1968), Pasemaster Mase (b. Vincent Mason, 1970)
FIRST ALBUM RELEASE: *3 Feet High and Rising*, 1989
MUSICAL STYLES: Rap, hip-hop

De La Soul formed in the late 1980's and immediately gained attention by developing their own unique brand of rap music. While most hip-hop groups were influenced primarily by "old-school" artists such as Grandmaster Flash and Kurtis Blow or by the newer and angrier sound of Public

Enemy, De La Soul drew inspiration from pop music, jazz, reggae, and psychedelic music. The result was a more laid-back sound with clever, humorous rhymes that seemed to have as much in common with 1960's psychedelia as it did with 1980's urban rap.

Rising. De La Soul (French for "of the soul" or "from the soul") was formed in the late 1980's by three high school friends whose stage names reflected the whimsical style that would characterize their first album: Kelvin Mercer became Posdnous (an inversion of "Sound-Sop," the name he used as a disc jockey), while David Jolicoeur renamed himself Trugoy (a backward version of yogurt, one of his favorite foods) the Dove.

De La Soul's first demo tape led to a contract with Tommy Boy Records in 1988. Their debut album, *3 Feet High and Rising*, was released the following year and immediately caught the attention of critics and the listening public. While De La Soul did not abandon the funk and soul roots of rap music, they did add a diverse collection of other musical influences to the mix, including jazz, reggae, and psychedelic rock. With casual rhymes that preached peace instead of street violence and samples drawn from such unusual sources as a French-lesson cassette and television, the group created a revolutionary sound that many critics believed would lead hip-hop music in a new direction. Indeed, the album prompted the formation of such alternative-rap groups as PM Dawn, Basehead, and Digable Planets. In 1989, a collective of East Coast rap groups calling themselves the "native tongues" school appeared, with De La Soul at their center. Other members of the collective included the Jungle Brothers, A Tribe Called Quest, and Queen Latifah.

Changes. Although the prediction that *3 Feet High and Rising* would cause a widespread revolution in hip-hop music was derailed by the rise of gangsta rap in the 1990's, the album did lead to an unexpected change in the way hip-hop music was composed. The song "Transmitting Live from Mars" contained a sample of the Turtles' 1968 single "You Showed Me," which prompted former members of the Turtles to file a lawsuit against De La Soul. The case was settled out of court, but it

set a precedent that forced future rap bands to obtain permission before they used samples from other songs. Besides changing the way that many groups worked, it also delayed the release of many albums that had already been recorded, including De La Soul's *De La Soul Is Dead*.

De La Soul Is Dead (1991) drew mixed reactions from a public that was expecting more light-hearted music from the band. Many were disappointed to find that the new album had a heavier sound and contained songs about such serious topics as incest and drug abuse. Despite the album's dark tone, however, it was only slightly less popular than its predecessor. De La Soul's third album, 1993's *Buhloone Mind State*, had a more intense sound than either of the previous albums but marked a return to the off-kilter experimentation of their debut. Despite strong reviews, the album did not appeal to an audience that had become interested in the more straightforward urban rhymes of gangsta rap. De La Soul's *Stakes Is High* (1996) was likewise released to critical acclaim but failed to divert attention away from the dominant gangsta sound.   —*Douglas Long*

SELECT DISCOGRAPHY
■ ALBUMS
3 Feet High and Rising, 1989
De La Soul Is Dead, 1991
Buhloone Mind State, 1993
Stakes Is High, 1996

SEE ALSO: Grandmaster Flash; Public Enemy; Queen Latifah; Turtles, The.

For the Record

On their debut album, De La Soul introduced concepts such as the D.A.I.S.Y. Age (Da Inner Sound, Y'all) and Dan Stuckie (a feeling of ease, relief, and ecstasy, as in "Sit back, take a luuden, and everything will be Dan Stuckie"), prompting some critics to refer to the trio as a neohippie band.

The Dead Kennedys

ORIGINAL MEMBERS: Jello Biafra (b. Eric Boucher, ca. 1959), East Bay Ray, Klaus Fluoride, Ted (b. Bruce Slesinger)

OTHER MEMBERS: Darren H. Peligro

FIRST ALBUM RELEASE: *Fresh Fruit for Rotting Vegetables*, 1980

MUSICAL STYLES: punk

Formed in San Francisco in 1978, the Dead Kennedys combined hardcore punk rock and a relentless indictment of right wing politics and organized religion to become one of the most successful West Coast punk bands. Bored with the country rock so prevalent in his hometown of Boulder, Colorado, in the early 1970's, Jello Biafra searched for bands outside the mainstream such as Iggy and the Stooges, MC5, 13th Floor Elevators, and the Nazz. It was a concert by the Ramones that finally convinced him to form his own band.

Fueled by a furious instrumental assault and the quavering vocals of Biafra, the Dead Kennedys' first album, *Fresh Fruit for Rotting Vegetables* (1980), was a smorgasbord of social and political diatribe. Much of the band's best work was on their debut, including "Drug Me," "California Über Alles," "Holiday in Cambodia," and "Kill the Poor." In 1981 the Dead Kennedys formed their own record label, Alternative Tentacles, and began releasing albums by unknown punk artists. The following year they released their second full-length album, *Plastic Surgery Disasters* (1982). One critic described this frenetic album, which included the songs "Terminal Preppie," "Winnebago Warrior," and "Moon over Marin," as "punk at its best, musically and lyrically."

Legal Difficulties. After a long hiatus, the Dead Kennedys released *Frankenchrist* (1985), which be-

The Dead Kennedys' Jello Biafra (Michael Ochs Archive)

For the Record

After attacking state governor Jerry Brown in the vitriolic "California Über Alles," Jello Biafra ran for mayor of San Francisco in 1979. Calling for Market Street businessmen to wear clown suits downtown, he finished fourth out of ten candidates.

came their most controversial album. The music was inferior to their earlier albums, and the band had lost much of its edge in the postpunk landscape, but a poster insert of H. R. Giger's painting *Landscape #XX* caused an uproar. The poster, which featured repetitive rows of genitalia engaged in sex acts, was deemed pornographic and led to a legal suit against the band for distributing pornography to minors. Though the long court case ended in a hung jury and was dismissed, the band broke up in 1987 just after releasing *Give Me Convenience or Give Me Death*, a compilation of their most accessible material.

With the demise of the Dead Kennedys, Biafra continued his political activism in a series of spoken-word albums and college lecture tours. One of his most popular pieces was "Grow More Pot," an argument in favor of the industrial use of hemp. He also continued to run Alternative Tentacles as an outlet for bands who were deemed too risky for the traditional corporate music industry.

—*John Powell*

SELECT DISCOGRAPHY
■ ALBUMS
Fresh Fruit for Rotting Vegetables, 1980
In God We Trust, Inc., 1981 (EP)
Plastic Surgery Disasters, 1982
Frankenchrist, 1985
Bedtime for Democracy, 1986
Give Me Convenience or Give Me Death, 1987
   (previously released material)

SEE ALSO: Black Flag; Ramones, The.

Deep Purple

ORIGINAL MEMBERS: Ritchie Blackmore (b. 1945), Jon Lord (b. 1941), Ian Paice (b. 1948), Rod Evans (b. 1945), Nick Simper (b. 1946)
OTHER MEMBERS: Ian Gillan (b. 1945), Roger Glover (b. 1945), Glen Hughes, David Coverdale (b. 1949), Tommy Bolin (1951-1976)
FIRST ALBUM RELEASE: *Shades of Deep Purple*, 1968
MUSICAL STYLE: Rock and roll

Ritchie Blackmore (guitar), Jon Lord (keyboards), and Ian Paice (drums) were the founding members of Deep Purple, who came together on February 19, 1968. This trio were survivors of a failed attempt to form a band called Roundabout led by former Searchers drummer Chris Curtis. Lord had been a member of the Artwoods, and Paice had played with the Maze, whose lead singer, Rod Evans, soon joined Deep Purple. Nick Semper from Johnny Kidd and the Pirates became the bass player.

Modeling their sound and choice of material after the U.S. group Vanilla Fudge, the band signed contracts in England with Parlephone and in the United States with the short-lived Tetragrammoton Records partially owned by comic Bill Cosby. During May, 1968, in Pye Studios in London, the group recorded *Shades of Deep Purple*, a debut album revealing the band's three strong suits: Lord's classically trained keyboard work, Blackmore's hard-rock guitar, and Evans's deep, bassy vocal delivery. The album's opening instrumental track, "And the Address," showcased the trademark Lord organ sound that would dominate early group albums, as well as Blackmore's distinctive lead lines later described as a precursor to heavy metal.

The group's first single, "Hush," written by American Joe South, was released in the summer of 1968 and quickly became a Top-10 hit. In December, the group issued its experimental follow-up album, *The Book of Taliesyn*. This album also featured a Top-10 single written by an American, "Kentucky Woman," a cover of the Neil Diamond hit. The album featured a long jam version of "River Deep, Mountain High," a hit by Ike and

Tina Turner that other rock artists also covered, including the Animals and Harry Nilsson.

Not yet confident in their compositional skills, the group's first three albums were largely covers of standard hits, featuring medleys of Beatles tunes on each release. While the band was building a fan base for their dramatic performances, critics were often unappreciative. In 1971, Lillian Roxon only devoted two sentences to Deep Purple in her highly personal, widely read *Encyclopedia of Rock*. Still, some material foreshadowed the group's future. One original track on the second album cowritten by Lord and Evans, "Anthem," featured string arrangements by Lord. Lord's interest in merging classical with rock sounds expanded in *Deep Purple* (1969), the last album with Evans and Simper, with strings and woodwinds taking a larger role in the production.

Second Generation. Vocalist Ian Gillan and bassist Roger Glover of Episode Six replaced Semper and Evans who were fired in 1969, and Deep Purple underwent substantial change. This would be the lineup most associated with the group name. They established their own record label in England, Purple Records, and signed with Warner Bros. in the United States. The group's future albums were all original music with all of the group's members sharing writing credits, which would be a source of dissension in later years.

This lineup debuted with Lord's final attempt to mix classical music with rock, 1970's *Concerto for Group and Orchestra*, recorded live with Britain's Royal Philharmonic Orchestra. It became immediately evident that Deep Purple now featured one of the most distinctive singers of the era, a presence with both energy and a vocal range uncommon in rock. Gillan impressed composer Andrew Lloyd Webber and his lyricist partner, Tim Rice, who signed him for the title role in the first recording of the 1970's musical *Jesus Christ Superstar*. This coup gave the group helpful publicity for their next studio effort, *Deep Purple in Rock* (1970). While not a major seller, the record yielded the single "Black Night," which reached number 2 in England.

The group's fortunes rose dramatically with 1971's *Fireball*, from which "Strange Kind of

Woman" was drawn as the next single. It was the next album, however, *Machine Head* (1972), which took the group to its highest level of popularity, with "Highway Star" and "Space Truckin'" becoming audience favorites in live shows. "Smoke on the Water," a narrative based on the group's experiences recording *Machine Head* in December, 1971, at the Grand Hotel in Montreux, Switzerland, became an international smash hit.

In 1972, the two-record live album *Made in Japan* was a major seller as one of the first successful import sales. The next studio offering was *Who Do We Think We Are* in 1973, which continued the heavy trends of the three previous recordings, with "My Woman from Tokyo" becoming the group's last Top-10 single. "Mary Long," a criticism of censorship in England, was the group's most obvious attempt at social commentary, and the song caused minor controversy in Britain.

Third Generation. In 1973, after illness and arguments over songwriting credits, Gillan and Glover left the band. The bass position was filled by Glen Hughes from the band Trapeze. The group then held widely publicized auditions for a lead vocalist, ultimately giving the slot to unknown singer David Coverdale. The new, mellower Deep Purple quickly released two new albums, *Burn* (1974) and *Stormbringer* (1974), but interest in the band had waned. In 1975, Blackmore left to form Ritchie Blackmore's Rainbow, a group clearly imitating the hard-rock sounds of middle-period Deep Purple.

New guitarist Tommy Bolin from the James Gang dominated 1975's *Come Taste the Band*, but Bolin's more soulful, lighter touch on the guitar was not what fans expected or wanted. It seemed clear the fire had finally left the surviving founders of the band, with Lord and Paice contributing little to the album's compositions. In 1976, Deep Purple formally disbanded, a few months before Bolin died of a heroin overdose.

Aftermath. In 1984, the second lineup of Deep Purple reunited for *Perfect Strangers* (1984) and *The House of Blue Light* (1987). Recurring animosity between Gillan and Blackmore led to their intermittent membership in the 1990's. For *Slaves and Masters* (1990), former Rainbow lead singer Joe Lynn Turner was temporary vocalist. In 1994, Joe Satriani filled in for Blackmore. Gillan returned for *The Battle Rages On* (1993) and *Purpendicular* (1996), on which Steve Morse joined Blackmore on guitars. The band again tried to climb the singles chart with 1996's "Don't Hold Your Breath," "Sometimes I Feel Like Screaming" and 1997's "Hey Cisco." While reviewed in *Billboard* magazine, the singles failed to renew the group's previous fortunes.

Some band members had success outside Deep Purple. In 1972, Rod Evans joined with former members of Iron Butterfly and the Johnny Winter Band to form Captain Beyond, an ensemble that had one chart hit, "Thousand Days of Yesterday (Time Since Come and Gone)." David Coverdale formed the highly profitable Whitesnake, and Paice and Lord earned brief critical attention for their team-up with Tony Ashton in the short-lived Paice, Ashton, and Lord. Blackmore's reputation earned him a place as a founding father of heavy metal, particularly influencing guitarist Eddie Van Halen. In 1991 and 1992, anniversary editions of *Deep Purple In Rock*, *Fireball*, and *Machine Head* were issued on compact disc, each album augmented by studio conversations, alternate takes, and singles recorded during the compilation of each album. —*Wesley Britton*

SELECT DISCOGRAPHY
■ ALBUMS
The Book of Taliesyn, 1968
Deep Purple, 1969
Concerto for Group and Orchestra, 1970
Deep Purple in Rock, 1970
Fireball, 1971

Machine Head, 1972
Made in Japan, 1972
Who Do We Think We Are, 1973
Burn, 1974
Stormbringer, 1974
Come Taste the Band, 1975
Perfect Strangers, 1984
The House of Blue Light, 1987
Nobody's Perfect, 1987
Slaves and Masters, 1990
The Battle Rages On, 1993
Come Hell or High Water, 1994
Purpendicular, 1996

SEE ALSO: Led Zeppelin; Van Halen.

Def Leppard

ORIGINAL MEMBERS: Joseph Elliott (b. 1959), Richard Savage (b. 1960), Peter Willis (b. 1960), Stephen Clark (1960-1991), Richard Allen (b. 1963)
OTHER MEMBERS: Philip Collen (b. 1957), Vivian Campbell (b. 1962)
FIRST ALBUM RELEASE: *On Through the Night*, 1980
MUSICAL STYLES: Rock and roll, hard rock, heavy metal

Def Leppard changed the way heavy-metal music sounded. Their songs were melodic, with guitars that were prominent but not shrill. Choruses were memorable and singable, with larger-than-life production. In essence, the group created its own genre—pop metal—which appealed to a broader audience and became the blueprint for countless other metal bands.

In the Beginning. Def Leppard came together in Sheffield, a northern England city best known for its steel. In 1974, three fourteen-year-old Tapton Comprehensive School students formed Atomic Mass. Rick Savage played bass, Pete Willis was the guitarist, and Tony Kenning was the drummer. Willis's acquaintance Joe Elliott became the singer three years later, though he had never sung before. The lineup was completed when Steve Clark joined as second guitarist in 1978.

Elliot changed the name of the band to Deaf Leopard. (The spelling was later amended to Def Leppard.) The quintet rehearsed and wrote songs in an abandoned spoon factory. In November, 1978, Def Leppard released an eponymous extended-play single on the band's own Bludgeon Riffola record label. During that time drummer Kenning was replaced by fifteen-year-old drummer Rick Allen. Extended-play single sales and live performances attracted fans and the media, who embraced the band as forerunners of a movement called the new wave of British heavy metal. Def Leppard signed a worldwide record deal with Phonogram on August 5, 1979.

The Road to Stardom. The band's first album, *On Through the Night*, was released in March, 1980. They toured the United States for the first time and received better reception than in England, a trend that would continue throughout their career.

Def Leppard met their future mentor and producer Robert John "Mutt" Lange during the recording of their second album. Lange changed the way the band wrote and recorded, and he created the sound that would make Def Leppard superstars. He recorded each instrument separately, often taking apart a riff and building it note by note. He would change melodies or speeds and overdub vocals and instruments into a wall of sound.

The birth of MTV was instrumental in boosting sales of *High 'n' Dry*, released in 1981. Because the fledgling music channel had a limited library, a video featuring these young, attractive faces immediately went into heavy rotation.

Times of Crisis. During the recording of *Pyromania*, released in January, 1983, founding member Willis was asked to leave the

band. He was replaced by Phil Collen, a London-born veteran of London-based bands Dumb Blondes and Girl (another band that had been part of the new wave of British heavy metal). The concept videos for *Pyromania* featured choreographed staging, a sense of humor, and many closeups of the band. This, coupled with extensive touring, resulted in album sales of over ten million copies.

Just before the recording of Def Leppard's next album, an automobile accident severed drummer Allen's left arm at the shoulder. While in the hospital, Allen suggested drumming with his left foot and his right hand. Fitted with electronic drum pads, cymbals, and foot pedals, Allen joined the recording of *Hysteria*, which was re-

Def Leppard in 1987: Rick Allen, Rick Savage (front); Steve Clark, Joe Elliott, Phil Collen (rear) (AP/Wide World Photos)

For the Record

Def Leppard drummer Rick Allen's father had to cosign Allen's worldwide record deal because Allen was only fifteen years old. Allen's older brother accompanied the band on early tours both as a road manager and a chaperone.

leased in August, 1987. The record was the pinnacle of the band's career and sold more than fifteen million copies.

On January 8, 1991, guitarist Clark was found dead in his apartment in London. His death was an indirect result of his long-standing battle with alcoholism; he was thirty years old. Clark had contributed approximately 90 percent of Def Leppard's music over the years. His last effort would be six songs that appear on *Adrenalize*. The album was recorded as a four-piece band and released in March, 1992.

The video for the first single, "Let's Get Rocked," was the first to use the newly developed technology of computer animation. It garnered three MTV Video Music Award nominations in 1992. The band then recruited Irish-born Vivian Campbell, formerly of Whitesnake and Dio, to preserve the two-guitar approach that was an integral part of their sound.

In 1993, Def Leppard released *Retro-Active*, a compilation of rare tracks. By this time the band's popularity was waning as heavy metal made way for grunge music. A 1996 album, *Slang*, was released without fanfare. However, in terms of sales, Def Leppard is one of the most successful heavy-metal bands in music history. —*Deirdre Rockmaker*

SELECT DISCOGRAPHY
■ ALBUMS
On Through the Night, 1980
High 'n' Dry, 1981 (rereleased in 1984 with two extra tracks)
Pyromania, 1983
Hysteria, 1987

Adrenalize, 1992
Retro-Active, 1993
Vault: Def Leppard's Greatest Hits—1980-1995, 1995 (compilation)
Slang, 1996

SEE ALSO: Bon Jovi.

John Denver

BORN: Roswell, New Mexico; December 31, 1943
DIED: Monterey Bay, near Pacific Grove, California; October 12, 1997
FIRST ALBUM RELEASE: *Rhymes and Reasons*, 1969
MUSICAL STYLES: Country, folk, pop

John Denver, born Henry John Deutschendorf, Jr., was the son of an Air Force pilot, a fact that would greatly influence the course of his life. As a military dependent, he moved to Japan, Oklahoma, Arizona, Alabama, and Texas during the early years of his life. Encouraged by his mother, Denver began his musical training as a member of the Tucson Boys' Choir. After his grandmother gave him a 1910 Gibson guitar, he became obsessed with folk music during his teen years. He tried to join a band while still in high school, but his parents refused to consider the idea. In 1961, he enrolled at Texas Tech University in Lubbock and majored in architecture, supplementing his income, whenever possible, by performing with a group called the Alpine Trio. He eventually left the university in 1964, relocating to Los Angeles in the hope of breaking into the music business. Once in California, he began using the stage name John Denver and joined the group Back Porch Majority. In 1965, he replaced Chad Mitchell in the renamed Chad Mitchell Trio, a group with whom he recorded and toured the college circuit for nearly four years.

Denver's first big break in the music industry came when his song "Leaving on a Jet Plane" was recorded in 1967 by Peter, Paul, and Mary. The song, which established him as a songwriter, became a number 1 hit for the group, the last before they disbanded. Denver's first solo album, *Rhymes and Reasons,* was released in 1969 by RCA records.

The Music Legend. In the 1970's, Denver's singing career reached its zenith. Although often criticized for his bland lyrics, he produced a string of hits that included "Rocky Mountain High," "Sunshine on My Shoulders," "Thank God I'm a Country Boy," and "I'm Sorry." "Take Me Home, Country Roads," written with Bill and Taffy Danoff, became his first million-selling single in 1971. His albums *Back Home Again* (1974) and *Windsong* (1975) peaked at number 1. His 1973 *John Denver's Greatest Hits* album stayed in the Top 200 for more than three years and sold more than twenty million copies. In 1974, *Cashbox* magazine named him the number-one album seller and artist. He was also named Entertainer of the Year in 1975 by the Country Music Association. Denver started his own label, Windsong, in 1975. Starland Vocal Band, one of the first groups to sign with his new label, had a number 1 hit for two weeks with "Afternoon Delight" in 1976.

A regular on television, Denver frequently appeared on talk shows and starred in at least one television special per year from 1974 to 1981. *An Evening with John Denver* won an Emmy Award for Outstanding Comedy-Variety or Music Special. In 1975, he began his film career, appearing in a remake of the 1939 classic film *Mr. Smith Goes to Washington.* Two years later he appeared with George Burns in the film *Oh, God!* He went on to host the Grammy Awards ceremonies in 1978, 1979, and 1982.

By the 1980's, despite having produced a total of fourteen gold and eight platinum albums, Denver's popularity had begun to wane. His last big hit, "Perhaps Love," a duet with opera singer Placido Domingo, was released in 1981. *Some Days*

John Denver (Paul Natkin)

Are Diamonds, also released in 1981, was his last gold album. Despite his failing popularity, however, Denver continued to record and perform. He appeared annually on television specials and at music events until his death.

The Humanitarian. Always fascinated with politics, Denver began his active involvement at the national level as a staunch supporter of politician George McGovern's unsuccessful presidential campaign. He went on to became interested in environmental causes and world affairs. He eventually constructed a solar-powered house near Aspen, Colorado, and made feature-length films about world hunger, traveling worldwide to support his favorite causes. His first trip to Africa was as a member of a fact-finding delegation sent by President Jimmy Carter to tour African countries suffering from droughts and starvation. He later noted his horror at the conditions some children faced in Africa. An increasing interest in world affairs eventually led to a tour of the then-Soviet

Union in 1984. He later returned to Moscow to record a duet single, "Let Us Begin" (1986), with a popular Russian singer. He went back to the Soviet Union once more in 1987 to perform a benefit concert for victims of the 1986 Chernobyl nuclear disaster. In 1984, he wrote a song for the Olympics, "The Gold and Beyond," which he performed at the Winter Games in Sarajevo. His tour of China in 1992 was the first by a Western artist, and he went on to perform in Vietnam in 1994. Harmony Books published his autobiography, *Take Me Home*, in 1994, a critical look at his life and career. In 1993, he became the first nonclassical musician to receive the Albert Schweitzer Music Award for humanitarian work.

Plagued by an ongoing divorce, Denver was arrested in 1993 on drunk driving charges in Colorado. He pleaded guilty, although denying guilt in his autobiography, and was fined and sentenced to probation.

An Untimely Death. As the son of a pilot, Denver had expressed an interest in flying since his youth. A board member of the National Space Institute, he volunteered to fly on the United States space shuttle but was denied the request. The Soviet Union responded by offering to let him fly in its space shuttle for ten million dollars, but he did not accept. A licensed pilot who flew jets, aerobatics planes, and gliders, Denver became increasingly intrigued by aerodynamics. Undaunted by a 1989 airplane accident in which the 1931 aircraft he was piloting spun around while taxiing on the runway, he continued to fly. In 1997 Denver was not so lucky when the experimental plane he was flying, a single-engine two-seater built from a kit, ran out of fuel and crashed into Monterey Bay off the coast of California. Denver,

who died upon impact, was fifty-three years old. Toxicology test results found no evidence of alcohol or drugs in his system.

—*Donald C. Simmons, Jr.*

SELECT DISCOGRAPHY
■ ALBUMS
Poems, Prayers, and Promises, 1971
Rocky Mountain High, 1972
John Denver's Greatest Hits, 1973
Back Home Again, 1974
I Want to Live, 1977
Seasons of the Heart, 1982
Different Directions, 1991

SELECT AWARDS
Record World, named Top Male Recording Artist, 1974, 1975
Country Music Association Entertainer of the Year Award, 1975
Grammy Award for Best Musical Album for Children for *All Aboard!* 1997

SEE ALSO: Peter, Paul, and Mary.

Depeche Mode

ORIGINAL MEMBERS: Vince Clarke (b. 1960), Andrew Fletcher (b. 1961), David Gahan (b. 1962), Martin Gore (b. 1961)
OTHER MEMBERS: Alan Wilder (b. 1959)
FIRST ALBUM RELEASE: *Speak and Spell*, 1981
MUSICAL STYLES: Pop, alternative, grunge

Depeche Mode is primarily known for their electronic music that utilizes synthesizers. They became early experts at sampling sounds and mastering, and they were one of the earliest bands to use remixing for single releases. They have sampled everything from the cry of an African pygmy to a hydraulic drill and have incorporated these sounds coherently into their music. According to the band members, they are interested in pushing musical limits with sounds, not just instruments. Because they have been considered a pop band, their experimentation has not always been accepted by critics, but audiences have liked

For the Record

John Denver's first *Greatest Hits* album (1973), with sales of more than twenty million, was the largest-selling album ever released by RCA Records.

it. Depeche Mode has never sold many records in the United States, but they have been selling out U.S. arena shows since the 1980's.

The Early Band. The members of Depeche Mode, which is French for fast fashion, all grew up in Basildon, England, a working-class suburb of London. The founding members, Vince Clarke, Martin Gore, and Andrew "Fletch" Fletcher had been experimenting with different instruments and different bands since high school but found their niche with synthesizers about the time they solidified their band structure by adding singer David Gahan, another friend from Basildon.

In the early days of Depeche Mode, Clarke was the designated leader of the band, mainly because he took the initiative, but also because he was the songwriter. Clarke left the band in late 1981. He went on to form Yaz and Erasure, both successful groups.

Upon Clarke's departure, at which point most people foresaw the end of the band, the remaining members divided responsibilities. Gore took over the songwriting duties, proving that he was fully capable of producing good pop songs. Gahan became even more important as the promotional front man. Fletcher became, as his bandmates labeled him, "the backbone" of the band. His natural interest in the band's business management came to exceed his musical interests. Alan Wilder, Clarke's replacement, has been considered the only true musician in Depeche Mode. He was the only member to have any traditional music training. However, the individuals' distinct roles have been advantageous to the longevity of the band.

Stardom. Depeche Mode's initial success occurred in the postpunk new Romantic movement in Great Britain in the late 1970's. Depeche Mode gathered a strong local following by 1981 and was being courted by important music companies. They signed with Daniel Miller, founder of independent music label Mute Records, who offered Depeche Mode an opportunity to record their music according to their interests. By the time of the release of their first album, *Speak and Spell* (1981), they had already made it to the Top 20 on the British charts and had appeared on television's *Top of the Pops.* On this album were included their previous single releases, "New Life" and "Just Can't Get Enough," two very light pop songs written by Clarke that were well liked by teen listeners.

After Clarke's departure, the three remaining members recorded *A Broken Frame* (1982), feeling they had something to prove in recording their second album. Gore proved his songwriting ability with the popular "Meaning of Love" and the ballad "See You." *Construction Time Again* (1983), Depeche Mode's third album, this time with the contributions of Wilder, was so named because of all the time

Depeche Mode (Paul Natkin)

that the members of the group and Daniel Miller spent on construction sites sampling the sounds. The uses of such harsh noises gave this album a rough-sounding edge unlike the previous albums. This use of unusual sound is apparent on "Everything Counts"; the disparaging chorus, "The grabbing hands grab all they can, everything counts in large amounts," overlies the harsh percussion of clanking metal pipes and hammering. Some critics have credited this album as heralding the industrial music of the late 1980's.

Some Great Reward (1984) was Depeche Mode's strongest album to date. The single "People Are People" was their first big hit in the United States. *Some Great Reward* yielded two singles that were popular more for the controversy they caused than for the music. First came "Master and Servant," about a sadomasochistic relationship, and then "Blasphemous Rumors," about the irony between the survival of a suicidal girl and the accidental death of a religious one. "Blasphemous Rumors" angered the British religious community with its chorus, "I think that God's got a sick sense of humor." Both of these songs were nearly banned by the British Broadcasting Corporation (BBC) and received virtually no airplay due to their lyric content.

Commercial and Critical Success. Their most critically acclaimed album of the 1980's was *Black Celebration* (1986). By the time they recorded *Black Celebration*, they were already a well-established band, but they had little credibility. They had their fans, and since they felt they would never have the good opinion of critics, they reached new heights of dark cynicism with *Black Celebration*. The title song is an ode to the bleak rituals that accompany daily working-class life. The controversial "Question of Time" is about corruptive influences on a young woman. Many songs on this album did not please Britain's censors, but critics were more enthusiastic about the music.

Music for the Masses (1987) is a strong album that is best known for a song that did not appear on it. Depeche Mode did a cover version of the American classic "Route 66," mixed it with their song "Behind the Wheel," and released it as a single. It became the theme song for the U.S. leg

For the Record

On March 20, 1990, the day of the release of *Violator*, the members of Depeche Mode agreed to make an in-store appearance at a record store in Beverly Hills, California. By the time the band members were to appear at nine P.M., the crowd had swelled to some ten thousand people packed on the sidewalks around the store. Before ten P.M. riot police were called to control the crowd.

of their "Music for the Masses" tour. At the end of this tour Depeche Mode played to a record sixty-five thousand people at the Rose Bowl arena in Pasadena, California. This concert was filmed by noted director D. A. Pennebaker and made into a feature film, *101*.

Holding Steady in the 1990's. Their 1990 album, *Violator*, again irritated the religious community because of the first single released, "Personal Jesus." The theme of the song, only marginally related to Christianity, is that people typically seek a savior in their personal relationships. Many leaders in the religious community did not interpret it that way, however. One of the more endearing songs Depeche Mode has produced is "Enjoy the Silence." The chorus, "All I ever wanted/ all I ever needed is here in your arms/ words are so very unnecessary/ they can only do harm," is sung by Gahan backed by a soft beat and synthesized strings. While touring for *Violator*, Gore surprised many fans and critics by playing an acoustic-guitar version of the song "Personal Jesus."

Songs of Faith and Devotion (1993) was a strong follow-up to *Violator*. When the band came together to record *Songs of Faith and Devotion*, they did so with the intention of incorporating some new styles of music, including grunge. "I Feel You," the first single, has Depeche Mode's telltale sampling of harsh sounds and is mixed with gritty vocals. The early Depeche Mode shows itself on songs such as "Walking in My Shoes." This album was well received by fans but was largely overlooked by critics.

Transitions. This album marked the end of Depeche Mode as a foursome. Wilder left the band in 1995 to pursue a solo career. Depeche Mode did not record another album until 1996. *Ultra* (1997) did not meet with the success of its predecessors. The music was characteristically Depeche Mode, with a little more severity and less self-mockery than their previous work. The single release, "Barrel of a Gun," while a good song, is not challenging in the way that "Never Let Me Down Again," from *Music for the Masses*, or "Black Celebration" are.

In 1998, Depeche Mode released *The Singles 1986-1998* as a companion to their previous single collection, *Singles 1981-1985*. They included new material on this album as well.   —*K. L. A. Hyatt*

SELECT DISCOGRAPHY

■ ALBUMS

Speak and Spell, 1981
A Broken Frame, 1982
Construction Time Again, 1983
Some Great Reward, 1984
Singles 1981-1985, 1985
Black Celebration, 1986
Music for the Masses, 1987
101, 1989
Violator, 1990
Songs of Faith and Devotion, 1993
Songs of Faith and Devotion Live, 1993
Ultra, 1997
The Singles 1986-1998, 1998

SEE ALSO: Cure, The; Duran Duran; Ministry; Smiths, The / Morrissey.

Devo

ORIGINAL MEMBERS: Jerry Casale, Mark Mothersbaugh, Bob "Bob I" Mothersbaugh, Bob "Bob II" Casale, Alan Myers
FIRST ALBUM RELEASE: *Q: Are We Not Men? A: We Are Devo!* 1978
MUSICAL STYLES: Pop, new wave

Formed in Akron, Ohio, in 1972, Devo is composed of Kent State University graduates. Details of the band's biographies before they joined Devo have been intentionally obscured in an attempt to maintain their stage image as futuristic automatons. Jerry Casale and Mark Mothersbaugh stand as the main creative force driving the admittedly tongue-in-cheek group. Called by one music critic "a new-wave version of Kiss," Devo's theatrics, stage imagery, and marketing are as important as their music. Devo's musical style, which combines mechanical sounds, robotic rhythms, and aharmonic major-chord progressions meshed with the standard pop music structures, set the precedent for the techno and industrial bands which would follow.

Devo's songs deal with such issues as the pursuits of apemen, rubber workers, and other "de-evolved" humanity and carry the message that humankind is in a state of genetic and cultural de-evolution into a state of corporate-enforced blandness. Devo performed in uniforms consisting of inverted plastic crimson flowerpots as helmets, plastic hairpieces, and yellow plastic industrial costumes. The Devo stage show included appearances by Booji Boy, a demented Kewpie doll who is the band's mascot, and dancing pinheads. Devo also set precedents in its use of film and video in rock music before MTV made video a necessity for marketing music.

We Are Devo! At Kent State University, Mark Mothersbaugh and Bob Casale studied art while they explored the world of college rock music of the early 1970's, first performing in public in 1973 on campus. In the fall of 1975, they regrouped to build a band based on a self-invented musical philosophy (and the name for their band) which they called "de-evolution," meaning, literally, the sound of things falling apart. The Mothersbaugh brothers, the Casale brothers, and Myers then produced a ten-minute film short entitled *The Truth About De-Evolution* which was a prize winner at the 1975 Ann Arbor (Michigan) Film Festival. The group began to play area clubs, shortened the band's name to Devo, and released their first single, the double-A sided "Jocko Homo"/"Mongoloid," on their own Booji Boy label in 1977.

"Satisfaction." Later in 1977, Devo released their second single on Booji Boy records, "Satisfaction." Their quirky, robotic cover of the Rolling Stones classic led to Devo being championed by such artists as David Bowie and Iggy Pop. Devo's sound inspired the title of Neil Young's 1979 album *Rust Never Sleeps*, and they later appeared in the tour film of the same name. Stiff Records took note of the band's success and rereleased Devo's first two singles in the United Kingdom, where "Satisfaction" reached number 41, and "Jocko Homo" reached number 51 on the British charts.

As a result of the successful Stiff singles, Devo was signed by Virgin Records in the United Kingdom and Warner Bros. in the United States. In 1978, the band went to Germany with producer Brian Eno to record their first album, *Q: Are We Not Men? A: We are Devo!* Due in part to a rigorous touring schedule, the album reached number 12 on the British charts. In 1979, with Ken Scott producing, *Duty Now for the Future* was released, yet it reached only number 49 on the British charts.

"Whip It Good." In 1980, Devo returned to the studio. With Robert Margouleff serving as producer, the band recorded *Freedom of Choice* which delivered their commercial breakthrough in the form of their first gold single, "Whip It." "Whip It" peaked at number 14 on the U.S. singles charts. In its wake, *Freedom of Choice* climbed to number 22 on the album charts. "Whip It" marked the strongest commercial success Devo would enjoy. In 1981, Devo returned to the studio where they self-produced the album *New Traditionalists* which failed to produce a hit single and rose to number 24 on the U.S. album charts and reached only number 50 on the British charts.

"Working in a Coal Mine." Late in 1981, Devo crawled back onto the U.S. singles chart with a remake of Lee Dorsey's "Working in a Coal Mine" for the sound track of the 1981 film *Heavy Metal*. In December of 1982, Devo released the Roy Thomas Baker-produced album, *Oh No! It's Devo*, which reached number 47 on the U.S. album charts. In 1983, "Theme from *Doctor Detroit*," for the 1983 film of the same name, reached number 47 on the singles charts. In 1984, Devo continued

Devo in 1981 (AP/Wide World Photos)

its tradition of remaking rock classics when they released their version of Jimi Hendrix's "Are U Experienced" on *Shout.*

After *Shout,* two years would pass before Devo released another studio album. The band released muzak versions of their hits, *E-Z Listening Muzak* (1981) and *E-Z Listening Muzak, Volume 2* (1986), for mail-order purchase only. *E-Z Listening Disc* (1987) was a compilation of these designed to fill the gap left by the lack of a new studio album. In 1988, the band released their first album on the Enigma label, *Total Devo.* Before Enigma collapsed, the band managed to release *Smooth Noodle Maps* in 1990. As Enigma sank, Devo was put on hiatus, and the group began to look for other engagements. The first of what would be many such opportunities came when actor Paul Reubens convinced Mark Mothersbaugh to provide the musical score for his upcoming television show *Pee Wee's Playhouse.*

Mutato Muzika. In 1990, it appeared that Devo had hung up their yellow suits and red plastic hats for good. Four volumes of greatest hits were released. As time passed, most of the band began to work at Mark Mothersbaugh's composing corporation Mutato Muzika, which produced successful commercial jingles, film (1995's *Mighty Morphin Power Rangers*) and television scores (*Rugrats, Beakman's World, Liquid Television*), and musical scores for theme park rides. Devo's appearances appeared to have been completely relegated to memory and virtual reality with the release of *Devo Presents the Adventures of the Smart Patrol,* a CD-ROM

For the Record

How seriously did Devo take itself? The British magazine *New Music Express* attempted to sum them up by suggesting that Devo saw themselves as "mirror-image representatives to the proletariat of the vegetable kingdom—song and dance men miming the plight of the human race in the modern world."

game created by Mark Mothersbaugh, Jerry Casale, and Inscape.

Lollapalooza. In 1996 and 1997, Devo returned to the stage to headline a number of performances of the alternative music festival Lollapalooza. Billed as "The Godfathers of Alternative Rock," Devo achieved "retro-hip" status as bands such as Nirvana ("Turnaround") and Soundgarden ("Girl U Want") have recorded cover versions of Devo songs. New future incarnations of Devo should surprise no one, as Devo was known to appear as Dove, the Band of Love, leisure-suit-clad crooners who occasionally would serve as Devo's opening act.   —*B. Keith Murphy*

SELECT DISCOGRAPHY
■ ALBUMS
Q: Are We Not Men? A: We Are Devo! 1978
Duty Now for the Future, 1979
Freedom of Choice, 1980
New Traditionalists, 1981
Oh No! It's Devo, 1982
Shout, 1984
E-Z Listening Disc, 1987
Greatest Hits, 1990
Smooth Noodle Maps, 1990

SEE ALSO: Eno, Brian.

Neil Diamond

BORN: Brooklyn, New York; January 24, 1941
FIRST ALBUM RELEASE: *The Feel of Neil Diamond,* 1966
MUSICAL STYLES: Pop, rock and roll

Through more than thirty years of pop and power ballads, Neil Diamond has provided the sound track to a wary post-Woodstock generation surviving marriages, divorces, and suburbia. The statistics are staggering: 110 million records sold, more than eight hundred sold-out performances, and more than fifty Top 100 hit singles. His concerts are almost as famous as his songs—*Rolling Stone* magazine even referred to him as the Jewish Elvis Presley and, as with "the King," tribute bands ply the stages, emulating his glitzy pop showmanship.

Neil Diamond (Columbia/Neal Preston)

later become his permanent home. Despite appearances at record hops and radio stations, the one release, "At Night," backed by "Clown Town," went nowhere.

Convinced his future lay behind the scenes instead of on the stage, Diamond leased an office on Broadway, for thirty-five dollars per month, where he could devote all his time to writing. He described the setting in the liner notes for his 1998 boxed set *In My Lifetime:* "For . . . two years, outfitted with an upright piano and a pay telephone [I didn't have credit for a regular phone account], I put up a little desk in an available corner of a tiny storage room above the Birdland Jazz Club and called it home."

It was during this time that he met producers Jeff Barry and Ellie Greenwich, which led to a contract with Bang Records. One of the first demos recorded during the Bang session was "Cherry, Cherry." Though a more polished version was later recorded, it was the demo that made his first album, *The Feel of Neil Diamond*, and became his first hit single.

He continued to write for other artists as well, penning "Sunday and Me" for Jay and the Americans and the number 1 hit "I'm a Believer" for the Monkees. He also toured as part of the Dick Clark Caravan, which included Tommy Roe and Billy Joe Royal. The teenage fans who flocked to the shows inspired the song "Girl, You'll Be a Woman Soon," remade in 1994 by Urge Overkill for the cult film *Pulp Fiction*.

The Uni Years. Diamond ended his relationship with Bang in 1968, when they did not consider his song "Shilo" commercial enough for single release. Seeking greater artistic freedom,

The Beginnings. Diamond was born in Brooklyn, New York, in 1941. He was working in his father's haberdashery when he received a guitar for his sixteenth birthday. Lessons followed, which led to songwriting. Still, after high school, Diamond went on to study medicine at New York University on a fencing scholarship but dropped out just six months before graduation. The reason was a fifty-dollar-per-week songwriter position with Sunbeam Music in New York's legendary Tin Pan Alley.

His first recording contract was with Dual records; he and high school friend Jack Parker recorded the Everly Brothers-inspired "What Will I Do" as Neil & Jack. A single record contract with Columbia followed in 1961, the label that would

he signed with MCA subsidiary Uni Records in 1968. His first album on that label, *Touching You, Touching Me*, started a string of gold records that would remain unbroken for twenty-two years. *Touching You, Touching Me* featured concert standard "Holly Holy," as well as covers of songs by such diverse artists as Ricky Nelson and Joni Mitchell.

His second Uni release was an ambitious, African-inspired concept album called *Tap Root Manuscript* (1970). The album produced Diamond's first number 1 single, "Cracklin' Rosie," a rollicking tribute to cheap wine, and the Top-20 single "He Ain't Heavy. . . . He's My Brother," later covered by the Hollies. The focal point, however, was "The African Trilogy," a seven-song musical suite that filled side 2 and featured the joyous "Soolaimon" as its centerpiece.

Two more albums followed; *Stones*, in 1971, and the 1972 release, *Moods*, which included "Song Sung Blue," Diamond's second number 1 single. That year, he became the first pop artist to play Broadway, selling out twenty shows at the Winter Garden Theater. He also released his best-selling album to date, *Hot August Night*, a passionate live performance.

The Big Time. A 4.5 million dollar, ten-album contract brought Diamond to Columbia Records in 1973, where he would remain throughout the 1980's and 1990's. The contract, which at the time was the largest for any artist, brought criticism for label president Clive Davis. Diamond immediately repaid their investment with the film sound track *Jonathan Livingston Seagull* (1973), a release that outperformed both the book and the film of the same name.

Diamonds first regular album on the new label was *Serenade*, in 1974. In many ways, *Serenade* seemed a continuation of *Jonathan Livingston Seagull*, containing many of the same themes, and included the song "I've Been This Way Before," which was intended for the sound track but not completed in time.

The 1976 follow-up was another concept album, *Beautiful Noise*, which dramatized his early years in New York as a Tin Pan Alley songwriter. It was produced by guitarist Robbie Robertson, and

For the Record

Neil Diamond's solo version of "You Don't Bring Me Flowers" originally appeared on his 1977 release, *I'm Glad You're Here with Me Tonight*. Barbra Streisand loved the song enough to record it for her next album, *Songbird*. Both versions were recorded in the same key and were similar enough that an enterprising disc jockey, Gary Guthrie, was able to splice the two versions. The resulting "duet" sounded so good that it prompted Diamond and Streisand to go into the studio and record the real thing.

earned Diamond an invitation to the Band's swan song performance, the "Last Waltz." In 1977, he attempted to reclaim the magic of *Hot August Night* with the live *Love at the Greek*. Five years of experience made Diamond a more polished performer, and he was unable to recapture the raw beauty that marked the first concert.

Adult Contemporary. Diamond's next three studio albums mark his shift from pop to easy listening. *I'm Glad You're Here with Me Tonight* (1977), *You Don't Bring Me Flowers* (1978), and *September Morn* (1979), filled the airwaves and produced hit singles, most notably the 1978 duet with Barbra Streisand on "You Don't Bring Me Flowers," which reached number 1.

In 1980, Diamond branched out into acting with the title role in the remake of *The Jazz Singer*. He composed and performed the film's multiplatinum sound track, which included the Top-10 singles "Love on the Rocks," "America," and "Hello Again," all Top-10 singles. Diamond continued to record throughout the 1980's, releasing four studio albums, accompanied by a pair of compilations and another live album, *Hot August Night II*. Though his fans remained loyal, only the title song from 1982's *Heartlight*, inspired by the film *E.T. The Extra-Terrestrial*, reached the Top 10.

In 1993, Diamond returned once more to his

New York roots with *Up on the Roof: Songs from the Brill Building*. The cover album paid tribute to the songs and songwriters of the 1950's and 1960's and featured top songwriting teams such as Gerry Goffin and Carole King, Barry Mann and Cynthia Weil, Jerry Leiber and Mike Stoller, and Burt Bacharach and Hal David. Critics wondered if the album might have been better had he chosen to record the songs he had written during his Tin Pan Alley days.

In 1995, Neil Diamond received his thirty-first gold album, placing him second behind Elvis Presley for male solo artists with the most gold records. He also continued to branch out as a performer, traveling to Nashville to record the 1996 release *Tennessee Moon*. All but one of the songs was written with a country collaborator, and the Diamond standard "Kentucky Woman" received a southern makeover.

In 1998, Diamond released the boxed set *In My Lifetime*. The three-compact-disc retrospective features thirty-seven of his hit singles and sixteen early demos, including early singles "What Will I Do," "At Night," and a 1980 live recording of "Hear Them Bells," the first song he ever wrote.

—*P. S. Ramsey*

SELECT DISCOGRAPHY
■ SINGLES
"Cherry Cherry," 1966
"Girl, You'll Be a Woman Soon," 1967
"Sweet Caroline," 1969
"Holly Holy," 1969
"Cracklin' Rosie," 1970
"I Am . . . I Said," 1971
"Song Sung Blue," 1972
"Play Me," 1972
"Longfellow Serenade," 1974
"You Don't Bring Me Flowers," 1978 (with Barbra Streisand)
"America," 1981
"Heartlight," 1982
■ ALBUMS
Just for You, 1967
Touching You, Touching Me, 1969
Tap Root Manuscript, 1970
Hot August Night, 1972

Jonathan Livingston Seagull, 1973
Beautiful Noise, 1976
You Don't Bring Me Flowers, 1978
The Jazz Singer, 1980
The Best Years of Our Lives, 1988
Up on the Roof: Songs from the Brill Building, 1993
Tennessee Moon, 1996
As Time Goes By: The Movie Album, 1998

SELECT AWARDS
Grammy Award for Album of Best Original Score Written for a Motion Picture for *Jonathan Livingston Seagull*, 1973

SEE ALSO: Band, The; Everly Brothers, The; Hollies, The; Mitchell, Joni; Monkees, The; Streisand, Barbra.

Bo Diddley
(Ellas McDaniel)
BORN: McComb, Mississippi; December 30, 1928
FIRST SINGLE RELEASE: "Bo Diddley"/"I'm a Man," 1955
MUSICAL STYLES: Rhythm and blues, pop, rock and roll

Despite the profound influence his wild musical experimentation had on American popular music from rhythm and blues to rap, Bo Diddley's fame has only recently begun to equal his significance as an innovator and inspiration to other musicians. Many who first learned of him as a rock-and-roll pioneer from the 1950's would be startled to discover that he continues to be a successful working musician many decades after his record "I'm a Man" shook the musical world, establishing his reputation as a talented songwriter and an original performer.

Beginnings. Born in the Deep South of McComb, Mississippi, Ellas Bates (renamed Ellas McDaniel on adoption in infancy by his mother's cousin Gussie McDaniel) moved to Chicago when he was six. Raised strictly by his churchgoing cousin McDaniel, Ellas studied violin in the Ebenezer Sunday School Baptist Band from the age of seven. He picked up the nickname "Bo

Bo Diddley (Archive Photos/Frank Driggs Collection)

Diddley" during a brief but successful flirtation with boxing and kept it as his stage name.

Bo decided he wanted to play guitar when he heard John Lee Hooker's "Boogie Chillun" at the age of twelve, and when his sister bought him a guitar he took to it immediately. He tuned it to suit himself (a style which turned out to be Sebastopol, or open-D, tuning: D, A, D, F#, A, D, low to high) and tried out all the different sounds he could make. His unique rhythmic style adapted well to this tuning and allowed impressive stylization and flourishes from a boy whose hands were already too big for fancy fretwork. His background in classical music and violin gave him a sound musical foundation with which to experi-

ment while creating the musical style and beat which was to become a driving influence of funk, rock and roll, and later, less directly (and less to his liking), rap.

Trendsetting. Diddley wasted no time forming a band, starting out on street corners and moving quickly on to clubs. His trademark sound relied heavily on maracas, harmonica, and his unique guitar technique, with its innovative blend of overloaded amplification and tremolo sustain. In the spring of 1955, Diddley released his first double A-side, "Bo Diddley"/"I'm a Man," introducing the "CHINKA CHINK-a-CHINK, a-CHINK-CHINK" beat, which changed rock and roll forever. It was an immediate rhythm-and-blues hit, and Diddley was soon playing the Apollo Theatre in Harlem, New York, and *The Ed Sullivan Show* on television. He sang the blues for Chess Records for years, and though he did not cross over to white audiences as successfully as labelmate Chuck Berry, numerous white stars covered his hits "I'm a Man," "Mona," and "Who Do You Love."

Diddley's performing persona was no less trendsetting than his music, and his threatening yet comic style and signifying style of boastful storytelling left its mark on everyone from the Rolling Stones to later rap artists. His vigorously suggestive performances and assaultive rhythms were a revelation to young audiences and a cause of worry to their parents. He was accused of inciting immorality with double entendres about "something in my pocket" in "I'm a Man."

Elvis Presley was among the first, and far from the last, to take notice of, imitate, and profit immensely from Diddley's style. While Diddley himself was largely restricted to the rhythm-and-blues charts due to his skin color, his rhythms, songs, and performance style were re-created ("covered") in performances by hugely popular white performers such as Buddy Holly, the Everly Brothers, Elvis Presley, the Rolling Stones, the Yardbirds, Ronnie Hawkins, and many more. Diddley explains, "I was a rock-and-roll artist before rock and roll existed. The only reason they named it rock and roll was the white brothers started playing it. The white radio stations in America didn't want to start playing black music but they didn't have sense enough to know that these white artists were covering songs that some black dude had wrote."

Going Strong. Diddley was still performing and going strong in the late 1990's, playing his signature rectangular guitar in his Stetson hat and thick, horn-rimmed glasses and working on albums. He also made more than a few media appearances, including a Nike commercial with Bo "Bo Knows" Jackson and a cameo as a pool player in the video of George Thorogood's "Bad to the Bone."

Diddley has penned concertos and has made his own guitars and electronic instruments, including a "Super Stick": an unusual looking, vaguely guitar-shaped instrument with two drum synthesizers and buttons that produce a wide variety of sounds, including tom-tom, snare drum, bass drum, and cowbell. Diddley built his original signature rectangular guitars himself, and he built "a new thing called the GuitDrum. That's a guitar and a drum machine together, for the guy who wants to play a bar mitzvah. He don't need to bug a drummer. He just takes it and does his thing." Even as Diddley enjoyed creating and playing such electronic instruments, he warned against the rising dependence on electronic wizardry in music today. "I'm against all that stuff where a guy just sits back and pushes a button. We should not rely on transistors. We should learn to play our instruments, so if you're plugged up to something and the sucker quits working, you can take an acoustic guitar and make the gig so you can pay your rent. I learned that a long time ago, bro."

Diddley has been increasingly concerned with social issues, visiting local schools to preach to teens about the hazards of drugs and the importance of obeying their parents, and writing songs about the plight of the homeless, such as the title track of his 1993 album *This Should Not Be.*

—*Jean McKnight*

For the Record

"Say Man," the only Diddley song to crack *Billboard*'s pop chart (reaching number 20 in 1959), came about more by accident than design. One day he and Jerome Green were singing and fooling around with their instruments in a recording studio, thinking they were alone. It happened, however, that Diddley's producer, Leonard Chess, and a sound engineer were taping them. Afterward, according to Diddley, they pieced the tape together, "took all the dirt out of it, and came up with 'Say Man.'"

SELECT DISCOGRAPHY
■ SINGLES
"Bo Diddley"/"I'm a Man," 1955
"Who Do You Love"/"I'm Bad," 1956
"Hey Bo Diddley"/"Mona," 1957
"Say Boss Man"/"Before You Accuse Me," 1957
"Hush Your Mouth"/"Dearest Darling," 1958
■ ALBUMS
Bo Diddley in the Spotlight, 1960
Bo Diddley Is a Lover, 1961
Bo Diddley's a Twister, 1962
Bo Diddley Is a Gunslinger, 1963
Surfin' with Bo Diddley, 1963
Hey! Good Lookin', 1965
500% More Man, 1965
The Originator, 1966
The Black Gladiator, 1970
Another Dimension, 1971
The London Bo Diddley Sessions, 1973
Give Me a Break, 1988
Breakin' Through the BS, 1989
The Chess Box, 1990 (boxed set)
Rare & Well Done, 1991
This Should Not Be, 1993

SELECT AWARDS
Rock and Roll Hall of Fame, inducted 1987
Rhythm and Blues Foundation Lifetime
   Achievement Award, 1996

SEE ALSO: Berry, Chuck; Clash, The; Domino, Fats; Everly Brothers, The; Haley, Bill; Lennon, John; Lewis, Jerry Lee; Little Richard; Rolling Stones, The.

Ani DiFranco

BORN: Buffalo, New York; September 23, 1970
FIRST ALBUM RELEASE: *Ani DiFranco*, 1989
MUSICAL STYLES: Rock and roll, folk rock

Singer-songwriter Ani DiFranco has been called a "folkie in punk's clothing." Her intensely loyal fans respond to the artist's unflinching, uncompromising approach to music and to life; she has not commercialized her songs to make them more accessible to the mainstream. DiFranco's determination to remain an independent artist, despite the courting of major labels, has provided her with the freedom to be so bold.

Learning Years. DiFranco grew up in Buffalo, New York, and was playing Beatles songs in area clubs by the age of nine. The child prodigy gave up music for a few years to study dance but returned to it as a teenager and was soon writing her own songs. Her musical inspirations included many of the top solo artists of the time, such as Suzanne Vega, Michelle Shocked, and Christine Lavin, for whom DiFranco's guitar teacher arranged performances in Buffalo. In the process, DiFranco met the artists and learned from them. In fact, she remembers, "quite a few of them stayed at my family's house. . . . I got to know . . . a bunch of singer-songwriters." She began writing songs because it was a popular thing to do during the time period.

Success in New York City. Her family deteriorating, DiFranco began living independently while still a student at Buffalo's Visual and Performing Arts High School. She performed locally for a while after graduating then moved to New York to attend the New School of Social Work. Before long, a self-released cassette of original material began drawing attention, especially among feminist audiences. DiFranco soon found herself performing for an expanding circle of listeners. She began playing concerts in surrounding states and soon dropped out of school to perform full-time.

Career underway, DiFranco founded her own record label, Righteous Babe, and released her original cassette as the album *Ani DiFranco* (1989). It sold briskly at concerts among fans taken with her spartan folk style and hard-hitting personal statements on social issues, especially those important to women. The singer-songwriter released *Not So Soft* through Righteous Babe in 1991 and increased her touring, tirelessly crisscrossing the country in her Volkswagen Beetle. Hard work resulted in the development of a strong fan base and even a cult following, as DiFranco loyalists began sporting extreme hairdos, tattoos, and pierced bodies similar to their idol.

Fiercely Independent. DiFranco built upon her early success by releasing two more albums,

Ani DiFranco (Paul Natkin)

1992's *Imperfectly* and 1992's *Puddle Dive*. Both displayed the work of a more mature artist and sold extremely well. Righteous Babe was quickly becoming a cottage-industry powerhouse and receiving national media attention. Major labels began courting DiFranco, but she remained fiercely independent, choosing artistic control rather than financial and political compromise.

In the years following *Puddle Dive*, DiFranco's career continued to progress. She continued to release albums through Righteous Babe and toured almost constantly. *Not a Pretty Girl* (1995) received considerable notice from the national media, and 1996's *Dilate* even made *Billboard*'s album charts, a triumph for a recording on an independent label. A live album, *Living in Clip*, followed in 1997, while 1998 brought her greatest artistic achievement, *Little Plastic Castle*.

DiFranco's various albums reveal her to be a compelling artist musically. Her earliest outings were minimalist, focusing exclusively on her voice and rowdy guitar playing. Later releases still prominently featured these musical ingredients, but other instruments were gradually added, to the point that 1998's "Little Plastic Castle" included everything from horn stabs and pump organ to concertina and talking drum.

Folk Roots, Punk Sensibilities. Much like fellow artist Beck, DiFranco has paired her folk roots with a contemporary approach to create a distinctive style. In her case, she turned to the hard-edged sounds of punk for inspiration. One might consider a folk-punk blend a bizarre combination, but the artist has found a fundamental similarity between the two styles: "Similarly to punk, [folk is] of people. It's subcorporate music."

Lyrically, DiFranco's music has been aimed at mature audiences, since she sings frankly about such issues as rape, abortion, sexism, and sexual orientation. Her songs about the last of these, such as "Light of Some Kind," have attracted the most attention from both fans and the media. Generally speaking, DiFranco's strongest songs have dealt with social issues of one form or another, earning her the label of "issues" artist and revealing her folk orientation.

DiFranco's lyrical candor has helped shape her

For the Record

Ani DiFranco has said of her guitar playing, "My style comes out of survival techniques; years of playing in load bars where you have to figure out some way of making people turn around and shut up and listen."

public persona. Some lines from her song "32 Flavors" reflect the price DiFranco has paid for her forthrightness and the success it has brought: "And God help you if you are a phoenix and you dare to rise up from the ash/ A thousand eyes will smolder with jealousy while you were just flying past."

Musical Talent. DiFranco's guitar playing has received quite a bit of attention. It can seem barbaric at times, but a closer listen reveals an accomplished, inspired instrumentalist. The strumming on "Light of Some Kind" has been called "spasmodic" and "arhythmic," yet it expresses the anxiety felt by the subject of the song in a manner not possible with more serene strumming.

DiFranco has had an impact on fellow singer-songwriters, the world of folk music, and the independent music industry. She has shown that an artist can be true to herself and still find considerable success in the world of popular music.

—*David Lee Fish*

SELECT DISCOGRAPHY
■ ALBUMS
Ani DiFranco, 1989
Not So Soft, 1991
Imperfectly, 1992
Puddle Dive, 1992
Like I Said, 1993
Out of Range, 1994
Not a Pretty Girl, 1995
More Joy Less Shame, 1996
Dilate, 1996
Living in Clip, 1997
Little Plastic Castle, 1998

SEE ALSO: Indigo Girls, The; Morissette, Alanis.

Celine Dion

BORN: Charlemagne, Quebec, Canada; March 30, 1968

FIRST ENGLISH-LANGUAGE ALBUM RELEASE: *Unison*, 1990

MUSICAL STYLES: Pop

A French-Canadian singer with international appeal and fame, Celine Dion has been one of the top pop vocalists of her generation. Performing since her early teens, Dion has created hit albums with hit singles in her native language (French) and in English. She would be a pop music sensation during the 1990's, growing more popular with every new release.

Biography. Celine Dion grew up in Charlemagne, Quebec, Canada, a rural French-Canadian town outside Montreal. The youngest of fourteen children, Dion began performing at a very early age. Her entire family was musical, and by age five she was singing with her siblings in a restaurant and club operated by her parents. By her early teens she was performing, managed by her future husband Rene Angelil. Her success came quickly, and at fifteen years of age she was well on her way to becoming a superstar in Canada and France. In 1991, Dion's international appeal widened extensively with the release of the theme song to the Walt Disney film *Beauty and the Beast*. The duet with Peabo Bryson put her name on the international pop charts and began her rise to the top of the pop music world.

The 1990's. Since the release of her first English-language album, *Unison* (1990), Dion has taken the pop music world by storm. She has recorded many hit songs written by the top pop songwriters and producers of her generation. *Celine Dion* (1992) produced four hit singles and included songs written by Prince and Diane Warren. *The Colour of My Love* (1993) had two major hit singles including songs written by David Foster and Diane Warren. In 1996, the release of *Falling into You* saw recordbreaking sales. *Let's Talk About Love* (1997) continued in the same genre as her previous releases. It includes a song written and performed with the Bee Gees, duets with Barbra Streisand and Luciano Pavarotti, and the title track written by Bryan Adams, Jean-Jacques Goldman, and Elliot Kennedy.

Sound-Track Sensation. Dion has been one of the most sought-out voices for contributions to film sound tracks, due to her reputation as an outstanding ballad singer. Her first successful motion-picture recording came in 1991 for Disney's *Beauty and the Beast*. The duet with Peabo Bryson hit number 9 on the charts and "Beauty and the Beast" was also released on her album *Celine Dion*. This was the beginning of many successful film sound-track recordings. She also performed "When I Fall in Love" for the 1993 film *Sleepless in Seattle*, released on *The Colour of My Love*, and "Because You Loved Me" for 1996's *Up Close and Personal*, released on the album *Falling into You*. This streak of successful hit singles connected with motion pictures continued with the release of the album *Let's Talk About Love*. "My Heart Will Go On (Love Theme from *Titanic*)," from the 1997 film, sold millions of copies worldwide and made Dion's name a stable feature on music charts.

A Place at the Top. Dion's career has seen many hit records, awards, and firsts. She was the first Canadian to have a gold single, "D'Amour Ou D'Amitié," in France, and she was only fifteen years old at the time. She was the first female singer to have two hit singles selling more than one million copies each in the United Kingdom: "My Heart Will Go On (Love Theme from *Titanic*)," and "Think Twice." She has won numerous awards all over the world for her music. In 1996 she won seventeen awards, which included two Grammy Awards for Album of the Year and Best Pop Album for *Falling into You*. She also received four Juno awards, the Canadian equivalent to the Grammy Award, for International Achievement, Best-Selling Album (*Falling into You*), Best-Selling French-Speaking Album (*Live á Paris*), and Female Vocalist of the Year. The album *Falling into You* went to number 1 in eleven different countries and sold more than ten million copies in the United States.

The highlight of Dion's career was recording a duet with Barbra Streisand for her album *Let's Talk*

About Love. In 1993, Dion became the National Celebrity Patron for the Canadian Cystic Fibrosis Foundation, tirelessly raising money for the cause. She would also own a chain of restaurants throughout Canada with her husband and manager Rene Angelil. —*Stephanie Brzuzy*

SELECT DISCOGRAPHY
■ ALBUMS
Incognito, 1987
Unison, 1990
Celine Dion, 1992
The Colour of My Love, 1993
D'eux, 1995 (known in the United States as *The French Album*)
Falling into You, 1996
Live á Paris, 1996
Let's Talk About Love, 1997

SELECT AWARDS
Juno Awards for Album of the Year for *Unison* and Female Vocalist of the Year, 1990
Juno Award for Single of the Year for "Beauty and the Beast," 1992
Grammy Award for Best Pop Performance by a Duo or Group with Vocal for "Beauty and the Beast," 1992 (with Peabo Bryson)
Juno Award for Female Vocalist of the Year, 1994
World Music Award for Best-Selling French-Canadian Artist, 1995
Grammy Awards for Album of the Year and Best Pop Album for *Falling into You,* 1996
World Music Award for World's Overall Best-Selling Recording Artist, 1997

SEE ALSO: Carey, Mariah.

For the Record

Since 1992, more than fifty million of Dion's albums have been sold worldwide. *Falling into You* has sold more than twenty-five million copies since its release.

Dion and the Belmonts / Dion

Dion and the Belmonts
ORIGINAL MEMBERS: Dion DiMucci, Fred Milano (b. 1939), Carlo Mastrangelo (b. 1938), Angelo D'Aleo (b. 1940)
FIRST SINGLE RELEASE: "We Went Away," 1957

Dion
BORN: Bronx, New York; July 18, 1939
FIRST SINGLE RELEASE: "Lonely Teenager," 1960
MUSICAL STYLES: Rock and roll, doo-wop, folk

Dion and the Belmonts were the quintessential late 1950's, urban street-corner, singing group. Based in the Bronx, New York, directly north of Manhattan, the group of Italian-American teenagers initially gathered wherever and whenever they could (especially anyplace with an echo) to blend their voices in harmony, often without instrumental accompaniment. They signed a record deal and recorded both up-tempo songs about being in love and softer ballads including show tunes.

Doo-Wop. The basic style of Dion and the Belmonts' music is now called doo-wop, so named because the background singers would support the lead vocalist (either in harmony or counterpoint) with nonsense phrases such as "doo-wop," "bop-sh-bop," or "ditta-dum-ditta-dit." When the style was popular, however, it was simply called rock and roll or group harmony singing, and Dion and the Belmonts were among the most popular and most creative of the many groups that dotted the doo-wop landscape.

The Belmonts' career lasted only a few years, though, from 1957 to 1960. After that, Dion DiMucci broke off from the group to begin a solo career, and the Belmonts continued on without him. Dion (he was known only by his first name) went on to great success as a solo rock artist, recording several songs that became classics. He then was absent from the charts for five years, only to return in the late 1960's as a folksinger. He would have a sporadic career, emerging next as a contemporary Christian artist, then eventually returning to his rock-and-roll roots.

The Beginnings. According to Dion, in order to survive in his tough hometown of the Bronx, a teen either had to join a gang or a singing group. He chose the latter route, and it became profitable. He was always interested in music. At age eight he began playing guitar, and by age fifteen he was performing on television. In 1957, Dion was taken to a recording studio by a family friend and placed with a group he had never met, the Timberlanes. They recorded a couple of songs, but the record did not succeed.

When the record company, Mohawk, asked him to return, Dion brought a group of his own friends, Carlo Mastrangelo, Fred Milano, and Angelo D'Aleo. They called themselves Dion and the Belmonts, taking the group's name from one of the local streets, Belmont Avenue. Nothing came of the group's first single, but they were then signed to another label, Laurie Records, and in 1958 recorded a song called "I Wonder Why." It made the national charts and sent Dion and the Belmonts on their way to success.

The group was touring with Buddy Holly, Ritchie Valens, and the Big Bopper in early 1959. On one cold night in Iowa, Dion opted to take the bus to the next stop instead of a small plane. Holly, Valens, and the Big Bopper were killed when the plane crashed. Only a few months later, Dion had his next hit, "A Teenager in Love." It would become a rock-and-roll classic. The group's next hit, in late 1959, was the ballad "Where or When," originally performed in 1937 for the musical *Babes in Arms*. The record went to number 3 on the charts and proved that Dion and the Belmonts were not limited to playing rock and roll. For a follow-up song, they recorded the 1940 *Pinocchio* classic "When You Wish upon a Star."

Splits, Then Hits. In late 1960, Dion and the Belmonts decided to go their separate ways. Simply calling himself Dion, the singer had an immediate hit with "Lonely Teenager." His real breakthrough came in 1961 when he recorded "Runaround Sue," a classic rocker about a girl who dates other men behind her boyfriend's back.

"Runaround Sue" became Dion's first and only number 1 record, and he followed it up with a number 2 hit that has also become a classic, "The Wanderer." This time, it was the man who ran around: "I roam from town to town/ I go through life without a care." The record later became the inspiration for a book by Richard Price (later a 1979 film) called *The Wanderers*.

Dion continued to produce hits in the early 1960's: "Lovers Who Wander," "Ruby Baby" (a

Dion and the Belmonts (Archive Photos/Frank Driggs Collection)

For the Record

Although he grew up in the heart of New York, and his primary musical influences were rhythm and blues and early rock and roll, Dion was also a big fan of country singer Hank Williams. Dion has said that he based some of his "self-pity" songs on themes that were present in Williams's songwriting.

cover of a Drifters song), "Donna the Prima Donna," and others. It was the pre-Beatles era in rock and roll, and handsome male solo singers were very popular. Dion was a "teen idol," but unlike many of the others he did not have a soft image that appealed only to young girls; Dion was streetwise and tough, and his records spoke to males as well. As for the Belmonts, they did not enjoy the same level of success as Dion, but they did fairly well. Their biggest hit was "Tell Me Why," an up-tempo doo-wop song, in 1961.

The Comeback. After 1963, Dion disappeared from the music scene while he experienced drug problems. He spent five years recovering, and when he returned to music he was a completely changed artist. Sporting long hair and wire-rimmed glasses, Dion had dropped the teen-idol guise and become a folk-rock singer. Playing acoustic guitar and singing blues and message tunes, he had been moved by the same social and political changes that were affecting others of his generation.

Dion's comeback hit was "Abraham, Martin and John" (1968), a tribute to the assassinated President Abraham Lincoln, civil rights leader Martin Luther King, Jr., and President John F. Kennedy. Although the song was written by Dick Holler, Dion added an extra verse about Senator Robert F. Kennedy, who was slain just prior to Dion's recording of the song. It reached number 4 on the charts.

Dion never had another chart hit, but he did not vanish entirely from the music scene. After

reuniting for a concert with the Belmonts in 1972, Dion reinvented himself. Having undergone a religious conversion, he began recording contemporary Christian, or gospel, albums, which were quite well received by fans of that style. He avoided his old rock-and-roll and folk songs for many years, but finally, in the late 1980's, Dion made peace with his past and began singing his old hits again. He also recorded several new albums and appeared in concert regularly, treating his fans to music from all points of his career.

—*Jeff Tamarkin*

SELECT DISCOGRAPHY
Dion and the Belmonts
■ SINGLES
"I Wonder Why," 1958
"A Teenager in Love," 1959
"Where or When," 1959
Dion
■ SINGLES
"Lonely Teenager," 1960
"Runaround Sue," 1961
"Wanderer, The," 1961
"Ruby Baby," 1962
"Donna the Prima Donna," 1963
"Drip Drop," 1963
"Abraham, Martin and John," 1968

SELECT AWARDS
Rock and Roll Hall of Fame, inducted 1989 (Dion)

SEE ALSO: Beatles, The; Drifters, The; Holly, Buddy / The Crickets; Valens, Ritchie; Williams, Hank.

Dire Straits / Mark Knopfler

Dire Straits

ORIGINAL MEMBERS: Mark Knopfler (b. 1949), David Knopfler (b. 1951), John Illsley (b. 1949), Pick Withers
OTHER MEMBERS: Alan Clark, Hal Lindes, Terry Williams
FIRST SINGLE RELEASE: "Sultans of Swing," 1978

Mark Knopfler

BORN: Glasgow, Scotland; August 12, 1949
FIRST ALBUM RELEASE: *Local Hero*, 1983 (sound track)
MUSICAL STYLES: Rock and roll, country rock

The son of a Scottish architect, Mark Knopfler, the central figure in Dire Straits, was born in Glasgow, Scotland, in 1949. A few years later he moved with his family, including younger brother David, to Newcastle-upon-Tyne in northern England. During his early years, Knopfler listened to Scottish border songs, the skiffle sounds of Lonnie Donegan, early rockabilly, Chuck Berry, and Bob Dylan. He became interested in the blues of B. B. King, Muddy Waters, John Lee Hooker, and Howlin' Wolf. This eclectic range of influences later were revealed as a hallmark of Knopfler's work, as he progressively merged musical genres from the American Delta to traditional Celtic instrumentations.

Early Years. After working as a warehouseman, journalist, and English teacher, Knopfler formed his first pub band, the Brewer's Droop, in Leeds, England. In 1977, Knopfler formed Dire Straits in Deptford, England, naming the band after the financial situation in which the group found themselves. The original lineup included Knopfler (guitar, songwriter), his younger brother David (guitar), John Illsley (bass), and Pick Withers (drums).

Throughout their first year, the band toured constantly, fighting an uphill battle in the climate of punk bands then popular in British clubs. Then, London disc jockey Charlie Gillett discovered them and introduced the unusual group to his listeners. As a result of Gillett's efforts, Dire Straits signed with Vertigo Records and released their first single, "Sultans of Swing." The semiautobiographical narrative was first a hit in Holland and England in 1978, before U.S. label Warner Bros. backed the band with major promotional funds. After this campaign, in March, 1979, the debut song reached number 2 on the U.S. charts.

The band's first album, *Dire Straits* (1978), was produced by Muff Winwood, a former member of the Spencer Davis Group and brother of Traffic headman Steve Winwood. The album showcased the group's distinctive, gentle, bluesy sound dominated by Mark Knopfler's laid-back vocals, song craftsmanship, and guitar lines similar to those of Eric Clapton. Knopfler's lyrics were an original mix of English imagery with U.S. country-and-western idioms, a formula evident in "Sultans of Swing," "Down to the Waterline," and "Where Do You Think You're Going?"

Dire Straits quickly sold seven million copies, and the band enjoyed a popularity among fans who normally avoided the prevailing rock music of the era. However, the next single, "Lady Writer," was a relative failure, as was the band's next album, *Communiqué* (1979), which sold only three million copies and fared poorly with critics.

Top of the Pops. Deciding to pursue a solo career, David Knopfler quit the group. After the recording of *Making Movies*, he was replaced by Hal Lindes of the band Darling. *Making Movies* (1980) was the album that elevated Dire Straits into its most successful period. Clearly influenced by the style of Bruce Springsteen, the fuller, larger sound on *Making Movies* resulted in a string of singles beginning with the complexly arranged and produced "Tunnel of Love" and "Romeo and Juliet." The band was assisted by top session players on *Making Movies*, notably Roy Bittan, keyboardist for Springsteen's E Street Band. Session musicians would contribute to later albums as well, among them Omar Hakim, Joop de Korte, Mel Collins, Mike Mainieri, and Randy and Michael Brecker. Keyboardist Alan Clark was added to the band after *Making Movies*.

Subsequent singles included the seven-minute "Private Investigation," "Twisting by the Pool," and "Portobello Belle." These artfully arranged hits and the innovative videos produced for them demonstrated the group's adeptness at crafting tunes aimed at the newly growing MTV market.

Brothers in Arms (1985) was the group's high-water mark, slickly produced by Knopfler. It contained the band's biggest-selling single, "Money for Nothing" (which includes Sting singing the phrase "I want my MTV"). The video for the song featured computer graphics and redrawn footage that helped make MTV a household word. The global hit was followed by other singles, including the Cajun-flavored "Walk of Life," subsequently recorded by Cajun performer Charles Mann. The group supported the album with a two hundred date tour which pushed the band's sales above fifteen million total copies. It was estimated that one-tenth of New Zealand's population attended their concerts, and one in ten British households owned a copy of *Brothers in Arms*. The album was number 1 for nine weeks in the United States, and it stayed on the British charts for three years. By this time, Dire Straits had grown into a nine-piece onstage outfit, including two or three guitars, two keyboards, percussion, and saxophone.

When former Mann drummer Terry Williams replaced Withers, Knopfler and Illsley were the only founding members remaining for the

Dire Straits' Mark Knopfler (Lissa Wales)

group's last studio project, the poorly received *On Every Street* (1991). The group continued to have success in the live arena, such as their appearance at the 1985 Live Aid benefit concert and their 1988 appearance at Nelson Mandela's birthday concert at London's Wembley Stadium. In 1991, the band went on a two-year tour which exhausted Knopfler. After releasing the live *On the Night* (1993), Knopfler decided to disband the group indefinitely to pursue solo projects.

Side Tracks. Mark Knopfler's outside interests were ignited when Bob Dylan asked Knopfler and Withers to play on his 1983 *Infidels* album, which Knopfler also produced. Later production work for Knopfler included albums for Randy Newman, Aztec Camera, and Willy de Ville. In 1984, Knopfler wrote Tina Turner's comeback hit, "Private Dancer," and later wrote songs for Eric Clapton ("Setting Me Up") and Mary Chapin Carpenter ("The Bug"). He worked with the Celtic band the Chieftains and served as session guitar player for Waylon Jennings, Sonny Landreth, and other friends.

Knopfler also scored sound tracks for films such as *Local Hero* (1983), *Cal* (1984), and *The Princess Bride* (1987). While working on *Cal*, Knopfler met keyboardist Guy Fletcher, whom Knopfler employed on every project afterward, from the last Dire Straits productions through his first solo album, *Golden Heart* (1996).

Knopfler's solo work also included the 1990 *Neck and Neck*, a Grammy Award-winning collection of guitar duets with Chet Atkins. Based around vocalist Brendan Croker, Knopfler gathered together old pub friends and produced the informal band the Notting Hillbillies, hoping to be able to play smaller clubs than Dire Straits could manage. Their 1990 debut album, *Missing . . . Presumed Having a Good Time*, was a disappointment, and the group disbanded.

Knopfler's first official solo album, *Golden Heart* (1996) received much critical attention, earning praise for the singer's fusion of Cajun, Celtic, country, and rock styles. The music was a return to the spirit of Dire Straits, but Knopfler stated he had no plans for a reunion.

—*Wesley Britton*

SELECT DISCOGRAPHY

■ ALBUMS
Dire Straits, 1978
Communiqué, 1979
Making Movies, 1980
Love over Gold, 1982
Local Hero, 1983 (Knopfler, sound track)
Alchemy, 1984
Brothers in Arms, 1985
Money for Nothing, 1988
Neck and Neck, 1990 (Knopfler with Chet Atkins)
On Every Street, 1991
Golden Heart, 1996 (Knopfler solo)

SELECT AWARDS
Grammy Award for Best Rock Performance by a
    Duo or Group with Vocal for "Money for
    Nothing," 1985
Grammy Award for Best Music Video, Short
    Form, for *Dire Straits: Brothers in Arms*, 1986

SEE ALSO: Dylan, Bob.

The Dixie Dregs. *See* Steve Morse

Willie Dixon

BORN: Vicksburg, Mississippi; July 1, 1915
DIED: Burbank, California; January 29, 1992
FIRST SINGLE RELEASE: "Sweet Louise," 1940 (with
    the Five Breezes)
FIRST SOLO ALBUM RELEASE: *I Am the Blues*, 1970
MUSICAL STYLES: Blues, rhythm and blues

Willie Dixon rose from humble origins to become
one of the most influential blues and rock lyricists
of all time. His songs have been performed by
numerous artists around the world. He was also
an accomplished bassist whose solid playing un-
derscored many recordings.

Early Years. Vicksburg, Dixon's birthplace, is
located on the edge of the Mississippi Delta region
and was the second largest city in the state. Many
famous blues singers, most notably Charley Pat-

ton and Robert Johnson, hail from the Mississippi
Delta, and young Dixon was exposed to the blues
early in his life. He heard Patton and Little
Brother Montgomery, for example, in one of the
local Vicksburg establishments, Curley's Barrelhouse. Dixon recalls that Montgomery was always
friendly to the children who used to gather outside the barrelhouse to hear his piano playing.

When musicians traveled through Vicksburg,
Dixon would always go to hear them. Dixon's
music was influenced by a stint during the early
1930's with the Union Jubilee Singers, a gospel
group from whom he learned the rudiments of
harmony singing. It was also during this time that
he began to write poetry; his first poem was entitled "The Signifying Monkey."

Not all his experiences were positive during
these early years. When he was around twelve years
old, Dixon was arrested for stealing plumbing

Willie Dixon (Paul Natkin)

fixtures from a house and was sent to the Ball Ground County Farm (a prison farm). There he was exposed to blues music in its most elemental form: the hollers (improvised work songs of African Americans) of the convicts as they worked in the fields. In *The Willie Dixon Story* (1989) he says, "That's when I really learned about the blues. I had heard 'em with the music and took 'em to be an enjoyable thing but after I heard these guys down there moaning and groaning these really down-to-earth blues, I began to inquire about 'em. I would ask guys why they sang these tunes. . . . I really began to find out what the blues meant to black people."

Going to Chicago. Chicago was a popular destination for southern African Americans, since many saw the northern cities as a way out of the poverty of the Deep South. Dixon had visited his sister in Chicago when he was in his teens, but in 1936 he moved there permanently. The move gave him a chance at a career in boxing. He was a big man and he won the Illinois State Golden Gloves Award in 1938. It is possible that Dixon could have continued as a professional boxer, but he began to play the upright bass and joined a singing group, the Five Breezes. A member of the group, Leonard "Baby Doo" Caston, finally persuaded Dixon to give up his boxing career for music, and in 1940 they recorded "Sweet Louise," Dixon's first record.

Under normal circumstances, Dixon's musical career probably would have developed rapidly. However, the 1940's were a troubled time because of World War II. Many young men were drafted into the Army and went to Europe or the South Pacific to fight in the war. Dixon, though, declared himself a conscientious objector. As a result, he was arrested and spent about ten months in jail for resisting the draft. After the war, Dixon returned to his musical career and formed the Four Jumps of Jive and the Big Three Trio, the latter of which included Caston.

The Hoochie Coochie Man. Dixon's career took off in the 1950's. In 1951 he began working for Chess Records and continued with them as a producer, session musician, talent scout, and songwriter for the next twenty years. Dixon acted

For the Record

"I feel that if the proper songs get to the various people of the world, it helps their mind to concentrate on what's going on in the world and this will give you a better communication. That's the real meaning and the real good of the blues, a better education and understanding among all people."
—*Willie Dixon*

in a similar capacity at Cobra Records, where he helped shape the sounds of Magic Sam and Otis Rush. It was in 1954 that perhaps the most important event in his career occurred. Two well-known blues singers, Muddy Waters and Howlin' Wolf, recorded versions of Dixon songs: Wolf recorded "Evil" and Waters recorded "I'm Your Hoochie Coochie Man." These songs had the clever phrasing and wry humor that characterized many of Dixon's lyrics. For example, "I'm Ready," another Dixon song, contains the following verse: "I gotta axe handle pistol on a graveyard frame/ That shoots tombstone bullets wearing balls and chain/ I'm drinking TNT, smokin' dynamite/ I hope some screwball starts a fight." Both "Evil" and "I'm Your Hoochie Coochie Man" were hits, and Waters and Wolf recorded many more Dixon songs throughout their careers.

The popularity of the Chicago blues artists was modest by today's standards. In the 1960's, however, many rock bands from England embraced the blues and became interested in Dixon's songs. Artists such as the Rolling Stones, Led Zeppelin, Cream, and John Mayall's Bluesbreakers recorded versions of Dixon songs. Through the work of these artists, his songs finally gained well-deserved attention on the world music scene.

Unfortunately, Dixon did not always receive the proper credit and royalties for his creative output. In 1985, he initiated legal action against Led Zeppelin over their song "Whole Lotta Love," which was derived from Dixon's song entitled "You Need Love." This dispute was finally settled in 1987. Sadly, this lack of recognition for black artists was common in the 1950's and 1960's. For example, despite Dixon's long and fruitful association with Chess Records, he gained the rights for his own songs from Chess only by taking legal action.

Blues Heaven. In 1987, Dixon founded the Blues Heaven Foundation, an organization dedicated to increasing awareness of the blues and to gaining proper recognition for blues artists whose work was never properly credited. According to Dixon in *The Willie Dixon Story* (1989), this latter purpose is the most important because "We've got to correct some of the past mistakes. . . . If we can just get to some of the people that know they inherited millions through the blues, we can help some of the blues people's children or grandchildren to reap some of the benefits." For Dixon, it was in these later years of his life that he finally received the recognition he deserved. He was honored by induction into two halls of fame, and in 1988 his album *Hidden Charms* won a Grammy Award. The clever and sometimes humorous lyrics of Dixon's songs, which were recorded by so many great artists, were instrumental in bringing the heart and soul of the Mississippi Delta to listeners around the world.

—*Robert Clifford*

SELECT DISCOGRAPHY
■ ALBUMS
I Am the Blues, 1970
Catalyst, 1973
What Happened to My Blues? 1976
Hidden Charms, 1988
The Chess Box, 1988 (compilation)

SELECT AWARDS
Blues Foundation Hall of Fame, inducted 1980
Grammy Award for Best Traditional Blues Recording for *Hidden Charms*, 1988
Rock and Roll Hall of Fame, inducted 1994

SEE ALSO: Allman Brothers Band, The; Clapton, Eric; Cray, Robert; Cream; Guy, Buddy; Hooker, John Lee; Howlin' Wolf; King, Albert; King, B. B.; Led Zeppelin; Raitt, Bonnie; Rolling Stones, The; Waters, Muddy.

DJ Jazzy Jeff and the Fresh Prince

ORIGINAL MEMBERS: Fresh Prince (b. Willard Smith, 1968), DJ Jazzy Jeff (b. Jeff Townes, 1965)
FIRST ALBUM RELEASE: *Rock the House*, 1987
MUSICAL STYLE: Rap

Dubbed by one critic as "bubblegum" rap at its best, the music of DJ Jazzy Jeff and the Fresh Prince was considered irrelevant by many streetwise rappers. Nevertheless, the duo's goodtime lyrics won over a mainstream audience resistant to themes of drugs and violence, and this popularity eventually vaulted the Fresh Prince to stardom in television and films.

Rocking the House. Jeff Townes and Will Smith had been performing individually since they were preteens, Townes spinning records and Smith rapping. They met at a house party in 1981 and soon formed a partnership, making records in Townes's basement. Their debut album, *Rock the House* (1987), failed to make the Top 40, but when Jive Records bought out their contract and had success with "Girls Ain't Nothing but Trouble" (released three weeks before Smith graduated from high school), Smith turned down a scholarship to the prestigious Massachussetts Institute of Technology in order to pursue a career in the record business.

The group's second album, *He's the DJ, I'm the Rapper* (1988, number 4), was a pioneering work. Though dismissed by hardcore rappers, it helped bring the urban genre to the American heartland. It was one of the first Trap albums to reach a mass audience, going triple platinum, and was named Best Rap Album at the American Music Awards. Its hit single, "Parents Just Don't Understand"

For the Record

"Ring My Bell" (number 20, 1991) was a remix of Anita Ward's 1979 number 1 hit.

(number 12) was the first rap piece to earn a Grammy Award (1988), for Best Rap Performance.

The duo's third album, *And in This Corner . . .* (1989), reached number 39 on the album charts and sold more than one million copies. They followed it up with the platinum *Homebase* (1991), which went to number 12 on the charts and included the group's biggest single, "Summertime" (number 4). "Summertime," which sampled Kool and the Gang's "Summer Madness," hit number 1 on the rhythm-and-blues charts and earned DJ Jazzy Jeff and the Fresh Prince a second Grammy for Best Rap Performance by a Duo or Group.

Smith's Star Appeal. Meanwhile, Smith had been pursuing a successful television career. After a chance meeting with producer Benny Medina, early in 1990 Smith was chosen to star in *The Fresh Prince of Bel-Air* (1990-1996), a sitcom about an East Coast ghetto youth adopted by his wealthy black California family. Townes was also featured occasionally as Smith's friend. It performed consistently well and served as a showcase for his acting talent. Though it never made the Top 10, it was one of the few shows widely watched by both black and white audiences. Smith's winning personality and solid talent led to significant motion-picture roles in *Six Degrees of Separation* (1993), *Bad Boys* (1995), and *Independence Day*, the summer hit film of 1996.

Though Smith and Townes continued to work together, as early as 1992 Smith was planning to leave the music business in order to concentrate on acting. The duo's final album, *Code Red* (1993), featured a harder edge and proved that Smith had real talent, though it was not a commercial success (number 64). It nevertheless spawned the hit "Boom! Shake the Room" (number 12).

Continued Solo Success. Smith's broad appeal was further solidified when he starred in *Men in Black*, the blockbuster summer comedy of 1997, and earned a Grammy Award for Best Rap Solo Performance singing the title song. Later that year he released his first solo album, *Big Willie Style*, which went double platinum and rose to number 10 on the pop album chart. In addition to "Men in Black" it included the number 1 hit "Getting Jiggy Wit It" and featured Larry Blackmon and Cameo, Camp Lo, and TLC's Left Eye on three tracks.

—John Powell

DJ Jazzy Jeff and the Fresh Prince at the 1992 American Music Awards (Archive Photos/Fotos International/Bob Grant)

SELECT DISCOGRAPHY
DJ Jazzy Jeff and the Fresh Prince
■ ALBUMS
Rock the House, 1987
He's the DJ, I'm the Rapper, 1988
And in This Corner . . . , 1989
Homebase, 1991
Code Red, 1993
Greatest Hits, 1998 (compilation)
Will Smith
■ ALBUMS
Big Willie Style, 1997

SELECT AWARDS
American Music Awards for Best Rap Artist and
    Best Album for *I'm the D.J., He's the Rapper*,
    1988
Grammy Award for Best Rap Performance for
    "Parents Just Don't Understand," 1988
Grammy Award for Best Rap Performance by a
    Duo or Group for "Summertime," 1991
Grammy Award for Best Rap Solo Performance
    for "Men in Black," 1997 (Smith)

SEE ALSO: TLC.

Dr. Dre

(Andre Young)
BORN: Los Angeles, California; February 18, 1965
FIRST ALBUM RELEASE: *The Chronic*, 1992
MUSICAL STYLE: Rap

Considered to be the moving force behind what
is known as West Coast gangsta rap, Dr. Dre performed with and produced some of the rap industry's most famous and infamous voices. His first
solo album, *The Chronic* (1992), molded funk classics and rap into yet another new genre known as
gangsta funk. Dre, along with Suge Knight,
founded Death Row Records and one of the most
influential and profitable genres of popular
music.

Compton. Andre Young was raised in Compton, a neighborhood south of downtown Los Angeles where poverty, drugs, and violence were the
norms. Young's break from the ghetto came in the

form of music. In 1981, after hearing the work of
rapping pioneer Grandmaster Flash, Young
changed his name to Dr. Dre (in honor of basketball star Julius "Dr. J" Erving) and began making
rap tapes in his bedroom for friends.

In the mid-1980's, Dre became a founding
member of Niggaz With Attitude (N.W.A.) along
with O'Shea "Ice Cube" Jackson. N.W.A., which
Rolling Stone called the Sex Pistols of rap, are
credited with creating hip-hop's gangsta sound,
which is funky, powerful, and often vulgar and
violent. In hip-hop music, the producer/DJ has
the most influence on the band's sound, and
Dre's production work was the driving force behind the gangsta sound. He produced Eric "Eazy-
E" Wright's "Boyz-n-the-Hood," considered to be
the first gangsta single, and still had his hands on
the controls when N.W.A.'s 1991 album *Efil4zag-*

Dr. Dre at the 1995 MTV Video Music Awards (Manny
Hernandez/Archive Newsphotos)

gin reached the top of the album charts in the United States.

Deep Cover. After *Efil4zaggin*, N.W.A. fell apart. In 1992, Dre released his first solo effort. Entitled "Deep Cover," the single was credited to "Dr. Dre Introducing Snoop Doggy Dogg." Dre, in an attempt to divorce himself from Eazy-E's Ruthless Records, founded, along with Suge Knight, Death Row Records, which Dre called "the Motown of the '90's." In 1992 Dre released his first solo album, *The Chronic*, which utilized samples from classic Parliament/Funkadelic funk songs and wove these around lyrics filled with standard but chilling gangsta threats and vulgar language. *The Chronic* was an immediate success, reaching number 3 on the American album charts and eventually selling over three million copies. That success launched Dre's rap protégé Snoop Doggy Dogg to stardom and created the gangsta funk genre of rap. *The Chronic* included such hit singles as "Nuthin' but a 'G' Thang," "Dre Day," and "Let Me Ride" (featuring funk pioneer George Clinton).

Dre's success continued through the end of 1993 and into 1994. In December of 1993, Snoop Doggy Dogg's solo album, *Doggy Style*, was released. With Dre as producer, *Doggy Style* became the first debut album to enter the charts at number 1. In time, *Doggy Style* sold over four million copies. In the spring of 1994, Dre was named the Best Rap/Hip-Hop Artist and the Best New Rap/Hip-Hop Artist at the American Music Awards. One month later, he won a Grammy Award for the Best Rap Solo Performance of the year for "Let Me Ride." Dre continued his success as a producer with the 1994 soundtrack for *Above the Rim*, which was released on Death Row Records and peaked at number 2 on the album charts. Dre also produced a wide variety of acts for Death Row, ranging from Tupac Shakur to Warren G.

Dre Day. Near the end of 1994, Dre found himself in jail for a parole violation. He was on parole for breaking a fellow producer's jaw in 1992. Upon his release from jail, he announced plans to reunite with former N.W.A. rapper Ice Cube. The reunion produced only one single, "Natural Born Killaz," which was used in the

sound track for the short film *Murder Was the Case* (1994), which starred Snoop Doggy Dogg. In 1996, Dre sold his stake in Death Row Records to Knight, who was in jail after pleading no contest to assault charges, and formed a new label, Aftermath Records. Dre's first release on the new label, *Dr. Dre Presents . . . The Aftermath* (1996), was a compilation of new and established rap stars that showcased Dre's production as well as his rapping talent on the single "Been There Done That."

—*B. Keith Murphy and Hanif Stubbs*

SELECT DISCOGRAPHY

■ ALBUMS
The Chronic, 1992
Above the Rim, 1994 (sound track)
Back N Tha Day, 1994 (remixes of pre-N.W.A. material)
Concrete Roots: Anthology, 1994 (compilation of pre-N.W.A. material)
Dr. Dre Presents . . . The Aftermath, 1996

SELECT AWARDS
Grammy Award for Best Rap Solo Performance for "Let Me Ride," 1993
American Music Award for Best Rap/Hip-Hop Artist, 1993

SEE ALSO: Ice Cube; N.W.A.; Snoop Doggy Dogg.

Dr. John
(Malcolm "Mac" Rebennack)
BORN: New Orleans, Louisiana; November 20, 1940
FIRST ALBUM RELEASE: *Gris-Gris*, 1968
MUSICAL STYLES: Rhythm and blues, funk, jazz, rock

Dr. John was among the artists most influential in spreading New Orleans rhythm-and-blues music. He blended the New Orleans keyboard sound with rock and thus introduced it to new audiences in the United States and Europe. He first made a name for himself in the late 1960's with some very distinctive New Orleans styles, including traditional Mardi Gras dress and tunes. He persevered

Dr. John (Ken Settle)

bennack was impressed by the originality of Longhair's playing and later credited Longhair as one of the key influences on his career.

While attending Jesuit High School, Rebennack frequented the J&M studio of family friend Cosimo Matassa and listened while Little Richard recorded his first albums. He especially loved the great piano players in the studio's house band. Rebennack started his professional career as a guitarist, playing in two high school bands and as a backup session player at the J&M studio. Playing guitar in the studio in the late 1950's when New Orleans rhythm and blues was really popular, he received plenty of work. In 1959, he recorded a single of his own, "Storm Warning," on Rex Records, but it was not successful.

During this period, segregation was still in force throughout much of the South. Playing with black bands sometimes forced the white Rebennack to hide in the back of the bus and to try to "pass" for black. Nevertheless, he continued working with African Americans. Moreover, to pay back the black musicians who had taught him so much, he helped organize an artists' cooperative label called All For One Records, which featured primarily black musicians. Taking such actions and frequently performing with African Americans sometimes drew criticism from other white musicians.

Rebennack's tendency to help others nearly ended his career in 1961. He tried to get a friend out of a fight in Jacksonville and was shot in the hand, nearly severing his index finger. The finger was repaired, but playing guitar was difficult. For a while Rebennack played bass. Eventually, bandmate James Booker gave Rebennack lessons on the organ, and that and the piano soon became his instruments of choice.

into the 1990's as a successful musician, both critically and commercially, by incorporating more jazz and pop into his repertoire.

The Beginnings. Dr. John was born Malcolm John Rebennack, Jr., in 1940, and nicknamed Mac. His mother was a model and his father owned a record store. Mac's extended family, which included several pianists, introduced him to the joys of live music. Perhaps most important, his Aunt Andree showed him the Texas boogie. Furthermore, when Mac, Sr., serviced jukeboxes, young Mac would accompany him to clubs to replace the records, exposing Mac to all of the most popular music.

On one occasion he joined his father on a trip to a black club called the Pepper Pot to fix the public address system. An older African American man was playing the piano with a unique style that Rebennack had never seen. It was Professor Longhair, and he gave Rebennack a few pointers. Re-

A New Life. In 1964 Rebennack's first marriage ended and his drug use became a serious problem. After time in a detoxification program at a hospital, he moved to California, where his mother and sister lived, to rebuild his life. In the mid-1960's, Rebennack found work in studio recording sessions in Los Angeles, with help from fellow New Orleans native Harold Battiste. California in the mid-1960's was the setting for the wild and creative period that would see the rise of Janis Joplin, the Doors, Jimi Hendrix, and the Grateful Dead. Rebennack sensed an opportunity to make his mark.

Back in the 1950's in New Orleans, Rebennack had been impressed by a black musician named Prince Lala, who practiced Voodoo rituals. Rebennack believed that Voodoo and other Mardi Gras traditions could be forged into a very powerful act. With encouragement from Battiste he decided to create a new stage persona: Dr. John Creaux the Night Tripper. The character was loosely based on a real doctor, John Montaine, a black from Nigeria who had been a Voodoo guru in New Orleans for thirty years in the nineteenth century. Rebennack's sister had studied the original doctor's life and passed on the details.

So Rebennack became Dr. John and started working on an album and a stage act. In 1968, the album, *Gris-Gris*, was released. The act featured Dr. John singing and playing a piano lit by a giant candelabra; he would wear a long robe and a feathered headdress and be backed by singers and dancers in elaborate costumes. A particularly striking woman named Colinda would writhe around the stage with a snake. The hypnotic beat and chorus of the backup singers on songs such as "I Walk on Gilded Splinters" made Dr. John's original act one of the most intriguing of the late 1960's. He started to spread New Orleans sounds around the country, and he became respected overseas.

During a European tour in 1970, Dr. John hired temporary replacements for several of his regular band members who could not get passports. Dissatisfied with the replacements' performance, he soon fired several of them. By the time he reached England, he had only his drummer and backup singers. Both Mick Jagger and Eric Clapton had been impressed by Dr. John's first album, and they agreed to join him for some recording sessions.

Commercial Success. Returning to the United States, Dr. John experienced conflicts with his manager Charlie Green. Severing ties with him, Dr. John decided to record an album of simpler New Orleans rhythm-and-blues classics. The album, *Dr. John's Gumbo* (1972), featured a version of "Iko Iko" that was based on an old New Orleans number, "Jockomo," made famous by Sugar Boy Crawford in the 1950's. It was Dr. John's first hit. *Gumbo* had benefited from the assistance of another talented New Orleans musician, Aaron Neville, and they continued to work together on the Doctor's next project.

Dr. John continued to move away from his Voodoo persona into more straightforward rhythm and blues, and in 1973 he released the album *In the Right Place*. It included his biggest hit, "Right Place, Wrong Time," which made it to number 9 on the charts. "Such a Night" reached number 42 and would become a highlight in Dr. John's live performances. By the mid-1970's, Dr. John had carved out a solid niche for himself in American music as a master of a unique blend of New Orleans rhythm and blues, rock, and funk.

Legacy and Later Career. Dr. John demonstrated that the New Orleans sound could be

For the Record

After his finger was shot during a brawl around the early 1960's, Dr. John temporarily switched to playing bass. He later recalled what happened while he was working in a Dixieland band: "I borrowed an upright bass from a guy in my band. But when I played it, my finger bled so much that the blood was ruinin' the guy's strings. So I switched to Fender [electric] bass. I introduced the instrument to the Dixieland world."

successful among both fans and critics. He branched out in the 1980's, recording a solo piano album, a blues album, and a jazz album. His 1989 album of old standards, *In a Sentimental Mood*, earned a Grammy Award for his duet with Rickie Lee Jones on "Makin' Whoopee." In the 1990's he remained one of the caretakers of New Orleans music, still touring and recording. While remaining in the public eye in commercials for Popeye's restaurants, he continued to play with and support young New Orleans musicians. Partly because of Dr. John, people around the world appreciate the spice of New Orleans music and the talent of New Orleans musicians.

—*Andy DeRoche*

SELECT DISCOGRAPHY

■ ALBUMS
Gris-Gris, 1968
Dr. John's Gumbo, 1972
In the Right Place, 1973
Dr. John Plays Mac Rebennack, 1981
The Ultimate Dr. John, 1987 (compilation)
In a Sentimental Mood, 1989
Mos' Scocious: The Dr. John Anthology, 1993
    (compilation)
Anutha Zone, 1998

SELECT AWARDS
Grammy Award for Best Jazz Vocal Performance, Duo or Group, for "Makin' Whoopee," 1989 (with Rickie Lee Jones)

SEE ALSO: Jones, Rickie Lee; Neville Brothers, The / Aaron Neville.

Fats Domino

BORN: New Orleans, Louisiana; February 26, 1928
FIRST SINGLE RELEASE: "The Fat Man," 1950
MUSICAL STYLES: Rhythm and blues, rock and roll

Antoine "Fats" Domino was one of the most popular rock-and-roll singers of the late 1950's and early 1960's, with more than thirty Top-40 songs. His boogie-woogie-influenced piano playing and his band's hard-driving beat combined with his

warm, lightly accented, distinctive voice and his jolly persona helped make him even more popular.

The Beginnings. Antoine Domino was born in New Orleans in 1928 and soon gained the nickname of "Fats." Coming from a family of musicians (his father was a violinist, and an uncle played jazz trumpet) and nourished by the rich musical culture that also produced Professor Longhair, Huey "Piano" Smith, and zydeco music, he soon learned to sing and play piano, making his first public appearance at the age of ten. As a young man, he suffered a factory accident that almost severed his hand, but he kept exercising until he could play the piano again.

He soon joined trumpeter-bandleader Dave Bartholomew, who was known for his original arrangements and would cowrite most of Domino's songs. In 1949 Domino was discovered by Lew Chudd, the president of a new label called

Fats Domino (Archive Photos)

Imperial Records, who immediately signed him to a contract. Domino first hit the rhythm-and-blues charts in 1950 with his signature song, "The Fat Man." For the next few years he was a local phenomenon, writing and performing songs like the bluesy "Going to the River" (later recorded by Chuck Willis), the Voodoo-influenced "Hey, La Bas," and "Every Night About This Time," on which he introduced the piano triplets which were to become an integral part of his music.

In 1955, Domino reached wider national attention with "Ain't That a Shame" (called "Ain't It a Shame" on the label). In the usual practice of the times with successful songs by black artists, another label released a cover version, by Pat Boone, with as close to the original arrangement as possible behind the singer's comfortably Caucasian voice. The Boone version sold better, but Domino had reached the attention of the American public.

Stardom. Domino's next few records, "Poor Me," "Boll Weevil," and "All by Myself," did not make the national charts, but in early 1956, his rollicking "I'm in Love Again" went to the Top 10. The flip side offered what was to become a frequent Domino practice, an uptempo revival of an old ballad, in this case the 1930's paean to domesticity "My Blue Heaven." It was also popular.

Two more revivals, "When My Dreamboat Comes Home" and "Blueberry Hill," kept Domino on the charts in 1956, and they were followed by an original, "Blue Monday," which encapsulated the blue-collar experience of working hard all week for a single day of pleasure (followed by a hangover).

Like "Ain't That a Shame," "I'm Walkin'" (1957) was covered by a white performer (Ricky Nelson in his move from sitcom child star to singer), but the original also received airplay and sales, as did its flip side, "What's the Reason I'm Not Pleasin' You?" Another two-sided hit followed: The sardonic ballad "Valley of Tears" offered an interesting contrast with the uptempo romance of "It's You I Love," but both reached the Top 10. After these, however, Domino's sales slid for a while. "When I See You" and "Wait and See" were only moderate hits. He performed the title song in *The Big Beat* (1958), a typically plotless

For the Record

Though Fats Domino was born in the United States, the language he grew up speaking was French.

§

All of Domino's eight children's names begin with the letter *A*.

rock-and-roll film in which he also got to sing "I'm Walkin'."

Ready, Willing, and Able. Late in 1958, Domino returned to the Top 10 with a song which, in retrospect, can be seen to emphasize an aspect of his work that went unremarked at the time: eroticism. Sex was a constant subtext in Domino's work, though at that time it was considered a taboo subject for overweight black men. It was revealed as early as the almost explicit promise of satisfaction in "All by Myself" or the directness of "Blueberry Hill." In 1958 Domino was directly promising a "Whole Lotta Loving." Although almost any vagueness and omission of words was then considered suggestive, "Whole Lotta Loving" allowed the audience to fill in the blanks in "Got a whole lot of . . . to do." The follow-up, "I'm Ready," adopted the popular 1950's musical trope of being "ready, willing, and able to rock and roll all night," with the unstated possibility of other physical activities. (In his prime, Domino would conclude his live act by pushing his piano across the stage with his stomach and thighs.)

The 1960's. "I'm Ready" was followed by another two-sided hit, with the cheery uptempo "I'm Gonna Be a Wheel Someday" backed by the insistent beat of "I Wanna Walk You Home." "Walking to New Orleans" represented Domino's last visit to the Top 10, with "Three Nights a Week" and "My Girl Josephine" almost reaching those heights. In the 1960's, however, Domino's sales fell. In 1961, there was a flurry of interest in "Let the Four Winds Blow," a song he had written for Roy Brown years earlier but now recorded himself. Then, as Ray Charles did, he turned to country-and-western music, recording Hank Williams's "Jambalaya" and "You Win Again," but these were only mildly successful. A move from Imperial to ABC-Paramount did not improve sales.

After a few years out of the spotlight, Domino returned in 1968, when Warner Bros. released an album in which he revived some of his old favorites and recorded newer material, most notably a cover of the Beatles' "Lady Madonna" that made it seem as if the song had been written for him.

Off the charts for many years, Fats Domino continued to perform, particularly in Las Vegas. His son, Antoine Domino (one of eight children) has followed in his father's footsteps as a singer and piano player.

History and Influence. Fats Domino is believed to have sold more than 65 million records. He also played piano on records made by many of his fellow New Orleans musicians, such as Lloyd Price and Smiley Lewis. His influence is ubiquitous, from a young singer named Ernest Evans changing his name to "Chubby Checker" to his work with contemporary and later New Orleans musicians such as Allen Toussaint, saxophonist Lee Allen (who played on many Domino records), and the Neville Brothers. —*Arthur Hlavaty*

SELECT DISCOGRAPHY
■ SINGLES
"The Fat Man," 1950
"Going to the River," 1953
"Ain't That a Shame," 1955
"I'm in Love Again," 1956
"When My Dreamboat Comes Home," 1956
"Blueberry Hill," 1956
"Blue Monday," 1956
"I'm Walkin'," 1957
"Whole Lotta Loving," 1958
"I'm Gonna Be a Wheel Someday," 1959
"Lady Madonna," 1968
■ ALBUMS
Fats Domino—Rock and Rollin', 1956
Just Domino, 1963
Fats, 1970
They Call Me the Fat Man—Antoine "Fats" Domino: The Legendary Imperial Recordings, 1990
Christmas Is a Special Day, 1993

SELECT AWARDS
Rock and Roll Hall of Fame, inducted 1986
Grammy Award for Lifetime Achievement, 1987

SEE ALSO: Berry, Chuck; Little Richard; Neville Brothers, The / Aaron Neville.

Donovan
(Donovan Philip Leitch)
BORN: Glasgow, Scotland; May 10, 1946
FIRST SINGLE RELEASE: "Catch the Wind," 1965
MUSICAL STYLES: Folk, folk rock

Although generally associated with the "British invasion" of U.S. popular music in the mid-1960's, Donovan succeeded in carving out a nearly unique niche for himself on both sides of the Atlantic Ocean. Emerging from the poverty and urban squalor of Maryhill, an economically depressed section of Glasgow, Scotland, Donovan embraced music as a means of escape and eventually excelled as a musician, singer, songwriter, and producer. One of the most interesting aspects of Donovan's talent was the variety of topic matters he drew upon in writing his both introspective and extroverted songs. His record sales and concert appearances declined markedly in the early 1970's, but respect for his talent and a growing recognition of his influence on modern musical and social history have cemented his respected place in popular culture.

The Beginnings. Donovan's family moved to a neighborhood near London while he was an adolescent, and eventually he finished secondary school. An indifferent student, Donovan attended a local college for one year but then left to pursue a musical career. In 1964, he began making public appearances, mostly at pubs and folk clubs. Performing mainly his own material, he accompanied himself on the acoustic guitar and harmonica and was frequently joined by an enigmatic kazoo player known only as Gypsy Dave. Economic survival was always a challenge, however, and Donovan often worked as a waiter when not hitchhiking across the United Kingdom trying to find music jobs. The money situation was severe enough that he apparently resorted briefly to crime and was convicted for stealing food and cigarettes, leading to a brief jail term.

While appearing at the Southend in Essex, England, Donovan caught the eye of professional music producers Peter Eden and Geoff Stephens, both of whom agreed to manage his stalled career. By early 1965, the singer was making demo records in London that led to a contract with the small recording company Pye Records. Television, however, was the medium which brought him national fame and led to the success of his first released record, "Catch the Wind." Talent scout Bob Bickford was so impressed with Donovan that the latter was signed to appear on the program *Ready, Steady, Go*, which was tremendously popular throughout the United Kingdom and enjoyed the reputation of showcasing the best of young musical talent. Donovan so impressed the program's

viewers and producers that he appeared on the program for three straight weeks, an unprecedented occurrence. By mid-1965, having accrued a hit record ("Catch the Wind" reached number 4 on the British charts), national media exposure, and a recording contract, Donovan appeared positioned for stardom.

Sunshine Superman. For several years, Donovan had been an admirer of U.S. folksinger and trendsetter Bob Dylan. Many critics had faulted Donovan for supposedly emulating every aspect of Dylan's public persona, a criticism which struck the former's fans as cruel and unfair. The two met in March of 1965 during Dylan's British tour and formed a lasting amiable relationship. In July of 1965, Donovan scored his second hit record, "Colours," signed a U.S. distribution agreement with Hickory Records, and experienced his first tour of the United States. He was seen on several nationally broadcast U.S. television programs and

Donovan (Archive Photos)

For the Record

Donovan had an obviously strained relationship with Epic Records producer Mickey Most, hiring and firing him at least four times.

§

Paul McCartney provided the whispered lyrics to "Mellow Yellow," and Donovan sang on the Beatles' classics "Yellow Submarine" and "All You Need Is Love."

performed a well-received set at the legendary Newport Folk Festival. Donovan developed a friendship with Joan Baez, with whom he was seen at several protest marches, and also was close to the Beatles, especially Paul McCartney. He was becoming something more than just popular; he was respected and admired not just for his substantial music talent but also for his poetic writings, social conscience, and peace advocacy.

Recording Classics. In terms of both record sales and social impact, Donovan was a giant on the music scene. His first antiwar protest song, "Universal Soldier," was one of his few hits written by someone else, in this case American Indian Buffy Sainte-Marie. From that point forward, though, his best-selling records were all his own compositions. In September, 1966, the singer enjoyed his first chart topper in the United States, "Sunshine Superman," a song about whose meaning many people speculated, although Donovan claimed it was simply about his courtship of a young woman named Linda Lawrence, who later became his wife.

Three months later, "Mellow Yellow" became his next million seller and was more thoroughly studied and analyzed than any of his previous recordings. The song's apparently nonsensical lyrics were claimed to be about abortion, electric sex toys, drugs, or any other topic the public could imagine.

The next two years did not produce any recordings of the magnitude of his 1966 smashes, al-though he stayed busy with nearly constant touring. Several songs did do reasonably well, such as "Epistle to Dippy," "There Is a Mountain," "Wear Your Love Like Heaven," and "Jennifer Juniper," all of which reached the U.S. Top 25. In late 1968, "Hurdy Gurdy Man," a mystic and largely incomprehensible song, became his top-selling record in two years. In May, 1969, Donovan reached the Top 10 list for the last time with the lengthy, sing-along anthem "Atlantis." Although several much smaller hits would follow in the next few years, by the early 1970's the musical and political times had changed to such a degree that Donovan's mixture of aestheticism, pacifism, and introspection no longer seemed as relevant or interesting.

Legacy. Donovan was part of one small but growing musical tradition, and he largely created another. As a talented singer-songwriter, he was a direct artistic descendant of Hank Williams and Buddy Holly. At the same time, Donovan combined the tortured soul of a nineteenth century Romantic poet with the desire for social justice found in the reformers of the Progressive Era to produce a type of folk music that centered on both internal and external factors. Later performers such as Tracy Chapman, Jewel, and many others have followed in his path.

—*Thomas W. Buchanan*

SELECT DISCOGRAPHY

■ SINGLES
"Catch the Wind," 1965
"Sunshine Superman," 1965
"Mellow Yellow," 1966
"Hurdy Gurdy Man," 1968

■ ALBUMS
Sunshine Superman, 1966
Mellow Yellow, 1967
Like It Is, Was, and Evermore Shall Be, 1968
    (compilation)
Barabajagal, 1969
Donovan P. Leitch, 1970 (compilation)
Troubador: The Definitive Collection 1964-1976,
    1992 (boxed set, compilation)

SEE ALSO: Beatles, The; Chapman, Tracy; Dylan, Bob.